WOMEN UNDER STRESS

WOMEN UNDER STRESS

Donald Roy Morse, D.D.S., M.A.
Associate Professor
Department of Endodontology
Temple University School of Dentistry
Philadelphia, Pennsylvania

M. Lawrence Furst, Ph.D., M.P.H.
Associate Professor
Division of Behavioral Sciences
Temple University Health Sciences Center
Philadelphia, Pennsylvania

VNR VAN NOSTRAND REINHOLD COMPANY
NEW YORK CINCINNATI TORONTO LONDON MELBOURNE

Copyright © 1982 by Van Nostrand Reinhold Company

Library of Congress Catalog Card Number: 81-11654
ISBN: 0-442-26648-0

Manufactured in the United States of America

Published by Van Nostrand Reinhold Company
135 West 50th Street, New York. N.Y. 10020

Van Nostrand Reinhold Limited
1410 Birchmount Road
Scarborough, Ontario M1P 2E7, Canada

Van Nostrand Reinhold Australia Pty. Ltd.
17 Queen Street
Mitcham, Victoria 3132, Australia

Van Nostrand Reinhold Company Limited
Molly Millars Lane
Wokingham, Berkshire, England

15 14 13 12 11 10 9 8 7 6 5 4 3 2 1

Library of Congress Cataloging in Publication Data

Morse, Donald R.
   Women under stress.

   Includes index.
   1. Women—Mental health. 2. Stress (Psychology)
3. Stress (Physiology) I. Furst, Merrick L.
II. Title. [DNLM: 1. Stress, Psychological.
2. Women—Psychology. WM 172 M884w]
RC451.4.W6M67   616.89'05'088042   81-11654
ISBN 0-442-26648-0   AACR2

Foreword

The word "stress" has entered our common vocabulary only in the past ten years. Before this, for most of us, "stress" meant force applied to inanimate objects, as demonstrated in a physics class, or referred to human reactions to cataclysmic events, such as natural disasters or wars.

Today it is generally recognized that stress is an inescapable part of life and that the accumulation of many small stresses (as well as an occasional traumatic event) can create a "stress load" that can wear down the system and leave an individual prone to physical and emotional illness. Such everyday stress can also prevent the individual from leading a pleasant and fulfilled life.

With stress now recognized as an important factor in determining health and well being, it would seem a logical next step for researchers to examine the particular stresses that confront women. The widespread concern about women's inferior social roles, which has led to much-needed political action, has seldom led to consideration of the *total* picture of female stress in our society. This has most likely occurred because of the inherent difficulty of such an undertaking. In addition to their own specific difficulties, women share many problems in common with men and there is considerable overlap between male and female stress (environmental pollution, for example, does not discriminate between sexes), and women's unique stresses are so diverse that they encompass a broad spectrum of problems falling within the fields of medicine, dentistry, sociology, psychology, anthropology, criminology, nutrition, and many others.

When Doctors Donald Morse and Larry Furst set out to write about the specific stresses of women in our society, my initial reaction was: "This is an impossible subject to tackle! Women's stress is a subject as broad as life itself." And, indeed, in some respects, it is. Nevertheless, these two male authors have succeeded in organizing a vast array of information regarding the physiological, emotional, and social stresses that affect women in particular, and, in so doing, have created not only a highly readable book but one that is informative even to the expert in the stress reduction field.

I teach a course on the Humanistic Management of Stress at Princeton University; I deal with stress management in corporate settings in my role as consultant to industry; and I spent a number of years researching, writing about, and teaching one of the most effective stress reduction techniques I knew of—a modern form of meditation. Despite my familiarity with this field, on reading Morse and Furst's book, I came across some new and important information concerning the stresses that confront women.

It is perhaps not surprising that these authors are able to be as objective and empathic as they are when presenting the woman's point of view with respect to stress. Both of them are highly experienced in the area of stress management and are well known for their pioneering work combining meditation with hypnosis and for being the first research team to study the use of meditation for pain control. I have long been interested in their work and am particularly pleased to see that they have presented a wealth of relevant material in a manner that can be easily understood by the untrained person. The point of view they present in this book is remarkably unbiased, with no single cause of women's stress emphasized at the expense of another, and the "outer" causes of stress in women and the inner causes stemming from women's own *reactions* to growing up female in our society are given equally careful attention.

The result is a well-rounded and absorbing book, complete with sound advice on what to do *about* the stress encountered. It is my hope that many women of today will read it; it should be truly helpful.

Patricia Carrington, Ph.D.
Department of Psychology
Princeton University
Author of *Freedom in Meditation*
(Doubleday)

Problems such as these are considered in this book. Also emphasized are effective methods of coping that are geared to women. Special consideration is given to the problems of the working woman. Some of the stress-inducing situations, problems and conflicts include: separation from mother, the perils of puberty, premenstrual tension, the Oedipus (Electra) complex, marital stress, maternal stress, staying single, menopause, aging, sexual freedom, the ethnic minorities, family and career, the woman athlete, women in religion, women's liberation, dieting, drinking and pill-popping, and assertion and aggression.

While the subject is scientific and thoroughly researched and documented, it is presented in down-to-earth terms. Some humor is included to help lighten the reading load. An anxiety evaluation form is presented and the book concludes with a holistic female stress-control assessment questionnaire.

The rationale for us as male researchers to write about females is based on our strong interest in female stress. The authors have engaged in several investigations of stress-related phenomena manifested by women. We have given courses for women such as "Women in the Business World" and the "Two-Career Couple," and regularly speak to women's groups. In addition, we have had many women as clients, patients and subjects—and seem to have been instrumental in helping them achieve control of their stress-related problems. There are also precedents in reverse. For example, *The Sensuous Man, The Male Mid-Life Crisis, Men In Love* and *The Hite Report on Male Sexuality* are books about men authored by women.

We would like to thank Mr. Alex V. Mucha, Director of Visual Education, Temple University School of Dentistry, for the photography. A special thank you is extended to Ms. Kathy Conboy, Mrs. Nissie Segal, Ms. Joan Austin, Ms. Chris Haeussler, Dr. Lorraine Herrenkohl, Dr. Patricia Carrington, and the numerous other women who have helped us in the awareness of the diversity of female stress. We particularly want to thank our wives Diane and Norma for bearing with us and helping us understand marital stressors. Thanks are also given to Ms. Susan Munger, Senior Editor, Mr. Robert Baird, Director of Publicity, Ms. Chris DiSimone, Publicity, Ms. Alberta Gordon, Managing Editor, and Mr. Sam Prosser, National Sales Manager, all of the Van Nostrand Reinhold Company, for their sincere cooperation in the publication of this book.

DONALD ROY MORSE
M. LAWRENCE FURST

Preface

Many books have been written about stress and its management but almost none have emphasized the special and specific stress that affects women. The problems of men have been the main consideration. For example, much has been written on the stressful "male" jobs held by the physician, the dentist, the accountant, and the air traffic controller.* Countless references have been made to the male-oriented stress-related diseases such as heart attacks and ulcers. Moreover, stress-control methods have been discussed with men in mind.

Consider the jogging and exercise boom as exemplified by books such as *The Complete Book(s) of Running* by James Fixx and the *Aerobics* books by Kenneth Cooper. Meditation books follow suit with the several Transcendental Meditation (TM) books and *The Relaxation Response* by Herbert Benson. All of these are male-authored and primarily consider the masculine approach to stress management.

Undoubtedly, women have stressful experiences in common with men. Anxiety, guilt and frustration are not the privileged province of either sex. Women and men alike often indulge in the negative stress coping methods of overeating, smoking, drinking and "pill-popping." Still, women have special stress-related problems. Just to emphasize this, in a recent issue of *The Philadelphia Inquirer* (Sept. 26, 1980) which highlighted national news briefs, of the five headlines, three were related to female stress. The headlines were as follows: (1) Forty-two percent of female federal workers report sexual harassment; (2) An intrauterine device should no longer be used by women, a company says; and (3) Four female soldiers at Fort McPherson in Atlanta were discharged this week by the Army because of alleged homosexual "tendencies and acts."

* In contrast, some "female" jobs are held by the teacher, the salesclerk, the waitress, the social worker, the nurse, the dental hygienist, and the librarian.

Contents

PART IV   WOMEN'S SEXUALITY

PART V   WOMEN AND ENVIRONMENTAL PRESSURES

PART VI   STRESS MANAGEMENT FOR WOMEN

WOMEN UNDER STRESS

PART 1
INTRODUCTION

In the first chapter, which encompasses this section, a fictionalized version of a case history of a woman's stress-laden life is presented. Several stressful situations are developed and resolved. This chapter serves to introduce the theme of women under stress.

PART 1
INTRODUCTION

In the first chapter, which encompasses this section, a fictionalized version of a case history of a woman's stress-laden life is presented. Several stressful situations are developed and resolved. This chapter serves to introduce the theme of women under stress.

1

Born to be a Woman:
The Saga of Roberta*

The tattered sign—The Newcastle Home For Senior Citizens—was creaking in the wind. Viewing it, Roberta knew that the sign's state was a reflection of her own condition. She, too, was run-down and weatherbeaten, but it hadn't always been that way. Roberta was once young and vibrant. That seemed like ages ago, and maybe it was. Roberta pondered her fate: Was she just one of the unfortunates, or was it something else? Was her aging and deteriorated condition the Lord's revenge or was it just bad luck? Could it have been changed or was it inevitable? Was it the drugs, her diet or did it start earlier? Maybe it was the result of her birth—of being born a female—a woman emerging in a man's world . . .

Robert Gardiner was in the prime of his life; in his mid-thirties and a self-proclaimed, self-made man. Robert's parents were escapees from a pogrom in Poland. (At the detention center on Ellis Island, in the late 1800s, the authorities couldn't determine the spelling of the family name which sounded something like "Gardinsky." So it was fortuitously changed to the pronounceable WASPish surname Gardiner.)

Robert's parents instilled in him a burning desire to get ahead. He grew up in the teeming East Bronx and labored hard. Robert worked two and three jobs at a time and eventually achieved financial success. He was bright but the family's monetary plight had prevented him from attending college. Robert made it anyhow; and now he had a lot going for him. He

* This is a fictionalized version of a complex case history. Names and places have been changed and dramatic overtones have been added. The tale is basically true and serves to introduce many of the stressors (i.e., stress-causing factors) to which females are particularly prone.

was considered to be "tall, dark and handsome," had an engaging personality, and possessed a probing mind.

Thus, it was no accident that Robert rose quickly and effortlessly in the business world. His present position was first vice president of the Faber Dress Manufacturing Company of New York. Robert was also an athlete. He had always excelled in swimming, handball and soccer, although his first love was baseball. His overriding goal as a teen-ager had been to be a professional baseball player. Life's exigencies thwarted that ambition. Robert had to settle for the business world and a once-weekly $8 as a Saturday afternoon semipro centerfielder.

Robert's intense drive affected his physical condition. In his youth, he had experienced curious attacks which had plagued him periodically. They took the form of sudden spells of knifelike cramps in his abdomen, accompanied by nausea and heart palpitations. During these periods, he had difficulty in eating. Now, as an adult with heavy business responsibilities, he was experiencing the attacks more frequently. An exploration of his abdomen, ordered by the family physician, failed to reveal anything of a suspicious nature. Regardless of cause, the attacks continued. Strangely, Robert was not bothered at work, but only when he arrived home.

Home, for Robert, was a luxurious Tudor house in suburban Westchester County, New York. He shared it with a beautiful (and docile) wife, Evelyn, and an equally docile (and homely) dog, Mitzi. Apart from his intestinal problems, Robert felt fulfilled except for one missing ingredient. He was at a genetic dead-end; he had no child to meet his need for immortality. It wasn't for lack of trying. The Gardiners had been married for eight years and during that time they exceeded the reported "average-of-nine-times-per-month for American couples." They tried every method, every position but to no avail. They visited physicians, psychiatrists, and men of the cloth. (In the process, subjecting themselves to tests and inquiries that removed the last vestiges of civilization and dignity.) Moreover, the Gardiners had employed everything from a hundred-and-one positions to prayer but they just had no luck. They were resigned to a childless marriage until they learned that their application for adoption was approved. The day the adoption papers came through, they celebrated and Evelyn got drunk—and pregnant.

Evelyn was elated but Robert was ecstatic. He knew that he was going to have a son. His son would get it all, and without the sweat and strain that he had had to endure. "Robert, Jr." would surely outdo his dad; he would become a "pro"—a major league centerfielder.

Robert never had a doubt—the unborn child was a boy. A decorator was hired and the guest bedroom was transformed into a bright blue little boy's room. "Robbie-to-be" even had his first baseball glove, bat and ball neatly stacked at the side of the crib.

Evelyn was a passive, husband-pleasing female. Whether it was Robert's influence or her own desire, Evelyn firmly believed that she, too, wanted a boy. For nine months she was coddled and catered to. Robert did not let her take one false step. Then after several premature visits to the hospital, the prolonged period of labor began. The delivery was difficult and protracted; both mother and child barely pulled through. Evelyn lay exhausted on the bed and was hardly cheered by her doctor's words, "Mrs. Gardiner, you have a lovely baby daughter." And so Roberta Gardiner began life as an unwanted female.

"Senior citizen, my foot!" exclaimed Roberta, "The place is nothing but an old folk's prison, a final, pointless end to a frustrating life." Roberta had been an achiever, a hard worker. She had left her mark and now was dropped off; "no deposit, no return." Sad, solitary and single, Roberta was left to spend her final days in the same manner as when her life began; she was still an unwanted female. . .

Robert Gardiner would not be foiled. He wanted a son; he *needed* a son. If he couldn't have a son, he would do the next best thing. He would treat his daughter as if she were a son. She would be given all the advantages of the male. Thus, Roberta became one of the boys and it started with sports. Even before she was old enough to walk, the lessons began. A tiny bathtub swimmer; a little girl cuddling a lightweight soccer ball. Roberta progressed to softball and handball. Roberta even packed a mean left hook that was feared by many of her male contemporaries.

Roberta's training didn't stop with sports. From the time she learned to read, Roberta was instructed in the art of salesmanship. A business background for a budding beauty. With her beautiful teeth and natural smile, Roberta learned the effectiveness of nonverbal communication. Although she was destined to operate in a man's world and was given the masculine approach to sports and employment, her femininity shone through. Roberta was developing into a lovely young woman. It didn't happen without some disturbing signs. At age four, Roberta didn't know about "penis-envy" but she knew she was different. One day Roberta had accidentally walked into the boys' bathroom and found out that the guys stood up to urinate. Roberta thought that she was a late developer but soon found out that girls were left out on that score.

At eleven, her breasts began to bud and for a while she was "one up" on the boys. But her breasts got in the way during many of her athletic endeavors. Still, Roberta considered that it was an even exchange. The guys had to wear jock straps to contain their genitals; she had to wrap her bust into a bra. Thus, both sexes had their trials and tribulations.

At twelve, Roberta had her first bleeding episode. Menstruation was one burden the guys didn't share. She was embarrassed and angry when the cramps prevented her from playing up to par or even caused her to miss a game. Roberta didn't dare tell the boys the truth and she had no close girl friends in whom to confide. Roberta was considered strange by both sexes. The boys tolerated her for her athletic skill; the girls shunned her for being a "tomboy." Many thought she was a "lezzie," but Roberta had the usual heterosexual teen-age sexual fantasies and desires. She was an outstanding female athlete, but no one except her father really cared. And for him, the attention he gave was out of desperation. The Gardiners' single successful reproductive venture was never repeated and Roberta remained an only child.

Robert was relentless in his pursuit of Roberta's perfection. Not only was she instructed in athletics and salesmanship, Roberta was expected to be excellent in scholastics. Roberta reluctantly responded by becoming an "A-grubbing" student. Despite these achievements, happiness eluded Roberta. Aside from her problems with her peers, Roberta had an unloving mother. Her mother, Evelyn, felt inadequate as a woman. After all she had only one child, and a daughter at that. Evelyn Gardiner's life was tied up with her house and husband. To keep a clean, well-decorated home, to prepare interesting and satisfying meals, and to support her husband's career—those were Evelyn's mundane goals. She once was a beauty but now she cared little for her appearance. And to her, self-actualization was a foreign term. Evelyn was deeply religious and believed in the irrevocable Will of God. In her religion, God spoke *through* and *to* the male: Abraham, Moses and the other Prophets, they were all men. God himself was a male figure. When Evelyn went to the synagogue, she sat in the side balcony (i.e., the "female" gallery). Women had their place and Evelyn knew hers. And having an only daughter didn't help.

Evelyn's belief system had a negative effect on her constitution. She turned into a frail, inadequate, sad-looking woman who experienced daily spells of acute anxiety. While talking, Evelyn would stop and forget what she was going to say. At first she thought she was just forgetful, but soon these experiences became extremely distressing. At times the memory lapses actually caused her to feel physically ill and the presence of her unwanted daughter didn't improve her disposition or condition.

Evelyn did not love Roberta for many reasons. First and foremost was the simple fact that "Roberta" was not "Robbie." Secondly, she felt that

Roberta had "ruined" her insides. Of course, the reason that Evelyn had no further children was not really related to her internal anatomy, but no doctor could ever convince Evelyn on that point. Although she heard that breast-feeding was best, the very thought of breast-feeding her daughter was abhorrent to Evelyn. Roberta had to be content with bottles and pacifiers. In fact, Roberta saw very little of her mother. The Gardiners had a sleep-in "nanny" named Eloise. The main reason Roberta developed into a "normal" child was because of Eloise's affection. Evelyn gave Eloise a free hand with Roberta and Eloise remained with Roberta through the crucial next fifteen years.

Evelyn had other reasons for not loving her daughter. She neither appreciated her intelligence nor her athletic pursuits. Evelyn was also jealous of Roberta's good looks. Evelyn herself was a mass of contradictions. She hadn't wanted a daughter, but when she had a daughter, she permitted her husband to raise her daughter as a son. She was understandably disturbed because her daughter was "unladylike," but she did nothing to make Roberta into a "lady." Evelyn wouldn't admit it but there was a touch of "Electra" jealousy present.* Roberta and her dad got along *too* well. Yet even here, Evelyn was ambivalent. She wanted to please Robert so she tolerated Roberta, but she was upset over their closeness.

In spite of it all, by the age of sixteen Roberta blossomed into a well-developed, attractive young woman. She was also a straight-A student and could hit a fast ball with the best of them. But these were mixed blessings. Athletically, she was too good for the girls and they disliked her. She occasionally got into a game with the guys but they really didn't appreciate her intrusions into "manly" sports. Even on a one-to-one basis Roberta had her problems. At that age, Roberta was unaware of the popular beliefs of the time, that a girl should never show that she was a better athlete than the boy she was dating, or that a young "lady" should not appear more knowledgeable than her masculine companions. The result was that while Roberta scored well scholastically and on the playing field, she "struck out" on all her dates. However, Roberta had one big advantage; she wasn't tied to her mother's apron strings and could develop on her own (independent of her father's push). So Roberta concentrated on scholastics and athletics. In college, as a business major she made Dean's list and earned varsity letters in softball, basketball and track. Still, the beaux were scarce—and scared.

Roberta went on to graduate school. She earned a business degree from Columbia and, with her father's influence, she entered the business world

* By definition, the Electra complex implies a desire for the father and feelings of hostile rivalry toward the mother.

of the Faber Dress Manufacturing Company. Robert Gardiner was a superb salesman. He skillfully skirted the line between assertion and aggression and he taught Roberta his many skills. Yet men tended to misconstrue Roberta's assertiveness as aggression, and her firm behavior "turned off" several of her colleagues. Being raised with a masculine emphasis, Roberta found it difficult to play the role of the sweet, passive female. She was caught in a classic "double-bind." For even in business, the female role was supposed to be subservient to the male; and with subservience she could not advance.

At the age of twenty-six, Roberta was physically, intellectually and athletically gifted, but with it all she was still single. Had she lived fifty years later, she probably would have enjoyed her life as a successful single business executive and female sports star. But those were the days when it was considered an oddity for a woman to have such a life-style. To be twenty-six and still single was judged to be a failure for a woman—an unfulfilled female; and Roberta was definitely unfulfilled.

Roberta now belonged to the "rocking chair" set. One of her few current pleasures was to set her withered old body in perpetual motion as she lay back on the only decent rocker remaining at The Newcastle Home. That once firm, agile body now had to depend on an external force to set it in motion. As Roberta rocked, the grandfather clock chimed twelve times announcing the arrival of lunch. The usual bill-of-fare was bland and tasteless. Roberta couldn't care less. Even eating had lost its enjoyment. It had been years since food had any special taste for her. Roberta's thoughts soon turned away from food. She thought about all her previous acquaintances and the fact that now she had none. There were other similar cast-offs in that large waiting room but Roberta felt alone. She looked around at that roomful of decrepit humans; most were women. They were sitting around awaiting the inevitable. Some were simply staring out into space; and others, while apparently sleeping, were twisting and turning or snoring. There were a few who showed greater signs of life: a glance at a magazine; a game of solitaire; a stare at the TV set. One thing was certain, the place was no beehive of activity; and Roberta was once so very active. . .

Roberta might not have been fulfilled as a married woman, but between the softball games and business meetings, she was certainly keeping active. Then one day while sliding into second base, she sprained her left big toe, and that's how Roberta and Stephen met.

Stephen Blatterfein was a thirty-two-year-old chiropodist. Stephen also had had his share of frustrations. His father, Joseph, was motivated much as was Roberta's father. He, too, wanted a son who would become a star athlete. Stephen's mother, Gloria, wanted a son who would become a "doctor." Stephen obliged them both by emerging as a male but that's where his obligations ceased. He flopped out of the birth canal weighing in at twelve pounds, six ounces. Stephen spent the next thirty-two years of his life engaged in the "battle of the bulge." But Stephen's love for food surpassed his desire to touch his toes. As the weight increased, Stephen's athletic promise proportionately decreased. His father Joseph fumed, but mother Gloria smiled as their child attacked his books with a vengeance. Unfortunately, the attack was vigorous but not sufficiently effective; Stephen did not get into medical school.

Gloria and Stephen then considered alternatives. Gloria had sound teeth, had no back problems and didn't need glasses, but she had really bad feet—so Stephen became a foot doctor.

Stephen had good hands, a pleasant personality and a poor sense of smell . . . three assets for a foot doctor. Subsequently, he developed a fine practice in North White Plains. Stephen was a poor businessman and his outside investments were disastrous. So even with a sound practice, he had financial problems. Stephen liked his patients, especially the women. He empathized so well with his woman patients that many thought he was effeminate but that was not the case. On the other hand, Stephen did not exactly generate sexual appeal. Although he was reasonably good looking, his rotund appearance and athletic deficiencies put him in poor stead with the women he desired, and women with similar physical proportions "turned him off." So on occasion Stephen sought sexual gratification on a paying basis. Even those occasions were rare: once at age eighteen (along with his first "drink"); a second at age twenty-one (when he legally came of age); and two last occasions when he reached his twenty-sixth birthday. Then when he was thirty-two, Stephen met Roberta.

Roberta's ailment was minor; a sprained toe. Since Stephen's next patient canceled, he had sufficient time to tend to the injury and become acquainted with Roberta. They "hit it off" well. Roberta was athletic, business-wise, intelligent and attractive. Stephen was unathletic, had a poor business sense, and was not overly bright (a "perfect" match).

All his life, Stephen had been dominated by his mother, so he was accustomed to being around a powerful woman. Roberta was definitely a powerful, dominant woman. Roberta wasn't enthralled by Stephen's physical appearance but she believed (as so many women do) that her influence could effect a change for the better. They were both looking for a way out; that is, wanting to escape unhappy homes. They were also eager to increase their sexual opportunities. Neither set of parents was particularly overjoyed by the match, but Roberta and Stephen decided, for a change, to take charge. And so they were married in a simple religious ceremony on a cold March day.

Roberta had been dozing, but the sound of her name startled her. Why was she hearing her name? Where was it coming from? She even doubted if it were her name and she hardly remembered who she was. A tap on the shoulder returned Roberta to the present. There was a call, a telephone call. It was for her, from her daughter, Lisa. After a few fumbling minutes, Roberta managed to reach the one public phone in the large waiting room at The Newcastle Home.

The voice on the other end was faint or at least that's how it sounded to Roberta. She used to hear so well; and once it was important to understand the words. But now—what did it matter? "Hello, mom, how are you? We all miss you so much. I really intended to see you today but Jim had to work this weekend and the other car is in the shop. I definitely will come next Sunday. How do you like the place? The grounds are really beautiful; you must love to look at them. And the owner seems like such a nice man. Oh! There's the front doorbell, gotta go. See you soon. Love ya! Bye."

"Love ya!—crap! I gave her the best years of my life and for what. For an occasional call and once-a-month fifteen-minute visit. That's gratitude. But what can you expect? I got nothing from my mother and I get nothing from my daughter and my husband wasn't much better". . . .

Roberta Gardiner and Stephen Blatterfein didn't exactly have an ideal marriage, but judging by present standards it wasn't too bad. Roberta and Stephen had a fashionable home built in North White Plains. It was fifteen minutes by car to his downtown office and forty-five minutes by train to her Manhattan office. Life was going reasonably well for both of them when one morning two years after they had moved into their new home, Roberta felt strange. She noticed some small physical changes about one week after her period was due. Two weeks and one dead rabbit later her suspicions were confirmed—she was pregnant!

Roberta's stint in the business world had been beneficial. Being so often around men taught her how to deal with them. Roberta no longer was naive in her dealings with a "man's world" (both in business and personal relationships). And she really was enjoying her independence and the sense of importance it gave her. But Roberta wanted to be a mother. So when her daughter Lisa was born, Roberta vowed not to repeat her parent's mistakes. Her child would be treated as a "real" girl and would be handled with tender, loving care. However, it didn't take long for Roberta to become disgusted with "diapers, dishes and dustpans."

Although Stephen's practice was expanding and the money was not being dissipated as heretofore (Roberta's business experience came in handy here), Roberta became restless. She missed the excitement of business maneuvers and the exhilaration of her daily swimming sessions. So when Lisa was two years old, Roberta hired a sleep-in maid and renewed her contact with the outside world.

Using her father's influence as before, Roberta was rehired by the Faber Dress Manufacturing Company. All went well except for an unexpected problem: Roberta was plagued by guilt—the guilt of the working woman leaving a young child at home. Little Lisa's behavior didn't help either. Temper tantrums, crying fits and regular bed-wetting episodes resulted in the forced resignation of three live-in maids within six months. Yet, Roberta wouldn't return to full-time motherhood.

Since Roberta was now a business executive (third vice president), she often attended the business*man*'s luncheons. Roberta tried to escape and decrease her guilt by increasing the liquid intake at these luncheons. The alcohol tended to diminish the gloom, but she became mentally sluggish and her athletics suffered as well. Had Roberta any other recourse? Who could she turn to? She wouldn't talk to her mother—she was too angry with her. She couldn't talk to her father—she was too proud for that. And she couldn't talk to her husband—Stephen turned to *her* for help. Hence, Roberta was left talking to the bottle.

Fifty years later, Roberta did get some sort of help. Gerald, the maintenance man, hung up the phone and elbow-supported Roberta on her way back to the rocker. As she walked, the bones creaked and the joints ached. Roberta wondered if her brittle bones and rheumatism was another feminine curse. Having now reached the chair, she was soon back in motion. The pendulous movements were conducive to another escape. She merely had to close her eyes . . .

Roberta's strong will prevailed and she was able to overcome her alcohol addiction. She was less successful in her bid to get Stephen to become athletic and lose weight. She forced him to try vigorous exercises, various diets, and psychiatric consultations. Roberta even withheld sex as a weapon in the war against his excessive poundage, but nothing worked. After a frustrating period, she just gave up and concentrated her activities on the dress manufacturing business.

Stephen also gave up on his physical problems but the consequences were costly. He became depressed over his weight, his aging ("middle-age blues"), recurrent fatigue and lack of will power. He started complaining of "nervous tension" and pains throughout his body (especially in his lower back). Stephen had problems of endurance which were getting progressively worse. He even had difficulties in concentration so that he could often only work for half a day. His digestion suffered primarily because of excessive eating and insufficient exercise. Although a "doctor" himself, Stephen lacked common sense; he rationalized that his overweight resulted from a naturally sluggish metabolism. He spent much of his time lying down. At times, fear "paralyzed" his stomach. Stephen had a feeling of intense pressure squeezing his gut. He thought it was gas building up without any outlet, but usually the gas escaped; and when it escaped, it was often from opposite ends with an explosive release. The embarrassment was bad enough, but it also interfered with his professional practice and the little lovemaking that had remained with Roberta.

One April afternoon, Roberta was discussing a new account with a sales associate, Bruce Dernier. He was about Roberta's age, married and the father of three young children. Bruce was a handsome man, reasonably intelligent, and could occasionally talk informatively about nonbusiness matters. Roberta and Bruce had had business meetings on many occasions during the last three years. This day she was feeling somewhat depressed (thinking about Lisa and Stephen). She and Bruce were having lunch in a French restaurant on Manhattan's West Side. It was a beautiful Spring day, and the conversation and wine added to the romantic setting.

Ten years before, it wouldn't have occurred to Roberta to have an affair, but now the idea was inviting. The feeling was reciprocal. Bruce found Roberta to be attractive, attentive and animated. In these last few years, Roberta had become skilled in the art of "turning on" a man. This affair proved to be a providential escape for Roberta—at least for a while.

After the first interlude, Roberta was so overwhelmed by guilt that she consulted a psychiatrist. She was relieved to find that she could say what was on her mind without value judgements being expressed by the psychiatrist—she felt ashamed and guilty enough already. Roberta admitted to a need to feel like a woman, as she had not had extramarital sexual relations merely to punish her husband. The circumstances of her life at that point were such that she felt she had no choice. The frustrations had increased to the point that she simply needed to be touched, held and talked to by another warm human being.

While Roberta felt she had used Bruce for her own purposes, Bruce also had been "using" her. That is probably why the two of them had gotten along so well (after a dismal start). The morning after the first occasion, Roberta awakened to find a "person" next to her in a hotel bed and she panicked. She couldn't wait to get him out of there. When he finally left, amid protestations of "love," she literally tore up her undergarments and dumped them in the wastebasket. Even though she ordinarily preferred baths, Roberta immediately jumped under the shower. She just couldn't stand to have "contaminated" bath water circulating about her. Although she repeatedly washed her hair and body, she felt that if she could only peel off her skin then perhaps she could restore herself.

Although Bruce had called her shortly thereafter and pleaded that it was not a "one-night stand," Roberta couldn't immediately face him. She also swore that if he so much as hinted to her husband of their liaison, she would deny it all and, moreover, see to it that he lost his job at "Faber." Nevertheless, after a period of time and self-examination at the psychiatrist's office, she finally accepted her needs and renewed their relationship.

Fortunately for Bruce, the relationship had been of advantage. Actually, he had been worried over his recent impotence. Perhaps it was lack of desire, but he felt that the inability to hold an erection was destroying him. In fact, he had considered suicide as an alternative. The anxiety resulted in a diarrhea which led to drug treatments by various medical specialists who evidently had not realized that they were dealing with a "neurosis." One beneficial result of Bruce's affair with Roberta was the spontaneous disappearance of the impotence and the diarrhea. He also kept his job; not a word was spoken to Stephen.

Dr. Stephen Blatterfein's fondness for food and abhorrence of exercise finally proved fatal. Two months after Roberta's first illicit escapade, she returned home at six o'clock to greet her husband. The greeting never took place. That morning, in his sleep, Stephen had succumbed from a massive heart attack. Since Roberta had to go to New York, she left as usual before Stephen had awakened. She hadn't thought it odd that phlegmatic Stephen failed to respond to her early morning "peck" before she left and he always felt relatively cold. But he must have been dead for at least an hour. So at the age of thirty-two, Roberta found herself a widow . . . a widow riddled with guilt over her daughter, her husband and her affair.

Getting no consolation from her mother Evelyn, Roberta sought out her father. Roberta "poured out" her heart to him and, as she cried, out came the guilt, the frustrations, the anxiety and the anger. The revelations were too much for Robert and rendered him immobile. Unfortunately, the "mobility" never returned. Robert's heart "froze," the result of a massive outpouring of adrenaline.

Jolted back to the present by a sharp, sudden stab of deep chest pain, Roberta reacted quickly to her "aching" heart. She took a small white pill and placed it under her tongue. The pill was nitroglycerine; the condition was angina. Roberta was apparently protected against heart disease for many years because of her female sex and athletic pursuits. Now Roberta was succumbing to the cumulative excesses of alcohol, drugs, fatty foods, stress and the inevitability of old age. Physically and emotionally, her heart had gone "bad". . .

When Stephen and Robert died, Roberta went into a state of shock. For the first time in her life, she lost control. For a short period, the three women—Evelyn, Lisa and Roberta—tried consoling one another. As some compensation for the double deaths, the life insurance payouts left Roberta and Evelyn financially secure. When the exchanged consolations did not prove effective, Roberta looked outwardly for help. Psychotherapy aided for a while. Roberta tried to improve her relationships with both her mother and daughter. But the years of mutual resentment between Evelyn and Roberta proved insurmountable. Roberta tried harder with Lisa. Whenever possible, she was home when Lisa returned from school. It wasn't enough. Lisa—left without a father or grandfather, with a working mother and an unloving grandmother—was readily influenced by her peers. She soon turned to smoking, drinking, and indulging freely in "sex."

Roberta would have been a "natural" for the yet unborn women's movement. Her early development as an independent woman made her ready and eager to get involved with women's rights. But first she had to restore order at home.

Lisa was informed in no uncertain terms that she would be provided for, but only if she "straightened out." Evelyn sold her house and moved in with Roberta and Lisa. A "big, brave and bold" sleep-in maid was hired. The truce seemed to work. Lisa improved her grades and "cooled" her social improprieties. Evelyn took up crocheting and sewing, and gossiped with her cronies. Roberta was promoted to second vice president in the organization, marched with the women, and retained her sanity.

Roberta remembered once reading about senility and its association to aging. Now as she was approaching eighty years of age, she knew it was happening to her. It wasn't too difficult recalling incidents from the deep past but what happened five minutes ago was another story. Not that anything important happened five minutes or even five days ago, but it disturbed her that her once infallible memory was slipping. The anxiety over the memory loss was far greater than the true loss. She was now having these mental blocks added to her other infirmities. One consolation, Roberta rationalized, it couldn't last forever. . .

With some semblance of family order restored, Roberta decided she was not going to remain in the business world forever. Her interest in women's rights kindled a political flame. While still maintaining her business connection, Roberta entered politics by obtaining a position on the local town council. Achieving some success in that effort, she also successfully became Deputy Mayor. By now, Roberta had been bitten by the political "bug." Since she had sound financial resources, Roberta invested heavily in the next political campaign and emerged a winner—she was elected Mayor of White Plains! Having achieved her first major political goal, Roberta kissed the business world goodbye. She now became involved with the stress-producing intrigues of the world of politics. It was no picnic. Roberta feuded with the (male) fire inspector, argued with the (male) police chief, admonished the (male) sanitation head, fired the (male) water commissioner and was blessed with the "male" executive psychosomatic ailment, peptic ulcers. She didn't fare much better with the only female head, the education commissioner. Roberta used her partly for consultations and consolation with respect to the male-related problems, but the education commissioner was not left unscathed. Roberta "attacked" her for the deficiencies of the school system.

Meanwhile, back at home, another "shocker" developed. Lisa decided that the time of tranquility was over. Thus, at the tender age of seventeen she eloped with a salesman. Although Roberta had an Orthodox Jewish background, she only gave "lip service" to her religion. When she found out that Lisa had eloped, that was bad enough, but when informed that her husband was not Jewish—that was a disaster. From that time on Roberta "found" religion and Lisa was treated as an outcast . . . at least for a while.

"Religious" Roberta was waiting to meet her maker. She now believed in a personal God who would take her by the hand and deliver her from her miseries. In her earthly life, Roberta had very little true love. Maybe in death, she would find some heavenly love. At least she would have peace, or so Roberta believed . . .

Nancy was born to Lisa and Roberta became a grandmother. Of all the females in this matriarchal line, the only semblance of affection that developed took place between Roberta and Nancy. It also brought back peace to the household. Roberta finally realized that she could do nothing about Lisa's out-of-the-faith marriage to Jim. Jim was a lot like Roberta's father. He was an ambitious businessman and a fine athlete. Jim wanted a son and he, too, got a daughter. Roberta did her best to circumvent a continuance of the vicious cycle. She interceded by accepting Jim, forgiving

Lisa and adoring baby Nancy. It almost worked. For years she showered gifts and affection on Nancy and a strong mutual attraction resulted. But petty jealousies were aroused and soon the typical mother-in-law/son-in-law conflicts took place. Nancy, with her unconscious "Electra" feelings surfacing, was torn between her "daddy" and her "nanna." Roberta lost again and the relationship "cooled."

Throughout all these years, Roberta had been relatively healthy. When menopause arrived, Roberta's body responded with an almost complete collapse. She developed arthritis, osteoporosis, high blood pressure and angina, and the peptic ulcers perforated. So in the twilight of her years, Roberta was introduced to modern medicine. As a result, she became a "pill-popper." Roberta also had "pyorrhea" that had been developing undetected in her jaws for years and her vision began to fail. By now her political career was on the wane. She lost in a bid for the governorship and her money supply was "drying up." In addition to the huge sums she used for the political campaigns, Roberta had unwisely invested in land, oil wells and speculative stocks. (Contrary to her usual investments in the past where she had been conservative and paid attention to "business.") At the age of sixty-six, Roberta again faced the world. This time it was with bifocals, dental plates and a few hundred dollars.

With the assistance of social security, a pension from the Faber Dress Manufacturing Company and some support from her daughter, Roberta was able to maintain an apartment for five years. She tried her hand at senior citizen activities but found few rewards. Roberta's physical health deteriorated even more and now her mental capacities began to decline. Finally, she was unable to fend for herself and Lisa had her taken to The Newcastle Home for Senior Citizens.

Roberta Gardiner Blattenfein was dying. Her father's last "gift" to her was a genetic predisposition towards a "coronary." At the age of eighty-two, Roberta had a severe heart attack. It was delayed in coming but, as was the case with her father, the first attack was the last. (At least she was saved from a lingering death.)

Lisa and Nancy were at her deathbed. Lisa said, "She was such a wonderful mother." Nancy said, "She was such a wonderful grandmother." But Roberta died of a "broken" heart.

PART II
STRESS: CAUSES
AND CONSEQUENCES

We all know about stress, or do we? In Chapter 2, the focus is on the nature of stress. The discussion includes stressors, the individual makeup, and the stress response with emphasis on women. Chapter 3 delves into the bodily ills that result from stress and how they affect women. Diseases considered include: heart attacks; cancer; depression; headaches; ulcers, asthma; rheumatoid arthritis; and ulcerative colitis. In Chapter 4, stress-related disorders of interest to females are covered. Disorders considered include: alcoholism; smoking; drug addiction; obesity; anorexia nervosa; divorce; and suicide.

2
Stress: What Is It?
How Does It Occur?

There are three aspects to the stress concept. The first is the causative factors known as *stressors*. The second relates to how these factors are perceived, and is known as the *individual makeup*. The third is the physiological and psychological changes and is known as the *stress response*. In Box 2.1, a dramatized version of a true incident serves to highlight these three aspects of the stress concept.

STRESSORS

There are three types of stressors: physical, psychological and social.[1] Physical stressors are external factors such as drugs, pollutants, bacteria, radiation, trauma, noise and exercise. Joanna had been exposed to the physical stressor (i.e., the noise in her office) but she had adapted well to it. However, the quiet sound of footsteps was a more imposing physical stressor (i.e., because it was involved with a psychological stressor: anxiety).

Psychological stressors are intense emotions and include: anxiety; fear; frustration; guilt; worry; anger; hate; jealousy; sadness; self-pity; and inferiority feelings. People often become accustomed to physical stressors such as was the case with Joanna and the office noise, but psychological stressors are usually more damaging because of their chronic nature.

Psychological stressors can either be self-induced, brought on by physical stressors, or intensified by physical stressors. When Joanna had been working for a while and realized that it was late, quiet and dark, she began to worry and became frightened. Nothing had changed in the external environment but her perceptions had altered. Later when Joanna heard definite new sounds such as the footsteps, that physical stressor intensified

Box 2.1. Stress After Hours.

Joanna was working late. Everyone had gone for the evening except Frank, the night watchman. He had peeked in a few minutes earlier, saw Joanna at her desk, gave a quick nod, and left. Joanna rarely worked late, but the Emerson account had a tight deadline and it had to be met by morning. So she stayed.

Now there was silence, utter stillness and suddenly Joanna became frightened. She had been conditioned to the noises of the office—the typewriters, the copying machines, the office chatter—but the present quiet and emptiness, that was fearsome. Joanna was a mature business-woman but was now reduced to acting like a fearful child: afraid of the silence, apprehensive about the dark, and frightened of the unknown. Psychologically, she was seeking safety—the security of her mother's bosom or the comfort of her husband's arms. But her mother and husband were elsewhere, and the silence became unbearable.

Joanna had been working at her desk with the only illumination coming from a small fluorescent lamp. To help counteract her fear, she flipped on all the room light switches. The sound of silence was transformed by the fluorescent and incandescent lamps into a buzzing hum. It was a warm summer day and the air conditioning system had been on continuously throughout the day. Now, amazingly, the heretofore almost silent purr of the blowers became a deafening roar. The walls and ceilings also got "into the act" and began to crackle. Then a loud pounding began. Joanna looked outwardly but the sound came from within; it was her heart and it thumped and thumped. . .

There was another "thump"; it was coming from the stairs—and it sounded like a man's footsteps! Joanna knew the sound of watchman Frank's steps; it definitely was *not* Frank. No one should be in the building, she thought. "I must be quiet," Joanna told herself but her body wouldn't cooperate. She was afraid: her breaths were coming in gasps, she was sweating profusely, and she felt light-headed and dizzy.

Joanna's father had trained her well; she was a top-notch, well-conditioned athlete. So instead of fainting, Joanna removed her shoes, crawled to a hall closet and grabbed a metal rod resting there. The door opened, Joanna swung mightily, the figure toppled, and *then* Joanna fainted. The next day's evening edition of the *New York Gazette** had a small item buried on page 13. The headline read: "Woman Business Executive Clobbers Robber."

* Name changed for anonymity.

the psychological stressor, anxiety, and she easily might have panicked. Fortunately, because of her mental conditioning and physical training, Joanna reacted rapidly and positively.

The third kind of stressors are social stressors. They are externally induced and result from the interaction of a person with the environment. The most severe social stressor is the death of a loved one. (Remember from Chapter I how Roberta lost her husband and father in quick succession?) Another major social stressor is forced retirement. (Remember when Roberta was forced into a nursing home, that was her death knell?) These unforeseen stressors are difficult to prepare for and even more difficult to cope with.

There are many physical stressors but noise is one that mothers are faced with throughout the growing years of the children. It begins with the newborn's first scream at delivery. Crying is the infants' primary attention-seeking method. Whether the mother nurses the child or uses the bottle, nighttime interruptions by the crying child routinely awaken her from a sound sleep. This kind of interruption is akin to the jolt of an alarm clock. Husbands do not ordinarily get up to heed the screaming infant. They may use the excuse of being the breadwinner who requires uninterrupted sleep in order to hold the job. In some households, the husband may move to a separate bedroom to insure his peace and quiet.

Times are changing though, and some wives insist that the husbands alternate with them in answering the call of the crying child.

Jumping ahead a few years, during weekdays from about 3:00 P.M. on, in most households the housewife/mother is faced with a triple array of noise stressors. First, there is the telephone. This is primarily a factor in the home with teen-age girls since they tend to spend hours on the telephone. The second and third noise stressors are the sounds of the television and stereo. Teen-agers may spend a daily total of thirty minutes in eating, forty-five minutes in homework and five hours in TV watching and listening to "rock" and "disco."

Working women are often faced with another noise stressor: the pounding of the typewriter keys. Although women are now entering "male" occupations, many women still have secretarial positions and typing is often a "key" requirement. The sounds of the typewriter are definitely not conducive to relaxation.

Psychological stressors are not in the specific province of either sex, but there are certain kinds to which women appear to be more susceptible. One specific example is anxiety.[2-4]* Fear is brought on by realistic expectations of pain, danger, or disaster. Anxiety, in contrast, is an irrational fear and

* An excellent book on this subject is DeRosis, Helen. *Women and Anxiety,* New York: Delacorte Press, 1979.

may be brought on by some external event. (Remember Joanna's reaction to the silence and darkness?)

There are two types of anxiety.[5] The first is *generalized trait anxiety* in which an individual experiences anxiety as a personality characteristic or as a stable aspect of her* life. Some women who are treated as "second-class citizens" both at home and in the working world develop this kind of anxiety. It is related to the many obstacles placed in the path to their success. Many women are ill at ease in competitive situations and they become anxious whenever they are forced to make decisions. There is some evidence to show that women are more susceptible than men to anxiety and tend to react to it by passive-avoidance behavior.**[6,7] Men, on the other hand, are more apt to respond to anxiety in a more aggressive manner which may be based on the Y (male) chromosome and the male hormone testosterone.*** (See Figure 2.1)

The second kind of anxiety is *transitional situational anxiety*. In this type, an individual who is normally in control becomes anxious because of a specific event or set of circumstances. (Do you recall that in the day-to-day business world, Joanna was in control? The nighttime situation with its accompanying silence and darkness was the trigger that temporarily regressed Joanna back to the dependency role of a child and she became quite anxious.)

The women's movement may have created transitional anxiety for some women. Suddenly asserting their independence may temporarily cause women anxious moments. Of course, there are many men, too, who cannot handle independent decisions. Yet, it had always been considered "normal" for women to become unsettled and cry when faced with potentially stressful decisions, though not "normal" for men.

Crying, as is discussed later in the book, is actually a beneficial stress release mechanism. In our society, men aren't supposed to cry. Rather than show apprehension and shed tears, they often hold in their feelings. If that were to become a patterned response, it could lead to either hypertension (i.e., high blood pressure) or peptic ulcers. Other men hide their fear by becoming angry or aggressive but this is generally only an illusion of strength. The end result is distress and eventual disease. Hence, although it

---

* In this book, to stress the relevancy to women, when speaking generally, the female pronouns *she* and *her* are used rather than the common male pronouns *he*, *his* and *him*.

** Although women report themselves as being more anxious than men, it may be that they are just more willing than men to admit to their feelings. Maccoby, E. E. and Jacklin, C. *The Psychology of Sex Differences.* Stanford, Calif.: Stanford University Press, 1974.

*** A good review and current study on testosterone and aggression is found in: Oliveus, D., Mattsson, Å., Schalling, D., and Löw, H. Testosterone, aggression, physical and personality dimensions in normal adolescent males. *Psychosom. Med.* 42:253–259, 1980. A recent corroborative study on hormones and male aggression is: Reinisch, J. M. Prenatal exposure to synthetic progestins increases potential for aggression in humans. *Science* 211:1171–1173, 1981.

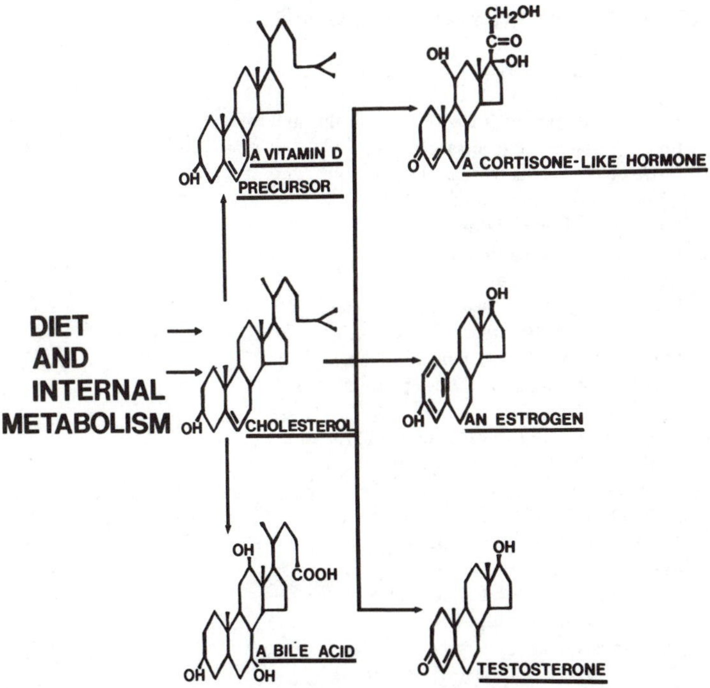

Fig. 2.1 Cholesterol and its derivatives. Eating animal fats such as are found in milk, beef and eggs is a dietary means of getting cholesterol into the blood stream. Cholesterol is also produced during internal metabolism from acetates. (See Chapter 3 for types of cholesterol.) Cholesterol may contribute to coronary heart disease but it is also a precursor of important body substances. For example, the bile acids are needed for fat absorption, enzyme action and intestinal movement. Vitamin D is needed for bone metabolism. Cortisone is one of the major stress hormones. Aldosterone (not shown) is related to cortisone and is involved in water and salt metabolism. Estrogen is the major female sex hormone. Progesterone (not shown) is related to estrogen and is another major female sex hormone. (See Fig. 6.1.) Testosterone is the principal male sex hormone.

is considered "effeminate" to cry, the crying response is preferable to the "bottled up" or angry feelings to which men are prone.[3] To help assess your personal anxieties, see Table 2.1 and rate your own anxiety level.

There are all types of *phobias* (abnormal, illogical, and exaggerated fears). Common ones are acrophobia (fear of heights), claustrophobia (fear of confinement) and nyctophobia (fear of the dark). Agoraphobia, nominally a fear of open places (from the Greek *agora*—the open marketplace) is actually a fear of leaving the home. The agoraphobic syndrome is estimated to affect two in every thousand Americans and occurs about twice as often in women as in men.[9] The importance of this syn-

TABLE 2.1. Count Your Anxieties: The Fewer The Better.

___ I'm a constant worrier.
___ My "nerves" often get to me.
___ Troublesome thoughts frequently run through my mind.
___ I have problems concentrating.
___ I often picture frightening scenes.
___ I don't think too much of myself.
___ I have a hard time making a decision.
___ I find it difficult to stick to a job.
___ I'm usually not happy.
___ I frequently hear my heart pound.
___ I get recurrent chest pains (but my heart is fine).
___ My stomach frequently tenses up.
___ I often get nauseous without apparent cause.
___ The same is true for diarrhea.
___ I frequently have trouble catching my breath.
___ At times, I feel as if I were smothered.
___ I sigh a lot.
___ I often feel dizzy without knowing why.
___ The same is true for fainting.
___ I get a lot of headaches.
___ I perspire even when it is not hot outside.
___ I blush over minor things.
___ Little things make me cry.
___ Often I "freeze up" instead of reacting.
___ I have a tendency to fidget.
___ I frequently feel jittery all over.
___ I often pace around.
___ I get tired very easily.
___ I have trouble getting to sleep and staying asleep.
___ My appetite is not good.
___ I frequently stutter or have problems in talking to people.
___ I get chills when it is not cold outside.
___ TOTAL: To help decrease the number, see Chapters 20–23.

drome cannot be underestimated since it literally prevents some women from leaving their homes and stops them from going to school or work.

Another psychological stressor that may have been induced as the result of the women's movement is *frustration*. Frustration results when a person is blocked from achieving a goal and feels annoyed, confused or angry. The closer the individual is to reaching the goal when the blockage occurs, the greater is the resultant frustration.

It has been stated that married women find their position in society to be more frustrating and less rewarding than that of married men.[4] A man typically has two possible sources of gratification, his family and his work. Women usually have only one, the family. Even when a married woman works, she often has a less satisfactory job and generally has to take care of the housework. Aside from the marriage situation, women have frustration of an even more intense nature when they have to choose between two important goals. The choosing of either alternative results in frustration in regard to the other.[10] Two goals that women often have to choose between are personal desires and satisfying others. A diagrammatic representation of five ways to react in choosing either of these two goals is shown in Figure 2.2. Let us consider these five alternatives.

1. If a woman chooses self-satisfaction and ignores other people (egotistical behavior) she may achieve some goals but she inspires resentment from others. This behavior is more frequent with goal-oriented males, but as women "climb the business ladder" they may choose this frustrating mode of behavior.

2. If a woman chooses helping others and ignores her own goals (altruistic behavior), she is frustrated because of a lack of personal achievement. Even the rewards gained from helping others are few and infrequent. Many women previously followed this alternative, what with sacrificing for their husband's career, their children's schooling, and the family's health (usually to the detriment of their own).

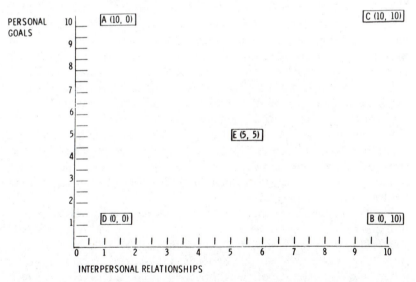

Fig. 2.2 The paths to frustration. (Adapted from a presentation by Rodney Napier at the Philadelphia Society of Periodontists in Philadelphia, 1977.) A(10.0) = the "egoist;" B(0,10) = the "altruist;" C(10,10) = the "wheeler-dealer;" D(0,0) = the "hermit;" E(5,5) = the "compromiser." (From Morse, D.R. and Furst, M.L. *Stress for Success: A Holistic Approach to Stress and its Management.* New York: Van Nostrand Reinhold Co., 1979. Reprinted with permission.)

3. Some people believe that they can be all things to all people including themselves. They become frustrated because they cannot maximally please both themselves and others. Men who attempt this are known as "wheeler-dealers." Women don't often behave in this manner.

4. Some women simply give up. They bury their heads in the ground (the "ostrich") and forget about pleasing themselves or others. But they are maximally frustrated because they please no one, not even themselves.

5. Many women traditionally have followed this fifth mode of behavior —the compromise. This is also frustrating since some worthwhile self goals are sacrificed and some important people may not be pleased.

To resolve the dilemma about self-satisfaction and pleasing others, women should be selective. If the personal goals are important, women should work towards them but others should always be considered. If the goals are less important, it may be more prudent to first consider others.

Remember when Roberta (see Chapter 1) had to choose between being a "good" mother and pursuing a business career? This common problem of many of today's working women is considered in Chapter 14.

Other psychological stressors that women have been prone to are *shame* and *inferiority feelings*. It has been observed that women's former position of economic and social inferiority provided an objective basis for their feelings of inferiority and shame.[3] The housewife/mother position had been considered subservient to the male role of economic provider. Also, women were taught at an early age not to expose themselves in public for fear of embarrassment. The evolutionist Charles Darwin was aware of this when he said, "Women blush much more than men."[11] However, this is all changing and the concept of "letting it all hang loose" may make shame a thing of the past (at least for some women).

Women have also been taught early in life not to express *anger*. As a result, anger and related emotions are often suppressed. This may lead to stress-related disturbances as adults. Although there may be problems with shouting and screaming, it is usually more beneficial to vent anger than to hold it in. (See Chapter 21.)

Severe social stressors that are especially traumatic to women are death of a spouse and divorce. There are more widows than widowers. One of the principal reasons is the greater susceptibility of the male to sudden death from heart attacks. When this happens, the married woman is suddenly thrust into widowhood, often without any preparation. This severe life-change event[12] can precipitate mental and physical problems. ("When Stephen and Robert died, Roberta went into a state of shock. For the first time in her life, she lost control.")

Divorce negatively affects both women and men, but often women are more traumatized by the event.[13] First, it usually comes as a shock to the woman; hence, it acts as a more severe social stressor. Second, since the man is generally involved with business and legal matters, he is in a better position to deal with the business aspects of the divorce (which is actually the termination of a legal contract). Third, since the man is usually the breadwinner, even though he generally has to pay alimony, he is more accustomed to managing money. The traditional woman is often unsure of financial management and the monetary requirements of the family. For example, she may be at a loss on how to establish credit. At that stressful time, legal advice often is bewildering and confusing. Fourth, since one of the main reasons for divorce is male infidelity (although the cycle is changing), the man has already been in the position of seeking love and counsel from "the other woman." The newly divorced woman is suddenly thrust into single status. She now has to contend with managing the family's financial affairs, raising the children, and still find the time and desire to compete with single women and widows for "eligible males." Considering all this, divorce is generally a more severe social stressor for women. (See Chapters 4 and 7)

THE INDIVIDUAL MAKEUP

Individuals vary greatly in how they react to the same stressors. For instance, tuberculosis is caused by the tubercle bacillus (an infectious bacterium); an example of a physical stressor. (See Chapter 3) An illustration: If six women walked into a room saturated with tubercle bacilli, possibly two of them would develop tuberculosis, another two might show no clinical signs of the disease (i.e., they would be carriers), and the remaining two could remain completely unscathed (i.e., they would be immune). In short, six women are facing the same severe physical stressor and yet there are three divergent reactions. Still, even those who didn't come down with the actual disease would probably show signs of stress because of the anxiety induced by the fear of contacting that dread disease. (Even here, there are variable reactions.) The reason for the apparent biological variability lies in the differences of the makeup of the several women. In analyzing individual makeup we must consider personalities, traits and attitudes, genetic factors and environmental conditions.

Personality

Personality is a group of specific behavioral patterns which reflects thoughts, attitudes, and emotions as an individual adapts to various life situations. However, doubt exists over whether there is such a stable concept as a personality.[14] Also, many aspects of personality, especially as they relate to women, may be culturally influenced. Nevertheless, let us consider some personality "types" that may be prevalent in women.

Introverts and extraverts were first classified as such by Carl Jung, one of Freud's disciples.[15] Extraverts are the "blow-hards" and their stress-release mechanism of "blowing off steam" tends to be temporarily beneficial—if not to others, at least to themselves. Introverts are individuals who withdraw internally and "seethe." This negative stress-release method may be more common with unliberated women.

The obsessive-compulsive individual is the perfectionist type who pays strict attention to minor details. Any change from the accustomed routine is distressful. Although there is some evidence that men have more obsessions and compulsions than women,[1] many housewives are compulsive about the cleanliness and orderliness of their homes. On the other hand, the "aggressive" or "explosive" personality is usually a male who tends to lose control when faced with minor stressors.[1]

Another personality type well-represented among "repressed" women is the "passive-dependent."[14] Such a woman is sad, shy, submissive, afraid to offend, rarely expresses independent judgement, and holds in her emotions. In contrast, the "sociopathic" or "antisocial" personality is well-represented among aggressive males.[1] They easily become frustrated and may harm other people as a stress-release mechanism. (Unfortunately, women are often on the receiving end of this hostile activity.)

Up to the present, the "noncompetitive" personality had been usual in female circles.[14] This woman constantly avoids competition or any other potentially stressful encounter. When forced to compete, she often manages poorly. Contrast this with the "narcissistic" personality. This individual is frequently a man (e.g., the perpetual "spoiled brat"). He expects others (particularly women) to subordinate their desires to his pleasures so that he would always be considered first. The "narcissistic" female is the "prima donna." She, too, expects others to cater to her whims and is ineffective in stressful situations.

The "hysterical" personality historically was considered to be a woman (Freud, and his teacher Joseph Breuer, attributed this phenomenon to the female) and hysteria is diagnosed mainly in women.[1]* The hysterical person tends to seek out physical stressors that cause suffering and pain. She may have an unconscious need to be hurt (masochism).

There are certain disease-profile personalities. Such people are prone to develop specific stress-related diseases. The most well-known disease-profile personality is the "Type A personality."[16] The type A is often a male who is a competitive achiever with feelings of time urgency, hostility, and aggressiveness. He tends to suppress fatigue and tries to control his en-

---

* Hysteria has a latin derivation and means womb.

vironment. As a result, he is prone to developing high blood pressure and coronary heart disease.

The opposite type is the "Type B personality." This individual is described as passive, restrained, not ambitious or aggressive, and resistant to hypertension and heart disease. Women are well represented in this category. However, with the advent of women's liberation and the emergence of women into the competitive business world, type A's are beginning to be found more frequently among women.[17] (One might say that Roberta tended toward the type A personality.)

There are many kinds of cancer and many possible causes; yet there appears to be a "cancer personality."[18] Such individuals are considered to be low-geared; with few outbursts of emotion and retaining feelings of isolation from their parents that began in childhood. These people are also described as being depressed before the onset of the cancer. Here too, women are well-represented especially with respect to breast and genital tract cancers.

Another related personality type is the "depression-prone personality."[19] These individuals are described as being outwardly happy, conscientious, and hardworking, but inwardly they are tormented. As is discussed in the next chapter, depression is becoming established as a major female disorder. The relationship between depression and cancer may be one of the reasons for the large increase in female cancers. This was known ages ago; the second-century physician Galen was reported to have said that women with *melancholic* dispositions (i.e., depressed) were more inclined to develop breast cancer than women with a *sanguine* temperament (i.e., happy outlook).[20]

Another well-known disease personality is the "ulcer personality."[21] This individual is often male, with these characteristics: continually leans on others; desires to be fed; seeks close body contact with others; represses anger; and tends to be prim, tidy, mild-mannered, conscientious, inhibited, and punctual. With many women now entering the stressful "male" occupations, the female incidence of heart attacks and ulcers appears to be on the increase.[22,23] (It may be recalled that Roberta was rewarded with ulcers and a final fatal coronary.)

A stress-related disease personality associated with women is the "rheumatoid arthritis personality."[24] These women are described as being unhappy in the traditional female sex role. They are considered to be perfectionists who are self-sacrificing, punctual, tidy, and orderly; and they are easily frustrated. However, a recent study failed to support this hypothesis.[25] (Roberta was turned away from the traditional female sex role as the result of her father's early "push." She, too, succumbed to rheumatoid arthritis: "As she walked, the bones creaked and the joints ached. Roberta wondered if her brittle bones and rheumatism was another female curse.'')

Another stress-related disease often observed in women is the "ulcerative colitis personality."[26] These women are described as having problems both at home and at work. They are considered to be mild, prim and proper, well-mannered, restrained, conscientious and dependent upon others (which are often men).

A final "disease" personality frequently found in females is the "migraine headache personality."[27] According to some studies, such a woman is hypersensitive to stressful situations. She is identified as someone who has obsessional-perfectionist traits, repressed hostility, and a great deal of "bottled-up" resentment. Other studies have shown that such women who experience migraine frequently suffer from anxiety and depression.[28]

Traits and Attitudes

Some investigators note that personality is not a constant, and yet certain characteristics may be relatively fixed. These characteristics are referred to as traits and attitudes. Others consider that traits and attitudes tend to be patterned with some people, but they may be modified. At any rate, studies have shown that specific traits and attitudes can be associated with the development of specific stress-related diseases. In general terms, positive attitudes allow people to cope better with stressors (e.g., see the "sunny side of life"; think positively; have the "will to live"; see Chapter 20). In contradistinction, negative attitudes can lead to distress and disease.

Let us now look at the findings of some studies on attitudes and resultant diseases, with emphasis on women.[29-31]

A woman who feels "nagged at" tends to develop acne; she who feels neglected may come down with asthma; a perpetually frustrated female is prone to develop eczema (a skin rash); she who feels mistreated may wind up with hives; a woman who needs constant physical proximity of others but fails to receive it can get neurodermatitis (another skin disease). The woman who feels she is being restrained, develops rheumatoid arthritis; and she who wants to escape is prone to backaches. Although these associations were uncovered by competent investigators, these are tendencies and many other factors are important in the development of stress-related diseases.

Genetic Factors

While the previously discussed personalities, traits, and attitudes have a genetic basis, they are primarily environmentally controlled. Still, other aspects of the individual makeup are basically genetic. These are now considered.

Age. During normal development, certain age periods are more stressful than others. (See Chapters 5-9) Let us now consider a few examples.

In Roberta's case, her early years in a family which had planned for a boy were stressful. Nevertheless, the ages from five to ten are often less stressful than the teen-age years. During the latter years, the young girl is faced with a host of physical and environmental changes (e.g., developing breasts; onset of menstruation).

In adult development various stressful encounters take place.[32,33] Some particularly stressful periods for women are: (1) when daughters leave home; (2) the struggling years of marriage; and (3) the mid-life crisis. Older individuals have a diminished resistance to physical stressors such as infection and trauma.[34] (Roberta knew that the sign's state was a reflection of her own condition. She, too, was run-down and weatherbeaten . . .")

Sex. The XX chromosomes (i.e., those that genetically determine the female sex), estrogen (see Figure 2.1) and the noncompetitive, stay-at-home, family-raising life-style of some females, have combined to make women generally more resistant than men to many stressors. For example, recent studies show that estrogen helps protect women against heart attacks[6,35-39] and infectious diseases.[40] (See Chapter 3)

Women may also manage other stressors better than men. Recent studies have shown that during the reproductive years, when faced with challenging psychological and social stressors, females produce less stress hormones (discussed shortly) than do males.[41,42] This may make women less susceptible to stress-related diseases such as hypertension, heart attacks, and ulcers. (See Chapter 3)

Yet it is not "a bed of roses" for women. Other recent findings reveal that many women as compared to men have exaggerated emotional responses to social stressors such as loss of a job, moving, marriage, and divorce.[43] It has been hypothesized that these responses are partly related to certain differences in male and female brains. Although studies on sex differences in human brains are controversial, some of the recent findings are of interest.*[44,45]

* Almost all of the studies comparing female and male brains have been done on rats; and the differences reported were in nervous tissue, primarily in areas of the hypothalamus. The only relationship found with behavior was with respect to sexual activity; e.g., "lordosis" (passive sexual position) associated with "female" brains, and "mounting" behavior associated with "male" brains. Goy, R. W. and McEwen, B. S. *Sexual Differentiation of the Brain: Based on a Work Session of the Neurosciences Research Program.* Cambridge, Mass.: MIT Press, 1980; Maclusky, N. J and Naftolin, F. Sexual differentiation of the Central Ner-

Biochemical differences between female and male brains that affect perception are used to explain women's greater emotional responses. Using electroencephalographs (i.e., EEG; measures brain waves) and computers to analyze the brain's electrical response to stimuli (known as "evoked potentials"), researchers have found that the response was greater for women as compared to men for all three of the senses examined. Vision was tested by flashing lights; sound by repeated tones; and tactility by an electric shock on the forearm.[43]

However, these responses do not prove that women react more emotionally or even that emotional reactions are necessarily "bad." In fact, recent evidence shows that crying is a favorable coping method.[46] On the other hand, with women entering "male" occupations there may be an increase in the female incidence of stress-related diseases such as heart attacks and ulcers.[22,23,47] (See Chapter 3) In addition, around menstruation time, many women react poorly to stressors.[48] (See Chapter 6)

Environmental Conditions

There are several environmental agents that affect the individual's makeup. These factors help determine one's ability to respond to stressors. They include: fatigue; diseases; diet; drugs; occupation; location; family and social structure; fitness (physical and mental); emotional stability; and the ability to relax. Let us now consider these as they relate to women.

Diet. People who are undernourished are prone to vitamin deficiency diseases. For example, undernourishment is associated with the disease, anorexia nervosa.[49] (See Chapter 4) This condition occurs mainly in teen-age girls. These young women are extremely susceptible to stress-related disease, and have poor resistance to infection and other stressors. (See Box 2.2)

Drugs. Many female teen-agers are addicted to colas, cigarettes, candy, alcohol, and drugs. Various drugs, and particularly alcohol, interfere with the body's immune mechanism. This can result in a poor response to bacterial stressors which leads to serious disease. Regular cigarette smoking may result in dangerous diseases such as lung cancer and heart disease. One other effect of cigarette smoking is to deplete the body's content of vitamin C.[50] This can also affect the host response to infection and delays healing. Within the last few years, cigarette consumption has made the most rapid gains among teen-age girls.[51]

---

vous System. *Science* 211:1294–1303, 1981. A more simplified explanation of male-female brain differences is found in: McBroom, P. Why can't a woman think more like a man (and vice versa)? *Philadelphia Inq. Today Mag.* 10–19, Feb. 15, 1981.

Box 2.2.   Diet, Drugs, Drinking and Disease.

The author (DM) had a patient who may have been suffering from anorexia nervosa. She was eighteen years old and was undergoing routine root-canal therapy on an upper right first premolar tooth. Her medical history revealed nothing unusual, and aside from the fact that she was extremely thin, she appeared normal. She had been treated over the course of two visits and no tooth-related problems developed. A microbiological culture taken from the tooth's root canal showed the absence of infection. The patient was scheduled for completion of the case the following week.

During the interval, DM went to a dental convention in Los Angeles. As soon as he arrived at the hotel, a long distance phone call was received from his covering dentist. The young woman had been hospitalized with a high fever (104°F), a severe cellulitis (spreading infection of the cheeks), and other signs of intense infection. She was treated with millions of units of penicillin (the indicated procedure in this instance), and she made a rapid recovery. On DM's return, the case was successfully completed. On follow-up, the patient revealed some previously withheld information. She disclosed that she had been on a "crash" diet consisting of colas, salads, and very little else of substance. She admitted to sleeping less than five hours a night, and indulging freely in drugs and alcohol.

This case is a dramatic example of how a poor diet, combined with a lack of sleep, "pill-popping," and drinking, can cause a relatively minor stressor to result in a serious, near-fatal condition.

Occupations. Women's occupations can be extremely stressful. From the housewife/mother to the business executive (à la Roberta), stress is always staring women in the face. (See Chapters 13–19) Let us now highlight some of these stressful occupations and their particular stress-related problems.

The housewife/mother typically has the task of raising the children, balancing the budget, keeping the house clean, feeding and clothing the family, catering to the husband's associates, being a lovable wife, and trying to stay slim and beautiful.

Teachers have to discipline as well as teach. Secretaries may have to put up with noisy typewriters, abusive clientele, sexual advances, and insufficient salaries.

Nurses do much of the "nitty-gritty" work without the fanfare and the glory. Dental hygienists "scrape and polish" and are rarely permitted to do more complicated procedures.

Housekeepers and chambermaids engage in menial labor and get few rewards. And prostitutes have to be concerned about police raids, personal safety, disease transmission, payoffs, maintaining their appearance, and responding to the demands of their customers.

Many women are newcomers in the ranks of the employed and they are often the first to be laid off. The loss of a job is a severe social stressor, especially to a woman who may have been unsure of her working capabilities. Studies have shown that the newly unemployed often come down with stress-related conditions such as hypertension, heart attacks, strokes, and ulcers.[52,53]*

Location. Where one lives and works is also related to stress. There are more stressors associated with city living than with residing in the suburbs or rural areas. Just consider these accompaniments of the slums of a typical center city: drug addicts; noise; air pollution; graffiti; cramped quarters; lack of sunshine; and teen-age gangs.

For the suburban housewife, life can also be stressful. Some of the mundane problems are: "keeping up with the Jones'"; the teen-agers' whereabouts; and the "housing development boredom" syndrome.

Family and Social Structure. Marriage can be almost as stressful as divorce for some women. It has been said that, "Marriage is a stress-reducing mechanism for men and a stress-producing one for women."[54] However, the stigma of not being married used to be even more stressful for a woman. To be an "old maid" was a fate to be avoided at all costs. As a result, some women married the first man who proposed; others waited longer but still got married out of desperation. ("To be twenty-six and single was considered to be a failure for a woman . . . an unfulfilled female, and Roberta was definitely unfulfilled . . . Roberta wasn't enthralled by Stephen's physical appearance but she believed . . . that her influence could effect a change for the better. They were both looking for a way out . . .")

Nowadays, "living together" is popular, and not all women have that strong drive to get married. But, as is discussed in Chapter 7, living together does have its problems. Being single or socially isolated may not be as healthful as being married or having friends. Studies have shown that singles have a higher incidence than do married people of stress-related disorders such as cancer and suicide.[54,55] "Loners" are more likely to die prematurely than women with many friends.[56]

Severe social stressors such as the death of a loved one may have less of an impact on a deeply religious woman who believes in the "will of God." However, according to the concept of *Locus of Control,* people who

---

* An Ohio woman was recently fired from her clerical job for alleged incompetence. She filed suit claiming that the incident caused her to suffer a nervous breakdown. Norris, E. Stress: Employers, insurers feel the pains of spreading occupational ailment. *Bus. Insur.* **3,** 58, Nov. 10, 1980.

believe that whatever happens to them is the result of luck, fate or "superior beings" (these individuals are categorized as "externals") generally react poorly to stressors.[57] At the other extreme are the "internals" who believe that they exert some control over the environment and what may happen to them. Such people generally react well to most stressors. Most women do not fall into either of these extremes but, until recently, they did rely on men for some control of their environment (e.g., financial support; and the "knight in shining armor").

Fitness. Physical and mental fitness is very important in the management of stressors. Being prepared helps insure successful coping. Rape is a serious problem in today's Western society.[58] Formerly, many women shied away from physically preparing themselves to help ward off an attack. Yet physical educators have shown that women can defend themselves effectively as well as perform admirably in many physical activities formerly considered to be only within the capabilities of a male (e.g., basketball; track and field; and wrestling). The key is that the motivated woman takes the time and makes the effort to train. Large muscles aren't absolutely necessary nor does engaging in body-building mean that a woman will develop large unsightly muscles. (The late Marilyn Monroe was a weight lifter, and Bo Derek of the movie *10* fame trains with weights.)[59] (See Chapters 17 and 21)

Mental preparation is also of major importance. Many women are realizing this and are "training their minds." Colleges are now showing large enrollments of women who had interrupted careers because of family "pressures." Not only are the women going back to school in increasing numbers, but many are excelling and are using their newly acquired skills to help them cope with the "stress of life."

Emotional Stability. Being emotionally stable is a key factor in the management of stressors. The female has often been characterized as acting emotionally in contrast to the rationally acting male. Of course, this is a gross distortion since there are emotional men and cold, calculating women. Even so, tears are an effective weapon for many women in stressful situations.[46]

With the advent of women into the professional and business world, other approaches are now more frequently taken. Some of these positive methods are: being calm in the face of adversity; smiling instead of frowning or crying; tempering criticism with praise; and most important, thinking before acting.[60] "Ignorance may be bliss" but learning and preparing are much better. ("Roberta's stint in the business world had been beneficial. Being around men so often had taught her how to deal with them. Roberta no longer was naive in her dealings with the masculine sex . . .")

Relaxation. If one can learn to relax, then stress can be managed and counteracted successfully. Specific methods of relaxation geared to women are discussed in Chapter 20.

THE STRESS RESPONSE

The third component of stress is the stress response.* The stress response is composed of the physiological and psychological reactions of the body that result from the interaction with a stressor. As discussed previously, there are certain stressors, and genetic and environmental factors, that primarily affect females. But the changes that constitute the stress response occur similarly in both sexes.**

Physiological Changes

First, let us briefly review the major physiological reactions.[1] When the body is activated by a stressor, an unknown signal alerts the hypothalamus (a gland in the midbrain). The signal may come from the front part of the brain (frontal cortex).[61] The hypothalamus then activates two primary systems. The first one is the hypothalamus-anterior pituitary***-adrenal cortex**** axis (H-AP-AC). The end result is the release of cortisone and related compounds. (See Figure 2.1) The second system alerted by the hypothalamus is the sympathetic division of the autonomic nervous system (i.e., the "automatic" nervous system; see Figure 2.3) and the adrenal medulla.**** Substances released are the catecholamines, adrenaline (epinephrine) and noradrenaline (norepinephrine; see Figure 2.4). A diagrammatic representation of the two systems of the stress response is shown in Figure 2.5.

When the body is in a stressful situation, all unnecessary functions are shut off. The principal reason for the release of the stress hormones***** (i.e., cortisone, adrenaline, and noradrenaline) is to prepare the body to fight or run (i.e., the "fight or flight" response). Therefore, the collective results of the action of these hormones are the following:[60,62-64]

---

* In this section, a simplified version is presented. For a more detailed description, consult: Morse, D. R. and Furst, M. L.: *Stress for Success: A Holistic Approach to Stress and its Management.* New York: Van Nostrand Reinhold Co., 1979.

** It is appropriate at this point to mention that although the authors have emphasized the differences in stress between women and men, there are more similarities than differences between the sexes.

*** Known as the master gland.

**** The adrenals are small paired glands that lie on top of the kidneys. The adrenal cortex is on the outside of the gland while the adrenal medulla is within the gland.

***** Hormones are chemical messengers that are carried in the blood stream from one body site to another.

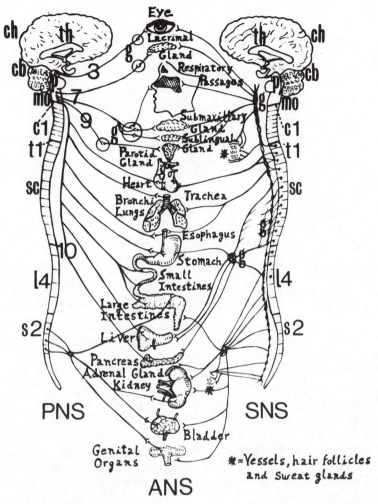

Fig. 2.3 The autonomic nervous system (ANS). The ANS is divided into the parasympathetic nervous system (PNS; cranial-sacral) and the sympathetic nervous system (SNS; thoracolumbar). The SNS is activated during stress and the PNS during relaxation; and their reactions are generally opposite in effect. Both systems are integrated with the CNS (brain and spinal cord). Brain parts are: ch = cerebral hemispheres; th = thalamus; cb = cerebellum; p = pons; mo = medulla oblongata. The spinal cord (sc) divisions are: c = cervical; t = thoracic; l = lumbar; and s = sacral. The cranial nerves involved with the PNS are: 3 (oculomotor); 7 (facial); 9 (glossopharyngeal); and 10 (vagus). Nerve cell bodies and connections between nerves are found in structures called ganglia (g).

PNS	STRUCTURE	SNS
constricts	pupil of eye	dilates
contracts	eye muscle (ciliary)	relaxes
stimulates	lacrimal (tear) gland	inhibits

(cont.)

PNS	STRUCTURE	SNS
stimulates large amount of watery saliva	respiratory passages salivary glands; submaxillary sublingual parotid	inhibits small amount of thick saliva
contracts muscles	trachea, bronchi and lungs	relaxes muscles
inhibits	heart	accelerates
	blood vessels of skin	constricts
	sweat glands	secretion
	hair follicles	contraction
activates	esophagus, stomach and intestines	inhibits
	liver and pancreas	increases activity
	adrenal medulla	secretion of adrenaline primarily
constricts muscles	kidneys and bladder	relaxes muscles
increases activity	genital organs	inhibits activity

(From Morse, D.R. and Furst, M.L. *Stress for Success: A Holistic Approach to Stress and to Management.* New York: Van Nostrand Reinhold Co., 1979. Reprinted with permission).

1. The activity of the gut is slowed down; digestion does not have priority at this time.

2. The production of glucose (blood sugar) is turned on; required for energy.

3. The breathing rate is increased; opens up more respiratory sacs. The chest is expanded which allows for increased intake of oxygen (for energy) and expulsion of the waste gas, carbon dioxide. Under stress, less oxygen is generally supplied to the skeletal muscles of women than of men. This is related to three factors in the female: (a) lower total body hemoglobin (oxygen-containing blood compound); (b) smaller lung capacity; and (c) lesser blood volume.[6]

4. The heart is stimulated to pump faster and more vigorously. Women generally react with a faster heart rate than do men.[6]

5. The blood pressure is raised. Women usually react with a lower blood pressure rise than do men.[6]

6. Blood is transferred from the gut to the heart and skeletal muscles; these last three activities (4–6 above) are necessary to get the oxygenated and glucose-rich blood to the muscles for effective action.

7. The nerves that "fire off" the muscles and make them more excitable are activated. The muscles "tense" (partial contraction) and become "braced for action."

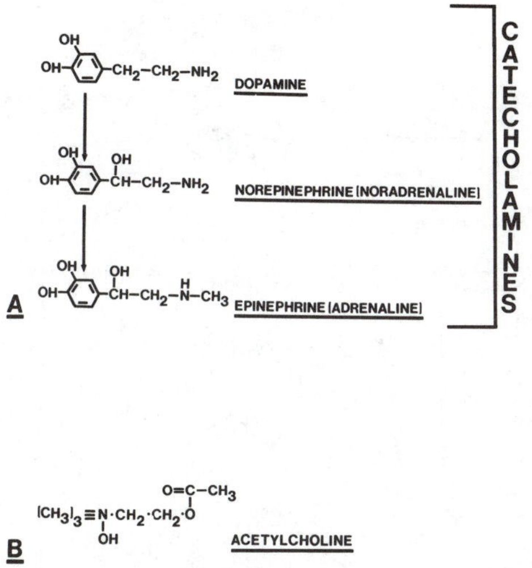

Fig. 2.4 The hormones of the autonomic nervous system. A. The catecholamines. Dopamine acts as a neurotransmitter (nerve messenger) in the brain. Norepinephrine (noradrenaline) and epinephrine (adrenaline) also act as brain neurotransmitters but are principally involved as stress hormones. Norepinephrine is primarily a mediator in the sympathetic nervous system (but 20% of this hormone is derived from the adrenal medulla). Epinephrine is principally derived from the adrenal medulla. B. Acetylcholine. Acetylcholine is a mediator of both skeletal muscles and the parasympathetic nervous system. (See Fig. 2.3.) It is activated during the relaxation response. (See Chapter 20.)

8. The sweat glands are turned on to rapidly remove waste products.

9. The pupils are dilated to allow for sharper vision (provided that there is adequate light).

10. The other sense organs such as smell, hearing and touch are activated. (Remember when Joanna was under stress, how the sounds of the office suddenly became magnified?)

11. The flow of saliva is decreased; saliva is part of the digestive system and is not needed at this time; hence, its release is slowed down, especially from the parotid glands (i.e., those opposite the cheeks).[62,76]

12. The blood circulation to the skin is closed down; this causes blanching.

13. There is an increased tendency of the blood to clot; it has been hypothesized that closing down the skin circulation would prevent excessive blood loss and increased clotting would also decrease blood loss. For example, you would be under stress in a fight. Should you get cut, the release of stress hormones would reduce the blood loss.

14. The inflammatory response is turned off to better prepare the body to take care of the major problem (i.e., the stress-causing situation). In

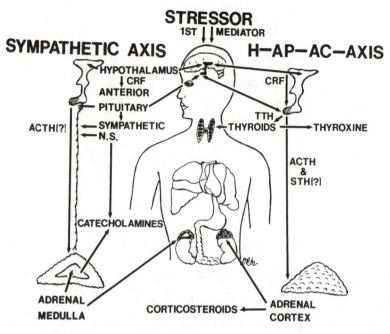

Fig. 2.5 Major physiological changes of the stress response. CRF-corticotropin releasing factor: ACTH = adrenocorticotropic hormone; TTH = thyrotropic hormone, STH = somatotropin; and symph. n. s. = sympathetic nervous system. The stressor activates the 1st mediator which turns on both the sympathetic axis and the H-AP-AC (hypothalamus-anterior pituitary-adrenal cortex) axis. CRF is released and activates the anterior pituitary, which in turn releases ACTH, STH and TTH. ACTH activates the adrenal cortex to release the syntoxic steroids (anti-inflammatory; e.g., cortisone) and possibly the adrenal medulla to release the catecholamines. STH apparently activates the adrenal cortex to release the catatoxic steroids (pro-inflammatory; e.g., aldosterone). TTH induces the thyroid to release thyroxine. The sympathetic nervous system and the adrenal medulla are also activated to release the catecholamines (epinephrine [adrenaline] and norepinephrine [noradrenaline]). (See text for details of the actions resulting from the release of these various stress hormones.)

reducing inflammation, cortisone deactivates the thymus gland and lymph nodes, which are important organs in the immunological responses; i.e., responses that fight infection and cancer cells. Cortisone also curtails the function of the body defensive cells, including polymorphonuclear leucocytes (PMN's for short), lymphocytes (white blood cells), and macrophages (large scavenger cells).[63,64] Catecholamines also possess an anti-inflammatory action. If these responses were continually occurring, it is possible to spread infection and cancer. (See Chapter 3)

15. Pain is inhibited. Another reaction that is observed during the stress

of a fight or competitive game is the decrease in pain perception. This is apparently related to the release of ACTH (a major hormone) by the anterior pituitary gland. The ACTH is released along with morphinelike substances called endorphins. Endorphins have been shown experimentally to block pain.[65] Thyroxine from the thyroid gland (found in the midneck region) is another major hormone released during stress. Thyroxine and other thyroid hormones increase the body's metabolism. This activity is necessary for normal stress responses in which an active, alert body is essential (as in fighting and fleeing). Chronic stress in a susceptible individual could lead to hyperthyroidism. (See Chapter 3)

If the stress response is severe enough, the parasympathetic division (i.e., the "vegetable" response) of the autonomic nervous system assumes an important role. (See Figure 2.3) Acetylcholine is the involved hormone. (See Figure 2.4) During stress, the normal role of this division is to dampen down excessive reactions by the sympathetic division. For example, it would tend to lower the blood pressure and slow down the heart rate. In some individuals, when the stress response is severe, the parasympathetic division becomes dominant. The end result may be a very slow heart rate, low blood pressure, shallow breathing, low blood sugar, nausea, dizziness, and fainting.[66]

The stress response is normal and is a necessary means to cope with physical dangers. It was an important response for our cave-dwelling ancestors when they had to fight a foe or flee from a wild animal. However, in today's world, the response is often triggered by self-induced psychological stressors (e.g., guilt, anxiety, anger, and frustration). When it becomes repetitive and chronic, bodily damage occurs.

There are three kinds of stress response.[1] If the stress response is essential for the day-to-day reactions of a woman to her environment and results in the maintenance of an internal steady state (known as homeostasis), it is called *neustress* (neu = neutral). For instance, neustress occurs when one breathes, walks, and performs other vital body activities. If the stress response is deleterious and potentially disease-producing, it is described as *distress* (dis = "bad" or negative). Constantly being anxious can result in a sustained rise in blood pressure which is probably related to the release of hormones such as cortisone, adrenaline and noradrenaline.

If the stress response is beneficial and results in improved physical and mental functioning, it is labled *eustress* (eu = "good" or healthy). For example, robust regular stressful exercises such as jogging may result in pleasurable bodily sensations and a lowered blood pressure (that is, after a few months).

Distress and eventual disease can result from prolonged or repetitive stress responses. Some possible outcomes are the following:

1. Continual action of cortisone, adrenaline, and noradrenaline in the gut in shutting down digestion may cause irritation of the gut lining and result in ulcers.[1]

2. Repetitive activity by the stress hormones raises blood pressure and could cause the blood pressure "thermostat" in the hypothalamus to be "reset" at a higher level and result in hypertension.[67]

3. The increased tendency of blood clotting that occurs during stress might precipitate coronary or cerebral (brain) clots and result in a heart attack or stroke.[1,68]

4. Although diabetes is partly genetically determined, the continual release of glucose as the result of stress hormonal activity could help bring on or aggravate the diabetic condition.[1,69]

Men and women basically have the same physiological changes during stress but not everyone shows all of the previous reactions. Some people can have repeated stress responses without serious consequence. During stress, some individuals respond primarily by more rapid breathing; others react principally with a rise in blood pressure; still others show a faster heart rate; and there are those whose principal sign is sweating of the palms. (See Box 2.3)

Even with physiological responses, women seem to be at some advantage. As mentioned previously, the results of studies showed that women

Box 2.3. Different Strokes For Different Folks.

In one of our studies at Temple University, we found that certain individuals showed practically no change in skin resistance (a measurement of sweat-gland activity) regardless of the stressful stimuli.[70] (Incidentally, that is one reason that the lie detector, which relies heavily on skin resistance changes, is not universally applicable. Some people can lie without "sweating." It has not yet been determined whether women or men have the "edge" in this department.)

Two recent studies support the observation that there are different types of stress responses. One study showed more beneficial stress responses (e.g., lower blood pressure; slower heart rates) when participants exercised while expressing feelings of happiness and extreme pleasure as contrasted to when they exercised and reported feeling angry, afraid or sad.[71]

Another study showed less oxygen consumption (which would indicate less stress) when subjects meditated while riding on a stationary bicycle as compared to doing the same exercise without meditating.[72]

produce less of the stress hormones than men during stressful encounters.[1,41,42] This may be an additional reason for the lower incidence of hypertension and heart attacks among women and may also account for their lower rate of ulcers. Women may also differ slightly from men in the psychological changes induced by stress.

Psychological Changes

When people are under stress, they have particular subjective feelings and observable actions. Some people feel "nervous." They may tremble, fidget, or even shake (i.e., the results of excessive muscle activity). Other actions that often occur are squinting of the eyes, pursing of the lips, clenching of the hands, and gritting of the teeth. Stressed individuals may feel giddy, "high," confused or even appear to be drunk. Often mood changes occur. Some people report "chills running up and down the spine." All of these symptoms and signs are related to the release of the stress hormones.[1]

The rapid heart rate of stress can induce heart palpitations. The digestive changes occurring during stress may cause "a sinking feeling in the gut." Catecholamine action on the sweat glands can cause excessive nervous sweating and can also lead to body odor.

The action of adrenaline and noradrenaline on the skin blood vessels can cause cold, clammy hands, cold feet, a ghostlike facial appearance, and even the opposite rebound effect, blushing. Blushing seems to occur more readily with females, at least with the previously mentioned repressed group. Blushing is often indicative of embarrassment or guilt. Mark Twain aptly described it: "Man is the only animal that blushes. Or needs to."*

With anger, which is more of a male trait, a person can appear very pale ("white with anger") or flushed ("red with rage"). These actions are also related to the catecholamines. The vasoconstriction or shutting down of blood vessels causes the pale reaction (i.e., the ghostlike appearance). This is principally caused by adrenaline (in the early stages) and noradrenaline. The vasodilatation or opening up of blood vessels causes the red reaction (i.e., the flushed face and blushing). This is primarily a rebound reaction caused by adrenaline.[73]

There have been some interesting studies on the differing reaction from these hormones.[74] In "fighting" animals such as lions, tigers and bears, noradrenaline is the principal stress hormone produced. Consequently, it has been given the pseudonym, the "aggression" hormone. In "frightened" animals such as deer and rabbits, adrenaline is the main stress hormone produced. Hence, it has been nicknamed, the "fear" hormone.

* From Pudd'nhead Wilson's New Calendar.

Several years ago, experiments were performed in which it was found that noradrenaline was produced principally under the emotion of anger, while adrenaline was produced primarily during anxiety and depression.[74] Consequently, the popular version of the sex differences in emotions may be related to those differences. Thus, the angry male may pump out more noradrenaline and the anxious female may produce more adrenaline (although this has not yet been definitely established).[75]

SUMMARY

There are three basic types of stressors: physical, psychological, and social. Physical stressors are generally the least damaging unless they are severe and repetitive (e.g., noisy typewriters). Psychological stressors are usually the most damaging since they can be self-induced and are repetitive (e.g., anxiety, anger, guilt, and frustration). Social stressors, such as the death of a loved one, can cause the most damaging single stressful response.

The reaction to stressors is modified by each individual's particular makeup. The individual's makeup includes personality factors (e.g., the passive-dependent woman who holds in her emotions), genetic factors (e.g., the heart attack-resistant female), and environmental factors (e.g., the housewife/mother).

As a result of the interplay between the stressor and the individual makeup, a rather specific set of physiological and psychological changes occur; i.e., known as the stress response. These changes result primarily from the release of the major stress hormones: cortisone, adrenaline, and noradrenaline. But there are individual variations in the stress response relative to the kind, severity and frequency of the stressor and the makeup of the individual.

If the stress response is basically neutral, but essential for bodily function, it is called neustress. If the stress response is damaging, it is designated as distress. If the stress response promotes improved physical and psychological functioning, it is known as eustress. In the next chapter, we examine stress-related diseases with special significance to women.

REFERENCES

1. Morse, D. R. and Furst, M. L. *Stress for Success: A Holistic Approach to Stress and Its Management.* New York: Van Nostrand Reinhold, 1979.
2. Flor-Henry, P. Gender, hemispheric specialization and psychopathology. *Soc. Sci. Med.* **12** (3B):155–162, 1978.
3. Lewis, H. B. Sex differences in superego mode as related to sex differences in psychiatric illness. *Soc. Sci. Med.* **12** (3B): 199–205, 1978.

4. Gove, W. R. Sex differences in mental illness among adult men and women: An evaluation of four questions raised regarding the evidence on the higher rates of women. *Soc. Sci. Med.* **12** (3B):187–198.
5. Evans, F. J. The placebo response in pain reduction. *Adv. Neurolol.* **4**:289–296, 1974.
6. Martinson, I. M. and Anderson, S. Male and female response to stress. *In* Kjervik, D. K. and Martinson, I. M. (eds.), *Women in Stress: A Nursing Perspective.* New York: Appleton-Century-Crofts, 1979, pp. 89–95.
7. Gray, J. A. and Buffery, A. W. H. Sex differences in emotional and cognitive behavior in mammals including man: Adaptive and neural bases. *Acta Psychologica* **35**:89–111, 1971.
8. Goy, R. W. and McEwen, B. S. *Sexual Differentiation of the Brain: Based on a Work Session of the Neurosciences Research Program.* Cambridge, Mass.: MIT Press, 1980.
9. Marks, I. M. Agoraphobic syndrome (phobic anxiety state). *Archs. Gen. Psychiat.* **23**:538–553, 1970.
10. Miller, N. E. Liberalization of basic S-R concept: Extensions to conflict behavior, maturation and social learning. *In* Koch, S. (ed.), *Psychology: A Study of a Science,* Vol. 2 New York: McGraw-Hill Book, 1959, pp. 196–292.
11. Darwin, C. *The Expression of the Emotions in Man and Animals.* London: John Murray, 1872, p. 311.
12. Petrich, J. and Holmes, T. H. Life changes and onset of illness. *Med. Clin. N. Am.* **61**:825–838, 1977.
13. Gordon, V. C. Women and divorce: Implications for nursing care. *In* Kjervik, D. K. and Martinson, I. M. (eds.), *Women in Stress: A Nursing Perspective.* New York: Appleton-Century-Crofts, 1979, pp. 260–275.
14. Mischel, W. *Introduction to Personality,* Second Ed. New York: Holt, Rinehart & Winston, 1976.
15. Jung, C. G. *Psychological Types.* New York: Harcourt, Brace & World, 1923.
16. Friedman, M. and Rosenman, R. H. *Type A Behavior and Your Heart.* New York: Knopf, 1974.
17. Waldron, I.: Type A behavior pattern and coronary heart disease in men and women. *Soc. Sci. Med.* **12** (3B):167–170, 1978.
18. Le Shan, L. An emotional life-history pattern associated with neoplastic disease. *Ann. N. Y. Acad. Sci.* **125** (3):780–793, 1966.
19. Sword, R. O. The depression-prone personality: Almost "too good" to be true. *Dent. Surv.* **53** (3):12–18, 1977.
20. Pelletier, K. R. *Mind as Healer Mind as Slayer: A Holistic Approach to Preventing Stress Disorders.* New York: Dell Publishing 1977.
21. Arehart-Treichel, J. Can your personality kill you? *New York Magazine* **10**:62–67, November 28, 1977.
22. McKeown, P. Women paying price for joining man's world. *Philadelphia Eve. Bull.*: A1, 4, May 14, 1980.
23. Pflanz, M. Sex differences in abdominal illness. *Soc. Sci. Med.* **12** (3B):171–176, 1978.
24. Moos, R. H. and Solomon, G. F. Psychologic comparisons between women with rheumatoid arthritis and their non-arthritic sisters. *Psychosom. Med.* **27**:150–164, 1965.
25. Spergel, P. Ehrlich, G. E., and Glass, D. The rheumatoid arthritic personality: A psychodiagnostic myth. *Psychosomatics* **19**:79–86, 1978.
26. Grace, W. J., Wolf, S., and Wolff, H. G. *The Human Colon.* New York: Paul B. Hoeber, 1951.
27. Cohen, M. J., Rickles, W. H., and McArthur, D. L. Evidence for physiological stereotyping in migraine headaches. *Psychosom. Med.* **40**:344–354, 1978.

28. Ziegler, D. K. Headache syndromes: Problems of definition. *Psychosomatics* **20**:443–447, 1979.
29. Grace, W. J. and Graham, D. T. Relationship of specific attitudes and emotions to certain bodily diseases. *Psychosom. Med.* **14**:243–251, 1952.
30. Graham, D. T., Lundy, R. M., Benjamin, L. S., Kabler, J. D., Lewis, W. C., Kunich, N. O., and Graham, F. K. Specific attitudes in initial interviews with patients having different psychosomatic diseases. *Psychosom. Med.* **24**:257–266, 1962.
31. Holmes, T. H., Jaffe, J. R., Ketcham, J. W., and Sheehy, T. F. Experimental study of prognosis. *J. Psychosom. Res.* **5**:235–252, 1961.
32. Sheehy, G. *Passages: Predictable Crises of Adult Life.* New York: Dutton, 1976.
33. Gould, R. *Transformations.* New York: Simon & Schuster, 1978.
34. Gallagher, J. C. and Nordin, B. E. C. Calcium metabolism and the menopause. *In* Curry, A. S. and Hewitt, J. V. (eds.), *Biochemistry of Women: Clinical Concepts.* Cleveland: CRC Press, 1974, pp. 145–163.
35. Stumpf, W. E., Sar, M., and Aumüller, G. The heart: A target organ for estradiol. *Science* **196**:319–320, 1977.
36. Colburn, P. and Buonassisi, V. Estrogen-binding sites in endothelial cell cultures. *Science* **201**:817–819, 1978.
37. Hartung, G. H., Foreyt, J. P., Mitchell, R. E., Vlasek, I., and Gotto, A. M., Jr. Relation of diet to high-density-lipoprotein cholesterol in middle-aged marathon runners, joggers and inactive men. *N. Engl. J. Med.* **302**:357–361, 1980.
38. McGill, H. C., Jr., Anselmo, V. C., Buchanan, J. M., and Sheridan, P. J. The heart is a target organ for androgen. *Science* **207**:775–776, 1980.
39. Shaw, L. The spasm theory of heart attack. *Prevention* **31**(10):106–110, 1979.
40. Klebanoff, S. J. Effect of estrogens on the myeloperoxidase-mediated antimicrobial system. *Infect. Immun.* **25**:153–156, 1979.
41. Frankenhaeuser, M., von Wright, M. R., Collins, A., von Wright, J., Sedvall, G., and Swahn, C. G. Sex differences in psychoneuroendocrine reactions to examination stress. *Psychosom. Med.* **40**:334–343, 1978.
42. Collins, A. and Frankenhaeuser, M. Stress responses in male and female engineering students. *J. Hum. Stress* **4** (2):43–48, 1978.
43. Goleman, D. Special abilities of the sexes: Do they begin in the brain? *Psychol. Today* **12** (11):48–59, 120, 1978.
44. Kolata, G. B. Sex hormones and brain development. *Science* **205**:985–987, 1979.
45. Carter, C. S. and Greenough, W. T. The brain: Sending the right sex messages. *Psychol. Today* **13** (9):112, 1979.
46. Shatzman, M. Shedding new light on the fine art of crying. *Philadelphia Eve. Bull.* BK. 24, June 13, 1980.
47. Editorial. Heart risk less in some working women. *New York Times:* C2, April 15, 1980.
48. Warnes, H. Premenstrual disorders: Causative mechanisms and treatment. *Psychosomatics* **19**(1):32–40, 1978.
49. Shiner, G. Anorexia nervosa studied at several centers. *Res. Resources Reporter* **4**(5):1–7, 1980.
50. Riccitelli, M. L. Vitamin C: A review and reassessment of pharmacological and therapeutic uses. *Conn. Med.* **39**:609–614, 1975.
51. *Smoking and Health: A Report of the Surgeon General.* Washington, D. C.: U. S. Department Health, Education, and Welfare, Public Health Service, 1979, p. A–14.
52. Barmash, I. *Welcome to Our Conglomerate--You're Fired!* New York: Delacorte, 1971.
53. Lewis, H. R. and Lewis, M. E. *Psychosomatics: How Your Emotions Can Damage Your Health.* New York: The Viking Press, 1972.

54. Kinzer, N. S. *Stress and the American Woman.* New York: Ballantine Books, 1980.
55. Le Shan, L. An emotional life-history pattern associated with neoplastic disease. *Ann. N. Y. Acad. Sci.* 125:780–793, 1966.
56. Editorial. Loneliness really can kill you. *Philadelphia Eve. Bull.* 23, December 15, 1977.
57. Rotter, J. B. Generalized expectancies for internal versus external control of reinforcement. *Psychol. Monogr.* 80:1–28, 1966.
58. Ledray, L. E., Lund, S. H., and Kiresuk, T. J. Impact of rape on victims and families: Treatment and research considerations. In Kjervik, D. K. and Martinson, I. M. (eds.), *Women In Stress: A Nursing Perspective.* New York: Appleton-Century-Crofts, 1979, pp. 197–217.
59. Anonymous. Hollywood stars tell of health and beauty secrets that keep them in tiptop shape. *The Star* 35, October 7, 1980.
60. Selye, H. *Stress Without Distress.* Philadelphia: J. B. Lippincott, 1974.
61. Skinner, J. E. The brain: Heart-attack trigger. *Psychol. Today* 14(2):124, 1980.
62. Morse, D. R., Schacterle, G. R., Furst, M. L., and Bose, K. Stress, relaxation and saliva: A pilot study involving endodontic patients. *Oral Surg.* In Press, 1981.
63. Selye, H. *The Stress of Life,* Second Ed. New York: McGraw-Hill Book Co., 1976.
64. Kopin, I. J. Catecholamines, adrenal hormones and stress. In Krieger, D. T., and Hughes, J. C. (eds.), *Neuroendocrinology.* Sunderland, Mass.: Sinauer Associates, 1980, pp. 159–166.
65. Cory, C. C. Newsline: Pain: The promise of drugless pain control. *Psychol. Today* 12(12):26–27, 1979.
66. Schlesinger, J., Barzilay, J. Stryjec, D., and Almog, C. H. Life threatening "vagal reaction" to emotional stimuli. *Isr. J. Med. Sci.* 13:59–61, 1977.
67. Eliot, R. S. *Stress and the Major Cardiovascular Disorders.* Mount Kisco, N. Y.: Futura, 1979, pp. 1–15.
68. Glass, D. C. Stress, behavior patterns and coronary disease. *Am. Sci.* 65:177–187, 1977.
69. Bradley, C. Life events and the control of diabetes mellitus. *J. Psychosom. Res.* 23:159–162, 1979.
70. Morse, D. R., Martin, J. S., Furst, M. L., and Dubin, L. L. A physiological and subjective evaluation of meditation, hypnosis and relaxation. *Psychosom. Med.* 39:304–324, 1977.
71. Schwartz, G. E. The brain as health care system: A psychobiological foundation for stress and behavioral medicine. Read before the Symposium on Stress and Behavioral Medicine, New York, December 3–4, 1977.
72. Benson, H., Dryer, T. and Hartley, L. H. Decreased VO_2 consumption during exercise with elicitation of the relaxation response. *J. Hum. Stress* 4(2):38–42, 1978.
73. Goodman, L. S. and Gilman, A. *The Pharmacological Basis of Therapeutics,* Fifth Ed. New York: Macmillan Publications, 1975, pp. 483–495.
74. Funkenstein, D. H. The physiology of fear and anger. *Sci. Am.* 192(5):74–80, 1955.
75. Leshner, A. I. *An Introduction to Behavioral Endocrinology.* New York: Oxford University Press, 1978.
76. Morse, D. R., Schacterle, G. R., Esposito, J. S., Furst, M. L., and Bose, K. Stress, relaxation and saliva: A follow-up study involving clinical endodontic patients. *J. Hum. Stress* 7(3), In press, 1981.

3
Stress-Related Diseases:
With Women in Mind
(And Body Too)

INTRODUCTION

During acute stress situations (sudden, severe, and short-lived), it appears that the principal hormones released are adrenaline and noradrenaline.

Induced symptoms include heart palpitations, cold, clammy hands, chills, sweating, and giddiness. When stress becomes chronic, cortisone is the major hormone pumped out.[1] Chronic symptoms of stress include weakness, fatigue, malaise ("run-down" or queasy feeling), appetite loss, and stomachaches. Both acute and chronic stress can lead to stress-related diseases but most diseases are associated with chronic stress. Yet some people can be exposed to either acute or chronic stressors and not come down with any symptoms or diseases. For example, a severe stressor such as the radiation leak at Three Mile Island induced stress-related symptoms in most of the surrounding population. "After the accident, what Three Mile Island workers feared most was not the leaking radioactivity, but losing their jobs."[2] Similar reactions have been reported with the Love Canal chemical pollution leak. However, some individuals—because of their positive outlook or better stress tolerance—had no untoward physiological or psychological responses.

It is also an enigma why the same or similar stressors result in different symptoms or diseases in various individuals. The "weak organ" theory offers one possible explanation.[3] It is based on the notion that people have inherent weakness in specific organs or body sites. For instance, weakness of the hair follicles predisposes toward baldness; weak lungs make asthma a likely possibility; and a poorly performing intestinal tract favors ulcer development.

Which disease or symptoms occur also depends upon the type of autonomic nervous system response that predominates: Some individuals react to stress with an accelerated rise in blood pressure; others show a marked increase in heart rate (women generally have a smaller blood pressure rise but more rapid heart rate under stress);[4] and still others have the opposite reactions of falling blood pressure and slowed heart rate. The latter individuals would show the symptoms of dizziness and fainting.

Another puzzle is related to stress-related symptoms, diseases, and death. One would think that the gender that had more reported symptoms, illnesses, intake of drugs, and physician and hospital visits would also show more debilitating diseases and a higher mortality rate. Yet, the opposite is true. Women show all the manifestations of being sicker than men, yet consistently have been shown to have fewer heart attacks and to live longer than men.*[5-7] One reason is that women are generally more concerned than men with their symptoms and more willing to follow their doctors' advice.[6] Why they tend to live longer is discussed shortly.

In Box 3.1, a study which attempts to uncover the association between stress and symptoms is presented.

Bearing in mind the variability of stress-related symptoms and diseases, let us now consider these conditions with the focus on women. We begin with the major stress-related diseases, those of the cardiovascular system.

CARDIOVASCULAR DISEASES

The major stress-related diseases are those of the cardiovascular system with coronary heart disease, cardiac arrhythmias, hypertension, and angina pectoris of principal importance. The diseases of the cardiovascular system kill more people than all others combined. Up to now, for women there has been a much lower incidence of these diseases, particularly coronary heart disease. Let us look into the possible reasons for this discrepancy and consider future trends.

Coronary Heart Disease

Coronary heart disease (ischemic heart disease; heart attack) is the "Number One" killer for men in the United States. A recent estimate is that in a single year, 1.3 million Americans (combined women and men) will have coronary heart disease. Of those, about 675,000 will die, with 175,000 of them being premature (i.e., before age sixty-five).[8] Surveys in

---

* According to the U.S. Census, of the fifty-nine causes of death listed, in fifty-seven of them men have a higher rate; only diabetes mellitus and pernicious anemia are higher in women. (Williams, J. H. *Psychology of Women: Behavior in a Biosocial Context.* New York: W. W. Norton & Co., Inc., 1977, p. 119.)

Box 3.1. Psychosomatic Words.

With respect to stress and symptoms, we have completed a study on personality and words selected for meditation.* Subjects meditated with the words selected as "best," "worst," and "most neutral." As part of the study, the seventy-two subjects were asked to describe their subjective bodily sensations while meditating with each word. Many words induced pleasurable sensations such as warmth, floating sensation, tingling, lightness, and heaviness. For example, "love" induced warmth more than any other word. Negative words such as "vomit," "ice pick," "coronary," "nerve," and "gas" frequently brought forth unpleasant symptoms. These symptoms included: nausea; stomachache; headache; neckache; shoulderache; pain in legs; dizziness; heart palpitations; coldness; numbness; gagging; muscle twitches; itching; crying; and sweating.

As might be expected, "vomit" induced the most unpleasant sensations with the most frequent symptom being nausea. But the strange thing was that some subjects actually did well with negative words. For instance, for some people "vomit" induced feelings of floating, lightness, warmth, and tingling.

These results reinforce the "weak organ" theory since symptoms relate to different parts of the body for different individuals. The study also demonstrates that merely repeating a "sound" for five minutes can induce psychosomatic symptoms. Hence, the relationship of psychosomatic diseases to emotions may now be understood in part.

As far as sex differences and symptoms are concerned, our findings reinforce other studies that show women report more symptoms. On the average, each male subject reported three symptoms during meditation; for the women, the average was five reported symptoms.

the United States and Great Britain have shown that there are between three and six male deaths for every female one (under the age of seventy).[9,10] However, this pattern may be changing as attested to by a recent, limited one-year study showing a male-to-female ratio of 1.65 to 1.0 of coronary heart disease (both fatal and nonfatal cases).[11] There also has been a recent (unexplained) decrease in the overall death rate from heart attacks.[12]

Coronary Thrombosis. With most cases of heart attacks, the coronary blood vessels show atheromatous, cholesterol-rich deposits around the walls of the blood vessels causing considerable narrowing. This, in turn,

* Morse, D. R. and Furst, M. L., Psychosomatic effects of words used for meditation. *J. Am. Soc. Psychosom. Dent. Med.* In press, 1981.

makes a thrombosis (i.e., a clot) much more likely with subsequent death of the associated heart muscle (myocardial infarction).[1] In a recent study, it was observed that the female hormone, estrogen (see Figure 2.1) binds in the endothelial (innermost) lining of blood vessels (see Figure 3.1).[13] Estrogen may exert a protective shield against the development of the cholesterol-rich atherosclerotic plaque that occludes coronary arteries and leads to a heart attack.

Estrogen appears to stimulate scavenger cells to remove blood fats.[4] A major fat implicated in coronary thrombosis is cholesterol. (See Figure 2.1)

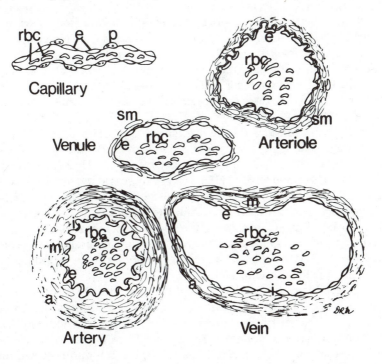

Fig. 3.1 Blood vessels. Cross section of five types of blood vessels beginning with the smallest (capillaries) and ending with the largest and thickest (arteries). rbc = red blood cells (erythrocytes); e = endothelial cells (the innermost lining cells); p = pericyte; sm = smooth muscle cells; i = intima, innermost layer of veins and arteries; m = media, middle muscular layer of arteries and veins (it is thickest in arteries); a = adventitia, outmost layer of arteries and veins (it is thickest in veins). Atherosclerotic plaque can attach to the intima of coronary arteries and can lead to a heart attack. Oxygen (O_2)-rich blood goes from the arteries to the arterioles, then to the capillaries and finally into the tissues. Carbon dioxide (CO_2), the waste gas, goes from the tissues to the capillaries and then to the venules and veins. (From Morse, D.R. and Furst, M.L. *Stress for Success: A Holistic Approach to Stress and its Management.* New York: Van Nostrand Reinhold Co., 1979. Reprinted with permission.)

Cholesterol is found in the bloodstream in three forms: very low-density lipoproteins (VLDLs); low-density lipoproteins (LDLs) and high-density lipoproteins (HDLs).[14] VLDLs and LDLs constitute the "bad" type of cholesterol since they seemingly can develop into the atherosclerotic plaque that clogs coronary arteries. VLDLs and LDLs are apparently derived from saturated fat foods such as eggs, milk, cheese, butter, and beef. However, they can be produced by the body and there is considerable controversy over whether they can be adequately reduced merely by decreasing saturated fats in the diet.[15]

Most government agencies recommend a low fat diet to help prevent heart attacks but a recent report by the Food and Nutrition Board of the National Research Council opposed that viewpoint.[16] Nevertheless, in almost every society yet studied researchers have found that the more fat and cholesterol in the diet, the higher the blood cholesterol level and the higher the death rate from coronary artery disease.[15-18]* In addition to the diet, LDLs also increase during stress and as the result of cigarette smoking.[14,19]

The HDLs are considered to be the "good" type of cholesterol. They apparently help clear the coronary blood vessels of the VLDL- and LDL-type cholesterol and in that way exert a protective effect against heart attacks.[14,20] The blood level of HDLs can be increased by: vigorous exercise (e.g., running; racquetball);[14] ingestion of vitamin C;[21] lecithin;[22] polyunsaturated fats;[23] moderate alcohol intake (e.g., one or two glasses of wine daily); losing weight (for the obese); and the curtailing of cigarette smoking.[14] But the bonus for women is that they naturally have a higher blood level of HDLs than men. Estrogen appears to be instrumental in stimulating the high level of HDLs.[24]

It has been hypothesized that the clot that occludes the coronary arteries (that have been narrowed by atherosclerotic fatty deposits) is composed primarily of platelet-fibrin substances (their normal function is to induce blood clotting after a wound).[25] As discussed in Chapter 2, activation of the sympathetic nervous system (SNS; see Figure 2.3) during stress, causes the release of the catecholamines (see Figure 2.4). The catecholamines tend to cause clumping of blood platelets and hasten the rate of arterial damage, both of which can lead to coronary thrombosis.[26] Here also women may be at an advantage, as studies have shown that while under stress, women produce less of the catecholamines than do men.[27,28]

---

* In a recent study of 1,900 middle-aged men, it was corroborated that lipid composition of the diet affects serum cholesterol concentration, and high blood cholesterol increases the risk of fatal coronary heart disease. (Shekelle, R. B., Shyrock, R. D., Oglesby, P., Lepper, M., Stamler, J., Liu, S., and Raynor, W. J. Jr. Diet, serum cholesterol, and death from coronary heart disease, *N. Engl. J. Med.*, **304:**65–70, 1981.)

The common drug, aspirin, is known to inhibit platelet formation and may help prevent heart attacks.[29,30] Several studies now under way are testing this hypothesis. If aspirin does tend to prevent heart attacks, this may be another advantage for women as evidence has shown that women are more conscientious than men in their intake of drugs.[7]

Coronary Spasm. Recently, it has been found that sudden contraction of the coronary arteries can cause spasm with subsequent necrosis of the surrounding heart muscle. This can cause sudden death of the individual. Although most coronary blood vessels that become spasmodic show evidence of previous atherosclerosis and thrombus formation, in 10 to 25 percent of the cases, the coronary arteries appear to be perfectly normal. The direct cause of the spasm is not known although it is triggered by the sudden release of calcium into the blood vessels. It is known that activation of the SNS (see Figure 2.3) primes α-adrenergic receptors in the coronary arteries which results in calcium release and subsequent spasm. As previously mentioned, stress is a potent activator of the SNS. With women producing less of the catecholamines, theoretically they have a lower probability of developing coronary artery spasm.[27,28]

Another factor implicated in coronary vessel spasm is magnesium. Studies have shown that low levels of magnesium in the heart are associated with a high incidence of spasm. High levels of magnesium appear to be protective possibly by preventing the influx of calcium into blood vessels.[31] Women naturally have a higher concentration of magnesium than do men.[32] Another factor in spasm occurrence is the release of the component thromboxane (A_2) from clumping blood platelets. To counteract its formation, aspirin has been used as well as the drug, Anturane.® [25] The effectiveness of these drugs has not yet been definitely determined.[30] One group of drugs that appear to be effective against spasm is the calcium antagonists (e.g., nifedipine).[33] Once again, women's conscientiousness in the intake of drugs would be an asset if aspirin and nifedipine prove to be effective in preventing spasm and sudden death.

Myocardial Infarction. Heart muscle death occurs beyond the point of coronary artery blockage. The blockage can be related to atherosclerosis, thrombosis or spasm. The death of the heart muscle is known as myocardial infarction.[1] Studies have shown that a sudden release of catecholamines, as during stress, can cause a unique, severe type of damage to the heart muscle (i.e., ruptured muscle fibers). This can result in sudden death even in an individual with normal coronary blood vessels.[1] Again, women may be somewhat protected. First, they produce less catecholamines.[27,28] Second, in an animal study it was found that estrogen binds in the atria and auricles of the heart.[34] (See Figure 3.2.) "This suggests that estrogen has a direct effect on the atrial myocytes (muscle cells*) through which its protective action may be mediated."[34]

Cardiac Arrhythmias

Cardiac arrhythmias are abnormal heart rhythms. There are two principal types, atrial and ventricular. Ventricular arrhythmias are more serious and can be a cause of sudden death. They can also develop following heart attacks. Recent evidence shows that emotional stress-inducing factors can induce ventricular arrhythmias. The proposed pathway is via massive catecholamine release by activation of the SNS.[35,36] Once again, women's lesser release of catecholamines may be protective.[27,28]

Hypertension

Hypertension is the "Number One" risk factor for coronary heart disease and cerebral stroke.[1,37] In several animal and human experiments, it has been shown that psychological stressors cause sustained elevations in blood pressure. The psychological stressors, frustration and anxiety caused the highest increases in blood pressure and the elevations were sustained.[1,26] Remember from the previous chapter that many women are particularly prone to those stressors.** However, here too the catecholamines are instrumental in inducing sustained rises in blood pressure. And women produce less catecholamines under stress and consequently have lesser increases in blood pressure.[27,28] Another factor that may account for the lower blood pressure rise in women is estrogen. Estrogen appears to reduce the occurrence of hypertension in females.[34]

Angina Pectoris

In angina pectoris (pain in the chest), the coronary arteries have partial occlusion. The surrounding heart muscle does not get sufficient oxygen. The occlusion may be the result of atherosclerotic plaque but it can be inten-

---

* Authors' insertion.

** It was also discussed in the previous chapter that many women have to face noise stressors repeatedly. A recent study revealed that even if noise causes no ear damage, it can still lead to elevations in blood pressure which may predispose toward hypertension. Peterson, E. A., Augenstein, J. S., Tanis, D. C. and Augenstein, D. G. Noise raises blood pressure without impairing auditory sensitivity. *Science* 211: 1450–1452, 1981.

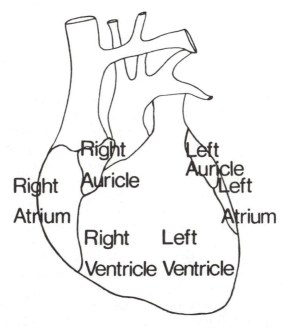

Fig. 3.2 The chambers of the heart. The auricles are appendages on the outside of the heart above the atria. The blood is pumped from the atria to the ventricles. (From Morse, D.R. and Furst, M.L. *Stress for Success: A Holistic Approach to Stress and its Management.* New York: Van Nostrand Reinhold Co., 1979. Reprinted with permission.)

sified by spasms.[38] Angina is often a precursor to a heart attack but it may also follow a heart attack. In some angina patients, heart attacks never occur. Women have a much lower incidence than men of heart attacks but they are equally affected with angina.

Risk Factors

The principal protection that women have against heart attacks and strokes is related to genetic and early developmental factors (i.e., the XX female chromosome; and estrogen). But heart-attack incidence and mortality is also related to environmental factors. Let us look at these risk factors as they relate to women.

Hypertension. This has already been discussed. One nutritional factor that causes sustained rises in blood pressure is salt.[39] (Hence, it is a good idea to avoid salting food.)

Race. Blacks have a higher incidence of hypertension and coronary artery disease than Caucasians. This is also true for black women as compared to white women. This is partly genetic, but may be primarily related to social and family factors which are less favorable for many blacks.[40,41]

Cigarette Smoking. Cigarette smoking is an important risk factor for heart attacks.[42] Cigarette smoking has the following negative effects in relation to heart disease: (1) increases flow of adrenaline; (2) accelerates heart rate; (3) constricts blood vessels; (4) increases tendency for blood to clot; (5) elevates blood levels of fatty acids and LDLs; and (6) produces carbon monoxide-hemoglobin which prevents the carrying of oxygen to needed blood vessels of the heart and brain.[14,43,44]

Unfortunately, women's cigarette smoking is on the upswing. But even here there is an interesting finding. Women tend to smoke for a different reason and in a different manner than do men.[10,42] "Women tend to light a cigarette particularly when under tension, whereas men light up mainly when they are understimulated or bored"; "the more nervous person (i.e., the woman*) plays more with the cigarette and spends less time steadily smoking it"; and "women inhale less than men."[10] These findings are from Great Britain but, if they are replicated in the United States, this too would help explain the lower incidence of heart disease, even among smoking women.

High Serum Fats. We have already discussed the dangers of high levels of LDL-cholesterol and the controversy surrounding high intake of saturated fats. Eating high-fat foods may be dangerous as it can lead to obesity.

Obesity. Obesity increases the risk of hypertension and heart attacks. It also increases the risk for diabetes, kidney diseases, and backaches.[37] Even with all of her gender advantages, if a woman is overweight, she greatly increases her chance of getting a heart attack. Fortunately, many women are weight conscious.

Diabetes. The presence of diabetes mellitus (discussed later) increases the risk of getting a heart attack.[10]

Lack of Exercise. Recent evidence shows that aerobic exercise (e.g., running; swimming; bicycling) appears to lower the probability of getting a heart attack.[14,43] Many women are now participating in jogging, tennis, aerobic dancing, and similar activities. (See Chapter 21)

* Authors' insertion.

Stress. Psychological stressors (e.g., anxiety; frustration) are capable of inducing high blood pressure, increased blood clotting, ventricular arrhythmias, and coronary artery spasm. As discussed in Chapter 2, life-stress events (social stressors) such as death of a spouse or even winning a lottery can induce sudden death from heart attacks.[44] Consider this item that appeared in *The Philadelphia Bulletin:* "Dies after winning. Harry Johnson, 56, a woodworking teacher at a school in Droylsden, England, died of a heart attack Tuesday, the day after he collected $1.6 million won in a football lottery."[45]

Does the stress engendered by women working outside the home promote heart attacks? The evidence is equivocal. As discussed in Chapter 2, type A behavior (i.e., hard-driving; competitive; aggressive; impatient) is primarily descriptive of the male and is associated with a high frequency of heart attacks.[46] However, this behavior is becoming more frequent among women entering competitive jobs and professions. Type A women have higher educational and occupational status than type B women. Nevertheless, the evidence has not shown that type A women suffer more fatal heart attacks than type B women.[42,47] In a recent study, it was found that single working women were less likely to get heart disease than were housewives.[48] For married working women in general, no special risk was found. Specific categories of married working women did have an increased risk of heart attacks. They were women with three or more children and women in clerical jobs who were married to blue-collar workers. But for the majority of working women, no specific risk was found. Again, it is probably related to the protective effect of lower production of catecholamines and the presence of estrogen.[27,28]

Coffee Drinking, Alcohol Intake, and Sugar Ingestion. There have been some studies reported showing that high coffee[49] and alcoholic beverage drinking,[1] and high sugar intake[50] can increase the risk of getting a heart attack.

It would be helpful to women to moderate their intake of these beverages and sugar. Drinking and overeating can lead to obesity which is a definite risk factor for heart attacks.

Birth-Control Pills. Oral contraceptives that contain estrogen cause increased platelet activation and also stimulate other blood clotting factors.[51,52] Apparently, naturally occurring estrogen doesn't lead to increased blood clotting or women would probable have a higher incidence of heart disease than they do. Women taking the estrogen-containing birth-control pills have an increased risk of heart attacks.[53,54]* When either women or men are given estrogen, the risk for heart attacks varies. With women taking replacement estrogen, the risk for heart attacks generally decreases.[55] With men given estrogen (usually for prostate cancer), there is usually an increased risk of heart attacks.[56] Thus, naturally occurring estrogen reacts differently than estrogen employed for therapy.

Oophorectomy. When a woman's ovaries are removed, there is usually a greater risk for coronary heart disease.[55] Whether this is related to removal of female hormones or to behavioral changes is not known.

Age. For both females and males, with advancing age, the risk of heart attacks increases. With women, from the time of menopause onward when estrogen levels dramatically decrease, women become just as susceptible as men to the development of heart disease.[34] ("Jolted back to the present by a sharp, sudden stab of deep chest pain, Roberta reacted quickly to her aching heart.")

CEREBRAL STROKE (CEREBRAL VASCULAR ACCIDENT)

Cerebral vascular accidents are a major cause of sudden death in both women and men, although they are more common in men.[37,52] The causes of cerebral vascular accidents are similar to coronary heart disease; i.e., atherosclerosis, hypertension, and stress.

CANCER

Cancer is the second leading cause of death in the United States.[52] The relationship of stress to cancer is less clear than that of stress to heart disease. Nevertheless, recent evidence indicates that the onset of cancer is often preceded by severe life-change events as well as chronic psychological stressors.[57] (See "cancer personality" in Chapter 2.) The life-stress studies show that most patients report anxiety, depression, hopelessness, and grief prior to the appearance of the tumors.[26,57-59] However, these reports are retrospective (i.e., backward looking) analyses of prior feelings which may be distorted by the current disease. In one prospective (i.e., forward look-

---

* Women who appear to have the greatest risk are birth control users who smoke cigarettes and are over the age of thirty. Associated Press. Pill a health plus, doctor contends. *Philadelphia Inq.* 3-A, Dec. 24, 1980.

ing) study, where people's attitudes were analyzed before they got sick, it was found that individuals who developed cancer were often "low-geared." They had few outbursts of emotion and felt isolated from their parents.[59] In a major retrospective study of women cancer patients, widowed women had the highest cancer mortality rate and divorced women the second highest rate.[60] In another prospective study, people who had significantly higher depression scores in a personality test developed a greater incidence of cancer than those individuals who had a low depression score on the same test.[59]

How stress can cause cancer is not known, although it has been hypothesized that the stress activation of the H-AP-AC system with release of cortisone can inhibit the activity of macrophages and lymphocytes (i.e., body defensive cells).* If these defensive cells are prevented from acting, tumor cells could multiply and form a cancerous lesion.[61]

In one animal study, it was found that mice developed tumors more quickly in a stressful atmosphere than in a protected environment.[57] In another study, mice subjected to inescapable stress (i.e., electric shocks) had a greater incidence of cancer and a shorter life span than mice subjected to escapable stress or no stress at all.[62] Considering the animal studies and the human research, it appears that stress can affect the development of cancers.

The major female cancers are those of the breast and female genital tract. Let us consider them first before going on to lung cancer.

Breast and Female Genital Tract Cancer

Several studies have shown that women who repress their feelings, especially anger, have a greater chance to develop breast cancer than benign breast tumors.[57,63,64] Other studies have shown that the loss of a loved one, habitual use of denial, and the occurrence of depression often precede the development of breast cancer.[63] In one retrospective study, women who had a recent emotional loss and feelings of "hopelessness" showed a significantly higher incidence of cervical cancer than women who did not have those experiences.[57]

An animal study showed that female mice who were separated from their young had more breast tumors than female mice that stayed with their young. It was hypothesized that the tumors seem to come with despair.[26]

---

* Inhibition by cortisone of macrophage anti-tumor function was recently shown in an animal experiment. Pavlidus, N. and Chirigos, M. Stress-induced impairment of macrophage tumoricidal function. *Psychosom. Med.* 42: 47–54, 1980.

Considering the evidence, in order to help prevent the onset of breast cancer, women should not hold in their feelings—especially anger—and try not to become depressed. It would also be helpful if married women had healthy husbands (widows fare poorly) and happy marriages (divorcees also have a higher risk). Judging by the results of those who have had spontaneous cures from breast and female genital tract cancer, it might be better to maintain a hopeful outlook, to let out one's feelings, and to employ methods such as hypnosis, meditation, and imaging to help the body fight the tumor cells.[61,65] (See Chapter 20) One (male) investigator stated that it was the "bitchy" women who vented their anger who had the best chance of recovery as contrasted to the "good" women who followed all instructions (often to their graves).[66] Of course, it is still essential to have standard medical treatment.

The association between birth control pills and the incidence of heart attacks has already been discussed. Studies have shown that high estrogen-containing oral contraceptives, as well as estrogen given for replacement therapy increases the chance of endometrial and liver cancer.[67-69]

There is often stress before and after breast cancer surgery. Before undergoing radical mastectomy (breasts, lymph nodes, and associated tissues are removed) as opposed to simple mastectomy (breasts removed), a second opinion should be sought. There are conflicting studies on whether it is essential to remove all the associated tissues (i.e., makes both reconstruction and arm movements more difficult).[70]

There are two principal stressors after mastectomy. The first is similar in all individuals who have had cancer treatment: the fear of recurrence. The other major stressor with respect to breast cancer surgery is the worry that the woman would no longer be "feminine" with the absence of her breast(s). However, artificial breasts and plastic surgery can be quite helpful in this regard. Psychotherapy and family therapy is often necessary to help the postmastectomy woman restore her self-confidence and her self-image.[71]

In a recent study of postmastectomy women, depression was usually found, with 25 percent of the women contemplating suicide.[72] Most of the problems stemmed from the changed sexual relationship between the wife and her husband. For instance, 25 percent of the women said that they no longer were seen naked by their husbands (and this was almost two years after surgery). It was observed that husbands who visited their wives in the hospital tended to have fewer problems coping with the consequences of their wives' surgery.

Similar problems can occur in posthysterectomy women. (See Chapter 8) A case report of a woman's fight against breast cancer and how she effectively coped in the postmastectomy period is presented in Box 3.2.

Box 3.2. Making It After Mastectomy by DM.

This night I was to lecture on stress management to a suburban Philadelphia organization composed of pre- and postmastectomy women. The group leader had a special story. She came to the United States from England over twenty years ago, but still speaks in that impeccable British way.

This is Victoria's* story. As a result of her upbringing, Victoria was taught to trust and respect doctors. Hence, when she found a gynecologist in whom she had confidence, Victoria stuck with him through the delivery of her two children and her own yearly check-ups. After eighteen years of regular visits to this same doctor, Victoria felt reassured when he diagnosed the lump in her breast as no more than a "sore muscle."

Three years later the lump was still present and her confidence began to wane. At this point, she went to her family physician to have him check out the pain she was now experiencing in her breasts. He thought it was caused by "cysts" and referred her to a surgeon to make sure of his diagnosis and reevaluate the still present lump.

The surgeon questioned Victoria about the lump and was both amazed and appalled when she informed him that the gynecologist originally diagnosed it as a sore muscle. Needless to say, a subsequent biopsy confirmed that the "sore muscle" was actually cancer—and the breast and adjacent nodes were removed.

When Victoria went home from the hospital, she was happy to be alive but the psychological impact was more than she could handle. She couldn't face the reality of being without a breast. For three days, Victoria wouldn't take off her clothes. And the thought of a shower in the nude was unbearable. At last, she did take a shower— but with her eyes closed and her daughter holding a towel about her. Then Victoria, a formerly full-breasted woman, looked in the mirror . . . and was devastated.

Through all this, Victoria had a supportive husband and family, and that helped enormously. She inquired about a postmastectomy group in the local area and discovered that there was none. Still the search was not completely unproductive; it produced one firm friend and that friendship helped put Victoria back on her feet. By the end of that first year, she had won a malpractice suit against the gynecologist and had the breast reconstructed.

Just when Victoria felt that the worst was over, she discovered another lump; fortunately, this one proved to be benign. At this point, Victoria decided that life was so precious that she would savor every day. She also was motivated to help other women get the aid that she had never received. So Victoria founded the community's first postmastectomy organization.

Thus, it was two years later that I was asked to speak to thirty smiling, wonderful women who had faced and dealt with the most serious kind of stressor—the specter of death. And thanks to people like Victoria, many more women will be smiling for many years to come.

* Name changed for anonymity.

Lung Cancer

Lung cancer is the leading cancer among men and it is causally related to cigarette smoking.[42,52] Lung cancer is also increasing among women but not as fast as would be expected from the increased smoking done by women in the last decade. Women appear to have a greater resistance to lung cancer than do men and, as discussed under heart diseases, it is probably related to their lesser degree of inhaling cigarettes, the fewer number of cigarettes smoked, and their tendency to put out the cigarettes before reaching the end.[10,42] According to the available evidence, one reason for this discrepancy between women's and men's smoking habits is that women smoke as a stress-relieving method.[10] Men generally smoke for the "macho" image, because it was the "in" thing to do as a teen-ager, and because they need oral stimulation.[10]

Studies on men have shown that individuals who get lung cancer tend to have repressed feelings.[62] The results would probably be similar for women. It would be beneficial for women to give up smoking, not hold in their feelings, and use positive stress-coping methods. (See Chapters 20–23)

DEPRESSION AND OTHER MENTAL DISEASES

Depression

As just discussed, depression may be causally related to cancer. And, as is covered shortly, depression is a key factor in diseases and disorders such as: migraine headaches; myofascial pain-dysfunction syndrome; alcoholism; divorce; suicide (the latter three are discussed in the next chapter); premenstrual tension (discussed in Chapter 6); and menopausal problems (discussed in Chapter 8).

But what is depression? Depression encompasses a whole host of disorders that range from prolonged sadness (that often goes unreported) to severe manic-depressive psychosis (that requires psychiatric treatment and hospitalization). In between are the majority of depressive cases that are seen by psychiatrists and psychologists as the most frequent mental illness. These cases include two major types of depression, reactive, and endogenous.[72] Reactive ("external") depressives tend to have their depression precipitated by life-stress events such as marital arguments, marital separation, loss of a loved one, and serious personal illness.[72–75] (See "depression-prone personality" in Chapter 2)

Endogenous ("internal") depression occurs without any obvious stressful antecedents (although these may just not be detectable). The endogenous type is more severe and borders on psychosis. It is associated with a relative or absolute deficiency of released noradrenaline (see Figure

2.4) at central nervous system synapses (connections between nerve cells) which is related to an increase in the enzyme monoamine oxidase (MAO).[72]

Regardless of the category, women are more prone to depression than are men.[72-80] Whether this is related to genetic or environmental factors is not known, but almost all reports show that depression is as prevalent in women as coronary heart disease is in men. Some possible reasons for the higher female incidence of depression are:

1. Women are not taught to show anger; they are brought up to control their emotions which leads them to internalize their feelings.

2. Girls have a greater dependency upon their mothers than do boys; they are usually provided with fewer opportunities for independence and individualization.

3. In adult life, women may become dependent upon their husbands or lovers for support and emotional attachment; when a loss of the person she is dependent upon occurs (as with divorce or death), the woman may then go into a state of depression.

4. Women get treatment for their symptoms of both physical and mental diseases more than do men; hence, more female cases are reported.

5. The menial housewife role tends to foment depression.

6. Even when women work, their role is often subservient to men or dependent upon them.

7. Married women who are working usually have the menial housework to do, and may feel guilty about leaving the children at home.

8. Most of the reported studies on depression have been done by men; there may be male bias in labeling more women than men as being depressed.[72-80]

An indication that women are not innately more depressed than men comes from a recent study. When female and male stereotypic roles were exchanged with wives working rather than being housewives, the men actually scored higher in depression.[80]

Irrespective of the reasons for the high female incidence of depression, it is imperative that women take all possible means to prevent and treat depression. This includes: (1) demanding equal rights with men in employment; (2) having husbands assume a fair share of the household chores; (3) preferably entering therapy with female therapists who can empathize with their special problems; (4) not depending upon negative coping methods such as drinking, overeating, smoking, and drug intake*;(5) being wary of the use of birth control pills since studies have shown that pill use may

---

* On occasion, antidepressant medications are indicated for severe cases of depression but they should be taken under strict medical supervision and only for as long as is necessary.

precipitate depression;[127] and (6) using positive coping methods such as meditation, running, and taking vacations. (See Chapters 20–23)

Other Mental Diseases

For other mental disorders such as schizophrenia, paranoia, and the neuroses, the relationship to stress is less apparent. Nevertheless, studies do show an increased occurrence of life-stress events prior to the onset of schizophrenia and neuroses.[73] One of the breakdown products of stress-induced adrenaline release can cause hallucinations.[81] Women do not have a greater incidence than men of these disorders, but some studies have shown a higher incidence amongst women of anxiety, phobias, and hysteria.[78]

The advice given for the prevention and control of depression also holds true for these diseases.

MUSCLE-RELATED CONDITIONS

As previously discussed, one of the physiological responses of stress is partial muscle contraction. With chronic psychological stressors such as anger, anxiety, worry, and frustration, the involved muscles can form "knots" and pain results.[37] If this occurs in the scalp, tension headaches may be experienced. In the mouth, the resulting conditions are known as clenching, bruxism, and the myofascial pain-dysfunction syndrome. With chronic partial muscle contraction, one can also get a "pain in the neck," a shoulderache or a backache.

Headaches

There are two major kinds of headaches related to stress, migraine and tension.

Migraine Headaches. As discussed in Chapter 2, there is a "migraine personality," but not all migraine sufferers have those personality traits (i.e., obsessional-perfectionist; orderly and rigid; repressed hostility; and restrained resentment).[82-84] Recent studies have shown that headache sufferers (both migraine and tension) have similar patterns of high anxiety, depression, hysteria, and obsessive-compulsion.[82] Studies agree that most migraine headache patients are women.[83,85] In a recent study it was estimated that "25 percent of women and 10 percent of men have migraine."[83] In another study, 70 percent of migraine sufferers were women.[85]

Migraine is definitely stress-related. Migraine sufferers experience headaches from life-change events such as moving, changing jobs, taking vacations, and the arrival of weekends. The headaches often occur during the time when the people relax (as during vacations and weekends). Anxiety-producing situations also induce attacks. Other causative factors are: (l) premenstrual and menstrual times (see Chapter 6 for a discussion of premenstrual tensional syndrome); (2) the use of extrinsic estrogen for replacement therapy (often given at menopause; see Chapter 8); and (3) the taking of birth control pills.[83]

Drinking alcoholic beverages and eating chocolate also can precipitate bouts of migraine. Migraine has a genetic component (based on the evidence that it tends to occur in families).

It was stated earlier that estrogen is important in heart disease prevention for women. As far as migraine headaches are concerned, it seems that both natural estrogen (which increases during the menstrual period) and extrinsic estrogen (given in replacement therapy and found in oral contraceptive pills) is instrumental in precipitating the headaches. The estrogen induces platelet (small blood particles) aggregation which sets the stage for release of chemicals that eventually cause the arteries of the scalp to dilatate (open up) excessively and pain results.[84]

How does one cope with migraine? First, try to avoid stressful situations. Second, if at all possible, only take estrogen when it is essential for medical reasons. Third, try to control attacks by employing relaxation methods, although attacks may occur during periods of relaxation. Finally, use medications only when the other methods are unsuccessful.

Tension Headaches. As is well known, tension headaches are often preceded by anxiety-producing situations; and women are the most common sufferers. In one study, 78 percent of the reported cases of tension headaches were in women.[85] There is no apparent family history (as is the case with migraine.)[85] The mechanism of action for tension headaches is different from that for migraines. With migraine, vasodilatation occurs; with tension headaches, vasoconstriction (closing down of blood vessels) of the scalp occurs. There is excessive muscular contraction of the scalp muscles and the vasoconstriction causes a lack of oxygen. The combined effect results in pain.[85]

Coping with tension headaches means dealing with psychological stressors such as anxiety. One should avoid or evade anxiety-producing situations and, when not possible, one should try to see the positive side of the situation. (See Chapter 20) Other effective methods are the use of relaxation, massage, and chiropractic. (See Chapters 20 and 21) Drugs such as minor tranquilizers (e.g., Valium) and analgesics (e.g, aspirin) can be temporarily effective but it is important not to become dependent upon drug therapy.

The Oral Conditions[86]

These include clenching and bruxism and the myofascial pain-dysfunction syndrome.

Clenching and Bruxism. Clenching is prolonged, intense contact of opposing teeth without any grinding movement. Bruxing or gritting is similar but the teeth come together in a grinding motion. Both conditions are considered to be responses to physical and psychological stressors (e.g., anxiety, frustration, and anger) and are often found in people with latent aggression and psychiatric problems. Bruxism frequently occurs in angry, hostile and dependent individuals. (However "normal" people can also be bruxers.) Local factors that help precipitate attacks are faulty "fillings" and improper bite relationships. Many times, people are unaware of their clenching and grinding habits until they are told about them by their sleeping companions.

If repeated, clenching and bruxing can lead to excessive tooth-related problems, and overdevelopment and spasms of the muscles of mastication (i.e., the chewing muscles).* Pain occurs and can spread to the neck (neckache), head (tension headache) and the jaw joints (temporo-mandibular joints; known as myofascial pain-dysfunction syndrome).

Clenching and bruxing can result from the stress response (as discussed in Chapter 2). The muscles of mastication are activated as are the other extrinsic body muscles used in fighting and running. Our cave-dwelling ancestors actually had a need for activating the biting and chewing muscles. For biting is an effective means of fighting if one has strong teeth and jaw muscles. Teeth are no longer regularly used as a weapon, although women may use their nails and teeth when attacked. However, the physiological activation of the jaw muscles still occurs in many people under stress.

Dental investigators at the College of Medicine and Dentistry of New Jersey report that 80 percent of the cases of bruxism occur in women.[87] Again, this statistic may be related to: (1) women acting upon their symptoms more than men and going to the dentist; and (2) the life-style of most women in which they are taught to "hold in their feelings."

* A recent study confirmed that bruxists have significantly higher muscle tension in the masseter muscles (a major chewing muscle) than do people who do not grind their teeth. Rao, S. M. and Glaros, A. G. Electromyographic correlates of experimentally induced stress in diurnal bruxists and normals. *J. Dent. Res.* **58:**1872–1878, 1979.

Myofascial Pain-Dysfunction Syndrome (MFPDS). This is a syndrome involving dysfunction in the muscles of mastication and the temporomandibular joints (i.e., those at the angle of the jaws). There is often evidence of concomitant stressors in the patient's life such as anger, anxiety, illness, death of a loved one, and marital, work-related, or financial problems. The patients are often depressed and may have a history of intestinal tract diseases such as colitis, gastritis, and ulcers. Clenching and bruxism are often precursors of or are associated with MFPDS.

Just as with clenching, bruxism and headaches, reported cases of MFPDS are much higher in women. Clinicians at Fairleigh Dickinson University Dental School stated that their myofascial pain-dysfunction clinic is attended mostly by women. Typical women patients are highly "disciplined" with a tendency to grind or clench their teeth.[88]

The cause of MFPDS is probably the same as for the other muscle-related conditions.* Biofeedback, meditation, and self-hypnosis for relaxation of the muscles, and psychotherapy and applied kinesiology to improve muscular function, have been employed effectively as treatments.[89] For prevention, it would be helpful to use the methods discussed under tension headaches.

Shoulderaches and Neck Pains

As a result of chronic psychological stressors, partial muscle contraction can spread from the head and jaws into the neck and shoulders causing intense pain in those areas. In some people, the muscle contractions originate in the neck and shoulders. Relaxation therapy should prove helpful. (See Chapter 20)

Backache

Pains in the back are among the most common of all physical ailments. They may be caused by improper lifting or disease states, but often are induced by chronic muscle spasms set in motion by repetitive psychological stressors.[90] Many individuals who develop backaches tend to be angry, resentful, competitive, and apprehensive. They are considered to be constantly on guard but afraid to act.[91] In addition, there is some evidence that low back pain occurs in individuals who have suffered severe life-stress events such as death of a spouse, marital separation, or divorce.[92,93]

* As is the case with bruxism, a recent study showed that MFPDS sufferers have significantly higher muscle tension of the masseter muscles than do control subjects. Mercuri, L. G., Olson, R. E. and Laskin, D. M. The specificity of response to experimental stress in patients with myofascial pain-dysfunction syndrome. *J. Dent. Res.* **58**:1866–1871, 1979.

Women do not appear to be more susceptible to back pain than men. However, child-bearing may promote back trouble because of the extra load and postural changes. Relaxation therapy, exercise, massage, chiropractic, osteopathy, and orthopedic treatments are often helpful in management. (See Chapters 20 and 21)

ULCERS

There are various kinds of ulcers, but the ulcers that most people think about and which concern us are the peptic ulcers.[94] There are two types, gastric (stomach) ulcers and duodenal (first part of the small intestine) ulcers. Recent estimates indicate that over 20 million Americans will get an ulcer at some time during their life-span, with about 6,000 dying from the complications.[95] Of the two types, the duodenal ulcer is four times as common.

The actual cause of these ulcers is not known, but the crater results from the combined action of hydrochloric acid (normally destroys bacteria that are swallowed, and also helps in the digestion of food) and pepsin (a protein-digesting enzyme). The two main complications of peptic ulcers are bleeding and perforation (i.e., penetration of the ulcer through the wall of the digestive tract permitting the contents to pour out into the body cavity).

As discussed in Chapter 2, there appears to be an "ulcer personality." However, not everyone who represses anger, leans on others, and tends to be prim, proper, and punctual gets a peptic ulcer.[96] Nor do all ulcer patients have these characteristics.

Although there are other factors involved, such as heredity and diet, stress is undoubtedly important in the development of peptic ulcers. Animal studies have shown that rats subjected to physical and psychological stressors develop severe intestinal ulcers.[26,81,97] In an experiment with monkeys, the monkey who pressed the lever to turn electric shocks "on" or "off" (i.e., the "executive" monkey) developed ulcers.[98] Conversely, the monkey who also got shocks but didn't have to make decisions didn't get ulcers. In these studies, it was observed that more ulcers were found when the stressors were intermittent rather than continuing. Another observation with rats was that unpredictable shocks caused more ulcers than did predictable shocks.[99] Hence, "decision-making" and "unpredictability" are associated with ulcer development (at least in animals).

With humans, studies have shown that peptic ulcers are often found in people who suffer repeated psychological stressors such as anger, hate, guilt, frustration, and hostility.[81,91,100] Duodenal ulcers have occurred following major life-stress events such as air raids in Great Britain and marital separation.[3,101] Individuals such as air traffic controllers who must make instantaneous life-and-death decisions, have a higher incidence of peptic ulcers than do airport workers not involved in such decision-making.[102]

In Chapter 2, it was mentioned that cortisone released during stress could be a factor in the etiology of peptic ulcers. Hence, quiet ulcers can "flare up" when patients are given cortisonelike drugs.[37] There is also some evidence that hypersecretion of gastric acid is mediated by the parasympathetic nervous system (PNS; see Figure 2.3) and could contribute to the ulcer formation.[101]

Men have a high incidence of ulcers, but recently women have begun to "catch up," possibly related to their increased employment in stressful jobs. (See Box 3.3) In one study, it was found that the higher the women's employment level the greater was the number of women dying from peptic ulcers.[103]

Box 3.3.   Ulcers Throughout the Ages.

The "sexual" history of peptic ulcer disease makes a fascinating story. From about 1860 to 1905, there was an excess of perforating ulcers in young women as compared to young men in both Great Britain and Germany. Although there were many possible explanations given (e.g., women had a different diet; they drank vinegar to lose weight; and they took laudanum as a sedative), a most interesting explanation was given by H.B.M. Murphy.[10] He equated the high female excess of ulcers with the use of tight corsets. "At the beginning of the 19th century these had been out of fashion, but they returned with the Bourbon restoration in France and new mass production methods led to their use by all classes." These corsets were reinforced by heavy layers of clothing. Murphy suggested that the tightness of the corsets restricted blood supply and since immobilization can produce ulcers in animals, it could conceivably occur in human females as well.

In 1908 the Mayo clinic reported about twice as many males as females with ulcers (i.e., women in the United States didn't "take" to corsets as much as their European counterparts). The male rate rose dramatically within the next two decades, so that by the 1930s the ratio was an extraordinary nineteen to one in favor of males. Since then the rate has been declining and the female rate has been rising, so that now it is about two to one in favor of the male.[95]

The constant striving of the male in business and as the breadwinner may have had something to do with the dramatic rise in male ulcers. Women's changing roles may be a factor in the higher recent incidence of female ulcers. It is hoped that women will not try to achieve parity with men in this regard.

Ulcers can be managed by diet, drugs, surgery, and relaxation methods.[95-101] But the best advice is: reduce stress; avoid arguments; decrease conflicts; don't get aggravated; and practice meditation or self-hypnosis. (See Chapter 20)

DIABETES MELLITUS[37,52,104]

Of all diseases in the United States, diabetes mellitus is among the top five killers. There are two main types of diabetes mellitus, juvenile (insulin-dependent) and adult-onset. "Juvenile" is the more severe and requires daily injections of insulin for patient survival. Adult-onset diabetes generally occurs later in life, is less severe, and usually can be controlled by diet. Formerly, it was treated by drugs but most diabetologists now find diet control is as effective with fewer side effects. The tendency toward contracting either form of diabetes is inherited but "juvenile" shows a greater genetic predisposition.

Stress has never been shown to be a direct causative factor of either type of diabetes. But there is evidence that stress can intensify pre-existent diabetes or can convert prediabetes to clinical diabetes.[105] Stress can also induce diabetic crises.[52,106] Remember from Chapter 2, that both cortisone and the catecholamines released during stress cause a rise in blood glucose. If this is repeated regularly and sustained, it could lead to diabetes in susceptible individuals.

The occurrence and exacerbation of adult-onset diabetes has been antedated in many cases by major life-stress events.[105] In a recent study, it was observed that with juvenile diabetics, life-stress events caused more problems in the management of their disorder than did life-stress events with adult-onset diabetics.[107] It has been already mentioned that diabetes is related to obesity and is one of the risk factors for coronary heart disease. Currently, there is a slight increase in mortality rate in female over male diabetics. In the past, the mortality rate was variable. (See Box 3.4)

In terms of coping with diabetes, it makes good sense: to avoid stress-producing situations; to follow a controlled diet; to take insulin if required; to practice relaxation techniques; and to get sufficient aerobic exercise. Recent studies have shown that regular aerobic exercise (e.g, running; swimming; bicycling) can allow for more efficient utilization of insulin and can possibly reduce the complications of juvenile diabetes.[108]

RHEUMATOID ARTHRITIS

Arthritis is inflammation of the synovial membranes of the joints of the body. There are many kinds but rheumatoid arthritis is a predominant

Box 3.4. Diabetes Throughout the Years.

As with peptic ulcers, the history of sex tendencies toward the development of diabetes is interesting. From the turn of the century through the 1920s, there was an excess of male deaths from diabetes. Then the sex differential changed and women began to die more frequently from diabetes than did men up through the 1950s. Recently, the trend has begun to reverse, but women still have a somewhat higher mortality rate.[108]

H.B.M. Murphy has another unique explanation for these changing rates.[10] Up to the 1920s, diet was the only way to control diabetes. Women of that time tended to follow the strict diet needed to control diabetes since they were concerned with slimness much more than men. (Women or men who had juvenile diabetes generally didn't survive.) It was in the 1920s that insulin became available and insulin injections then became the routine method for treating juvenile diabetes. Adult-onset diabetes was still treated by diet. Women of the time were less inclined than men to accept the painful and clumsy daily insulin injections. Women were also more reluctant to provide urine for analysis. On the other hand, men were not upset when asked to provide urine for analysis to a male doctor, and it was considered "manly" to take the self-administered daily injections. Hence, men's survival rate was better.

More recently, as a result of the women's movement, women have been made aware that they can take pain as well as or better than men. Women are now more open in talking about "female" problems and bring in urine samples as a matter of course. They often go to women physicians who give them more support. In addition, the newer forms of insulin are easier to administer and are more reliable. On the other hand, men are now more inclined to follow the strict diet that is required for adult-onset diabetic control.

One other factor which may account for part of the slight current increase in female diabetic mortality is the use of birth control pills. Although the taking of oral contraceptives has not been definitely shown to cause diabetes, studies have shown that taking the "pill" increases the blood glucose level which could be a forerunner of diabetes in susceptible individuals.[52]

type. The etiology is poorly understood but most investigators believe that it is an autoimmune, degenerative, chronic disease.[52] (That is, a long-standing debilitating type of disease in which the body's immune defense cells break down the body's own tissues.)

Although there is controversy over whether there is a distinct "rheumatoid arthritis personality" (as was discussed in Chapter 2), it is believed that stress is a factor in the onset of the disease. Some investigators consider "rheumatoids" to be individuals with "repressed hostility"; having interpersonal difficulties with parents; having authoritarian fathers and less loving mothers; more easily divorced since they are unhappy with their sex role; and having the characteristics of being self-sacrificing, orderly, punctual, tidy, and perfectionist.[59,109] However, a recent investigation found no specific personality traits that are associated with rheumatoid arthritis.[109]

Rheumatoid arthritis is becoming a women's disease. According to recent studies, four out of five rheumatoid arthritis sufferers are women.[59] And from 1-3 percent of the population in the United States suffer from rheumatoid arthritis.[52]

For symptomatic relief, effective methods include drugs (e.g., aspirin; cortisone) and relaxation therapy. (See Chapter 20) Learning not to "hold in" one's hostility feelings may also be beneficial.

ULCERATIVE COLITIS, DIARRHEA AND CONSTIPATION

Ulcerative Colitis

Ulcerative colitis is a chronic inflammatory disease of the mucosa of the colon (part of the large intestine). It is possibly caused by allergy or autoimmunity. As was discussed in Chapter 2, there seems to be an "ulcerative colitis" personality. Some characteristics of this individual are: obsessive-compulsion; dependent upon parents; becoming "hopeless" and "helpless" at loss of parents by rejection, separation, or death; and mild, well-mannered, punctual, inhibited, submissive, and conscientious.[52,110] Although not all ulcerative colitis victims have these attributes, stress certainly seems to be a factor in the acute exacerbation of the disease. The disease gets worse under conditions of anxiety, conflict, and stressful situations, many of which are either job-related or family-induced.

Ulcerative colitis is fairly common (about 200,000–400,000 sufferers in the United States, with approximately 25–30,000 new cases occurring each year). It is also more prevalent in females, with about 60 percent of the reported cases being women in both the United States and England.[52,110,111]

Sometimes the cases have spontaneous remissions. Most often drug therapy is helpful. For control of ulcerative colitis, job and family "pressures" should be reduced, and anxiety-inducing situations should be avoided. Meditation and self-hypnosis should prove helpful in reducing the acute "flare-ups." (See Chapter 20)

Diarrhea

Chronic diarrhea that is not related to any specific disease is known as the "irritable bowel syndrome." This condition is usually stress-related.[52] People who get repeated diarrhea have been described as: angry and hostile; filled with guilt feelings; and with a tendency toward panic.[91] The best treatment is prevention: being selective in eating and drinking; avoiding anxiety-producing activities; controlling emotions; and learning to relax. (See Chapter 20)

Constipation

As is the case with chronic diarrhea, non-disease-related constipation is stress-induced. Some people who suffer from repeated constipation have been described as being bored, grim, dejected, and depressed.[91] Constipation tends to become a vicious cycle. The importance of regularity and having at least two substantial bowel movements each day is a popular belief. When this fails to happen, people become stressed and the stress reaction may induce further constipation. The main problem with repeated constipation is that the straining that occurs can injure blood vessels and raise the blood pressure (with possible fatal consequences).

For control of constipation, one should eat high-fiber products, regularly exercise the lower body,[52] avoid stress-producing situations and learn to relax. (See Chapter 20)

RAYNAUD'S DISEASE

Raynaud's disease is a circulatory disturbance of the fingers and toes. It is characterized by ischemia (i.e., lack of blood) that is induced by cold or emotional stimuli. It often is exacerbated during the winter months. It appears that excessive SNS activity, as induced by stress, is primarily responsible. If the condition is untreated, gangrene can result with loss of the involved digits.

Although not common, Raynaud's disease is overwhelmingly a woman's disease. Women are affected five times as often as are men.[52] For control: cold should be shunned; warm mittens and socks should be worn in cold climates or during the cold season; cigarette smoking should be eliminated (smoking causes vasoconstriction in the digits); stress-producing situations should be avoided; and relaxation should be practiced. (See Chapter 20)

THROMBOPHLEBITIS

Thrombophlebitis is an inflammation of the veins that predisposes them toward blood clots. It often is found in the legs. Prolonged sitting and the intake of birth control pills can induce phlebitis.[52]

So far it has been noted that the taking of estrogen-containing birth control pills can increase the risk of getting: (1) heart attacks and stroke (clotting factor); (2) thrombophlebitis (clotting factor); (3) cancer; (4) diabetes (possibly); (5) migraine headaches; and (6) depression. However, one recent study didn't report finding an increased risk for these diseases in white American women.[112]

Stress can be a factor in the development of thrombophlebitis. The direct formation of the clots may be induced by catecholamines that are released during stress. The catecholamines activate the blood platelets causing them to aggregate (and induce clot formation). The incidence of thrombophlebitis is higher in females only when they are taking oral contraceptives.

For control: avoid long-term use of birth control pills; avoid anxiety-producing situations; and do not sit for long periods of time without exercising the legs.

ASTHMA AND OTHER ALLERGIC DISEASES

Asthma

Asthma is one of the most prevalent and serious allergic diseases. About 3 percent of the population of the United States are asthmatics. There is no difference in frequency by sex. Asthma has a genetic component but attacks are precipitated by exposure to allergens (e.g., dust; bacteria, foods; and drugs). Vigorous exercise, especially in hot, humid weather can bring on an attack. Cold weather can also bring forth symptoms. Stress is definitely a factor since emotional reactions can bring on severe attacks.[52]

There are two kinds of personalities that have been associated with asthma. In one kind, the asthmatic child tends to have overly protective parents and the attacks serve as a way of getting more attention. In the second kind, the asthmatic child tends to have unconcerned parents which contributes to the asthma.[59]

Unlike most of the other stress-related diseases where the SNS and catecholamines are key factors, asthma is precipitated by the PNS (see Figure 2.3) and released acetylcholine. (See Figure 2.4) In fact, asthma is relieved by adrenaline and cortisone (which are produced during stress).

For control: Allergens and anxiety-inducing situations should be avoided; one should dress warmly in winter; exercising in hot, humid weather should be avoided; and relaxation therapy can be helpful.[37,113] (See Chapter 20)

Other Allergic Diseases

Other allergic diseases involved with stress are chronic urticaria (hives), angioneurotic edema (allergic swelling), allergic rhinitis (hay fever) and vasomotor rhinitis (allergic cold). Since emotional factors can precipitate attacks, avoiding anxiety-producing situations and practicing relaxation techniques should prove beneficial. (See Chapter 20)

HYPERTHYROIDISM (GRAVE'S DISEASE)

Hyperthyroidism is a chronic disease of the thyroid gland in which there is excessive production of thyroid hormone (e.g., thyroxine). It is definitely related to emotional trauma although it appears to be an autoimmune disease. Remember from Chapter 2 that thyroxine is produced during stress. If this becomes chronic, hyperthyroidism could result in susceptible individuals.[81] In one animal study, it was observed that a breed of wild rabbits tended to develop hyperthyroidism after being frightened by a barking dog.[37] In human studies, it has been found that thyroxine levels markedly increase in: (1) hypnotized subjects imagining distressful situations; (2) soldiers recalling agonizing war incidents; (3) people discussing family problems; and (4) individuals watching a disturbing motion picture.[114] It has also been shown that hyperthyroidism occurs at times following severe psychological stressors and life-stress events.[52,81,105] Stress can also exacerbate the hyperthyroid condition.[52,106]

Hyperthyroidism is a disease of adult women. The incidence is about three cases per 10,000 adults per year in the United States and women victims outnumber men by a five to one ratio.[52] Some women who take thyroid pills for weight reduction (the rationale being that body metabolism will burn off excess weight) can develop symptoms of hyperthyroidism. People with a sluggish thyroid (i.e., hypothyroidism) also take thyroid pills. That, too, could induce a hyperthyroid state in an individual if that is not carefully monitored. To prevent acute attacks, women should take their medications and gain control over their anxieties. (See Chapter 20)

INFECTIOUS DISEASES

Introduction

Before the discovery of penicillin, infectious diseases were the great killers. There are many kinds of transmissible infections including pneumonia, tuberculosis, influenza, and the common cold. All are caused by specific microorganisms or viruses but, with each, stress plays a role. In Chapter 2, we discussed how the release of cortisone and catecholamines during stress causes an impairment of the host's immune and inflammatory responses. This, in turn, could allow microbes or viruses that were present to disseminate and multiply. Then the individual would come down with manifestations of the particular disease.

Women have a higher reported incidence of infectious diseases than men (i.e., primarily because of greater utilization of physicians). However, women have less serious complications.[5-7] This could be related to the following reason: one of the major microbe-fighting systems in the body is the myeloperoxidase-mediated antimicrobial system of the PMNs (i.e., one of the white blood cells). The PMNs phagocytize (engulf) microbes which are eventually destroyed. There is evidence that estrogen binds to the PMNs and stimulates the microbe-destroying activity.[115] This may help explain why women manage infections better than men.

The relationship of stress to infectious disease is especially relevant with tuberculosis.

Tuberculosis

Tuberculosis used to be a great killer. Nowadays, with good nutrition and use of combined antimicrobial therapy, it is rarely fatal. Tuberculosis is primarily a chronic lung disease. The causative agent is the bacteria Mycobacterium tuberculosis.

Although clinical cases of tuberculosis are greatly on the decline, infection* is common. Many people have been exposed to the tuberculosis bacillus, have it in their lungs, but don't come down with the disease. That is because their resistance tends to be high.

However, under conditions of stress, resistance breaks down and subclinical tuberculosis can become active. The release of cortisone during stress paralyzes the phagocytes that normally keep the tubercle bacilli in check. The microbes can then disseminate and cause the overt disease. For instance, when a patient has quiescent tuberculosis and is inadvertently given cortisone therapy, an acute "flare-up" may occur.[52] In a few studies, it has been shown that major life-stress events preceded the onset of tuberculosis.[105]

Tuberculosis incidence may have been higher in females[116] but the death rate is definitely lower in women.[52] Note that tuberculosis can cause amenorrhea. (See Chapter 6)

For control, it is important to: maintain good nutrition (see Chapter 22); avoid anxiety-inducing situations; avoid crowded conditions; and stay away from known tuberculosis carriers.

---

* Infection is presence of microbes in a tissue or body site, whereas infectious disease is a negative response by the host to the presence of the microbes. For example, the normal mouth is infected since millions of microbes are found in the saliva, but when conditions are "ripe" infectious disease such as gingivitis (gum disease) occurs. (See Figure 7.1)

Acute Coryza (The Common Cold)

The common cold is one of the most prevalent of all diseases, and is the most common transmissible disease. It is most prevalent in the winter; about 15 percent of the population per week is affected. Colds account for one-half of all absenteeism in business and industry.[52]

Although colds are caused by viruses and are transmitted by coughing and sneezing, stress is definitely a factor. Often when people feel "run down," they "catch" a cold. As is the case with the tubercle bacillus and tuberculosis, the viruses of the common cold are normally present but, in this case, they are in the nasal passages and throat rather than in the lungs. Stressors cause diminished resistance; the body's release of cortisone impairs the immune response and those same viruses or new ones then cause the clinical disease.

There is no difference in frequency by sex for the common cold. However, more women than men go to the physician for treatment of cold symptoms.[5-7] Treatment remedies are well-known but probably offer little beyond symptomatic relief (e.g., aspirin; decongestants; expectorants; and vitamin C).[119]*

Prevention is more important. One way is to stay clear of people with active colds. Another is to follow the advice on psychological coping methods, exercise, meditation, and nutrition offered in Chapters 20–23.

Influenza (La Grippe)

Influenza is an acute respiratory tract disease that results in symptoms out of proportion to its seriousness. It is caused by various strains of viruses. As discussed with the common cold, the reported cases of influenza in women are higher since women tend to make use of physicians' services more often than do men. However, they do not actually have a higher incidence than men and the complications are not as severe.[5-7]

Stress causes activation of the viruses, probably by the release of cortisone and catecholamines and their inhibition of the body's defense cells.[117,118] Treatment is symptomatic, with fluids, aspirin, and bed rest being the key components. There is some evidence that large doses of vitamin C can diminish the severity of the attacks.[119] Prevention is as described for the common cold.

---

* Aspirin and vitamin C shouldn't be taken together: aspirin diminishes the effect of vitamin C; vitamin C prolongs and intensifies the effect of aspirin. (Martin, E. W., *Hazards of Medication,* 2nd Ed., Philadelphia: J. P. Lippincott, 1978, p. 586.)

Infectious Mononucleosis ("Mono")

Infectious mononucleosis has recently been determined to be a virus disease. It typically affects young adults, often college-age people.

In college students, the peak incidence is early Spring and early Fall (right after vacations). "Mono" spreads rapidly under conditions of crowding and close personal contact ("the kissing disease").[52] It is of about equal incidence in both sexes but more female cases are reported. Although it is caused by a virus, lowered resistance is undoubtedly a factor. Stress is a major contributor to the lowered resistance. Other resistance-lowering factors are: lack of sleep; drug and alcohol intake; long hours of study; and poor diet.

Prevention is keyed toward eliminating the previously mentioned resistance-lowering factors and keeping out of crowds. The elimination of kissing is not seriously suggested but people should make close contact only when their resistance is high.

HYPOGLYCEMIA[52]

Hypoglycemia literally means low blood sugar. This condition can be found in patients with various diseases but we are primarily concerned with "spontaneous" or "functional" hypoglycemia in which there are no diseased organs. In this condition, there is often an excessive production of insulin. The insulin causes the glucose to be carried into the body's cells and this results in low blood sugar. In essence, this condition is the opposite of diabetes mellitus in which there is high blood sugar. Sometimes hypoglycemia can lead into diabetes. This can occur if the insulin-producing cells in the pancreas overwork and then "burn out." Then a lack of insulin can yield high blood sugar which can trigger diabetes.

Possible causes of spontaneous hypoglycemia are severe exercise, pregnancy, lactation, and stress. With exercise and stress, it may be a rebound phenomenon. The stress hormones result in glucose being "poured out" into the blood. Then glucose is brought into the cells by action of insulin. Insulin activity can become too effective and the blood sugar then gets quite low and symptoms of hypoglycemia develop.

Methods of control include psychotherapy and relaxation techniques. (See Chapter 20)

KIDNEY DISEASES

Although there are many types of kidney diseases, two have a particular relationship to stress. One is urinary tract inflammation and the other is enuresis (bed wetting).

Urinary Tract Inflammation

This disorder can be caused by infection and trauma, but psychological factors may be important. Some investigators have reported a personality picture of women who frequently come down with urinary tract inflammation. Such women are considered to be: passive; depressed; good natured to a fault; resigned to life's misfortunes; and victimized by others. Some of them may feign being dominant but still are passive and feel inadequate.[120]

Methods of control include: maintenance of good resistance (e.g., adequate sleep; good nutrition; and regular exercise); early treatment of infections to prevent serious complications; and avoidance of anxiety-producing situations.

Enuresis

Bed wetting is almost always psychological in origin. It occurs primarily in youngsters from four to fourteen years of age and is more common in boys than girls.[52] Prevention and treatment is primarily by psychotherapy but occasionally drugs are used as a temporary measure. Love and reassurance are the best antidotes.

ATYPICAL FACIAL NEURALGIA

Neuralgia literally means "ache" from a nerve. Most neuralgias are of unknown etiology. With atypical facial neuralgia, the patient's pain takes a bizarre, nonanatomic course. Hence, most investigators consider it to be a psychologically induced stress-related disease.[106] Atypical facial neuralgia is a disease with a high female incidence. Most reported cases are in perimenopausal women. Postmenopausal depression seems to be a factor in the onset of symptoms.[106]

Helpful control methods include psychotherapy and relaxation therapy. (See Chapters 8 and 20)

THE ADRENAL CORTEX DISORDERS: ADDISON'S DISEASE AND CUSHING'S SYNDROME

Remember from Chapter 2 that one of the primary systems in the stress response is the H-AP-AC axis. The "AC" component produces cortisone that, along with the catecholamines, are the major stress hormones. There are two relatively rare conditions related to under- and overproduction of the adrenal cortex hormones.

In Addison's disease, there is little or no production of cortisone. Hence, the people involved have a poor ability to cope with stress and regularly must be given supplemental cortisone. In contradistinction, Cushing's syndrome occurs from either an overproduction of cortisone by the adrenal cortex (usually caused by a tumor) or a supplementation of cortisone (used to treat various diseases).

Women have a much higher incidence of Cushing's syndrome than do men.[52] Cushing's patients also have negative responses to stressors. For example, they have problems with infection and often develop severe mood changes.

Both Addisonian and Cushing's patients must have their cortisone dosage carefully monitored during severe stressful incidents (e.g., prior to surgery) to prevent life-threatening complications.

GOUT

Gout is a hereditary disease of uric acid metabolism (involved in urine formation). It can form in various joints but the principal site is one of the big toes. Acute attacks are precipitated by: drinking alcoholic beverages; overeating; following an injury; and as the result of an emotional stress-producing involvement.[52,81]

The relationship of gout to stress is two-fold. First, in one study, it was shown that uric acid becomes elevated under certain stressful conditions.[121] Second, gout is a risk factor for the major stress-related disease, coronary heart disease.[122] Gout is generally a disease of older men who have led a life of "debauchery and intemperance."[15] To quote an old saying: "In the young, wine goes to the head; in the aged, it goes to the feet."

As is the case with coronary heart disease, women are much less susceptible to gout until the time of menopause. Hippocrates, the father of medicine, noted this: "Women do not take the gout until their menses be stopped."[52]

As far as management is concerned, prevention is the key: If you have the genetic tendency, don't be a glutton or an alcoholic, practice moderation, and avoid anxiety-producing situations.

SKIN AND HAIR CONDITIONS

There are various skin and hair conditions that can be exacerbated by stressful incidents. None of these are more frequent in either sex. The conditions are: neurodermatitis (a skin rash); wrinkled skin; alopecia (loss of hair on the head, face, arms, or legs); graying or whitening of hair; dandruff; and warts. According to one trichologist (i.e., a hair and scalp specialist), stress can cause all kinds of damage to hair including loss of hair, thinning of hair and slowed hair growth. Massage of the scalp can counteract the effects of stress by bringing extra blood, and its oxygen and nutrients, to the hair follicles. Scalp massage is also reported to be a wonderful tension-reliever.[123]

There is a definite cause for the appearance of warts. The papova virus lives inside epidermal cells (outer surface of the skin). Under anxiety-inducing conditions, the viruses multiply and produce the wart. Quite often warts continue to "crop up" until the underlying stress-inducing problems are resolved.[37]

MOUTH CONDITIONS

There are various mouth diseases and conditions that are affected by stress. These are generally not more frequent in one sex or the other.

Apthous and Herpetic Lesions

Apthous lesions are "canker sores." They are ulcers that are often found in the tongue, palate, gums, lips, and inside of the cheeks.

Herpetic ulcers are "cold sores" caused by a virus. They are usually found in the lips and gums. Both cold and canker sores often appear immediately after highly emotional periods.[86] Several studies have shown that canker sores are more frequent in women.[128]

The probable mechanism for the appearance of both cold sores and warts (as previously described) is that stress causes a rapid release of cortisone. This release inhibits the body's defenses and allows the viruses to multiply and cause the lesions.[37] Reducing stress should eliminate or decrease the severity of apthous and herpetic lesions.

Necrotizing Ulcerative Gingivitis

Many types of periodontal (gum and adjoining tissue) diseases exist but the one with the closest association to stress is necrotizing ulcerative gingivitis (NUG; Vincent's disease; trench mouth). Studies have shown that students before exams and soldiers during battle have a high incidence of NUG. Other studies show that NUG patients, as compared to controls, have high anxiety and increased blood pressure, respiratory rate, and pupillary dilation (indicating SNS activity).[37,86]

How stress affects the gums (gingiva) has been experimentally demonstrated. It has been shown that social and psychological stressors reduce oxygen concentration in the gingival tissues. The reduced oxygen (hypoxia) then causes degenerative changes in the tissues which show up as periodontal disease.[124]

Reducing stress and maintenance of good oral hygiene decreases the probability of re-infections.

Dental Caries (Dental Decay, Dental Cavities)

As mentioned in Chapter 2, one of the results of the stress response is decreased salivation (xerostomia). Studies have shown that under conditions of reduced salivation, dental decay increases. In animal experiments, stressed rats had increased caries as compared to nonstressed rats.[37,86,124] For humans, the time of maximum dental decay is the teen-age years. This is a period of high intake of "junk" foods. However, there are also associated psychological stressors that may induce decreased salivation (the effect of catecholamines) and impaired immune responses (the effect of cortisone). Together these effects would allow the microbes to multiply and produce "cavities."

Stress reduction should be a key factor in the prevention of dental decay. Since reduction of saliva promotes dental caries, increased salivation might reduce tooth decay. Saliva contains antimicrobial substances and the volume of fluid helps wash out bacteria from teeth crevices. Salivation increases before meals, when people are relaxed (as during meditation), and in anticipation of something pleasurable. Since sexual activity is something pleasurable, Darrell Sifford of *The Philadelphia Inquirer* inferred that "sex is good for your teeth."[125] (Well, Darrell, it may be true!)

Potpourri[37,86]

There are many other oral conditions that are stress-related. Tics are muscular twitches that become habitual and involuntary. They appear to be anxiety-induced and may be muscular expressions of psychological conflicts.

Psychological stressors such as anxiety, fear, and worry can precipitate certain oral habits. These include: thumbsucking; tongue thrusting; and nail-, lip- and cheek-biting. Altered taste sensations, and burning- and painful-tongue can occur in depressed people (usually women), and in individuals who have repeated emotional conflicts.

Over 90 percent of the cases of gagging are reported as being psychological in origin. Gaggers often express fears of suffocation or choking to death. Vague oral pain and paresthesia (numbnesslike sensation) have been reported to be induced by psychological stressors.

It can be seen that the mouth is a mirror of the body's stress. From gritting, grinding, and clenching to trench mouth and cavities, stress affects the mouth in a myriad of ways. By reducing stress, one may look forward to a "sound mouth in a sound body."

SEXUALLY RELATED DISORDERS

Of the sexually related disorders, oligomenorrhea, dysmenorrhea and premenstrual tension are covered in Chapter 6.

Impotence and infertility can either be related to organic conditions or psychological problems.[52] Quite often, anxiety, worry, and depression are involved in impotence. To determine the best course of action, it is important that diagnosis include medical and psychological approaches. In the past, the female had to suffer the shame and guilt even though it was the male who was impotent. Nowadays it is possible to get complete examinations without one or the other being assigned the blame.

If the problem happens to be psychological in origin, psychotherapy is obviously the treatment of choice. Statistics have shown that about 60 percent of the couples who are treated for infertility eventually have children.[126]

The major sexually transmitted (venereal) diseases are syphilis and gonorrhea. In these diseases, microbes are the principal causative factors with stress playing only a minor role. Within the last few years, another venereal disease has come into prominence. It is known as genital herpes. Just as is the case with oral herpes ("cold sores"), the ulcers are caused by a herpes simplex virus. The virus is transmitted during sexual intercourse and once it becomes established, it remains embedded in the body's cells with no known cure. Stress can cause an activation of the virus and then ulcers form (see Apthous and Herpetic Lesions under Mouth Conditions). It appears the more anxious one becomes about the recurrence of the sores, the greater is the chance that they will recur. Female virus carriers are under more stress than male virus carriers as the ulcers are visible on the male genitals but are hidden in the females internal genitals. Hence, the male can refrain from intercourse during active periods but the female may not be certain when she has active herpes. One saving grace is that genital herpes is not as serious as syphilis or gonorrhea.[129]

SUMMARY

There are many stress-related diseases of interest to women. Of major importance are the diseases of the cardiovascular system, cancer, depression headaches, bruxism, ulcers, diabetes, rheumatoid arthritis, and ulcerative colitis. Other stress-related conditions related to eating (obesity; anorexia nervosa) are covered in the next chapter, the stress-related disorders. The stress-related conditions, amenorrhea, dysmenorrhea, oligomenorrhea, and premenstrual tension are discussed in Chapter 6. Stress-related conditions related to menopause and aging are examined in Chapters 8 and 9.

REFERENCES

1. Eliot, R. S. *Stress and the Major Cardiovascular Disorders.* Mount Kisco, N.Y.: Futura, 1979.
2. Holland, J. Behavior: Fear and Trembling: Some myths exploded. *New York Magazine* 12:60, July 2, 1979.
3. Wolf, S. and Goodell, H. *Harold G. Wolff's Stress and Disease,* Second Ed. Springfield, Illinois: Charles C. Thomas, 1968.
4. Martinson, I. M. and Anderson, S. Male and female response to stress. *In* Kjervik, D. K. and Martinson, I. M. (eds.); *Women In Stress: A Nursing Perspective.* New York: Appleton-Century-Crofts, 1979, pp. 89–95.
5. Roskies, E. Sex, culture and illness: An overview. *Soc. Sci. Med.* 12(3B):139–141, 1978.
6. Mechanic, D. Sex, illness behavior and the use of health services. *Soc. Sci. Med.* (3B): 207–214, 1978.
7. Cooperstock, R. Sex differences in psychotropic drug use. *Soc. Sci. Med.* 12(3B): 179–186, 1978.
8. Glass, D. C. Stress, behavior patterns and coronary disease. *Am. Sci.* 65:177–187, 1977.
9. Anderson, T. W. Mortality from ischemic heart disease: Changes in middle-aged men since 1900. *J.A.M.A.* 224:336–338, 1973.
10. Murphy, H. B. M. Historic changes in the sex ratios for different disorders. *Soc. Sci. Med.* 12(3B):143–149, 1978.
11. Margolis, J. R., Gillum, R. F., Feinleib, M. Brasch, R., and Fabsitz, R. Community surveillance for coronary heart disease: The Framingham cardiovascular disease study. *Am. J. Cardiol.* 37:61–67, 1976.
12. Stallones, R. A. The rise and fall of ischemic heart disease. *Sci. Am.* 243(5):53–59, 1980.
13. Colburn, P. and Buonassisi, V. Estrogen-binding sites in endothelial cell cultures. *Science* 201:817–819, 1978.
14. Hartung, G. H., Foreyt, J. P., Mitchell, R. E., Vlasek, I., and Gotto, A. M., Jr. Relation of diet to high-density-lipoprotein cholesterol in middle-aged marathon runners, joggers, and inactive men. *N. Engl. J. Med.* 302:357–361, 1980.
15. Kolata, G. B. and Marx, J. L. Epidemiology of heart disease: Searches for causes. *Science* 194:509–512, 1976.
16. Brody, J. E. Panel reports healthy Americans need not cut intake of cholesterol. *New York Times.* 44, 597:A 1, 16, May 28, 1980.
17. Russek, H. I. and Russek, L. G. Behavior patterns and emotional stress in the etiology of

coronary heart disease: Sociological and occupational aspects. *In* Wheatley, D. (ed.), *Stress and the Heart*. New York: Raven Press, 1977, pp. 15–32.

18. Mann, G. V. Medical intelligence: Current concepts: Diet-heart: End of an era. *N. Engl. J. Med.* **297**:644–650, 1977.
19. Francis, K. T. Psychologic correlates of serum indicators of stress in man. *Psychosom. Med.* **41**:617–628, 1979.
20. Schaeffer, E. J., Anderson, D. W. Brewer, H. B., Jr., Levy, R. I., Danner, R. M., and Blackwelder, W. C. Plasma-triglycerides in regulation of H.D.L.-cholesterol levels. *Lancet* **2**:391–393, 1978.
21. Editorial. Vitamin C, HDL and a healthier heart. *Prevention* **30** (2):86–90, 1978.
22. Feltman, J. Lecithin cleans up cholesterol's dirty work. *Prevention* **30**(6):52–57, 1978.
23. Sherman, C. Jack Sprat had the right idea. *Prevention* **32**(2):133–142, 1980.
24. McGill, H. C., Jr., Anselmo, V. C., Buchanan, J. M., and Sheridan, P. J. The heart as target organ for androgen. *Science* **207**:775–776, 1980.
25. The Anturane Reinfarction Trial Research Group. Sulfinpyrazone in the prevention of cardiac death after myocardial infarction. *N. Engl. J. Med.* **298**:289–295, 1978.
26. Leff, D. N. Stress-triggered organic disease in this year of economic anxiety. *Med. World News* **16**:74–92, 1975.
27. Johansson, G. and Post, B. Catecholamine output of males and females over a one-year period. *Acta. Physiol. Scand.* **92**:557–565, 1974.
28. Collins, A. and Frankenhaeuser, M. Stress responses in male and female engineering students. *J. Hum. Stress* **4**(2):43–48, 1978.
29. Tanne, J. H. A newcomer in heart disease. *New York Magazine* **12**:75–84, December 17, 1979.
30. Kolata, G. B. FDA says no to Anturane. *Science* **208**:1130–1132, 1980.
31. Turlopaty, P. D. M. V. and Altura, B. M. Magnesium deficiency produces spasms of coronary arteries: Relationship to etiology of sudden death ischemic heart disease. *Science* **208**:198–202, 1980.
32. Shaw, L. The spasm theory of heart attack. *Prevention* **31**(10):106–110, 1979.
33. Antman, E., Muller, J., Goldberg, S., MacAlpin, R. Rubenfire, M., Tabatznik, B., Chang-seng, L., Heupler, F., Achuff, S., Reichek, N., Geltman, E., Kerin, N. Z., Neff, R. K., and Braunwald, E. Nifedipine therapy for coronary-artery spasm: Experience in 127 patients. *N. Engl. J. Med.* **302**:1269–1273, 1980.
34. Stumpf, W. E., Sar, M., and Aumüller, G. The heart: A target organ for estradiol. *Science* **196**:319–320, 1977.
35. Donlon, P. T., Meadow, A., and Amsterdam, E. Emotional stress as a factor in ventricular arrhythmias. *Psychosomatics* **20**:233–240, 1979.
36. Natelson, B. H. and Cagin, N. A. Stress-induced ventricular arrhythmias. *Psychosom. Med.* **41**:259–262, 1979.
37. Morse, D. R. and Furst, M. L. *Stress for Success: A Holistic Approach to Stress and its Management*. New York: Van Nostrand Reinhold 1979.
38. Neill, W. A., Wharton, T. P., Jr., Fluri-Lundeen, J., and Cohen, I. S. Acute coronary insufficiency: Coronary occlusion after intermittent ischemic attacks. *N. Engl. J. Med.* **302**:1157–1162, 1980.
39. Weinsier, R. L. Overview: Salt and the development of essential hypertension. *Prev. Med.* **5**:7–14, 1976.
40. Editorial. Hypertension more likely among less educated and blacks. *Med. World News* **19**(2):13, January 23, 1978.

41. Jenkins, C. D., Tuthill, R. W., Tannenbaum, S. I., and Kirby, C. Social stressors and excess mortality from hypertensive diseases. *J. Hum. Stress* **5**(3):29–40, 1979.
42. Waldron, I. Why do women live longer than men? *J. Hum. Stress* **2**(1):2–13, 1976.
43. Cooper, K. H. *The Aerobics Way.* New York: M. Evans, 1977.
44. Theorell, T. Life events and disease: Psychosocial precipitation of episodes of clinical coronary heart disease. *J. Psychosom. Res.* **23**:403–404, 1979.
45. Lewis, M. M. Dies after winning. *Philadelphia Eve. Bull.* NB 1, December 6, 1979.
46. Van Egeren, L. F. Social interactions, communications, and the coronary-prone behavior pattern: A psychophysiological study. *Psychosom. Med.* **41**:2–18, 1979.
47. Waldron, F. Type A behavior pattern and coronary heart disease in men and women. *Soc. Sci. Med.* **12**(3B):167–170, 1978.
48. Haynes, S. G. and Feinleib, M. Women, work and coronary heart disease: Prospective findings from the Framingham heart study. *Am. J. Public Health* **70**:133–141, 1980.
49. Jick, H., Miettiner, O. S., Neff, R. K., Shapiro, S., Heinonen, O. P., and Slone, D. Coffee and myocardial infarctions. *N. Engl. J. Med.* **289**:63–67, 1973.
50. Connor, W. E. and Connor, S. L. The key role of nutritional factors in the prevention of coronary heart disease. *Prev. Med.* **1**:49–83, 1972.
51. Dugdale, M. and Masi, A. T. Hormonal contraception and thromboembolic disease: Effects of the oral contraceptives on hemostatic mechanisms. *J. Chron. Dis.* **23**:775–790, 1971.
52. Beeson, P. B., Mc Dermott, W., and Wyngaarden, J. B. *Cecil Textbook of Medicine,* Fifteenth Ed. Philadelphia: W. B. Saunders, 1979.
53. Mann, J. I., Vassey, M. P., Thorogood, M., and Doll, R. Myocardial infarction in young women with special reference to oral contraceptive practice. *Br. Med. J.* **2**: 241–245, 1975.
54. Mann, J. I. and Inman, W. H. W. Oral contraceptives and death from myocardial infarction. *Br. Med. J.* **2**:245–248, 1975.
55. Higano, N., Robinson, R. W., and Cohen, W. D. Increased incidence of cardiovascular disease in castrated women. *N. Engl. J. Med.* **268**:1123–1125, 1963.
56. Blackard, C. E., Doe, R. P., Mellinger, G. T., and Byar, D. P. Incidence of cardiovascular disease and death in patients receiving diethystilbestrol for carcinoma of the prostate. *Cancer* **26**:249–256, 1970.
57. Holden, C. Cancer and the mind: How are they connected? *Science* **200**:1363–1369, 1978.
58. Hurst, M. W., Jenkins, C. D., and Rose, R. M. The relationship of psychological stress to onset of medical illness. *Ann. Rev. Med.* **27**:301–312, 1976.
59. Arehart-Treichel, J. Can your personality kill you? *New York Magazine* **10**:62–67, 1977.
60. LeShan, L. An emotional life-history pattern associated with neoplastic disease. *Ann. N.Y. Acad. Sci.* **125**:780–793, 1966.
61. Simonton, O. C. and Simonton, S. *Getting Well Again.* Los Angeles: J. P. Tarcher, 1978.
62. Sklar, L. S. and Anisman, H. Stress and coping factors influence tumor growth. *Science* **205**:513–515, 1979.
63. Greer, S. and Morris, T. Psychological attributes of women who develop breast cancer: A controlled study. *J. Psychosom. Res.* **19**:147–153, 1975.
64. Pettingale, K. W., Greer, S., and Tee, D. E. H. Serum IGA and emotional expression in breast cancer patients. *J. Psychosom. Res.* **21**; 395–399, 1977.
65. Weinstock, C. Recent progress in cancer psychobiology and psychiatry. *J. Amer. Soc. Psychosom. Dent. Med.* **24**:4–14, 1977.

66. Fogg, S. Scientists link cancer and emotionalism. *Philadelphia Eve. Bull.* NA 2, April 6, 1978.
67. Cole, P. Oral contraceptives and endometrial cancer. *N. Engl. J. Med.* **302:**575–576, 1980.
68. Neuberger, J., Nunnerley, H. B., Davis, M. Portmann, B., Laws, J. W., and Williams, R. Oral contraceptive-associated liver tumours: Occurrence of malignancy and difficulties in diagnosis. *Lancet.* **8163:**273–276, 1980.
69. Pfeffer, R., Arthur, M. and Henderson, B. E. A case-control study of menopausal estrogen therapy of breast cancer. *J.A.M.A.* **243:**1635–1639, 1980.
70. Editorial. More backing for conservative treatment of breast cancer. *Med. World News* **19(14):**63–64, July 10, 1978.
71. Fulman, R. The emotional scars. *Philadelphia Daily News* 72, April 19, 1979.
72. Paykell, E. S. Life stress, depression and attempted suicide. *J. Hum. Stress* **2(3):**3–12, 1976.
73. Rahe, R. H. Life change events and mental illness: An overview. *J. Hum. Stress* **5(3):**2–10, 1979.
74. Klerman, G. L. The age of melancholy. *Psychol. Today* **12(11):**36–43, 1979.
75. Arieti, S. Roots of depression: The power of the dominant other. *Psychol. Today* **12(11):**54–58, 92–93, 1979.
76. Scarf, M. *Unfinished Business: Pressure Points in the Lives of Women.* Garden City, N.Y.: Doubleday, 1980.
77. Lewis, H. B. Sex differences in superego mode as related to sex differences in psychiatric illness. *Soc. Sci. Med.* **12(3B):**199–205, 1978.
78. Flor-Henry, P. Gender, hemispheric specialization and psychopathology. *Soc. Sci. Med.* **12(3B):**155–162, 1978.
79. Gove, W. R. Sex differences in mental illness among adult men and women: An evaluation of four questions raised regarding the evidence on the higher rates of women. *Soc. Sci. Med.* **12(3B):**187–198, 1978.
80. Rosenfield, S. Sex differences in depression: Do women always have higher rates? *J. Health Soc. Beh.* **21(3):**33–42, 1980.
81. Selye, H. *The Stress of Life,* Second Ed. New York: McGraw-Hill Book Co., 1976.
82. Ziegler, D. K. Headache syndromes: Problems of definition. *Psychosomatics* **20:**443–447, 1979.
83. Kudrow, L. Current aspects of migraine headache. *Psychosomatics* **19:**48–57, 1978.
84. Cohen, M. J., Rickles, W. H., and McArthur, D. L. Evidence for physiological response stereotyping in migraine headaches. *Psychosom. Med.* **40:**344–354, 1978.
85. Friedman, A. P. Characteristics of tension headache: A profile of 1,420 cases. *Psychosomatics* **20:**451–461, 1979.
86. Morse, D. R. and Furst, M. L. Stress and the oral cavity. *In* Selye, H. (ed.), *Selye's Guide to Stress Research.* Vol. 2. New York: Van Nostrand Reinhold, 1981. In Press.
87. Editorial. Mysterious headaches may point to bruxism. *Dent. Prod. Rep.* 48, March 1976.
88. Editorial. Tensions cause MPD disorders in women. *J.A.D.A.* 92:893, 1976.
89. Gelb, H. Multidisciplinary management of the craniomandibular syndrome. *N.Y.S. Dent. J.* 46:190–195, 1980.
90. Norris, C. Is your back biting back? *Dent. Manag.* **17(11):**57–60, 1977.
91. McQuade, W. and Aikman, A. *Stress: What It Is, What It Can Do to Your Health, How to Fight Back.* New York: E. P. Dutton, 1974.

92. Nagi, S. Z., Riley, L. E., and Newby, L. G. A social epidemiology of back pain in a general population. *J. Chron. Dis.* **26**:769–779, 1973.

93. Leavitt, F., Garron, D. C., and Bieliauskas, L. A. Stressing life events and the experience of low back pain. *J. Psychosom. Res.* **23**:49–55, 1979.

94. Menguy, R. The prophylaxis of stress ulceration. *N. Engl. J. Med.* **302**:461–462, 1980.

95. Kaercher, D. Ulcer: What's your risk? *Better Homes & Gardens* **58**(6):16–18, 1980.

96. Weiner, H. *Psychobiology and Human Disease.* New York: Elsevier, 1977.

97. Miller, N. E. and Dworkin, B. R. Effects of learning on visceral functions–Biofeedback. *N. Engl. J. Med.* **276**:1274–1278, 1977.

98. Brady, J. V. Ulcers in "executive monkeys." *Sci. Am.* **199**(4):95–100, 1958.

99. Seligman, M. Chronic fear produced by unpredictable electric shock. *J. Comp. Physiol. Psychol.* **66**:402–411, 1968.

100. Wolf, S. *The Stomach.* New York: Oxford University Press, 1965.

101. Wolf, S., Almy, T. P., Bachrach, W. H., Spiro, H. M., Sturdevant, M. D., and Weiner, H. The role of stress in peptic ulcer disease. *J. Hum. Stress* **5**(2):27–37, 1979.

102. Cobb, S. and Rose, R. M. Hypertension, peptic ulcer and diabetes in air traffic controllers. *J.A.M.A.* **224**:489–492, 1973.

103. Pflanz, M. Sex differences in abdominal illness. *Soc. Sci. Med.* **12**(3B):171–176, 1978.

104. Hamilton, C. L. and Chaddock, T. Social interactions and serum insulin values in the monkey (Macaca mulatta). *Psychosom. Med.* **39**:444–450, 1977.

105. Petrich, J. and Holmes, T. H. Life changes and onset of illness. *Med. Clin. N. Am.* **61**:825–838, 1977.

106. Morse, D. R. *Clinical Endodontology: A Comprehensive Guide to Diagnosis, Treatment and Prevention.* Springfield, Ill: Charles C. Thomas, 1974.

107. Bradley, C. Life events and the control of diabetes mellitus. *J. Psychosom. Med.* **23**:159–162, 1979.

108. Pedersen, O., Beck-Nielsen, H., and Heding, L. Increased insulin receptors after exercise in patients with insulin-dependent diabetes mellitus. *N. Engl. J. Med.* **302**:886–892, 1980.

109. Spergel, P., Ehrlich, G. E., and Glass, D. The rheumatoid arthritic personality: A psychodiagnostic myth. *Psychosomatics* **19**:79–86, 1978.

110. Grace, W. J., Wolf, S., and Wolf, H. G. *The Human Colon.* New York: Paul B. Hoeber, 1951.

111. Gilat, T. and Rozen, P. Epidemiology of Crohn's disease and ulcerative colitis: Etiologic implications. *Isr. J. Med. Sci.* **15**:305–308, 1979.

112. Editorial. Medicine: Capsules: Reassessing the pill's risks. *Time* **115**(26):40, June 30, 1980.

113. Bloomfield, H. H., Cain, M. P., and Jaffe, D. T. *TM* Discovering Inner Energy and Overcoming Stress.* New York: Delacorte, 1975.

114. Lewis, H. R. and Lewis, M. E. *Psychosomatics: How Your Emotions Can Damage Your Health.* New York: Viking Press, 1972.

115. Klebanoff, S. J. Effect of estrogens on the myeloperoxidase-mediated antimicrobial system. *Infect. Immun.* **25**;153–156, 1979.

116. Burket, L. B. *Oral Medicine: Diagnosis and Treatment,* 3rd Ed. Philadelphia, J. P. Lippincott, 1957, pp. 380–383.

117. Gruchow, H. W. Catecholamine activity and infectious disease episodes. *J. Hum. Stress* **5**(3):11–17, 1979.

118. Mason, J. W., Buescher, E. L., Belfer, M. L., Artenstein, M. S., and Mougey, E. H. A prospective study of corticosteroid and catecholamine levels in relation to viral respiratory illness. *J. Hum. Stress* **5**(3):18–28, 1979.

119. Pauling, L. *Vitamin C, The Common Cold and the Flu*. San Francisco: W. H. Freeman, 1976.
120. Chertok, L., Bourguignon, O., Guillon, F., and Aboulker, P. Urethral syndrome in the female ("irritable bladder"): The expression of fantasies about the urogenital area. *Psychosom. Med.* **39**:1-10, 1977.
121. Rahe, R. H., Ryman, D. H., and Biersner, R. J. Serum uric acid, cholesterol, and psychological moods throughout stressful naval training. *Aviat. Space Environ. Med.* **47**:883-888, 1976.
122. Howard, R. B. and Herbold, N. H. *Nutrition in Clinical Care*. New York: McGraw-Hill Book Co., 1978.
123. Goodman, J. Don't let worries go to your head: Looking good. *Philadelphia Eve. Bull.* WA 4, March 16, 1980.
124. Manhold, J. H. Stress, oral disease, and general illness. *Psychosomatics* **20**:83-87, 1979.
125. Sifford, D. Stress hits in the mouth: There's a reason for that dry taste. *Philadelphia Inq.* 14-C, June 26, 1980.
126. Landers, A. Her "obsession" could ruin a second chance. *Philadelphia Inq.* 4-D, July 22, 1980.
127. Brown, G. M. Psychiatric and neurologic aspects of endocrine disease. *In* Krieger, D. T. and Hughes, J. C. (eds.), *Neuroendocrinology*. Sunderland, Mass.: Sinauer Associates, 1980, pp. 185-193.
128. Antoon, J. W. and Miller, R. L. Apthous ulcers—A review of the literature on etiology, pathogenesis, diagnosis and treatment. *J.A.D.A.* **101**:803-808, 1980.
129. Gottlieb, A. J., Zamkoff, K. W., Jastremski, M. S., Scalzo, A., and Imboden, K. J. *The Whole Internist Catalog*. Philadelphia: W. B. Saunders, 1980, p. 484.

4
Stress-Related Disorders:
From "Closet Alcoholics"
to
Suicidal Women

In Chapter 3, it was shown how stress can directly or indirectly cause many diseases in women. In this chapter, it is shown how women's *responses* to stress can cause certain diseases and disorders. The conditions and situations covered are: alcoholism; caffeinism; drug addiction; excessive smoking; obesity; "chewing"; anorexia nervosa; accidents; divorce; "running away"; business breakup; and suicide.

ALCOHOLISM

People drink alcoholic beverages for many reasons. In business, drinking is conducive to consummating deals (the two-martini business*man*'s lunch). This was primarily a male pastime, but with many women entering sales and promotional occupations, women are also ordering a few "rounds" at lunchtime. Men often have friendly drinking encounters at the neighborhood bar or pub. It used to be unseemly or "unladylike" for a woman to fraternize at a bar, but that, too, is changing.

Some people drink for health reasons and, as was mentioned in the last chapter under coronary heart disease, a moderate intake of alcoholic beverages (e.g., one or two glasses of wine daily) increases the protective HDLs.[1] Alcohol in moderate doses also has a relaxing effect; the vasodilatation gives a warm feeling.

Finally, and probably most important, people drink to escape daily stressors. To "drown one's troubles in drink" is a great American practice and one of the major stress-reducing outlets. Unfortunately, it is also one of the most damaging.

Excessive drinking or alcoholism is a serious problem. Ten million adult Americans are considered to be alcoholics or problem drinkers.[2] Excessive drinking can lead to: brain damage; cirrhosis of the liver; cancer; heart injury; and damage to the body's immune system.[2,3] Drinking can be considered a "death-defying act," being responsible for half of all traffic accidents, many suicides, and a high incidence of fatal drug reactions.

Chronic alcoholics have morbidity and mortality rates that are much higher than social drinkers.[4] Alcohol is a central nervous system depressant and interacts, sometimes fatally, with narcotics (like codeine), barbiturates (sleeping pills) and antianxiety agents (like Valium®).[5] Drinking is often to blame for business breakups, family strife and divorces.

Even with all of its attendant problems, drinking by males has always been tolerated in the United States. After all, it was "manly" to have a drink and if you happened to have "one too many" that was all right too. If things got too bad, then the boss or the family would often see to it that the man was treated since he was the breadwinner and needed in the business.

The drinking woman was another story. Most often it was a quiet affair done in the privacy of her home. And as long as the family wasn't disrupted too much, her drinking often went untreated. Even when women were flagrant drunkards, more often than not they were neither confronted nor arrested by police. They were either left alone (i.e., they usually weren't public nuisances) or were sent home.[6] Society often considered women problem drinkers to be either "bad" mothers or prostitutes. But, of course, neither characterization was true. Most women alcoholics, as stated before, drink at home and not in bars or hotels. And in one study, all mothers felt that the worst part of their problem was the guilt they felt about their children.[7]

The differences in female-male drinking patterns and arrest practices are reflected in the statistics. Until quite recently, there were about seven male alcoholics to every three female alcoholics.[8] But those were reported cases and, as mentioned previously, many female cases went unreported. Times are changing though; women are "coming out of the closet," at least with respect to their drinking habits.

Women are going to bars, liquor stores, and drinking at businesspeople's luncheons. A report by *Liquor Store Magazine* revealed that in 1962, women made up 29 percent of the liquor store customers. In 1974, they made up more than 50 percent of the customers.[9] Even the "housewife drunk" is getting more liberated and going in for treatment. In 1968, 22 percent of the members of *Alcoholics Anonymous* were women. In 1977, women comprised 29 percent of its membership.[9] As a result, women are creeping closer to men in the statistics. Now there are about six male alcoholics to every four female alcoholics.[8] In terms of numbers, there are over two million adult female alcoholics in the United States.[9]

Until recently, there wasn't too much known about female alcoholics. Most studies on alcoholism were restricted to males and often those of the lower socioeconomic level. The few studies of women concentrated on middle-class samples (i.e., women who could afford to be treated or women who had psychological support).[10,11]

Some recent findings are of interest:

1. People with antisocial personalities (i.e., who tend to be criminals) who drink are usually males.[12]
2. Women drinkers tend to have a history of depression.[12]
3. Married women who are employed generally have higher drinking rates than do single working women or housewives.[13]
4. Working women and short-term unemployed women regularly drink more than do long-term unemployed women.[13]
5. Frequency and volume of drinking is higher in more educated women; this is not true with men.[13]
6. There is an increasing incidence of women reporting to hospitals and clinics for treatment of mixed drug-alcohol abuse.[14]
7. There is a high rate of miscarriage (25–45 percent), abortion (15–33 percent) and having handicapped children (10–30 percent) for women alcoholics.[12]
8. Women alcoholics also have a high rate of mentally retarded children.[2] A specific syndrome known as the *fetal alcohol syndrome* (alcohol addiction) occurs in some children of alcoholic mothers.[15]*
9. Suicide attempts are higher in chronic alcoholic women than in chronic alcoholic men.[12]

Why people drink has been discussed; but specifically, why do women drink? Probably the main reason is they drink to escape daily stressors. The woman at home is engaged in nonstimulating work. This labor is beneath

---

* A possible way that alcohol can cause mental retardation in the unborn child was shown in a recent animal study. Alcohol intake during pregnancy caused marked abnormal changes in the hippocampus (a brain area) of the fetuses of alcoholic rat mothers. West, J. R., Hodges, C. A. and Black, A. C. Jr. Prenatal exposure to ethanol alters the organization of hippocampal mossy fibers in rats. *Science* **211**: 957–959, 1981.

the intellectual level of most married women who later become drinkers. Women in the job market often must fight sexism, sexual harassment, low salaries, and unstimulating and unrewarding business opportunities.

Married working women with children often have the dual role of competing in business and having to take care of the home and family. Leaving young children at home or in nurseries sets up additional guilt stressors. Also, it is not considered "ladylike" to let out stress by shouting, screaming, and stomping as do many men.

Considering all of this, it is no wonder that some women want to escape "in the bottle." But things are improving. Marriages and "living together" are becoming sharing arrangements. The husband and wife have equal responsibilities for the house and family while both work. Business opportunities are opening up for women in many formerly "male" occupations.

Women can break the drinking habit. Alcoholics Anonymous does an outstanding job, and techniques such as hypnosis and meditation may alter the drinking pattern. (See Chapter 20)

CAFFEINISM

The typical husband and wife generally start off the day with a cup of coffee. At work, many individuals join in for another institution, the "coffee break." If the woman stays at home, there are often other cups of coffee or tea that help her cope with the daily stressors. Boys and girls get "in on the act" too by drinking colas and cocoa, and eating chocolate bars and cakes. Caffeine is the common ingredient in all of these drinks and snacks. Although caffeine in moderation is an effective and pleasureable stimulant, in large amounts it can be dangerous. Many of us take large amounts without being aware of the quantity. An average cup of coffee contains 100 milligrams of caffeine; the decaffeinated brands have 3.5 milligrams. An average cup of tea has 50 milligrams, while a cup of cocoa contains somewhat less. The typical cola has about 20 milligrams of caffeine and a chocolate bar contains around 25 milligrams.[16]

Even one cup of coffee can act as a severe stimulant for some people and interfere with sleep. It may also stimulate urination (which can also interfere with sleep). According to some recent studies, coffee drinkers have increased risks for peptic ulcers, bladder cancer, and heart attacks.[16,17]*

---

* In a recent study from Harvard University, it was found that people who drink a cup or two of coffee a day are almost twice as likely as non-coffee drinkers to get cancer of the pancreas. As there was no association found between pancreatic cancer and tea drinking, it seems that caffeine (found in both coffee and tea) is not the culprit. The researchers suggested that further testing is necessary. MacMahon, B., Yen, S., Trichopoulos, D., Warren, K., and Nardi, G. Coffee and cancer of the pancreas. *N. Engl. J. Med.* **304**:630–633, 1981.

Box 4.1. Caffeinated Beverages By Sex.

In our study of personality and words selected for meditation (see Chapter 2), an interesting relationship was found. As part of the study, seventy-two subjects were questioned on their drinking habits. As far as alcoholic beverages were concerned, there were no noticeable differences between women and men. Most of the subjects considered themselves social drinkers. With respect to caffeinated beverages, on the average the female coffee drinkers had 3.6 cups per day; for the males, it was 2.2 cups per day. Tea drinkers drank less per day but, even here, the women drank more; an average of 2.5 cups a day as opposed to 1 cup daily for the men. Of course, a small sample such as this is not representative of national averages but it does give an indication that women may be drinking caffeinated beverages in a great enough amount to cause damage.

Taking several cups of coffee daily can lead to caffeinism. Symptoms are: nervousness; irritability; headache; insomnia; and dizziness. The individuals are highly anxious in many situations.[3] Paradoxically, caffeine withdrawal causes similar symptoms. A recent study revealed increased anxiety and muscle tension after abstinence in habitual coffee drinkers.[18]

Just as many women drink alcoholic beverages to cope with home and work-related "pressures," so, too, do they drink caffeinated beverages. It is difficult to get a true indication of coffee and tea drinking frequency by sex. In Box 4.1 some evidence is presented.

There does seem to be a problem with pregnant women and caffeine. Studies show that if pregnant women drink five or more cups of coffee a day (or its equivalent in tea or cocoa) they will substantially increase the risk of having babies born with birth defects (e.g., cleft palate; missing toes and fingers).[19] Studies have shown that 23 percent of all Americans who drink coffee consume five or more cups a day. Recently, the FDA warned pregnant women to either avoid or minimize caffeine intake.[20]

It would be advisable to drink coffee and tea in moderation. Even better, one should drink a decaffeinated variety or a noncaffeinated beverage (e.g., Postum®).

SMOKING

As is the case with drinking, people smoke for many reasons. At those same business*men's* luncheons, for a woman, lighting a cigarette (along with a cup of coffee) is often part of the closing ceremony. Smoking for

Box 4.2. "Kicking The Habit."

A good start is to join an organization such as *Smokenders*. Drugs work for some individuals and, interestingly enough, so do some foods. Researchers at the University of Nebraska Medical School found that cigarette smokers smoke primarily because of the craving for nicotine.[26] During smoking the nicotine from the cigarettes enters the bloodstream. Stress, alcoholic beverages, and acidic foods (e.g., meats) decrease the blood level of nicotine and make the cigarette smoker crave more cigarettes to maintain a given level. By eating alkaline foods, there is less nicotine lost and the smoker would require fewer additional cigarettes. The researchers found that by eating such foods or taking an alkaline drug such as sodium bicarbonate, smokers cut down the number of cigarettes smoked. The alkaline foods also made it easier for them to stop smoking entirely. Some popular alkaline foods are: spinach; lima beans; raisins; brewer's yeast; almonds; carrots; grapefruit; sweet potatoes; celery; tomatoes; and strawberrries.

Some other ways to break the cigarette habit include: behavior modification; hypnosis; and meditation. (See Chapter 20)

many teen-agers is a way to join the "in" crowd. As previously mentioned, teen-age girls are the fastest growing group of new smokers.[21]

Many people smoke for the pleasures derived which may be related to the sensual feel of the cigarette in the mouth. According to Freudian psychology, the mouth is a primal pleasure zone and many people smoke for oral gratification. Others are stimulated by the nicotine content.

A major reason people smoke is for stress relief. As with drinking, smoking is one of the major American stress-reducing outlets, and also one of the most dangerous. Firm evidence exists between cigarette smoking and the development of lung cancer, emphysema, and coronary heart disease.[21] According to a large prospective study of adult Americans, heavy smokers' mortality rate was more than double that of nonsmokers.[4]

Not only has there been a dramatic increase in the smoking habits of teen-age girls, but women in general have significantly increased their smoking. Increased deaths from lung cancer and heart attacks (even though not as high as in males) have attested to their new-found habit.[21]

The health-related problems with birth control pills have been previously discussed. One other study revealed that women who smoke and also take oral contraceptives have an increased risk of heart attack and brain hemorrhage.[23] Pregnant women who smoke tend to give birth to smaller babies than nonsmokers. They also have an increased risk of miscarriages, stillborns, and babies who die soon after birth.

Marijuana smoking is becoming more acceptable among women, but the health-related problems are not well substantiated. For pregnant women there may be damage to the chromosomes of the unborn child.[24] Unless absolutely essential, it is certainly not worth the risk to take any drugs during pregnancy. Breaking the cigarette habit is difficult but the attempt is worthwhile. (See Box 4.2)

DRUG ADDICTION

As previously discussed, people drink and smoke for many reasons. There are also reasons why people take drugs. A major reason is for the treatment of diseases (e.g., penicillin is life-saving in many infectious diseases). Another reason to take drugs is for the control of pain. For acute pain, as in the case of a severe burn or injury, narcotics are essential. For chronic pain, drug use is less indicated and often is kept up as a crutch.

Just as was the case with alcohol, nicotine and caffeine, narcotics can cross the placental barrier and negatively affect the fetus. Studies have shown that chronic use of narcotics by pregnant women can cause their offspring to become narcotic addicts at birth.[27]

Some individuals take drugs to help them fall asleep and remain asleep. Barbiturates are used in this regard. Dependency upon pills to overcome insomnia is foolish and dangerous. Excessive doses taken deliberately or accidentally can lead to respiratory depression and death. Barbiturates also interact dangerously with alcohol and pain pills.[5,14]

Students studying for exams and people wanting to lose weight often take amphetamines (e.g., "speed"). The stimulating effects may keep students awake, and "burn off" excess calories for the obese, but amphetamines are dangerous and psychologically addicting (i.e., habituating).[5]

Others looking for pleasure and excitement take drugs such as LSD, heroin, cocaine, and marijuana. But the effects are only temporary. And the drugs are strongly addictive with damaging side effects.

In this "uptight" society, the main reason people take drugs is for the control of anxiety and depression. In addition to drinking and smoking, taking pills such as Valium is a favorite American stress-relieving pastime. In fact, Valium is the "Number One" prescription drug.[28] Valium is popular because it is: (1) relatively safe; (2) effective in the control of anxiety; (3) a daytime sedative; (4) an effective sleeping pill; (5) an excellent muscle relaxant; (6) helpful in the control of seizures; and (7) an aid in the treatment of alcoholic withdrawal.[29] But Valium and tranquilizers can be dangerous if their use becomes habitual since they interact with other drugs and alcohol.[5,14,30,31] Recently, these drugs have been put under strict control by the FDA.[28,29] *

Who takes all these drugs? Men take more of the illegal addicting drugs such as heroin, marijuana, and cocaine.[8] Women are way ahead in the use of psychotropic drugs such as the major tranquilizers (e.g., Thorazine®), antianxiety agents (e.g., Valium), barbiturates (e.g., Nembutal®), antidepressants (e.g., (Elavil®) and amphetamines (e.g., Dexedrine®).[32] The FDA states that there are about 1–2 million female drug abusers in the United States.[33]

Why do women take all of these drugs? Numerous studies have shown that women report more symptoms than men; they go to physicians more frequently for those symptoms; they get more prescriptions from their physicians; they're more conscientious in filling the prescriptions than men; and they are more likely to get renewed prescriptions. Women also self-medicate for their symptoms more than do men.[32-34] We can only speculate on why this situation has occurred. Women probably take drugs for the same reasons as is discussed under *Alcoholism*. They are mainly treated by male physicians who often take the "easy way out" and write prescriptions. Nonliberated women are used to the authoritative role of the male physician and feel obliged to follow his counsel.[8]

Recent studies in the United States have identified nonworking married women as the largest group of tranquilizer users. In this case, being single is definitely advantageous since unmarried women take less tranquilizers and sedatives than do married women. The evidence also shows that the contemporary working woman (single or married) takes fewer tranquilizers and sedatives than the traditional housewife.[32]

Hence, the best advice for women is: Don't depend on drugs. If possible, get out of the household rut. Have your housewife duties shared if you are married or "living together." Whether single or married, seriously consider working in a job suitable to your needs and education. And learn the positive methods of stress control. (See Chapters 20–23)

OBESITY

People even eat for a variety of reasons. Of course, people "eat to live" but many also "live to eat." During that "business*man's* lunch," "weighty"

---

* At a recent meeting of the American Association for the Advancement of Science, a Canadian researcher gave evidence from animal experiments that Valium can promote the growth of existing cancers. A spokesperson for the manufacturer of Valium stated that there is no evidence for this association in humans. Kotulak, R. Valium may promote cancers, expert says. *Philadelphia Inq.* **16–A,** Jan. 8, 1981.

matters are covered and food and drink often add "weight" to the individuals concerned.

Eating can be pleasureable as well as an oral fixation. Some people are impelled to put things into their mouths, and what could be better than putting in something that tastes good. Finally, eating is a means of coping with stress. But in similar fashion to drinking, smoking, and drug ingestion, compulsive eating is a negative coping method and can also lead to obesity. Obesity can contribute to a number of diseases (e.g., coronary heart disease; strokes; hypertension; diabetes; kidney diseases; and back problems.[3,35]

In a major prospective study, it was found that obese individuals had a greater mortality rate than people whose weight was within average weight-height-body frame-adjusted limits. Obesity is a major health problem in the United States with up to 30 percent of the American population being overweight, and many of the obese being women.[35*]

A recent study showed that the obese are subject to severe ridicule, humiliation, and discrimination.[36] They were ranked lower than the physically handicapped, and negatively ranked along with drug addicts, alcoholics, homosexuals, and people with mental illness. The logic is that obesity (as with the other cases) is the individual's own fault. This discrimination is unjustified since obesity is a complex matter that is not simply caused by overeating and underexercising.

There are now national obese people's organizations (e.g., Fat Liberation Movement). These organizations are trying to decrease the harassment of the obese. However, it may be that the fat liberation organizations are doing a disservice when they advise the obese to try and *not* lose weight. It is not sound advice; the health consequences are too dangerous.

It is probably true that part of the health-related problems with obesity are induced by the stressors of our society and especially the alternating cycles of weight loss (i.e., fasting) and weight gain (i.e., feasting). Nevertheless, if one follows the advice given in Chapters 20–23, it is possible to lose weight, maintain the weight loss, and still cope positively with stress.

Obesity is primarily caused by overeating and underexercising but there are other factors involved. (See Box 4.3)

There are also social and ethnic factors that determine who becomes obese. Some examples are given in Box 4.4.

---

* Two recent papers summarizing known current evidence conclude that "desired" body weights should be revised upward by about 10 to 15 pounds. The data also suggests that being too thin can be just as dangerous as being too heavy. Even with the upward revision of "desired" body weight, obesity is still recognized as imposing a health risk (e.g., dangers of hypertension, diabetes, gall bladder disease and certain cancers). Lewin, R. Overblown reports distort obesity risks. *Science* 211:258, 1981.

Box 4.3. Fat Theories.

Fat people tend to have fat children. Part of this may be genetic but mostly it is social as even adopted children of the obese tend to become fat. A sluggish thyroid gland may contribute to overweight but it is rarely a major factor. Obese people may have a disturbed mechanism in their appetite-regulatory center in the hypothalamus. (See Figure 2.5) They may also have irregularities in an enzyme that controls blood triglycerides (fat compounds).[37] A recent finding is that the obese may have an excess of the hormone, beta-endorphin (also involved in pain control) that appears to induce a craving for sweet, fat foods. This hormone increases when people are in pain. Hence, it may be that some people eat when they are in pain.[38,39]

Another theoretical mechanism of why some fat people remain obese is that they have either less "brown fat" (i.e., small deposits of brown-appearing fat cells) or a decreased ability to burn brown fat, than do naturally lean people. In animal experiments, it has been shown that brown fat is an exceedingly powerful heat-producer. Some people with active brown fat mechanisms may be able to burn off excess calories as heat without gaining weight.[40]

Not to be outdone, researchers at Harvard have uncovered another mechanism. They have determined that an enzyme, ATPase, is a major factor in weight control.[41] This enzyme is involved in energy metabolism and people vary in the amount found in their blood. With a large amount of ATPase present, individuals burn more calories; hence, they can eat more. People who have little ATPase use up fewer calories and as a result, they gain weight.

Fat people can now eat without feeling guilty; they can have their pick of hypothetical explanations for why they've gained weight.

Controlling obesity is a major problem. In general, only from 5 to 20 percent of fat people can lose weight and keep it off after dieting.[35] Even with all the diet books around, no one diet has been found to be superior. Drugs such as thyroid pills and amphetamines may be temporarily effective but they can be dangerous.[5]

The same is true for intestinal bypass surgery af a means of taking off excess pounds. There are possible complications such as arthritis, rashes, kidney, and lung diseases.[42]* Another method that is temporarily effective

* A relatively new surgical procedure for obesity is called *gastroplasty*. It involves creating a small pouch at the top of the stomach to allow for the holding of a very small amount of food. When this small pouch fills up, the individual feels satisfied. The food then passes into the remainder of the stomach and digestion takes place. As the person is satisfied with less,

Box 4.4. Who Gets Fat.

There are interesting associations with obesity.[35] Americans of Irish, Scotch, and English descent tend to be thinner than Italian, Spanish, and German-Americans. Less-educated women tend to be heavier than more-educated women. Black women are usually heavier than white women, but black men are thinner than white men. As they climb the socioeconomic ladder, black men get heavier and black women get thinner. No association has been found between obesity and the speed of eating. Whether one eats slowly or fast doesn't seem to matter in terms of gaining weight. The sight and smell of food doesn't attract fat people any more than lean people. Fat people don't necessarily eat more than thin people.

There is some evidence that people who are fat as infants and remain fat have more fat cells than people who become fat as adults. The number of fat cells in obese children increase continuously from birth to ages fourteen to sixteen. Some fat people have many fat cells; others have very large fat cells; and still others have both large and numerous fat cells. What it all means is not really known.

is jaw-wiring. But this, too, causes complications such as dental decay, gum disease, and speech problems.

Behavior modification and hypnosis are effective for some obese people as are the organizations *Weight Watchers* and *Overeaters Anonymous.* A combination of aerobic exercise, small meals, and avoidance of late-night snacking is an effective means of controlling obesity. (See Chapters 21 and 22) Women normally have a built-in protection against heart disease. They should not jeopardize that protection by becoming obese.

CHEWING, BITING AND SUCKING

Instead of eating to reduce stress, some people engage in chewing, biting, and sucking. Chewing and biting can take many forms. Chewing tobacco and toothpicks are predominantly male activities; and women have a preference for hair pins. All forms of chewing, biting and sucking have their negative aspects. Chewing on fingernails, pencils, pins, and toothpicks can cause damage to the teeth and induce a faulty bite. Chewing on sugar-containing gum can promote dental decay and the gum can loosen fillings, "caps," and bridges. Some of the artificial sweeteners in sugar-free

she eats less and loses weight. The procedure is commonly known as *stomach stapling* and is considered less drastic than *intestinal bypass surgery.* Nevertheless, any surgery can have complications. Jenkins, M. Gastroplasty—shed weight surgically. *Courier-Post* **5B,** January 6, 1981.

gum have been implicated as carcinogenic (cancer-causing) agents. Tobacco chewing and spitting is unesthetic and it has health-associated problems (e.g., can lead to mouth cancer).[22,43] Sucking candy balls can cause damage to teeth and large candy balls have been known to get stuck in the throat.

For health and esthetic reasons, women should confine their chewing to foods.[44]

ANOREXIA NERVOSA

While obesity is found in women and men of all ages, the opposite condition, anorexia nervosa, is found almost exclusively in women. About 95 percent of the cases occur in females; 1 in every 200 female Americans in the twelve- to eighteen-year-old range are affected with anorexia.[45,46] Anorexia nervosa is a condition that combines extreme weight loss with appetite disturbances and amenorrhea.

Why females are affected more than males is not completely known. Conjectures are: (1) Males are usually larger and heavier and can lose a great deal of weight before they become malnourished and anorectic; and (2) culturally, thinness is emphasized more for females than males and thus may give the women a greater psychological risk.[46]

Why do women become anorectic? Here too, the answers are not readily forthcoming. Most investigators consider anorexia nervosa to be a psychologically induced disease. Yet, there are also social and biological factors. Biologically there may be disturbances in the hypothalamus (which contains the appetite-regulating center) and a lack of certain hormones. Luteinizing hormone (LH; which is important in ovulation) is markedly decreased; and the secretion of growth hormone (STH) is also impaired. It is not known whether these changes precede the illness or result from it.[46]

The social disturbances (social stressors) are usually related to the family, although "peer pressures" to be thin may also be a factor. Certain family traits have been found in typical anorectic nervosa cases. These include: (1) enmeshment (i.e., family members are overinvolved with each other); (2) overprotectiveness (found in areas of food, health, and facing the outside world); (3) rigidity (i.e., inability to adjust, for example, to the death of a family member);[47] (4) inability to negotiate conflict (i.e., child is enlisted by one parent against the other); and (5) frustration (i.e., parents are unable to change the child's behavior).[46]

However, the family may appear "normal" and the child can still develop anorexia. That is why personal psychological reasons are probably the most important. The teen-age female develops such a morbid fear of gaining weight and becoming fat that she becomes obsessive in her pursuit of thinness. She eats practically nothing and tends to exercise vigorously.

At first, she still feels hungry but suppresses the desire to eat. She may sublimate her lack of eating by collecting recipes and preparing elaborate meals for others.[46]

There are some anorectics that go on "eating binges" and then induce vomiting or take diuretics and laxatives.[46,48]* The compulsive drive makes the anorectic hyperactive until she is so emaciated that she becomes listless and immobile. The weight loss induces a vicious cycle because as the anorectic becomes thinner, she develops a distorted image of her body shape. The thinner she becomes, the heavier and wider she thinks she is; so she tries to lose even more weight.[49] And if she thinks she is not successful, she becomes depressed. Most anorectics are perfectionist "model" children who try to please everyone. Often they feel that they are not pleasing others, and a poor self-image results.

The anorectic develops amenorrhea and her sexual desires disappear. Soon her blood pressure falls, her body temperature drops and she has trouble falling asleep and staying asleep. If untreated, she is likely to die from malnutrition, starvation, or commit suicide because of the depression.[46,48]

Treatment of anorexia nervosa takes several paths. If the child is near death, hospitalization and tube feeding is mandatory. In order to overcome the depression and severe stress, antidepressives and tranquilizers may be temporarily employed. To correct the hormone imbalance, insulin may also be used temporarily.[45,46] In less severe cases, psychological and nutritional methods are often combined.

ACCIDENTS

Most stress-related accidents are those involving automobiles. Many accidents are caused by people who drive while either drunk, drugged, or mentally preoccupied. Accidents are also caused by people being emotionally aroused. It has been reported that 20 percent of all fatal automobile accidents involve drivers who have had upsetting emotional experiences within six hours of the fatal car crash. It was also found that one out of three accident victims was depressed prior to the accident.[50]

Related to emotional responses and accidents, an *accident-prone personality* had been formulated. The individuals are considered to be aggressive, angry and hostile, often with feelings of guilt, and tendencies toward self-punishment and suicide. They are also considered to be "impulsive doers," who tend to take on many challenges.[51]

---

* Induced vomiting by anorectics can cause permanent damage to their teeth. The acid vomitus can literally erode away the surfaces of the teeth, making for a very unattractive appearance. Brady, W. F. The Anorexia Nervosa Syndrome. *Oral Surg.* **50:** 509–516, 1980.

Even though women are reported to be more depressed than men, take more psychotropic drugs than men, and are increasing their intake of alcoholic beverages, statistics show that they are not involved in more fatal accidents. (Almost three times as many men as women are killed in motor vehicle accidents.)[32,52] It may be that men are typically more often drunk and are more reckless in their driving habits and that women tend to do their drinking at home.

Many accidents may be disguised suicides and, as is discussed shortly, men are more successful than women in suicides. Accidents are the second leading cause of death in teen-agers, and overall suicides are the third leading cause of death.[8]

Although women may have less fatal accidents, they should still try to avoid accidents by controlling their anxiety and depression, not taking drugs and alcohol, and remaining alert while driving.

DIVORCE

Divorce is one stress-related disorder in which there are an equal number of women and men affected. But as was discussed in Chapter 2 under social stressors, divorce is often more traumatic to the woman. For example, the incidence of depression is much higher in separated or divorced women than it is in separated or divorced men.[53] The incidence of divorce is mounting in the United States. Currently, the United States is the leading country in the world for divorce with more than 40 percent of new marriages ending in divorce.[54,55] Divorce is now multiplying at a faster rate than either new marriages or the general growth of the population.[54]

Seeds of divorce are sown in many ways, but often drinking, smoking, drug problems, and overeating are major factors. These negative coping methods are usually related to the man: being unfaithful; being unemployed; having poor financial resources; and possessing a bad temper. Other factors leading to divorce are: wife-beating; rape; incest; frigidity; loss of love; conflicting careers; and physical and mental incompatibility. Surprisingly, the 1980 Roper Poll of American Women's Opinions found that one of the greatest sources of friction that can lead to divorce was disputes over television shows.[56] Marital discord can lead to anxiety, frustration, guilt, and depression which can culminate in divorce.

Even though it is becoming easier to terminate an unhappy or impractical marriage, divorcees are still treated as substandard citizens. Part of this is related to the sanctity of the marriage vow. And when the marriage breaks apart, too often the woman has to bear the brunt of the blame. Stigma is often placed on the divorced and separated woman because she was "unable to keep her man." When the divorced woman tries to head up the family, it formerly had not been considered a "normal" family. It was given descriptions such as "broken," "disintegrated," "disorganized," "deviant," and "pathological." (Currently with about 50% of families being single parent, this is no longer the rule.) The divorced woman is also considered to be an easy "prey" in sexual matters, or she is described as being out to seduce other women's husbands. As a result, the divorced woman and her children may suffer social ostracism.[57]

All of this creates a great deal of stress for the separated or divorced woman. She often suffers from self-blame and subsequent depression which can lead to drinking, drug ingestion, chain-smoking, compulsive eating, accidents, and suicide attempts.[8]

Anxiety and guilt also occur, especially when the divorced woman has to work, maintain the household, and be a mother and "father" to the children. Even though there are now cases occurring where the father gains custody of the child (à la the movie, *Kramer vs. Kramer*), the single-parent family is still typically headed by a woman. Guilt tends to occur as the woman is torn between her sexual desires and the needs of her children. The divorced woman may have ambivalent feelings toward men because of the failure of the marriage. She may not want to develop strong attachments, and yet may feel angry, depressed, and have a low self-esteem if she engages in casual sex.[58] Homosexual feelings may surface, and this too can cause anxiety and depression. However, the Lesbian relationship may be positive since some "marital hassles" are eliminated. On the other hand, the divorcee may give up men completely and devote herself to the family. Another route she may choose is to overeat, gain weight, and become unattractive to either sex. The various social and psychological stressors can then lead to stress-related diseases such as ulcers, migraine headaches, and bruxism.

All of this doesn't have to happen. With the advent of women's liberation and equal rights, women are now preparing for possible divorce *before* they get married. They are getting employed at an earlier age; they are learning about the business world; and they are making sure that they fully understand the marriage contract and how it can be terminated. Things can change and, as is discussed in Chapter 20, being prepared for eventualities is a major method of coping with stress.

It is also normal to grieve after a loss such as occurs with divorce, but the period of grief should be relatively short-lived (six to twelve weeks seems reasonable, dependent upon the length of the marriage).[8] The woman should also be realistic about blame. She should look out for herself even though she may love her family and her home.

Methods to deal with the stressors of divorce include: consulting with an attorney and a psychological counselor; practicing meditation or self-hypnosis; engaging in aerobic exercises; going to school; becoming employed; and getting involved in hobbies and other diversions. (See Chapters 20–23)

RUNNING AWAY

When marital stress reaches the breaking point, the legal solutions are separation and divorce. The illegal solution is "running away." Formerly, it was the husband who decided that he had "had enough" and left the family stranded. But recently there have been wives who have abandoned their families.[8] Why? One of the reasons may be related to the women's movement. Equal rights is interpreted as meaning equal opportunity to make and break marital arrangements. Another reason could be the emphasis in the seventies on "me first" and "looking out for number one."

Even though the phenomenon of the "runaway wife" or the "runaway mother" is increasing, society deplores such women. Society frowns on the runaway husband, the "deserter." But even here there is a distinction. The male has always been considered to be the adventurer. Although he may not be a "nice guy" if he leaves his wife and family, at least it's "understandable." On the other hand, for a mother to abandon her husband and especially her children is considered "unnatural." "How could a woman forsake her maternal instincts?" At least that's the way society reacts.

A runaway wife has her problems. In addition to the moral and ethical issues, there are legal entanglements. (She will probably be cut off financially, and lose child support and possibly visitation rights.) Once she is "loose in the world," unless she is well-trained, she'll probably have to settle for a low-paying job. And sexual harassment may be a problem. One way out of this dilemma is for easier divorces to be made available (e.g., 31 states now have some form of "no fault").

Before she makes her move, the wife who is considering "running away" should seek legal and psychological counsel.[59] (In Chapter 6, the plight of the runaway girl is discussed.)

BUSINESS BREAKUP

Business associations often break up for the same reasons that marriages dissolve. Possible reasons are: incompatibility between the partners; alcoholism; drug addiction; chain-smoking; unequal distribution of the workload and finances; and homo- or hetero-sexual liaisons involving secretaries, clients or partners' spouses.

With more women now entering the business world, there can be additional stressors. If the partnership or association involves men and women, there can be sexual liaisons, sexual harassments, and sexist discrimination. There may also be problems with unequal pay for women and unfavorable roles for the women in the association.

Problems can relate to the expected stereotypical behavior of men and women. For example, some characteristics attributed to males are: objective; innovative; unsentimental; independent; competitive; aggressive; task-oriented; and self-disciplined. On the other hand, women are supposed to be: sensitive, conforming; intuitive; passive; empathetic; dependent; nonaggressive; fragile; noncompetitive; inner-oriented; other-disciplined; subjective; and interpersonally oriented.[60-62]

Furthermore, in interpersonal communications, men and women are supposed to have different ways of behavior. For example, males are purported to: demonstrate positive attitudes; be objective; give more information; initiate interactions; be on the task/goal dimension; talk more frequently; use more words; and interrupt more frequently. Women's ways of reacting are described as: responding to interactions; being opinionated; expressing warmth and helpfulness; being on the social-oriented dimension; withdrawing from unpleasant interactions; talking and acting less as men talk more; and communicating negative attitudes.[62,63]

If women don't happen to follow these expected behaviors, it could be disastrous for the business arrangement. Fortunately, with greater understanding that all of these behavioral patterns are socially shaped, there is increased likelihood that the future will see business arrangements succeeding or failing solely on the merits of the partners and the arrangements. Hopefully, stereotypical behavior expectations will become a thing of the past.

Another kind of business arrangement is the all female association. Here, too, problems can occur. Some women work better with other women; others find greater success working with men. As with the other associations, the arrangements should be decided or terminated on the basis of merit, not personality or sexual preference.

SUICIDE

Distress can lead to deviant behavior. When deviant behavior is turned outward, it can be considered sadistic. (See Box 4.5)

Box 4.5. The Sadistic Male and the Masochistic Female.

Sadism is considered to be cruel and pain-inflicting punishment toward others, while in masochism one derives pleasure from punishment either self-induced or induced by others. Sadism is considered to be a "male" trait. According to Helene Deutsch, a Freudian psychoanalyst, masochism is a normal condition for women that derives from their female biological functions such as menstruation, sexual intercourse, and childbirth. In these activities there could be a combination of pleasure and pain.

The masochistic attitudes derived from sexual reproduction are then transferred over to the nonsexual aspects of the women's lives. Hence, masochism becomes a manifestation of feminine qualities. Karen Horney believed that female masochism is derived from sociological factors such as: economic dependence of women on men; restriction of women to nurturing and charitable roles; blocking of outlets for ego satisfaction; and the concept that women are inferior to men. Howard Blum, a contemporary psychoanalyst, considers the female to be predisposed to masochism but says there is no evidence that she derives pleasure from pain. Also, masochism can appear in combination with sadism (i.e., sadomasochism).[64,65]

Sadistic behavior may be manifested in criminal activities such as torture, rape, arson, and murder. In activities such as these, men are far ahead of women although the proportions are changing.

The number of women in prisons and other correctional institutions has increased 81 percent from 1968 to 1973. Even so, there is still a huge surplus of males in jails (twenty-five to one in favor of males).[64] But more women are being arrested and sent to prison. Part of this is related to women's increasing liberation and equality as well as the increased drug and alcohol use by women. As women get more freedom, law-enforcement officials are becoming more willing to arrest and imprison them.[64]

When deviant behavior is turned inward, it is manifested as masochism (see Box 4.5) and suicide. *Conversion hysteria* is a psychiatric condition in which women far outnumber men.[66] Individuals with this affliction seek out physical stressors that cause pain and suffering. They apparently have an unconscious need to hurt themselves (i.e., masochism).[3]

The statistics on suicide are interesting. In almost all studies in various societies, women have attempted suicide more frequently than men, yet men have been more successful at it.[53] According to one review, women attempted suicide four times as frequently as did men. In contrast, men were successful three times as frequently as were women.[64] Why are there such differences? No one knows for sure. One far-fetched explanation for the females' lack of success in suicide is that the majority of attempts take place around the time of menstruation. During that time, women are supposed to be careless, absent-minded, thoughtless, unpunctual, and forgetful.[67] Hence, although they attempt suicide, they are rarely successful.

Most authorities don't consider women to have those aforementioned attributes during premenstruation and menstruation. (See Chapter 6) Rather they believe that attempted suicide and completed suicide are two different phenomena. Attempted suicide appears to be a "crying out" for help; it is a weapon to use when no other seems available and it appears to result from a sense of powerlessness. Attempted suicide is a reaction to the severity of life-stress events. It often follows adverse life events such as: loss of a parent or a spouse (either by death, desertion, or divorce); severe arguments with a spouse or lover; a serious personal illness; a serious illness of a close family member; and forced relocation of home or business.[68] Attempted suicide is closely related to depression.

Many of the disorders discussed in this chapter are related to depression and can lead to attempted suicide. The alcoholic, the drug addict, the obese, the anorectic, the chain-smoker, the divorcee, the runaway, and the failing business partner—all can become depressed, "cry out" for help, and when there is no response, attempt suicide.

More is known about attempted suicide than completed suicide because many attempted suicides are unsuccessful and hence, require hospital or emergency room admission. It is through interviews that investigators have learned that the cases are unsuccessful, not because of poor planning, but because of "half-hearted" attempts. The people really wanted help. Many of them also had associated personality disorders.[68] For example, some women attempt suicide as a way of "getting even."[69] It is their means of creating guilt or shame in others.

The phenomenon of attempted suicide has increased four-fold in the last thirty years.[68] In the United States, there is an attempted suicide once every minute of every day.[8] The most common methods employed are by drug overdose (e.g., barbiturates) and gas. Attempted suicide is primarily found in young women.

Completed suicide is a different phenomenon. It is the ninth leading cause of death in the United States.[70] On the average, every twenty-four minutes someone commits suicide in this country.[8] Most of the victims are older males. The primary methods used are physically destructive ones employing guns, knives, and ropes.[8,65]

Even though more men than women kill themselves, the ratios are changing. In 1950, the ratio was about 3.4 male suicides to each female suicide. In 1976 there were about 2.7 male suicides to each female suicide.[8] In the last few years, the overall suicide rate has greatly increased for females, while only slightly increasing for males.[65] The highest suicide rates are in divorcees; next are widows; then comes single women; and married women are last.

Why is there an increased rate of suicide in females? It may be related to the increased incidence of women in employment (especially in "male" occupations).[8] For instance, women medical students and physicians commit suicide at a rate four times higher than that of women in general in the United States.[8,71] Most of the woman physician suicide victims were younger than age forty, while male physician suicide victims were generally between the ages of forty-five and sixty-four.

Many women physicians claim that the high suicide rate for women results from the sexist obstacles in the medical profession. Others claim that women who go into medicine have traits that could lead to manic-depressive tendencies (i.e., intelligent; aggressive; determined; motivated; and nonreactive to negative responses).[71] These tendencies, in turn, could lead to suicide.

Women psychologists kill themselves at a high rate (three times that of the population at large). Women chemists also kill themselves at a disproportionately high rate.[8] Aside from the possible sexism in these professions, it may be that the small number of women involved had few ties and role models. That, combined with the fact that many of the women were unmarried and felt "pressured" to marry, could have added to their distress and depression. Those who were married might have been stressed from the simultaneous roles of professional and housewife.

Aside from the professions, women entering other "male" occupations may try to emulate male behavior. The successful male is often pictured as being assertive, compulsive, not adaptable, and unable to "roll with the punches." According to some studies, it is the nonadaptability of the achieving male when he reaches retirement that leads to the high rate of male suicide at that time.[71]

According to these studies, traditional women are considered to be experts at adapting to change. Those women's passivity and flexibility would be helpful at retirement and tend to prevent suicide. Women who emulate men's behavior while working, upon retirement may reach parity with men in suicide.[72] To be successful, a working woman doesn't have to "think like a man, act like a lady, and work like a dog." She can maintain "feminine" qualities of passivity, flexibility, and adaptability and still be assertive enough to be successful. In doing so the working woman may save a life—her own.

Some people think that there are justifiable suicides. That would be for individuals who are incurably ill and are in extreme pain. There is even a British society (The Society for the Right to Die with Dignity) that has published a booklet, *A Guide to Self-Deliverance,* which is a "how-to" handbook on suicide for the incurably ill.[73] The stress of agonizing, painful death may justify suicide.

There are other forms of suicide. These are of the slow variety. As described, the male, compulsive, aggressive behavior (i.e., the "Type A"; see Chapter 2) can lead to suicide at retirement, but just being a type A is a form of suicide in itself. Hard-driving behavior can contribute to a fatal coronary. Being a chain-smoker, drug addict, alcoholic, and compulsive eater are also forms of slow suicide since they can lead to fatal heart disease and cancer.

Of course, the best treatment for suicide is prevention. Slow suicide can be avoided by reducing or eliminating drugs of all sorts and cutting down on compulsive behavior. Suicide and attempted suicide can be reduced if one gets at the causes. Counseling would be a major help with the psychological problems. Furthermore, sexism must be eliminated.

As more women enter formerly male strongholds, their sense of isolation and unattachment will be reduced. This should diminish the number of suicides. As women get help in the management of the household from their husbands or male companions, that too should cut down the number of suicides. "Hot line" organizations, such as "Contact," can also be helpful with women who are suicidal. The telephone provides the ready means for crisis support. With the realization that holidays and Monday mornings (see Box 4.6) are depressing for the suicidal, extra operators are made available at those times.

Box 4.6. "Blue Mondays."

Interestingly enough, Monday is the leading day of the week for sudden death occurrences. According to one study, 75 percent of all fatal heart attacks that happen on the job occur on Mondays. Going back to work after a relaxing weekend may set up severe stress reactions with a massive release of adrenaline sending the heart into "shock waves." Suicides are also high on Mondays. The best recommendation is to enjoy weekends but also try to get an interesting, enjoyable job.[74]

CONCLUSION

There is a common thread that runs throughout this chapter; that thread is depression. Depression can lead to or follow: alcoholism; caffeinism; drug addiction; chain-smoking; obesity; anorexia nervosa; accidents; divorce; abandonment; business breakup; and suicide. By controlling the causes of depression, not being dependent upon drugs in any form, and trying not to emulate the male type A behavior, women can prevent most of the stress-related disorders.

In Part III, women's stress from birth to death is considered.

REFERENCES

1. Yano, K., Rhoads, G. G., and Kagan, A. Coffee, alcohol and risk of coronary heart disease among Japanese men living in Hawaii. *N. Engl. J. Med.* **297:**405–409, 1977.
2. *Healthy People: A Report of the Surgeon General.* Washington, D. C.: U. S. Department Health, Education, and Welfare, Public Health Service, 1979.
3. Morse, D. R. and Furst, M. L. *Stress for Success: A Holistic Approach to Stress and its Management.* New York: Van Nostrand Reinhold, 1979.
4. Breslow, L. and Enstrom, J. E. Persistance of health habits and their relationship to mortality. *Prev. Med.* **9:**469–483, 1980.
5. Morse, D. R. *Clinical Endodontology: A Comprehensive Guide to Diagnosis, Treatment and Prevention.* Springfield, Ill.: Charles C. Thomas, 1974.
6. Lundman, R. J. Routine police arrest practices: A commonweal perspective. *Social Problems* **22:**127–141, 1974.
7. Sandmaier, M. *The Invisible Alcoholics: Women and Alcohol Abuse in America.* New York: McGraw-Hill Book Co., 1980.
8. Kinzer, N. S. *Stress and the American Woman.* New York: Ballantine Books, 1980.
9. Horner, C. Women alcoholics: Bringing the facts out of the closet. *Philadelphia Inq.* 1-I, 2-I, August 3, 1980.
10. Beckman, L. J. Women alcoholics: A review of social and psychological studies. *J. Stud. Alcohol* **36;**797–824, 1975.
11. Schuckit, M. A. and Morrissey, E. R. Alcoholism in women: Some clinical and social perspectives with an emphasis on possible subtypes. *In* Greenblatt, M. and Schuckit, M. A. (eds.), *Alcoholism Problems in Women and Children.* New York: Grune & Stratton, 1976.
12. Schuckit, M. A. and Morrissey, M. A. Psychiatric problems in women admitted to an alcoholic detoxification center. *Am. J. Psychiatry* **136:**611–617, 1979.
13. Parker, D. A., Wolz, M. W., Parker, E. S., and Harford, T. C. Sex roles and alcohol consumption: A research note. *J. Health Soc. Behav.* **21:**43–48, 1980.
14. Schuckit, M. A. and Morrissey, M. A. Drug abuse among alcoholic women. *Am. J. Psychiatry* **136:**607–611, 1979.
15. Streissguth, A. P., Landesman-Dwyer, S., Martin, J. C., and Smith, D. W. Teratogenic effects of alcohol in humans and laboratory animals. *Science* **209:**353–361, 1980.
16. Manber, M. The medical effects of coffee. *Med. World News* **17:**63–73, January 26, 1976.
17. Maugh, T. H. II. Coffee and heart disease: Is there a link? *Science* **181:**534–535, 1973.

18. White, B. C., Lincoln, C. A., Pearce, N. W., Reeb, R., and Vaida, C. Anxiety and muscle tension as consequences of caffeine withdrawal. *Science* **209**:1547–1548, 1980.
19. Editorial. Crippled infants linked to caffeine. *Philadelphia Eve. Bull.* XB-10, November 18, 1979.
20. Sun, M. FDA caffeine decision too early, some say. *Science* **209**:1500, 1980.
21. *Smoking and Health: A Report of the Surgeon General.* Washington, D. C.: U. S. Department Health, Education, and Welfare, Public Health Service, 1979.
22. Morse, D. R. and Furst, M. L. *Stress and Relaxation: Application to Dentistry.* Springfield, Ill.: Charles C. Thomas, 1978.
23. Rensberger, B. Cigarettes and pill don't mix: The two may spark fatal hemorrhage. *Philadelphia Eve. Bull.* 36, August 23 1978.
24. Editorial. Lung cancer fact sheet. *Penn. Dent. J.* **47**(3):20, 1980.
25. Petersen, R. C. (ed.), *Marijuana Research Findings: 1976.* Rockville, Md.: U. S. Department Health, Education, and Welfare, 1977.
26. Yates, J. A diet to help you quit smoking. *Prevention* **31**(10):91–97, 1979.
27. Dinges, D. F., Davis, M. M. and Glass, D. Fetal exposure to narcotics: Neonatal sleep as a measure of nervous system disturbance. *Science* **209**:619–621, 1980.
28. McCarthy, C. Hazardous to health: Calmness drugs put under control. *Philadelphia Inq.* 15-A, August 12, 1980.
29. Colen, B. D. The valium explosion: All things to all people. *Philadelphia, Inq.* 1-G, 2-G, August 31, 1980.
30. Gordon, B. *I'm Dancing as Fast as I Can.* New York: Harper & Row, 1979.
31. Hughes, R. and Brewin, B. *The Tranquilizing of America: Pill-Popping and the American Way of Life.* New York: Harcourt, Brace, Jovanovich, 1979.
32. Cooperstock, R. Sex differences in psychotropic drug use. *Soc. Sci. Med.* **12**(3B):179–186, 1978.
33. *Tranquilizers: Use, Abuse and Dependency.* Pueblo, Col.: Consumer Information Center, Dept. 6546, 1979.
34. Dohrenwend, B. P. and Dohrenwend, B. S. Sex differences and psychiatric disorders. *Am. J. Sociol.* **81**:1447–1454, 1976.
35. Kolata, G. B. Obesity: A growing problem. *Science* **198**:905–906, 1977.
36. DeJong, W. The stigma of obesity: The consequences of naive assumption concerning the causes of physical deviance. *J. Health Soc. Behav.* **21**:75–87, 1980.
37. Editorial. Research focus: Role of enzyme in obesity studied. *Res. Resources Report.* **4**(5):10–11, 1980.
38. Collins, B. His research offers hope for the anti-fat pill. *Philadelphia Inq.* 1-K, 8-K, August 24, 1980.
39. Morley, J. E. and Levine, A. S. Stress-induced eating. *Science* **209**:1259–1261, 1980.
40. Wingerson, L. Study of rats fosters new obesity theory. *New York Times* C₂, March 18, 1980.
41. Goodman, E. And now . . . dieters' little helpers. *Courier-Post* 9A, November 4, 1980.
42. Sifford, D. Bypass surgery: Is weight loss worth long-term risk? *Philadelphia Inq.* 4-C, July 29, 1980.
43. Christen, A. G. The case against smokeless tobacco: Five facts for the health professional to consider. *J.A.D.A.* **101**:464–469, 1980.
44. Morse, D. R. and Furst, M. L. Stress and the oral cavity. *In* Selye, H. (ed.), *Selye's Guide to Stress Research,* Vol. 2. New York: Van Nostrand Reinhold, 1981. In Press.
45. Bhanji, S. Anorexia nervosa: Physicians' and psychiatrists' opinions and practice. *J. Psychosom. Res.* **23**:7–11, 1979.

46. Shiner, G. Anorexia nervosa studied at several centers. *Res. Resources Report.* 4(5): 1-7, 1980.
47. Avery, C. Girls who starve themselves are haunted by the dead, doctor discovers. *The Star* 8, October 7, 1980.
48. Ben-Tovim, D. I., Marilov, V., and Crisp, A. H. Personality and mental state (P.S.E.) within anorexia nervosa. *J. Psychosom. Res.* 23:321-325, 1979.
49. Ben-Tovim, D. I., Whitehead, J., and Crisp, A. H. A controlled study of the perception of body width in anorexia nervosa. *J. Psychosom. Res.* 23:267-272, 1979.
50. McQuade, W. and Aikman, A. *Stress: What It Is: What It Can Do to Your Health: How to Fight Back.* New York: E. P. Dutton & Co., 1974.
51. Dunbar, F. *Psychosomatic Diagnosis.* New York: Harper, 1943.
52. Waldron, I. Why do women live longer than men? *J. Hum. Stress* 2(1)2-13, 1976.
53. Gove, W. R. Sex differences in mental illness among adult men and women: An evaluation of four questions raised regarding the evidence on the higher rates of women. *Soc. Sci. Med.* 12(3B):187-198, 1978.
54. Brisco, C. and Smith, J. Psychiatric illness: Marital units and divorce. *J. Nerv. Ment. Dis.* 440:156-157, 1973.
55. Hetherington, E. M., Cox, M., and Cox, R. Divorced fathers. *Psychol. Today* 10(4): 42-46, 1977.
56. Preston, M. Television and divorce: Exit reality, spouse following. *Philadelphia Inq.* 1-G, 6-G, June 22, 1980.
57. Brandwein, R. A., Brown, C. A., and Fox, E. M. Women and children lost: Divorced mothers and their families. *Nursing Dig.* 4(1):39-43, 1976.
58. Gordon, V. C. Women and divorce: Implications for nursing care. *In* Kjervik, D. K. and Martinson, I. M. (eds.), *Women in Stress: A Nursing Perspective.* New York: Appleton-Century-Crofts, 1979, pp. 259-275.
59. Hoffman, S. Marital instability and the economic status of women. *Demography* 14(1):67-76, 1977.
60. Broverman, I. K., Vogel, S. R., Broverman, D. M., Clarkson, F. E., and Rosenkrantz, P. S. Sex-role stereotypes: A current appraisal. *J. Social Issues* 28:59-78, 1972.
61. Bardwick, T. and Donovan, E. Ambivalence: The socialization of women. *In* Gornick, V. and Moran, B. K. (eds.), *Women in Sexist Society.* New York: Basic Books, 1971, pp. 225-241.
62. Menikheim, M. L. Communication patterns of women and nurses. *In* Kjervik, D. K. and Martinson, I. M. (eds.), *Women In Stress: A Nursing Perspective.* New York: Appleton-Century-Crofts, 1979, pp.133-143.
63. Baird, J. E. Sex differences in group communication: A review of relevant research. *Quart. J. Speech* 62:179-192, 1976.
64. Williams, J. H. *Psychology of Women: Behavior in a Biosocial Context.* New York: W. W. Norton, 1977.
65. Blum, H. P. (ed.), *Female Psychology: Contemporary Psychoanalytic Views.* New York: International Universities Press, 1977.
66. Lewis, H. B. Sex differences in superego mode as related to sex differences in psychiatric illness. *Soc. Sci. Med.* 12(3B):199-205, 1978.
67. Pollitt, J. Sex difference and the mind. *Proceed. Royal Soc. Med.* 70:145-148, 1977.
68. Paykel, E. S. Life stress, depression and attempted suicide. *J. Hum. Stress* 2(3) 3-12, 1976.
69. Durkheim, E. *Suicide.* Glencoe, Ill.: Free Press, 1951.
70. Editorial. Life span is 73 years, a new high. *Philadelphia Eve. Bull.* A 15, May 19, 1979.

71. Rockmore, M. From the top: Why are doctors so suicide prone? *Philadelphia Sunday Bull.* Mag. 16, March 19, 1980.
72. Elias, M. The human angle: Men will succeed, even if it kills them. *Philadelphia Sunday Bull.* WA 3, February 10, 1980.
73. White, A. and Leo, J. Behavior: How to commit suicide: A British society causes a furor with a guide on the right to die. *Time* **116**(1):49, July 7, 1980.
74. Anonymous. Monday really is a killer. *The Star.* 9, October 7, 1980.

PART III
WOMEN'S STRESS:
FROM BIRTH
TO DEATH

Women have varying degrees of stress throughout their lives. It begins with the first scream at birth; it ends with the last dying gasp. In between there is stress associated with childhood, puberty, mid-life, menopause, and old age. In Chapter 5, the stress from being a woman in a man's world is highlighted. Topics covered include: from preconception to birth; the first few years; the Oedipus (Electra) complex, penis envy; and symbiosis versus separation. Chapter 6 examines the events from puberty through the "twenties." Subjects discussed are: masturbation; menarche; premenstrual tension; dysmenorrhea; and amenorrhea. The "middle years" is the theme of Chapter 7. Topics reviewed include the stress from marriage and childbirth, and the possible complications from being single. In Chapter 8, the changes occurring with menopause are covered. Chapter 9 is involved with the stress of aging and dying.

5
Breaking The Umbilical Cord: Momma's Little Girl Faces The World

FROM PRECONCEPTION TO BIRTH

The male biological advantage begins before birth and is "downhill" after that. There are millions of sperm produced with all of the male's genetic material in each sperm head. Out of the many millions produced, the odds are good that one will survive to penetrate and fertilize an egg. Females produce only one egg at a time, and if it is defective, it is necessary to wait for the next ovulation for a possible conception to occur.

There are from two to four times as many male as female fetuses formed (based on stillborn evidence). However, there is a tremendous loss of male fetuses so that at the time of birth, there is just a slight male advantage (i.e., 106 males for every 100 females). From that time on, more males die than females; that is, from childhood to old age.[1,2] Why this occurs is not completely understood. It may be related to: (1) the biological disadvantage of the male Y chromosome (may be due to the incompatibility between some male fetuses and their mothers); (2) the benefits of the double "dose" of the female X chromosome (XX has more and a greater variety of genetic material than XY);[3] (3) the possible advantage of estrogen in preventing heart disease and infectious diseases (as discussed in Chapter 3); (4) the relative aggression of the male (partly related to the Y chromosome and testosterone; and partly socially conditioned) which makes him more likely to be involved in stress-related activities; [4,5] (5) the passive life-style of the traditional woman (primarily culturally determined) which may help protect her against heart attacks and the effects of the stress involved in aggressive behavior;[6] and (6) the concept that the basic and apparently more stable human form is the female. (See Box 5.1.)

Box 5.1   The Biologically Superior Female.

> The genetic determination of sex is dependent upon the sex chromosomes.* In each cell of the body, except for the sperm and ova (eggs), there are twenty-three paired chromosomes. One of each pair comes from the father and one comes from the mother. Twenty-two pairs are responsible for the various body characteristics and are known as autosomes. The other pair is the sex chromosomes and is designated as XY in the male and XX in the female. The sperm of the male contains twenty-two autosomes and either an X or Y chromosome, but there are more Y chromosomes found in sperm cells. The egg of the female contains twenty-two autosomes and an X chromosome. The fusion of the sperm and egg forms a zygote with either an XX genetic sex, a female, or an XY genetic sex, a male. Since there are more Y-bearing sperm, more male zygotes are formed. The X chromosome is one of the largest of all chromosomes while the Y is one of the smallest and does nothing of importance except to trigger the formation of the male testes (sperm- and testosterone-producing structures).
>
> If a Y chromosome is present in the zygote (XY), then the undifferentiated gonad (sex organ) develops as a testis. If the Y chromosome is absent (XX), the embryonic gonad develops into an ovary (female egg-producing structure.) If the zygote shows an XO pattern (a rare condition, known as Turner's syndrome in which there is an X either from the female or male parent and an "O" representing the absence of a sex chromosome), it develops as a female, although without ovaries.
>
> An embryonic gonad develops into a functioning ovary if there is a second X from the male or female but it doesn't need a second X in order to develop female characteristics (as is the case in Turner's syndrome).[7] What this means is that in order to be a male, something must be added (i.e., the Y chromosome). In order to have female characteristics, it is not essential for something to be added (i.e., a second X). One could interpret this by saying that the prototype human reproductive matrix is female.
>
> The next major determinant of sex is the influence of sex hormones. The fetus has a dual potential embryonic reproductive system. It is composed of the wolffian ducts which normally develop into male reproductive structures and the mullerian ducts which normally develop into female reproductive structures. Which way development goes depends upon the fetal testes and their two hormones, *mullerian inhibiting substance* and *testosterone*. (See Figure 2.1) Development is not dependent upon the ovaries and the ovarian hormones. For example, if a genetic male (XY) has

*Chromosomes contain genes which, in turn, are made up of DNA, the genetic material that is responsible for all the inherited characteristics of the individual.

no mullerian inhibiting substance, the mullerian ducts will develop into a uterus and oviducts. Hence, the embryo will be a male with female structures. In a normal male, the mullerian ducts degenerate and testosterone causes the wolffian ducts to develop into male reproductive structures.

If a genetic male (XY) has no testosterone produced, the wolffian ducts will not develop into male reproductive structures and the embryo will develop female genitalia. Normally, a female (XX) has functioning ovaries that produce female hormones such as estrogen that facilitates the development of the female reproductive structures. But just as is the case with the sex chromosomes, something must be added (i.e., testosterone) to have further male development. Without testosterone, the embryo develops as a female.[8] There is even some embryological evidence that the penis and scrotum are derived from an originally female precursor. Thus, the penis starts out its life as a clitoris and the scrotum comes into being as an outgrowth of the labia majora (outer lips of the vagina).[9] (See Figure 10.1)

Recent studies have shown that there are sexual differences between female and male brains.[5] Here, too, testosterone is necessary for the formation of the male-type brain. Without added testosterone, the brain develops into the female form. Hence, the female brain could be considered to be the prototype.

These findings add great support for the concept that the basic human pattern is female.[9] Perhaps the Bible was wrong, since it now seems more likely that Adam should have been formed from one of Eve's ribs! Even the English language is confused on the prototype form. Consider that *female* is derived from *male*; wo*man* is derived from *man* and the names given to our species are *human* and *homo* sapien, meaning wise *man*.

THE FIRST FEW YEARS

Physical Factors

It was previously mentioned that the female may have biological advantages in stress and survival related to the XX chromosomes and the sex hormones (primarily estrogen). However, being reared as a female may be of even greater importance. There have been cases of females who began life as males (XY) with functioning male genitalia and male sex hormones (androgens). Because of natural or human error these biological males in infancy either lost their penises or had clitorislike penises. They were then reared as females and given estrogen therapy. These children looked like, acted like, and were considered to be, females.[10]

It would be interesting to note if these reassigned females had stress-related diseases and disorders in the same manner as males or females. Since there are too few of these cases to get a valid sample, one can only conjecture. Judging by the increased incidence of stress-related disturbances in women who follow the male role model (i.e., in business, sports and politics), it may be that much of the women's stress protection is related to the typical female life-style.[6] Let us now consider the stresses from growing up in the female gender.*

Being brought up as a girl is a great start in life. The extremely high prenatal death rate of male fetuses was previously noted. The trend continues since 33 percent more boys than girls die in the first year of life in this country.[11] Not only do more boys than girls die in the first year but they suffer many more emotional, neurological, and physical defects. In one study of 15,000 children, of 248 possible abnormalities, 65 percent had a higher prevalence among males. Only 26.6 percent had a higher incidence in females.[2] The main advantages for male infants are that they are heavier and longer, and have a greater lung capacity at birth. Soon after birth they also have a higher caloric intake than female infants.[3]

Infant girls have other advantages at birth. They have stronger bones and a more advanced development of the central nervous system.[3,12] These factors may also partly explain why in one study of infants at thirteen and one-half months, girls were superior to boys on both mental and motor tests.[13] At the age of two and one-half years, a study showed that infant males had a higher incidence of neurological disorders and a significantly lower IQ than did infant females.[14]

So far as survival and emotional, neurological, and physical defects are concerned, infant girls are vastly superior to infant boys. Although there are genetic and other environmental components to those disabilities, stress is certainly a factor. In the first few years of life, girls continue their lead over boys in central nervous system maturity. They develop motor skills earlier than boys. One specific example is in bladder control. In a national study in Great Britain of seven-year-old children, 12.1 percent of the boys were still wetting their beds as compared to 9.7 percent of the girls.[15] Certainly in that aspect, the girls had less stress.

As was discussed in Chapter 3, with respect to stress-related diseases, women fare better than men throughout their life spans. However, the mental disturbances (such as anxiety neurosis, depression, and hysteria) are more frequent in females than males. These disturbances may begin in in-

---

*Sex is generally considered to be biologically determined. Hence, an XX child with female hormones and female reproductive organs is a member of the female sex. Gender is environmentally determined. It has to do with how the child is reared. Usually, genetical and environmental determination run along the same path and sex and gender are the same (e.g., female). However, there are cases where castrated males (XY) are given female hormones and then are reared as females. They would then be biological males but of the female gender.

fancy, but whenever they occur they are related to the different ways that boys and girls are reared (discussed later).

Mental Factors

There have been several studies on infants to determine whether males and females respond differently. Behaviors examined included: irritability; smiling; fear; anxiety; and dependency. The results were inconclusive. However, there was a stronger tendency for mothers to have close interpersonal bonds with their daughters, while encouraging separation, autonomy, and exploration in their sons.[3]

CHILDHOOD

Intelligence

As infancy merges into childhood (beyond three years of age), certain sex differences emerge. Although the ages vary for the traits, in general girls do better than boys in verbal ability and boys are favored in mathematical and spatial ability. In most tests of general intelligence (twenty-nine cited), the majority of studies showed no difference between young girls and young boys. In those in which there were clear differences, ten favored girls and only one favored boys (although in those that favored girls verbal ability might have been more important).[4] Verbal ability includes vocabulary, speech fluency, understanding language, comprehension, and reading achievement.[3] Considering the superiority of young girls in verbal ability, one might conjecture that they would do better than young boys in stressful situations in which speaking and understanding are important (probably the majority of stressful situations).

Social and Psychological Factors

There have been several studies comparing young girls and boys on psychological and social behaviors. The areas investigated were: fear and anxiety; dependency; aggression; and nurturance and maternal behavior. These are all related to stress.

Fear and Anxiety. In Chapter 2, the differences between fear and anxiety were discussed. However, in most of the studies of young children no distinctions were made between these two psychological stressors. In twenty-six studies of self-reports of fear and anxiety of children aged six and over, with seventeen of them sex differences were found (the girls reporting greater fear and anxiety in most of them.)[4] Young girls may be more fearful than young boys or, as is the case with adult females, they may be more apt to reveal their feelings than are boys (considered further under *Freud and Company*).

Dependency. Dependency deals with several types of behavior such as help-seeking, social interactions with peers and adults, proximity to peers, and frequency of contact with teachers. Although there are varying dependency definitions in the various studies, the results of most of them find young girls to be higher than young boys on measures of dependency.[16] Being dependent, if not overdependent, may be beneficial in terms of stress management. Seeking help can be an advantage in dealing with stress situations. On the other hand, if young girls are too dependent, they are not self-sufficient, can't cope with stress situations, and must be taken care of.

Aggression. Aggression implies threatening behavior or behavior with the intent to hurt or injure someone. It includes verbal as well as physical abuse. Most studies show that young boys are more aggressive than young girls. The sex differences begin around age two and are found in cross-cultural samples.[3,4,17] Boys have been found to be higher in both physical and verbal aggression.[17] Although there are definitely social factors in regard to aggression (e.g., girls are encouraged to be nonaggressive while boys may be rewarded for aggressive behavior), studies have shown that aggression is partly related to levels of male hormones, specifically testosterone.[4,10]

There is a syndrome in girls called, the *adrenogenital syndrome,* in which through an error of metabolism, the girls have male hormones that affect the development of their genitals. In studies, it was found that these "androgenized" girls displayed characteristics described as "tomboyism." They were vigorously active in outdoor and boys' sports, and had little interest in playing with dolls or baby-sitting. They were not considered to be aggressive in the sense of being threatening or hostile to others.[10] Boys' aggressive behavior often is threatening and assaultive toward others.[3] However, aggression is certainly not an advantage for the male as far as stress is concerned. The young male's aggressive behavior is generally carried on into adulthood and may be partly responsible for the high male death rate from heart attacks, suicide, murder, and war.

Nurturance and Maternal Behavior. Nurturance is defined as a willingness to give comfort and care to others, especially those in need such as the sick, the infirm, the young, and the aged. Nurturance has traditionally been considered to be part of maternal behavior. In most societies, little girls receive early training in nurturant and maternal behavior and maintain that role throughout their lives.[3] Since testosterone can affect male aggressive behavior, it is believed by some that the female sex hormones such as estrogen can promote nurturant and maternal behavior. However, this has never been determined for humans, and as is discussed under *Freud and Company*, in some societies males participate actively in nurturant and maternal behavior.

In terms of distress and stress-related disease, it appears that the traditional nurturing female is less prone to distress than is the aggressive male.[6,32] In the next section, the reasons for the different sex behavior in young females and males is presented. But first let us return to infancy with Sigmund Freud.

FREUD AND COMPANY: FROM INFANCY TO PUBERTY

Freud and Female Psychology

Sigmund Freud is not well-loved by the feminist movement because of his negative treatment of female psychology, but it is necessary to investigate the Freudian concepts to help understand the development of female stress.[18] According to Freud, during the first year of life the mouth is the primary erotogenic zone and the child derives its pleasure by sucking (i.e., *the oral stage*). During the second and third years of life, the anal region becomes an erotogenic zone as the child gains control of, and pleasure in, the retention and expulsion of feces (i.e., *the anal stage*). Between three and four years of age, the child finds gratification in the genitals (i.e., *the phallic stage*). Around the age of six until the time of puberty, overt sexual displays cease (i.e., *the latency stage*). At puberty, a resurgence of sexual impulses occurs (i.e., *the genital stage*). Freud maintained that the development of girls and boys was similar and of bisexual nature until they reached the phallic stage when the Oedipus complex is manifested.

The Oedipus Complex (Electra Complex; see Box 5.2). Both infant girls and boys have their mother as their principal love object. During the phallic stage, the boy becomes sexually attracted to his mother and considers his father as a hated rival. This sets up anxiety in the male child. He soon learns that his mother and other females do not have a penis as he has, and he believes that theirs was cut off or is missing. This sets up further anxiety as he fears that his secret sexual desires for his mother and

Box 5.2.   Oedipus Rex.

Oedipus Rex was a fifth-century B.C. drama written by the Greek playwright Sophocles. In the story, Oedipus is abandoned as a boy to prevent a soothsayer's vision from coming true. The vision is that Oedipus will kill his father and marry his mother. However, Oedipus is rescued and later on in life he fulfills the prophecy by unknowingly slaying his father and marrying his mother. The Electra story is less well known but it is basically the reverse situation with the woman marrying her father. Most psychoanalysts use the term Oedipus complex for both male and female versions although occasionally Electra complex is used for the female aspect.

hatred for his father might cause his penis to be cut off. According to Freud, either emasculation or castration anxiety causes the young male child conflict and distress. To resolve these difficulties, the Oedipus wish, the castration anxiety and pleasures of masturbation are all relegated to the unconscious (i.e., repressed) during the next stage in development, the latency stage. The boy then begins to identify with his father and his masculinity and at puberty enters the genital stage and psychosexual maturity. Young girls also go through an Oedipus (Electra) complex but first they must make a great discovery.

Penis Envy.[3,19-21] When the young girl enters the phallic stage, she too finds the joys of masturbation. However, she soon discovers that she doesn't have a penis like her brother or other little boys. She then becomes envious of the male penis. Freud believed that the little girl perceives that she has been emasculated and castrated, and thus, develops a feeling of inferiority. When she discovers that all girls and women lack a penis, she becomes contemptuous of her own sex. Freud believed that as an adult, penis envy results in jealousy, which is considered to be an important female trait.

When the young girl becomes angry at lacking a penis, she then blames her mother for the unfortunate result. She transfers her sexual energy (libido) to her father and her mother is then considered as the rival. Since she cannot get a penis she substitutes that desire for the wish to have a child. By equating the penis with a child, she resolves her penis envy and is then ready to develop normally as a woman.

Problems may occur that thwart normal development. Before discovering the boy's penis, the little girl was satisfied with clitoral masturbation. Now that she has become envious of the male penis, she is dissatisfied with her small clitoris. She subsequently represses her sexual desires. According to Freud, this sets the stage for adult neuroses.

Another possible problem can occur if the young girl refuses to believe in her emasculation and castration and continues in her clitoral masturbation. This leads to the *masculinity complex*. The young girl clings to a fantasy of being a man. This could lead to her acting as a man or developing into a homosexual.

According to Freud, young girls have a much more stressful transition than young boys towards adult development. First, boys retain their original love-object, their mother, through the Oedipus period. Girls have to transfer their love from their mother to their father. Second, the boys' masturbation pleasure object and their sex object during the genital stage always remains as the penis. Young girls again have to change, from the active clitoris for masturbation to the passive vagina during the genital stage. Freud did not believe that infant girls had any vaginal stimulation.

As do young boys, young girls also repress their sexual problems during the latency period. These include the Oedipus wish for their father, penis envy and clitoral masturbation. Freud believed that at puberty, clitoral stimulation becomes passive as sexuality is transferred to the vagina. If a woman retained clitoral stimulation to achieve orgasm, Freud considered her to be psychosexually immature.

Freud believed that the tremendous problems females had in achieving their sexual identity could account for their lower sex drive and for the frequency of female frigidity. Motherhood is helpful for the woman because of its role in overcoming penis envy. Of special joy is the mother-son relationship. The mother then, by a second-hand arrangement, can have the sought-after penis. Freud also believed that penis envy could lead to the female traits: narcissism* (a self-preoccupation which results in a great need to be loved); vanity (women had to place a great value on their physical charms to compensate for their lack of a penis); and shame (its original role was to conceal the lacking penis). Finally, Freud believed that because young girls didn't have a threat of emasculation and castration as did young boys, they never had to abandon their sexual interest in their father. Since they had less "pressure" to abandon their Oedipus wishes than did young boys, they would develop less morality and "traits of civilized mankind." Hence, adult women according to Freud, had a little sense of justice and a weak interest in social affairs.

Before one recoils with distaste at Freud's apparent "put-down" of the female genitalia, and of women in general, let us consider a few things.

*Narcissus was a mythological Greek character who fell in love with his own image after seeing it reflected in a pool of water.

First, whether or not one agrees with Freudian views, the widespread dissemination of these views has made many women cognizant of them. Therefore, women who believe in these concepts, or who have been influenced by them may feel inferior, and become envious and jealous of males. Of course, if Freud was completely wrong as some writers believe, then it is essential to get at the truth if that is possible, to help overcome the female's stress. This is covered shortly. But let us now try to understand why Freud came to his conclusions.

Freud's concept of female psychology was a product of his own background and times. He lived in a patriarchal society (still basically true today) and women's place was considered to be in the home and with the children. Women in general were apparently content with that role. There was generalized ignorance about the nature of sexuality and this was especially true for women's sexuality. (Who could have known about such things as multiple orgasms?) And Freud was actually never content with his concept of female sexuality. He didn't include it in his first writings on human sexuality and he stated that he felt that it would be modified in time. How these views have changed is now considered.

Deutsch's Modifications[22]

Helene Deutsch was one of Freud's disciples but she differed with him on some concepts of female sexuality. She considered penis envy to be no more than a secondary tendency and an outgrowth of general envy that affected both young girls and boys (e.g., being envious of a new child).

In Freud's version of the Oedipus complex, the young girl abandons her mother for her father. Deutsch believed that girls never completely abandon their mothers and, if the ties are kept too close, this can be the cause of a great deal of women's later distress. To be fully developed emotionally, separation from the mother eventually must be achieved. Deutsch also felt that the infantile period was not dominated by sexual urges since the child was busy with trying to master and understand the environment. Deutsch considered that right from birth sexual differences between females and males occured. She also believed that after puberty the vagina became functional when activated by the male.

Like Freud, Deutsch considered that clitoral masturbation would interfere with vaginal receptivity. Deutsch believed that female frigidity was common and based on: (1) continual clitoral stimulation which interfered with vaginal sensation; or (2) a previous early sexual trauma. Deutsch also contended that women's sexuality was less important in their life-styles than was the sexuality of males. She felt that sexual energy could be diverted to reproductive functions and mothering. Deutsch was a firm believer in the passivity of the female as contrasted with the activity of the male. Although Deutsch differed with Freud in the importance and role of penis envy and the detachment from the mother as the object of love, she basically was in agreement with Freud in his other concepts of female sexuality. Hence, Helene Deutsch has borne the brunt of feminine criticism.

Another psychoanalyst who departed slightly from Freud's position was Erik Erikson.

Erikson's Spaces

Erik Erikson trained with Helene Deutsch and is mostly known for his concept of the psychosocial stages of man's life cycle. As was the case with Freud, he too was not overly concerned with female development. However, he did make some interesting contributions. Erikson studied the play constructs of young boys and girls.[23] He found that boys erected buildings and towers that had the potential to fall apart. There were cylinders and cones (protruding objects). In contrast, girls built interior peaceful scenes consisting of furniture groupings and low enclosures such as gates and vestibules. Sometimes male or animal intruders forced the females in the scenes to hide. By analogy, Erikson associated these constructions with sexual anatomy. Thus, the males emphasized active, erectile and penis-like objects and the females emphasized protected, receptive vagina-like openings that had the threat of forceful intrusion.

Erikson accepted the notion of penis envy but he did not take it to mean that the young female desired the missing organ. Rather it was a representation that the child would feel despair if her empty space was left open and unfilled. According to Erikson, the design of the female body was such that the womb and vagina was her *inner space*. The inner space made her different from the male and set the stage for her life role which he considered to be that of taking care of the human infant. The male, in contrast, was destined for *outer space* which in adult life gives him great freedom for a multitude of possible roles. It certainly appears that Erikson's concepts are hardly any more acceptable to the feminist movement than are those of Freud. Recent studies of Erikson's concepts have failed to support his conclusions. In a study by Caplan, preschoolers were used as subjects. There were no sex differences found in the frequency of construction of towers and enclosures.[24] In a second study by Hopkins, coeds at a large urban university were the subjects. The results showed that "outer space" identity was emphasized more than "inner space" identity for college-level females.[25]

Another investigator who challenged Freud's concepts was Karen Horney.

Horney's Views[26]

Karen Horney began her career as a Freudian psychoanalyst but she diverged greatly from Freud's viewpoints on female psychology. Horney emphasized the cultural influence upon female development. She believed that Freud's concepts of penis envy, masculinity complex and female inferiority were biased, unsubstantiated and derived from a male point of view. Although Horney acknowledged that penis envy could occur, she downgraded its importance and Freud's idea that it could persist into adulthood and affect a woman's entire life. Horney believed that some girls could have a masculinity complex but not as an unresolved culmination of penis envy. Rather it was just an illusion of maleness to cover up the young girl's desire to escape the imposed female role. However, the escape into maleness does cause a great deal of distress to the female. For the girl has to adapt herself to values that are foreign to her (i.e., acting like a male). This may make the girl feel inadequate. Horney believed that the female's role is equivalent to that of a slave to a master (i.e., the male). That is the reason why young girls are envious of males. They know right from birth that there are different alternatives and opportunities for males and females. Girls could become mothers and housewives; and boys had unlimited opportunities. No wonder girls are envious, feel inferior and try to emulate males.

Horney reaffirmed a concept that had lain dormant. She "put the shoe on the other foot" and stated that young boys were envious of young girls because they (the boys) could not become pregnant, couldn't deliver a child and couldn't nurse a child. She suggested that young boys had *breast envy*. According to Horney, the female clearly is biologically superior (as supported by current findings). But the knowledge of female superiority is so disturbing to boys that they repress it. It is then transformed to the opposite concept that the female is inferior. Horney said that the reason the male's *femininity complex* is less common is that in this patriarchal society, the male has many opportunities for creative and diversified achievement. This can compensate him for his inability to bear and sustain life.

Women's subordinate role is caused by the ideologies foisted upon them about their nature (e.g., being weak, emotional, and unsuited for independent activity). No wonder women feel inferior and may develop masochistic traits. Obviously, the ideas of Karen Horney are more palatable to feminists and appear to be related to women's psychological stress-related problems such as anxiety and depression.

Another woman psychoanalyst who joined in the battle against Freud's concept of female psychology was Clara Thompson.

Thompson's Focus[27]

Clara Thompson was a Freudian-trained psychoanalyst influenced by Karen Horney and Alfred Adler (one of Freud's disciples). She believed that sex is not an important aspect of the child's growth. The most important feature is interpersonal relationships and that forms the basis for the child's identity. In infancy, the relationships are with the mother; as a young child the relationships are with the child's peers. The child learns about closeness and separation in her dealings with others. From them, she finds out about happiness, sadness, competition, and cooperation. Sex enters the picture only in adolescence. Thompson elaborated on Horney's view of penis envy. She considered that penis envy and all of its Freudian consequences (such as jealousy, inferiority feelings, and a weak sense of justice and interest in social affairs) were based on the cultural adaptations women had to make in Western society. Young female children were not envious of the male penis but of the male's independence and lack of limitations. The female child felt inferior because of her socially based inferiority; she couldn't take on high-status social roles because right from the start her future role was given to her (e.g., given dolls to dress, feed, nurse, and put to bed).

Thompson did not concur with Freud on the transfer of the penis envy to the concept of having a baby. She believed that motherhood was an important function in itself and had nothing to do with penis envy. Thompson also negated Freud's rationale for the masculinity complex (i.e., the woman's refusal to accept her emasculation and castration). She said women acted like men in order to move out of their sheltered roles as mothers and housewives. As the young child has no female role models to emulate, she necessarily has to follow the male model.

Freud was being battered and soon others joined the battle. One combatant was the female anthropologist, Margaret Mead.

Mead's Influence

Margaret Mead, a noted anthropologist, has been one of the most influential females in the women's movement. She studied primitive societies and from them learned that the cultural influences apparently were the major ones in delineating sex roles. Mead found the behavior of three tribes that she studied to be of special interest.[28] In the *Mundugumor* tribe, the children of both sexes were brought up in an aggressive and ruthless manner. Nurturing and maternal behavior had minimal importance for the females as well as the males. In the *Arapesh* tribe, the reverse occurred. The children of both sexes were brought up to be concerned with nurturing and maternal behavior. Aggression was frowned up and cooperation was the rule.

In the *Tchambuli* tribe, the children were trained in roles completely the opposite of those found in Western societies. The little girls were brought up to be curious and free to maneuver, manipulate, and explore. They developed into adults who took control of the affairs of the tribe. The little boys spent their time in "feminine" activities such as gossiping. They developed into adults who devoted themselves to unimportant affairs in ceremonial houses.

Another important finding of Mead's was that in societies such as in Western civilizations and the Tchambuli tribe where there are appropriate behaviors strictly determined for each sex, that deviants will develop. Individuals who cannot or will not conform to the norms for their sex emerge and emulate the behavior of the opposite sex. This can lead to a great deal of distress as, for example, in our society with transvestites (discussed in Chapter 12).

Finally, Mead considered that Freud's concept of penis envy was merely a culturally based belief.[29] There are biological differences between males and females but most of the female child's problems are based on the rigid sex role determined by Western societies.

Now let us return to a subject that Helene Deutsch considered as potentially stress-provoking for the female, the concept of separation from mother.

Mother and Daughter

Nancy Friday recently authored a best-selling book, *Men In Love,* but she is mostly known for her pioneering review of the problems encountered between daughters and mothers relative to *symbiosis* and *separation.* Using her own mother-daughter experiences plus interviews with more than two hundred women and several men, she wrote the best-selling book, *My Mother/ My Self.*[30] Notable authorities in the field who helped in the formulation of symbiosis and separation include: the aforementioned Helene Deutsch; the eminent psychoanalyst, Margaret Mahler; psychiatrist Richard Robertiello; psychotherapists Elizabeth Janeway and Leah Schaefer; sex researcher Wardell Pomeroy (involved in the Kinsey reports); psychiatrist Mio Fredland; anthropologist Lionel Tiger; child psychiatrist Aaron Esmon; psychologist Judith Bardwick; and physician Sirgay Sanger.

Many of the stress-related problems that young females encounter as adults result from their mothers' negative admonishments. Consider these examples: "No! No! You shouldn't do that!"; or "Good little girls don't act that way." Such pronouncements are often in regard to sexual activities. The little girl has her hand slapped when she fondles her clitoris or even approaches it. "No!" mother says when the young girl runs after boys; or "Wait until you're older." Suppressing the child in her initial sexual expectation, can lead to her becoming a passive adult, a woman who looks to others to take care of her sexual and general needs.

The young girl is led to believe that erotic feelings must be tied to motherhood. Sex outside of marriage or motherhood is perceived as a danger. Sex is hidden, denied, or suppressed. The female child is overprotected; she can't hear "dirty" jokes, see obscene pictures, wear her skirt too short or act in an "unladylike" fashion. She tends to fear sex as something potentially hazardous; even her mother doesn't appear to be a sexual creature. In fact, her mother may seem to be sexless.

Quite often the young girl only sees her mother as a nurturant and protective woman; her mother's sex life is so hidden from her that it appears to be nonexistent. The female child is taught that sex is part of marriage and motherhood but she learns very little about the true nature of sex. Sex is supposed to be connected in some way with love and that's what the female's role is all about: to love her husband, her children, her whole family.

The young girl should see her parents not just as mother and father but also as warm and loving adults concerned with each other's feelings. (That doesn't mean that the child should witness the primal scene or other sexual activities, but she should see her parents holding hands, kissing and exchanging pleasantries with each other.)

The female child's Oedipus strivings toward father are usually thwarted. "Get off daddy's lap!; Leave daddy alone!; Can't you see he's busy?" There is evidence that the young girl whose attention to daddy is rejected repeatedly (either by mother's or father's activities) often becomes a fearful, frigid woman who is afraid to take risks. Certainly the mother or father shouldn't encourage incestuous relationships but little things from father like a smile, a squeeze, a hug, or pleasant, loving conversation can help the girl develop into a woman with pride and identity.

Another source of stress with the female child is her attachment to her mother. Early in life, the young boy is given his freedom; he goes out and plays with the boys; and he can be rough, tough, and independent. The young girl is always watched closely: "Don't go out in the street!" Be careful!"; and "Come right home!" The daughter knows that she belongs with her mother and must not "break the strings" or pull too hard. Symbiosis is the technical term for the close reciprocal relationship between mother and child. It is important for infants of both sexes. Symbiosis gives them a secure base from which to develop and teaches them love. But the child must learn after a while to venture out on her own.

One example of how symbiosis can cause distress in the young girl is *school phobia*. In reality, in most cases of school phobia, the young girl is not phobic about school; she is just afraid to leave her mother's side. She is afraid that by leaving mother, she will leave love. But the young girl must establish her own identity, develop her own self-reliance, and become an individual. If not, she forever remains "tied to her mother's apron strings." She may move out, secure employment, get married, and have children but if she doesn't achieve a sense of independence, she may never gain self-confidence. She may either go back to mother in any and all crisis situations or be completely dependent upon her husband.

A young girl requires symbiosis as much as she requires separation. Without sufficient symbiosis, she develops into an insecure adult, a woman who lacks interest in trying different things. She often marries the first man who asks her, takes a safe, nonchallenging job instead of trying for an interesting career. Without symbiosis, a female may develop an exaggerated attention toward herself. She didn't enter into symbiosis with her mother so that as an adult she becomes narcissistic or vain.

Even when young girls appear to enter into symbiotic relationships with their mothers, the symbiosis may only be partial. There is evidence that boy babies generally get direct physical expression of their mother's love while girl babies get indirect love and approval via smiles and words. The physical way is more effective; the indirect way tends to show ambivalence. If this indirect activity is continued, it reinforces the girl to be passive, not actively seeking and touching. That may explain why little girls become better verbally in school than little boys; they are used to verbal cues from home. That may also explain why little girls are such "good" students. They may act in class like "quiet robots," but inwardly they may be disturbed. The authors found that this behavior may carry over into adult life as it was observed in female dental hygiene students (discussed in Chapter 16). Young girls need physical expression of love as much as young boys.

Symbiosis cannot last forever and separation from mother is essential for mature development. It should take some form by the age of three and one-half years. The child should be given its own space and time to develop; from toilet training to genital discovery. When the young girl can learn the joys of achievement by herself; when she is not thwarted in all her desires; when she learns sex and mothering can be separate; when she becomes aware that marriage and the family is not the only choice for a female—she can then become a healthy nonneurotic adult. She can then like herself and be proud of herself.

THE YOUNG GIRL'S STRESS

Let us now put forth an integrated approach on stress in young girls. First of all, it should be emphasized that regardless of the viewpoint (e.g., following Freud, Deutsch, Horney, or Friday) most young girls appear happy and unstressed. They seem to be enjoying life whether or not they are influenced by ideas such as penis envy, Oedipus, masculinity, and symbiosis and separation.

Psychological stressors come into play as girls become young women. As the song says "You've got to be taught to hate," and as we've observed this readily applies to fear as well. For instance, let us consider the dental situation. As long as they have not heard "horror stories" from their parents or friends, young children actually enjoy their dental visits and look forward to returning to the office. The same is true for physicians and hospitals provided that the approach is honest and straightforward. Young children have great imaginative powers and are readily hypnotizable. That can enhance the pleasant experience in doctors' offices. Our clinical impression is that there are no sex differences in terms of fear and anxiety.

Considering the effects of emotional trauma on young girls, there are certain acceptable ways of behavior to prevent anxiety, depression and stress-related diseases and disorders as adults. Undoubtedly, there are biological differences between males and females and, as has been emphasized throughout this book, from a stress and mortality viewpoint these differences strongly favor females. Therefore, young girls should be brought up knowing that being female has special advantages.

Young girls should also be informed that they have another great advantage over males: they can bring forth life and nurse children. The males can only be surrogate mothers in these respects. In addition, daughters should be brought up to know that they can go beyond the motherhood experience. They can enter any career as long as they have the desire and ability. Young females should be informed that: (1) they need not marry nor have children; (2) they can have children without getting married; or (3) they can have homosexual relationships.

In order for girls to enter male-dominated professions and careers, they must be informed of potential pitfalls. Some girls would not like those conditions and might be happier as wives and mothers. On the other hand, they might prefer the "female" occupations such as nursing, teaching, and clerical sales. The important thing is that young girls should not be limited in their choices; they should be given feasible options.

With respect to sexual matters, there, too, it is important to be frank and realistic. Young girls should not be thwarted in their early masturbating activities and should be informed about their sexual anatomy.[31] (See Figure 10.1) Young girls should learn that "mothering is a proud profession," and that sex and love in marriage can be a wonderful combination. However, they should also be informed that sex can be enjoyable by itself and it is not inherently evil. Yet, young girls should be made aware of the realities of rape, wife-beating, and the fact that it is the female who becomes pregnant. Mother and daughter are two of a kind and the symbiotic relationship can be wonderful for both. But daughters should be given more freedom than most mothers generally grant them. Early in life girls should be allowed to explore and investigate.

Studies have confirmed that daughters who are able to separate early from their mothers can gain confidence in their coping abilities, and as adults are more willing to take chances for valued goals.[3] Young girls must also be shown that emotions are to be vented, not repressed. This is especially true of anger and frustration. Little girls don't have to be prim and proper all the time; if they are, they will probably emerge as anxious and depressed adults. As is discussed in Chapters 2 and 21, it is often more beneficial to let out one's feelings than to suppress them. And girls are often taught to hold in their feelings at a very young age.

All in all, it seems that this is a great time to be a young female. Girls still have all their biological advantages and now they have many more possible choices in life. Unlike many of today's liberated women, the new young female generation has female role models to follow.

REFERENCES

1. Lerner, I. M. *Heredity, Evolution and Society.* San Francisco: W. H. Freeman, 1968.
2. Singer, J. E., Westphal, M. and Niswander, K. R. Sex differences in the incidence of neonatal abnormalities and abnormal performance in early childhood. *Child Develop.* 39:103–132, 1968.
3. Williams, J. H. *Psychology of Women: Behavior in a Biosocial Context.* New York: W. W. Norton, 1977.
4. Maccoby, E. E. and Jacklin, C. *The Psychology of Sex Differences.* Stanford, Calif.: *Stanford University Press,* 1974.
5. Goy, R. W. and McEwen, B. S. *Sexual Differentiation of the Brain: Based on a Work Session of the Neurosciences Research Program.* Cambridge, Mass.: MIT Press, 1980.
6. Elias, M. The human angle: Men will succeed even if it kills them. *Philadelphia Sunday Bull.* Mag. 16, March 19, 1980.
7. Erhardt, A., Greenberg, N. and Money, J. Female gender identity and absence of fetal hormones: Turner's syndrome. *Johns Hopkins Med. J.* 125:237–248, 1970.

8. Jost, A. A new look at the mechanism controlling sex differentiation in mammals. *Johns Hopkins Med. J.* **130**:38–53, 1972.

9. Sherfey, M. J. *The Nature and Evolution of Female Sexuality.* New York: Random House, 1972.

10. Money, J. and Ehrhardt, A. *Man and Woman, Boy and Girl.* Baltimore: The Johns Hopkins University Press, 1972.

11. Garai, J. E. and Scheinfeld, A. Sex differences in mental and behavioral traits. *Genetic Psychol. Monogr.* **77**:162–299, 1968.

12. Kagan, J. The emergence of sex differences. *School Review* **80**:217–227, 1972.

13. Braine, M. D. S., Heimer, C. B., Wortis, H., and Freedman, A. M. Factors associated with impairment of the early development of prematures. *Monogr. Soc. Res. Child Develop.* 31 Ser. No 106, 1966.

14. Cutler, R., Heimer, C. B., Wortis, H., and Freedman, A. M. The effects of prenatal and neonatal complications on the development of premature children at two-and-one-half years of age. *J. Genetic Psychol.* **107**:261–276, 1965.

15. Pringle, M. L. K., Butler, N. R., and Davie, R. *Eleven Thousand Seven-Year Olds.* London: Longmans, 1966.

16. Mischel, W. Sex typing and socialization. *In* Mussen, P. H. (ed.), *Carmichael's Manual of Child Psychology.* New York: Wiley, 1970.

17. Whiting, B. B. and Pope, C. P. A cross-cultural analysis of sex differences in the behavior of children aged three through eleven. *J. Soc. Psychol.* **91**:171–188, 1973.

18. Freud, S. *An Outline of Psychoanalysis.* New York: W. W. Norton, 1949.

19. Strouse, J. (ed.), *Women and Analysis.* New York: Grossman, 1974.

20. Blum, H. P., (ed.), *Female Psychology: Contemporary Psychoanalytic Views.* New York: International Universities Press, 1977.

21. Wittkower, E. D. and Robertson, B. M. Sex differences in psychoanalytic treatment. *Soc. Sci. Med.* **12**(3B):219–222, 1978.

22. Deutsch, H. *The Psychology of Women: A Psychoanalytic Interpretation.* Vols. 1 and 2. New York: Grune & Stratton, 1944, 1945.

23. Erikson, E. H. The inner and the outer space: Reflections on womanhood. *Daedalus.* **93**:582–606, 1964.

24. Caplan, P. Erikson's concept of inner space: A data-based reevaluation. *Amer. J. Orthopsychiatry* **49**:100-1-8, 1979.

25. Hopkins, L. B. Inner space and outer space identity in contemporary females. *Psychiatry* **43**:1–12, 1980.

26. Horney, K. *Feminine Psychology.* New York: W. W. Norton, 1973.

27. Green, M. R. (ed.), *Interpersonal Psychoanalysis: The Selected Papers of Clara Thompson.* New York: Basic Books, 1964.

28. Mead, M. *Sex and Temperament in Three Primitive Societies.* New York: William Morrow, 1935.

29. Mead, M. On Freud's view of female psychology. *In* Strouse, J., (ed.), *Women and Analysis.* New York: Grossman, 1974.

30. Friday, N. *My Mother/My Self: The Daughter's Search for Identity.* New York: Dell Publishing, 1978.

31. Lerner, H. F. Parental mislabeling of female genitals as a determinant of penis envy and learning inhibitions in women. *In* Blum, H. P. (ed.), *Female Psychology: Contemporary Psychoanalytic Views.* New York: International Universities Press, Inc. 1977, pp. 269–283.

32. Sifford, D. Age of dissent: For retired couples, togetherness can be the biggest strain. *Philadelphia Inq.* 2-D, February 19, 1981.

6

The Juvenile Years: From Eleven Through Twenty

The young girl has fun and games for the most part. Playing house, dressing dolls, jumping rope, and going to school; there's not too much stress in those activities. The first day at school was a little rough, but by the time she's ten or eleven that's "old hat."

Of course, there are those unconscious things working on her mind (you know, the nemeses: Oedipus; penis envy; the masculinity complex), but now she is oblivious to them. She's having too much fun. Just when she's really beginning to enjoy her complication-free life, the young girl becomes a young woman—she reaches puberty.

PUBERTY

Puberty signals the start of adolescence and all of a sudden, stress hits the new teen-ager with a whole host of physical, social, and psychological changes. Let us now look at these potential stress-producers.

Right from the start, boys have physical evidence of their sexual nature, the obvious penis. Young girls have a vulva, clitoris, and vagina of which they usually have very little awareness. Then about the age of eleven, their breasts begin to bud, and this is the first evidence of "becoming a woman." Other changes follow soon including: appearance of pubic hair; an increase in the rate of growth; a redistribution of body contours toward the feminine form; a slight deepening of the voice; and a mild increase in skin pigmentation.[1] Depending upon the child's preparation, she may or may not become upset at these visible body changes.

Internally, the ovaries and uterus become larger and more active and, about one or two years later (usually between twelve and seventeen years of age), the first menstruation occurs (known as menarche).

MENARCHE

The age of menarche has decreased progressively in Western countries over the past few decades. This has been ascribed to superior nutrition and health care. The timing of menarche is related to the regulatory activity of the hypothalamus in stimulating the anterior pituitary gland to start the female menstrual cycle (see Figure 6.1).* The start of menstruation can be a matter-of-fact occurrence, or it may be extremely stressful, leaving indelible scars. If the mother treats it in a negative way, the daughter will probably have problems from that time on. If the mother is objective and realistic, and explains menstruation as a normal, natural occurrence, the chances are excellent that the daughter will not develop future physical and psychological problems. Menarche and menstruation have received very bad publicity. The reviews started centuries ago. Some examples are given in Box 6.1.

Until recently, many mothers and daughters had a great deal of confusion about their body openings. They often confused the urethra, vagina, and anus, even considering them as one opening (e.g., they were lumped together as areas of waste disposal; feces, urine and menstrual blood).[5] (See Figure 10.1). If mothers pass this attitude onto their daughters, undoubtedly the young women will not think positively about menstruation. It would bring back fears associated with wetting the bed and soiling the sheets (activities of elimination over which the young girl may have had no control).

Some mothers become anxious when their daughters begin to menstruate. This anxiety can be transferred to the daughter. There may even be a tinge of jealousy and Oedipus rivalry here.[7]

Most women remember their first menstruation because of the associated trauma. It is hoped that future generations of young girls reaching menarche will have few recollections about the incident because of the natural way it was managed.

The first few "periods" tend to be sparse and irregular, but then the typical cycles begin. Before the menstrual period begins, most females feel

* Many women are engaging in vigorous athletic activities (see Chapters 17 and 21). According to some recent research, if young girls engage in strenuous physical activity, it could delay the onset of menstruation. The concept is that at the age of menarche, girls need a body-fat content of about 17 percent. Vigorous activity may reduce the body-fat content to lower levels and thereby interfere with menstruation. Gunby, P. What does exercise mean for the menstrual cycle? J.A. M.A. 243:1699, 1980.

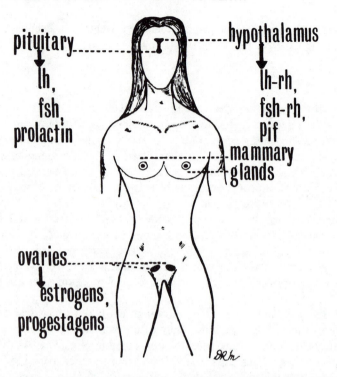

Fig. 6.1   The female hormone system. The female hormone system is geared toward reproduction. Hence, egg release (ovulation), fertilization and impregnation are enhanced by hormonal action. The hypothalamus releases FSH–RH (follicle-stimulating hormone releasing factor), which activates the anterior pituitary gland to release FSH (follicle-stimulating hormone). FSH stimulates growth and development of the ovaries and the ovarian follicles (in which the eggs are found). The hypothalamus also releases LH–RH (luteinizing hormone releasing factor), which activates the anterior pituitary gland to release LH (luteinizing hormone). LH is needed for final development of the mature follicle to cause the release of the egg (ovulation) and to produce the corpus luteum (formed from the follicle after the egg release). Estrogens are formed from the ovarian follicles, and progestagens are formed from the corpus lutea. Estrogens have many functions related to female characteristics and body structure; they are needed for maturation of the follicle, ovaries, corpus luteum, and mammary glands and to maintain pregnancy. Progestagens are essential for the control of reproductive activity, for morphological development of the mammary glands and to maintain pregnancy. During pregnancy other hormones are produced; relaxin from the corpus luteum (prepares tissues for delivery of the fetus) and chorionic gonadotropin (HCG) from the placenta (needed for maintenance of pregnancy). A final hormone released from the hypothalamus is PIF (prolactin inhibitory factor). It turns off the activity of prolactin (PRL, lactotrophic hormone; LTH, luteotrophic hormone). Prolactin is turned on when PIF is not released. This occurs during pregnancy when prolactin is needed for milk formation in the mammary glands. Estrogens and progestagens have feedback activity on the hypothalamus and anterior pituitary to regulate the release of LH and FSH. For example, FSH and LH are turned off by high estrogen and progestin levels produced during pregnancy. (A fertilized egg

Box 6.1 The Curse.

In 77 A.D., the Roman author Pliny stated the following about menstruating women: "If they happen to approach a vessel of wine, be it never so new, it will presently sour . . . Let them handle any grasses, they will die . . . The very bees in the hive die. Iron and steel presently take rust, yea, and brass likewise, with a filthy, strong and poisoned stink if they but lay hand . . ."[2] Many ancient societies and major religions had severe pronouncements against menstruating women. The ancient Persians considered a menstruating woman to be the work of the devil; she could never look at the sun and a sacred fire, or talk to a man. If a woman menstruated for longer than four days, she was given one hundred lashes and kept secluded. The Incas of South America forbade menstruating women from entering sacred temples or sacrificing to the gods. The ancient Siberians made their menstruating women wear special hats to protect the heavens against pollution.[3]

Hindu law stated that a menstruating woman was not allowed to gaze at anyone, even her own children. In Moslem law, menstruation was considered to be a "hurt and a pollution." In the Hebrew Old Testament, there is a statement that men are forbidden to touch menstruating women.[3]

In many cultures, menstruating women are forced to live apart in special menstrual huts, dark cells, narrow cages, or hammocks. These customs can be found in tribes from Northern India, East Africa, Ceylon, Borneo, New Zealand, and Brazil.[1,3-6] In some Australian aboriginal tribes, menstruating women are forbidden to touch anything used by men. In the Dogan East African tribe, a menstruating woman is supposed to bring misfortune to everything she touches.[3] In one South African tribe, there is a belief that cattle will die if even one drop of menstrual blood touches their feet. To prevent this, menstruating women must walk on special paths over which cattle do not pass.[1]

Millions of women were burned as witches from the fifteenth to the eighteenth century. Witches supposedly had menstrual "pacts with the devil." Witches were considered to have the same type of strange powers that Pliny the elder ascribed to menstruating women.[4] For example, witches were supposed to sour wine, ruin crops, rust iron and put curses on men. This may have been how menstruation and the "curse" became synonymous.

is present, and no more follicles which have eggs are needed.) This system is active from puberty to menopause. In males, the system is similar except that androgens (e.g., testosterone) are produced by the testes instead of the ovaries. In addition, sperm are produced instead of eggs. (From Morse, D.R., and Furst, M.L. *Stress for Success: A Holistic Approach to Stress and its Management.* New York: Van Nostrand Reinhold Co., 1979. Reprinted with permission).

different, and often the sensations are not pleasant. These "feelings" have been combined and are known as the premenstrual tensional syndrome (premenstrual tension).

Premenstrual Tensional Syndrome

A whole host of clinical manifestations have been described as occurring prior to the onset of menstruation. These are collectively known as the premenstrual tensional syndrome. The manifestations include: anxiety; depression; bloated feelings of the abdomen; nervousness; lethargy; irritability; headaches; dizziness; nausea; fainting; palpitations; backache; joint pains; breast pain; swelling of the face and extremities; acne; skin rash; hypoglycemia; sinusitis; sore throat; mastitis; eye disorders; asthma; epilepsy; excessive sleeping; and excessive thirst and appetite. Almost an equal number of additional signs and symptoms have been reported, so this is indeed an amazing array of manifestations for one clinical condition.[8-10]

In addition, some women have been reported to act in a bizarre way during this time as evidenced by an increase in suicides, psychiatric hospital admissions, accidents and criminal acts. Schoolgirls also have been reported to have behavioral and scholastic problems during the premenstrual period.[8,11,12] From 25 to 100 percent of women are affected with some of the manifestations of the premenstrual tensional syndrome.[13] Premenstrual problems are one of the most common reasons for American women to consult their physicians.[3]

Premenstrual tension results from a combination of hormonal, psychological and social changes. At the premenstrual time, there is a relative decrease in estrogen and progesterone (see Figure 2.1) and an increase in MAO activity. (See *Depression* in Chapter 3.)[14] As previously mentioned, MAO is much higher in the blood of psychiatrically depressed people as compared to nondepressed individuals.[15] Hence, the increased MAO level at premenstruation may be associated with the depression seen in some females at that time. MAO level is lowest at the midpart of the cycle, at the time of ovulation (when many women feel fine).

During premenstruation, there may also be excess secretion of some other hormones such as prolactin, aldosterone, and cortisone (all are produced during stress).[10,16] Some women who tend to bloat, retain sodium and water at that time.[10]

Studies of psychological factors have shown that life-stress events and subjective attitudes often cause exacerbation of symptoms at the premenstrual time. The reported factors include: increased family quarrels;

fearful attitude toward menarche and menstruation; poor self-experiences of menstruation; poor acceptance of the female psychosexual role; and a feeling of being unable to cope with life's daily routines.[10] In one study it was shown that undesirable life-stress events (such as loss of a job) were associated with increased premenstrual symptoms.[17] In other studies, women who had neurotic tendencies and negative attitudes toward menstruation had a high incidence of premenstrual tensional symptoms.[10] A recent study has shown an association between women with anxious personality traits and premenstrual tension.[57]

There is evidence that expectation is an important part of the symptomatology in the premenstrual tensional syndrome. In one study, an investigator was able to demonstrate significant differences in symptoms between women who thought that they were in the premenstrual stage* as compared to women who believed that they were in the midperiod of their cycles.[18] Ironically, both groups were about one week before the start of their menstrual periods. In another study, no association was found between women's moods and the period of the menstrual cycle. The women did not have more negative feelings during the premenstrual period.[19]

Being in good physical and emotional health is associated with fewer problems during the premenstrual period. In one study, women who were in good emotional health didn't have greater complaints during the premenstrual phase.[19] In another study, physically fit women athletes were found to be less prone to premenstrual tension.[20] It has also been found that working women, women in nontraditional roles, and androgynous women (i.e., women who combine masculine and feminine traits) have less premenstrual tensional symptoms than do traditional women.[21]

There are many possible treatments for this syndrome including:tranquilizers; antidepressants; vitamins (pyridoxine and A); progesterone; estrogen; bromocriptine[1] (suppresses prolactin); and birth-control pills (decreases symptoms in some women).[10,22] However, prevention is preferable to therapy. Positive preparation of the daughter by her mother before menarche is a start in the right direction. Keeping physically fit is another positive step. And not worrying or anticipating problems will help reduce the symptoms.

Psychotherapy often proves helpful, and relaxation therapy should prevent the onset of anxiety, depression, and pain (see Chapter 20).

At the start of menstruation there may be other problems. A major one is dysmenorrhea.

---

* The women were deceived into thinking that an amazing new scientific technique allowed the investigator to accurately determine when they were in the premenstrual stage.

DYSMENORRHEA (MENSTRUAL CRAMPS)

Menstrual cramps are not life-threatening, but they are painful. They are also prevalent (affect from 30 to 50 percent of menstruating women).[23] Dysmenorrhea can be caused by organic conditions (e.g., fibroid uterine tumors) but it is usually not related to any known disease.

The usual symptoms of dysmenorrhea are: painful pelvic area cramps; nausea; vomiting; diarrhea; headache; fatigue; and nervousness. The cramps are generally absent for the first few menstruations and they tend to diminish after the birth of the first child or after the age of twenty-five.[24]

Menstrual cramps are similar to labor pains, and uterine contractions are believed to be responsible. Recent studies have implicated prostaglandins as the initiating factor in both the uterine contractions and the other manifestations of dysmenorrhea. Prostaglandins are potent chemicals produced at various body sites. They have several actions but are often involved in inflammation. Studies have shown that in women with dysmenorrhea, there is often an overproduction of prostaglandins by the uterus (verified by high prostaglandin concentration in menstrual fluid). In women with dysmenorrhea, there is generally strong pressure in the uterus and a high frequency of uterine contractions, all of which can add up to pain.[23] Nausea, vomiting, headache, and diarrhea can also be caused by prostaglandin action (stimulates smooth muscle contraction at those sites).

Why some women suffer more from menstrual cramps than others is not known, although there are genetic factors (relative to prostaglandin production) as well as psychological factors.[1,24,25] As is the case with premenstrual tension, social and psychological stressors can affect body hormones and stress could increase the levels of prostaglandins.[26]

It has been estimated that dysmenorrhea causes the loss of 140 million working hours per year.[23,25] Although it is probably just a small minority, it is possible that some females under stress may intentionally or unintentionally exaggerate the intensity of their monthly cramps. This could give them an opportunity to relax or even seek some indulgence (i.e., secondary gain).[17]

As prostaglandins apparently initiate dysmenorrhea, research had proliferated on the use of prostaglandin inhibitors to counteract the symptoms of dysmenorrhea. Drugs used are nonsteroidal (different from cortisone), anti-inflammatory compounds (e.g., indomethacin; naproxen).[23,25,26] Although aspirin has some antiprostaglandin activity, it has not proven effective.[23] Oral contraceptives indirectly suppress prostaglandins and that may be why they tend to alleviate menstrual cramps. Alcohol also is believed to have antiprostaglandin activity.[3]

Side effects for the various drugs are minimal with the exception of high doses of indomethacin (can cause headaches, mood disturbances and gastrointestinal upsets).[23] The negative side effects of oral contraceptives and alcohol have previously been discussed.

In summary, it is believed that, as is the case with premenstrual tension, a positive psychological attitude would be helpful in the control of dysmenorrhea. Psychotherapy may be advantageous in that regard. Good preparation in the mother-daughter relationship would also tend to diminish the severity of the cramps. Relaxation therapy during painful periods can only be helpful.

Now that we've considered the menarche, premenstrual tension and dysmenorrhea, let us investigate other aspects of menstruation.

MENSTRUATION

Once a female reaches menarche and after a few short and irregular periods, she then enters into thirty or forty years of regular monthly menstrual periods. Most studies describe distressing symptoms during the premenstrual phase but, with some women, these symptoms persist for several days into the menstrual period.[27] With other women, there are no changes that relate to either premenstruation or menstruation.[19]

There is some evidence that female sexual arousal is heightened during the premenstrual and menstrual periods when progesterone and estrogen levels are low.[28,29] Anecdotal reports indicate that women who have sexual relations or masturbate during those times often relieve their menstrual cramps and other menstrual symptoms.[7,21,28]

As discussed, MAO levels increase during the premenstrual period. They remain elevated during menses and this could account for some women's depression during that time.[14] It is not only women who are "hypochondriacs" who report distressful symptoms during menstruation. In a recent study, it was found that "quite healthy women can suffer physical and emotional discomfort during menstruation."[30] Another finding in that study was that women who were judged "high" in feminine qualities (as determined by a questionnaire) reported more severe symptoms of menstrual discomfort than did women considered high on masculine traits. It was also found that women who knew more about menstruation had more positive feelings toward it.[30]

One psychological problem with some women during menstruation is related to the period itself. Going back to their earlier fears about soiling the sheets or losing fecal control, the fear of staining can be quite disturb-

144 III / WOMEN'S STRESS: FROM BIRTH TO DEATH

ing. Women may feel humiliation (a severe psychological stressor) if they stain or if they believe that their odor is bad. But it doesn't have to be that way. Current protective pads are quite effective and there are products to overcome unpleasant odors. There are generally no problems associated with the use of sanitary napkins or tampons, but some dangers associated with the latter have recently been reported. (See Box 6.2) However, the advertising for sanitary napkins may, in effect, peddle anxiety as well as pads when it suggests this will bring "an end to the worries about *that time.*"

Attitude is also quite important in regard to menstruation. In one study, it was found that women who were less anxious and "moody" during their periods and who tried to ignore taboos against sex and swimming, tended to bleed less.[33]

Finally, by learning to relax one can overcome many menstrual-related problems. Centuries ago women voluntarily withdrew during menstruation to a quiet place for periods of contemplative meditation.[3] Women have a biologically programmed time period where self-hypnosis, meditation, and other forms of relaxation would permit them to enjoy the "woman's friend."

Let us now consider when menstrual periods cease or are irregular.

AMENORRHEA

Amenorrea is the absence of menstruation after puberty without the occurrence of pregnancy. It can be related to known causes such as ovarian or uterine disease, the intake of psychotropic drugs, and strenuous physical exercise.[1] But of all the menstrual-related syndromes, amenorrhea is the one most involved with stress. It has been hypothesized that the accumulation of stress-induced catecholamines disrupts the cyclic menstrual activity.[34,35] Stress has also been shown to cause an elevation of prolactin levels which could interfere with the normal female hormone cycle.[26]

Life-threatening or catastrophic social stressors may cause an abrupt cessation of menstruation.[36] Studies have shown that depressed women and women undergoing psychotherapy are prone to amenorrhea. Women who regularly change homes or travel frequently may also develop psychogenic amenorrhea.[36] In one study, 25 percent of a group of American young women training in Israel developed amenorrhea for a period of three months.[37] Young women leaving home for an out-of-town school for the first time often have a number of missed periods.[26]

Young females who suffer from anorexia nervosa (see Chapter 4) and women on "crash" diets who rapidly lose weight often develop amenor-

Box 6.2. The Deadly Tampons.

There are about 50 million American women who use tampons and almost all find tampons to be effective and safe. In a very small percentage of cases, women who use tampons develop a serious condition known as *toxic shock syndrome*.[31,32] From January to October, 1980, there were 480 cases of this syndrome recorded by the U.S. Center for Disease Control. Most cases occurred in white middle-class females under the age of thirty with more than 90 percent of the cases beginning during menstruation. Major symptoms are: a high fever; a sunburn-like rash; diarrhea; vomiting; and a sudden drop in blood pressure which often results in shock. Shock can result in death (40 of the 480 reported cases were fatal).

No one is certain of the cause but the consensus is that the common pus-producing bacteria, Staphylococcus aureus is an important factor.[58] This bacteria produces a toxin that typically results in carbuncles, boils, and abscesses. The belief is that the S. aureus grows in the protected environment of the vagina and the poisonous toxin is spread throughout the system. The FDA is conducting tests to determine if this proposed mechanism actually occurs. About 7 percent of women harbor the S. aureus microbe, but very few of them come down with toxic shock syndrome (about 3 of every 100,000 menstruating women per year).* Undoubtedly, as with other infectious diseases, stress plays a part in lowering the body's resistance and allowing the microbes to multiply.

To prevent this condition, women should endeavor to follow the stress-coping methods discussed in Part VI. There have been no reported cases of toxic shock syndrome with the use of sanitary napkins or minipads. Hence, women who either have had symptoms of the syndrome, had a previous bout with it, or who don't want to take a chance of getting toxic shock syndrome, could use either of those two protective methods.

An executive of Tampax, Inc. (which produces almost half the country's share of tampons) stated that in forty years of clinical testing, his company has had no direct knowledge of the disease.[31] Just recently, the FDA has had one manufacturer recall all of its tampons (*Rely*, Proctor and Gamble, Cincinnati, Ohio).[32]

In case any signs or symptoms of the syndrome develop, a physician should be notified immediately. Antibiotics are partly effective and can reduce the risk of reoccurrences.

* A recent estimate by the FDA is that 10–15 per 100,000 is the more accurate figure. (Editorial. Update on toxic shock syndrome. *FDA Drug Bull.* 10(3):17-18, 1980).

rhea.[38] Amenorrhea has developed following electroshock therapy and during imprisonment in concentration camps.[26]

In terms of treatment, suppressing prolactin by drug therapy (e.g., bromocriptine) has been shown to be effective. However, since amenorrhea is usually stress-related, reducing stressors is the most logical and safest method. If the anxiety-inducing situations cannot easily be reduced or eliminated, reassurance by the therapist or physician should help in the return of normal menses.

Other stress-related female reproductive conditions are oligomenorrhea and anovulation.

OLIGOMENORRHEA AND ANOVULATION

Both oligomenorrhea (irregular menses) and anovulation (failure to ovulate) can be related to stress.[35,36] Women who have irregular periods can become amenorrheic during severely stressful times. Stress can also trigger excessive bleeding during regular menstrual periods and may occasionally be responsible for bleeding between periods. However, organic reasons (such as ovarian cysts) should always be thoroughly checked out for these episodes. As with amenorrhea, psychological counseling would be helpful. There is another interesting condition in which menstruation ceases. It is known as pseudocyesis.

PSEUDOCYESIS (FALSE PREGNANCY)

Pseudocyesis is a conscious but erroneous belief that one is pregnant. The condition is often stress-induced. The women are considered to be in conflict between their desire for pregnancy and their fear of it. Hostility and immature dependency in relationship to their mother may cause anxiety, depression, and a fear of pregnancy and its outcome. However, being pregnant helps fulfill their dependency and succorant needs. Pseudopregnancy temporarily resolves the conflict.[1,37,39]

These women usually show all the signs and symptoms of being pregnant including: amenorrhea; weight gain (including an expanding abdomen); breast changes; and a positive pregnancy test (probably related to stress-induced release of the female hormone LH).[39,40]

Psychotherapy is most important in this condition. Once the patient is assured that she is not actually pregnant and is perfectly normal otherwise, then the usual sequellae are: disappearance of morning sickness and other pregnancy symptoms; the return to normal size of the abdomen; and the resumption of regular menstruation.[36]

With some young girls, instead of becoming amenorrheic, stress affects them in another manner: they simply run away.

RUNNING AWAY

In describing stress-related disorders in Chapter 4, the phenomenon of adult women deserting their families was discussed. Now let us consider the factors that cause teen-agers to run away. In the last chapter, we looked into the Oedipus (Electra) complex in which there was an attraction between young girls and their fathers. A recent study analyzing the reasons for adolescent girls running away showed that one of the principal reasons was to escape incestuous relationships between themselves and their fathers or father substitutes.[41]

Other reasons given were: (1) to escape family quarrels and "tensions"; (2) to search for a better life, a better situation or a better home; (3) to be free to have sexual relations with a boy (usually older than themselves); (4) to solve personal "tensions"; and (5) just to have a chance to rest and relax away from the continual conflicts of home.

Most young girls who ran away were drug abusers, sexually active, and depressed. The thought of going back to school could have increased their depression since most of the runaway episodes occurred in June and December (i.e., before and during holidays). Almost all of the runaway girls had sympathetic girl friends. Hence, it was clear that the girls needed support, much of which was absent in their home situations.

Management of the problem of the runaway girl is dependent upon effective individual psychotherapy and family therapy. Also, methods are needed to overcome drug dependence (e.g., "halfway" houses).

Running away accounts for a high proportion of female juvenile delinquency, and it is one of the major reasons why young females are referred to juvenile courts. Other "crimes" that cause teen-age females to appear in court are sexual delinquency, truancy and incorrigibility. Boys are much less frequently referred for such offenses; they generally follow adult male behavior and commit crimes such as burglary, larceny, and car theft.[42] Regardless of the offense, female teen-agers are far less likely to engage in illegal activities (probably related to their following the "norm" for the feminine role).[1]

Adjusting to being a teen-ager doesn't necessitate such drastic alternatives such as running away, or becoming amenorrheic. Let us consider some of the normal teen-age "pressures" and how they are managed.

MASTURBATION

The teen-ager has two avenues for sexual activities. The first and easiest is masturbation. The second, sexual intercourse, is occurring at a younger age with this generation of female teen-agers and it is becoming widespread (discussed shortly). Masturbation does not have the taboos it once had, but still many teen-age girls do not openly discuss the subject with their mothers or peers. In Victorian times, masturbation was considered evil. It was known as the "solitary vice" and engaging in it was supposedly associated with serious disease, mental derangement, and future childbirth complications.[1,43,44] To prevent masturbation, it was not unusual in Victorian times to excise the clitoris of young girls.[44] Fortunately, such radical thinking and treatment has ceased.

Although young children occasionally masturbate, deliberate and frequent masturbation begins in prepuberty and early puberty years. According to the Kinsey report, 85 percent of females had reached their first orgasm through masturbation as compared to 70 percent for males.[45,46] As was discussed in the last chapter, the mother's attitude toward masturbation can affect: the daughter's feelings about the activity; her self-image; and her sexuality. An open discussion by the mother with her prepuberty or puberty daughter will help dissipate many of the fears, anxieties, and guilt feelings that otherwise might develop concerning masturbation. A young girl who feels good about her personal anatomy will feel good about herself and be better prepared to enter into sexual relations.

MEETING BOYS

With the advent of sex education in many schools, young girls have a much better knowledge about sexual matters than do former teen-agers (and even some of their mothers). With the current sexual freedom, it is not unusual for teachers and principals to be dealing with the results of this new-found knowledge and freedom—teen-age pregnancies. The other damaging result of sexual freedom in young girls is that they are being afflicted with sexually transmitted diseases such as syphilis, gonorrhea, and herpes vaginalis. Birth control and disease prevention methods are being taught in sex education classes. It is hoped that female teen-agers will "lend an attentive ear." It would be quite unfortunate if the current openness of mothers with their daughters about sexual matters and the new wave of sexual freedom led to an increase in unwed teen-age mothers, abortions and venereal diseases. There is a great deal of distress associated with these unfortunate consequences.

One recent report attests to the fact that these problems are becoming prevalent. In Washington County, Maryland (population of 100,000), the current year (1979) teen-age birth rate rose 25 percent from the previous year. It is estimated that in the summer of 1980, a quarter-million teen-age American girls became pregnant[47] and within the next few years one out of five teen-agers will become mothers.[48]

Yet there are still some positive signs. Even with the new sexual freedom, teen-age girls are not becoming more promiscuous* than previous generations. Although there is an increased frequency of premarital sexual intercourse among teen-agers and women in their twenties, there is no increase in the number of partners involved. (With a greater number of male partners, there is a greater chance to contact some kind of venereal disease.) Most young women are having relations with only one or two partners. Of those females who had premarital sexual intercourse, in both the Kinsey report (1953) and a more recent Playboy survey (1973), approximately half of the women had only a single partner—and he was the man they expected to marry. Thus, the current generation of female teen-agers may still be able to manage their stress-related sexual problems in a positive way. In addition to sexual anxieties, the young female has other potential problems with which to cope.

FROM PIMPLES TO POT

The teen-age time is known as the "awkward age." As the body develops, there are many changes including pimples, voice changes, and redistribution of anatomical contours. Some of these may be temporarily upsetting. But as these changes are also happening to the young woman's peers, the shared problems are easier to manage. The knowledge that the "awkward age" is only temporary should make it easier for coping. Changes are occurring in drug and alcohol habits as well. As was discussed in Chapter 4, smoking is increasing rapidly for adolescent females. Many more young women are also becoming involved with drugs and alcohol.

As with sex education, courses in health education are given early in the school curricula. Emphasis is on the negative aspects of alcoholism, cigarette smoking, and drug intake. Hopefully, young women will be in-

* The term promiscuous is used to describe behavior in which there is widespread sexual activities, often with several different partners over a prolonged period. Many people consider it a sexist term since it is almost never used to describe male behavior. It is generally used for females with the strong implication that they are acting "bad" or in an emotionally disturbed manner (Scarf, M. The promiscuous woman. *Psychol. Today,* **14**(2): 78–87, 1980). Recently, it has been proposed that this behavior may have some positive benefits (Talese, G. *Thy Neighbor's Wife.* Garden City, New York: Doubleday & Co., 1980).

fluenced by these courses and by the holistic health movement.[50] Holistic health emphasizes the importance of taking care of one's own body and getting natural "highs" from practices such as meditation and jogging.[51,52] Holistic health also promotes the ideal body-weight concept as do some health education courses. Women are generally concerned about their appearance, and being neither overweight nor underweight; i.e., an important component of "looking good." Teen-age girls often go on "eating binges" and "crash diets," neither of which are beneficial. They also have a tendency to eat calorie-rich, nutrient-poor junk foods.[53] As a result, youngsters may be caught between obesity and anorexia nervosa (see Chapter 4). As is discussed in Chapters 21 and 22, eating properly and exercising regularly are the main components to insuring a healthful, firm figure.

The teen-age girl is also thinking about her future. Will it be marriage, a career or both? Will she have children? The female adolescent in today's Western society has more options than were previously available including the possibility of entering "male" occupations.

It used to be that young women would strive to get married and have many children. It was considered prestigious and worthwhile to be fertile and have a large family.[54] Nowadays it is still essential to have children for society in general but because of economic pressures such as inflation, recession, and high unemployment—and because women want to lead a life of their own without always being pregnant—young married (or "living together") women are content with small families. Therefore, the growing teen-ager if she wants to stay "old-fashioned" will probably have fewer children and still be able to have more freedom and less stress (see Chapters 13 to 18).

As was discussed in the last chapter, young girls are higher in verbal ability than are young boys. They often do well in school and are rewarded with good grades. As a teen-ager, other values creep in such as physical attractiveness, being popular, dating boys, and having good social skills. There is stress associated with both being beautiful and popular and being unattractive and unpopular. The beautiful young woman may be so busy being popular that her grades suffer. Teachers often favor attractive-looking students, so these students may have added "pressures" to perform well since they know they will be called upon. If the young women are so busy with dates and other outside activities, they may not have the time to adequately prepare for school.

On the other hand, the unattractive unpopular young woman may channel her energies into being an excellent student. Although she may suffer distress as a result of her appearance, she often compensates for it in other ways, such as in studies.[55]

Regardless of outside activities, with most young women there is still the general "pressure" to conform to the feminine model of getting married and being a housewife. Hence, many girls don't do justice to their innate intelligence and go to college, or don't opt for careers for which they have innate abilities. Competition has always been a negative word in the female vocabulary and some young women are loath to compete for grades. Yet many females do go on to college and aspire for careers, but even here some of them feel they have to compromise in their choice of careers. This can cause some young women to avoid success in certain careers primarily because they want to avoid anxiety.[56]

Interestingly enough, this may be the same reason why the results of enrollment at one large Southeastern state university showed that most females still opted for careers in traditional female occupations.[1] The majors with high female enrollments were: Early Childhood and Elementary Education; Dance; Speech Communication; Nursing; Rehabilitative Counseling; and other programs in the College of Education. This was a few years ago and changes are in the offing. For example, ten years ago there were only a few females in the "freshman" class at the University of Pennsylvania Dental School. In the current "freshman" class (1980), almost one-third of the students are female. Times are definitely changing, and with proper sharing of female-male roles, today's young woman has a bright future.

In the next chapter, we cover one of the young woman's decisions—marriage or bachelorhood.

REFERENCES

1. Williams, J.H. *Psychology of Women: Behavior in a Biosocial Context.* New York: W.W. Norton, 1977.
2. Pliny the Elder, *Natural History.* Quoted in Dobell, E.R. The new wisdom about menstruation. *Redbook,* p. 202, March, 1979.
3. Dobell, E.R. The new wisdom about menstruation. *Redbook* 199–206, March, 1979.
4. Frazer, J.G. *The Golden Bough.* New York: Macmillan, 1951.
5. Weideger, P. *Menstruation and Menopause: The Physiology and Psychology, the Myth and the Reality.* New York: Knopf, 1976.
6. Shuttle, P. and Redgrove, P. *Wise Wound: Eve's Curse and Everyman.* New York: R. Marek, 1978.
7. Friday, N. *My Mother/Myself: The Daughter's Search for Identity.* New York: Dell Publishing , 1978.
8. Parlee, M.B. The premenstrual syndrome. *Psychol. Bull.* **80**:454–465, 1973.
9. Dalton, K. *The Premenstrual Syndrome and Progesterone Therapy.* Chicago: Year Book Med. Publ., 1977.
10. Warnes, H. Premenstrual disorders: Causative mechanisms and treatment. *Psychosomatics* **19**:32–40, 1978.

11. Zola, P., Meyerson, A. T., Reznikoff, M., Thornton, J. C., and Concool, B. M. Menstrual symptomatology and psychiatric admission. *J. Psychosom. Res.* **23**:241–245, 1979.
12. Banks, M. H. and Beresford, S. A. A. The influence of menstrual cycle phase upon symptoms recording using data from health diaries. *J. Psychosom. Res.* **23**:307–313, 1979.
13. Moos, R. H. The development of a menstrual distress questionnaire. *Psychosom. Med.* **30**:853–867, 1968.
14. Grant, E. C. G. and Pryse-Davies, J. Effects of oral contraceptives on depressive mood changes and on endometrial monoamine oxidase and phosphates. *Br. Med. J.* **3**:777–780, 1968.
15. Broverman, D. M., Klaiber, E. L., Vogel, W., and Kobayashi, Y. Short-term versus long-term effects of adrenal hormones on behaviors. *Psychol. Bull.* **81**:672–694, 1974.
16. Selye, H. *The Stress of Life*, Second Ed. New York: McGraw-Hill Book Co., 1976.
17. Siegel, J. M., Johnson, J. H., and Sarason, I. G. Life changes and menstrual discomfort. *J. Hum. Stress* **5**(1):41–46, 1979.
18. Ruble, D.N. Premenstrual symptoms: A reinterpretation. *Science* **197**:291–292, 1977.
19. Abplanalp, J.M., Donnely, A.F., and Rose, R.M. Psychoendocrinology of menstrual cycle: 1. Enjoyment of daily activities and moods. *Psychosom. Med.* **41**:587–604, 1979.
20. Timonen, S. and Procope, B. Premenstrual syndrome and physical exercise. *Acta Obstet. Gynecol. Scand.* **50**:333–337, 1971.
21. Kinzer, N. S. *Stress and the American Woman.* New York: Ballantine Books, 1980.
22. Herzberg, B. and Coppen, A. Changes in psychological symptoms in women taking oral contraceptives. *Br. J. Psychiatry* **116**:161–164, 1970.
23. Marx, J. L. Dysmenorrhea: Basic research leads to a rational therapy. *Science* **205**:175–176, 1979.
24. Lennane, K. J. and Lennane, R. J. Alleged psychogenic disorders in women—A possible manifestation of sexual prejudice. *New. Engl. J. Med.* **288**:288–292, 1973.
25. Editorial. A drug to ease menstrual cramps. *Newsweek* **63**, July 9, 1979.
26. Reichlin, S., Abplanalp, J. M., Labrum, A. H., Schwartz, N., Sommer, B., and Taymor, M. The role of stress in female reproductive dysfunction. *J. Hum. Stress* **5**(3):38–45, 1979.
27. Dalton, K. *The Premenstrual Syndrome.* Springfield, Ill.: Charles C. Thomas, 1964.
28. Masters, W. H. and Johnson, V. E. *Human Sexual Response.* Boston: Little, Brown, 1966.
29. Hite, S. *The Hite Report.* New York: Macmillan Publishing, 1977.
30. Chernovetz, M. E., Jones, W. H., and Hansson, R. O. Predictablility, attentional focus, sex role orientation, and menstrual related stress. *Psychosom. Med.* **41**:383–388, 1979.
31. Associated Press. Tampons are linked to a rare disease. *New York Times* 17, June 28, 1980.
32. Medicine. Toxic Tampons: One product is recalled. *Time* **104**, October 6, 1980.
33. Paige, K. Women learn to sing the menstrual blues. *Psychol. Today* **7**(4):41–48, 1973.
34. McMann, S. M. and Moss, R. L. Putative neurotransmitters involved in the discharging gonadotropin-releasing neurohormones and the action of LH-releasing hormones in the CNS. *Life Sci.* **16**:833–852, 1975.
35. Lachelin, G. C. L. and Yen, S. S. C. Hypothalamic chronic anovulation. *Am. J. Obstet. Gynecol.* **130**:825–831, 1978.
36. Askel, S. Psychogenic amenorrhea: Diagnosis by exclusion. *Psychosomatics* **20**:357–359, 1979.
37. Shanan, J. Brzezinski, H., Shilman, F., and Sharon, M. Active coping behavior, anxiety,

and cortical steroid excretion in the prediction of transient amenorrhea. *Behav. Sci.* **10**:461–465, 1965.

38. Vigersky, R. A., Anderson, A. E., Thompson, R. H., and Loriaux, D. L. Hypothalamic dysfunction in secondary amenorrhea associated with simple weight loss. *N. Engl. J. Med.* **297**:1141–1145, 1977.

39. Katchadourian, H. and Lunde, D. *Fundamentals of Human Sexuality,* Second Ed. New York: Holt, Rinehart & Winston, 1975.

40. Yen, S. S. C., Rebar, R. W., and Quesenberry, W. Pituitary function in pseudocyesis. *J. Clin. Endocrinol. Metab.* **42**:132–136, 1976.

41. Reilly, P. P. What makes adolescent girls flee from their homes? An analysis of 50 such girls studied at Boston Juvenile Court. *Clin. Pediatr.* **17**:886–893, 1978.

42. Chesney-Lind, M. Juvenile delinquency: The sexualization of female crime. *Psychol. Today* **8**:43–46, 1974.

43. Haller, J. S. and Haller, R. M. *The Physician and Sexuality in Victorian America.* Urbana, Ill.: University of Illinois Press, 1974.

44. Sherfey, M. J. *The Nature and Evolution of Female Sexuality.* New York: Random House, 1972.

45. Kinsey, A. C., Pomeroy, W. B., and Martin, C. E. *Sexual Behavior in the Human Male.* Philadelphia: W. B. Saunders, 1948

46. Kinsey, A. C., Pomeroy, W. B., Martin, C. E., and Gebhard, P. H. *Sexual Behavior in the Human Female.* Philadelphia: W. B. Saunders, 1953.

47. Glen, M. and Shearer, C. Urgent: The high cost of no sex ed. *Philadelphia Inq.* 9A, July 7, 1980.

48. Phipps-Yonas, S. Teenage pregnancy and motherhood: A review of the literature. *Am. J. Orthopsychiat.* **50**:403–431, 1980.

49. Hunt, M. *Sexual Behavior in the Seventies.* Chicago: Playboy Press, 1974.

50. Slinkhard, L. and Maccoby, N. Pilot study of smoking, alcohol and drug abuse prevention. *Am. J. Publ. Health* **70**:719–721, 1980.

51. Morse, D. R. and Furst, M. L. *Stress for Success: A Holistic Approach to Stress and its Management.* New York: Van Nostrand Reinhold, 1979.

52. Pelletier, K. *Holistic Medicine: From Stress to Optimum Health.* New York: Dial Press, 1980.

53. Benowicz, R. J. *Vitamins & You.* New York: Grosset & Dunlap, 1979.

54. Ritvo, S. Adolescent women. *In* Blum, H. P. (ed.), *Female Psychology: Contemporary Psychoanalytic Views.* New York: International Universities Press, 1977, pp. 127–137.

55. Stein, A. H. and Bailey, M. M. The socialization of achievement orientation in females. *Psychol. Bull.* **80**:345–366, 1973.

56. Horner, M. S. Toward an understanding of achievement-related conflicts in women. *In* Stacey, J., Gereaud, S., and Daniels, J. (eds.), *And Jill Came Tumbling After: Sexism in American Education.* New York: Dell, 1974.

57. Awaritefe, A., Awaritefe, M., Diejomaoh, F.M.E., and Ebie, J.C. Personality and Menstruation. *Psychosom. Med.* **42**:237–251, 1980.

58. Cohen, M.L., and Falkow, S. Protein antigens from Staphloccocus aureus strains associated with toxic-shock syndrome. *Science* **211**:842–844, 1981.

7
The Twenties, Thirties, and Forties: Choices and Decisions

INTRODUCTION

Although more choices related to marriage and careers are open to females, most women still get married. However, the number of new marriages is dropping off in the United States. Women are getting married at a later age and nonmarital living together arrangements are increasing at a tremendous rate.[1] In addition, being a single woman is achieving a new status with a legitimate life-style of its own.[2] Nevertheless, at least according to one recent study of six hundred Chicago-area women, most of the respondents considered the three most important roles of a woman to be mother, wife, and homemaker.[3] Given this information, let us first consider the stressors involved in the traditional marriage.

TRADITIONAL MARRIAGE

Some consider the act of marriage as a return to symbiosis for the female; the changing of the ties and dependency from the mother to the husband.[4] It is not necessarily an advantage for the woman to make that switch. It has been said that marriage induces stress in women and reduces stress in men.[5]

Men can still do most of the same things they've done before marriage. They can work, engage in athletics, go to sporting events, and watch TV. They have the additional advantages of having someone prepare the meals, wash their clothes, and fulfill their sexual needs. Women, in contrast, find that they are burdened with extra jobs that they were ill-prepared for such as cooking, cleaning, washing floors, darning socks, and ironing clothes.[6] Their educational abilities are downgraded by these mundane tasks. In addition, they are expected to be the sweet, adorable, loving wife. No wonder marriage can be stressful for the female.

One of the causes of distress is change. Most women consider marriage to be one of the biggest changes in their lives.[3] For some, the change is beneficial; for others it is not. Some women believe that they become more tolerant, patient, and sharing, and learn to be more independent. Others feel that they lose their freedom; going from independence to dependence and greater responsibilities.[3] The taking of a "second family" that could include in-laws, his relatives, and children from a previous marriage may be stressful to some women.

Another potential source of stress for the married female is lack of financial control. Most often the husband is the principal breadwinner and controls the finances, although the wife may be "in charge" of family expenses. Lack of power can be quite stressful to the married woman. Often the husband makes the final choice of where to live, when and where to take vacations, and when to move.

It is true that many more women are working. More than half of all adult women work, and 60 percent of them are married.[1] However, in many families, the wives income is an "extra" and not the major source of family finances. And, as such, her "power" is still relatively insignificant. The reasons for women working and the problems attendant in the various career choices are considered in Chapters 13–18.

Another source of stress in the traditional marriage is sexual. Nowadays, premarital sexual activities are more prevalent in females, and if current trends continue premarital sexual intercourse will be the norm.[6] The newly married female may find it more difficult to confine her sexual activities to one partner if she is used to a varied experience before marriage.[7] In essence, she would be in the same situation as males have been for many decades. That may be the reason why alternative kinds of marriage and sexual arrangements are now becoming more prevalent (e.g., "open marriage," "living together," and communes; discussed shortly). On the other hand, married women may be caught in a bind. They may believe in many women's liberation ideas such as equality between the sexes in jobs, schools, politics, and sports, but they are firmly opposed to sexual freedom outside of marriage for either the woman or man.

A major source of marital stress is the drudgery of being a housewife. As this is really an occupation, although a nonremunerative one, the stress of being "only a housewife" is covered as one of the female occupations (see Chapter 13). Not every female considers the traditional marriage to be

Box 7.1.   Aisha Seishin.

Even though traditional marriage causes some distress to females in Western countries, in Japan married women really have their problems. Consider the results of this Japanese survey. Married Japanese men were asked: "If you were driving along a highway and an earthquake occurred, whom would you phone first?" Only 9 percent of the men surveyed answered that they would first phone their wives. Thirty-seven percent stated that they would first phone their employers. The investigators conjectured that the results showed that a large segment of the Japanese male population value their jobs more than their wives. Japanese married women are well aware of their husbands' stringent devotion to business. They call it "aisha seishin" and consider it to be a primary cause of marital unhappiness and disagreement, and a key factor in divorce. Job loyalty is an integral component of Japanese culture.

Recently, the Japanese prime minister's office took a poll of single Japanese women. Some results were: 25 percent of the single women said that they didn't want to get married because it was not the road to fulfillment; 62 percent of them expected to get married, but only 12 percent of them expected any happiness out of it. The majority of Japanese single women realized that the Japanese wife ranked low in the pecking order.[9]

stressful. For instance, the concept of the traditional marriage is still strong in the younger female generations of certain ethnic groups such as Italian-American, Jewish-American and Eastern European-American. In these groups, surveys have found that 80 percent of the young generation consider marriage and children to be more important than a career.[8] In other cultures, marriage can be a problem. For an example of severe marital stress, see Box 7.1.

One way to overcome some of the potential problems of the traditional marriage is the adoption of "open marriage."

OPEN MARRIAGE

When one thinks of open marriage, the first idea that comes to mind is that one is free to have extramarital sex. Although this may be part of the open marriage contract, there are several other potentially favorable components to this alternative form of marriage. The major premise is that there should be equal freedom and identity for both partners.[10] In terms of equality, the roles of husband and wife should be flexible so that both household chores and financial support can be shared by both partners. Each spouse should be able to fulfill her/his own identities. Privacy for partners is important.

They shouldn't have to do things together all of the time. There should be open and honest communication between the spouses. Living should be for now; not mired in the past or deferred until retirement. There should be respect and integrity for each other.

All this sounds fine, but a potential problem could be related to the freedom of each partner to have outside companions. With respect to extramarital affairs and open communication, it has been the clinical experience of one of us (MF) that jealousy and distrust expressed by the individuals making up the couples can occur and wreck the other advantages of open marriage. However, it would be advantageous for trust, equality, flexibility, identity, privacy, and living for now to be incorporated into traditional marriages. That would certainly reduce the stressors of marriage for most people. Another alternative to the traditional marriage is "living together."

LIVING TOGETHER

Living together with a man outside of the traditional bonds of matrimony has these advantages for the woman: (1) She keeps her name and identity; (2) the arrangement can be terminated without harassing legal battles; and (3) as a single person living together with a man, she and her partner would pay less income taxes than they would as a married couple (according to current income tax laws).[11]

Yet living together has certain disadvantages. One is that the relative ease of termination also provides for very little financial and emotional security for the woman.* Another potentially stressful problem is that children born in these arrangements often suffer psychological stressors. Although the woman thinks she'll get a better deal, studies have shown that in the "living together" arrangements women still do the bulk of the housework, even when both partners work.[12]

Two recent alternatives to the couple living together are: singles' societies and group (multilateral) marriage.

SINGLES' SOCIETIES

In this kind of arrangement, each person remains single but all live together in the form of society. However, some studies have shown that here, too,

---

* However, the recent financial settlement in the Marvin and Marvin case showed that judges are now considering that with the termination of the arrangement, women are entitled to monetary compensation. Special report. Battle of the sexes: Men fight back. U.S. *News & World Report* 50–54, December 8, 1980.

there is role assignment on the basis of sex. The societies still cater to men since the men have the option of doing most of the pursuing and selection from the eligible females.[2]

MULTILATERAL (GROUP) MARRIAGE

In this arrangement, there is a marriage of at least three people each of whom is "married" to at least two other members of the group.[13] The commitment that each shares with the other is considered to be equivalent to the traditional marriage. Some of the spouses, in fact, have legal marriage contracts with one member; others have none. Studies of these groups have revealed some interesting observations:

1. Most members were interested in personal growth opportunities and in having a variety of sexual partners.
2. Psychological tests showed that the female participants had greater sexual needs than did the male members.
3. There was a great deal of shared roles with some men taking care of children and doing housework and some women having careers.
4. The work which no one else wanted to do usually was done by the least assertive and most order-minded individuals (which most often were women).[13]

So even here the women don't generally get a "fair shake."

One other group arrangement is communes.

COMMUNES

There are many different kinds of communes based on religion, philosophy, drugs, gender, and family. They are often relatively unstable and the membership tends to fluctuate.[14] There are all sorts of marital and non-marital arrangements. Sexual mores range from monogamy to complete openness in either heterosexual, homosexual, or mixed arrangements. Overall, women's roles seem to be similar to those in traditional marriages; the women are still primarily concerned with housework and child care.[1] One thing that all these arrangements have in common is that the "wife" often becomes a mother.

Let us now consider the stressors of pregnancy, childbirth, breast-feeding, and the start of a family.

MOTHERHOOD

The usual sequence is: First a wife; next a housewife; and then a mother. In recent times the stages are often switched with pregnancy or motherhood coming before marriage or homemaking. And there are now many single women who become mothers without the benefit of either marriage or living together arrangements.

Becoming pregnant, especially for the first time, is one of the greatest changes in a woman's life and, as change induces stress, it can be one of the most stressful periods for a woman. With most changes in people's lives, decisions are arrived at after careful consideration. With pregnancy, "It is a truism that no woman really decides to get pregnant; it just happens."[15] However, nowadays there is no such thing as an immaculate conception; there is at least the knowledge that after sexual intercourse pregnancy may be a natural consequence.

There are certain reasons why women contemplate motherhood:

1. The marriage is "coming apart at the seams," and the belief is that a child will supply the "glue" to repair the damage. Although this may be temporarily effective, it often fails to restore an unhappy marriage. Once the child leaves home, the marital crisis resurfaces. This is exemplified by the high rate of divorce among middle-aged and older couples.[15]

2. Being a mother is the thing to do for a "real" woman. This is exemplified in psychoanalytic writing (e.g., Deutsch's conception of womanhood as a progression from childhood to motherhood,[16] and Erikson's identification of "inner space" with motherhood as being the key role for women).[17] According to Freud, being pregnant is a substitute for the missing penis.[18] Religion traditionally maintains the importance of motherhood. Pope John Paul II recently stated that women express their true nature by bearing children.[19] Nevertheless, with the growing importance of the women's movement, many married women are realizing that having children is not the only path to fulfillment. Women who have children only because it's "the thing to do," often have a great deal of resentment.

3. Having children is a method of achieving a sense of immortality; one's genes are continued in another life through one's children. This ego-centered reason does have some merit, but if the children turn out in an unfavorable mold, then disappointment and even hate can result.

4. Children are necessary for the survival of humanity and especially of the particular ethnic group. Undoubtedly, if people didn't believe this, the human race would disappear and so would separate cultures. The Judeo-Christian creeds consider it to be a moral duty to have children, and being unfertile is considered to be a curse.[1] However, as with the second reason given above, having this as a major motive for motherhood can be a later source of stress.

5. Children are a source of fun and happiness. They complete a family

and add a sense of joy and wonderment to life. They are mysterious and novel and challenging. They can fulfill affiliative needs and they inspire competence, creativity, and feeling of achievement for mothers. Nevertheless children can also be a source of aggravation and distress. They are constantly in need, require continual attention, reduce one's freedom of activity and flexibility, and can be a source of friction between husband and wife (e.g., divided loyalties).

6. Children are a source of economic power. They can help in the household or family business, usually at reduced or nonexistent wages. They are also of value for the country's economy, providing needed labor. Here, too, this is a "mixed bag." Children often resent being unpaid laborers, and this can cause marital and family strife. In highly industrialized societies such as the United States, the economic value of having many children is low. Hence, the benefit to the country may be minor.

7. Children will take care of their mothers when they get old. If this was the usual case, it would be wonderful to have care and consideration from loving children as one ages gracefully. Unfortunately—à la Roberta in Chapter 1—women are often left to spend their declining years in nursing homes.

In order to have children for any of these aforementioned reasons, it is necessary to become pregnant, and pregnancy can be either a highly stressful time or a wonderful experience. Not all women who want children can or want to become pregnant. Some women really want to become pregnant, but their intense desire along with anxieties about pregnancy causes their hormonal system to become unbalanced and they can't become pregnant.[6] For all of these women adoption may be the preferred route, but even so, someone had to become pregnant in the first place.

Let us now consider the stressors of pregnancy.

PREGNANCY

Pregnancy can be considered another stage in the continuing symbiotic relationship of women. The female starts off life in symbiotic relationship with her mother which continues through early childhood. It periodically returns or is never severed in adulthood. It is reaffirmed in marriage, and with pregnancy, symbiosis is renewed in the most direct manner.[18] Symbiotic relations with her mother for the pregnant woman may increase the stress of pregnancy. If the pregnant women hears "tales of doom" from her mother, then her pregnancy is more likely to be filled with anxiety.[6] Also, if she becomes too dependent upon her mother for advice, this can negatively affect her attitude.[1]

The first stressful aspect of pregnancy is the missed menstrual period. As discussed in the last chapter, amenorrhea can occur for several reasons and a missed period is not a fail-safe sign of pregnancy. It is also possible to have bleeding episodes during the first trimester of pregnancy. Nevertheless, a missed period is often an indication of pregnancy. It can bring tears of joy or extreme anger depending upon the woman's desire to become pregnant.

Another early potential stressful aspect of pregnancy is *morning sickness*. Nausea alone or in combination with vomiting occurs in about 75 percent of pregnant women.[1] Increased levels of female hormones play a major role in morning sickness but there are undoubtedly some psychological components to the condition. In one study, *pathological vomiting*(hyperemesis) occurred in pregnant women who had repeated severe life-stress events (social stressors) as contrasted to nonvomiting pregnant women who did not have many stressful episodes.[1] A second pregnancy-related condition that is quite prevalent is *pregnancy gingivitis*. Related to the increased levels of progesterone and immunosuppressive factors during pregnancy, the body's ability to fight infection decreases. One of the key areas in which this shows up is the gingiva (gums).[20] Pregnant women often have bleeding, swollen, and tender gums. Although this is brought on by pregnancy-induced hormonal changes along with stressful factors, having dental care and maintaining good oral hygiene (e.g., brushing, flossing, use of interdental stimulators, and oral irrigation devices) can greatly reduce the incidence and severity of pregnancy gingivitis.[61] (See Figure 7.1 for examples of this condition.)

Other potentially disturbing early pregnancy symptoms are increased fatigue, sleepiness, and urination.[1] These can be somewhat annoying but are unimportant. However, as stress can exacerbate the diabetic condition or can convert a prediabetic into a diabetic (as discussed in Chapter 3), it would be important to have a glucose tolerance test for diabetes if the increased urination continued.

During the second trimester, the woman's waistline enlarges and her abdomen begins to protrude. This can be stressful for the new mother, especially if she is especially concerned about her figure. Most well-adjusted women can adapt to the changing body contours as they know it lasts for no longer than nine months. However, there may be some bouts of stress-induced compulsive eating which, as was discussed in Chapter 4, can lead to obesity. Eating too much during pregnancy can result in obesity after delivery.

Women's mental attitudes are usually quite good at this time. Calmness and euphoria can occur and are partly related to the high levels of female hormones. In contradistinction, along with the high levels of estrogen and

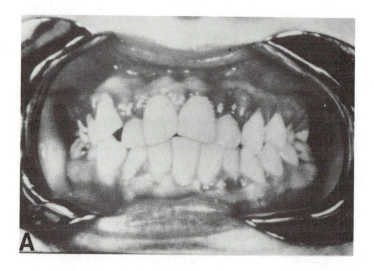

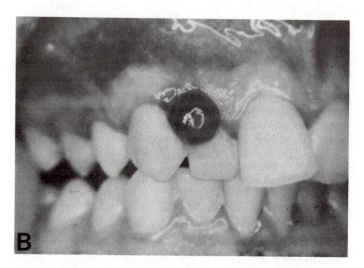

Fig. 7.1. Pregnancy-associated gingival changes. In the first trimester, the rising progesterone level can trigger inflammatory changes in the gingiva (gums) in some women. Although progesterone is important, the resultant inflammation is also dependent upon the presence of local irritants such as calculus (tartar).

A. Pregnancy gingivitis—A widespread inflammation of the gums.

B. A pregnancy tumor—A localized swelling of the gums (*Courtesy of Dr. Dave Litwack, Philadelphia, Pa.*)

progesterone, there are decreased levels of noradrenaline.[1] As was discussed under depression, with low noradrenaline levels, there may be increased clinical depression. With some pregnant women, low noradrenaline levels are associated with high depression scores.[1]

In the last trimester, the breasts enlarge and get sore, the kicking infant can be annoying and cause back pains and sleep interruptions, and sexual activity is greatly interfered with. At that time the woman can even consider the fetus to be an enemy who is injuring her kidneys or womb.[21] Other complications of pregnancy in this trimester such as *toxemia* and *preeclampsia* (in the third trimester, a persistent diastolic blood pressure of 90 millimeters or more in a nonhypertensive woman) may be stress-related.[6,22] The body is at its greatest distortion and the woman feels most dependent in the third trimester. She may become impatient and want to "get it over with."[21]

One investigator considers pregnancy to be a gradually unfolding crisis that has labor and delivery as the final stage and greatest peak.[23] Let us now consider the stress from childbirth.

CHILDBIRTH

Childbirth can be stressful because of: (1) the pain involved in labor and delivery; (2) the delivery taking place (usually) in a hospital where there is sickness and dying present; (3) a fear of the unknown, since for many it is the first trip to a hospital; (4) the treatment by primarily male obstetricians who may tend to downplay the woman's role in the delivery process;[24] (5) the administration of general or spinal anesthetics along with various other drugs that can be upsetting in themselves and generate fear of death or bodily damage for both mother and child; (6) the sudden temporary loss of the child; (7) the isolation in a foreign environment; and (8) being treated by strangers without the benefit of a husband's (lover's) or family's comfort and support.

Childbirth is not always distressful. In fact, some women report feelings of intense pleasure (euphoria) during childbirth. This could be related to the discovery of the naturally occurring hormone beta endorphin in the placenta. This hormone has antipain (analgesic) and antianxiety effects. A recent study has shown that endorphins increase in the mother throughout pregnancy with a sharp increase just before parturition.[25] Endorphins also apparently act as "happiness hormones" for some women during childbirth.[26]

Stress during pregnancy can have an effect on the delivery, the mother's health, the developing fetus, and the unborn child.* One study assessed married pregnant women of similar age, race, and social status that had deliveries in the same hospital. The results showed that those women who had the most social stressors and the least social support (as measured by closeness with husband, family, and community) had about three times the frequency of complications of pregnancy and delivery.[27] The deleterious effect of stress on labor and delivery has been corroborated in other studies.[22] In one study, experimentally induced stress caused intense uterine contractions in pregnant women.[1]

In another study, women who had life-stress events in the week preceding the onset of labor had premature labor.[28] The life-stress events included a sudden substantive decrease in income, and serious illness in family members. Other women who had continuing financial worries for many months also had premature labor. In other studies it was shown that both cortisone and adrenaline (stress hormones) can affect uterine contractions that occur during labor.[29,30]

Other research has shown that women with high anxiety levels had a three to four times greater incidence of postpartum hemorrhage (excessive vaginal bleeding within the first day after birth) and pre-eclampsia than did women with normal anxiety levels.[22] This is of special importance as those two complications of pregnancy are principal causes of serious illness and death for the delivering mother,

The cumulative stressors of pregnancy can affect women mentally after childbirth. In Chapter 3 we discussed the high incidence of depression in females. One severe type of depression can occur after childbirth and is known as *postpartum depression*.[6] It is more frequent after the first child and may be related to: (1) the sudden drop in levels of estrogen and progesterone;[1] (2) the tremendous responsibility of taking care of a helpless infant; (3) the lack of child-care preparation; (4) the interference in sexual relations with the husband; and (5) the woman's own feeling of inadequacy.

Psychological stressors during pregnancy may also be partly responsible for stillborn babies. This was assumed to be a contribution to the higher incidence of stillborn babies for illegitimate as compared to legitimate births.[31] Stress can also contribute to infertility and habitual abortion.[22] As mentioned in Chapter 4, drinking alcoholic beverages, smoking cigarettes and taking drugs can cause stillborn and defective babies.[32] Alcohol, caffeine and nicotine cause increased levels of catecholamines (adrenaline and

---

* Two excellent reviews on the effects of stress on pregnancy are: Herrenkohl, L.R. The anxiety-prone personality: Effects of prenatal stress on the infant. In Matthew, R.J. (ed.), *The Biology of Anxiety*. New York: Elsevier/North Holland, 1981; Spezzano, C. Prenatal Psychology: Pregnant with questions. *Psychol. Today 15* (5): 49–57, 1981.

noradrenaline), and alcohol and nicotine cause increased levels of cortisone.[32] As the catecholamines and cortisone are stress hormones, it can be seen how there may be interactions between maternal stress and drugs in causing birth defects.

In a recent study, it was found that the pregnant mother's use of amphetamines, marijuana, and LSD can be damaging. The offspring had a higher than average incidence of stillborn births and congenitally malformed babies.[33]

Women judged to be fearful about themselves and their babies and who were considered high in tension, depression, and withdrawal were found in one study to have babies of lower weight than women who were not so emotionally involved.[1] In another study, women scoring high in "hypochondria" and "neuroticism" also had smaller babies than normal scoring women.[34]

Stress during pregnancy can also cause the birth of babies with congenital deformities, cleft palates, and mental retardation.[35] The mechanisms for the stress-associated effects are not known, but there is some indication that stress causes a delay of respiration in the newborn. In animal experiments, it was shown that maternal stress causes a decrease in testosterone (see Figure 2.1) production in male fetuses and that might affect the newborn's behavior.[36]

With many women delaying marriage and childbirth for years, there is the possibility of them becoming pregnant when they are well into their forties. Since all of the female's ova (eggs) are present in immature form in her ovaries from birth, these eggs will have age-changed by the time they are ready to be fertilized. The age changes may cause the development of defective offspring. (Sperm are continuously produced and as a result do not show age changes although they may have other deficiencies.) This may account for the higher incidence of mongoloid (Down's syndrome) children born to older women.[1] Therefore, if women want to raise a family and have a career, they may elect to begin the family in their late twenties or early thirties. That would help reduce the stress resulting from giving birth to a mongoloid child (although mongoloid children can be a source of love).

One final stressor relating to childbirth is the method of delivery. There has been a three-fold increase in Cesarian deliveries in the last ten years in the United States (up to 15 percent of all deliveries).[37] One rationale that is given for this increase is that both doctors and mothers want to be certain that the newborn are as healthy as possible. Hence, if there are any suspicions of problems such as prolonged labor, or breech position, the tendency has been to quickly perform a Cesarian delivery.

Another reason for the increase is the physicians' fear of malpractice suits if a defective child is born. A third reason is that women who have had previous Cesarians are automatically given another Cesarian delivery (over 99 percent of the cases).

With original Cesarians, there was a vertical incision and subsequently a scar formed. Follow-up vaginal deliveries could have caused rupture of the scar with the possibility of death or serious complications to both child and mother. However, currently, a low horizontal incision is employed and the scar formed from the incision is very unlikely to rupture with future vaginal deliveries.[37]

There is greater stress from Cesarian deliveries as compared to vaginal deliveries. The death rate for mothers from Cesarian delivery is twice as high as from the conventional vaginal delivery. In addition, there is a greater risk of maternal infection following Cesarian than vaginal deliveries. Other stress-inducing factors associated with Cesarian delivery are: (1) generally, the husband is not present in the delivery room; (2) home delivery is not possible; and (3) the child is generally separated from the mother immediatedly for observation in special nurseries. Moreover, recent studies have not verified that babies delivered by Cesarean section are healthier than conventionally delivered babies. For all these reasons, women should be given a greater say in the method of delivery.

Once the child is born the mother may be ready to nurse, which in itself can be stress-inducing.

BREAST-FEEDING

Breast-feeding is undergoing a new surge of interest as part of the concept of returning to natural methods. However, nursing can induce stress for several reasons:

1. Swollen, tender breasts and cracked nipples may occur from nursing.
2. Being tied down to the baby's feeding schedule can be upsetting.
3. Husbands may complain because of the inconvenience and lack of attention.
4. Anxiety may develop about sagging breasts resulting from nursing.[1]
5. There may be anxiety about whether or not the baby is getting sufficient milk.
6. Anxiety can affect the production of milk by upsetting the production of prolactin and other female hormones. This can result in the woman wanting to nurse and then being unable to do so (induces further anxiety).

7. The anxious woman who has trouble nursing often has a colicky baby that keeps her up all night.[6]

The advantages of breast-feeding are:

1. A warm relationship can develop between mother and child.
2. The child is receiving natural mother's milk rather than cow's milk.
3. Breast milk confers temporary immunity against certain infectious diseases.[1]
4. The woman may get a positive feeling as a "successful" mother.

However, there is no firm evidence that bottle-fed babies are less healthy or well-adjusted than breast-fed babies.[1]

Once the child is born, regardless of whether she is breast-fed or bottle-fed, the new mother has a whole new life-style. Let us now consider the stressors of the new mother.

THE PROBLEMS OF THE NEW MOTHER

Studies have shown that young married couples without children are happier than those with young children. Happiness decreases with the birth of the first child, and then increases as the children grow older and increases further after they leave home.[1]

One of the major problems contributing to stress for the new mother is the lack of help in doing a myriad of tasks including: feeding the child; changing diapers; doing the food shopping; washing and ironing clothes; cleaning the house; preparing meals; and being a loving wife. It has been suggested that "every woman needs a wife,"[6] and that suggestion seems appropriate.

Another stressor for the new mother is guilt. If she goes back to school or work, and even if she is fortunate enough to have "help," the new mother often suffers pangs of guilt. If a child is born before the parents are economically secure, stress is increased because of the interaction of other factors such as insufficient finances, in-law problems, inadequate housing, and health problems. In Box 7.2, an example of stress associated with motherhood in another culture is given.

Now that we've looked at the stress that can result from pregnancy, childbirth, nursing, and taking care of the new child, let us consider ways to decrease that stress.

Box 7.2.   The Stress From Pregnancy and Motherhood in Other Cultures.

There are many stressors associated with pregnancy, childbirth, and motherhood in Western countries, but in other cultures the stress, compared to our standards, seems to be much worse. The pregnant *Borneo* native (in tropical Africa) leaves her husband and stays with her mother for two years. The rationale is that by being isolated from her husband and in the safety of her mother's care, the destructive wishes that the husband or wife might have against the child would be thwarted.[18]

Just as menstruating women are kept isolated in many primitive cultures (see Box 6.1), so, too, are women who are in labor. Consider the *Kadu Gollas* of India who place their women in labor inside isolated huts. The women are considered impure and must remain in the huts for three months, or until they are permitted to return by the gods.[1]

In our culture there are no taboos against having sexual relations while the mother is nursing. In fact, many couples have sexual intercourse throughout the pregnancy. In many primitive cultures, sexual relations are forbidden both during pregnancy and while the child is being nursed. Consider the problems of the *Abysin* women of Paraguay. They nurse their children for up to three years, and during all that time they are not allowed to have intercourse with their husbands (or any other males).[38] In other primitive cultures, sexual relations are encouraged during pregnancy. The belief is that the sperm provides food for the growing fetus.

PREPARING FOR MOTHERHOOD

The new trend in pregnancy and childbirth is preparation. Here is a partial list of the ways that pregnancy, childbirth, and the new mothering experience can be rendered less stressful:

1. Instructional preparations are made for the husband and wife in regard to all aspects of pregnancy, childbirth, breast-feeding and other components of maternal care. This is done with pamphlets, books, movies, and regular meetings with other couples.[39]

2. Some young couples even acquire a dog to help prepare them for the responsibilities that come with caring for another living creature.[15]

3. Young couples often become involved with newborns and infants of friends to further acquaint themselves with the care of a new child.

4. The young couples develop friendships with other couples who have pregnant wives and "nervous" husbands. This can help in sharing experiences and concerns.

5. The use of "natural," "prepared," or "participating" methods of

childbirth (e.g., Dick-Read and Lamaze methods) are encouraged. The woman is taught to reduce "tension," fear, and pain and is trained in techniques of muscular relaxation, deep chest breathing, and rhythmic breathing. The methods stress the participation of the husband in the training, labor, and delivery. The women can have auxiliary means of anesthesia if they desire, but many use these relaxation techniques exclusively. Hypnosis is also becoming quite popular as an alternative to general anesthesia and spinal anesthesia.

6. Husbands are permitted to participate in labor and delivery.[62]

The literature shows that the results of this kind of preparation are extremely positive. The reports reveal: less pain; less need of medication; shorter labor; fewer forceps deliveries; greater pleasure in the birth experience; feelings of more active control in the delivery; and less anxiety and stress.[40-42]

To make motherhood a continuing positive experience, there must be continual support from the husband, other family members and friends. It is important that help be provided for the new mother/housewife or else all the positive benefits of pregnancy and childbirth will be lost.

Sometimes the wife not only does not get help, she gets "beaten."

BATTERED WIVES

One of the few male advantages is that they are, on the average, physically stronger than females. Unfortunately, some males abuse this advantage by using physical violence against their wives. The passive obedient image of feminity has for decades been ingrained in Western cultures, and partly because of this image married women have been tolerating a lot of abuse from their husbands (or live-in mates). Because of their low self-image, some women may marry or stay with inadequate or unworthy men who then, because of their own inadequacy, resort to beating their wives.[43] Being beaten once, often causes a battered woman to feel more inadequate. In addition, she becomes afraid for the safety of herself and her children. There also may be the fear of loneliness if she leaves her husband.[43] Sometimes women hope things will get better and, therefore, tolerate beatings.[44]

But changes are coming. With the advent of the women's movement and women's consciousness-raising groups, women realize that they can and should fight back, and recently some women have been doing just that. They have been "beating up" their husbands. However, in almost all of the cases investigated the husband beatings were in the form of retaliation.[45]

Whenever there is wife beating there is often associated alcoholism, drug abuse, unemployment, criminal behavior, and financial and sexual problems.[43,46] To reduce the physical and psychological stressors of wife beating, the woman victim has several recourses:

1. Physical fitness is important for women. In this violent society where rape, wife beating, incest, robbery, and murder are becoming commonplace, it is essential that women learn methods of self-defense. Body building, karate, judo, calisthenics, and running are a few of the principal practical methods.

2. Consultation may be helpful. Marriage counseling, psychotherapy, and family therapy are methods to bring the partners together provided that they will both attend the sessions. Often the husbands refuse to attend and the wives may feel frustrated and powerless. Individual psychotherapy can be important for the wives to overcome their fears of confronting their husbands. It would also prove beneficial for battered wives to enroll in an assertiveness training program.

3. Physical separation is important. There is no reason (including "love") that women should allow themselves to continually get beaten. It might be advisable for the woman to simply take her belongings and leave. First separation, and then divorce. If the woman cannot go to close family or friends, there are temporary shelters available. If she is physically and psychologically abused, hospitals have services available to take care of the battered woman.[43,46]

4. Legal action should be taken if the woman was hurt physically, psychologically, or both. The time to "grin and bear it" is long past. No woman should allow herself to be abused just because she is afraid to act. There are female activist organizations and government agencies that will assist the battered wife and help reduce the distress from this violent activity.

Some women find the stress resulting from having young children to be intolerable. As discussed previously, this can lead to alcoholism, drug abuse, chain smoking, compulsive eating, depression and suicide. It can also lead to child beating.

CHILD ABUSE

Marriage is a great change in a woman's life; childbirth is another major change. The new wife/housewife/mother faces an array of changes, each with its own potentially stressful aspects. Taking care of a helpless infant, especially if she cannot understand its problems, can cause overwhelming stress to the new mother. Waking up from a deep sleep to the sound of a screaming infant sets up the "fight or flight" alarm reaction. This acute stress response, if it happens once, is disturbing enough. But when a woman has to be repeatedly startled and has the sole responsibility for managing the problem (i.e., the screaming infant), it is understandable why some women cannot cope.[15]

"Why is he screaming?"; "I just fed him!"; "I rock and rock and rock her until I'm falling asleep, but she still cries!"; "Every minute I'm changing diapers!"; "Why does he spit out everything I feed him?" . . . and so on. These are some of the infant-related stress-inducing problems of the new mother. If the stress reaches the breaking point, the woman reaches disequilibrium and either beats the child, abandons the child, or may even kill the infant. Although there are no firm figures since many cases go unreported, it has been estimated that in the United States there are 2 million cases of child abuse per year with between 500 to 1000 of them resulting in death.[47]

As with wife beating, there are generally associated problems of alcoholism, drug addiction, depression, unemployment, financial, and sexual stressors and the woman's own poor self-image.[47] Life-stress events such as loss of a job or sudden financial loss can precipitate child abuse.[48]

Wife beating, and being a victim of child abuse, can also precipitate child-beating.[47] The woman, left with no easy alternatives, displaces her anger on to the child.

Child beating does not only happen with a mother and a new infant.* It can occur when there is more than one child in the family. Possible causes are: (1) too many mouths to feed; (2) children interfering with the mother's housework; (3) children not attending to their chores; (4) children getting into entanglements with other children; and (5) children upsetting the mother's marital relations.[49]

Aside from being a victim herself, there are other reasons why a woman beats her child. Two reasons are lack of preparation for motherhood and lack of support (related to low salaries and unemployment). As discussed previously, the new mothers should receive instruction in all phases of taking care of an infant. Unfortunately, many cases of child abuse occur with unplanned and unwanted children.[47] But the mother must learn that the child is not to blame.

---

* Husbands can get "riled" and beat their children as well as their wives, but mothers are more responsible for abuse than fathers, probably because of their greater time with the children. Josten, R. Child abuse. *In* Kjervik, D. K. and Martinson, I. M. (eds.), *Women in Stress: A Nursing Perspective* New York: Appleton-Century-Crofts, 1979, pp. 218–236.

It is also essential that she receive help in child care. There is nothing innate about a woman that says only she is qualified to wake up at night, to change diapers, and to feed and rock the child. The husband, even if he is the sole breadwinner, should help his wife in all phases of child care. Studies have shown that many women who abuse their children: rarely belong to social groups (e.g., church or synagogue; PTA); have few friends; and are often isolated from their families. Therefore, it is important that mothers receive support from others in addition to their husbands.[47]

Most women love their children, and when a child is lost, the stress may be unbearable.

LOSS OF A CHILD

In the first year of life, crib death is the major cause of death; after that, the various forms of cancer (including leukemia) are predominant.

With crib death, one minute the child is healthy and the next minute the child is dead.[63] Sudden death such as occurs with crib death and motor-vehicle accidents is especially traumatic for the mother. There is no time for preparation. This is the time when a mother needs all the help she can get. She and her spouse can console each other but they must have help from family, friends, the clergy, psychiatrists, and psychologists. Even so, the grief may be overwhelming. One way that couples who have suddenly lost a young child partially compensate is by having another child.

Cancer in a young child is still generally a death sentence. With the use of chemotherapeutics in various combinations along with radiation and surgery, it is possible to prolong life for years. But in most cases, the child eventually dies. The stress of a mother with a very sick or dying child is in some ways worse than the stress associated with sudden death. At least, in the latter, the end is swift. With cancer, and especially leukemia, there are "ups and downs." There is cause for optimism followed by extreme pessimism. Some days the child appears perfectly healthy, other days she may be almost comatose. There is also the isolation of the child—generally in a hospital away from family and friends.

The young child is almost always most intimate with her mother. When she is sick or dying, her needs are magnified. The biggest stressor for the child is fear, fear of loss of mother, family, friends, home, and belongings. There is also fear of the unknown (the hospital with its strange equipment and people). The mother must help overcome these fears and at the same time still try to keep some semblance of order with herself and the family.

To help alleviate some of the distress associated with a dying child, it is helpful if the parents and child see each other continually. A study done at a major city hospital showed that there was better adjustment and a decreased incidence of problems when parents and child were in constant contact.[50] Even better results are found when the child can be treated at home. In one study, three-fourths of the cases had the parents act as primary care-givers in the terminal stages of the disease.[51] The families had the support of a home-care nurse and the option of returning the child to the hospital, but most chose to keep the child at home.

Grief and loneliness are the major consequences of the death of a child. There are no easy remedies, but as was discussed with the child dying suddenly, support from others is essential and having another child can be renewing. The mother who must take care of a handicapped, retarded, or chronically ill child also needs a great deal of support.[52] Positive coping methods for stress discussed in Part VI would also be of benefit to grieving mothers who must manage handicapped, sick, or dying children.

Whether it is childbirth or the loss of a child, some women have to face the consequences alone. Let us now consider the plight of the single mother.

THE SINGLE MOTHER

A woman can be a single mother as the result of: teen-age pregnancy; being raped; having sexual relations as a consenting adult; getting divorced and maintaining custody of the child; becoming a widow; and adopting a child.

Pregnancy for single girls ages fifteen to seventeen has almost doubled from 1966 to 1975.* The probable reasons for this increase are frequent sexual activity and greater public acceptance of unmarried pregnancy.[15] Although some of the pregnant teen-agers elect abortion, and others give their new babies up for adoption, many of the single adolescent parents keep their children. As discussed in Chapter 6, the stressors of adolescence are many. To have the added burden of being a single mother may be too much to manage. Fortunately, most often the girls' parents give a great deal of support to the teen-age mother. Most of the teen-agers accept motherhood but it is not their first choice. Evidence shows that although teen-agers are aware of birth-control methods, unrealistically many of them practice contraception only after the birth of their children.[15] It is clear that sex education has to be improved and become more widespread if the trend of increasing teen-age mothers is to be reversed.

* In a recently released report from Johns Hopkins University, it was revealed that pregnancies among teen-age females between the ages of fifteen and nineteen have risen steadily from 28 percent in 1971 to 32.5 percent in 1979. O'Brien, P. Study: Teen pregnancies increasing. *Philadelphia Inq.* 3-A, October 17, 1980.

Other females, generally in their twenties and thirties elect to become single parents because they may want the joys of mothering without being tied down to a marriage. As they often choose this voluntarily, generally they are well prepared for motherhood. Some of these women live alone, some live with a man or a woman, others live with their parents, and still others live in singles societies or communes.

Many of these single mothers have full-time jobs. In order for them to cope with parenting and working, it is essential that they have help either from friends, parents, child-care facilities or day workers. They may also have to lower their standards in housework and meal preparation.[6]

Women who are separated, divorced, and widowed and have children are generally less well prepared for the role of single mother than are the never-married mothers. This is related to the trauma involved in their becoming a solo parent. There are many solo parent groups, such as *Parents Without Partners,* who can help the single mother cope with the stressors of motherhood.

Nowadays many women elect to stay single and choose a career over marriage and motherhood.

THE SINGLE WOMAN

It used to be "better dead than unwed," and to be an "old maid" or "spinster" was considered to be a horrible fate. But today being single is not considered to be socially undesirable. Even women who do get married are prolonging their single years. Since 1960, 33 percent more women between the ages of twenty and twenty-four have remained single.[1] Women today are entering many "male" occupations as well as increasing their numbers in women's traditional fields. (See Chapters 13–18) With the sexual revolution, women are engaging in more frequent sexual relations with greater freedom. Birth control is widely practiced and abortion is legal; hence, the fear of pregnancy is decreased. (See Chapters 10–12 for a further discussion of women's sexuality.) Women can now remain single, and have some of the benefits of marriage without the legal ties. When women have good jobs, they are more likely to stay single. Unemployed women and women with less prestigious and lower paying jobs get married more frequently.[53]

With the resurgence of the women's movement has come a greater acceptibility of the single woman and her life-style.[2]* There are also many single women's groups where the stressors of being single are discussed.(See Box 7.3) Women now take instruction in varied fields such as automobile

* An excellent new book on this subject is: Barkas, J. L. *Single in America.*New York: Atheneum-Scribners, 1980.

Box 7.3.   Whatever Happened To The Men?

Liberated women in their thirties and forties are "making it" in the business and professional world, but are finding problems in meeting men.[60] At work, if they go out with "fellow" employees or employers, they find their careers may suffer (à la the Bendix corporation affair). At singles bars, most of the men can be categorized into these types: (1) men who are looking to get married because of their need for a substitute mother; (2) men who are married who are looking for an affair; (3) single men who are looking for fast results (into bed tonight and out by morning); (4) good-looking, intelligent men who happen to be gay; (5) eligible men who happen to be impotent; (6) good-looking men who are bores; (7) intelligent men who are unattractive; (8) men who appear to have it all, but shy away from commitments; and (9) men who make commitments but are looking for younger women.

There are several reasons for the lack of eligible men:

1. Some men are terrified by today's liberated women and don't know how to act in their presence. They also prefer a less intelligent woman who will make them seem important.

2. In 1979, there were 17,334,000 women in the U. S. between the ages of twenty-five and thirty-five. In the same age bracket, there were only 16,719,000 men. Hence, the statistics work against these women.

3. Recent estimates list the male population as being 13 percent homosexual. In Philadelphia alone, there are about 200,000 gays.

4. The marriage gradient is against these women. Men in their forties and fifties tend to marry women in their twenties and early thirties. Women who look to marry older men find fewer men available, and even those often have physical incapacities.

5. Intelligent, attractive men often stay away from singles bars. Women can't meet these men unless friends arrange "blind" dates.

The solution to this problem is not easy. Some women are going out and marrying men who are less accomplished and less interesting than themselves. Other women are having children by men who are noncommittal, but are otherwise "top-notch." Still others are giving up on men altogether and going out with other women. One possible saving grace for the single woman who wants to get married, is the emergence of androgynous men who can be warm, loving, understanding, and committed to marriage (discussed shortly).

From the foregoing, it would appear that the bulk of women's stress has to do with men. Be that as it may, one is forced to the conclusion that women will make it anyway.

mechanics, home mortgages, the stock market, assertiveness training, home repairs, self-defense, and stress management. They are learning to cope with the problems that may occur with being a single woman. An important aspect of these courses is to instruct women on how to become less dependent on men for technical and emotional help. One way for women to be less dependent upon men is for them to adopt some of the male's traits. One way for men to become more understanding of women's problems is for them to adopt female traits. There is a new movement afloat in trying to get men and women to change in this way. It is called psychological androgyny.

PSYCHOLOGICAL ANDROGYNY

Men are supposed to be independent, aggressive, unemotional, adventurous, and self-confident. But they are also judged to be cruel, vicious, and implacable. In contrast, women are described as being emotional, excitable in minor crises, conceited, talkative, dependent, easily influenced, passive, less aggressive and assertive, and less adventurous than men. But they are also judged to be more caring and kind.[6,54] Of course, these descriptions are male-oriented and outmoded, but many people still consider them to be partly or completely accurate descriptions.

The concept of psychological androgyny is that by combining the best "masculine" and "feminine" qualities we can have individuals who are kind, tender, compassionate, and caring. At the same time they can be assertive, competitive, adventurous, and self-confident.[55]

Androgynous individuals should be concerned with both "the corporation" as well as the feelings of the workers. They should enhance the prestige of the university as well as understand the students' problems. Such individuals will be able to teach children to be loving and understanding as well as good competitors. They should be equally capable of taking part in business board meetings and washing dishes at home.

It seems that women are more likely to acquire the better "male" traits while men find it against their "macho" image to become nurturant and caring.[56-58] But times are changing and with more androgynous people developing, the stress for both single and married women will decrease.[59] The stress should also decrease for men who adopt this behavior.

As women get into their fifties, other problems crop up. These are covered in the next chapter.

REFERENCES

1. Williams, J. H. *Psychology of Women: Behavior in a Biosocial Context.* New York: W. W. Norton., 1977.
2. Moran, R. The singles in the seventies. *In* DeLora, J. S. and DeLora, J. R. (eds.), *In-*

timate Life Styles: Marriage and its Alternatives. Pacific Palisades, Calif.: Goodyear, 1972.

3. Lopata, H. Z. *Occupation: Housewife.* New York: Oxford University Press, 1971.
4. Friday, N. *My Mother/My Self: The Daughter's Search for Identity.* New York: Dell Publishing, 1978.
5. Bernard, J. The paradox of the happy marriage. *In* Gornick, V. and Moran, B. K. (eds.), *Women in Sexist Society: Studies in Power and Powerlessness.* New York: Mentor Books, 1971, pp. 145-162.
6. Kinzer, N. S. *Stress and the American Woman.* New York: Ballantine Books, 1980.
7. Hunt, M. *Sexual Behavior in the Seventies.* Chicago: Playboy Press, 1974.
8. Rosof, F. Family is still first for many ethnic women. *Philadelphia Inq.* 1-G, 2-G, June 22, 1980.
9. Shearer, L. Parade's special intelligence report: First loyalty. *Philadelphia Sun. Bull. Parade* 7, June 15, 1980.
10. O'Neill, G. and O'Neill, N. *Open Marriage.* New York: Avon, 1972.
11. United Press International. Court: Tax due for undoing "I Dos." *Philadelphia Daily News* 4, August 7, 1980.
12. Coffin, P. The young unmarrieds. *In* DeLora, J. S. and DeLora, J. R. (eds.), *Intimate Life Styles: Marriage and its Alternatives.* Pacific Palisades, Calif.: Goodyear, 1972.
13. Constantine, L. L. and Constantine, J. M. Group and multilateral marriage: Definitional notes, glossary, and annotated bibliography. *Family Process.* **10:**157-176, 1971.
14. Veysey, L. Communal sex and communal survival. *Psychol. Today* **8**(8):73-78, 1974.
15. Rising, S. S. Childbearing: Its dilemmas. *In* Kjervik, D. K. and Martinson, I. M. (eds.), *Women in Stress: A Nursing Perspective.* New York: Appleton-Century-Crofts, 1979, pp. 116-132.
16. Deutsch, H. *The Psychology of Women: A Psychoanalytic Interpretation.* Vols. 1 and 2. New York: Grune & Stratton, 1944, 1945.
17. Erikson, E. H. The inner and the outer space: Reflections on womanhood. *Daedalus* **93:**582-606, 1964.
18. Kestenberg, J. S. Regression and reintegration in pregnancy. *In* Blum, H. P. (ed.), *Female Psychology: Contemporary Psychoanalytic Views.* New York: International Universities Press, 1977, pp. 213-250.
19. U. P. I. Pontiff says motherhood is woman's true ministry. *Philadelphia Eve. Bull.* NB 3, March 13, 1980.
20. Lopatin, D. E., Kornman, K. S., and Loesche, W. J. Modulation of immunoreactivity to periodontal disease—associated microorganisms during pregnancy. *Infect. Immun.* **28:**713-718,1980.
21. Jessner, L., Weigert, E., and Foy, J. L. The development of parental attitudes during pregnancy. *In* Anthony, E. J. and Benedek, T. (eds.), *Parenthood.* Boston: Little, Brown, 1970, pp. 209-244.
22. Crandon, A. J. Maternal anxiety and obstetric complications. *J. Psychosom. Res.* **23:**109-111, 1979.
23. Chertok, L. *Motherhood and Personality.* London: Tavistock, 1969.
24. Corea, G. *The Hidden Malpractice.* New York: William Morrow, 1977.
25. Gintzler, A. R. Endorphin—mediated increases in pain threshold during pregnancy. *Science* **210:**193-195, 1980.
26. Editorial. Flair: The doctor is in: "Euphoria"during childbirth. *Philadelphia Daily News* 23, September 4, 1979.
27. Editorial. Uncle Sam believes. Part II: Lifestyle improvement can help us all lead longer, happier lives, says this unusual government report. *Prevention* **32** (6):122-130, June 1980.
28. Newton, R. W., Webster, P. A. C., Binu, P. S., Maskrey, N., and Phillips, A. B.

Psychosocial stress in pregnancy and its relationship to the onset of premature labour. *Br. Med. J.* **2**:411-413, 1979.

29. Burns, J. K. Relation between blood levels of cortisol and duration of human labour. *J. Physiol.* **254**:12p, 1976.

30. Lederman, R. P., Lederman, E., Work, B. A., Jr. and McCann, D. S. The relationship of maternal anxiety, plasma catecholamines and plasma cortisol to progress in labor. *Am. J. Obst. Gynecol.* **132**:495-500, 1978.

31. James, W. H. The effect of maternal psychological stress on the foetus. *Brit. J. Psych.* **115**:811-825, 1969.

32. Weathersbee, P. S. and Lodge, J. R. Alcohol, caffeine and nicotine as factors in pregnancy. *Postgrad. Med.* **66**(3):165-167, 170-171, 1979.

33. McCary, J. *Human Sexuality*. New York: D. Van Nostrand, 1973.

34. Murai, N. and Sato, T. Psychological study on pregnancy—relationship of maternal emotional characteristics to body weight gain of newborn infants. *J. Japan. Psychosom. Soc.* **11**:25-29, 1971.

35. Crandon, A. J. Maternal anxiety and neonatal wellbeing. *J. Psychosom. Res.* **23**:113-115, 1979.

36. Ward, I. L. and Weisz, J. Maternal stress alters plasma testosterone in fetal males. *Science* **207**:328-329, 1980.

37. Kolata, G. B. NIH panel urges fewer cesarean births: The "once a cesarean, always a cesarean" dictum is not valid. *Science* **210**:176-177, 1980.

38. Saucier, J. F. Correlates of the long postpartum taboo: A cross-cultural study. *Curr. Anthropology* **13**:238-249, 1972.

39. Standley, K., Soule, B., and Copans, S. A. Dimensions of prenatal anxiety and their influences on pregnancy outcome. *Am. J. Obstet. Gynecol.* **135**(1):22-26, Sept. 1979.

40. Henneborn, W. J. and Cogan, R. The effect of husband participation on reported pain and probability of medication during labor and birth. *J. Psychosom. Res.* **19**:215-222, 1975.

41. Norr, K. L., Block, C. R., Charles, A., Meyering, S., and Meyers, E. Explaining pain and enjoyment in childbirth. *J. Health Soc. Behav.* **18**:260-275, 1977.

42. Doering, S. G., Entwisle, D. R., and Quinlan, D. Modeling the quality of women's birth experience. *J. Health Soc. Behav.* **21**:12-21, 1980.

43. Valenti, C. Working with the physically abused woman. *In* Kjervik, D. K. and Martinson, I. M. (eds.), *Women in Stress: A Nursing Perspective*. New York: Appleton-Century-Crofts, 1979, pp. 187-196.

44. Gaylord, J. J. Wife battering: A preliminary survey of 100 cases. *Brit. Med. J.* **1**:194-197, January 25, 1975.

45. Straus, M. Victims and aggressors in marital violence. *Amer. Behav. Sci.* **23**:681-704, 1980.

46. Roy, M. (ed.), *Battered Women: A Psychosociological Study of Domestic Violence*. New York: Van Nostrand Reinhold, 1978.

47. Josten, L. Child abuse. *In* Kjervik, D. K. and Martinson, I. M. (eds.), *Women in Stress: A Nursing Perspective*. New York: Appleton-Century-Crofts, 1979, pp. 218-236.

48. Blair, J. and Duncan, D. F. Life crisis as a precursor to child abuse. *Publ. Health Rep.* **19**(2):110-115, 1976.

49. Terr, L. A family study of child abuse. *Am. J. Psychiatry* **127**:665-671, 1970.

50. Goldfogel, L. Working with the parent of a dying child. *Amer. J. Nursing* **70**:1675-1679, 1970.

51. Martinson, I. M. Loss of a child: Two case studies. *In* Kjervik, D. K. And Martinson, I.

M. (eds.), *Women in Stress: A Nursing Perspective*. New York: Appleton-Century-Crofts, 1979, pp. 330–336.

52. Burdin, R. L. Measuring the effects of stress on the mothers of handicapped infants: Must depression always follow? *Child Care Health Dev.* 6(2):111–125, 1980.

53. Bernard, J. *Women and the Public Interest: An Essay on Policy and Protest*. New York: Aldine-Atherton, 1971.

54. Menikheim, M. L. Communication patterns of women and nurses. *In* Kjervik, D. K. and Martinson, I. M. (eds.), *Women in Stress: A Nursing Perspective*. New York: Appleton-Century-Crofts, 1979, pp. 133–143.

55. Bem, S. L. Sex-role adaptability: One consequence of psychological androgyny. *J. Pers. Soc. Psychol.* 31:634–643, 1975.

56. Sifford, D. In search of completeness: Taking a cue from women. *Philadelphia Inq.* 3-B, June 16, 1980.

57. Sifford, D. But where are the "new men"? *Philadelphia Inq.* 1-K, 7-K, July 20, 1980.

58. Sifford, D. "Amalgamation" could benefit men and women alike. *Philadelphia Inq.* 4-D, July 22, 1980.

59. Kaplan, A. *Psychological Androgyny: Further Considerations*. New York: Hum. Sciences Press, 1979.

60. Carey, A. The sad plight of single women. *Philadelphia Inq. Today* Mag. 14–16, 22–24, November 30, 1980.

61. Sydney, S. B. Treating pregnancy related gingival problems: A case report. *Dent. Surv.* 56(12):46–48, 1980.

62. Beck, N.C. and Siegel, L. J. Preparation for childbirth and contemporary research on pain, anxiety, and stress reduction: Review and critique. *Psychosom. Med.* 42:429–447, 1980.

63. Behavior, More SIDS clues: Vitamins and heat. *Science News* 117(24):379, January 14, 1980.

8
The Problems of the Fifties

INTRODUCTION

In the late forties or early fifties, another potential crisis occurs in the life of women; they reach menopause. During this time period, many women undergo a major surgical procedure (i.e., hysterectomy) and various minor surgical procedures (such as tooth extractions). It is also during these years that children grow up and depart, leaving the mother and father alone (the "empty nest" syndrome). Quite often the husband is sick (may be a heart attack, stroke, or cancer) and the wife must take care of him. During this time period, many women lose their husbands and become widows. All of these events are stress-inducing and are now considered.

MENOPAUSE

For many decades, menopause had been considered one of the most stressful periods in a woman's life. For once ovulation and menstruation ceased, a woman could no longer become pregnant and fulfill her biological role in life.[1] So society considered that it would be "normal" for women to become sick and despondent at this time of their lives. The names given to this period of desperation were "menopausal syndrome" and "climacteric syndrome." Symptoms and signs of this syndrome were described as: anxiety; depression; feelings of inferiority and hopelessness; insomnia; forgetfulness; and most commonly hot flashes, chills, sweats, and palpitations.[2-5] Other changes discussed were increased and decreased sexual desires, weight gain, and osteoporosis (porous bone that is more prone to fracture).[6,7] Increased sexual desires were considered to be more stressful since it was thought that post-menopausal women should become oblivious of sex.[6]

Most of the diagnoses were made as the result of women consulting their physicians for special problems occurring at the time of menopause. For women reaching menopause who didn't seek medical advice, no information about symptoms was available. Also, many women were conditioned to expect problems during menopause, so it was possible that much of the distress was psychosomatic. Another factor was that other changes occur at the time of menopause which could be ascribed to the menopausal syndrome. These changes are related to: children moving out ("empty nest" syndrome); taking care of ill husbands; becoming a widow; retirement from a job; and noticeable age changes.[8] Yet it was realized that not all women felt anxious and depressed at menopause. Some actually felt relief and had renewed vigor.[9]

The current concept of the menopausal syndrome is quite different. Most investigators believe that only a small percentage of women develop the varied manifestations just described. The majority of women have positive attitudes toward menopause because of: (1) elimination of the fear of pregnancy; (2) loss of the annoyance of menstruation; (3) improved sexual relations; (4) increases in energy; and (5) feelings of well-being.[8]

Nevertheless, there are definite changes that occur during menopause, and these changes can cause physiological and psychological effects that necessitate medical consultations for about 25 percent of women.[10] The primary changes seen are hot flashes, and episodes of perspiration (e.g., night sweats). Other changes reported are: fatigue and difficulties in sleeping; palpitations and dizziness; anxiety; irritability; nervousness and depression; headaches and body aches; atrophic changes in the vagina; and osteoporosis.[6,10-12] Some of these changes are related to the decreased secretion of estrogen and progesterone by the ovaries.[10] Blood levels of the other female hormones, follicle stimulating hormone (FSH), and luteinizing hormone (LH), increase and reach a maximum two to three years after menopause. The increase of these hormones may be related to the incidence of hot flashes and sweating.[10,13]

The estrogen levels usually decrease gradually, and the menstrual periods generally become erratic in both flow and regularity. These changing patterns can begin months or even years before menses actually ceases. The hormonal changes may be responsible for the mood changes, anxiety, and depression that occur in some women.[6,7,10]

Studies have shown that even among women who don't consult physicians, there is a relatively high incidence of hot flashes and sweating episodes. About 40 to 75 percent of women experience hot flashes and 25 to 40 percent of women have sweating episodes during the menopausal period.[5,6] The hot flashes usually occur in the face and neck area but can be widespread. They generally last for between 15 seconds and 5 minutes. They are characterized by a deep red color and a feeling of heat which is followed by occasional chills or tingling sensations in the fingers and toes. Hot flashes may be accompanied by a blush or red splotches.[6,7] Women have reported that warm outside temperatures, and states of excitement and stress predispose to the onset of hot flashes.[6,14] For many years estrogen has been used to control these episodes, but there are negative side effects from estrogen therapy. Exogenous estrogen increases the risk of cancers of the uterus and breast.[7,15,16]

Although there are no controlled studies, case reports have shown that vitamin E (800 I.U. per day for about a week) greatly reduces the incidence of hot flashes.[7] Fatigue commonly occurs in about 50 percent of women in the perimenopausal (around the time of the usual cessation of menopause) period, but it has not been definitely correlated with the onset of menopause. Insomnia is also quite prevalent in menopausal women, and it may be related to the night sweats.[6] Palpitations and episodes of dizziness are also fairly common. They have been reported as accompanying the hot flashes.[5,6]

Anxiety, irritability, nervousness, and depression occur in anywhere from 10 to 90 percent of menopausal women.[5,6,11] However, these psychological manifestations are not clearly related to menopause, although there are some interesting theoretical conjectures. For example, in one study, the low levels of estrogen during menopause were correlated with low levels of the amino acid tryptophan in the blood of depressed menopausal women.[17] Tryptophan has been shown to be effective against anxiety and depression. In the body it converts to the hormone serotonin which helps induce relaxation and sleep.[7,18]

In Chapter 6, it was stated that low levels of estrogen are correlated with high levels of MAO and depressive episodes at premenstruation. Since there is evidence that the depression of menopause is more prevalent in women who have had previous bouts of depression, there may be some chemical relationship to menopausal depression. Nevertheless, it is believed that mood changes, anxiety, neuroses, and depression are primarily psychologically induced. Generally, traditional women who consider the female's role to be childbearer, are the ones who suffer most of these manifestations.[6] Attesting to this, it has been observed that working women have fewer menopausal problems including depression than do nonworking women.[19,20,55]

Somewhat less than 50 percent of perimenopausal women report symptoms such as headache, aches in bones, joints and muscles, and tingling of extremities. No correlations have been found between these symptoms and menopause.[6]

Atrophic changes occur in the vagina and surrounding tissue in about 50 percent of women in the perimenopausal period.[10] Undoubtedly, these changes are related to reduction in estrogen since they have been ameliorated by exogenous estrogen.[21] However, as mentioned previously, there are dangers associated with estrogen replacement therapy. Problems related to the atrophic changes are vaginal pain, bleeding, itching, and irritation. To alleviate these causes of distress, estrogen-containing vaginal creams and lubricants have proven beneficial. One method that has been advocated is regular sexual intercourse. The rationale is that regular intercourse increases lubrication and maintains the vagina's ability to expand.[22]

Osteoporosis is quite prevalent in postmenopausal women. There is a definite link between estrogen deficiency and calcium deficiency, and the development of postmenopausal osteoporosis. Calcium and phosphorus are lost from bones and this makes them weaker and more prone to fracture.[23] There is less calcium absorbed in the intestines and more calcium excreted in the urine.[24]

Stress may also be a factor in the development of postmenopausal osteoporosis. Both thyroxine and cortisone are released during the stress response (see Chapter 2) and both have been shown to cause bone resorption (eating away of bone). Studies have shown that both thyroxine- and cortisone-treated postmenopausal women have increased bone resorption.[23] Hence, it is conceivable that stress (which causes the release of those hormones) could accelerate the osteoporosis of menopause. Estrogen has been given for osteoporosis and has been effective in many cases.[22] However, vitamin D and calcium have also proven effective and are generally considered to be safer.[6,23,24]

Heart disease is more frequent for women after menopause. As discussed in Chapter 3, estrogen seems to afford a natural protection for women against coronary heart disease. With menopause, the low levels of estrogen are apparently insufficient to continue that protection. Blood concentrations of cholesterol increase markedly at menopause and there are increases in diastolic blood pressure (the lower and probably more important figure in the blood pressure ratio).[25] The increased cholesterol is principally of the injurious LDL type (see Chapter 3).[7] Another fat group implicated in heart disease is the triglycerides, and this also increases in the blood of postmenopausal women.[26] The results of a major study in heart disease in Framingham, Massachusetts showed that none of the 2873 women involved had a heart attack before menopause. After menopause (ages 45–54), heart disease became a common occurrence.[27] As discussed in the prevention of heart diseases (see Chapter 3), there are many methods to help prevent heart attacks (such as ingestion of lecithin, vitamin C, and magnesium, along with exercise and reduction in fat intake).[7]

Menopause does not have to be a time of distress. A positive attitude along with good nutrition, an active life-style and regular exercise can make this a time of joy rather than a time of despair. Freedom from pregnancy and menstruation along with less ties at home can make menopause a rewarding time rather than an ending of womanhood.[28] Sometimes menopause is surgically induced; this is considered next.

HYSTERECTOMY

There are several potentially stressful procedures that are related to operations on women's reproductive organs. The least traumatic is *dilatation and curettage* (D&C). It is performed to remove residual infections, degenerative tissue, and benign tumors. It is also used for abortions.[8,29]

A D&C does not affect menstruation, the ability to have children, or the onset of menopause. A *tubal ligation* (tying the tubes) is a voluntary operation that women undergo for the purpose of terminating childbirth capacity. It prevents the union of sperm and egg, and causes only minor anatomical changes and negligible effects on menstruation and menopause. As tubal ligation is generally an elective procedure with minimal body change, it rarely causes any psychological or physical problems. Variations on tubal ligation are *laparoscopic sterilization* (minilaparotomy) and *reversible sterilization*. The former is a more recent procedure and has had good results; the latter allows the possibility of a "change of heart." These procedures also cause relatively minor psychological and physical problems.[30,31]

A *total hysterectomy* is a major surgical procedure that involves the removal of the uterus (the womb; see Figure 8.1). If only the body of the uterus is removed, it is called a *partial* or *subtotal hysterectomy*. A total hysterectomy is the more common procedure. Removal of the ovaries is called *oophorectomy*. If both ovaries are removed it is called *bilateral oophorectomy*. Removal of the ovaries and uterus is known as a *complete hysterectomy,* or a *panhysterectomy*.

Hysterectomy results in cessation of menstruation and the ability to have children. Ovulation still continues and menopause occurs at about the same time or a few years earlier than expected.[29,32] If a woman had bleeding problems during menstruation (dysfunctional bleeding), that will stop after

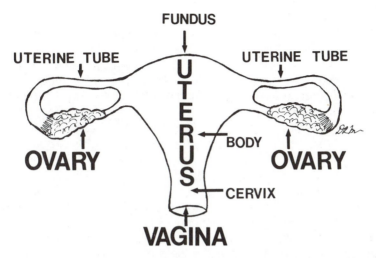

Fig. 8.1. Diagrammatic representation of the female reproductive system. The ovaries form the ova (eggs) and elaborate estrogen and progesterone. A mature egg is released in the middle of the menstrual cycle and passes into the uterine tube (oviduct-ovary part, fallopian tube-uterine part). If sperm are present, fertilization can take place in the fallopian tube. The fertilized egg is propelled into the uterus and is implanted in the inner wall (the endometrium). If sperm are not present or fertilization does not occur, the egg is released along with the break-down products of the endometrium. This event is known as menstruation. It ceases after menopause. Hysterectomy (removal of the uterus) results in cessation of menstruation and the ability to have children. However, ovulation still occurs and menopause usually comes around the expected time. Oophorectomy (removal of the ovaries) along with hysterectomy causes: cessation of menstruation; an inability to have children; and the onset of menopause. With tubal ligation, all genitally-related functions occur normally except the released egg cannot be fertilized.

a hysterectomy. But as ovulation continues and estrogen and progesterone are released, premenstrual tensional syndrome symptoms can still occur (see Chapter 6).

As a result of the operation, there is a transient hormonal imbalance. This can result in temporary appearance of hot flashes, which can be treated successfully with exogenous estrogen.[29]

When bilateral oophorectomy is done alone or along with hysterectomy (i.e., complete hysterectomy), then this induces cessation of ovulation, menstruation, and the ability to have children, along with a sudden onset of menopause. Menopause occurs because the major structures that release female hormones (estrogen, progesterone) are the ovaries. Once they are removed, ova (eggs) are no longer produced and the hormones that coordinate the monthly cycle are of insufficient amount to have any effect. The complete hysterectomy is by far the most traumatic and stressful of the female reproductive system operations. (See Box 8.1)

Of the various types of hysterectomies, the most frequent is the total hysterectomy. This operation is one of the most commonly performed surgical procedures in the United States. In 1975, there were about 725,000 hysterectomies done, and it is estimated that almost one-half of all American women past the age of forty will be advised to have a hysterectomy.[29] There are many reasons that physicians give for suggesting a hysterectomy, but the most usual one is because of the presence of benign tumors of the uterus (known as fibroids). It has been estimated that over 40 percent of all women past the age of forty have fibroids.[33] Often they cause no symptoms and require no treatment. Even with symptoms, if treatment is delayed, the lesions tend to decrease in size after menopause. Sometimes if the symptoms persist, the tumors can be removed intact without the necessity of a hysterectomy. One of the major reasons given for removal of the uterus is to prevent cancerous changes in fibroids. However, only between 0.01 and 0.05 percent of all fibroids removed are cancerous.[29] Hence, fear of cancer should not be a sufficient reason to perform a hysterectomy.

Box 8.1. Coping with Complete Hysterectomy.

Phyllis* was thirteen years old when she had her first menstrual period. For many years following that, every time she had her period, Phyllis developed cramps, nausea, headaches, backaches, and bloating. Her periods were erratic; sometimes she skipped periods for months, other times the flow was extensive. Partly as a result, Phyllis had depressive episodes whenever her period was imminent. When she got married, Phyllis tried to have children but to no avail. She later found out that her uterus was tipped to the left side. Several months ago, Phyllis had a complete medical examination. Her obstetrician discovered ovarian cysts and uterine fibroids. It was decided that a complete hysterectomy would be done. This decision was based on the severe menstrual problems, and the lately increased hemorrhage, and the presence of cysts and fibroids.

For the first three weeks after the operation, Phyllis was extremely depressed. With the use of estrogen on a temporary basis and regular psychotherapy sessions, Phyllis was able to overcome her depression. She and her husband have now adopted two children, and the cramps, headaches, and bleeding are a thing of the past.

* Name changed for anonymity.

Uterine bleeding and adenomyosis (an enlargement of the uterus related to lining changes) can often be treated successfully by curettage without the necessity of hysterectomy.

An essential indication for hysterectomy is the presence of cancer of the uterus and adjacent organs. About 20 percent of all hysterectomies are done to remove cancerous tissue. The presence of precancerous lesions of the uterus is also given as an indication for hysterectomy.[29]

Hysterectomy is being performed for sterilization, cancer phobia, hypochondriasis, ectopic pregnancy, and other conditions. Research reports indicate that about 35 percent of all hysterectomies are unnecessary.[29] As discussed before, in many cases either curettage, tubal ligation, psychotherapy, or no treatment can be just as effective.

Psychological responses to hysterectomy can be overwhelming.[34] This is especially true if the surgery is either for cancer, or is done without the woman's full understanding of the implications. Some women are "browbeaten" into having the work done by being told that it is "all rotten inside" and must be "cleaned out," or it is useless to have your tubes tied as "your womb would only go bad like a dead tooth without a nerve and you would have to have it out later."[35] There is some evidence that women of low socioeconomic background are "talked into" a hysterectomy when less severe procedures would do. Some physicians may suggest hysterectomy over tubal ligation and a D&C because of the better financial remuneration for hysterectomy.[29] To help prevent these occurrences, women should learn more about their bodies and the different procedures, and if they have any doubt, they should insist on a second opinion.[56]

On the other hand, there are some women who have hysterectomies as a protest against male domination. With their wombs removed, they no longer feel burdened by childbirth and menstruation. Undoubtedly, sexist exploitation by some male physicians must stop, but not to the detriment of a woman's own body.

The most common psychological response to hysterectomy is depression, with about a 30 percent occurrence.[29,36] According to the results of one study, there are 2.5 times more referrals to psychiatrists for treatment after hysterectomy than after any other surgical procedure.[37] Women with a previous history of depression or prior emotional breakdown are more prone to be depressed after hysterectomy. Other factors that tend to promote unfavorable psychological responses for posthysterectomy women are: (1) high anxiety and neurotic levels prior to the surgery; (2) poor relationship with their mothers; (3) fear about future sexual activities; and (4) poor preparation for the surgery.[29]

Some women must have hysterectomies (e.g., the presence of uterine cancer). For them, it is essential to eliminate some erroneous ideas about the procedure and its after-effects. First, there is no lowering of sexual desire and ability to have sexual relations. For many women "sex" is better since there is no fear of pregnancy and no need to worry about "periods." If the ovaries are removed, there are no problems with premenstrual tension.[38]

There is about a 20 to 25 percent incidence of posthysterectomy urinary tract infections, but this is temporary and can be effectively treated with drugs.[35] Headache is another frequent temporary symptom that can be alleviated with drugs.[36] Hypnosis may be effective to control these headaches. Weight gain has also been reported as a frequent occurrence after hysterectomy.[39] This can be controlled with diet and exercise. Here, too, hypnosis may be effective. Many women also report fatigue and weakness.[40] These symptoms are also short-lived and may be reduced by rest and meditation. We've already discussed the transient incidence of hot flashes that often occur in about 50 percent of women.[37]

Women who must have their ovaries removed along with the uterus (i.e., complete hysterectomy) must have greater preparation because of the sudden appearance of menopause. This is especially true if it occurs when the woman is relatively young and still has the desire to have children. However, it should be emphasized that the woman's health is more important than having children. Furthermore, she should be alerted that adoption is a feasible alternative and sexual relations will not be impaired. The woman also has new-found freedom to engage in a great many work- and non-work-related activities.

Although there is a physical distance between the mouth and uterus, there are similar considerations with respect to disease and removal of body parts. Let us now consider tooth extractions.

TOOTH EXTRACTIONS

As discussed previously (see Chapter 5), there is great (Freudian) significance attached to the mouth. It is the first erotic zone, and people who always must have something in their mouths may be "arrested" at the oral stage of development. The teeth symbolize potency and strength. The cavelike shape of the mouth is symbolic of the vagina.[41] Some women patients subconsciously equate dental treatment with rape since it is an invasion of an important pleasure zone.[42] Teeth are symbolic of youth and beauty. Consider the Miss America smile. When teeth are lost or extracted that is taken as a sign of aging.

Hysterectomy is one of the most common major operations; tooth extraction is the most common minor operation. Just as there are many needless hysterectomies, so, too, are there many needless extractions. Although teeth are not as critical as the uterus or ovaries, they do have important physiological and psychological implications for women. Teeth are essential for digestion, speech, esthetics, biting, and kissing. When women reach menopause, and are concerned with maintaining themselves as attractive and active females, it can be disarming if they are told that they must lose their teeth. The authors have spoken to many menopausal women as part of their continuing studies on stress, as well as in private practice. One of the greatest fears the patients report is the fear of tooth loss or extraction. Some of the worst nightmares are related to having teeth fall out.

There are several reasons for the great fear of tooth loss:

1. Teeth are the hardest and most durable structures in the body. When they are lost or must be extracted, one loses an important part of oneself.
2. Women are now aware that dentures are never as functional as one's own teeth. Teeth are essential to proper digestion and during the menopausal time, women may begin to develop digestive problems.
3. Teeth are symbolic of beauty. They maintain the contours of the face. When they are lost, the face sags and becomes aged in appearance. Bridges and dentures can only partly compensate for this appearance.
4. Without natural teeth, there is interference with proper speech.
5. Women's weapons have been considered to be their teeth and nails. Biting is a problem without natural teeth.
6. Teeth are essential for kissing and other aspects of love-making.
7. Finally, losing teeth is symbolic of aging; to stay young, it is essential to keep teeth for a lifetime.

Although root-canal therapy and periodontal treatments are more expensive than extractions, it is more expensive to extract teeth and replace them with bridges.[43] Teeth have great importance, well beyond the function of chewing, and most often they can be saved. Before women allow their teeth to be extracted, they should seek a second opinion. Over the last ten years, in the office of the author (DM) about 75 percent of the patients referred for root-canal therapy have been women.

Other dental conditions that frequently occur during the menopausal period are myofascial pain-dysfunction syndrome and atypical facial neuralgia (discussed in Chapter 3). In order to help alleviate those conditions and prevent extractions, it is important for women to see their dentists regularly, to question them about intended extractions, and practice good oral hygiene. That way, a woman can smile right through the menopause.

It may be difficult to smile when the children leave home. Let us now consider the "empty nest" syndrome.

THE "EMPTY NEST" SYNDROME

For years, mothers struggle to see that their children grow up "right." Parents scrimp and save for the children's education and careers, and then one day they awake to find the "nest" is empty. The children grow up, get married themselves, or leave for a job and then mom and dad again are just two. Suddenly, they no longer need the big house. When the rooms are cleaned and clothes get picked up, the mess doesn't return within minutes. Breakfast is no longer a "rush-rush" procedure and husband and wife can sit quietly and sip their coffee. But the change for the woman at home can be just as stressful as is retirement for the working man. Just as depression can be brought on by menopause and hysterectomy with their potential crises, so too can the "loss of the brood" bring on depressive episodes.[8] The "empty nest" syndrome is especially traumatic to the traditional woman who had no other career except that of housewife and mother. In Chapter 2, social stressors were considered. Studies have shown that a daughter or son leaving home is one of the major social stressors.[44] The stress would be more severe when all the children left home.

To reduce the impact of the "empty nest" syndrome, women must realize that it is a potentially constructive time.[54] There is more freedom for vacations and hobbies, an opportunity to begin a new career, and privacy for affection. Many women find that they can do the things they always planned but never had the required time for. Some become writers, a few become artists, and many go back to work or college and really enjoy their new-found interests. Even though the children leave, there is still plenty of opportunities to see them and to help them.

Unfortunately, most women feel that once the children leave home, they neglect their mothers and are undutiful and unloving. However, the children have lives of their own and generally feel that their parents are overly demanding of them (see Box 8.2).

With many women now having full-time jobs, another severe social stressor occurs when forced retirement takes place. That generally occurs at age sixty-five or seventy and is discussed in the next chapter. But in the middle years, many women are confronted with a very serious life-stress event: a sick husband.

Box 8.2. Neglected Mothers.

In a recent study of parents and their grown-up children's attitudes in the New York City area, the following was found: Jewish mothers felt themselves to be the most neglected; Catholic mothers were next; and the women who felt least neglected were WASP women.[45] According to the survey, the children who had the greatest amount of guilt for not seeing their mothers often enough, were the sons of Jewish mothers. Even so, the Jewish mothers were telephoned the most frequently. Maybe their "pressures" helped in getting a response. One positive result of the survey was that only a very small minority of the people were entirely out of touch with each other. Thus, as long as the phone and fast transportation is available, the "flock" can still keep in communication, even if all involved are not completely satisfied.

THE SICK HUSBAND

When a man has a serious illness, he has a great amount of stress. He is out of work and unable to provide for his family. He has the fear of dying and the worry of physical and psychological impairment. These anxieties and fears are generally transferred to his wife. The woman must be supportive and protective of her husband. She has to try and encourage him and help him but not allow him to be overdependent. As a result, the woman often neglects or denies her own needs and can become overwrought and suffer severe anxiety and depression.

In a recent study on psychosocial adaptation of wives following their husband's heart attacks, it was found that 25 percent of the women suffered anxiety and depression.[46] Some women reported that they did not want to disturb their husbands for fear that a "wrong word" might kill them. As a result, there was decreased communication and increased marital estrangements. The wives, in turn, suffered anxiety and depression. In another study of wives of post-heart-attack men, one-third of the women suffered anxiety and depression.[47] Many of them reported that if they showed concern, they were accused of being overprotective. On the other hand, if they became less involved, they were chastised for being noncaring. These and other studies revealed that if good family relations existed before the serious illness, then adjustment of husbands and wives was good afterward. Wives who were very dependent upon their husbands had the greatest problems in adjusting to their new situations. They couldn't get support from their seriously ill spouses, and lacking this help, they tended to collapse emotionally. The problem was compounded because physicians and hospital staffs were only concerned with the sick husbands, and the wives were afraid to draw attention away from their spouses.[46-48]

There are several ways to counteract the stress of wives who have seriously ill husbands. These include: hospital-based educational groups for spouses; group-therapy sessions for spouses; couples therapy groups for depressed spouses and their husbands; individual psychotherapy for the wives; and family therapy.[46,49,50] If this kind of support is given to the wives of ailing men, then when the husbands recover, they will have healthy wives with whom to share years of mutual love and support. If the husband does not recover, the wife then must face life without him as a widow.

WIDOWHOOD

It is a startling statistic, but about two-thirds of all married women will eventually become widows.[51] According to the Holmes-Rahe Social Readjustment Scale, which rates the stress impact of life-stress events, the most severe life-stress event is the loss of a spouse.[44] Even though other family members may die first (see *Loss of a Child* in the previous chapter), for most women the first experience with death in the family is the loss of a husband (except for aging parents). And very few women are prepared to face such a loss.

After the husband's death, grief inevitably follows. There are considered to be three stages of grief. These are *shock* (impact), *realization* (recoil), and *readjustment* (recovery).[51] Although there may be variations, in the first stage of shock, there is great distress. The woman may feel bewildered and collapse. She often refuses to accept the reality and employs the defense mechanism of denial to help cushion the shock. The woman may feel life is not worth living. This stage can last from one day to as much as six months or more.[51]

In the stage of realization, the awareness of what happened is brought to consciousness. The woman may want to join her husband in death or she may feel extreme anger toward him for leaving her. The widow may feel lost at this time, without goals and with a loss of self-esteem. During this period, which can last anywhere from one month to a year, the woman often feels lonely and depressed.[52] She may also have intense feelings of guilt. The guilt may occur because she felt she didn't do enough to prevent her husband's death or it may be guilt over her extreme dependence on her late husband.

In the recovery phase, which can be between three months and two years following the death, the woman continues to feel the loss but she is now better able to cope with it. The grieving process is normal and essential but it should be completed between one and two years following the loss if the woman is to maintain her own life and health.[53] The grieving widow should receive support throughout the whole period of grief. She should be physically comforted in the beginning and allowed to express her thoughts and feelings to others. By recalling her life together with her husband, the widow should be able to break the emotional ties in order to live her own life. If the woman has strong religious beliefs, these can give her comfort and support. A priest, minister, or rabbi can be a great source of solace at this time.

After the initial consolation, the widow needs companionship to help guide her into decisions and solve problems.[8] It is important that friends emphasize that the widow can cope, that her husband would want her to carry on, and that there are many things that she can and must still do. Just as there are support groups for the obese, divorcees, single women, rape victims, and women alcoholics, so, too, are there widow-to-widow groups.[52] The empathy received from other widows is important in helping the new widow recover. By being active, the widow can learn that life is still meaningful.

As the fifties head into the sixties and seventies, women begin to think about getting old. The stressors of aging are covered in the next chapter.

REFERENCES

1. Osofsky, H. J. and Seidenberg, R. Is female menopausal depression inevitable? *Obst. Gynecol.* **36**:611–615, 1970.
2. Deutsch, H. L. *The Psychology of Women: A Psychoanalytic Interpretation.* Vols. 1 and 2. New York: Grune & Stratton, 1944, 1945.
3. Hoskins, R. G. The psychological treatment of the menopause. *J. Clin. Endocrin.* **4**:605–610, 1944.
4. Kupperman, H. S., Wetchler, B. B., and Blatt, M. H. G. Contemporary therapy of the menopausal syndrome. *J.A.M.A.* **171**:1627–1637, 1959.
5. Neugarten, B. L. and Krainer, R. J. Menopausal symptoms in women of various ages. *Psychosom. Med.* **27**:266–273, 1965.
6. Dyer, R. A. M. Menopause: A closer look for nurses. *In* Kjervik, D. K. and Martinson, I. M. (eds.), *Women In Stress: A Nursing Perspective.* New York: Appleton-Century-Crofts, 1979, pp. 303–318.
7. Yates, J. How nutrition helps menopause. *Prevention* **32**(5):150–156, 1980.
8. Williams, J. H. *Psychology of Women: Behavior in a Biosocial Context.* New York: W. W. Norton, 1977.
9. Sherman, J. *On the Psychology of Women.* Springfield, Ill.: Charles C. Thomas, 1971.
10. Wilding, P. Biochemical changes at the menopause. *In* Curry, A. S. and Hewitt, J. V. (eds.), *Biochemistry of Women: Clinical Concepts.* Cleveland: CRC Press, 1974, pp. 103–110.

11. Thompson, B., Hart, S. A., and Durno, D. Menopausal age and symptomatology in a general practice. *J. Biosoc. Sci.* **5**:71-82, 1973.
12. Feeley, E. and Pyne H. The menopause: Facts and misconceptions. *Nursing For.* **14**(1):74-86, 1975.
13. Chakravarti, S., Collins, W. P., Forecast, J. D., Newton, J. R., Oram, D. H., and Studd, J. W. W. Hormonal profiles after the menopause. *Brit. Med. J.* **2**:784-787, 1976.
14. Reitz, R. *Menopause: A Positive Approach.* New York: Penguin Books, 1979.
15. Hoover, R., Gray, L. A., Cole, P., and MacMahon, B. Menopausal estrogens and breast cancer. *N. Engl. J. Med.* **295**:401-405, 1975.
16. Ross, R. K, Paganini-Hill, A., Gerkins, V. R., Mack, T. M., Pfeffer, R., Arthur, M., and Henderson, B. E. A case-control study of menopausal estrogen therapy of breast cancer. *J.A.M.A.* **243**:1635-1639, 1980.
17. Editorial. Tryptophan and depression. *Brit. Med. J.* **1**:242-243, 1976.
18. Wurtman, R. J. and Growdon, J. H. Dietary enhancement of CNS neurotransmitters. *In* Krieger, D. T. and Hughes, J. C. (eds.), *Neuroendocrinology.* Sunderland, Mass.: Sinauer Associates, 1980, pp. 59-66.
19. Kinzer, N. S. *Stress and the American Woman.* New York: Ballantine Books, 1980.
20. Bart, P. Depression in middle-aged women. *In* Gornick, V. and Moran, B. K. (eds.),- *Women in Sexist Society: Studies in Power and Powerlessness.* New York: Basic Books, 1971, pp.163-186.
21. Maddison, J. Hormone replacement therapy for menopausal symptoms. *Lancet* **1**:1507, 1973.
22. Dresen, S. E. The sexually active middle age adult. *Am. J. Nursing* **75**:1001-1005, 1975.
23. Gallagher, J. C. and Nordin, B. E. C. Calcium metabolism and the menopause. *In* Curry, A. S. and Hewitt, J. V. (eds.), *Biochemistry of Women: Clinical Concepts.* Cleveland: CRC Press, 1974, pp.145-163.
24. Heaney, R. P., Recker, R. R., and Saville, P. D. Menopausal changes in calcium balance performance. *J. Lab. Clin. Med.* **92**:953-963, 1978.
25. Weiss, N. S. Relationship of menopause to serum cholesterol and arterial blood pressure: The United States Health Examination Survey of Adults. *Am. J. Epidemiol.* **96**:237-241, 1972.
26. Shibata, H., Matsuzaki, T., and Hatano, S. Relationship of relevant factors of atherosclerosis to menopause in Japanese women. *Am. J. Epidemiol.* **109**:420-424,1979.
27. Gordon, T., Kannel, W. B., Hjortland, M. C., and McNamara, P. M. Menopause and coronary heart disease: The Framingham study. *Ann. Int. Med.* **89**:157-161, 1978.
28. Weideger, P. *Menstruation and Menopause: The Physiology and Psychology, the Myth and the Reality.* New York: Knopf, 1976.
29. Finck, K. S. The potential health care crises of hysterectomy. *In* Kjervik, D. K. and Martinson, I. M. (eds.), *Women In Stress: A Nursing Perspective.* New York: Appleton-Century-Crofts, 1979, pp. 276-302.
30. McCary, J. L. *Human Sexuality.* New York: D. Van Nostrand, 1973.
31. Speidel, J. J. and Mc Ann, M. F. Mini laparotomy—A fertility control technique of increasing importance. *Adv. Planned Parenthood*13(2):42-57, 1980.
32. Masters, W. H. and Johnson, V. E. What young women should know about hysterectomies. *Redbook* 48-50, January 1976.
33. Gray, M. The Changing Years: The Menopause Without Fear, Second Ed. Garden City, New York: Doubleday, 1981.
34. Kaltreider, N. B., Wallace, A., and Horowitz, M. J. A field study of the stress response syndrome: Young women after hysterectomy. *J.A.M.A.* **242**:1499-1503, 1979.

35. Raphael, B. The crisis of hysterectomy. *Austral. New Zealand J. Psychiatr.* **6**:106–115, 1972.
36. Richards, D. H. A post-hysterectomy syndrome. *Lancet* **2**:983–985, 1974.
37. Barker, M. G. Psychiatric illness after hysterectomy. *Brit. Med. J.* **2**:91–95, 1968.
38. Krueger, J. C., Hassell, J., Goggins, D. B., Ishimatsu, T. Pablico, M. R., and Tuttle, E. J. Relationship between nurse counseling and sexual adjustment after hysterectomy. *Nurs. Res.* **28**:145–150, 1979.
39. Dodds, D. T., Potgieter, C. R., and Turner, P. J. The physical and emotional results of hysterectomy. *S. African Med. J.* **35**:53–54, 1961.
40. Williams, M. Easier convalescence from hysterectomy. *Amer. J. Nursing* **76**:438–440, 1976.
41. Hall, C. S. *A Primer of Freudian Psychology.* New York: World Publishing, 1954.
42. Morse, D. R. and Furst, M. L. *Stress and Relaxation: Application to Dentistry.* Springfield, Ill.: Charles C. Thomas, 1978.
43. Morse, D. R. *Clinical Endodontology: A Comprehensive Guide to Diagnosis, Treatment and Prevention.* Springfield, Ill.: Charles C. Thomas, 1974.
44. Holmes, T. H. and Rahe, R. H. The social readjustment scale. *J. Psychosom. Res.* **11**:213–218, 1967.
45. Wolfe, L. When was the last time you called your mother? A "New York" magazine survey of readers and their parents. *New York Magazine* 47–54, May 7, 1979.
46. Stern, M. J. and Pascale, L. Psychosocial adaptation post-myocardial infarction: The spouse's dilemma. *J. Psychosom. Res.* **23**:83–87, 1979.
47. Skelton, M. and Dominion, J. Psychological stress in wives of patients with myocardial infarction. *Br. Med. J.* **2**:101–103, 1973.
48. Anthony, E. J. The impact of mental and physical illness on family life. *Am. J. Psychiat.* **127**:138–146, 1970.
49. Holub, N., Eklund, P. and Kennan, P. Family conferences as an adjunct to total coronary care. *Heart Lung* **4**:767–769, 1975.
50. Mc Gann, M. Group sessions for the families of post-coronary patients. *Supervisor Nurse* **7**(2):17–19, 1976.
51. Albrecht, M. E. The experience of widowhood. *In* Kjervik, D. K. and Martinson, I. M. (eds.), *Women In Stress: A Nursing Perspective.* New York: Appleton-Century-Crofts, 1979, pp. 319–325.
52. Silverman, P. The widow-to-widow program: An experiment in preventive intervention. *Mental Hyg.* **53**:336–337, 1969.
53. Blank, R. H. Mourning. *In* Kutscher, A. H. (ed.), *Death and Bereavement.* Springfield, Ill.: Charles C. Thomas, 1969, pp. 204–206.
54. Lucas, L. Hatching a new life in the empty nest. *Prevention* **32**(9):166–170, 1980.
55. Polit, D. F., and LaRocco, S. A. Social and psychological correlates of menopausal symptoms. *Psychosom. Med.* **42**: 335–345, 1980.
56. The Boston Women's Health Book Collective *Our Bodies, Our Selves.* New York: Simon & Schuster, 1979.

9
Onward From the Sixties

INTRODUCTION

As women reach the sixties, they often become concerned with aging. Aging is inevitable, but it is better than the ultimate alternative and it can be positive and enjoyable. Some stress-related problems of aging are: changes in physical appearance; decrease in energy; loss of strength; slow reaction time; memory loss and senility; greater susceptibility to disease; increased intake of drugs; poor vision, hearing, smell and taste; loss of teeth; decreased sexual activity; loneliness; forced retirement; loss of power and status; and depression. Let us consider these in turn.

PERSONAL APPEARANCE

With aging, there is an increase in collagenous connective tissues and cross-linkages.[1] This makes tissues stiffer, less resilient and, in skin, causes an increase in wrinkling. Many women are concerned with wrinkles. Part of this is related to the mass media with its emphasis on youth and beauty. But women don't have to try to keep up the appearance of youth to achieve their own self-esteem. As more women have careers and are less dependent upon men, they will find that it is not imperative that every wrinkle is covered or removed, and every gray hair is pulled or hidden. However, part of the wrinkling changes result from poor circulation, and proper exercise and massage can keep the skin and its associated muscles firm. There are anecdotal reports to the effect that proprietary vitamin E skin creams can help the skin maintain its tone and reduce wrinkling. Even though there is some question about carcinogenic (cancer-inducing) properties of some hair dyes, the improvement in physical appearance for some women attained by hair dyeing would seem to be justified.

Women who can afford it and who are stressed by wrinkles and aged appearances can have plastic surgery to help them look young again.

DECREASE IN ENERGY

Nutrients tend to be delivered more slowly to aging tissues and waste removal from these tissues is decreased. Oxygen intake and the basal metabolic rate also decreases.[2] As a result, older people tend to be more readily fatigued. But there are athletic women who are fit in their nineties. These energy-related changes occur gradually, and if a woman stays in condition and has a healthful diet, she will hardly notice any loss of energy. (See Chapters 21 and 22.)

LOSS OF STRENGTH

Although women are not usually concerned with strength, there is a loss of muscle fibers and decrease in actual size of muscles with age.[3] Here, too, the changes are gradual and can be greatly reduced if women remain physically active.

SLOW REACTION TIME

Aging changes occur in the brain and central nervous system which causes decreases in size and loss in number of neurons (nerve cells). These changes, along with others, may be partly responsible for the slow reaction time and slow learning of the aged.[2] Yet women, as well as men, can still react well and be successful in regard to learning new tasks and information. The key is to delay or reduce the incidence of atherosclerosis (see Chapter 3). Other helpful methods are: reduce the intake of alcohol (damages and kills brain cells); get sufficient exercise (increases the circulation and functioning of the brain); and keep mentally alert. Recent studies have shown that people can learn well, even in advanced age.[4,5] It just takes them a little longer to learn. In fact, there is evidence that the average seventy-year-old often does better than young people in "power" tests.[6] (Power tests allow sufficient time to answer the questions.)

MEMORY LOSS AND SENILITY

With many old people there is a memory loss for recent events along with an accentuated recall of past events.[2-5] This is partly caused by the aforementioned brain and nervous system changes but is accelerated by atherosclerosis, alcoholism, and lack of physical and mental activity. The same preventive measures discussed under *Slow Reaction Time* would apply here.

Senility is a manifestation of a degenerative brain disease known as *Alzheimer's disease* (a specific degeneration of the brain cells). Early signs are: (1) general forgetfulness; (2) mood changes going from elation to depression, along with periods of anger; and (3) memory lapses that tend to increase in number and duration. Senility affects about 5 percent of people past sixty-five and 15 percent of those over eighty. It may be genetically programmed, but high blood pressure and cerebral atherosclerosis may hasten its onset. There is no known cure and that is why prevention of the nongenetic factors is important (see *Slow Reaction Time*).

SUSCEPTIBILITY TO DISEASES

With aging there is (1) a decrease in the number of normal functioning cells; (2) an increase in degenerative changes in cells; (3) a decreased nutrient and gaseous exchange; (4) a decreased functioning of endocrine glands (those that produce hormones); (5) an impairment of the immune system (fights infections and tumor cells); (6) disturbances in the heart and circulatory system (less blood pumped and slowing down of the circulation); (7) decreased functioning of the kidneys (problems in urination); and (8) a reduced activity of the sexual organs.[2,3,5,8,9] These changes can result in increased susceptibility to infections, cancer, heart attack, stroke, diabetes, kidney diseases, and arthritis. Yet none of these are inevitable. By exercising, eating well, not smoking, drinking little, taking a minimum of drugs, keeping mentally active and having a positive attitude, it is possible for women to live into their nineties with a minimum of disturbances.[10,11]

INTAKE OF DRUGS

One of the biggest problems with aging is drug intake. As previously discussed in Chapter 4, women take many more prescription drugs than do men, and with aged women this is even a greater potential source of stress. The elderly currently make up about 10 percent of the U.S. population but they consume about 25 percent of all prescription drugs. These drugs are given for chronic conditions such as heart disease (remember that postmenopausal women become just as susceptible as men to heart attacks) and diabetes (also high in older women). Estrogen is prescribed for perimenopausal symptoms.

The more drugs individuals take, the greater is the risk of drug interactions and untoward reactions. People over the age of sixty are admitted to hospital emergency rooms for adverse drug reactions in twice the frequency as are people under the age of sixty.[12] Because of the impaired defenses of the elderly (as previously described), drugs have a greater effect on them. Hence, there is an increased chance of side effects or adverse drug reactions.

Many times elderly women are given drugs for anxiety and depression. These drugs could often be avoided if there was sufficient counseling given to these women. About 25 percent of psychotropic drugs (e.g., Valium, antidepressants) are given to people over the age of sixty-five for conditions such as the loss of a husband.[13] However psychotherapy is the treatment of choice.

Sleeping pills are abused by the elderly. They receive 40 percent of all sleeping pills prescribed.[13]Women are still receiving frequent prescriptions for estrogen. Estrogen is currently the fifth most frequently prescribed drug.[14] Many patients are given heart disease drugs such as digitalis, nitroglycerine, and antihypertensives. It is not that the latter drugs shouldn't be prescribed, but often physicians and patients alike don't take into consideration other drugs being prescribed or over-the-counter medications being taken. One other drug-related problem with the elderly is errors in taking pills (occurs in about 40 to 60 percent of older individuals). They either take the wrong dose, take the pill at the wrong time, or forget to take the pill entirely. One study showed that 47 percent of the patients forgot to take their medicine; 10 percent took the wrong amount; and 20 percent didn't know why they were taking the drugs in the first place.[12] Some older patients take the wrong dose or pill because they have trouble reading the labels. One other problem with the elderly is their tendency to exchange drugs with friends. They also may increase or decrease the dose themselves without medical consultation.

To help avoid some of these problems, here is some advice for older women:

1. Don't take drugs unless they are absolutely essential. (Seek a second medical opinion if necessary.)
2. Keep a list of all drugs you take and when they are taken. Let your physician, dentist, and pharmacist know about your drug regimen.
3. Write down the instructions and side effects for each drug taken so that you can be prepared for untoward reactions.
4. To help you know your medicines, use a different color tab for each bottle.
5. Don't borrow or lend out drugs.

6. If you are feeling better, let your doctor know so that your dependency on the drugs can be reduced.

IMPAIRMENT OF THE SENSES

Vision, hearing, smell, taste, touch, and speech all decline with age. The colors blue, green, and violet become more difficult for older people to distinguish. Hearing loss occurs, but it is mainly in the upper frequencies.[2,3] One positive aging change is that the teeth often become less sensitive to cold and sweets.[15] In terms of perception, the aged require more time to receive and interpret complex figures. These aging changes don't have to induce stress for the following two reasons.

One is that the changes are usually gradual which allows time to adjust. Secondly, modern medicine has developed effective methods to help with the various impairments. For example: Eyeglasses, contact lens and hearing aids are effective; and periodontal (gum treatment), endodontic (root canal), and crown and bridgework therapies can all relieve dental conditions. Taking time to perceive and react to problems is generally beneficial. It allows one latitude to make less stressful decisions.

SEXUAL ACTIVITY

After menopause, there are certain changes in the female genital organs. As previously mentioned, there is atrophy of the vagina and reduction in lubrication. Orgasms are less intense and fewer, and the contractions may be somewhat painful.[16] However, there is no reduction in the desire to have sexual relations. The biggest problem may be lack of available men. In the sixty-five to seventy-four-year-age bracket, there are about seventy-two males for each hundred females. After the age of seventy-five, the ratio is sixty-three males to one hundred females.[17] There are four times as many widows as widowers. Two-thirds of the men past 65 are married, while only one-third of the women are married. Even when there are available men, many of them are impotent. Seventy-five percent of the impotent males in one study were over fifty years of age.[16] Another factor working against older women is that even when older men are sexually active, they tend to look for younger partners.

With less opportunities available, some older women choose masturbation as a sexual outlet.[18] Some choose other women for homosexual relations, while still others are content not to engage entirely or have an occasional sexual involvement. As a result, women have less active sex lives than men of comparable age.[16]

Of the various stress-related age changes, this is one of the most difficult for women. One helpful aspect would be for women to take up the theme from *My Fair Lady* in reverse and state, "Why can't men be more like women?" The move toward androgyny in males, and men becoming actively involved in exercise programs, meditation, balanced nutrition, and positive psychological approaches should result in the next generation of men living longer and being satisfied with their spouses (and hopefully, vice versa). This should result in fewer divorces and fewer widows. Then women who prefer men may have more opportunities to have an active and enjoyable sex life as they age.

LONELINESS

Being isolated and lonely is one of the great fears of older women (à la Roberta in Chapter 1). Women with many social contacts were shown to be less lonely and isolated and lived longer than women with few social contacts.[19] Sources of social contact included husbands, close friends, relatives, church membership, and both formal and informal group associations.

Older women don't have to be lonely and isolated. According to recent surveys, loneliness among women over sixty-five is no greater than loneliness among younger women. Most older women are not shunted off into nursing homes. Only 4–5 percent of women over sixty-five go into nursing homes.[6] Many of them who do go into homes have neither husbands, children nor near relatives. Most older women remain in their own communities, near their families and friends. Some women voluntarily move into residential communities that have excellent services that they cannot obtain at home (e.g., health care, transportation, and residential facilities). However, there is often a family conflict when a decision has to be made whether or not the mother is competent enough to manage her own affairs. A recent study showed that parent-caring is becoming a principal source of stress in family life.[6]

In order to avoid feelings of loneliness and isolation, women should maintain social contacts throughout their lives, even if they must be made in residential communities rather than in their own homes.

FORCED RETIREMENT

Now that women are entering the business and professional world in large numbers, it is fortunate that they will have less problems with forced retirement than was the case heretofore. Compulsory retirement by age sixty-five has now been outlawed, and this can only be helpful to the older woman. In Holmes and Rahe's Social Readjustment Rating Scale, retirement is one of the major life-stress events.[20] By remaining active, which includes part-time or full-time jobs, women can reduce the stress of aging. Active older women generally have more self-esteem and a better outlook toward the future than do inactive women.[5]

LOSS OF POWER AND STATUS

In Western societies, the aged lack power and status. When the children leave and the husband dies, traditional women no longer have status in the family. Working women who have retired have a sudden loss of income and power. Each of these changes are major social stressors.[20] Women who are used to working either in the home, the outside world, or both, may find the "relaxation" and "recreation"of retirement, to be boring and frustrating. To counteract the loss of power and status, the older woman should engage in sports, hobbies, part-time employment (even if it is voluntary), community activities, social gatherings and sex.[3]

DEPRESSION

Forced retirement or the breaking of family ties can lead to social isolation and loneliness which can, in turn, bring on depression. Older women tend to become depressed when they feel they have lost something of importance such as a husband, a job, or contact with their children. This can result in the loss of self-esteem and the feeling of having nothing to live for.[16]

To overcome depression, older women must maintain their self-esteem. They must feel that they can still contribute to society and themselves. Something they can do is develop a new profitable hobby (à la Grandma Moses) or even do volunteer work in a neighborhood hospital.

COUNTERACTING THE STRESS OF AGING

One way to decrease the stress of aging is to be fit when the golden years arrive. To help achieve this, women should follow these rules throughout their lives:[10]

1. Sleep between seven and eight hours a night.
2. Regularly eat breakfast.
3. Don't snack with junk foods between meals.
4. Maintain a normal body weight.

5. Exercise regularly.
6. Don't be an alcoholic; one or two glasses of wine a day may be beneficial.
7. Do not smoke.
8. Have positive attitudes. ("See the glass as half full rather than half empty.")[3]
9. Practice a relaxation method regularly.[3]

As senior citizens, women can enjoy their twilight years: by maintaining their interest in life; by keeping active, having hobbies, retaining an alert mind; and by not looking at the obituary page in the local newspaper.[21] Women can get help from other women throughout their lives whether it is in regard to divorce, pregnancy, rape, smoking, overeating, or drinking. And as they age, other women are there to help and lobby for them as well. Organizations such as the *Gray Panthers,* the *American Association of Retired Persons,* and *The National Council of Senior Citizens* lobby for federal and local support for the elderly. There are also many local senior organizations for older women. With the help of others and their own initiative, the sixties and beyond can be an exciting time of life for today's "young" old women.

DYING

Dying can be made less stressful. Clinical reports have shown that when people are dying and they are conscious, the last few hours or days on earth can be made more pleasant if they have learned methods of deep meditation or self-hypnosis. By being in a self-imposed trance, or having someone else guide them into an imaginary idyllic place or time, the transition from life to death can be placid and even euphoric.[22]

Now that we have covered the ages of a woman's life, in the next chapter let us consider one of the more important aspects of living, sexuality.

REFERENCES

1. Sinex, F. M. The biochemistry of aging. *In* Spencer, M. G. and Dorr, C. J. (eds.), *Understanding Aging: A Multidisciplinary Approach.* New York: Appleton-Century-Crofts, 1975, pp. 21–39.
2. Wolff, K. *The Biological, Sociological, and Psychological Aspects of Aging.* Springfield, Ill.: Charles C. Thomas, 1959.
3. Morse, D. R. and Furst, M. L. *Stress for Success: A Holistic Approach to Stress and its Management.* New York: Van Nostrand Reinhold, 1979.

4. Butler, R. N. and Lewis, M. I. *Aging and Mental Health: Positive Psychosocial Approaches.* St. Louis: C. V. Mosby, 1977.
5. Dibner, A. A. The psychology of normal aging. *In* Spencer, M. G. and Dorr, C. J. (eds.), *Understanding Aging: A Multidisciplinary Approach.* New York: Appleton-Century-Crofts, 1975, pp. 67–90.
6. Hall, E. and Neugarten, B. Acting one's age: New rules for old. *Psychol. Today* **14** (4):66–80, 1980.
7. Rockmore, M. From the top: Myths and truths about senility. *Philadelphia Sunday Bulletin* Mag. Sect. 10, July 8, 1979.
8. Kolata, G. B. The aging heart: Changes in function and response to drugs. *Science* **195**:166–167, 1977.
9. Marx, J. L. Hormones and their effects in the aging body: Changes in the working of the endocrine system have been linked to some of the diseases that diminish the quality of later life. *Science* **206**:805–806, 1979.
10. Belloc, N. B. Relationship of health practices and mortality. *Prev. Med.* **2**:67–81, 1973.
11. Woodruff, D. *Can You Live to Be 100?* New York: Chatham Square Press, 1977.
12. Bullard, S. Drugs and the elderly. *Fort Lauderdale News/Sun-Sentinel.* Lifestyle Today 1D, 6D, January 6, 1980.
13. Gaeta, M. J. and Gaetano, R. J. *The Elderly—Their Health and the Drugs in Their Lives.* Dubuque, Iowa: Kendell/Hunt, 1977.
14. Pfeffer, R., Arthur, M., and Henderson, B. E. A case-control study of menopausal estrogen therapy of breast cancer. *J.A.M.A.* **243**:1635–1639, 1980.
15. Morse, D. R. *Clinical Endodontology: A Comprehensive Guide to Diagnosis, Treatment and Prevention.* Springfield, Ill.: Charles C. Thomas, 1974.
16. Williams, J. H. *Psychology of Women: Behavior in a Biosocial Context.* New York: W. W. Norton, 1977.
17. Puner, M. Will you still love me? *Hum. Behav.* **3**:6, 42–48, 1974.
18. Masters, W. and Johnson, V. Human sexual response: The aging female and the aging male. *In* Neugarten, B. (ed), *Middle Age and Aging.* Chicago: University of Chicago Press, 1968.
19. Shaw, L. A personal road map for longer life. *Prevention* **31**(9):73–78, 1979.
20. Holmes, T. H. and Rahe, R. H. The social readjustment scale. *J. Psychosom. Res.* **11**:213–218, 1967.
21. Editorial. Shadow of death over aging. *Science* **207**: Editorial Page, March 28, 1980.
22. Bahson, C. Guided imagery and hypnosis in the care of patients with chronic illness. Presented to the Philadelphia Society of Clinical Hypnosis, Philadelphia, May 6, 1979.

PART IV
WOMEN'S
SEXUALITY

Nowhere is stress more apparent for a woman than in the area of sexuality. In Chapter 10, the stressors of heterosexuality are considered: from Victorianism to multiple orgasm; from premarital relations to extramarital affairs. Another consideration is methods of birth control including the pill, the diaphragm, the IUD, the condom, and abortion. The sexual dysfunctions are also discussed. Chapter 11 is concerned with the violent sexual abuses, incest, and rape. In Chapter 12, the focus is on alternative sexual relationships such as homosexuality, bisexuality, transvestism, and transsexuality.

10
Heterosexual Stress

INTRODUCTION

Until recently, the woman's role in sexual intercourse was judged to be that of the passive partner whose main function was to satisfy the man's needs. The woman was led to believe that the less she knew and did about sex the better it was for her. The "ideal" female was considered to be "undamaged goods," a virgin who would be given untarnished to her husband. The sexually aware, worldly-wise male would then teach her all she had to know about sex. Most often that was simply to be ready to help him achieve orgasm when *he* wanted it. Her needs were considered either nonexistent or unimportant. Men were encouraged to learn all they needed to know about sex before marriage by having as many sexual partners as possible. The more they had, the better was their social acceptance among other males and even among women. Obviously the men had to find some women for their sexual initiation and expertise. These women were denigrated. They were called "loose," "fast," prostitutes, "easy lays," or whores. The men "scored"; the women "put out." Scoring was akin to a sporting event, the more the men scored the better. "Putting out" was a negative "trait"; the more women "put out," the lower the esteem they had among other women and men. Women who enjoyed sex with a number of men were considered to be nymphomaniacs, "nymphos" or promiscuous. Men who had many sexual encounters were "macho," the envy of the other guys; there was no such thing as a promiscuous man.

This "double standard" was promulgated during the Victorian age, and became part of morals and manners. As such, many mothers did (and still do) instill into their daughters a fear and rejection of sex. The young girl was given a contradictory message. She was told that sex is "bad"; all sources of sexual stimulation should be shunned including masturbation and "petting." On the other hand, sex in marriage for procreation is "good," but a "good girl" doesn't try to lure a husband by sexual contrivances. She must be modest, passive, and not show passion. The result was that many women had sexual relations only to become pregnant. In order to cut down on male lust, the newly married were advised to have separate bedrooms.[1] Women had all the problems with none of the pleasures. Birth control was unknown except by withdrawal or abstinence, and the results showed that many women frequently became pregnant. In 1800, each woman in the United States averaged seven children.[2]

Currently, based on the Kinsey report,[3] the work of Masters and Johnson,[4] the Playboy survey (analyzed by Morton Hunt),[5] and the research of Helen Kaplan,[6] it is known that women can be sexually stimulated to a great extent. Just as is the case with incidence of disease and mortality rate, most women are vastly superior to most men in sexual responsiveness. Women tend to prolong their sexual enjoyment much longer than men, and women are capable of multiple orgasms while men need rest and recovery between orgasms. Let us first consider the sexual response in women. Then the various potential stressors of heterosexuality are examined and finally, contraception methods and sexual dysfunctions are discussed.

THE SEXUAL RESPONSE

For many years it was believed, based on psychoanalytic theory, that women could achieve two orgasms; one was clitoral and the other was vaginal. Freud considered that in infancy the vagina was dormant, and that clitoral orgasm was the only kind. With puberty, vaginal orgasm replaced the infantile clitoral kind. A woman who persisted with clitoral orgasm, generally achieved through masturbation, was considered sexually immature and frigid.[7] Based on the research of Masters and Johnson it is now generally maintained that there is just one kind of orgasm for women. It is physiologically the same regardless of who is the stimulator and which part of the body is stimulated.[4]

Penile, finger, vibratory, and other kinds of intravaginal stimulation can affect the minor lips (labia minora), the clitoris, and the lower vagina as a functional unit. (See Figure 10.1) There are four phases of sexual stimulation.[4,8] The first stage is *excitement*. Physical and psychological stimulation can bring on this state. Although women are more sensitive to touch than are men, they can also be aroused by sight and even sexual pictures.[8] During the excitement state, vaginal fluid appears and increases in amount and the heart rate and blood pressure accelerate. The next state is *plateau* which in women can last for twenty minutes or more. There are many genital

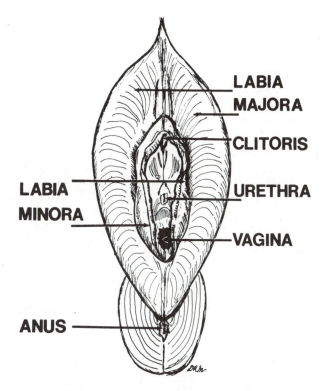

Fig. 10.1.   A representation of the external female genital structures. The urethra is the external opening of the urinary tract and liquid wastes are disposed of through this opening. The
vagina is the external opening of the female reproductive tract. Through it, sperm are introduced, menstrual products are eliminated, and a new born child is delivered. The anus is the
inferior external opening of the gastrointestinal tract. Through it, solid wastes are disposed.
The labia ("lips") serve to protect the external openings of the urinary and reproductive
tracts.

changes related to engorgement of blood. There is also an increase in heart
rate, blood pressure, and breathing rate. Muscles of the abdominal, inter-
costal (between the ribs), and rectal areas contract (occasionally).

The third stage is *orgasm* in which there are cervical contractions
(orgasmic platform), and contractions of the uterus. The heart rate, blood
pressure and breathing rate increase further, and there are involuntary contractions of the various muscle groups. This stage can be repeated in some
women who are capable of multiple orgasms. The fourth stage is *resolution*. This takes between ten and twenty minutes. The heart rate, blood
pressure, breathing rate, and muscle activity return to normal. With men,

generally the blood pressure rise is most rapid in excitement, plateau and orgasm and the entire sexual response is of shorter duration.

In Chapter 21 we discuss the advantages of aerobic exercise. A prolonged sexual response with its aerobic activity could be considered a method of aerobic exercise for women. Unfortunately, most men do not prolong the duration for a long enough time to derive positive cardiovascular benefits. However, being fit does have its advantages sexually.

Studies have shown that maximum heart rate, blood pressure, and breathing rate during sexual intercourse is lower (more efficient) in trained individuals.[9-11] They would also have more endurance and less fatigue. By engaging in calisthenic and body-building exercises, women as well as men would have better development of abdominal and gluteal muscles and could maintain greater activity of those muscles during sexual relations. It could be considered that sex is not only fun but also a means of keeping in condition at least for women and men with good control. As a form of aerobic exercise, sexual activity, if prolonged and repeated could be an aid in weight loss and maintainance of a good figure.[12] Sex could then be considered as good exercise, a figure aid, and a positive stress-coping method. However, sex under duress is stressful. Let us now look into the stressors of sexual activity.

STRESSORS OF SEXUAL ACTIVITY

Although the Victorian age is gone and there is a sexual revolution, many women are not completely liberated in their sexual thinking and activities. Masturbation is still rarely admitted to and discussed. Most mothers don't encourage premarital sexual activity for their daughters. Nevertheless, premarital relations have increased. Of the women born before 1900, three out of four were virgins before marriage.[3] Nowadays, three out of four women have had premarital sexual relations.[5]

One of the principal stressors for a woman about to engage in sexual intercourse for the first time is the fear that it will hurt. It used to be thought that an intact hymen* was a cardinal sign of virginity and proof that the girl was "pure." However, the hymen can rupture during normal childhood activities as well as from horseback riding. Even if there is an intact hymen, penetration by the penis during coitus generally causes only slight pain and bleeding.[2]

Because of the negative input received from their mothers, young women engaging in premarital sex relations can have feelings of guilt. But evidence

* The hymen is a thin membrane that covers the vaginal opening. It has no known function.

shows that these feelings don't prevent subsequent premarital sexual activities, and most often the guilt feelings abate in time.[13]

Years ago women were seemingly satisfied in assuming the passive sexual role, and even today there are women who can live a complete life with minimal or no sexual stimulation. Many nuns apparently have that conviction. Nowadays, women may become stressed if they don't achieve orgasm during each sexual experience. And, with the knowledge about multiple orgasms, some women feel cheated if they only have one orgasm. But just as people differ in their personalities and attitudes, so do they differ in their orgasmic potential. Some women have "minimal" orgasms with a peak of low intensity. Others have "multiple" orgasms with higher peaks of intensity and longer resolutions. Still others have orgasms with high peaks of intensity and rapid resolutions.[4] Other women rarely achieve orgasm and yet still report sexual satisfaction.[5]*

All four types can be satisfying to the individual concerned and none is inherently better than any other. The ability to achieve orgasm is not innate. It can be learned and improved upon. Women are learning rapidly. Studies have shown that the rate of women achieving orgasm has doubled in the last thirty years.[5]

Kinsey found that women's sexual peak occurs at about the age of thirty and stays primed for at least the following ten years.[3] Males reach their prime between the ages of fifteen and twenty.[14] Most women marry men somewhat older than themselves. From a sexual vantage point they might be better off marrying younger men.

It used to be thought that women should suppress their sexual needs in deference to those of their male partners. Nowadays it is believed that the partners should concern themselves with the needs of the other. But this can be very frustrating for a woman who has been brought up to be a caring and concerned person. She inevitably tries harder. Another aspect is that "Looking Out For Number One"[15] has meaning in sexual relations as well as with other realities. Men have always looked out for themselves sexually. It is time that women let men know what pleases or displeases them. Then they should try to arrange the relationships so that they achieve satisfaction at least as often as their male partners. Reticence is not beneficial. Men are not innately sexually knowledgeable and need to be guided. In this way, sexual relations can be mutually beneficial.

* Although women do not get sick from not having orgasms, there is evidence that some women who are sexually frustrated develop uncomfortable feelings of pressure in the pelvic area. When a woman is sexually aroused, blood rushes into the pelvic area and if it is not "pumped out" with orgasm, it remains and causes congestion and symptoms. Orgasm causes the symptoms to disappear. Sifford D. How much sex does a woman need? *Philadelphia Inq.* 2–D, February 26, 1981.

Another cause for stress is related to the time needed for sexual arousal. Although most women usually take longer to get aroused and reach orgasm than do men, this is not always the case. Some women get "turned on" quickly and rapidly achieve orgasm. Others take longer and need "atmosphere." Circumstances can vary those behaviors and neither is innately right or wrong.

Other stressors are related to divergent methods of sexual activity such as oral-genital, oral-anal, and anal intercourse. Studies by Kinsey,[3,14] Hunt [5] and others [13] have shown that these methods are achieving greater popularity because of their sensuousness and as means of birth control. For example, in the 1940s anal intercourse was rarely reported, but recent findings indicate that 25 percent of married women under the age of thirty-five have experienced anal intercourse.[5]

Just because more people are "doing it" doesn't necessarily mean that all forms of sexual activity are "right" for all women. Women should have the freedom to choose their own sexual pleasures. On the other hand, they shouldn't feel that anything is inherently "dirty."*

Another concern is whether or not to limit one's sexual activity to a single partner. In 1925, 50 percent of the married men and 26 percent of the married women had one extramarital sexual experience by the age of 40.[3] By 1974, the incidence of extramarital sex had risen slightly and it was mainly accounted for by females under the age of twenty-five.[5] Most recently, a *Cosmopolitan* magazine survey of 106,000 females revealed that 50 percent of the married women admitted to having an extramarital affair.[16]

Occasionally, extramarital sex can improve a marriage.[17] In the *Cosmopolitan* survey, 42 percent of the married women who had an affair said it had no effect on their marriage, 34 percent said it helped their marriage, and 25 percent said that it harmed their marriage.[16]

For men, engaging in extramarital affairs can be harmful to their health. There is evidence that extramarital sexual activities by married men (women were not investigated) can lead to severe elevation in both heart rate and blood pressure. Such activity, especially with new partners can be extremely stressful and has been implicated in most cases of sudden death during sexual intercourse.[18] In one study it was found that heart attacks during extramarital sex were related to the following compounding

---

* A recently popular (in some circles) sexual diversion is *sadomasochism*. In this extreme form of sexual foreplay, women and men allow themselves to be spanked, whipped, tied in chains, battered and bruised. Although some people go to parlors to receive these services without follow-up sex, it generally occurs as part of a sexual encounter. Needless to say, this is not the type of sexual activity that has a high following. Leo, J. Sexes: Stomping and whomping galore. *Time* 73–74, May 4, 1981.

stressors: A strange or new partner; a heavy meal taken with alcoholic beverages; intense guilt feelings; and a fear of detection.[19] Women rarely get heart attacks from extramarital acts; they primarily become burdened with guilt feelings. Possibly in the next few years, with more women working in stressful occupations, the incidence of postsexual intercourse heart attacks will increase in women. Partly related to the incidence of extramarital sex, is the finding that the divorce rate in the United States has doubled between the years 1965 and 1975.[13]

Group sex and mate swapping* are not widespread. Figures indicate that only about 2 percent of the married population engage in "mate swapping," and less than 1 percent of married women have had sexual relations with other partners in the presence of their spouse.[5]

Regardless of the type of sexual activity, women appear to be more disturbed by outside distractions than are men. However, there are differences with women in this regard. In a study comparing orgasmic women with nonorgasmic women, it was found that the orgasmic women were much less disturbed by outside noise than were the nonorgasmic women.[20] The women who regularly achieved orgasm also were more satisfied with a variety of sexual positions than were the nonorgasmic women. The orgasmic women liked "sex for sex's sake." They looked to "sex for recreation" rather than only "sex for procreation."

Not all women enjoy sex for recreation. In fact, a recent survey found that among married women, sex was not the favorite activity. (See Box 10.1)

Whether women enjoy sex for fun or to have children they are concerned with not getting infected and not being constantly pregnant. In that regard let us now consider contraception methods.

Box 10.1.   Wives Prefer Reading to Sex.

A survey was taken on leisure-time preferences of a random sample of middle-class married couples in a Southeastern city.[21] The husbands and wives were asked to select their favorite leisure activities from a list of ninety-six possibilities. The majority of men picked "engaging in sex" as number one, followed by "attending athletic events," and "reading books." Most women ranked "reading books" first. "Sex" was a distant second, just nosing out "sewing for pleasure" by one percentage point. Perhaps younger married women might have different preferences.

* In male chauvinistic circles, this is known as "wife swapping."

CONTRACEPTION

Although contraception methods have been emphasized in recent years with the coming of the pill, methods to prevent pregnancy were practiced for centuries (see Box 10.2). Birth control is primarily a concern and responsibility of women. Many women object to this and rightfully so. But even if men took a greater role, if contraception fails, it is women who would suffer the direct consequence and most of the stress. Considering this, let us examine the stress potential of the current kinds of contraceptive methods.

Abstinence

Abstinence from sexual intercourse is a widely practiced method of birth control. However, this does not mean that all sexual activities are not performed, only sexual intercourse is forgone. Other noncoital methods are used such as: petting to orgasm; mutual masturbation; fellatio and cunnilingus (oral sex); and anal intercourse. Masturbation and nocturnal emission ("wet dreams") are either self-induced or naturally occurring. While all of these techniques add to the variety of the sexual experience and the potential enjoyment, there may be associated anxiety and guilt if routine sexual intercourse is continually avoided. One advantage of abstinence is its effectiveness for birth control. One method of partial abstinence is less predictable; that is, the rhythm method.

Box 10.2.   Birth Control Throughout History.

Historically, birth-control methods have been practiced throughout the ages. One of the most prevalent methods was abstinence. The early Christians advocated abstinence for both moral reasons and character building. St. Paul put it this way: "It is good for a man not to touch a woman."*
The Christians believed that conservation of sperm was equivalent to conservation of energy, and thus the abstaining male would live longer and have fewer diseases.[2] This belief is still held by the Hindus.

All during the nineteenth century, abstinence was advocated both for moral and religious reasons. Probably little thought was given to the negative effect of multiple pregnancies on women. As the concept was that sex was needed only for procreation, it was a woman's moral duty to have several children, but sex for pleasure was frowned upon. Hence, the practice of abstinence was more for reasons of sanctity than for limiting the number of births. Malthus (1776–1834), who was one of the first advocates of birth control to defuse the population explosion, favored abstinence as

* I Corinthians 7:1.

an effective method. In the Victorian era, upper-class women were supposed to abstain from sex unless they were to have children. The men, as usual, had it better since they could have their "sex" with lower-class prostitutes.

Abstinence was not the only measure used. There were several crude techniques including the stuffing of rags into the vagina, and the intravaginal introduction of chemicals to slow down or kill the sperm. Such chemicals included honey, sodium carbonate, and a paste of crocodile dung. Casanova's method was to take one-half of a squeezed lemon and insert it over the front of the uterus (theoretically the acid would kill the sperm). With some women, he also placed a "gold ball" in the vagina to physically block the passage of sperm.[2,22]

Although not specifically advocated as birth-control methods, these measures discussed by a thirteenth-century bishop were judged to cause failure of conception: (1) the women laying on top of the man (the sperm would fall out); (2) the female arising, jumping up and down or sneezing soon after intercourse (the sperm would dislodge); and (3) the woman urinating after intercourse (the force would dislodge the sperm and the acid would kill the sperm; it was not realized that the urethra and vagina had separate openings).[23]

Fallopius, a sixteenth-century physician, was credited with inventing the condom which was originally devised to prevent syphilis. His condom was made of linen; soon others made of catgut followed. Casanova, to protect his image as a great lover, also used condoms, but he used them to prevent the pregnancy of his partners. The big event of the 1876 Philadelphia Centennial was the introduction of the first vulcanized rubber condom.[13]

Diaphragmlike devices were also known. One was introduced in the 1870s and was known as a "womb veil." Others of various designs followed. One looked like a long-stemmed mushroom and was known as a "stem pessary." Contraceptive potions were taken for ages. David Defoe of Robinson Crusoe fame wrote of women taking "purgations, potions and poisons."[23]

As can be seen, there were no paucity of birth-control methods attempted but success was questionable considering the high rate of pregnancies. Throughout the ages, the burden of birth control fell upon the women, with the possible exception of the condom and that was originally designed to prevent the male's "catching" syphilis from wayward women.

The Rhythm Method

The rhythm method, which is advocated by the Catholic Church, is based on abstinence during the woman's fertile period, which is generally about three days during the middle of the menstrual cycle. Unfortunately, the time of ovulation, when a woman is fertile, is not too predictable. Studies have shown that two-thirds of women have irregular periods so that the calendar rhythm method is not reliable.[2] The temperature rhythm method is based on a slight temperature drop at the time of ovulation followed by a rise of a half-degree or more. It, too, is not that reliable as some women have very slight temperature changes, and many women don't want to take the time and effort to prepare daily temperature charts.[24] Using the rhythm method can induce stress because of its unreliability (considered to be about 70 percent effective) and the extra burden of daily calculations.[25] Most Catholic women choose to decrease the stress from uncertainty regarding contraception by using more effective contraceptive methods.[26]

Having sexual intercourse around the time of menstruation is also not foolproof since conception occasionally can occur during that time period. Although women who breast-feed tend to have a temporary absence of menstruation (postpartum amenorrhea), having coitus during that period is also not a safe method of birth control for the following three reasons: (1) Not all women have postpartum amenorrhea. (2) If women do have a delay in menstruation, ovulation will occur about two weeks before the renewed "period," and they would be fertile during that time.[2] (3) There are no reliable statistics on the effectiveness of this method.[25]

One other not too reliable method of partial abstinence is coitus interruptus.

Coitus Interruptus (Withdrawal)

In this method, the male withdraws from the vagina just before he has an ejaculation. This technique is particularly stressful for the female because:

1. The women must rely on the man having enough control to prevent his ejaculation within the vagina.
2. With some men, the Cowper's glands, which secrete mucous lubricating fluid before ejaculation, contain sperm. Hence, even without intravaginal ejaculation, viable sperm can penetrate and cause conception.
3. Some men can have a partial ejaculation and not be aware of it.
4. If the man ejaculates close to the vulva, motile sperm may find their way into the vagina.[2]

If a woman has to worry about all these possibilities, this would probably decrease her enjoyment and reduce her orgasmic potential. Nevertheless, there are men who are very effective with coitus interruptus (it has

been estimated to be about 80 percent effective).* They can delay ejaculation until the woman achieves orgasm. With respect to this method, the best advice for women is to get to know your partner(s).
Another not too effective method is douching.

Douching

Douching after sexual intercourse has been tried with just about everything (e.g., tap water, vinegar, herbs, and wines). Tap water is effective in killing sperm, but the sperm travels so rapidly into the cervix that the douche often fails to reach them. A woman who relies on douching would be increasing her stress level since it is only about 65 percent effective.[2,25]
Another popular but questionable method is the use of chemicals.

Foams, Creams, and Jellies

These sound like desserts but are in reality chemical methods used to destroy and inhibit sperm. They are supposed to be placed inside the vagina a few minutes prior to ejaculation and should be repeated before subsequent ejaculations. When used alone they are better than douches and are considered to be anywhere from 75 to 95 percent effective.[2,25] They are even more effective when used in combination with condoms and diaphragms.

Condoms

Nowadays, the condom (penile sheath, prophylactic) is made of thin rubber or sheep intestines to allow for protection against venereal disease and containment of the sperm, and still allow for effective sexual stimulation of the penis. It is the best method available (aside from abstinence) to protect against venereal diseases. The use of the condom is also a very effective contraceptive method and is considered to be about 95 percent successful.[25] The major disadvantage is that the placement of the condom disrupts the continuity and spontaneity of the lovemaking. For the male, condom use, even with the very thin rubber type, still somewhat impedes the sensitivity of the penis. But considering the other advantages it is still an excellent method. The condom is the only male method of contraception (aside from withdrawal); it doesn't require a medical examination or a fitting; and it is relatively inexpensive. That is why it is the most popular method of birth control.

* A recent study at Johns Hopkins University revealed that coitus interruptus is the most popular method of birth control with teen-agers, and for them, it is the most unreliable. O'Brien, P. Study: Teen pregnancies increasing. *Philadelphia Inq.* 3-A, October 17, 1980.

The problems with condoms are minor. One is that occasionally they are either defective or old and can tear. If this occurs inside the vagina, then conception is possible. The other problem with condom use is that the penis must be firm and erect for the condom to be placed over it. Sometimes ejaculation occurs before placement. Other times the lovemaking becomes so passionate that the partners forget about the application of the condom.

When the condom is used with foam or jellies, then contraception approaches 100 percent.[25] Considering that venereal diseases are quite high in teen-agers (5–10 percent of the population) and that the use of the condom and foams and jellies require neither prescriptions nor medical examinations, it would be a great advantage if teen-agers used these methods in combination. Their combined use also emphasizes the concept that contraception is a shared responsibility of females and males.[25] Parents might argue that the use will increase their children's sexual activity, but it is better to prevent conception than to have abortions and teen-age mothers. Also, studies of teen-agers have shown that contraceptive use does not determine whether or not they will have sexual relations. Quite often teen-agers have been quite experienced sexually before they decided to use contraception methods.[27]

One relatively effective method of contraception requires a physician's help; that is the diaphragm.

The Diaphragm

A diaphragm is a shallow thin rubber cup placed in a flexible ring. It is fitted by a physician to cover the cervix and prevent the entrance of sperm. This mechanical barrier is enhanced by the use of chemical creams or jellies that kill sperm and also act as lubricants.

The stressful aspect of diaphragm use is, as with the condom, the realization that there must be disruption of the lovemaking to insert the device. If advanced planning is done, then there is no interruption. However, some women don't like to plan ahead for sexual activities; it compromises the spontaneity. In fact, when they repeatedly prepare for sex by inserting a diaphragm or use some similar method, some women develop a "prostitution anxiety."[28] For them there is the conflict between engaging in either marital, premarital, nonmarital, or extramarital sex, and being a moral or "nice" woman.

They may also have the problem of not wanting to become pregnant and at the same time not wanting to plan ahead for contraception. This double bind could cause them to avoid contraceptions like the diaphragm, become pregnant, and then worry about whether or not to have an abortion.[25] The best thing for a woman to do is to make a decision one way or the other regarding her sexual activities and contraceptive methods. Then she should not worry over the correctness of the decision.

Two other possible problems with diaphragm use are: the diaphragm may be incorrectly inserted; and it can slip during sexual intercourse. Nevertheless, if a diaphragm is correctly inserted and used regularly it can be a highly effective means of birth control (about 90 percent successful).[2,25]

Another more permanent insertion method also requires medical intervention. This is the intrauterine device (IUD).

The IUD

IUDs are effective contraceptive devices that are made of plastic or metal and are inserted semipermanently into a woman's uterus. They act to prevent the implantation of a formed zygote on the wall of the uterus. They are about 98 percent effective.[2,25] Some have antifertility agents such as progestagen or copper incorporated. The major advantage of the IUD is that it obviates planning ahead. There are also no daily pills to take, diaphragms to insert, or calendars to watch. Once it is in place, it can be ignored (except for periodic examinations or unless symptoms develop) and it allows the woman to enjoy her sexual activities without being concerned with conception.

There are some possible problems with the IUD. First, as the IUD is a foreign substance it can act as an antigen and be rejected (happens about 10 percent of the time in the first year). However, about 40 percent of those rejected "take" on the second try.[29] Cramps and bleeding can occur after insertion of the IUD, but this is generally a temporary reaction. If incorrectly placed, the uterus can be perforated and severe infections can occur. This is rare but it is a consideration for women who contemplate this method of birth control. Some women cannot tolerate the regular IUD but the copper type is smaller and may be better managed.[25] The latest model of the copper IUD is reported to cause less expulsion, bleeding and pain than the previous models.[30]

Recent evidence has uncovered some additional possible problems with the IUD. The National Women's Health Network asked in a lawsuit that A. H. Robins Company recall their type IUD, the Dalkon shield. The contention is that the string tail could erode and increase the risk of infection and sterility. The company denies the allegation.[43] On another front, researchers at the University of Texas Medical School have uncovered evidence that calcium builds up on IUDs and causes pelvic infection. The calcium deposits appear to be the body's response to the foreign substance (the IUD). The calcium layer acts as a site for actinomyces bacteria to grow and this can lead to the virulent infection, actinomycosis, which can result in sterility. To prevent calcium build-up, the researchers advocate IUD replacement every two years.[44]

The IUD along with birth-control pills have become very popular in the last ten years. Currently, about 15 million women use them in the United States.[25]

Oral Contraceptives

There are many varieties of oral contraceptives but they are principally a combination of synthetic progesterone (Progestagen) and synthetic estrogen. The pills act to initiate pregnancy-like hormonal changes and prevent the maturation of the ova (eggs). They also tend to prevent implantation of a fertilized ovum on the uterine surface and act to impede sperm invasion in the uterus.[2]

The pill has been both a boon and a bust for women. The major advantage of birth-control pills is that they are a very effective contraceptive method (over 98 percent successful).[25] Like the IUD, it allows sex to be completely separated from procreation. The advantage over the IUD is that there is no surgical implantation. The disadvantage is that the pills have to be taken on a daily basis without fail, or else conception can occur (presuming that sexual intercourse takes place).

We have already mentioned in Chapter 3, the major problems with long-term use of birth control pills (e.g., the possibilities of uterine and liver cancers, blood-clotting disorders, stroke, headaches, and depression). Most of these negative changes are related to the estrogen content of the oral contraceptives. Newer "pills" have been marketed with a lower estrogen content, and fewer side effects. Nevertheless, women must realize that when hormones (as in the oral contraceptives) are introduced into the body on a regular basis, there can be negative reactions. Women should consider this in their evaluation of methods of birth control. Apparently not all women are that concerned with the negative effects of the pill. In that recent *Cosmopolitan* survey of 106,000 women, 40 percent of them said that they still used the pill for birth control.[16]*

* There is also some recent evidence that the pill is not too much of a health risk for many women. A researcher at the National Center for Disease Control stated that for women under the age of 30, the pill is relatively safe and most advantageous for birth control. Evidence shows that the pill reduces the incidence of benign breast tumors, benign ovarian cysts and iron deficiencies. The women at the greatest risk from taking the pill are women over 30, especially if they smoke. Associated Press. Pill a health plus, doctor contends. *Philadelphia*

Many women ask, "Why isn't there a male pill?" This is a reasonable question and the male pill is under investigation. Right now there is no currently effective and safe pill available. Also, even if there were a male pill available, the woman still runs the risk of pregnancy and she would have to be certain the man took his pill.[25]

Another problem with oral contraceptive use is that it has diminished the use of the condom. This has caused an increase in the incidence of venereal disease (VD) since the pill offers no such protection. In Sweden the government began a campaign to encourage the widespread use of the condom and, partly as a result, the incidence of VD has declined.[13]

If a woman has any concern about being infected she should go to a physician. Syphilis, gonorrhea, and other venereal diseases are generally easily managed with antibiotics when they are treated early.

Birth control can also be managed after the fact. One way is with "day-after pills." These contain high levels of estrogen and are meant to be taken for five to seven days. The pills commonly cause nausea and other side effects and therefore shouldn't be routinely used for contraception.[25]

The other major postintercourse method of birth control is abortion.

Abortion

Abortion means the termination of the fetus before it is considered viable (generally regarded as being before the onset of the seventh month).[2] As the result of the U.S. Supreme Court decision of 1973, abortion has become the principal method of postcoitus birth control and is one of the most frequently performed operations (over 1 million per year).[2,25]

Although it is popular now, abortions have been performed throughout the ages. (See Box 10.3) Currently, there are various methods to induce abortion. *Menstrual extraction* (menstrual aspiration or induction) is the removal of the endometrial lining of the uterus, and the embryo (if present) via the vagina. It can only be done in the first four weeks of pregnancy. The advantage of menstrual extraction is that it is an office procedure and relatively nontraumatic, both physically and psychologically. It can also be done without the necessity of confirming the pregnancy.[33]

Another effective new method is the use of *prostaglandins*. These chemical substances are self-administered as vaginal suppositories and are

---

Inq. 3-A, December 24, 1980. Even the danger of blood clotting may be reduced according to the findings of a Duke University researcher. A factor known as plasminogen activator is involved in clot breakdown. This factor increases in the blood of women who exercise regularly. Although his results are not finalized, the investigator suggests that women who take the pill should exercise vigorously for $\frac{1}{2}$ hour, three times a week (see Chapter 21). Kolata, G. B. Exercise, blood clots, and the pill. *Science* 211: 913, 1981.

Box 10.3   Abortion Throughout the Ages.

Five thousand years ago, the Chinese used mercury to induce abortions. Other primitive methods that were used in antiquity included herbs and drugs of all sorts that were either ingested or injected directly into the uterus. Women were also advised to jump up and down and use other forms of violent exercise. If these didn't work, then beating and stomping on the woman's abdomen was attempted.[31] A primitive Hawaiian tribe used an abortion stick, which was a sharp pointed curved wooden utensil, designed to be introduced into the vagina.[2]

When one considers the crudeness of these methods plus the absence of anesthesia, it is apparent that women were forced to undergo extreme torture in order not to bear children. Maybe it was a blessing in disguise that the ancient Hebrews ruled that abortion was only permitted to save a mother's life, and the Christians forebade abortion under any circumstances.[32] Some women might have considered that it was better to deliver a child than to suffer through the available crude methods of abortion. Even with the pain, and the disapproval of the church, abortion was practiced in an illegal form for centuries. The desire not to have unwanted children and the ability to have sexual relations without childbirth forced many women to attempt abortion. Since there were no really effective methods of birth control, abortion became the principal method of preventing childbirth.

Up to the time of the Supreme Court decision in 1973, many women who agreed to abortion had to worry about the illegality of the procedure and had fears related to unsanitary conditions and incompetent operations. In addition, there was possible guilt about the death of the fetus. With abortion now being the law of the land, women no longer have to be concerned with the legality aspect or the safety of the procedure.* Currently, when done within the first twelve weeks, abortions are among the safest operations.[25]

highly successful.[34] It is hoped that they will soon be available for home use by women. The side effects are transient episodes of uterine pain and vomiting and diarrhea.[25]

From the fourth to the twelfth week of pregnancy, the usual methods of abortion are *uterine aspiration* (similar to menstrual extraction) and *dilatation and curettage* ("D & C"). After twelve weeks, more extreme surgical methods are done along with prostaglandin infusion. *Saline (salt)-induced* abortions are also done in some clinics during this time period.[35] Abortions

* With the passage of the Hyde amendment, lower-income women no longer receive government financial support for abortions; hence, they find themselves in a monetary bind. There is also the possibility that an amendment to prohibit abortion except to save the mother's life might eventually pass and become the law of the land.

are performed because of rape, incest, danger to the life of the mother, knowledge of a malformed fetus, and primarily to prevent unwanted pregnancies.[25]

Although many women have guilt feelings or feelings of regret or grief before or soon after they have an abortion, follow-up studies have shown that after several years "no regrets" is the most typical response.[25] In addition, since the advent of legalized abortion there has been a major decline in: deaths and complications from illegal abortions; rates of illegitimate births; and infant mortality.[36]

Aside from abstinence, the most effective way to prevent childbirth is to become sterilized.

Sterilization

In Chapter 8, we discussed the sterilization methods and the various types of hysterectomy. As mentioned before, the most traumatic is the complete hysterectomy in which the ovaries and uterus are removed. Vasectomy is the male sterilization procedure. Tubal ligation and vasectomy are relatively simple surgical procedures, and each can generally be completed in less than a half-hour. Attesting to the popularity of these new methods, it is now estimated that about 15 percent of couples in the United States use sterilization as a contraceptive method.[25]

Even though these are reversible sterilization techniques, they are not yet perfected. Therefore, the decision for or against sterilization must be carefully weighed. Women should never undergo sterilization unless they are certain they do not want any more children. Unfortunately, with the present high divorce rate, "today's certainty may be tomorrow's doubt." A newly married woman might want to have additional children with her new husband. However, some women want to be freed of the burden of having more children whether or not they get divorced and remarried. For many women, the emotional and financial rewards of not having additional children are well worth the price of sterilization.

In some cases, the problem is not having too many children but rather not being able to have any children or being able to achieve sexual satisfaction.

SEXUAL DYSFUNCTION

Sexual dysfunction is a catch-all term that includes general sexual dysfunction, frigidity, orgasmic dysfunction, vaginismus, premature ejaculation, and organic dysfunction. Impotence and infertility were discussed in Chapter 3.

General Sexual Dysfunction

General sexual dysfunction is the scientific term for what is generally known as frigidity. However, in psychoanalytic terminology, frigidity is usually limited to orgasmic dysfunction. Women who have general sexual dysfunction either are afraid of sexual relations, have no sexual desire, find sex revolting, consider sex a chore, can't get sexually stimulated or have a low self-esteem.[2,37,38]

Orgasmic Dysfunction

Orgasmic dysfunction is the inability to achieve orgasm. From a Freudian viewpoint, a woman suffering from frigidity never achieves vaginal orgasm because her sexuality is fixed at the immature childhood clitoral stage. The frigid woman is supposed to have unresolved penis envy.[39] The findings of Masters and Johnson show that there is only one kind of orgasm, although it can be achieved either by clitoral or vaginal stimulation.[40] Undoubtedly, some frigid women are envious of men and their cultural advantages, but it is not necessarily penis envy (see Chapter 5).

Some women never achieve orgasm; others can achieve orgasm under certain circumstances; while still others can achieve orgasm only by masturbation. All women do not achieve orgasm and it is considered possible for women to have sexual pleasure without having orgasm.[20]

Vaginismus

In vaginismus, the muscles surrounding the outer third of the vagina contract tightly whenever anything attempts to penetrate the vagina. This relatively rare condition can occur in sexually nonresponsive women and occasionally in women who are sexually active and orgasmic. Any penetration causes pain and results in frustrating sexual relations.[2]

Male Sexual Dysfunction

Sexual dysfunction in the male is primarily premature ejaculation. Other problems are inability to maintain an erection and inability to achieve penetration. A woman who attempts having coitus with a male afflicted with these dysfunctions would be stressed because of her own failure to achieve satisfaction. Therefore, for her own benefit she should insist that the man obtain treatment. If he refuses, the woman should consider an alternate sexual partner, unless she is otherwise satisfied with the relationship.

Organic Sexual Dysfunction

Surgery or illness affecting the genitals can cause sexual dysfunctions.[37] However, a more frequent cause of inadequate sexual relations is fear of heart attack in the male with heart disease. Studies have shown that the male-on-top position is not more stressful than the man-on-bottom position (as was formerly believed). A general rule of thumb which has recently been verified is that if the patient can climb two flights of stairs without symptoms, then he can resume sexual activity with his usual sexual partner. This should reduce the stress for male cardiac patients and their partners.[41]

Etiology

Most cases of sexual dysfunction are related to these factors: (1) repression of sexuality in childhood; (2) shame and guilt about the sex act; (3) fear of failure, performance anxiety, fear of rejection or fear of not being able to please a partner; (4) anxiety about "letting go" and losing control; (5) anger, fear or distrust of men; (6) previous unpleasant sexual relations with men; (7) lack of strong emotional ties in previous relations; and (8) inadequate stimulation by partner.[4,37]

Treatment

There are two main approaches to treatment. One, the formerly traditional method, is psychoanalysis in which the underlying causes are probed (usually childhood repression).[39] It is a long-term approach but can be effective. The other method is sex therapy which has been popularized by the work of Masters and Johnson.[4,40] Here the relief of symptoms is the purpose of the therapy; underlying causes are not generally probed. Sex therapy involves the patient (often male and female together) in exercises and tasks to help overcome the psychological problems that have induced the dysfunction.[4,40] Helen Kaplan, a renowned woman psychiatrist, offers a combined approach of treating symptoms and attempting to deal with the unconscious etiology.[6]

Sex therapy is generally considered to be effective. Masters and Johnson report an overall cure rate of 80 percent,[40] although recent investigators question the validity of some of their statistics.[42]

Women who have problems in achieving orgasm, tolerating coitus or enjoying sexual relations may be anxious, frustrated, worried, and angry. In other words, they can be under stress. Sex therapy, which can be considered a form of psychotherapy, is a means to help them resolve their stressful sexual problems. It may be of particular advantage for women to have sex therapy by a woman therapist.[37] Depending upon the person and the particular problem, therapy can be on an individual basis, with the sexual partner, or as part of a group.

It has been found that meditation or self-hypnosis are useful methods to induce deep relaxation and help alleviate the anxiety about the sexual act. They also help block out distractions such as noise and personal problems which can interfere with the sexual performance.

One thing that can definitely interfere with the sexual performance is when the act is forced. This is covered in the next chapter where rape and incest are considered.

REFERENCES

1. Haller, J. S. and Haller, R. M. *The Physician and Sexuality in Victorian America*. Urbana, Ill.: University of Illinois Press, 1974.
2. Williams, J. H. *Psychology of Women: Behavior in a Biosocial Context*. New York: W.W. Norton, 1977.
3. Kinsey, A. C., Pomeroy, W. B., Martin, C. E., and Gebhard, P. H. *Sexual Behavior in the Human Female*. Philadelphia: W. B. Saunders, 1953.
4. Masters, W. and Johnson, V. *Human Sexual Response*. Boston: Little, Brown, 1966.
5. Hunt, M. *Sexual Behavior in the Seventies*. Playboy Press, 1974.
6. Kaplan, H. S. *The New Sex Therapy*. New York: Brunner/Mazel, 1974.
7. Kleeman, J. A. Freud's views on early female sexuality in the light of direct child observation. *In* Blum, H. P. (ed.), *Female Psychology: Contemporary Psychoanalytic Views*. New York: International Universities Press, 1977, pp. 3–27.
8. Huerter, R. Female sexuality. *In* Kjervik, D. K. and Martinson, I. M. (eds.), *Women in Stress: A Nursing Perspective*. New York: Appleton-Century-Crofts, 1979, pp. 96–115.
9. Hellerstein, H. K. and Friedman, E. H. Sexual activity and the post-coronary patient. *Arch. Intern. Med.* **125:**987–999, 1970.
10. Nemec, E. D., Mansfield, L., and Kennedy, J. W. Heart rate and blood pressure responses during sexual activity in normal males. *Am. Heart J.* **92:**274–277, 1976.
11. Stein, R. A. The effect of exercise training on heart rate during coitus in the post myocardial infarction patient. *Circulation* **55:**738–740, 1977.
12. Smith, R. *The Dieter's Guide to Weight Loss During Sex*. New York: Workman Publishing, 1978.
13. Reiss, I. L. Heterosexual relationships of patients: Premarital, marital and extramarital. *In* Green, R. (ed.), *Human Sexuality: A Health Practitioner's Text*. Baltimore: Williams & Wilkins. 1979, pp. 83–97.
14. Kinsey, A. C., Pomeroy, W. B., and Martin, C. E. *Sexual Behavior in the Human Male*. Philadelphia: W. B. Saunders, 1948.
15. Ringer, R. J. *Looking Out for #1*. New York: Fawcett Crest Books, 1977.
16. Wolfe, L. The sexual profile of that Cosmopolitan Girl. *Cosmopolitan* 254–257, 263–265. September, 1980.
17. Hunt, M. *The Affair*. New York: New American Library, 1973.
18. Wagner, N. N. and Sivarajan, E. S. Sexual activity and the cardiac patient. *In* Green, R.

(ed.), *Human Sexuality: A Health Practitioner's Text.* Baltimore: Williams & Wilkins, 1979, pp. 193-200.

19. Editorial. The penalty of sin. *Exec. Fitness Newsletter*, Sample, Issue 1, 1977.

20. Shope, D. F. *Interpersonal Sexuality.* Philadelphia: W. B. Saunders, 1975.

21. Newsline. Sexuality: It says here wives prefer reading to sex. *Psychol. Today* 13(3): 17, 1979.

22. Himes, N. E. *Medical History of Contraception.* New York: Gamut Press, 1963.

23. Wood, C. and Suitters, B. *The Fight for Acceptance.* Aylesbury, England: Med. Tech. Publ. Co., 1972.

24. McCary, J. L. *Human Sexuality.* New York: D. Van Nostrand, 1973.

25. Diamond, M. Sex and reproduction: Conception and contraception. *In* Green, R. (ed.), *Human Sexuality: A Health Practitioner's Text.* Baltimore: Williams & Wilkins, 1979, pp. 59-80.

26. Westoff, C. F. and Jones, E. F. The secularization of U. S. Catholic birth control practices. *Fam. Plan. Perspectives* 9:203-207, 1977.

27. Fordney-Settlage, D., Baroft, S., and Cooper, D. Sexual experience of younger teenage girls seeking contraceptive assistance for the first time. *Fam. Plan. Perspectives* 5:223-228, 1973.

28. Bardwick, J. Psychological factors in the acceptance and use of oral contraceptives. *In* Fawcet, J. T. (ed.), *Psychological Perspectives on Population,* 1973.

29. Westoff, L. A. and Westoff, C. F. *From Now to Zero: Fertility, Contraception and Abortion in America.* Boston: Little, Brown, 1971.

30. Thiery, M., Van Der Pas, H., Van Os., W. A. A., Tanber, P. F., Dombrowicz, N., MacDonald, J. S., Haspels, A. A., Drogendijk, A. C., Van Kets, H., and Boogers, W. Three years experience with the ML Cu 250, a new copper-wired intrauterine contraception device. *Adv. Planned Parenthood* 13(3):35-40, 1980.

31. Bates, J. E. and Zawadzki, E. S. *Criminal Abortion.* Springfield, Ill.: Charles C. Thomas, 1964.

32. Hall, R. E. (ed.), *Abortion in a Changing World.* New York: Columbia University Press, 1970.

33. Watson, W. B., Menstrual regulation: The method and the issues. *Studies Fam. Plan.* 8:250-278, 1977.

34. Dillon, W. P., Chaudhuri, G., Hurd, M., and Lippes, J. Evacuation of the uterus by intravaginal PGE2 suppositories: A comparison of clinical effectiveness. *Adv. Planned Parenthood* 13(3):30-34, 1980.

35. Robins, J. A clinical comparison of intra-amniotic prostaglandins F2 alpha and intra-amniotic hypertonic saline for mid trimester pregnancy termination. *Adv. Planned Parenthood* 13(2):27-34, 1980.

36. Kinzer, N. S. *Stress and the American Woman.* New York: Ballantine Books, 1980.

37. Rosenbaum, M. Treatment of sexual concern by the primary care female clinician. *In* Green, R. (ed.), *Human Sexuality: A Health Practitioner's Text.* Baltimore: Williams & Wilkins, 1979, pp. 277-286.

38. Rosoff, L. Helping women find their sexuality. *Philadelphia Inq.* 1-I, 2-I, August 3, 1980.

39. Moore, B. E. Psychic representation and female orgasm. *In* Blum, H. P. (ed.), *Female Psychology: Contemporary Psychoanalytic Views.* New York: International Universities Press, 1977, pp. 305-330.

40. Masters, W. H. and Johnson, V. E. *Human Sexual Inadequacy.* Boston: Little, Brown, 1970.

41. Wagner, N. N. and Sivarajan, E. S. Sexual activity and the cardiac patient. *In* Green, R.

(ed.), *Human Sexuality: A Health Practitioner's Text.* Baltimore: Williams & Wilkins, 1979, pp. 193–200.

42. Zilbergeld, B. and Evans, M. The inadequacy of Masters and Johnson. *Psychol. Today* **14**(3):28–43, 1980.

43. The Scene: Home, health, family finances. P.S.: About the Dalkon shield. *Philadelphia Inq.* 13-A, January 9, 1981.

44. The Scene: Home, health, family finances. Birth control: IUD change advocated. *Philadelphia Inq.* 2-D, March 5, 1981.

11
Violent Sex: Incest and Rape

INTRODUCTION

In the last ten years, there has been a tremendous increase in the reported incidence of incest and rape. For example, in that recent *Cosmopolitan* magazine survey of 106,000 women, 10 percent of them said they had engaged in incest.[1] However, most incest cases are probably not reported. A recent Los Angeles survey extimated that 90 percent of all incest goes unreported.[2] It is believed that incest occurs in one out of ten families in the United States.[3]

In 1976, FBI statistics showed 65,000 forcible rapes in the United States.[4] This was an increase of 166 percent in the last 15 years.[5] Yet, that is only the tip of the iceberg. More recent estimates are that there are about half a million rapes occurring each year in this country.[5-7]

It used to be thought that the child molestor and sexual abuser was the stereotypical "dirty old man" flashing his genitals, or the stranger offering candy, but most cases of childhood sexual abuse occur with family members.[2] In that aforementioned *Cosmopolitan* survey, 47 percent of the women who reported incest stated that it involved a brother. Thirty-one percent had incestual relationships with their father and 22 percent had incest with their uncle.[1]

A similar relationship exists with rape. Although there are undoubtedly rapes committed by complete strangers, recent statistics reveal that more and more women are being raped by people they know or with whom they have had an acquaintance.[8] And most rapes take place in the victim's own home, not in a dark, dingy alley.[7,9] In addition, it is now legal in several states for a woman to prosecute her husband for rape.[10]

With this introduction on incidence, let us begin with a discussion of the stress from incest.

INCEST[2,3]

Incest often starts off as an innocent flirtation; e.g., the young girl sitting on the man's lap. This then can lead to casual touching of the breasts and genitals. Finally, genital penetration is attempted. The child may first be primed with alcoholic beverages or sweets. Since the child is often quite young, she may not even realize that anything is wrong or abnormal. Although incest often starts off innocently, and may even be mutually pleasurable, it usually turns toward coercion and violence.

Sexual abuse generally goes hand-in-hand with child abuse (see Chapter 5), and abusing parents have often been abused themselves as children. In fact, incest often runs in families over generations.

There are certain patterns in incest families:

1. The father is often an alcoholic and prone to violence.
2. The mother is frequently absent from the home (may be divorced, separated or working).
3. The mother may be chronically ill or depressed.
4. The mother is often passive and nonassertive.
5. The parents do not have a good sexual relationship.
6. The mother is not affectionate with either her husband or the daughter.
7. The father and daughter are often together and may even share the same bed.
8. The father is hostile toward outsiders.
9. The daughter may play the "little mother" role in the family because of her mother's absence or incapacity.

Quite often the parents deny the incest; the family may have a secrecy bond. The usual reasons are:

1. They are afraid of shame, embarrassment, and humiliation if the truth comes out.
2. They fear the husband (if he is the perpetrator) will leave and the family will break up.
3. They are concerned that the daughter will be taken from the family.
4. They need money, and if the father is the perpetrator and goes to jail, the family will lose income.
5. There is the worry that there will be retaliation by the perpetrator.
6. They fear negative reactions, blame and ostracization by relatives and friends.

The female victim of incest is also reluctant to talk because she: (1) fears being punished; (2) is afraid no one will believe her; (3) feels isolated from her friends; (4) feels ashamed and humiliated; (5) blames herself and feels guilty; (6) feels confused about how it got started; (7) fears hostility and rejection from other members of the family if she reports the incident; and (8) doesn't understand the nature of the act (i.e., can't differentiate incest from affection).

However, incest should be uncovered because if not stopped it tends to be repeated and there are harmful effects to the child. The young girl often develops feelings of guilt and low self-esteem, and fear of sexual relations. She may become an alcoholic; a drug addict; severely depressed; suicidal; a prostitute; or engage in criminal activities. Approximately 70 percent of the women in prisons throughout the United States were victims of incest or sexual abuse as children.[3]

If there is incest in the family, it generally is up to the mother or older sibling to report it. The police should be notified and groups such as *Women Against Rape* (WAR) are most helpful in getting or giving counsel, obtaining legal advice, and helping to maintain the safety of the child. WAR has a twenty-four-hour "hot-line" and has good rapport with the municipal police authorities.

Freud postulated the Oedipus (Electra) complex in which young girls and boys were attracted to the parents of the opposite sex (see Chapter 5). These natural flirtations are generally not dangerous but they can be the seed of incest. That is why it is important to prevent incest. Certain things to bear in mind are:

1. Children should be taught that no one, including "mommy" or "daddy" has a right to touch their bodies sexually.
2. Children must be informed that they should not take bribes, such as candy and toys in exchange for not telling the truth about things done to them.
3. Children should be told that they will not be punished if they tell when they have been touched sexually by anyone.
4. Young girls should not be permitted to sleep in the same room or bed with their fathers. They should also not be left alone with their uncles, grandfathers, or other relative if there are any suspicions about sexual activities.

Not all women who have had incestuous relations as children become psychologically disturbed adults. Programs such as those by WAR are very helpful, and psychotherapy often allows the women to return to completely normal lives. It is important for the victims of incest to have an empathetic therapist, one who understands and can deal with the deep emotional impact.[11] A woman therapist possibly can deal better with an incest victim's problems.

Let us now consider the stress from rape.

RAPE

Introduction

Rape has always been considered morally wrong when it occurred between members of the same group. Historically though, rape was permitted or even encouraged when it was done to outsiders. Thus, it was "natural" for conquering armies to rape the women of the vanquished; it was allowable for masters to rape their slaves; and members of one tribe were permitted to rape members of another tribe.[8] Although this kind of rape still occurs, it is more generally frowned upon by society. Unfortunately, individual rape up until very recently was considered to be a crime in which the victim was often blamed. The concept was that "she asked for it," or "if she didn't flaunt herself no one would have bothered her." Also, the following beliefs were prevalent: "Nice girls don't get raped"; "a woman can't be raped unless she is willing"; and "women enjoy a secret desire to be raped."

The fact is that rape is not primarily a sexual act; it is an act of violence and no one is immune, from children eighteen months of age to eighty-eight-year-old grandmothers.[9] Furthermore, most reports indicate that rapists deliberately plan their attacks in advance.[12]

Most rapists are emotionally disturbed and violent, but they often appear to be functioning completely normally.[9] Usually they are of the same race as the victim and are generally young. The national average is eighteen years of age. The rapist is not often "starving for sex," but generally suffers from sexual dysfunction such as inability to achieve an erection. He is frequently either married or has a steady girl friend but his relationships with women are often shallow and may be violent. Almost all rapists have disorganized home lives. They often have no father and a sexually active mother. The typical rapist is angry at his mother for never giving him love or support. He tends to have an inadequate personality and harbors feelings of inferiority. But he tries to display a "macho" image. His "bad" relationship with his mother colors his feelings toward women in general. He rapes not out of sexual desire but out of anger, depression or frustration. Most rapists often pursue other criminal activities such as robbery and theft. The rapist typically acts as if he is in a trance and under questioning often denies he ever raped anyone.*[13]

A sexual assault is a violent act against the victim's will. The woman is forced to perform either genital, oral, or anal intercourse. She is subjected to coercion and beating. The woman's predominant feelings are fear of death, molestation, and bodily harm since she is threatened with either a knife, a gun, or other weapon. Her children or husband may be intimidated or threatened with harm if she does not comply. The woman has no time to prepare and feels helpless and powerless.[14] Studies have shown that not resisting is the safest choice since resisting victims are often more seriously injured (although there is some conflicting evidence on this point).[7]**

Physical Effects

Generally, the physical trauma is not too severe. There may be damage to the vagina and rectum, but the necessity for hospitalization is not frequent. Statistics show that pregnancy following rape is of low incidence (about 1 percent) and venereal disease occurrence is infrequent (about 4 percent).[5] To prevent pregnancy, high estrogen is given (diethylstilbesterol) for a few days. To prevent venereal disease, high doses of penicillin are usually given. The postrape woman may have sleep problems as the result of recurrent nightmares and also may be reluctant to eat regularly.[15]

When a woman has been raped and the rapist has left the scene, there are certain steps the victim should follow. These include the following:

1. She should not wash, douche or change clothes.
2. She should not touch anything except the telephone to call the police. The reason for this is not to destroy any evidence such as fingerprints, bite marks, hair, fingernail scratches, and bloodstains.

* To prevent repeat rapes by the rapist and to help him return to society in a more normal fashion, there are institutes giving group therapy to rapists. Such an organization is the Joseph J. Peters Institute of the Philadelphia Mental Health and Mental Retardation Program.

** A recent Philadelphia woman's retaliatory response underscored the point that resistance may be beneficial to the attempted rape victim. At about 12:40 A.M., the woman was returning home from walking a relative to the Broad Street subway. Less than 30 yards from her home, she was grabbed from behind by a stranger who began to rape her. She pushed him away, reached into her purse for her .38-caliber revolver and shot him in the leg. This did not deter him as he kept on coming towards her. Then she shot him again, killing him. Cunningham, D., and Terry, R. J. Man shot dead in rape attempt, city police say. *Philadelphia Inq.* 1-A-, 16-A, May 10, 1981.

3. She should call the emergency number of a woman's help group such as WAR to get needed counsel.

It is important for the victim to calm herself, and meditation and self-hypnosis would be helpful in that regard (see Chapter 20).

Psychological Effects

The psychological effects of rape are severe. The trauma is both immediate and of long-term duration and has been labeled the "rape trauma syndrome."[16] The immediate effects ("acute reaction") are shock, numbness, and disbelief. The woman appears dazed, confused and finds it difficult to make decisions. Her normal patterns are disorganized and disrupted.

From a few days to a week later, the victim begins to adapt ("outward adjustment"). She tries to block out and deny the experience. By repressing or postponing the feelings, the victim gives herself time to adjust to them. She attempts to return to normal activity and outwardly appears calm. In the weeks that follow, "integration and resolution" take place. But the process is painful. The woman feels the need to talk about the experience. She may feel angry at the assailant and may feel angry at herself. The woman may blame herself and may even believe the popular contentions that rape victims "ask for it" or "allow it to happen."[17] The victim may blame her specific behavior (e.g., "I shouldn't have walked alone"; or "I should have fought back"), and she may blame her character (e.g., "I deserve to be raped", or "I was so stupid").

A new study revealed that some instances of victims' blaming their own specific behavior may be helpful.[18] The victims who had that kind of self-blame (e.g., "I shouldn't have walked alone") were less depressed than victims who blamed their characters (e.g., "I was so stupid"). However, most investigators believe that rape victims should learn to realize that they were a victim and were not at fault.[7,17] Most victims often become depressed and some may become suicidal, but generally the women realize that they were not to blame.

The rape often affects the woman's sexual activities. She may initially withdraw from sexual contact but still needs physical closeness and comfort.[19] In time, the woman generally returns to normal sexual functions. The reaction of her husband (or lover) is the key. If he gives her support at this time, recovery can be smooth. Unfortunately, just at this crucial time the victim is often rejected by her husband (or lover) since he may have preconceived ideas regarding her role in the rape. The man may even downgrade the woman as his method of punishing her. Separation and divorce are not unusual following rape.[17]

Not only does the woman have problems at home, she is often harassed in the hospital, at the police station, and in court. If she decides to press charges, she has constantly to repeat her story and may be forced to defend her sexual life-style under questioning by doctors, policemen, and lawyers. She often feels that the medical staff, the police, and the jury do not believe her.[5,15,20]

Even when the rape victim goes to court and suffers all the humiliating experiences, she is by no means certain of a conviction. Until just a few years ago, only 40 percent of the rapists taken to court were convicted.[5]

It is for these reasons that many women have been reluctant to press charges. They may even try to hide the rape from their husbands (or lovers) and family. But the psychological repercussions are too severe and the cases should be brought to trial. In recent years, more realistic laws have been passed and police and hospital harassment has greatly decreased. Society is also beginning to realize that rape is a crime of violence and the women are innocent victims and should be protected.

Even with gentle handling and winning the legal battles, there is still long-term psychological trauma from rape. For weeks and months afterwards, there may ge a whole host of fears such as: fear that the attacker will return; fear of walking the streets alone; fear of crowds; fear of looking provocative; and fear of people walking behind them.[5,16] The woman may have crying spells, feelings of anxiety and irritability, and recurrent episodes of depression. As is the case with incest, victims may later on turn to prostitution.[5]

All of these negative responses can be decreased or eliminated if the rape victim receives positive support from her family, friends, the medical staff, and the legal authorities. One real advance in recent years has been the community action programs such as WAR. These organizations offer immediate counsel to the rape victim and her family. They insure proper medical and legal treatment and they offer follow-up support for years following the incident.

Let us now consider methods of preventing rape.

Rape Prevention

Rapes probably can never be completely prevented but there are ways to decrease the possibility of an attack or to thwart a would-be rapist. Although studies have shown that physically fighting back may only provoke the rapist more,[7] there are times when a rape victim has an opportunity to free herself or escape. That is why it is important for women to be in good physical condition and to learn self-defense techniques such as judo and karate. Women who are adept at running may even be able to escape. With respect to escaping, it is recommended that women not wear high heel shoes, since it is too difficult to run with them. A small packet of mace—which can cause temporary blindness—can be kept in a woman's handbag to be used in an emergency.

Nevertheless, often talking to the would-be rapist may be more helpful than trying to run away or fight back. A recent study at Temple University found that the following statements are *not* effective in "turning off" a potential rapist:[21] "Are you aware that they put people in jail for doing this?" "The cops are right around the corner!" "If you do this, my friends will find you and kill you!"

Those statements are too logical and generally not believable to the experienced rapist. Statements that might be effective work on the rapist psychologically by instilling doubt and fear. Such statements are: "I have cancer of the vagina and you'll catch it if you rape me!" "I have a bad case of syphilis!"

Curiosity-inducing statements are occasionally effective such as: "My name is Joan. What's yours? Let's get to know each other!"

Although it is hard to believe, rapists may have some moral sense. For them a statement such as, "I'm a virgin!" might work. It is a good idea to practice all these statements so that when you are in a crunch and make the statements, they sound natural and spontaneous.

To reduce the incidence of rape, here is some advice for these troubled times. If you are riding a bus or subway, especially during off hours, don't make yourself conspicuous; don't wear glistening jewelry and, if possible, don't look too attractive. (Rape is generally an act of violence, but sexual motivation should not be overlooked.) Before taking public transportation, it is a good idea to find out the schedules. That way you won't have to sit or stand outside waiting. If possible, have someone pick you up or take you to the bus or train. If you see someone in your path when you are walking (remember, high heels are *out*), walk assertively, keep your shoulders straight, act confident, and maintain eye contact. If you must walk alone on a route, try to check it out ahead of time during daylight hours. Look for potentially safe places such as an all-night supermarket and enclosed telephone booths. Running into a telephone booth, sitting on the floor and propping your legs against the closed door makes it difficult for someone to enter.[21] It would also be helpful to vary your routines; don't always follow the same path.

When returning home, always check carefully to see that no one is standing near your house. If there is someone around or something looks suspicious, don't go in. Either go to a neighbor's and call the police, or go directly to the police.

In your home, keep your doors and windows locked whenever you are alone. Close your curtains and shades in the evening. Placing objects on the inside window ledge can be helpful. If the window is forcibly opened, the noise will alert you.

Above all, don't let strangers into your home. Many times would-be rapists tell you they have had car trouble or have to go to the bathroom. Don't let them in even if they sound sincere, particularly if you happen to be alone.

Keep emergency numbers readily available in large print near each phone. Call friends or family every day so that they will be suspicious if you don't call. If you get obscene phone calls hang up immediately. If they recur, call the police.

When driving, keep car doors locked and the windows two-thirds closed. Park your car in well-lit areas and close to your destination. Always have your car keys in your hand when you are leaving a building to walk toward your car. Before you enter the car, be sure that no one is standing near it. If there is someone suspicious there, go back into the building and see if you can get an escort. If no one is available and you have any doubts, call the police.

If you are being followed in your car, don't go home. Go to a friend's, the police or an open business establishment. If you can't find any of these places, go to a well-lit area and honk your horn until someone comes out to you. Never pick up a hitchhiker and never hitch a ride.

If you are in an elevator and feel threatened, push the emergency button. If you are single, widowed, or divorced, have your telephone listing with only your first initial and last name. You may prefer to be unlisted. The same is true for mailboxes or on front doors.[22]

Baby-sitters can be raped and must be cautious. Potential baby-sitters should do the following:

1. Check out ads, signs, or bulletin boards and requests from people unknown to you. Don't baby-sit for strangers unless you have checked them out thoroughly beforehand.
2. Don't discuss your baby-sitting job in public; someone may overhear you and follow you to the destination.
3. When you do "sit", advise your parents of the name, address, and

telephone number, and when you are to be picked up. Your parents may want to talk to your employer first.

4. When your employer leaves, lock the home and check to see that all windows and doors are secured. Pull down the shades and close the curtains. Leave on the outside lights.

5. Have available emergency telephone numbers of: the police; the hospital; your employer's destination; and a neighbor.

6. Have your parents or a friend telephone you at a set time.

7. If the husband comes home before the wife, immediately call home and ask to be picked up.

8. If any unusual or obscene phone calls occur, hang up and call the police.

9. If anyone tries any sexual advances while you were baby-sitting, tell your parents or an adult friend. If no one is available, call the emergency number of a women's help group such as WAR.[23]

As some rapes occur with blind dates (i.e. "date rapes"), it is advisable to: (1) find out as much as possible about the man before going out with him; (2) don't be alone with him but insist on double-dating; (3) try to pick up clues from his behavior; and (4) learn and practice methods of self-defense.[24]

It is sad that in the 1980s one cannot walk the streets safely; that people are not civilized enough to offer peace of mind. The reality is something we have to live with, and, much as we deplore the situation, prevention and caution is what we have to work with.

Hopefully, by following these suggestions—and those given under *Incest*—cases of incest and rape will be committed less often and punishment will be meted out for these violent crimes. (See Box 11.1, a true story of a woman who experienced both rape and incest.)

In the next chapter, we discuss the problems of some other harassed females; the homosexuals, transvestites, and transsexuals.

Box 11.1: The Sad Saga of Julia.

Julia* is the oldest of five children. She started off life in impoverished surroundings in the slums of Trenton, New Jersey. When she was ten, her father walked out on the family. He had been an alcoholic but that was not

---

* In the spring of 1980, the author (DM) gave a lecture to a suburban Philadelphia *WAR* group. At the conclusion of the presentation, a young woman offered to tell him about her life. What follows is the result of that discussion. This is basically her story, except for the use of a pseudonym and minor changes in time and locale references.

unique; so were her mother and grandfather. Julia's mother had a secretarial job during the day and at night she was rarely home. The grandparents often came to visit during her absence.

One night when Julia was eleven years old, the grandparents came over for a visit. Mom had gone out "on the town" and grandma was sleeping upstairs. Grandpop called Julia over to sit on his lap and watch the falling snow flakes. He put his arm around her and let her smell his drink. The Scotch smelled strange, but "sort of nice." Julia liked her grandpop, so when he offered her a drink, she readily accepted it. No sooner had the drink touched her lips than grandpop had unzipped his pants. The sight of his penis frightened Julia, but she had always trusted her grandpop. Then in quick succession, he inserted his fingers and a banana into her vagina. Before she knew what was happening, he was inside her. Julia hated the feeling and was thoroughly confused. Her parents had told her nothing about sex and grandpop had always been kind to her. So she let him proceed. After a few agonizing minutes, he withdrew, and then miraculously produced a stack of three bibles. Julia, who had a strong Christian upbringing, had to swear on the stack never to tell a soul. Hence, at the tender age of eleven, Julia was introduced to alcohol, incest, and lying.

Soon after this incident, Julia's mother remarried. The new father fit the family pattern; he, too, was an alcoholic. Unlike Julia's real father, her stepfather hated her. And he showed his hatred; he regularly beat her up. Julia's mother also was a recipient of her new husband's fists during his alcohol-induced temper tantrums. After a couple of months of battering, Julia's mother took him to court and he was soon locked up. That second marriage lasted for less than six months.

Julia's mother couldn't be without a man. Well ahead of her time, she ignored marriage and "lived in" with a neighbor. Unlike the second husband, this man was affectionate and kind to both Julia and her mother. Then one afternoon, when Julia was in her fourteenth year, the mother's man friend invited Julia out for a pizza. After the pizza, he parked the car and forced her to engage in oral sex. Julia fought him, but she couldn't stop him. When she returned home, Julia felt frightened, guilty, and angry; frightened that he would do it again, guilty because of her "sin," and angry at herself for allowing it to happen. That night she had her first cigarette and her second drink, but this time it was continuous . . . she drank an entire bottle of wine.

Julia always loved her own father. Therefore, when he came over one morning (a few days after her sixteenth birthday) and asked her to come back with him, she jumped at the chance. When her father took her home, he made up for all the years of abandonment. He showered her with clothes, food, drink, and affection. Unfortunately, he, too, didn't know how to stop. That became Julia's second experience with incest. Her "loving" dad also introduced her to the joys of drugs. She went from "uppers" to "downers," and from pills to injections. Then, when Julia no longer pleased him, her father threw her out into the street.

Having no friends and having been rejected by her parents, Julia quit school and began to hitch-hike to Florida. When she reached Georgia, she was picked up by a truck driver. Without waiting for any amenities, he immediately pulled over to the side of the road and raped her. He then beat her, poured whiskey down her throat, covered her naked body with a paper bag, and drove off. Julia was soon picked up by a second truck driver, but this one was more humane; he took her to a nearby hospital. She was treated and discharged.

Left alone again, Julia now began a career as a prostitute. She still hated her sexual encounters, but she had no special skills except for her sexual "expertise," and she needed the money. She didn't stay in any one place, but traveled between Pennsylvania, Florida, and New York. When Julia was seventeen, she went to a fraternity party in a college town in upstate New York. She promptly was tossed into a waterbed and raped by three "frat" brothers.

For the next two years, Julia continued to work as a prostitute. In order to reduce expenses, she settled down in a small town in western Pennsylvania, and got herself a female roommate. At the tender age of eighteen, Julia became acquainted with lesbianism. Actually, Julia had her first enjoyable sexual relations during those years, but the joy was short-lived. She didn't take to her partner's introduction of group sex and mixed sex.

Finally, Julia "had it" and voluntarily went into a drug rehabilitation center and began consultations with a psychologist. One specific result of the psychological consultations was that Julia began to feel that her physical attractiveness might have initially drawn men toward her, but her tendency towards self-punishment drew her into the entanglements. At any rate, Julia made some changes. From the ages of nineteen to twenty-one, she was off both drugs and sex.

Julia, who is white, had been beaten, bruised and used by other whites all her life. So when she met a black man who treated her like a women, she "fell" for him. After going out with him on a few dates (a new experience for her), Julia got married. And for the first time in her life, she had sexual relations with a man and really enjoyed them. But this story doesn't end here.

Julia's husband is intelligent (had college training in psychology), but is physically disabled. He drinks, smokes reefers and beats his wife. He has also attempted suicide three times. When he's sober and off drugs, he and Julia have an idyllic marriage. But those periods are few and far between. Already Julia has been to a battered women's shelter—and last week she filed for divorce.

But as I look at her, I can't help but think Julia *will* make it. She has now become an active member of *WAR*. Although Julia smoked several cigarettes while revealing her story, she agreed to see a hypnotist-psychologist to try and stop her smoking. She has been off drugs and alcohol for three years now. Julia also has plans for the future. Ever since public school, she has been a good swimmer. Now she is teaching swimming at a neighborhood school, and has gone back to school herself. So at the age of twenty-three, Julia is starting to live again—but this time for *herself.*

REFERENCES

1. Wolfe, L. The Sexual Profile of that Cosmopolitan Girl. *Cosmopolitan* 254–257, 263–265 September, 1980.
2. Jensen, G. D. Childhood sexuality. *In* Green, R. (ed.), *Human Sexuality: A Health Practitioner's Text,* Second Ed. Baltimore: Williams & Wilkins, 1979, pp.47–57.
3. WAR. *Prevention Through Education: Incest/Molestation.* A WAR pamphlet. Collingswood, N. J.: WAR, P. O. Box 346, 1980.
4. U. S. Department of Justice. *Uniform Crime Report for the United States.* Washington, D. C.: U. S. Government Printing Office, 1976.
5. Ledray, L. E., Lund, S. H., and Kiresuk, T. J. Impact of rape on victims and families: Treatment and research considerations. *In* Kjervik, D. K. and Martinson, I. M. (eds.), *Women in Stress: A Nursing Perspective.* Appleton-Century-Crofts, 1979, pp. 197–217.
6. Editorial. Straight facts on rape and wife abuse. *Philadelphia Bull. 30B, June 12, 1980.*
7. Abarband, G. The sexual assault patient. *In* Green, R. (ed.), *Human Sexuality: A Health Practitioner's Text,* Second Ed. Baltimore: Williams & Wilkins , 1979, pp. 227–241.
8. Huerter, R. Female Sexuality. *In* Kjervik, D. K. and Martinson, I. M. (eds.), *Women and Stress: a Nursing Perspective.* New York: Appleton-Century-Crofts, 1979, pp. 96–115.
9 . WAR. *Prevention Through Education: Rape.* A WAR pamphlet. Collingswood, N. J.: WAR, P. O. Box 346, 1980.
10. Editorial Staff. Legal battle of the sexes. *Newsweek* 68–75, April 30, 1979.
11. Krieger, M. J., Rosenfeld, A. A., Gordon, A., and Bennett, M. Problems in the psychotherapy of children with histories of incest. *Am. J. Psychother.* 34(1):81–88, 1980.
12. Amir, M. *Patterns in Forcible Rape.* Chicago: University Chicago Press, 1971.
13. Sifford, D. Now, therapy for the rapist. *Philadelphia Inq.* 1–F, 7–F, July 6, 1980.
14. Grota, N. A., Burgess, A. W., and Holmstrom, L. L. Rape: Power, anger, and sexuality. *Am. J. Psychiatry* 134:1239–1243, 1977.
15. Peters, J. J. Social, legal and psychological effects of rape on the victim. *Penn. Med.* 78(2):34–36, 1975.
16. Burgess, A. W. and Holmstrom, L. L. *Rape: Crisis and Recovery.* Bowie, Md.: Robert J. Brady, 1979.
17. Brownmiller, S. *Against Our Will: Men, Women and Rape.* New York: Simon & Schuster, 1975.
18. Newsline. Rape: Self-blame can help. *Psychol. Today* 14(2):111, 1980.
19. Notman, M. and Nadelson, C. The rape victim: Psychodynamic considerations. *Am. J. Psychiatry* 133:408–413, 1976.
20. Medea, A. and Thompson, K. *Against Rape: A Survival Manual for Women.* New York: Farrar, Straus & Giroux, 1974.

21. Sifford, D. Specific ways to turn a rapist "off." *Philadelphia Inq.* 11-A, July 7, 1980.
22. WAR. *Prevention Through Education: Senior Citizens' Program.* A WAR pamphlet. Collingswood, NJ: WAR, P. O. Box 346, 1980.
23. WAR *Prevention Through Education: Guidelines for Babysitters.* A WAR pamphlet. Collingswood, N. J.: WAR, P. O. Box 346, 1980.
24. Chastian, S. The man you trust could be a "date rapist." *Philadelphia Inq.* 1-K, 5-K, November 30,1980.

12
The Sexual Minorities: Lesbians, Transvestites and Transsexuals

INTRODUCTION

Women who adopt life-styles other than the standard heterosexual role are subject to intense stress. Although there are many more male than female homosexuals, transvestites, and transsexuals, women who fit into any one of these categories often find harassment at home, in school and at work. Women homosexuals are the principal type and are considered first.

LESBIANISM

Homosexuality throughout the ages has been variously considered as a crime, a sin, a form of deviant mental behavior, a second choice sexual outlet, and a life-style. After much debate, the *American Psychiatric Association* (APA) in 1973, removed homosexuality from its classification as a mental disorder and paved the way for it to be considered merely as a life-style.

There really is no absolute concept of homosexuality, as homosexual behavior can take many forms. In childhood, homosexual experiences are quite common. Many adults have had a few homosexual adventures in an otherwise heterosexual life-style. Some individuals have homosexual experiences only when they are in unisexually segregated places such as prisons, schools, the military, nursing homes, monasteries, and nunneries.[1-3] Others are bisexual with sexual interests in both males and females.

Some women call themselves homosexuals more as a political rebellion than because of active sexual preference. There are also individuals who, because of the children, their spouses or friends, act heterosexually but are homosexual in their preference. There are also people who are heterosexual but have been labeled homosexual by others because of certain behaviors. For example, males who shy away from sports and physical activities may be labeled "queer" and women who engage in track and field may be labeled "lezzies."

Finally, there are those who are exclusively homosexuals. In the United States, the incidence of exclusive male homosexuality has been estimated to be anywhere from 3 to 10 percent of the adult male population. For females, the incidence ranges from about 1 to 5 percent.[4-7]

Female homosexuals are known as lesbians.* The sexual activities of lesbians is similar to that of the typical male-female sexual behavior, with a somewhat greater preference for cunnilingus.[8] Coitus is less often performed. When it is done, it is simulated with one woman lying on top of the other. They rub their bodies together (tribadism), or an artificial phallus (dildo) can be used.[7,8]

The typical caricature of the lesbian is that of a cigar-smoking, fiercely competitive, male-dressed female who possesses the most obnoxious aspects of a man's temperament.[8] This is contrary to the true picture of the female homosexual. It is true that some lesbians adopt male roles ("butch" or "dyke") but they do not usually adopt male aggressive tendencies. Other lesbians adopt female roles ("femme"); while many lesbians are not stereotypically either male or female.

Since homosexuality has such diverse aspects to it, theories of causality are not satisfactory. It is not clear whether homosexuality has a genetic or environmental basis. There is some belief that homosexuality is related to unresolved neurotic conflicts and childhood problems, but recent studies have not substantiated these assumptions.[1,2] One study did find that there were more former "tomboys" who became lesbians than those who remained as heterosexuals.[9]

Nevertheless, many people consider homosexuals as being "sick." This is even true with some physicians. A recent questionnaire to one thousand physicians revealed that most physicians believed that homosexuality could negatively affect an individual's health.[10] Yet findings have shown that homosexuals have the same type problems as heterosexuals. Lesbians do not have higher rates of psychological disorders than heterosexuals and there is no evidence of any greater incidence of organic diseases. They also

*The word is derived from Lesbos, one of the Greek islands and the home of the sixth-century B.C. poet, Sappho. She wrote love songs to her female students.

have the same kind of sexual problems as heterosexuals and undergo the same type of counseling and therapy.[1,2] Unlike popular belief, homosexuals are not filled with sexual thoughts all the time. They carry on their daily activities just as do heterosexuals. Lesbians are reputed to have lesser levels of sexual interest than male homosexuals and tend to be stressed about their sexual activities. Because of society's generally negative view of lesbian sex, lesbians may become fearful and furtive in their sexual encounters. With lesbian liberation, things have improved and many more women are openly acknowledging their sexual preferences.

The activist lesbian liberation movement has helped bring female homosexuality out into the open. Key demands are equality under the law and an end to discrimination in schools and occupations. Many lesbians have become active feminists. They consider that lesbians are subject to dual discrimination, both as women and homosexuals. The lesbian-feminists believe that women will never be truly liberated unless they are free from male domination in every aspect, including sexuality.[1] One source puts it this way, "The sexual satisfaction of the women independent of the man is the *sine qua non* of the feminist revolution."[11] In women's liberation meetings such as NOW (National Organization for Women), there are often conflicts between the lesbian contingent and the heterosexual ("straight") contingent in regard to relations with men.

Although homosexual activity is officially barred in prisons, overt homosexual families are found in several institutions for delinquent girls and women's prisons. There are formalized "weddings" of "male" lesbians ("butch") with "female" lesbians ("femme") and children are "adopted." The families even have "aunts," "uncles," and "siblings."[12] Homosexual activity is also barred in the military services. In a recent case, some women that were sailors received a Naval discharge hearing on the ground that they were lesbians.[13]

One group of lesbians who really have had stress problems are lesbian mothers. They have the triple stressors of being a woman, a single parent, and a lesbian. In battles for custody of the children, most courts have found that lesbians, because of the very nature of their sexual preference, are unfit mothers.[14] Recently, some lesbian mothers have been receiving support. A New Jersey state appeal court returned two young girls to the custody of their lesbian mothers. The court ruled that the mere fact of one parent's homosexuality should not be the determining factor in awarding custody to the other parent. Legal custody cases are stressful for heterosexual parents, but even more so for lesbian mothers. They are forced to publicly disclose their sexual preferences. These lesbian mothers now have support organizations to help them in their decisions. For example, in

Philadelphia there is a group called *Custody Action for Lesbian Mothers* (CALM). CALM provides legal counsel and emotional support to lesbian mothers. Most often they advise them to stay out of court since the judge's decision could be worse than an out-of-court settlement.* Another supportive style for lesbian mothers are communities of lesbian mothers and their children.

Lesbian mothers are not innately better mothers than are heterosexual mothers, but neither are they necessarily worse. There does not seem to be a higher incidence of homosexual offspring in families run by lesbian mothers than there is in families managed by heterosexual mothers.[15]

Another group of lesbians that society pictures as having a bleak outlook are the older lesbians. But recent findings do not support that contention. In fact, older lesbians may do better in some ways than older heterosexual females. For one thing they have an easier time finding sexual partners (because of the higher male mortality).[16] They also maintain their sexual relationships longer (probably related to better availability of partners).

Another finding is that they have few problems in establishing friendships. Many older heterosexual women had prior friendships with men, but these diminished with age because of the lack of available older men. Lesbian women tend to have strong friendships which are predominantly with other lesbian women. Hence they often are not as lonely as are heterosexual older women. The older lesbian women do not tend to maintain strong family ties. This may also be helpful as older heterosexual women often suffer severe stress from the loss of family ties. Lesbian women may also suffer stress from the loss of family ties but they had a long time to acclimate to the loss. It was found in a recent study that lesbians with the highest self-esteem had the weakest sibling ties. They compensated by having strong friendships.[16]

With the older lesbians there were found two life-styles. One group was composed of feminists. They tended to be single, active in organizations, and enjoyed collective living. The other group, composed of traditional lesbians, were non-feminists, lived as couples, and were not active in organizations. Both groups tended to cope well.[16]

Some women who were heterosexuals all their lives became homosexual when they moved into nursing homes. One reason is that in nursing homes, women tend to outnumber men by a five to one ratio. However, with these

---

* This was affirmed at the highest level in a recent decision. The U.S. Supreme Court stated that a Kentucky Court of Appeals decision should be left intact. The court said that the child should be placed in the custody of the father, who had remarried, rather than remain with the mother who had a live-in lesbian lover. Carelli, R. Lesbian mother loses U.S. appeal. *Philadelphia Inq.* 4–A, April 21, 1981.

women, there is a lesser emphasis on sexuality and a greater emphasis on warmth and companionship.[3]

If lesbians are given the same opportunities to live, work, and play as are heterosexuals, they should be able to cope with stress at least as well. However, if they are continually harassed, they will always need extra support in coping with life's "pressures." Masters and Johnson believe that many homosexuals can be "cured."[17] Whether or not lesbians should try to become "straight" should be their own choice. Lesbians have many means to help them in their decision-making including books, lesbian consciousness-raising groups, and psychological counseling.

Another group of individuals who are faced with stressful decisions are the transvestites.

TRANSVESTITES

Transvestites are individuals who wear the clothes of the opposite sex and become sexually aroused as a result. They generally began their cross-dress behavior as young children, between four and six years of age. They prefer the activities and companionship of members of the opposite sex. The cross-dress and cross-preference behavior in boys is given the derogatory term "sissy." The sissy is the boy who avoids athletics, plays with girls, prefers dolls to erector sets, and occasionally wears dresses. Girls who play with boys, wear pants all the time, are very athletic and engage in activities such as climbing trees are known as "tomboys." Tomboyism is common in young females who often receive social rewards from their friends for behaving like boys. "Tomboys" may be considered by their peers as adventurous and "daredevils," but tomboyism generally has little consequence on girls' future behavior.

On the other hand, feminine behavior in young boys is frowned upon and occurs much less frequently than does masculine behavior in girls. When it does occur and is extensive, it is much more likely to lead to transvestitism and transsexual behavior.[18] The reasons for the difference in male and female tendencies to take cross-roles are not completely known, but may be related to these factors. Both genders identify with their mothers from the time of birth. Boys may have a more difficult problem because they have to change identification from mother to father. Girls shouldn't have this problem since they always identify with their mother.

If boys are not athletic and don't enjoy male clothes and activities, they can never maintain a female life-style as a male. In contrast, girls can partake in male-dominant activities, be rewarded for it, and still maintain their female identity. Wearing male-type clothes is now part of female fashion and hence, is also rewarded as being "chic."

Furthermore, during adolescence most girls find greater rewards in acting in a "feminine" manner and the "tomboy" girl often easily makes the transition. "Feminine" boys do not have the adolescent push to act in a masculine way and tend to retain their feminine nature.

The result of these male-female differences is that transvestitism is almost always a male behavior.[19] Occasionally, at adolescence some tomboys will not change to feminine behavior and find themselves erotically attracted to females. They adamantly refuse to wear dresses and may even assume a boy's name. Whether or not they develop into adult transvestites is not known, since these cases have not yet been followed.[18]

Transvestites have a great deal of stress. They are often frowned upon by heterosexual members of their own and opposite sex, as well as by homosexuals who get upset if they are confused with transvestites or transsexuals. Sometimes transvestites develop friendships with other transvestites, or join transvestite groups. The mutual support may be advantageous. However, the social isolation may make the transvestite even more stressed. Psychotherapy can be helpful, but if the transvestites are unhappy in their sex identity, then hormonal treatment and surgery may be elected. However, most transvestites are content with their sex identity.

TRANSSEXUALS

Transsexuals are individuals who have a long-standing, intense and insistent desire to transform their bodies into those of the opposite sex. They believe that they are victims of nature's faults. There are about 15,000 transsexuals in the United States. Four-fifths of them are males, but female transsexuals have recently been increasing.[20,21] The probable reasons for the majority of transsexuals being males are the same as those described for the male dominance in transvestite behavior. One additional reason is that it is easier to construct a cosmetically acceptable and functional vagina than it is to make a penis. But recently with the use of masculinizing hormones and improved penis reconstructive surgery, more women have become transsexuals.[22]

The desire to change sex generally begins in adolescence. The teen-age transsexual typically finds harassment at school. She may become so upset that she refuses to attend school unless she can do so as a male.[18] Although parents get extremely disturbed by this behavior, it would probably be beneficial to allow the teen-ager to go to school in her preferred gender role. There could be a trial period that would allow the girl to adjust to a male life-style before she receives hormones or surgery. Some teen-agers do well in their new roles, while others become disillusioned and return to their anatomical sex.[23] Psychotherapy can be helpful in either eliminating the transsexual behavior or in easing the passage towards the opposite gender.[24]

Johns Hopkins University Hospital was a pioneer in transsexual surgery, but it recently established a moratorium on doing any new cases as one study showed no basic long-range improvement from transsexual surgery. The hospital now limits its surgery to cases of hermaphrodites who have sexual organs of both sexes.[21]

Almost all transsexuals do not have any physical or biological evidence of opposite sex characteristics. They have the normal hormones and chromosomes for their anatomical sex. Basically then, transsexual identity is psychologically determined. That is why many investigators now believe that psychotherapy should be the treatment of choice, with the hope of restoring the patients to their anatomical sex.[24]

In addition, there are problems with the surgery. Quite often repeated operations are necessary. For example, the new organs may not function satisfactorily after a time, and there are often requests for surgery in different parts of the body to make the structures look anatomically more like those of the requested gender. Infection can also occur as a result of the surgery. Once the surgery is done, it is too late to change one's mind.

Considering the potential problems, before a woman decides on transsexual surgery, she should be thoroughly evaluated and informed. First, the woman should have an extensive trial period of psychotherapy to determine whether the motivation for the sex change is sufficient, or if she would be better off with her anatomical sex. Second, if it is determined that gender change is the intended course of action, then the woman should have a trial period in which she adopts the dress, mannerisms, and life-style of the male. If she is still convinced that she wants the sex change then she should be thoroughly informed about the pros and cons of hormonal and surgical treatments. Finally, there should be an extensive postsurgical adjustment period in which the "woman" receives medical and psychological support.

Recently, some institutions have been providing the female transsexual with all types of practical suggestions in how to live as a member of her new gender.[21] She is given instruction in everything from how to use a men's restroom to how to hit a baseball.

It is hoped that with the help of psychotherapy and support groups, and nonharassment by the public, the female transsexual will be able to reduce her stress and live in the life-style that she has chosen.

Regardless of a woman's sexual inclination she will either be a mother, work outside of the home, or do both. This is covered in Part V.

REFERENCES

1. Williams, J. H. *Psychology of Women: Behavior in a Biosocial Context.* New York: W. W. Norton, 1977.
2. Rosen, D. H. *Lesbianism: A Study of Female Homosexuality.* Springfield, Ill.: Charles C. Thomas, 1974.
3. Sifford, D. Helping the aged: A better finale. *Philadelphia Inq.* 2-D, June 19, 1980.
4. Kinsey, A. C., Pomeroy, W. P., and Martin, C. E. *Sexual Behavior in the Human Male.* Philadelphia: W. B. Saunders, 1948.
5. Kinsey, A. C., Pomeroy, W. P., Martin, C. E., and Gebhard, P. H. *Sexual Behavior in the Human Female.* Philadelphia: W. B. Saunders, 1953.
6. Hunt, M. *Sexual Behavior in the Seventies.* Chicago: Playboy Press, 1974.
7. Katchedourian, H. and Lunde, D. *Fundamentals of Human Sexuality,* Second Ed. New York: Holt, Rinehart & Winston, 1975.
8. Bell, A. P. The homosexual as patient. *In* Green, R. (ed.), *Human Sexuality: A Health Practitioner's Text.* Baltimore: Williams & Wilkins, 1979, pp. 98–114.
9. Saghir, M. and Robins, E. *Male and Female Homosexuality.* Baltimore: Williams & Wilkins, 1973.
10. Pauly, I. and Goldstein, S. Physicians attitudes in treating homosexuals. *Med. Aspects Hum. Sexual.* 4:26–45, 1970.
11. Johnston, J. *Lesbian Nation: The Feminist Solution.* New York: Simon & Shuster, 1973.
12. Giallombardo, R. *The Social World of Imprisoned Girls.* New York: Wiley, 1974.
13. United Press International. Boyfriends back gob with straight talk on sex. *Philadelphia Daily News* 20, August 7, 1980.
14. Hacker, K. Lesbians: Suddenly they're "unfit" mothers. *Philadelphia Sunday Bull.* 1 WA, 6 WA, August 12, 1979.
15. Green, R. (ed.), *Human Sexuality: A Health Practitioner's Text.* Baltimore: Williams & Wilkins, 1979.
16. Raphael, S. M. and Robinson, M. K. The older Lesbian: Love relationships and friendship patterns. *Alternative Lifestyles* 3(2):207–229, 1980.
17. Masters, W. H. and Johnson, V. E. *Homosexuality in Perspective.* Boston: Little, Brown, 1979.
18. Green, R. Children called "sissy" and "tomboy," adolescents who cross-dress, and adults who want to change sex. *In* Green, R. (ed.), *Human Sexuality: A Health Practitioner's Text.* Baltimore: Williams & Wilkins, 1979.
19. Prime, C. and Bentler, P. Survey of 504 cases of transvestism. *Psychol. Rep.* 31:903–917, 1972.
20. Pauly, I. B. Female Transsexualism. Part I. *Arch. Sex. Behav.* 3:487–507, 1974.
21. Restak, R. M. At issue: The sex-change conspiracy: The operation has become a $10 million growth industry . . . It seems clear that it is a drastic nonsolution. *Psychol. Today* 13(7):20–25, 1979.
22. Martino, M. *Emergence.* New York:Crown, 1977.
23. Newman, L. Transsexualism in adolescence. *Arch. Gen. Psychiat.* 23:112–121, 1970.
24. Davenport, C. and Harrison, S. Gender identity change in a female adolescent transsexual. *Arch. Sex. Behav.* 6:327–340, 1977.

PART V
WOMEN
AND
ENVIRONMENTAL
PRESSURES

Today's woman is faced with many choices. These are explored in this section. In Chapter 13, consideration is given to the stressors from the "traditional job" of the female, the housewife. Chapter 14 is an overview of women in outside jobs; it also focuses in on the stress from working and simultaneously raising a family ("superwoman"); and the problems of the dual-career couple are also considered. Chapter 15, is concerned with the lower-status female jobs, from "salesgirl" to "lady plumber." The traditional female professions is the topic of Chapter 16. In Chapter 17, the entrance of women into the male-dominated careers are considered as well as the woman professional athlete and her problems . The theme of Chapter 18 is the disadvantaged woman, encompassing the handicapped and retarded as well as the ethnic minorities. In this chapter we also consider women and the illegal professions: prostitution, larceny and others.

13

The Housewife:
Dealing with Doorbells,
Dustpans, Dinners,
and Dishes

INTRODUCTION

Traditionally, women have had three major roles in life. These are wife, mother, and housewife. In Chapter 7, we considered the stress from being a wife and a mother. In this chapter, we look into the stress from being a wife and a homemaker.

THE HOUSEWIFE STRESSORS

Being a housewife is one occupation that many women engage in at some time in their lives regardless of whether or not they have other jobs. Interestingly enough, women simultaneously do and do not consider being a housewife as an occupation. (See Box 13.1) Let us consider the reasons why.

Training

Being a housewife is one occupation that has no formalized training.* There are no instructional manuals for a prospective housewife to follow. Most women pick up some clues from their mothers and friends. There is

* There are some high-school courses given that discuss managing a household, and colleges do have home economics courses but women do not usually enroll in them just to learn to be a housewife.

Box 13.1. Occupation: Housewife.

The author (DM) has been practicing endodontics (root-canal therapy) for 19 years. Each new patient fills out a questionnaire, and one of the questions asked is: "What is your occupation?" Throughout all these years, it has been observed that married women who do not have an outside job invariably list their occupation as "housewife." Several of them listed it as "*just* a housewife." Some tried to enhance the prestige by calling themselves "homemakers." However, as soon as the married women obtained employment of any type, even if it was part-time or nonsalaried, they listed their occupation as whatever the job entailed; e.g., secretary, salesclerk, teacher, or nurse's aide.

All of these women were still housewives, but as soon as they got any other position, they instantaneously ceased listing "housewife" as an occupation or co-occupation. Several of the women who were housewives, obtained a job and were laid off. With a few of them there was an interval of several years between when they first came in for treatment and when they returned for subsequent treatment. Therefore, they were asked to fill out additional questionnaires. I then reviewed their earlier questionnaires and compared them to the current ones. It was noticed that the women listed their occupation as "housewife" in the first questionnaire, "secretary" (or other category) in the second questionnaire, and when they were unemployed, they again listed themselves as "housewives." All of the answers were given spontaneously. When the patients were informed about their responses, they were quite surprised, but they said it was understandable: Being a housewife is a profession that they didn't relish and of which they were not proud.

no such thing as a "natural" housewife that is akin to being a natural athlete nor is there any indication that working hard at it makes one a better housewife.

In one study, most women felt that they were inadequately trained to be housewives.[1] This is a definite source of stress since being prepared for a job is one of the best ways to reduce stress. When one is unprepared there is a greater incidence of frustration, anxiety and anger.[2]

Confusion

With most jobs, there are specific tasks and times set aside in which to perform them (see Box 13.2). In contrast, the housewife has no specific idea of tasks and times. Even if she does plan on doing certain activities at set times, she is often interrupted. Occurrences like screaming children, sales-

Box 13.2. A Time for Teeth.

In the author's (DM) office, patients are usually seen every forty-five minutes; surgery cases are generally done on Monday afternoons; and patients requiring hypnosis are typically seen at the end of the working day. Even when there are emergencies that can disrupt this schedule, there are times set aside in the schedule to handle those emergencies. The dental receptionist and assistants then have a general idea of tasks and times which reduces their stress.

men at the front door, telephone calls from friends, the dog barking to go out, the dishwasher flooding—all these can disrupt any continuity the housewife tries to set up. She is usually off schedule, behind time, and frustrated. The housewife is often confused about what to do first or which activity is most important. No wonder she is stressed at the end of the day.

Rewards

A housewife who keeps a meticulous household receives no more compensation than a housewife who rarely dusts and leaves the dishes undone until after dinner. Being a gourmet cook may be self-rewarding to a woman, and she may occasionally receive praise from her family. But financially she is no better off than the family that is fed "franks, burgers, and fries." Stress is always increased when an individual is not rewarded for her efforts. At least in terms of settlement for divorce, women are asking for some recognition for their homemaking contributions. Recent rulings have placed a financial value on a housewife's services.[3]

Boredom

One of the worst stressors is monotony.[2] Washing, folding, and ironing clothes, vacuuming, mopping, dusting, and food shopping . . . all are dull, repetitive, and boring chores. Even in the household where husbands share with the duties, they rarely partake in those activities. The man's chief role in helping the wife with "her" job is to take out the garbage, walk the dog, and maybe wash the dishes and pots.

Privacy

A principal way to reduce stress is to each day set aside periods of time to relax and exercise. With innovative businesses, there is built-in time for the workers to reduce stress. There may be relaxation breaks given or an exercise facility right in the business quarters.[2] The housewife with her day filled with scheduled and unscheduled interruptions rarely has the time or the opportunity to relax or take exercise breaks.

Household Help

There are various gradations of housewife. A woman with ten children and no outside help has to do everything herself. She is a housewife. Another woman with no children has a live-in maid, regular service people to wash the floors, clean the windows and vacuum the rugs. She goes to the beautician regularly and frequently relaxes at the country club. She, too, is a housewife. There is much ambiguity in the job because there are no criteria.[4] The women with all the help may call herself a housewife, but she would be under much less stress than the overburdened woman with the large family.

Qualifications

A pianist should be good with her hands; a ballet dancer needs strong legs; an air-traffic controller must be able to make instantaneous decisions; a homemaker needs no specific qualifications for her job. A college degree does not make for a better housewife. In fact, it might make for a worse housewife because of unused talents.

If a woman is unqualified for a job, she may be "fired." Housewives never get "fired," and they can't quit unless they elect for a divorce, a change of roles, or a sharing of roles. Knowing that there is no escape from a position can greatly increase stress.

Status

There are high-status professions such as medicine and law. There are lower status professions such as nursing and dental hygiene. And then there is the low status profession—the housewife. Because of the low status in being a housewife many women elect to "hang on the coattails" of their successful husbands in order to elevate their own status—to be known as "the woman behind the man." This can help reduce the stress of being in an occupation with low status, but it also reduces the woman's self-esteem. However, some women are satisfied with the role of being the spouse of a successful man. Others may be proud of their husbands but still make a name for themselves.*

Finances

One housewife responsibility in many households is to take care of the family finances—at least in terms of buying food, clothes, and household items. But even here the homemaker is often dependent upon her husband for the weekly allowance and a car to help her for shopping and errands (e.g., taking the kids for basketball practice or dancing lessons). The image of the housewife is also reflected in the car she drives. The housewife commonly drives around in an overloaded (with packages or kids) station wagon, while her husband may cruise around in a "snazzy" sports car. As far as the weekly allowance is concerned, there may be stress involved as the result of conflicts over how much money is needed. This is a special problem in these inflationary times.

Now that we've determined the stressors from being a housewife, let us consider the results of this stress.

THE RESULTS OF HOUSEHOLD STRESS

In Chapters 3 and 4 stress-related diseases and disorders were discussed. The typical housewife is susceptible to many of them especially agoraphobia (fear of closed spaces), alcoholism, drug addiction, compulsive eating, and "chain-smoking." Studies have shown that housewives have more psychological stress symptoms than do employed housewives and employed men. There is even a specific housewife condition known simply as *housewife's disease*. Symptoms of housewife's disease are: fainting, inertia, dizziness, hand trembling, heart palpitations, and extreme nervousness.[5]

Now let us consider methods of reducing household stress.

REDUCING HOUSEHOLD STRESS

There are mechanical and physical aids available that can make a housewife's life a little easier. Washers, dryers, dishwashers, microwave ovens—

---

* A good example is Marilyn Funt, former wife of Allen Funt, the millionaire creator of "Candid Camera." She recently wrote the successful book, *Are You Anybody?* In an interview she stated: "You can't hook onto somebody else's dream. It must be yours." Sifford D. She learned that a woman must dream her own dreams. *Philadelphia Inq.* 3-C, January 6, 1981.

all these can free up time to allow the housewife to be alone. Baby-sitters can also give a housewife some needed respite for relaxation, exercise, a trip to the beautician, or any other enjoyable daily diversion. A once weekly cleaning service or an employed housekeeper can reduce the number of chores the housewife must do.

For the women who does not want an outside job but doesn't enjoy being a housewife, there should be a sharing of roles in addition to time-saving appliances and part-time help. There is nothing innate about the duties of a housewife that limits the role to females. Even before a man and woman decide to get married, they should discuss sharing of household chores, mothering duties, and occupational roles. Men and women can alternate in cooking, cleaning, shopping, and even sewing. Many excellent surgeons and dentists who routinely suture difficult surgical openings with a variety of suturing techniques adamantly refuse to sew a button or darn a sock. (They plead "ignorance.")

If necessary, a sharing of roles should be incorporated into marriage contracts. To help offset the financial advantages of the working partner, whoever does specific household chores might be given extra financial remuneration.

The woman who wants a house, a family, and a career, should be given the same opportunity as her spouse to work outside the home, except for the time she is pregnant and possibly during the first few months after childbirth. The only way this can occur is for both partners to share in the household roles. It is to be hoped that with the development of androgynous people, a new profession will emerge—"the houseperson"—that can be engaged in by either a woman or man. The job may even gain a little more status along with some financial input.

Whether the husband is out working and the wife is home with the house and children, or vice versa, the time when they first meet each other at the end of the working day can be a particularly stressful period. This period, generally between 5:00 and 6:00 p.m., has been called "the arsenic hour."[6] The usual pattern is a husband who has had a hard day at the office and a wife who has had it "rough" between the housework and the kids. They meet each other and an explosion is inevitable. One way to forestall or evade the confrontation is to have a truce or "buffer period." It could be in the form of a glass of wine, a mutual meditation period, or simply a walk around the block. After this short interval, tempers could "cool off" and possibly the partners could see each other's viewpoint.

Related to the importance of a break there was an interesting recent study. Anxiety level tests were given to three groups of working men right after finishing work (about 5:00 p.m.) and again after arriving at home.[7]

The first group went to the neighborhood bar for a drink or two before going home. The second group stopped off at the health club, had a work-out and shower, and then went home. The third group proceeded directly home from work. The analysis showed that those who had an interruption either at the bar or the gym had significantly lower anxiety levels than those who went right home. Most likely the wives of those who were detained were less stressed as well. But to insure this, it is mandatory that the person at home be given the same opportunity to have a "work-out, drink, or relaxation break" as the working individual.

An overview of the working woman is the theme of the next chapter.

REFERENCES

1. Lopata, H. Z. *Occupation: Housewife*. New York: Oxford University Press, 1971.
2. Morse, D. R. and Furst, M. L. *Stress for Success: A Holistic Approach to Stress and its Management*. New York: Van Nostrand Reinhold, 1979.
3. Editorial. Legal battle of the sexes. *Newsweek* 68–75, April 30, 1979.
4. Williams, J. H. *Psychology of Women: Behavior in a Biosocial Context*. New York: W. W. Norton, 1977.
5. Oakley, A. *Women's Work: The Housewife, Past and Present*. New York: Random House, 1974.
6. Olson, K. *The Art of Hanging Loose in an Uptight World*. Greenwich, Conn.: Fawcett, 1974.
7. Sarshik, H. Taking a stress relief break. Read before the JCC Symposium in Stress Management, Cherry Hill, N. J., October 12, 1978.

14

The Working Woman:
An Overview

WHY ARE WOMEN WORKING?

Women have been entering the labor market at an increased rate in the last few years. More than half the adult women in the United States are now working.[1] What is the cause of this sudden influx? Let's consider the possibilities.

Inflation and Recession

The late 1970s and early 1980s have been a time of financial stressors for the average American household. With many lower- and middle-class families, the traditional concept of the husband working and the wife taking care of the house and children is not being followed. There is insufficient income to cope with the steep rise in prices. In many families the husband has more than one job and the wife is forced to go to work in order to supplement the family income. With the rising unemployment rate, many men are being laid off, and the burden of support is falling on the women.

Most women are working because of economic need, and this is attested to by statistics showing that two-thirds of all working women are either single, separated, divorced, widowed, or have husbands earning less than $10,000 per year.[2] About half the working women provide sole support for their families or have husbands earning less than $3,000 per year.[3] In addition, between the years of 1960 and 1974, 11 million additional women entered the labor market.[4]

In these situations, because of lack of sufficient training, many women, when they can get jobs are relegated to the "traditional" female positions. They take jobs as secretaries, typists, waitresses, bank tellers, telephone operators, salesclerks, or anything they can get.

Many college-educated women take their teaching certificates "out of mothballs," get recertified and go back to teaching. When people are obligated to do something, they often resent doing it. When they have little choice in deciding what they want or do not want to do, their anger and frustration mounts. And when they work at a job they do not enjoy, their stress increases even more.

In addition, in almost all these cases, the women are still expected to take care of the household and children, although they may get some help from their husbands. Considering the circumstances, going to work in these situations is certainly conducive to stress.

Feminism

With women's liberation, the concept is emerging that women should be freed from their traditional roles as housewife and mother. With the release of that bondage, women should be free to go out in the "man's working world." The concept is good, but many untrained women in their thirties, forties, and fifties have been caught in the whirlwind and have tried to get a job. As is the case with women being forced to go to work, these women are not often happy in the positions they obtain.

Sometimes some women get so enthused with women's liberation that they accept jobs for which they are not completely qualified.[5] Then they experience stress as a result of working too hard, putting in too many hours, or not feeling competent at the position. There is nothing wrong with aiming high but one of the cornerstones of stress management is to set realistic goals and gradually achieve one's ambition. Many men have fallen into the trap of "shooting for the stars" and "falling flat on their faces." Women should not follow that example. If a woman does not feel qualified for a position, rather than becoming embarrassed and stressed, she has two feasible alternatives: First, she can go back to school and prepare herself for the specific occupation. Second, she can take a position somewhat lower than she wants and prepare herself on the job for the better position.

Regardless of the type of job a woman obtains, unless she is assertive or has a liberated or androgynous husband, she finds that she still has the extra burden of caring for the children and maintaining the household. Younger women have it better. Those who are in high school or college are planning careers of their own choice. A recent survey found that only 9 percent of college female "freshmen" felt that women's activities should be limited to the household and family.[6] However, there can be a problem for that 9 percent. There are still some women who hear the calls of the feminist revolution but feel that they would rather be wives, mothers, and homemakers. In addition, there are women who are happy about working but who do not want to be crusaders or pioneers. Women should realize that being liberated means just that—having freedom of choice. Women should not feel stressed if they decide that they don't want to go along with the crowd.

Many women are now delaying either their marriages or having children in order to have the time to plan a lifetime career. One potential problem is not with the current twenty to thirty-five-year-old women who are doing this. The problem rests with current teen-agers who may later decide that they, too, want to postpone marriage and a family for a career. Many of today's teen-agers, caught in the new sexual revolution, have become pregnant and elected to keep their children. As teen-age mothers, they often have had support from their own mothers. But as liberated women in their late twenties or early thirties, they will need help to care for their children so that they can go on to school and plan a career. It is an extra burden with which they will have to deal, and it may prevent some women from furthering their education and careers.[7]

"Spending Money"

In many well-to-do families, women are going back to work so that they can have their own "spending money" ("pin money"). If they want a particular item of clothing, a personal item, or even a car, they don't have to be dependent upon their husbands for a handout. They can get it themselves. In this situation where the family does not need additional financial support, the wife can be selective about the job she takes and the duration of her employment. She may even set up a specialty shop or a boutique. Women in this position should not be as stressed as those in the previous situations. However, the husbands may frown upon their wives' working, claiming that the additional income is not helpful but only raises the family's tax bracket. If the men are not antagonistic toward their wives' employment, the men may tolerate it as a hobby or diversion. With that kind of support, working is not beneficial for these women's self-esteem or self-image.

Compensation

Housewives work at home for years with little appreciation and no financial rewards. Then they decide to get a job for any of the previous reasons or to just find out if they can be useful and be paid for it. After years of having little of no respect, it is a great psychological reward for women to find out that they can receive financial compensation for their efforts. However, after the initial euphoria, the position itself must be interesting enough or it becomes little more than a trade-off from one boring job (housewife) to another. As mentioned previously, if the woman was not previously trained, the choice of career is severely limited.

Breaking Up the Day

As we've emphasized, the role of housewife/mother is filled with boring tasks, continual interruptions, and frustration and anger. Some women decide to take a part-time job to break up the monotony and escape the chaos. When they return, they may feel more inclined to manage the household and family "pressures." However, if the women do not get any help they will return to the piles of work with less time to do it. This can only increase their stress.

Companionship

Housewife/mothers may have a problem carrying on a stimulating conversation with their young children. They also may become bored or dissatisfied with telephone "chit-chat" with friends and confrontations with salespeople. Getting a job can be a welcome relief. It may give the women a chance to make new acquaintances and be involved in new and interesting discussions. The housewife/mother in her new role can have various things to discuss with both her husband and friends.[8]

For the single woman, the companionship from work can be an especially rewarding aspect of having a job. For both married and single women, going to work can be a way of overcoming loneliness and a means of diversion which is important in stress management (see Chapter 3).

Preparation for the Future

With the current increased mortality rate of the male, many women are now realizing that some day they may be the family's sole breadwinner. Therefore, women are returning to school in large numbers to prepare themselves for careers. In fact, a report by the U.S. Census Bureau (August 24, 1980), revealed that, for the first time since World War II, the number of women attending college eclipsed that of men. The difference was primarily due to the women over thirty-five who were attending college to help them in the competition for jobs. A recent survey by the Commission on Civil Rights disclosed that for the same position, women require greater skills or educational background than men.[9]

Some women are getting jobs early in marriage, even if there are no financial pressures, so that they will have skills available for later use when they may be needed. If the women have time to prepare themselves, this can be rewarding. They can choose a job to their liking, try it out on a temporary basis and go back to school for further training if necessary. Many women are also preparing for a career before getting married. Therefore, they will have a career option for later years.

Achievement

For decades, women have been "brainwashed" into believing their sole role and destiny was to be a good mother and to manage a clean home. Many of these women were college-trained and yet their learning went for naught. Nowadays, women (as well as some men) realize that women's needs for achievement and recognition are just as strong as are men's. Women who were asked why they wanted to obtain skilled employment or start a career gave the following reasons: the need for status; the actualization of their potential; a high energy level; a desire to benefit society; a need for social contact; and an active orientation toward life.[10] Considering these findings, there is no reason that a woman should have her career aspirations thwarted in the embryonic stage just because she is married and has children. If single, she should have the same career opportunities as the male.

Power

There are all kinds of "power" including military, economic, sexual, and physical. Most women are not concerned with military power. Aside from a few weight lifters, gymnasts, and track and field stars, physical power is not high in women's priorities. As we've previously discussed, much to the male's chagrin, women are generally sexually more powerful than men. However, in the economic aspect, women have been powerless or noticeably weaker than most men.

Women have traditionally not been concerned with making money. Men have been interested in making "big bucks"; women have been afflicted with the "bargain syndrome."[11] They try to save cents; men try to make dollars. To achieve economic power, women must get involved with the economics of making money.

One way for women to overcome their dependency role and to learn the value and worth of money is to obtain a position that gives them a high salary and prestige. Women are now receiving a lot of help in learning the relationship of money to power. There have been several recent books published on this subject.[11-13]

Occasionally, women become more economically powerful than their spouses. This is fine for the women but the men may tend to feel inferior and powerless. (Some women may consider this a welcome switch.) This often occurs with media stars. If the males can't cope, they may become depressed, alcoholic, drug addicted, or suicidal. Another frequent occurrence is divorce (discussed further in this chapter with respect to the two-career couple). On the job, many men have trouble dealing with a powerful female boss but this, too, is a problem that men must face.

The "Empty Nest"

With the children gone and the large home sold, older women may find "time on their hands" and so they elect to go to work. They may find problems. Recent surveys have found that women over the age of forty-five receive less job counseling and testing and have lower earnings than younger women.[14] The younger women got better jobs and higher paid positions. The younger women received more diversified jobs while the older women primarily obtained traditional clerical jobs. Some states are now concerning themselves with the older woman seeking employment and are helping her with counseling, testing for aptitude, and job search.

WHAT KINDS OF JOBS ARE WOMEN GETTING?

Now that we've considered why women are working, let's look into the jobs they're getting. Within the last few years, there has been a tremendous increase in the number of women admitted into medical, dental, law, and other professional schools. These beginnings will not yet be reflected in the current number of women professionals. Also the governmental restrictions against sexual bias in jobs is slowly changing the pattern of women in former male strongholds. This, too, might not be reflected in the current job distribution. Bearing this in mind, here are some findings:

1. About 80 percent of working women were employed in low-level clerical and service jobs, or are performing "women's work" in factories.
2. Jobs that are more than 90 percent female include secretary, typist, telephone operator, and bank teller. In 1977, among jobs in 450

trades, only 2.2 percent were held by women. Two-thirds of the 16 percent of working women classified as professionals, are nurses and teachers. Of the workers earning between $3,000 and $5,000 a year, 63 percent are women. Of those earning more than $15,000 per year, only 5 percent are women. College-educated women average almost 40 percent less than their male counterparts.

3. In the United States, women in general earn about 60 percent of what men earn per year.[15,16] Throughout the world, women do even worse. Women make up slightly more than half the world's population. They account for two-thirds of the world's working hours but receive only one-tenth of world income and own about one-hundredth of the world's property.[17]

As bleak as this picture looks, there are changes occurring. There are federal "equal pay for equal work" laws and either by the threat of a lawsuit or an actual suit, women have slowly but surely been gaining parity with men. Just recently (August 1980), the Third U.S. Circuit Court of Appeals ruled that Title VII of the Civil Rights Act permits women to seek equal pay for doing jobs that are comparable, even though not identical, to jobs performed by men.[18] (See Box 14.1 for a brief history of women's inclusion in Title VII of the Civil Rights Act.)

The case that prompted this decision was a suit against Westinghouse Electric Corporation that stated female assembly-line workers were receiving less pay than male truck drivers even though their jobs were comparable. This decision may eventually make "female" jobs such as secretary and typist as financially rewarding as "male" positions such as plumber and carpenter.

Women are also opening up their own businesses in increasing numbers. And soon there will be many women physicians, lawyers, dentists, psychologists, and other professionals.

Box 14.1. Title VII Women.

In 1964, Title VII of the Civil Rights Bill was being considered. Howard W. Smith was Chairman of the Rules Committee of the U.S. House of Representatives at that time. He added the word "sex" to Title VII of that bill. It was widely accepted as a joke and as a device to divide the liberals and prevent the passage of the Civil Rights Bill. However, the "joke" backfired and the Civil Rights Act became law. Sex then stood alongside race and creed in not being allowed as a criterion in employment discrimination. Since then, other laws have been added and the legal basis for preventing sex discrimination is now on a firm basis.[19]

WHAT ARE WOMEN'S WORK-RELATED PROBLEMS?

Many women are finding out that getting the job is just the first battle; the war is not yet won. A major problem for mothers is securing child care to enable them to get out of the house and take the job. For newly employed women, many jobs are monotonous, uninteresting and low paying. But even if the positions were interesting, stimulating, and renumerative, there is often the problem of harassment, either sexual or sexist. Other problems are: becoming pregnant; difficulties in acting assertively rather than passively; geographic constraints; the lack of free time; and psychological stressors.

Child Care

Child care is a major problem for the working mother. Whether a woman employs a mother's helper, a baby-sitter, a housekeeper, a day worker or sends her child to a day-care center, there is often anxiety, worry, and guilt.[20] It is also a major expense. Several thousand dollars a year is the average cost and this amount must be subtracted from the women's salary to determine how much she is actually earning. That is why sometimes the woman's income may not be of any real financial benefit. However, in dual-career couples or families where the wife is the major wage earner, the child-care expense is a necessary cost.

Although many day-care centers do an exceptionally fine job, some women would prefer the child being at home in a one-to-one situation with a mother substitute. Some who work part-time have either their mothers or relatives watch the children or have a trade-off arrangement with a neighbor who also works part-time but on different days.

Another useful source for child care is the college "dropout." Some women have found that people who temporarily drop out of college and want room and board will be happy to act as mother's helpers.[21] Some potentially helpful changes for women are the inclusion of child-care benefits in some labor contracts, and the development of child-care facilities in some business establishments.[3]

Boredom

It is a common finding (by predominantly male researchers) that women are more satisfied than men with boring, insulated, low-status, and poorly paid jobs.[22] The usual explanation has been that work does not have the importance for women that it does for men since the woman's central roles are wife, homemaker, and mother. Feminists might frown upon such an explanation saying that traditional women just suppress their true feelings. Nevertheless, the majority of the female working force are forced to work in monotonous, low-status, low-paying jobs. To improve their job opportunities, many women are going back to school for further training or are entering "male" occupations.

Low Pay

As mentioned previously, the average working woman earns about 60 percent of what the average man earns.[16,23] In families run by a single parent, the man earns twice as much as the woman, and, in 1974, 41 percent of families headed by females were at the poverty level.[3]

Sexual Harassment

Sexual harassment for a woman can include: being asked to go to bed with a man; being touched without her consent; being given suggestions of physical intimacy by tone or description; hearing vivid descriptions of her body by men; being coerced to listen to sexual remarks or jokes; being shown pornographic pictures or movies; and being required to dress in a "sexy" manner when she was not previously informed that it was part of the job. Although there are no detailed figures available, surveys have indicated that about 80 percent of all working women get some form of on-the-job sexual harassment.[24]

Although most sexual advances are made by supervisory personnel, male co-workers also are guilty of this conduct. Women may feel reluctant to complain because of fear of loss of job, fear of retaliation by co-workers, and fear that they will not be believed. But these fears take their toll and result in stress-related disorders. Many sexually harassed women report problems such as migraine headaches and "nervous" stomachs.[24]

Women who feel that they have been sexually harassed can and should act, and they are getting various forms of support. *The Equal Employment Opportunity Commission* (EEOC) states that sexual harassment on the job is illegal, and it requires an employer to provide a working environment in which sexual harassment does not occur. There are women's groups that are becoming active in helping harassed women. These include: the *Women's Alliance for Job Equality* (WAJE), a Philadelphia-based outfit; and the *Working Women's Institute* of New York.

Specifically, here is some advice regarding sexual harassment:

1. Politely but firmly say "no" to all forms of sexual harassment.
2. Collect evidence if the harassment continues. Also make copies of any

favorable evaluations of your work so that your refusal of sexual advances doesn't lead to your being fired for "incompetent" work.

3. Speak to other female workers to find out if they, too, have been harassed. Try to line up support.
4. If the business is unionized, discuss the incidents with a union representative before making a formal complaint. This would help determine if you have a firm basis for action.
5. Discuss the matter with noninvolved management personnel.
6. If you have had no help and have obtained some corroborative support, file a complaint with the EEOC.
7. If the sexual advances have been physical in nature and are continuing, you can consider filing criminal charges.
8. The important thing is that if you enjoy the job aside from the harassment, but don't want the stress to continue, you must take action for your own peace of mind.*

Sexist Harassment

The other type of on-the-job harassment is more pervasive and harder to control; that is, sexism. Sexism basically is a belief that the male is superior to the female and has the right to keep her in a subordinate role. As long as men feel threatened by women "invading their realm," they may resort to sexist remarks or actions. There are two ways in which this may be changed. The first is for women to complain to their supervisors, employers or government agencies as was described above because sexist discrimination on the job is also illegal. The second is for women to demonstrate that they can perform as well as men or better. Possibly then the men will learn to control or eliminate their sexism.

Interestingly enough, although there is sexual harassment and sexist bias in employment, many women feel less stressed working for male employers than working for female employers. According to one informal survey most women prefer male bosses.[25] Reasons given were:

---

* An alternative viewpoint on sexual harassment was recently presented before a Senate committee by antifeminist crusader Phyllis Schlafly. She said, "Sexual harassment on the job is not a problem for virtuous women, except in the rarest of cases. Men hardly ever ask sexual favors of women from whom the certain answer is no. Virtuous women are seldom accosted. Nation. Asking for it? New view of sexual harassment. *Time* 29, May 4, 1981. Be that as it may, a federal appeals court has broadened the legal protections against sexual harassment. The U.S. Court of Appeals for the District of Columbia has ruled that sexual harassment, by itself, is a violation of the law and does not need further proof that the employee was penalized or lost benefits. Washington Post Service. Sex bias *per se* is illegal, D.C. court rules. *Philadelphia Inq.* 4-A, January 14, 1981.

1. There is a chemistry of attraction between the sexes.
2. Men are more stimulating and interesting.
3. Men deal better in positions of power.
4. Men are more secure and less jealous.

One reason for the male preference may be related to the lack of power and assertiveness of many women. With more women occupying management positions, they are becoming proficient in the art of interpersonal relations and then, conceivably they will be more frequently preferred as bosses by both females and males.[26]

Becoming Pregnant

It used to be common occurrence that when a woman began to "show," she was laid off and couldn't return to work for up to a year after the birth of her child. In fact, many employers would not hire a young married woman, an engaged woman, or a woman going steady, for fear that she would soon become pregnant. With the advent of many sick-leave benefits, pregnancy benefits were noticeably left out of most plans.

Interestingly enough, in many worldwide cultures, women work right up to the time of labor. This was revealed in a recent cross-cultural study of 202 societies throughout the world.[27] In about one-half of the societies, the women were back working at full capacity within two weeks after delivery. The United States is now falling into step with these other societies. With the passage of a new federal law, it is now illegal to refuse employment to a woman because she is or might become pregnant.[28] An employer is also forbidden to force the new mother to take an extended leave of absence if she wants to return to work. In addition, employees' health benefits must now cover pregnancy-related disabilities and reimburse for medical expenses related to pregnancy and childbirth as comprehensively as other medical expenses.

Pregnant women are now allowed to work for as long as they want or as long as their physicians say it is safe. They cannot be fired because the job is considered to be too difficult for a pregnant woman. They must be treated as if they had a temporary disability and if it is available, they must be given a less strenuous job until after childbirth. Considering all of this, the anxiety about being pregnant should be reduced for working women.

Assertiveness

Many women who have been passive all their lives find difficulties in acting assertively on the job. They may feel they will be considered less feminine if they act assertively. Some men have difficulty in dealing with an assertive woman but this is more of the male's problem. Again, it is usually related to the man feeling threatened. Women can be both assertive and feminine without becoming aggressive, and in doing so will reduce their own stress.[29]

Geographic Constraints

For the married woman teaching in an academic institution or working in an industry with nationwide branches such as General Electric or RCA, there is a problem related to job transfers. She is generally not mobile because of her husband's job and her children's ties (as well as her own). Therefore, she may lose out on promotions and better positions because of the lack of mobility.[30] Single women usually do not have this problem unless they have close family or personal relationships.

Lack of Time

Many married working women find that they have little free time. When they get home, they generally still have to do many of the household chores. Unless they get adequate help, they have little time left over for leisure-time activities. What often happens is that half of the weekend is devoted to household chores with only Sunday left for leisure. Saturday for the average family has become a day to run errands. Men are "pitching in" and finding the hazards of Saturday shopping.[31]

Psychological Problems

As the result of the various job-related problems, working women often come down with psychological disturbances. A recent study found that women with contemporary sex role orientations had more psychological problems than those who were oriented to the traditional roles of women.[32]

Nevertheless, the working woman with a traditional background has role conflict and stress that affects her in both her job and at home.[33] Job-related psychological stressors for the working woman are: fear of disapproval, either by men or other women; feeling of dependency on male coworkers or supervisors; need to submerge her own desires; fear of being aggressive or self-assertive and hence, being labeled unfeminine; fear of failure; and fear of success.[34]

However, this is a time of transition, and with more women getting into various positions working women should not have as many psychological problems and feel as isolated as they once did. They will have support from female co-workers as well as female supervisors. They will learn from female role models that:

1. Women can be assertive without being aggressive.
2. Women can be feminine, effective on the job, and not dependent.
3. Success or failure is nothing to fear since everyone has an occasional failure and success breeds success.

This holds true for school as well as in industry. In schools and universities there will be many more female costudents as well as instructors. If women get more support at home, they may be less inclined to feel guilty about leaving the children and housework and going out of the house for employment.

One new means of support for women is the development of women's networks.[35-37] Men have been using networks informally for years (the "old-boy network") and these have helped them to learn the "ins and outs" of getting ahead. The idea of networking is to help women (or men) become aware of the various problems or pitfalls in their quest for advancement. Networks are usually formed to give input on job and career opportunities. They can also be used to provide information about: managing job interviews; writing a "C.V." (résumé); listing references; speaking to supervisors; combining a business and homelife; setting up a boutique; filing complaints against discriminatory practices in schools and jobs; getting listings of nursery and child-care cooperatives; and finding out about the availability of consciousness-raising groups. Although men's networks are unofficial, there are now about 200 female networks nationally (as of 1980). A new book is available that lists all the women's networks throughout the country.[38] In the Philadelphia area, the organization is known as the *Philadelphia Women's Network*. Women pool their knowledge to help each other. Currently, the membership includes lawyers, publicists, financial analysts, corporate businesswomen, and even sculptors and dancers.[37] Networking is really a form of symbiosis—a mutual exchange program. It is a means of organizing and using friends, business associates and contacts. As such, it can only be beneficial to women who are trying to get ahead in the working world. Aside from networks, recent books are helping women enter and get ahead in the working world. Two worthwhile ones have been written by *Catalyst,* a nonprofit women's group devoted to helping women obtain a career.[39,40]

Now that we have considered the working woman in general, and the housewife in particular, let us look at the woman who tries to excel at both (i.e., the "superwoman"), followed by an examination of the dual-career couple.

"SUPERWOMAN": THE WOMAN WHO DOES IT ALL

Previously we've discussed the stressors of marriage, raising a family, running the household and having outside employment. These stressors are compounded when women try to do them all. Not only do some women try to do them all, they try for perfection. These women have created a new role model—"superwoman" or "supermom"—the woman who excels in everything.

Let us look at "superwoman's" characteristics.[5,10,41] First of all, she is an excellent housewife. Her kitchen is spotless; the floors gleam; the beds are always made; and dirty clothes are never to be seen. If one of the children rips her pants, "supermom" is ready with needle, thread and a patch. When it comes to car pooling, "supermom" has always got the old station wagon on call. Washing and ironing dad's shirts is another priority. After all, "supermom" can do it better than the local laundry, and she saves the family money as well. Going out to dinner? What for? "Supermom" can be depended upon to prepare gourmet meals at one-fourth the cost and she is cook, waitress, bus*boy*, and dishwasher all rolled up into one—and no tip is necessary!

"Supermom" is also a wonderful mother. She rushes the children to the doctor when they are sick and she comforts them when they are sad. She shops for their favorite foods, clothes, and toys. She helps them with their homework and their other problems. ("Of course, we can't bother dad; he's either too busy or relaxing from a hard day at work.")

Who sets the alarms to get the kids ready for school and to get dad off to work—why "supermom" of course! And who prepares breakfast for everyone, makes the beds, feeds the pets, and collects the garbage? You guessed it! It's "supermom" again. With everyone out of the house, the miraculous woman has a breakfast "on the run" and is off to work to continue her marvelous ways.

"Supermom" is tranformed to "superworker" when she arrives at the job. After all, she has to prove that she is as good as a man and is dependable as well. So "superwoman" is conscientious and acquiescent. Although she knows that she is being underpaid, she is happy to be out of the house and able to contribute to the household's finances. "Superwoman" is also "supertolerant" and she tries to ignore sexual harassment, sexist remarks, and being left out of "businessmen's" luncheons. She doesn't mind being a pioneer in her field and not having other female support on the job. After all, as "superwoman" she must be a "liberated" woman who is able to cope without collapsing.

Being "supermom" means that all of the housewife/mother jobs that were formerly done leisurely (???) throughout the day now have to be compressed into the few hours before and after work. And if necessary, this might mean a few hours less sleep at night. This extraordinary woman also must keep up her image as a wonderful wife; hence, when husband comes home she is transformed into "superwife." As such, she must be a loving and attendant companion to her hardworking husband. But if "super-mom" gets fatigued, if she starts to get tension headaches, anxiety attacks, or begins to feel depressed, she must suppress or deny them. After all, how can a "superwoman" get sick?

But "supermom/superwife/superworker" does get sick and does have a breakdown because just as there is no actual *Superman* there is no *Super-woman*. Women who try to be perfect in all situations and roles invite failure. In fact, there is a concept that "to be good in one role implies relative failure in another."[42] Hence, women who combine a career with motherhood place themselves in an untenable position where perfection is really not possible.

In order to prevent women from getting stress-induced ulcers, migraines or heart attacks, or becoming extremely anxious and depressed, here are some aids to prevent the "superwoman complex":

1. You must realize that you cannot do everything by yourself. Priorities have to be developed. If you must work and want to work, then other people have to take over some of the household/mothering tasks.
2. Perfection is simply not possible. You don't have to have the most spotless house on the block. But if it is in your nature that the house must be impeccably clean, then you must prevail on husband and children to do their share, or insist on household help.
3. Again in regard to work, you are entitled to the same consideration as the male employees. Do not be afraid to be assertive; don't feel that you have to meet all the (unreasonable) demands—just do the best that you can! Furthermore, don't endure harassment of any sort.
4. A real "superwoman" is a woman who gets "superenjoyment" out of life. To do that she has to have both a supportive family which is more that willing to do its share, and a considerate boss who realizes the potential problems of a working mother. Remember, you can't do it all indefinitely and you shouldn't even try.

Despite all that has been said, within reason, it is possible for a woman to successfully combine a career and motherhood.[43]

Now that we've discussed the stressors of being a housewife, and working in general, along with the problems of "superwoman," let us now consider the stressors of the dual-career couple.

THE DUAL CAREER COUPLE: A UNIQUE TYPE OF STRESS

Within the last ten years, there has been a tremendous increase in the number of families in which both husband and wife have careers.[43] The reasons for this upsurge, have been discussed earlier in this chapter under the reasons why working women are working. But the main reason is that women are now concentrating more on their career aims rather than being content with the housewife/mother role. They are looking for fulfillment rather than just a means to make some money. There are certain specific problems related to the dual-career couple. These are now considered.

PROBLEMS[44]

Overload

As was discussed in the last chapter, a woman cannot do it all. Whether it is the housework or the children, the partners must have an equitable sharing arrangement. Unlike the woman who works for spending money or to relieve boredom, the career woman has a position which is as important or more important than her husband's. Hence, the husband can't disagree to help the wife with her household/mothering chores. The chores are not the woman's but the family's and must be equally shared.

Role Reversal

In the traditional marriage, the wife—whether she's working or not— takes charge of the children's needs, such as taking them to the physician when they're sick, or going to teachers conferences to learn about the children's progress. In dual-career families, there may be role reversal with the husband doing these chores. The crucial determinant is the flexibility of the schedule. Whoever has a lower priority at the time should take care of the problem.

Mixed Priorities

In the last section, we discussed the traditional marriage where the mother works, but is still forced to take care of the family and household. But "supermom" generally cracks under the strain and winds up with stress-related disturbances. With dual-career couples, there may be mixed priorities. The husband may not want to do his share of household/mothering jobs or he may prefer only certain jobs. For example, he may wash the pots and put clothes in the washing machine, but he won't vacuum the rugs or wax the floors. One way out is for the couple to hire people to do the chores with which neither is happy (given that the finances permit it).

Money

In the traditional marriage, the husband who makes most of the money has most of the power. In dual-career couples, sometimes the woman has a more prestigious and a better paying position than the man. She may then try to wield her money weapon. For instance, the wife may want to buy a new car and let her husband drive the old car. Problems can arise when he has his money and she has her money. The best solution is when there is a pooling of money and a sharing of interests.

Jealousy

Jealousy of the other's career is usually not a problem with dual-career couples. This is especially true if each spouse has a career in a different profession or field and they are comfortable in their respective positions. When either of the partners is gaining success, they often receive support and praise from the other. Jealousy may appear if both partners are in the same profession and it is even more likely if they practice at the same location.

However, both partners may find the arrangement of working in the same place to be advantageous. For example, it can reduce automobile expenses and give them topics of mutual interest to discuss. On the negative side, being together so much can create friction; it is difficult to be on your best behavior twenty-four hours a day. Some couples work together only part time (e.g., either in stores or in sales) which overcomes the problem of being together too much. One rapidly growing part-time couple enterprise is the "house party" where goods such as Tupperware®, cosmetics, and vacuum cleaners are displayed and sold.[45]

Many wife and husband teams formerly found it extremely difficult to find employment together because institutions would not hire them both (a fear of nepotism). However, discrimination suits have changed the pattern, and now many married couples are working at the same place.

Job Offer

In dual-career couples, a major source of stress occurs when one of the partners gets a job or a promotion offer in another city. In the traditional family, it is the husband who gets the offer and the wife and children routinely follow if he decides to accept it and move. With the two-career couple, if it is the wife who has the "super" offer, what does the family do? There are a number of alternatives:

1. The woman takes the job and urges her spouse to leave his current position and try to find another one in the new city.
2. The woman takes the job and takes an apartment in the new city. The husband keeps his job and stays home; the wife comes home on weekends.
3. The wife takes the job and the husband keeps his. The family moves halfway between the two cities.
4. The woman takes the job. The husband refuses to leave his job or move. (That is, the couple gets divorced.)
5. The woman refuses the job and becomes "unliberated" because she feels her marriage is more important than her career.

All of these solutions occur and cause a certain amount of stress. Sometimes "the best solution is dissolution" (i.e., divorce) but often an amicable arrangement can be made.

The Family

If both members are career-oriented, they may decide to postpone raising a family. If the woman decides that her career is of paramount importance, then the couple may decide not to have any children. If children are present in a career-dominated family, they may suffer from lack of companionship and love. However, dual-career couples can combine a good home life and successful careers. As mentioned before, it takes mutual cooperation. The children of such a family often grow up as well or better than in a family where the mother doesn't go out to work. They often are proud of their working parents and become independent at an early age. The key thing is the "quality" time that parents give their children and not simply the quantity of time spent with them.

Happiness

Twenty-eight dual-career couples were asked to rate the amount of conflict they felt among four major roles: spouse; parent; career; and self-actualization.[46] Both women and men found the least conflict among the roles when: (1) their spouses supported them; (2) they had good self-esteem; (3) they had "profeminist" attitudes; and (4) they each had a high career commitment. The highly committed males who also had high career goals (i.e., aspired for advancement in their careers in addition to working hard at their careers) felt little conflict among their roles when they met the conditions (1) to (3) above. However, women who aimed for advancement in their careers even with meeting conditions (1) to (3) above had added conflict. The women who were satisfied with low career goals had the least conflict. This is probably related to the guilt and anxiety that many women still feel about neglecting their children, household, and wife roles. Hopefully, in time, women will learn to reduce those stressors.

Dual-career couples have some major advantages as well as some problems.

ADVANTAGES

Money

A major advantage is financial. If both members have lucrative positions, the dual salary will certainly enhance their life-style and allow them to do many more things than would be possible only if the husband was working, or if the wife merely had a low-status job.

Something to Talk About

In the traditional marriage, the husband comes home at the end of the work day and either remains silent about his day, "barks" out some choice epithets, or seriously tries to tell his wife about the daily occurrences. The wife has had her own problems and she, too, can respond in any of the same three ways. Usually, neither listens to each other and communication really becomes a problem.

With dual-career couples, both may feel that they have something important to talk about and there is a better chance that they will listen to each other, take turns, and try to give each other support.

Having a two-career marriage can be enjoyable and rewarding but the spouses must not go into it blindly. To reduce stress and its consequences, the individuals should carefully consider the advantages and disadvantages, and sometimes what seems to be an ideal arrangement turns out to be a disaster (see Box 14.2).

In the next chapter, we consider the stress for women from taking a position in one of the lower-status female jobs.

Box 14.2. Dual-Career Collapse.

She had a Ph.D. in Biology along with a tenured position at a big city university. He had a thriving law practice. Together they managed to enjoy their careers, and still share equally in caring for the children. Fortunately, they could afford a housekeeper, and she took care of most of the chores. They supported each other's careers. In fact, he was so excited about her getting a Ph.D. he practically gave out cigars.

The other day, before she left for work (he had already left), there was a knock on the front door. It was the sheriff and he presented her with a summons: It was a summons for a divorce—and she had 10 days to find a lawyer! In panic, she picked up the phone and called his office. He refused to speak to her. The message was relayed that all his talking would be done "through his attorney."

The unfolding story revealed his plans to marry a "young, blonde, recent college graduate." His wife-to-be was presumably sweet, coy, and simpering, and apparently had no career aspirations. She just wanted to be a homemaker—the kind of woman he always professed to detest!

We've all heard of closet homosexuals; by analogy, he was a closet male chauvinist.[47] The moral of this true story is that you can never tell what is really going on in someone else's mind or with someone else's marriage. The one saving grace for the woman is that she still has her career, her children and her pride, but it will probably be a while before she trusts another man.

REFERENCES

1. Williams, J. H. *Psychology of Women: Behavior in a Biosocial Context*. New York: W. W. Norton, 1977.
2. Thomas, J. Are women really afraid of money: Ignorant of money basics, most "save" but don't invest. *Philadelphia Inq*. WA-3, May 27, 1979.
3. Nelson, A. H. The women in the labor organization. *In* Carone, P. A., Kieffer, S. N., Krinsky, L. W., and Yolles, S. F. (eds.), *Women In Industry*. Albany, New York: State University of New York Press, 1977, pp. 10–42.
4. Krupsak, M. A. Women in employment. *In* Carone, P. A., Kieffer, S. N., Krinsky, L. W., and Yolles, S. F. (eds.), *Women In Industry*. Albany, New York: State University of New York Press, 1977, pp. 3–9.
5. Sifford, D. Backstage, superwoman is harassed and frustrated. *Philadelphia Inq*. 3-D, August 4, 1980.
6. Wilson, K. M. Today's women students: New outlooks, options. *Findings,* Educational Testing Service, Princeton, N. J., November 4, 1974.
7. Rindfuss, R. R., Bumpass, L., and St.John, C. Education and fertility: Implications for the roles women occupy. *Am. Soc. Rev*. **45**:431–447, 1980.

8. Janeway, E. *Man's World Woman's Place: A Study in Social Mythology.* New York: Dell Publishing, 1971.
9. Schmid, R. E. Sign of the times: More women than men in college. *Philadelphia Inq.* 2-A, August 24, 1980.
10. Hoffman, L. W. and Nye, F. I. *Working Mothers.* San Francisco: Jossey-Bass, 1974.
11. Chesler, P. and Goodman, E. J. *Women, Money and Power.* New York: William Morrow, 1976.
12. Ahern, D. D. and Bliss, B. *Economics of Being a Woman.* New York: Macmillan Publishing, 1976.
13. Auerbach, S. *A Woman's Book of Money: A Guide to Financial Independence.* Garden City, New York: Doubleday, 1976.
14. Pursel, D. E. and Torrence, W. D. The older woman and her search for employment. *Aging Work* 3(2):121-128, 1980.
15. Rule, S. The special groups: Women still knocking on the door. *New York Times National Recruitment Survey* Sec. 12: 43, October 12, 1980.
16. Kjervik, D. K. The stress of sexism on the mental health of women. *In* Kjervik, D. K. and Martinson, I. M. (eds.), *Women In Stress: A Nursing Perspective.* Appleton-Century-Crofts, 1979, pp. 144-156.
17. Wilder, B. Study: Women worse off: U. N. aims to ease their burden worldwide. *Philadelphia Inq.* 2-A, July 13, 1980.
18. Eisner, J. Court allows broader suits on sex bias. *Philadelphia Inq.* 1A-2A, August 5, 1980.
19. Davies, R. E. and Davies, H. C. Redress of grievances. *Ann. N. Y. Acad. Sci.* 323:197-209, 1979.
20. Harris, B. Two Lives, one 24-hour day. *In* Roland, A. and Harris, B. (eds.), *Career and Motherhood: Struggles for a New Identity.* New York: Human Sciences Press, 1979, pp. 25-45.
21. Curtis, J. *Working Mothers.* Garden City, New York: Doubleday, 1976.
22. Oakley, A. *Women's Work: The Housewife, Past and Present.* New York: Random House, 1974.
23. Moss, V. Financial problems of women. *In* Carone, P. A., Kieffer, S. N., Krinsky, L. W. and Yolles, S. F. (eds.), *Women in Industry.* Albany, New York: State University of New York Press, 1977, pp. 77-112.
24. Chastain, S. Sexual pressure still a hazard for working women. *Philadelphia Inq.* 1-I, 12-I, June 15, 1980.
25. Shearer, L. Parade's special intelligence report: Boss preference. *Parade* 13, April 27, 1980.
26. Bardwick, J. *In Transition: How Feminism, Sexual Liberation and the Search for Self Fulfillment Have Altered America.* New York: Holt Rinehart & Winston, 1978.
27. Simpson, P. Pregnant workers have a tough ally: Attitudes, policies in the working world are changing, thanks to the new baby law. *Parade* 31-32, May 20, 1979.
28. Houdek-Jiminez, M. and Newton, V. Activity and work during pregnancy and the post partum period: A cross-cultural study of 202 societies. *Am. J. Obstet. Gynecol.* 135(2):171-176, 1979.
29. Brothers, J. Work-related stress encountered by women. *Gloucester City Times* A-4, October 15, 1979.
30. Marwell, G., Rosenfeld, R., and Spilerman, S. Geographic constraints on women's careers in academia. *Science* 205:1225-1231, 1979.
31. Dundon, S. The incredible shrinking Saturday. *Philadelphia Inq.* 10-A, August 5, 1980.

32. Powell, B. and Reznikoff, M. Role conflict and symptoms of psychological distress in college educated women. *J. Consult. Clin. Psych.* **44**:473–479, 1976.
33. Miller, J. Schooler, C., Kohn, M. L., and Miller, K. A. Women and work: The psychological effects of occupational conditions. *Am. J. Soc.* **85**(1):66–93, 1980.
34. Moulton, R. Psychological challenges confronting women in the sciences. *Ann. N. Y. Acad. Sci.* **323**:321–335, 1979.
35. Daniels, A. K. Development of feminist networks in the professions. *Ann. N. Y. Acad. Sci.* **323**:215–227, 1979.
36. Welch, M. S. *Networking: The Great New Way for Women to Get Ahead.* New York: Harcourt, Brace, Jovanovich, 1980.
37. Kantrowicz, B. A network for women works on many levels. *Philadelphia Inq.* 1-F, 2-F, July 6, 1980.
38. Kleiman, C. *Women's Networks.* New York: Lippincott & Crowell, 1980.
39. The Staff of Catalyst. *What to Do with the Rest of Your Life.* New York: Simon & Schuster, 1980.
40. The Staff of Catalyst. *Marketing Yourself: Women's Guide to Successful Resumés and Interviews.* New York: C. P. Putman's, 1980.
41. Inglehart, A. P. *Married Women and Work: 1957 and 1976.* Lexington, Mass.: D. C. Heath, 1979.
42. Roland, A. and Harris, B. *Career and Motherhood: Struggles for a New Identity.* New York: Human Sciences Press, 1979.
43. Bryson, J. and Bryson, R. (eds.), *Dual-Career Couples.* New York: Human Sciences Press, 1978.
44. Sifford,D. How does spouse cope when the other's career begins to zoom? *Philadelphia Inq.* 1-C, 3-C, April 12, 1977.
45. Diamond, S. J. Big business takes a cue from Tupperware. *Philadelphia Inq.* 1-I, 5-I, August 24, 1980.
46. Cory, C. T. Newsline: Families: In two-career marriages, happy wives aim low. *Psychol. Today* **12**(6):28, 34, 1978.
47. Stein, L. A. Our town: The ideal marriage. *Philadelphia Inq. Today Mag.* 9, August 10, 1980.

15
White To Blue:
From Female Clerk
To
"Lady" Plumber

INTRODUCTION

In this chapter we address the stress for women in various fields, including white-collar clerical jobs, service positions, farming jobs, and blue-collar positions.

CLERICAL JOBS

The single largest field of employment for women is in the clerical field. There are currently about 11 million women employed in clerical work. Overall, female clerical workers earn about 60 percent of the salaries of male clerical workers. That is primarily because they work in the lower echelon of clerical jobs. Most women are employed as secretaries, stenographers, typists, switchboard operators, receptionists, file clerks, cashiers and bookkeepers.[1] Some women work their way up to becoming executive secretaries or administrative assistants, but there are still very few women who rise higher into management positions.[2] In contrast, when men take clerical jobs, these are frequently stepping stones to higher echelon positions.

SERVICE JOBS

The next largest category of female employment is in service jobs. The overall wages in service-related positions are the lowest of any category.

Female service workers earn about one-half the amount of male service workers. There are some women in higher echelon or higher-paying service jobs such as "policemen," enlisted women in the military, and insurance, but most of these fields are male-dominated.

Typical female service jobs are waitress, salesclerk, chambermaid, house-keeper, dental assistant, hospital worker, beautician, bank teller, telephone operator, and airline stewardess.

Even in hard times, door-to-door sales and its offshoot "house parties" remains a growing area. There are currently (August 1980) 4 million workers in this field. Most are part-time (90 percent) and the majority are women (80 percent). They sell items such as Avon® cosmetics and Tupper-ware® plastic containers. Even two-out-of-three Fuller Brush® "men" are females. Although people still slam doors in their faces, many others

Box 15.1.   The first female police class.

There were thirty women in uniforms of navy blue pants, light blue shirts and black ties and caps. They marched in perfect cadence on the drill field of the New Jersey State Police Academy in Sea Girt, New Jersey. The "lady cadets" then gave a demonstration of precision drills, boxing, judo, and calisthenics. It was graduation day for this unique class, the first all-female state police graduating class in the nation. The young women, rang-ing in age from eighteen to thirty, received their badges upon completion of a twenty-week training course considered to be one of the toughest state trooper training programs in the country.

When the class first began, it consisted of 104 women but most of them gradually dropped out. The principal reasons were the rigorous physical training, the high academic standards, and the long, intense hours of work. The women trainees had some other specific problems. For example, they could not run in the high-top shoes that were made for the male recruits. When they tried them, many developed ankle injuries. So they were given special athletic shoes for their daily five-mile run. Another problem was running in formation. The men ran in formation at one-arm's distance. When the woman recruits tried it, they tended to trip and fall down. However, at two-arms' lengths, they had no difficulties. The women were also given special assertiveness training. Women recruits managed weapons as well as the male recruits. As in other male fields in which women enter, there was initial negative reactions on the part of some males. The feeling was that females can't cope well in an emergency situation. However, the officers conducting the class stated that the women state troopers were physically and emotionally fit to do state police work. Another barrier has now been broken and women in the police ranks will no longer be limited to meter maids, street-crossing guards and clerks at police stations.[6]

enjoy the friendliness and cameraderie of the saleswomen, and either buy the products or host the parties.[3]

Ninety-five percent of household service employees are women, with more than 50 percent of them being black.[2] In hospitals, 75 percent of the health-care labor force is female.[1] Almost 70 percent of bank employees are women, but only 20 percent are bank officers.[4,5]

However, women are making inroads. For instance, in the broadcasting industry, many more women are becoming radio and TV announcers and disc jockeys, and women are well represented as "soundmen," producers, and assistant producers of TV and radio shows. There are also more women newspaper and magazine reporters. A blending of roles is occurring with beauticians and barbers; consider the many male beauticians and female barbers. The first all-female police class is discussed in Box 15.1.

ADVANTAGE OF CLERICAL AND SERVICE JOBS

The major advantages of these positions is the foreknowlege that they are traditional women's jobs. Women don't have to worry about being pioneers. There is a storehouse of knowledge about the jobs and women can easily "dig out" the required information. Most often they work with other women, or have friends, acquaintances, or family members who were employed in the same or similar jobs. Hence, there is no shortage of role models. Other women are also available for support, discussions, and simple gossiping.

For women who are not desirous of having a long-term commitment to a career, or do not want to spend a lot of time in preparing for a career, then these kinds of positions are advantageous. There is generally a more rapid turnover than in the professions such as teaching, nursing, and dental hygiene. Therefore, if necessary, the women could leave one job and later on obtain another position. However, continually changing jobs would make it difficult to remain employable.

DISADVANTAGES OF CLERICAL AND SERVICE JOBS

The major disadvantages of these jobs are: (1) the limited range of income; (2) the lack of suitable advancement; (3) the routine nature of the work; and (4) especially for the nontraditional jobs, problems of harassment (see Box 15.2).

This discussion of advantages and disadvantages is all relative. It depends upon individual needs and desires. What one woman would find to be boring or fear-provoking, another might find to be stimulating. For ex-

BOX 15.2:   The Female Soldier.

The United States Army has a current five-year goal to increase the number of enlisted women to 85,000 in a 765,000 member army. But the women are not "cooperating." Current studies (August 1980) show that 46.7 percent of female enlistees quit the service before their first hitch is completed. And forecasts predict that the rate of dropouts will increase even further.[7] Some possible causes for the high attrition rate for women soldiers are:

1. In the traditional jobs for women (e.g., clerk or medical orderly) the female soldiers often do little more than shuffle papers.
2. In the nontraditional jobs (e.g., maintenance, transportation, engineering) where 61 percent of the women are placed, the male soldiers have not been very cooperative or receptive.
3. Women in these positions often find themselves subjected to very close scrutiny.
4. Sexual harassment is a definite problem.

In order to get out of the service, women resort to various methods including: getting pregnant; going AWOL; becoming alcoholic or drug dependent; and demonstrating medical or personal hardship. Other women soldiers have complained that they did not get the training that they were promised.

At any rate it seems that many women are not finding the Army to be an equal opportunity employment career and are opting to try some civilian job instead. It is hoped that the Army will try to improve conditions and women soldiers will remain and maybe even reenlist.

---

ample, many new jobs are opening up for women as the result of the introduction of legalized gambling casinos in Atlantic City, New Jersey. Women are getting jobs as dealers, bartenders, and waitresses. The salaries are not high but the tips are very good. On the other hand, women report a high incidence of sexual harassment. Some women enjoy the "highly charged" emotional atmosphere at the gambling casinos. Other women find it to be stressful. One female occupation that can be both exciting and stress-inducing is that of the airline stewardess (see Box 15.3).

The best approach for a woman contemplating a position in any of the traditional blue-collar female fields is to consider the pros and cons of the particular job with the help of as many sources as possible (including friends, family, schools, and professionals). She should find out the duties and obligations, the criteria for advancement both in position and pay, and the various benefits. Then if she decides on the job and is hired, she should

BOX 15.3.   Stress in the sky.

The airline stewardess (hostess) has the opportunity to travel throughout the world and meet interesting passengers and airline personnel. This could be considered eustress (good stress). Companionship and support from female co-workers is readily available. The chance to meet airline pilots may either be an advantage or disadvantage depending upon the individuals involved. Potentially distressing aspects of the position are: (1) jet lag; (2) long hours; (3) short stays at stopover cities; (4) time "pressures" on the job; (5) possibility of hijackings; (6) possibility of a crash; and (7) sexual and sexist harassment by passengers.

Nevertheless, hostessing is often an exciting and interesting career that is relatively well paid. However, it is difficult to become a hostess since there are specific physical requirements and mandatory airline school attendance.

BOX 15.4.   Dental Assistant: The "Gal Friday."

One traditional female position is that of dental assistant. Depending upon the dental office, an assistant's duties can range from helping the dentist at the chair to greeting patients and "balancing the books." Dental assistants can take courses from three months to two years to learn their trade, or they can receive on-the-job training. Some assistants complete their schooling and find out that their dentist still insists on giving them additional on-the-job training. Dental assistants who take one- or two-year courses are eligible for certification after taking a test. There are now about 72,000 Certified Dental Assistants.[10]

In some offices, dental assistants are part of a large female office staff that includes chairside assistants, dental hygienists, dental receptionists, dental "rovers" (who clean up and prepare treatment rooms), and office managers. In other offices, the dental assistant may do it all and could be considered the "superwoman" of the dental profession.

Dental assisting is generally not a well-paid position. Certified dental assistants have the highest salaries. Dental assisting is not unionized but there is a national organization (American Dental Assistants Association), a national journal *(Dental Assistant)* and yearly meetings.

Dental assisting can be a rewarding occupation for the woman who enjoys: (1) meeting people; (2) developing personal relationships with healing professionals; (3) the opportunity to communicate with other health-care workers; (4) being in a generally relaxed atmosphere; and (5) having regular working hours. Many dental hygienists and female dentists received their impetus to go into the dental professions by first having a job as a dental assistant.

give it an unbiased trial period. If all is well, then the woman should consider herself fortunate since most people are not satisfied with their jobs. If she finds the job is not to her liking, then to avoid disappointment and stress, she should inform her employer. It would be wise to first have a commitment for another job before quitting the first, especially if there are financial problems. This seemingly commonsense advice is too frequently forgotten in the haste to leave an unfavorable job. It is true that stress can result from having an unenjoyable job,* but it is often more stressful to be unemployed. For example, when the Olin Chemical Works closed down its Saltville, Virginia factory, many of the newly unemployed came down with cases of stomach distress, alcoholism, and hypertension.[8] Studies have shown that employed women experience twice the amount of stress of male workers, but unemployed women report about four times more stress symptoms as do unemployed men.[9]

For an example of the advantages and disadvantages of a traditional female job, see Box 15.4.

FARMING AND BLUE-COLLAR JOBS

Throughout the world, women play an important role as semiskilled farm laborers. They work long hours in the fields doing tedious picking, carrying, and lifting chores. These positions are physically exhausting and mentally unstimulating. They are also seasonal. Women farm laborers are generally poorly paid. Another possible disadvantage is the ill effects of long hours of sunshine (potential for skin cancer and burns). Aside from earning some income, the only other possible advantage is the exercise that occurs from engaging in the various physical chores.

Blue-collar jobs consist of unskilled, semi-skilled, and skilled factory and nonfarm laborers, and skilled craftsmen and industrial workers. Blue-collar jobs make up 36 percent of all workers with 17 percent being women.[2] Women blue-collar workers earn about 50 percent of what males earn. They have the lowest status jobs such as checkers, packers, assemblers, sewers, and stitchers. Women are mainly employed in the apparels, textiles, and electronics industries.[9] Men generally have the higher status and better paying positions such as carpenters, electricians, plumbers, bricklayers, and mechanics. The meat industry has an interesting division of labor (see Box 15.5.).

* In a recent study, laborers, secretaries and office managers were found to head the list of jobs that apparently produce stress-related diseases. Laboratory technicians and waitresses were also found to be high-stress occupations. Most of these jobs had long working hours, boring and repetitive tasks, a fast-paced workplace and generated feelings of "pressure," "tension" and anxiety. They also provided no outlets for stress release. Chicago. Research says laborers, secretaries afflicted most. *Business Insurance* 59, November 10, 1980.

BOX 15.5.   Meat Stress.

Women are meat wrappers, while men are butchers. There are about 75,000 meat wrappers in the United States and Canada and most of them are women.[9] The argument used against hiring women as butchers is that they can't lift the heavy cuts of meat. Undoubtedly, there are some women who *can* lift the heavy loads just as there are some men who can't. In time, there probably will be more women butchers. But there are physical problems in being butchers (e.g., sliced fingers and strained backs). Even meat wrappers have to be careful about slips, falls, back strains, and nicks and cuts.[9] Most establishments have accident prevention programs to cut down the risks of injury.

Nationally, there has been a recent decrease in the number of blue-collar workers because of the recession, foreign competition, and phasing out of products. The decline has been in furniture, machinery, shipbuilding, transport, textiles, leather, shoes, equipment, and steel.[3] Nevertheless, women are entering blue-collar jobs in increasing numbers. There are two basic reasons for this:

(1) Primarily, legal pressures have forced businesses and unions to comply. Appropriately, the first woman ever was just added to the AFL-CIO executive council.[11] There are government constraints that can be withheld; there are consent and compliance decrees; and there are affirmative action programs. (2) In addition to the legal moves, women are learning that they have what it takes to enter many traditionally male fields. Tests have shown that women have the talents to enter into many male-dominated occupations such as radio and TV repairs, auto mechanics, business machinery repairs, aircraft mechanics, and household appliance repairs.[12]

As an example of the increased women's entrance into these fields, recently there was a 74 percent increase in one year in blue-collar jobs for women in Nassau County, New York.[4] Although women have had a small increase in the skilled crafts in the 1970's (about 3–5 percent), in the last few years they have been entering many more blue-collar fields.[2] Some of the fields with increased female participation include mechanics, plumbing and heating, and the truck, bus, and taxicab industries.[4]

When the Alaskan oil pipeline was laid down, there were 1,000 women who worked along with the 15,000 men. They worked the same 70-hour week and made the same $1000 per week salary. The construction industry employs the largest number of skilled trades workers of any industry in the United States. There are about 313,000 women employed in this industry. The breakdown is 113,000 in general contracting, 148,000 in special trades, and over 51,000 in heavy highway construction (1980 estimate).[13]

ADVANTAGES AND DISADVANTAGES OF
THE NONTRADITIONAL BLUE-COLLAR JOBS

Women entering the traditional blue-collar jobs have the same advantages and disadvantages as discussed under clerical and service jobs. The women coming into the former male bastions are developing other physical and psychological problems (see Box 15.6).

A specific problem has been the lack of union support. It has been difficult for women to get into some unions and win benefits equal to those of men. However, with governmental coercion, labor unions are beginning to cooperate and women are winning equal rights both on-the-job and in the labor union. They also have their own support groups to help them, such as the *Coalition of Labor Union Women.*

Women working in certain blue-collar jobs have had particular physical problems related to the environment and protective equipment. Women in construction must be aware of potential environmental problems such as: air pollution; noise; fire; shock; toxic chemicals; bad weather; dangerous tools, machinery and equipment; temperature extremes; and dangerous work methods. Protective equipment for the head, face, eyes, hands, feet, and other parts of the body is essential during various phases of construction. There is a national organization for women in construction, *The National Association of Women in Construction* (NAWIC), which helps in prevention and education for women construction workers.[13]

Women working in various factories, mines, and with specialized equipment, require personal protective equipment. This equipment includes items such as safety glasses, respirators, gloves, ear muffs, face shields,

BOX 15.6. Women, Mice and Bolts.

From a factory employing skilled workers, there is a report of a woman having had a mouse stapled to her machine. In another factory, a male co-worker used a wrench to tighten the bolts on a female worker's machine. They were tightened so securely that she could no longer operate the machine. In coal mines and automobile factories, women often report sexual harassment.

Women steel workers have also described harassment. However, they have found that *not* showing pain often helps. They laugh when they get hurt and they don't ask for help. Doing this, they state, earns the male worker's respect and the harassment tends to stop.[9]

Whether women would want to deal with harassment in this manner is another question. Undoubtedly, many women would prefer to let their supervisors know of the problems and if necessary, get legal help.

work shoes, hard hats, vests, aprons, coveralls, worksuits, and rain gear. Research and on-the-job reports have shown that in many industries the protective equipment was designed with the male in mind. Women have had safety-related problems because the equipment didn't fit well. Now with more women entering the various fields, improvements are being made in protective equipment for women.[14] But to prevent physical injury and psychological stressors, women should insist that the protective equipment they receive is suitable.

To work in the nontraditional blue-collar jobs is an exciting challenge to many women. It must be realized that many of these jobs are physically demanding. However, if women prepare themselves well, they may find such positions to be interesting as well as financially rewarding.

In the next chapter, we consider the traditional female professions.

REFERENCES

1. Jones, A. B. and Shapiro, E. C. The peak of the pyramid: Women in Dentistry, Medicine and Veterinary Medicine. *Ann. N. Y. Acad. Sci.* **323**:79–93, 1979.
2. Seidman, A. (ed.), *Working Women: A Study of Women in Paid Jobs.* Boulder, Colorado: Westview Press, 1978.
3. Diamond, S. Big business takes a cue from Tupperware. *Philadelphia Inq.* 1-I, 5-I, August 24, 1980.
4. Slotkin, F. Career choices/opportunities for women. *In* Carone, P. A., Kiefer, S. N., Krinsky, L. W., and Yolles, S. F. (eds.), *Women in Industry.* Albany, New York: State University of New York Press, 1977, pp. 194–219.
5. Eisen, E. N. Next: Women in the board room. *Philadelphia Eve. Bull.* NB 13–14, May 21, 1979.
6. McCrary, L. All-female state police class, 30 strong, goes marching in. *Philadelphia Inq.* 1-B, 2-B, June 28, 1980.
7. Hoffman, F. S. Nearly half of female recruits quit army early. *Philadelphia Inq.* 3-A, August 19, 1980.
8. Lewis, H. R. and Lewis, M. E. *Psychosomatics: How Your Emotions Can Damage Your Health.* New York: The Viking Press, 1972.
9. Nelson, A. H. The woman in the labor organization. *In* Carone, P. A. Kieffer, S. N., Krinsky, L. W., and Yolles, S. F. (eds.), *Women in Industry.* Albany, New York: State University of New York Press, 1977, pp. 10–42.
10. Peterson, S. (ed.), *The Dentist and the Assistant.* Saint Louis: C. V. Mosby, 1977.
11. Ullman, O. Woman named to AFL-CIO board. *Philadelphia Inq.* 3-A, August 22, 1980.
12. Fader, S. S. *From Kitchen to Career: How any Woman Can Skip Low-Level Jobs and Start in the Middle or at the Top.* New York: Stein and Day, 1977.
13. McPherson, A. "Constructing" recognition for female laborers. *Occupat. Health Safety* **49**(3):68A-68B, 1980.
14. Kaplan, M. C. Women and equipment: The female worker: Ignored by safety device manufacturers? *Occup. Health Safety* **49**(2):28–32, 1980.

16

The Traditional
Female Professions:
from Teacher to Librarian

INTRODUCTION

"Jill is a teacher, Jack is a professor; Jill is a nurse, Jack is a physician; Jill is a librarian, Jack is a scientist." As can be seen from the above, women's traditional professions have been rated a notch or two below the men's as far as status and money are concerned. The male-dominated professions entail greater responsibility and risk (e.g., higher malpractice insurance). Interestingly, there has been a recent reverse trend, possibly because of the lesser responsibility and still adequate prestige (e.g., more male nurses and male dental hygienists). Let us now consider the stressors of teaching.

TEACHING

From nursery school through senior high school, the ranks of teachers are well filled with women. Currently there are 2.2 million teachers in the nation's public schools and a high proportion of these are women. Women teachers are the backbone of our education system. Many of us can fondly remember a particular woman teacher who triggered off our career aspirations (see Box 16.1).

Teaching is a rewarding profession but there are several potential stressors. The school day doesn't end with student dismissal. There are exams to be prepared and graded as well as work assignments to be developed. Teachers often have to deal with undisciplined students and angry parents, and they may have to be somewhat subservient to the principal (who is usually a man).[1]

BOX 16.1. The Prime of Miss Primrose By DM.

It was the first day of English IV in my senior year at Dewitt Clinton High School in the Bronx. I was a science enthusiast having taken biology, chemistry, and physics. I aspired to someday becoming a dedicated researcher. And then I met Miss Primrose. She was a typical English teacher (tall and thin with thick horn-rimmed glasses and fast and furious in her speech). Miss Primrose was in her mid-forties and unmarried (no such thing as a Ms. in those days). Her English was impeccable and her love of the language knew no bounds. I had been a decent English student in my previous courses but had no special inclination toward either literature or creative writing.

In those days I hadn't the vaguest notion of hypnosis, but I became entranced by Miss Primrose. It was probably the "A" along with the enthusiastic comments on my first composition that did it. Whatever it was, I fell in love with both the English language and Miss Primrose (not necessarily in that order). In my senior year, I read and wrote and wrote and read. I went to the school and public libraries and took out "the 100 best novels of all time." I used to read in my bed with pencil, pad and dictionary as companions. I went from *Crime and Punishment* to *War and Peace*.

Years later, I was a bacteriology major at City College in New York. That summer I went to work as a waiter in Kutsher's Country Club in Monticello, New York. During my first week on the job, I saw an attractive young woman poring over "Word Power" in *Reader's Digest*. With typical male chauvanistic ego, I asked her if she would like some help with the word definitions. She agreed and was so impressed with my 100 percent rating that a few months later she consented to be my wife.

I have now written numerous scientific articles and several books. Even though I was fortunate in achieving my scientific ambition, I never lost my love for the written word. Thanks to you Miss Primrose, wherever you are.

Salaries are still not as good as in industry, but a far greater problem, especially in large public schools, is physical and sexual harassment. Discipline takes a large part of a teacher's time and aside from the loss of productive teaching there is the potential of physical danger.

In 1979, 110,000 teachers reported that they were attacked by students, an increase of 57 percent over the previous year. Twenty-five percent of all high-school teachers report that they had personal property stolen at school. Another problem: Although many teachers are desirous of teaching, many students don't want to learn. One New York panel found that in the years from 1968 to 1977, homework assignments were cut in half. The main reason was the students' refusal to do them. Television is considered to be one of the principal factors responsible.[1]

Other problems are: (1) the *New Math* (often confusing to the teacher and student alike); (2) "open classrooms" (often a mass of confusion); (3) the deterioration of the English language in deference to ethnic, native, and bilingual languages; (4) the lack of choice in textbooks; (5) meetings and paperwork; (6) forced busing with its attendant student fights and parent boycotts; (7) the policy of mainstreaming (all handicapped children, must, insofar as possible, be educated in the same classroom as other children); (8) the large-size classes (often 30 or more students); and (9) the loss of jobs (because of the declining birth rate).

As a result of these stressors many teachers are suffering from teacher "burnout." This is a stress-related condition of physical and emotional exhaustion. Some manifestations are: insomnia; inertia; ulcers; migraine; backaches; colitis; dizziness; recurrent colds; and even suicide.[1] For some teachers it is an occasional occurrence; for others it is an annual affliction, reaching its climax in late February. For still others, it never stops and they either end their lives or end their teaching careers. Some even become administrators.[2]

Many who leave don't return. For example, two out of three New York City school teachers who were laid off the previous year, when given the chance to come back, declined to return to classroom teaching.[2] In 1965, in a national poll, more than half of American teachers professed happiness in teaching. In 1980, less than one-third would become teachers if they had another chance.[1]

Rather than quitting, many teachers are forsaking the higher pay of center-city teaching and moving to the suburbs. Although there are problems in suburban and rural schools, there is less violence and a better opportunity to do pure teaching.

With all of its attendant problems, women do not have to abandon teaching. Many states are beginning to act with authority against violence and interference with teaching methods. Teacher conferences are taking place with the theme of overcoming teacher "burnout" (methods used are discussed in Chapters 20–23). Therefore, potential teachers should not give up. Now let us consider the stress from nursing.

NURSING

Nursing is the major traditional female profession in which the practitioner is automatically placed in a subordinate role. By the very nature of the position, the nurse in the hospital and office situation is attendant upon and answerable to the physician. Nurses take "doctor's orders" and follow them as requested. Yet nurses are the largest single body of health-care providers, constituting more than half of all the health-care workers. There are almost 1.5 million nurses in the United States with 98 percent of them being women.[3]

The subordinate role of nurses is derived from the historical introduction of nursing by Florence Nightingale during the Crimean War (see Box 16.2).

Since Nightingale's time nurses have continued to flatter physicians. There is an interaction known as the "doctor-nurse game".[5,6] According to the rules, there can never be open disagreement between the players. Of course, the nurse is the one who can never disagree with the physician. Another rule is that the nurse can never appear to be too intelligent in front of the physician. As a corollary, the doctor must always appear to be in control. The nurse's role is to take care of the physician because he is often "rushed," "overburdened," and "forgetful."[3] The nurse learns to care for the physician much like the secretary cares for her boss and the wife cares for her husband.[6] For a specific example of how the game is played, see Box 16.3.

Nurses have always been portrayed as conscientious, self-sacrificing, altruistic, compliant, quiet, humble, weak, and passive.[3,6] Exemplifying this is a 1976 thirteen-cent U. S. postage stamp featuring a nurse—Clara Maas. The comment written was, "She gave her life"; surely the ultimate form of self-sacrifice.[3]*

BOX 16.2.   The Nightingale Nurse.

> Florence Nightingale told her women followers only to assist the physicians on the battlefield with patient care when the physicians gave a specific request. Nightingale's success set up two patterns: (1) nursing was defined as women's work; and (2) nursing activities were contingent upon the physicians' approval.[3] Prior to Nightingale's intervention, nursing duties were primarily carried out by males.[4] Therefore, Florence Nightingale was forced to flatter the male's ego in order to introduce women as health-care providers.

* Recently, as part of their doctoral training in nursing, five women have undertaken a project to upgrade the image of nursing. In examining the media, they found four common stereotypical nurses: (1) the "absolute bitch"; (2) the "angel of mercy"; (3) the pure, innocent, naive, "good girl"; and (4) the "dumb, sexy, broad". The investigators believe that the feminist movement has affected nursing in a mixed way. On the positive side, it has encouraged nurses to be more outspoken. On the negative side, feminists tend to downplay the status of women nurses vis-a-vis women physicians and they encourage women to enter other "male" careers, which has resulted in a shortage of nurses. Sifford, D. Nurses battle to change negative views of their professions. *Philadelphia Inq.* 3–D, March 12, 1981.

BOX 16.3. The "Doctor-Nurse" Game

A physician gives a nurse "orders" for a renewal of the antibiotic *penicillin*. The nurse meekly reminds the doctor that the night nurse reported, and had charted, the occurrence of a severe allergic rash after the last penicillin regimen. The nurse suggests with bated breath, "Doctor, would you like to write an order for another antibiotic?" The physician responds "Thank you, Ann. I meant to change that to *erythromycin.*"

Nurses have to follow doctor's "orders," but sometimes the orders seem to be inane. For example, in many hospitals, a nurse cannot shampoo a patient's hair unless the request is given as a doctor's order.[7]

Nurses, like many other employed females, suffer sexist and sexual harassment on the job; everything from sexual advances from patients and physicians, to doctors sauntering into the nurse's station, lounging on the dispensary counter and engaging in sexist jokes with the nurses.[6] Other problems are: irregular shifts (sometimes working all night); and failure to use much of the detailed knowledge learned in school (i.e., they are "overeducated" for the routine procedures and are not permitted by the medical staff to perform other procedures for which they are trained).

As a result of their feelings of second-class status, many nurses develop stress-related problems. Nurses often are fearful of making mistakes, and are afraid to be chastised by physicians (male authority figures) or nurse supervisors.[6] Frustration is a common psychological stressor in nursing, and many nurses have repressed anger because they cannot report what they see, or know to be correct, for fear of reprisals. This leads to a fear of independent action.[7] As a result of their constantly taking orders and being compliant, many nurses have little confidence in themselves and develop a low self-image.

Just like the man who is angry at work and comes home and yells at his wife, so do some nurses take out their anger and frustrations. Of course, many nurses just internalize their stress and feel guilt as a result. However, others take it out on the ranks beneath them, the nurse's aides, the hospital orderlies, the secretaries, and occasionally even the patients. They may also have conflicts at home with spouses or family members. As was discussed with teachers, nurses also suffer from "burnout" and they suffer similar manifestations such as alcoholism, depression, marital conflicts, and suicide.[7] All of this has resulted in a high turnover rate for staff nurses and for nurses leaving the profession for other careers, including medicine (but that too can be stressful).

Yet it is not all bad. Nursing can and should be a rewarding profession.

Nurses can and should be able to take primary responsibility for health care and stress management in hospital situations. Nurses must be more assertive in order to improve their self-esteem. They should be proud of their knowledge and ability and not be afraid to use them. Of course, assertiveness is not aggressiveness and nurses should not deliberately try to antagonize physicians, administrators, or patients. Rather they should try to come to an understanding with the other health-care workers in delineating their role as being part of the health-care team, rather than a supporting, compliant branch. This can happen if: (1) nurses take more pride in themselves; and (2) physicians and administrators learn that a hospital and office cannot function without nurses. There are many courses available for nurses to help them overcome stress and become assertive. (See Chapters 20–23)

With all of the current interest in holistic health, the future will see less emphasis on treatment of disease. If nurses take the initiative, they can be a foremost part of the holistic health movement.

Let us now consider dental hygiene.

DENTAL HYGIENE

Up until the last few years, dental hygiene was a profession that was 100 percent female. As the result of equal opportunity employment laws, some males have been entering dental hygiene. For example, at Temple University within the last four years, there has been an average of one male student per class of sixty-five. Dental hygiene is a sought-after profession with currently about a five-to-one ratio of applicants to acceptances in the approximately 175 programs nationwide. There are now almost 6000 graduates per year as contrasted to about 2500 in 1970, and there are about 140,000 practicing hygienists.

As in the case with nurses and physicians, dental hygienists are subservient and answerable to dentists. They cannot practice alone (although some dental hygienists have taken the issue of independent practice to the courts). Their work must be under the direct or indirect supervision of a dentist. They are dependent upon the dentist for patient load, salary, fringe benefits, and equipment and supplies.

Nurses must accommodate a variety of physicians, administrators, technical personnel, and patients. Dental hygienists have an advantage in that regard as they are answerable only to one dentist and their patients (unless it is an office with multiple practitioners).

Dental hygienists may suffer from sexist and sexual harassment from patients and dentists but it is probably not widespread as there have been few

BOX 16.4. The Stressed Dental Hygiene Students.

Both of us have given courses to dental hygiene students for many years. Outwardly, we have found the young women to be ideal students: attentive, quiet, appreciative, and conscientious. This is in marked contrast to the predominantly male dental students who are on occasion noisy, inattentive, and unappreciative.

As part of our meditation and stress studies, we became interested in the word "feel" and its many meanings. In order to help ascertain the variety of meanings attached to "feel" we decided to give a question to be answered anonymously by the entire second-year dental hygiene class. Therefore, at the beginning of a lecture on stress management in dentistry, a card was handed to each student. On the card was written, "How do you feel?" The students were told to answer the question anonymously by the end of the lecture and leave the cards on the front desk. We expected to find an interesting result on the variety of meanings attached to "feel." What we did find was different and illuminating.

There were 112 distinct responses. The most common was, "I feel tired." This could be related to lack of sleep, overwork or boredom. Many of the responses were emotional. Some common ones were: "I feel worried" (5); "I feel frustrated" (4); "I feel anxious" (4); "I feel tense" (4); "I feel nervous" (3); "I feel stressed" (3); and "I feel uptight" (3).

As was expected, the responses to "How do you feel" were variable. The students' answers suggested many interpretations for "feel." What was not anticipated was the overwhelming "negative" perceptions of most of the students. Of the 112 responses, only 11 were either neutral or positive. The remaining 101 were decidedly negative. This unanticipated result gave an indication of the students' current assessment of their schooling and career. From previous discussions and a follow-up investigation, we found that dental students also reported being "pressured" during dental school.[9] Discussions with other educators and students from medical, law, osteopathy, nursing, and chiropractic schools show that they, too, have similar problems.

One positive recommendation seems warranted from this limited study: It may be beneficial for educators and employers to periodically have their students or employees respond to an anonymous "How do you feel?" questionnaire. The information might be useful in planning for improved conditions in the school or workplace.[10]

reports of incidents. Since there is a need for dental hygienists, a woman who experiences harassment can usually find another job where she will not find those problems.

There is one major problem that is not unique to dental hygiene; that is, boredom from doing repetitive procedures (i.e., comes from doing scaling and prophylaxis treatments repeatedly). Not to be outdone by teachers and nurses, dental hygienists also suffer from "burnout."[8] Some factors that predispose hygienists to burnout are:

1. They do repetitive procedures (see above).
2. They work continually at a high level of performance.
3. They set up "time pressures" in terms of how much work must be done for each patient in an allotted period.
4. They may not receive support from either patients, "fellow" workers, or dentists. Dental assistants often consider dental hygienists as "prima donnas." In many offices hygienists are told not to fraternize with patients. And in many practices hygienists feel that they are not appreciated by their dentists. They don't receive any strokes (i.e., a word of thanks; praise in the front of others; a meal out with "no strings" attached).
5. In many offices there is only one hygienist, one assistant, and one dentist. The hygienist may feel isolated and this is another factor that can predispose to "burnout."
6. Sitting in the same chair in the same room and in practically the same position can add to stress and increase fatigue.[9]

One factor that can contribute to later dissatisfaction for dental hygienists is their treatment in dental hygiene school (see Box 16.4).

Regardless of their "pressures" in school or on the job, most dental hygienists stay in practice and enjoy their work. Just like teachers and nurses, dental hygienists have access to courses in stress management, assertiveness training, and relaxation techniques (amplified in Chapters 20–23).[11]

THERAPISTS[12]

Therapists* are a diverse group of practitioners who are concerned with the management, generally on a team basis, of individuals with physical, mental or social handicaps, and disabilities. The impetus for the emergence of these relatively new specialties was the high number of injured veterans who returned after World War II. After the Korean and Vietnam wars, there were additional veterans entering civilian life who had suffered physical and mental impairments. Recently, with improved diagnosis and

* Therapists are found in the fields of education, art, music, dance, adaptive physical education, recreation, horticulture, manual arts, occupational therapy, physiotherapy, speech pathology, audiology, and rehabilitation for the blind.

patient awareness, there are many more children and adults who need the services of therapists. In this age of anxiety and depression, many people have drug-related disorders. In addition, with many individuals driving cars, planes, boats, and engaging in activities such as scuba-diving, sky-diving, water-skiing, cross-country skiing, and hang-gliding, accidents are increasing at an alarming rate. All of these factors have converged, and with the support of the federal, state, and local governments, have resulted in the development of the therapist movement.

Any one of the various therapy modalities can be an extremely rewarding career for a woman. The salaries are generally good and the opportunities for jobs are numerous and should be increasing. The major stressor is working with the retarded, handicapped, or impaired. Progress can be extremely slow with these individuals and frustrations can result. Nevertheless, the satisfaction of accomplishing something is worthwhile. Let us now consider the stressors of dietetics and nutrition.

DIETETICS AND NUTRITION[12,13]

In the broad umbrella of dietetics and nutrition there are three major careers that are involved directly or indirectly with nutrition. These are dietician, nutritionist, and home economist. Women are very well represented in these careers.

Dietitians provide nutritional counseling and care to individuals and groups. In addition, they develop menu patterns and supervise food service workers. Nutritionists counsel individuals or groups in sound nutritional practices designed to maintain and improve health. Home economists use knowledge acquired in homemaking as well as the biological, physical, and social sciences and the arts in order to promote the health and welfare of people and their families.

Since dietetics, nutrition, and home economics are traditional female fields related to women's roles as a homemaker and cook, some liberated women may not be favorably inclined toward them. However, there can be rewards occurring from helping people manage their lives better, and women entering these fields do not have to worry about breaking new ground. There are good role models and support is available from other practitioners. Let us now consider the stressors of counseling.

COUNSELING[12,13]

Counselors help individuals help themselves. They guide them in decision making, self-understanding, and life planning. There are four major types of counselors: school; employment; rehabilitation; and college career planning and placement.

School counselors are the largest counseling group. They work with students, their parents, teachers, community agencies, and various testing devices to help prepare students for careers. Employment counselors work with unemployed adults or people who want to change their jobs. They help them evaluate their potential and give them guidance for prospective job opportunities. Rehabilitation counselors provide guidance and career planning for the physically, psychologically, and socially impaired. Rehabilitation counselors either help the individuals get back to a former career or guide them toward a new career. College placement officers function to assist students in planning for careers; to help them get part-time and full-time jobs, and to counsel the potential college dropout.

The counseling fields may also be related to one of women's traditional roles, that of the helper. As such, this too may be frowned upon by some activist females. Nevertheless, these are good, interesting and diversified careers. The major disadvantage is that there is a great deal of competition for the available jobs. Let us now look into the stressors of social work.

SOCIAL WORKERS [12,13]

Social workers assist people, families, groups, and communities in understanding and solving problems. They use casework, group work, and community organizations. Social workers practice in a variety of settings such as hospitals, homes for the aged, clinics, nursing homes, mental health facilities, rehabilitation centers, correctional institutions, settlement houses, schools, public welfare agencies, state, county and city facilities, and voluntary or private agencies. There are well over 300,000 social workers and about two-thirds of them are women.

Social workers are also traditional women helpers. Yet, there are many women who do like to help and for them doing social work is rewarding. The major stressors are: (1) dealing with people in broken homes; (2) possibly working in unsafe areas such as the slums of a center city; and (3) the possibility of evening or weekend work.

Let us look at another major female occupation, librarianship.

LIBRARIANS [12,13]

There are various specialities in librarianship. In large libraries, librarians may specialize in user services (work directly with the public) and technical services (do cataloguing and acquiring of materials). In smaller libraries, librarians perform both services. There are almost 150,000 librarians and over 85 percent of them are women. Almost half the librarians are school librarians. About one-fifth work as college and university librarians and public librarians.

The major stressor from being a librarian is the silence of libraries. Two other potential stressors are the necessity for evening and weekend work and the stiff competition for positions. However, librarianship should continue to be a major female profession.

Let us now consider the stressors of the design professions.

DESIGNERS[13]

The design occupations encompass a variety of fields some of which are primarily female. The latter include: fashion design; interior design; floral design; modeling; and commercial art and photography.

Fashion designers design clothes; dressmakers make the clothes and fashion models display the clothes. Interior designers (decorators) make living, working and playing areas more attractive and functional. Floral designers assemble flowers into specific arrangements to express appropriate sentiments. Commercial artists create artwork to sell products. There are all kinds of photographers but commercial photographers, just as commercial artists, can use their work to sell products.

These various design occupations are relatively interesting and exciting work for women. However, each has its specific problems. Fashion design can be a highly remunerative profession but in times of recession, having fashionable clothes becomes less important, and fashion designers find their income decreasing greatly. Modeling also can be affected by recession and the work can be seasonal. Also, photographers' and artists' models have to be willing to pose in the nude.

Interior design can be very rewarding—to see a planned home arrangement come to life can bring psychological as well as monetary rewards. However, this field can also be negatively affected by an economic recession.

Floral design can be psychologically rewarding as people are generally appreciative of the designer's efforts. However, the salaries and chances for advancement are not too good, although enterprising women can become managers and even open up their own shops. The job opportunities are generally favorable and should remain so unless a severe recession occurs.

Both commercial artists and photographers must feel highly pleased if they are well received. However, here, too, in bad financial times, their services may not be required.

The design occupations in general can be interesting and exciting work, but women who want relatively secure work may not want to take the chance of entering occupations in which job security may fluctuate with economic conditions. However, for the woman who is willing to take a chance, design can be advantageous and enjoyable.

Now let us consider other exciting but insecure careers, those in the performing arts.

PERFORMING ARTS[13]

Many young women aspire to a glamorous career. It sounds ideal to be an actress, a singer, a musician, or a dancer. However, the reality is a different story. There is a tremendous amount of competition for these positions. Many aspiring performers have to take interim jobs as waitresses, bar maids, secretaries, teachers, or any other position they can get. Even those who are successful in obtaining a performing job, may find that there is no permanance to the position. In addition, the high salaries are reserved for the "stars" and many performers, even while working, have to supplement their incomes with part-time work in other fields. Another problem is the years of intense training that are required even before a woman can hope to enter her chosen field.

Overall, being a performing artist can be a highly rewarding career both from a psychological and financial viewpoint. But of all the potential careers for women, there is probably the greatest risk of not achieving success in the performing art fields. Probably the best balance for a talented woman is to be a performing artist either as a part-time position or as a hobby, while maintaining a secure job.

Another field that many women enter is art.

ARTISTS[13]

As with music, one can become a classical artist or a modern artist. In addition, a person can be a portrait painter, a cartoonist, or a medical or general science illustrator. (Commercial art has already been discussed.) Again because of the difficulties of obtaining employment or selling one's paintings, many artists teach to supplement their incomes.

If a woman paints or draws for her own enjoyment, this can be an excellent method to reduce stress. If she paints to sell her pictures and they remain on the shelf, this can be stress-inducing. If a woman sells her paintings, then the psychological effects can match the financial rewards.

Medical illustration is a good career for a woman who can draw well and accurately, is interested in science, and doesn't mind spending long hours working on intricate details. The future appears bright for this occupation. Instead of putting their feelings on canvas, some women write their feelings down on paper.

WRITERS AND POETS[13]

Writers and poets have the same kind of joys and regrets as do performing artists and artists. Writers can write for magazines or newspapers (either as a columnist or reporter) which are regular occupations. If writers attempt to write novels, short stories, or nonfiction books, they often find the chance of acceptance is limited. There are very few Helen Van Slykes or Nancy Fridays. Many authors write at their leisure while maintaining another career. Others teach English or creative writing while waiting for the "big break."

Writing is another psychologically rewarding career. It is a wonderful feeling to know that many other people are reading and, hopefully, being influenced by your written words. But writing and continually receiving rejection letters can be extremely frustrating. Writing as a hobby, though, can be fun and is also a means of reducing stress.

SUMMARY

There are many traditional careers that women can enter that offer interest and security. These include teaching, nursing, dental hygiene, social work, and librarianship. In contrast, other careers are more exciting but less secure. This is the case for the performing arts, art, and writing. The choice is up to each woman. Other choices of careers are described in the next chapter.

REFERENCES

1. Staff correspondents. Education: Help! Teacher can't teach. *Time* 54–63, June 16, 1980.
2. Gross, B. *Teaching Under Pressure*. Santa Monica, California: Goodyear, 1979.
3. Bush, M. A. and Kjervik, D. K. The nurse's self-image. *In* Kjervik, D. K. and Martinson, I. M. (eds.), *Women In Stress: A Nursing Perspective*. New York: Appleton-Century-Crofts, 1979, pp. 46–58.
4. Ehrenreich, B. and English, D. *Witches, Midwives and Nurses: A History of Women Healers*. Old Westbury, New York: Feminist Press at SUNY, 1973.
5. Stein, L. The doctor-nurse game. *Archs. Gen. Psychiat.* **16**:699–703, 1967.
6. Menikheim, M. L. Communication patterns of women and nurses. *In* Kjervik, D. K. and Martinson, I. M. (eds.), *Women In Stress: A Nursing Perspective*. New York: Appleton-Century-Crofts, 1979, pp. 133–143.

7. Weisenlee, M. Nursing's future role. *In* Kjervik, D. K. and Martinson, I. M. (eds.), *Women In Stress: A Nursing Perspective.* New York: Appleton-Century-Crofts, 1979, pp. 59–85.

8. Levin, A. Notes on a burned-out dental hygienist. *Dent. Hyg.* **54**(1):19,40–43, 1980.

9. Morse, D. R. and Furst, M. L. *Stress and Relaxation: Application to Dentistry.* Springfield, Ill.: Charles C. Thomas, 1978.

10. Morse, D. R. and Furst, M. L. The subjective aspect of feelings. *J. Am. Soc. Psychosom. Dent. Med.* In Press, 1981.

11. Stevens, M. M. Transcendental meditation and dental hygiene. *Dent. Hyg.* **54**(4):165–168, 1980.

12. U. S. Department of Labor. U. S. Department of Health Education and Welfare. *Health Careers Guidebook* Fourth Ed. Washington, D. C.: U. S. Government Printing Office, 1979.

13. U. S. Dept. of Labor. *Occupational Outlook Handbook, 1978–79 Edition.* Washington, D. C.: U. S. Government Printing Office, 1978.

17
Invading the Male
Strongholds:
From the Business World to
the Basketball Court

INTRODUCTION

The woman's liberation movement started it, then the government got into the act, and now a full-scale female invasion is under way. Women have set their sights on all those lucrative male-dominated careers and they have made rapid gains in the last few years. It has been a long, hard struggle, and for many the effort has been worth it. For others the toll in stress may not be worth the rewards. There may still be some truth in the old saying, "A woman has to be twice as good as a man to go half as far and get paid half as much."

At any rate, the "die is cast" and men must realize that they no longer have a monopoly in business, the professions, the military, politics, religion, and sports.

Let us begin with women in business.

BUSINESS

Women are entering the business world by "leaps and bounds." Many women are becoming accountants, buyers, real estate brokers, insurance agents, stock brokers, credit managers, hotel managers, book and magazine editors, bankers, and various types of administrators and executives. They are learning to advance up the corporate ladder. Women are also

306 V / WOMEN AND ENVIRONMENTAL PRESSURES

starting their own businesses. For example, the number of female-owned businesses increased by one-third in the United States from 1972 to 1977.[1]

There were 1.9 million self-employed women in 1979.[2] However, even with the sharp increase in numbers, the female-owned businesses only represented 7.1 percent of all the nations' business firms (excluding large corporations). The women's businesses totaled 6.6 percent of all receipts and only about .03 percent of all total business revenues.[3] The probable reason is that many of the women's businesses are of the small single-owner boutique type. Women may decide to "latch on" to the old American dream of owning their own business, but unfortunately the reality is that small shops require a lot of work and often little revenue is returned. Just as most women still enter traditional female jobs, so do most women open up traditional female shops. Typical women's businesses are: beauty salons; bridal boutiques; gift shops; card and candy shops; dress and shoe stores; sewing shops; dance studios; small restaurants; travel agencies; interior decorating shops; uniform stores; thrift shops; jewelry stores; pet shops; and dog-and cat-grooming boutiques.

However, recently, enterprising women with good business backgrounds are entering other businesses and finding some success. It is not unusual to see female owners of businesses such as TV and radio shops, record stores, stationery shops, upholstering businesses, and antique stores. Many other women are conducting businesses in their own homes. According to the Census Bureau, almost half the women-owned businesses are conducted from the home.[2] Women are doing everything from painting and rug weaving to consulting and treating patients.

Owning one's own business can be satisfying but it may also be stressful for these reasons:

1. There is *capital* that must be obtained. It used to be extremely difficult for women to obtain credit, but recently laws have made it easier for them to obtain money.
2. One must research the business to see if there is a definite *need* in the area.
3. An appropriate *site* has to be located.
4. The *rent* must be reasonable.
5. Trustworthy *employees* must be found.
6. The store must have good *security*.
7. The women must be capable of working *long hours*.
8. The women must be willing to deal with *complaining customers, touchy salespeople*, and sometimes inconsiderate *maintenance people*.

9. There can be problems of *credit checking, bounced checks,* and *late deliveries* of needed items.
10. There is the ever-present battle against *shoplifting.*
11. There is also the risk that even with the best intentions and abilities, the result may be a *failure.*

A woman who found that owning a boutique had more than its share of troubles is covered in Box 17.1.

Women who want to learn to become executives rather than just clerks are receiving support. Many young women are starting off by majoring in business rather than the traditional elementary education, or the formerly popular liberal arts and sciences. After they graduate, they can take any one of the numerous courses being given for women in the business world. When they are ready they can avail themselves of the firms that specialize in obtaining placement for female executives. There is a 45,000 member *National Association of Female Executive Women* that they can join.[4]

First they have to become executives, and currently there are only 5.5 percent of employed women who hold management or administrative positions.[5] In order to get ahead, women have to lay aside their passive role; they must learn to be assertive and not be willing to sit back and accept a subordinate role.

Other advice for women who want to "climb the corporate ladder" is:

1. Looking the part is important, so invest substantially in clothing.
2. When you are introduced to a man, offer him your hand since men often do not know whether or not to shake a woman's hand.
3. Let those concerned know that you are willing to work long hours and travel.
4. Have a career plan and then get exposure by making speeches and writing articles.
5. Let it be known that you are willing to take criticism.
6. Impress upon others that you are committed to your career and that your home life will not interfere with your job.
7. Be well organized and set priorities; learn to manage time effectively.
8. Learn the "territory"; be as familiar as possible with your field and the way others have advanced.[6]
9. Don't be upset by male negative attitudes. A recent survey of managers in the top five hundred industries and fifty largest banks and other companies revealed that white men have more bias toward women than toward nonwhites for management positions.[5] There may be some reason for the negative feelings of men. A recent study showed that female

BOX 17.1:   The Not So Chic Boutique.

The idea was great—to have her own boutique stocked with things she knew people would love. Hence, with the help of her partners, friends and bankers, she created a stylish little shop in Center City, Philadelphia. On display were items like "exquisite jam pots, mother-of-pearl soap dishes, and linen greeting cards." One early occupational hazard was broken fingernails and cut fingers resulting from hasty opening of arriving crates and packages. Another minor disaster was misplaced or lost invoices.

After "shelling out" some more money for insurance and a window logo, the grand opening was just one day away. That evening, one of the "help" set a case of Alfonso olives on a glass shelf in the gourmet department. The immediate response was a shattering of all the shelves and an aerial display of mustard and teriyaki sauce. The crash landings occurred in the "get well" cards and jigsaw puzzles. Retrieval of the crash victims wasn't the major problem—the odor was the principal problem. To help deodorize the shop, lavender water of the finest quality was poured over the grease spots that embellished the newly laid green carpet.

Once the store was officially opened, it would cater to people regardless of their work or home schedules. Thus, the hours were set from 8 A.M. to 11 P.M. (except a slightly later opening on weekends). As principal owner, she felt obligated to put in the "lion's share" of the hours. Hence, every day, her self-imposed hours were from 8 A.M. to 12:30 P.M., then a short break for lunch, and back again from 4 P.M. to closing time. For this devastating schedule, her "take home" pay was $100 per week.

Her life was the store. She was too tired for anything else. She also learned that things that sell in Europe may sit on the shelves in Philadelphia. Other depressing events were the arrival of damaged goods and the mass of unsold magazines.

When the shop was empty, that was dispiriting; when the shop was full that too was discomforting (she couldn't keep an eye on everyone). In fact, shoplifting became a major problem. Even when the shoplifters were caught, time had to be taken off to go to court and not one prosecution was successful.

Other problems developed: "weirdo" customers; feuding salespeople; and even the help was stealing merchandise. Then the competition arrived with similar items and larger stores.[11] All in all being your own boss and owning your own shop can be stressful but not everyone experiences such disasters.

managers had a lot more compassion and empathy when dealing with female employees than when dealing with male employees.[7]*

10. Try to be compensated at the same rate as males. Although older women executives receive less money than males, new female executives are reaching financial parity with men.[5]

11. Learn about sports and various teams. Businessmen love to talk about baseball, football, boxing, tennis, and golf. They also relate teamwork and sporting activities to the way they run their businesses. It certainly would help to get in the "inner circles" by becoming familiar with athletic events.

12. Develop self-esteem, self-confidence, a positive self-image and don't be afraid to take prudent risks.

13. Finally, in order to work well as an executive it is essential that you are in good physical and mental condition and use positive methods of coping with stress (see Chapters 20–23). If not, you may become one of those decision-making business executives who develops ulcers, heart attacks, and nervous breakdowns.[8] In fact, a recent Stanford University study found that female managers are much more likely than male managers to have nightmares and become depressed.[49]

One organization that is helping its members advance is the *National Association of Bank Women* (NABW). It is making a concerted effort to advance women in banking to positions of management. Almost 70 percent of bank employees are women, but most are clerks and tellers. Advancement is a slow process, but in 1979 there were 200 NABW women who had attained the rank of chairperson or president of a bank and there are about 35,000 women bank officers.

Women shouldn't jump at the chance of becoming bank executives. They must be willing and able to deal with irate customers, feuding tellers, board meetings with insecure males and the possibility of a bank robbery. On the other hand, banking hours are "nice" (although there's lots of work to do after hours).

Now that many more women are becoming managers and executives they are traveling more frequently. Women represent about 25 percent of the nation's business travelers. The ranks of female business travelers are currently growing at three times the rate of male travelers. As a result, changes

* The women's movement has spawned a men's liberation movement as a backlash. Part of the incentive for the new movement is the belief that males are being discriminated against in many job and school positions, in child custody cases, and in the military draft. This belief in turn can lead to negative male attitudes toward females. Special report. Battle of the sexes: Men fight back: Now it's "men's liberation" that's taking off. *U.S. News & World Report* 52–53, December 8, 1980.

are occurring in the travel industry to make the woman's trips less stressful. It used to be that women traveling alone were looked at strangely and treated with indifference by people such as waitresses, hotel desk clerks, and taxicab drivers. Nowadays, many hotel and motel innovations are being geared toward women. Examples are: (1) open, well-lit lobby bars rather than dimly lit secluded bars; (2) hotel rooms and lobbies with soft pastel colors; (3) improved room security with better locks and peepholes; (4) extended hours of takeout restaurant service (many women travelers prefer in-room meals); (5) escort service from the lobby, parking garage or dining room to the guest's room; (6) full-length mirrors, long closets, shower caps, skirt hangers, hair dryers, curling irons, ironing boards, and sewing kits in guest rooms; (7) a ban on employees addressing women as "dear," "honey," or by their first name; (8) and not automatically giving a restaurant check to an accompanying man.[10]

Regarding restaurant checks, it seems that waiters and waitresses are slow to learn about female executives and women's liberation (see Box 17.2 for details).

Some additional business fields that have seen a decided upsurge in female involvement in the last few years are purchasing, buying, merchandising, health services administration, communications, radio and television, publishing, and the stock market. In these and the aforementioned fields, there are great opportunities for advancement, security, and a good income. There is also a good chance for ulcers, hypertension, and heart attacks. The latter three are related to the "pressures" of the jobs caused by decisions, alienating people's feelings, fears of making mistakes, and trying to accomplish too much, too quickly. (See Chapters 20–23 for ways to

BOX 17.2.   I'll Take the Check.

In a recent study it was found that when a female "executive" takes a male to dinner, she rarely gets the check. Five research couples were involved and they ate seventy-three meals in various Phoenix area restaurants. In half of the occasions, the women took charge of ordering and responding to questions. Yet only five of the thirty-six "executive" women received the check. During one-third of the time, the situation was ambiguous with neither the male nor female apparently in charge. In all these cases, the women never received the check. When the man was clearly in charge, he automatically got the check. Interestingly enough, in all the cases waitresses were even more likely than waiters to give the man the check.[12]

overcome these potential stressors.) But now let us consider the stressors of science, engineering and college teaching.

SCIENCE[13]

Women have been in science for a long time, although their numbers have been few (e.g., Madame Curie). Now they are entering the sciences in greatly increased numbers. Women scientists, like men, work in either industry, teaching institutions, or for the government. Being a scientist is a prestigious profession, but it entails a great deal of preparation and hard work. To obtain a decent position and satisfactory income, it is necessary to have a doctorate degree plus years of experience. Scientists in their "ivory towers" either in colleges or industries are generally far removed from the hassles of the day-to-day working world. That is why scientists are generally rated as having low stress levels.[8] Not all scientists work in isolated laboratories. Some work outdoors in intriguing settings from the peaks of mountains to the depths of the oceans. Depending upon whether or not they enjoy interpersonal relations with various people, women scientists may be content working alone in laboratories or working together with others as part of a team.

Doing scientific work entails hours of intense concentration, often involved with fine details. Scientists who work in colleges generally have some teaching responsibilities in addition to their research activities. They may also have some administrative and service tasks.

The three major divisions of science are physical, life, and social. Physical scientists include chemists, physicists, and environmental (earth) scientists. In the environmental category are geologists, meteorologists, and oceanographers. Life scientists include general biologists, biochemists, physiologists, microbiologists, immunologists, cell biologists, and geneticists. Medical scientists (e.g., physicians, dentists, veterinarians, podiatrists) are also in the life-science category, but are discussed under *Medical Professions*. Mathematics can also be considered a science. All other sciences use mathematical formulations, and mathematics is used in various other fields such as computer science, statistics, and physics. The social science umbrella includes diverse professions such as sociology, psychology, anthropology, economics, geography, history, and political science.

Being a scientist is an exciting and challenging career for a woman today. Women who look to role models should find the best fields to enter are biology, chemistry, psychology, sociology, and anthropology (à la

Margaret Mead). Other women who enjoy challenges may want to enter the male-dominated fields of science such as physics, astronomy, mathematics,* and geology. One unique type of science now opening up to fe-

BOX 17.3.   Exercise Physiologist.

While climbing the executive ladder, men have often been tripped up by stress on the way to the top. Now women are taking the same climb and getting the same consequences. Many women are finding it to be even more stressful near the top because they have very little support. So in addition to the possibilities of ulcers, migraines, and coronaries, women quite often have loneliness to contend with.[14] What, you might question, does this have to do with exercise physiologists? The answer is simple. Exercise physiologists are being hired by many top business firms to act as directors of in-house exercise programs.[15] Exercise, as is discussed in Chapter 21, is an excellent means to cope with stress.

To be an exercise physiologist, one should get a bachelor's and master's degree in exercise physiology. At this time a doctorate is not essential, but in the future it would prove important. There are currently national certification examinations for program directors sponsored by the *American College of Sports Medicine*. Exercise physiologists work in collaboration with physicians to screen the subjects medically. They then set up programs with the help of physical educators and exercise technicians. The exercise physiologists perform diagnostic tests, develop exercise programs, and monitor the results. Most often these programs are run in commercial health spas, "Ys" and rehabilitation centers. But as previously mentioned, health programs are being set up for business executives right on the premises of the establishments. Women who enter this field cannot help but be impressed by the wonderful healthful effects of an exercise program, and they should become just as fit as the individuals with whom they are working.

With the tremendous interest in holistic health and self-help, the 1980s should certainly prove to be a time when exercise physiologists will be needed. The salaries are excellent and should get even better. And women exercise physiologists may get a great sense of satisfaction out of helping women executives cope with their stress.

* A recent study at Johns Hopkins University supports the contention that females have less innate mathematical ability than males. However, other research findings suggest that the major reason for males' mathematical superiority is the social "push." At any rate, more women are now entering the mathematical fields. Benbow, C. P. and Stanley, J. C. Sex differences in mathematical ability: Fact or artifact. *Science* 210: 1262–1264, 1980; Kolata, G. B. Math and sex: Are girls born with less ability? *Science* 210: 1234–1235, 1980; Schafer, A. T. Sex and Mathematics. *Science* 211: Editorial page, January 16, 1981.

males is exercise physiology (see Box 17.3). Let us now consider the stress of women engineers.

ENGINEERING[13]

Engineers design, develop, test, produce, operate, and maintain equipment and products. There are at least twenty-five specialties and eighty-five sub-specialties in engineering. Some major ones are mechanical, electrical, civil, chemical, aerospace, petroleum, biomedical, and nuclear.

Most engineers work in manufacturing industries. Others work in construction, public utilities, governmental agencies, colleges, and universities and various consulting services.

There are well over 1 million engineers making them, numerically, second only to teaching in the professions. Even though there are currently many more women engineering students than heretofore, women engineers account for less than 2 percent of the total.[13] A major reason has been the concept of engineering as being a male profession with the image of the "macho" engineer working on the construction site with his hard-hat in place.

Engineering is one of the best current professions from a financial standpoint and the future looks outstanding. Generally, engineers can get a good position with a bachelor's degree in engineering. Working conditions for most engineers are excellent, but some engineers spend part of their time at construction sites, in mines, or inside a factory. Engineers tend to change locations more frequently than most professions. There may be family moving problems. Even though there are not many women engineers, those women that become engineers are doing quite well. Current statistics show that engineering offers the highest starting pay for people with a bachelor's degree (about $24,000 in 1980[16]) and women are receiving higher initial salaries than are men. This is the only profession in which that is the case.[17] Women with "hard-hats" may become a more frequent sight in the 1980s.

Now let us consider the stress from college teaching.

COLLEGE AND UNIVERSITY TEACHERS

With most of the previous occupations, college and university teaching is one of the major employment options. Since college enrollments have gone down and probably will remain lower for the next decade, stiff competition is expected for many teaching positions, especially in the more prestigious schools. On the other hand, there are many new two-year junior and community colleges that will need teaching personnel (although the recent drop in numbers of junior high students may negatively affect the future need for teachers in these schools).

The most recent census finding reveals that more women than men are attending college. Most of these women are past thirty-five years of age and are attending school to establish their careers.[18] With more women attending school, this could make the job market in colleges and universities more fluid.

Women who want to become college teachers should be prepared to get a Ph.D. in their respective fields as the chances for advancement are slim without a doctorate.[13] Not too long ago in some departments there were no female teachers or, at best, a token representative. There is no longer overt discrimination because of governmental action and the efforts of women educational groups, such as the *American Association for University Women* and the *National Coalition for Women and Girls in Education.* However, there is still subtle discrimination, and advancement opportunities and salaries are still not as good for women as they are for men.

There are very few female full professors. Most women teachers are members of the "Triple A Club" (*A*ssistant Professor, *A*djunct Professor, and *A*ssociate Professor).[19] There has been a slight increase in women administrators but there are very few women deans or presidents. Most are members of another "Triple A Club" (*A*ssistant to the Dean, *A*ssistant Dean, *A*ssociate Dean).[20] In 1978, there were less than fifty women college presidents out of a total of more than 3000.[21]

Some women are suing for tenure and promotion but the legal battles take a long time and can be quite stressful.[22] Nevertheless, women are beginning to get their rights in academia.[23]

College teaching is an excellent, prestigious career for women who enjoy teaching, lecturing, writing, and doing research. Since there is much less of a discipline problem than in high schools, there is more time for pure teaching.

Nevertheless, some potential stressors include: (1) the "publish or perish" philosophy; (2) the necessity to achieve tenure for job security (and recently people have lost jobs even with tenure); (3) the necessity to attend regular departmental and school meetings; and (4) the need to do after-hours preparation and grading of examinations and theses. On balance, teaching in colleges and universities remains a favorable career for women.

Let us now look at the stress from law.

LAWYERS (ATTORNEYS)

Law is another former male stronghold that women have been entering in increased numbers in recent years. There are over 350,000 lawyers, and currently about 35 percent of the law students are women.[13] There are various specialties in law. The best known are criminal, civil, tax, labor, real estate, patent, corporation, international, and maritime. Law can also be used as an aid or preparation for other careers such as insurance, tax collection, credit investigation, claim examining, accounting, the judiciary, and politics.

There is keen competition in getting into law schools and many law firms consider class rank and the prestige of the law school as part of their hiring criteria. The bar exams that allow one to practice in various states can induce a great deal of stress. However, law is an excellent and prestigious career for women. One can practice part-time as a member of a law firm and can specialize in the particular area of primary interest. Lawyers generally do well financially, although it may take several years to become established. It is usually easier to get started in small towns than in big cities but in that case one must be willing to live and practice in a rural area.

As a self-employed practitioner, a lawyer can set her own fees, working hours, and vacation periods. A lawyer can also practice past the legal retirement age if that is one's inclination. However, law is a potentially stressful occupation. There may be long hours of intense studying. It is essential to be abreast of current legal decisions, and one must be willing to "pore over the books." There are numerous hassles in dealing with accused individuals, criminals, juries, judges, other lawyers, the media, and the public. There may be intense "pressures" during court trials and lawyers often have to hurry back and forth between their law offices, the courts and their homes.

Those women who are emotional may be upset over decisions going against their clients. However, being emotional may sometimes help influence jurors. To be a good lawyer, a women must enjoy working with all kinds of people—even those with whom she disagrees morally, politically, and emotionally.

There are undoubtedly some judges and other lawyers who are prejudiced against women lawyers. Once they realize that women are just as competent and probably more honest than many men, these practitioners will be more inclined to readily accept women lawyers.

THE HEALTH PROFESSIONALS[13,24,25]

Introduction

The principal health professions are medicine, dentistry, veterinary medicine, podiatry, osteopathy, chiropractic, optometry and pharmacy.

All health professionals have extensive preparatory schooling, have to pass state board examinations, and must outlay a substantial financial investment for both schooling and setting up of private practice.

Let us now briefly consider the stress for women in each of the major health professions.

Physicians

There are about 360,000 physicians in the United States and about 12 percent are women.[13,24] But the numbers are increasing as about 30 percent of the current medical students are women. In Great Britain, women constitute over 20 percent of the practicing physicians, and in the Soviet Union about 65 percent of the medical doctors are women.[26]

In addition to general practice, there are fifty-two specialities in medicine. Only about 20 percent of physicians remain in general practice. The practice of medicine is the most financially lucrative of all the professions, and specialists make substantially more money than general practitioners. The largest specialities are internal medicine, general surgery, obstetrics and gynecology, psychiatry, pediatrics, radiology, anesthesiology, opthalmology, orthopedics, dermatology, and family medicine.

Women tend to choose pediatrics, psychiatry, anesthesiology, internal medicine, and family medicine. Recently, there has been an upsurge in women choosing obstetrics-gynecology, which may be related to the women's movement (i.e., women taking care of themselves).

General surgery and the surgical specialities have generally been shunned by women.[26] Here, too, it seems that their nurturing, caring interest has caused women to gravitate to the more personal help-giving specialities of medicine.

Of all the health professions, the competition is the keenest to get into medical schools. Students are under intense pressure in their premedical courses in college, throughout their medical school training, and even during their practices. Constantly dealing with sickness and death can be devastating to some individuals. That may be the reason why many physicians have stress-laden lives and become drug addicts, alcoholics, chain-smokers, and caffeine addicts. They also have high rates of depression, divorce, and suicide.

Women medical students and physicians have even higher rates of drug addiction, alcoholism, and depression. They show an alarming four to one "advantage" over the general female population in suicides (see Chapter 4).

With the current large female enrollment in medical school classes, the negative responses should greatly decrease. Undoubtedly, there has been and still is sexism in medical schools but this will decrease as more women physicians get on medical school staffs and male teachers realize that women are just as capable as men.

With additional women teachers, women medical students will have more mentors and role models. The large female class should be able to lend support to its constituents. In hospitals, there are now more female staff physicians, chief residents and administrators. Therefore, women interns and residents should find hospital practice less stressful. As women climb to the top of the ladder in hospitals, they may find one additional problem (aside from sexism). That is, the disinclination of the predominantly female hospital staff (nurses, secretaries, receptionists, hospital workers) to be answerable to women physicians or administrators.[24]

Again, with an increased number of women doctors on staff, women staff employees will realize that female physicians are just as capable as males and worthy of their support.

There is no doubt that medicine is a difficult profession for a woman, but it is also extremely prestigious and rewarding. If a woman joins a group practice or partnership, she should have the opportunity of practicing part-time. There are many specialities in medicine and scientifically inclined women can choose one that appeals to them. If they don't like to deal directly with patients on a regular basis, they may go into pathology or radiology. If they enjoy children, they may choose pediatrics. It they do not want to regularly deal with life and death situations, they can opt for dermatology or opthalmology.

If they don't want to practice, they can become teachers or researchers. The path to an M.D. degree is stress-laden, but for the right person, the rewards justify the tribulations. Women doctors should definitely learn to reduce stress (see Chapters 20–23).

Dentists

Currently, there are about 125,000 dentists in the United States. Of these, slightly more than 3 percent are women.[13,24] For decades only 1 percent of dentists were women, but there has been a large recent increase in female dental students. In the current classes (1980) about 15 percent are women.[28]

The small numbers of practicing female dentists is in marked contrast to the ratio of female-to-male dentists in other countries. For example, the proportion of female-to-male dentists is seventy-one to twenty-nine in Russia, ninety-six to four in Lithuania and eighty to twenty in Finland.[29] In

Latin and South American countries there is a similar high proportion of female dentists.

Most dentists remain in general practice but there are eight recognized dental specialities. Dentistry is second to medicine in terms of financial remuneration, and dental specialists generally have higher incomes than general practitioners. Major dental specialities are orthodontics, oral surgery, periodontics, endodontics, and pedodontics. Women tend to practice general dentistry, pedodontics, orthodontics, and periodontics.There are very few women oral surgeons. The pattern is similar to the choice of specialties in medicine.

The competition to get into dental school is keen, but it is not as difficult as it is to get into U.S. medical schools. Nevertheless, people preparing to enter dentistry must commit themselves to hours of intense study both in college and dental school. Not to be outdone by physicians, dentists also suffer high levels of stress-related diseases and disorders.[30]

Female dental students, like their medical counterparts, report harassment in dental schools. Even with the increased numbers of women dental students, the problems will not disappear because there are very few female dental faculty members. Hence, mentors and role models are sorely lacking. But dental school male faculty members and administrators are beginning to realize that women are just as good dental students as men, and this will help reduce the woman dental students' distress.* For some specific examples of female dental students stressors, see Box 17.4.

Dentistry should be an excellent and prestigious profession for women. Dentists do not generally deal in life and death situations and they get few true emergencies. They can: set their own hours; take vacations when they are so inclined; live and work in excellent surroundings; and practice well past the normal retirement age. Women dentists are able to practice and raise a family if that is their desire. One major reason is that hiring domestic help and baby-sitters is within their financial means, and the flexibility of the hours allows them to return home when necessary.

Women dentists have an active support group: *The American Association of Women Dentists.* Eleanor Smeal, president of the *National Organization for Women* (NOW) thinks dentistry is an ideal profession for women. She stated at a recent hearing in Washington, "I think we could probably take over the profession if we were allowed to."[19] That probably won't happen, but there is no doubt that dentistry will become a highly desirable profession for women.**

* Had the situation been the reverse as in some other countries, the faculty might consider that male dental students (or medical students) are *just as good* as female dental (or medical) students.

** An up-to-date review of problems and rewards for women dentists can be found in several articles in the *Journal of the New Jersey Dental Association,* 52 (2), Spring, 1981.

BOX 17.4.   Women Dental Students.

One of the first problems female dental students found was the lack of adequate dressing areas and lavatories. Once classes started, they realized, like their male colleagues, that the dental school curriculum was a difficult one. But they didn't want to listen to all those sexist jokes or be shown those obscene slides. So they complained and got results. A memorandum came down from the dean's office stating that those policies had to be discontinued. So today, dental school is less sexist but also more serious.

One problem that starts in dental school and continues in practice is that of colleagues, teachers and patients addressing female dental students and dentists as "honey," "dear," or "sweetheart." A gentle admonishment often helps stop that practice.

Surprisingly, women dental students receive little support from the few women dental teachers. One student told us that the attitude of the women faculty is, "We had to work our 'butts' off to get where we did and so will you."

Women rarely become oral surgeons. Another female student gave us two reasons for this: She said, "I just don't have the strength to pull and yank all day long to try and remove a tooth." The second reason given was, "To position oneself to extract a tooth, it is generally necessary to cradle the patient's head in one's arms and most women don't want to wrap their arms around the male patients; we have enough sexual harassment as it is." But by the senior year, the serious female students were hardened and ready to go out into the remunerative, stressful world of clinical dentistry.

Veterinarians

There are approximately 35,000 practicing veterinarians and about 7 percent are women, but the numbers are changing rapidly.[13] Now almost 30 percent of the current classes (1980) are women.[24] Most veterinarians are in private practice. About one-third limit themselves to the treatment of small animals or pets; another third concentrate on cattle, poultry, sheep, swine, and horses; and the remainder treat both large and small animals.[13]

The concept of veterinary medicine as a "male" profession is related to the image of the strong, "macho" vet using his brute strength to hold down and treat large animals. But even in "large animal" practices brute strength is no longer necessary because of technical advances. More directly related to women is the increased public interest in small animal pets. This has augmented the need for "small animal" specialists and women are answering the call.

Veterinary medicine is the least family oriented of the medical professions. For example, many physicians and dentists come from families that already include physicians and dentists. Veterinary medicine has no such heritage; hence women don't have to break family barriers to become veterinarians.

There are only about twenty-five veterinary schools as compared to approximately sixty dental schools and one hundred twenty-five medical schools. Hence, the competition to get into veterinary school is fierce. Once women get into veterinary school, undoubtedly they receive the same type of harassment as occurs in medical and dental school, with the same prospects for improvement.

After graduating, they find that certain aspects of veterinary medicine are not easy. In private practice, there may be long and irregular hours. In rural areas, house and farm visits may be frequent, and they may have to work outdoors in inclement weather. But in small animal practices in urban and suburban areas, regular hours can be established, and the working conditions are generally excellent. In addition, veterinarians make a very good living and are highly respected in the community. All in all, veterinary medicine is an excellent profession for women; especially if they have a love of animals.

Podiatrists

There are about 10,000 practicing podiatrists in the United States, and less than 10 percent are women, but here, too, changes are occurring. In current classes (1980) in the five podiatry schools, there are about 30 percent women enrolled. Most podiatrists are in private general practice but there are six specialty areas.

The competition to get into podiatry school is not as intense as it is for medicine, dentistry, and veterinary medicine. However, one still must have the same kind of college background courses and do well in them.

Women in podiatry suffer the same problems as women in the other health professions, and the benefits are similar to those given for dentistry. One major advantage over the other medical professions is that podiatry is a noncrowded profession. With relatively few practitioners and an expanding public awareness of the need for foot care, podiatry should be an excellent field for many years. Women have a great opportunity to make their mark in the emerging profession of podiatry.

Osteopaths

There are less than 20,000 osteopaths in the United States and about 10 percent are women. There are only twelve osteopathy schools but the percentage of women is increasing as it is in the other health professions. Most osteopaths are family doctors, but there has been a recent trend for increased specialization. The osteopathic specialties are in the same fields as the major medical specialties.

Preparation, training, life-style, income, and problems in osteopathy are similar to those in medicine. Although it is not as difficult to get into osteopathy schools as it is to get into medical schools, the small number of osteopathy schools makes for keen competition for the available places. For those women interested in using manipulation as well as medical and surgical therapy, osteopathy may be advantageous. Great strength is not needed for osteopathic manipulation, so that phase of the practice should not dissuade women.

More people are becoming aware of osteopathic medicine and that should make osteopathy a continuing good career for women.

Chiropractors

There are currently about 25,000 chiropractors in this country with less than 10 percent being women. In the fifteen chiropractic colleges, the proportion of women students is about 25 percent. There is a growing public and governmental acceptance of chiropractic and even a reluctant acceptance by the established medical professions.

Although the most widely practiced method of chiropractic uses hand manipulation, there are newer "low-force" techniques available. Hence, it is no longer deemed essential or even beneficial to use bone crushing strength for manipulation.

The competition for places is increasing but it is still easier to get into chiropractic school than into other health science professional schools. Chiropractic has always had the image of being a man's profession but this image is changing. Women chiropractic students have the same problems as their colleagues in other schools but improvements are occurring.

For reasons similar to dentistry and podiatry, chiropractic can be a good career for women. One additional advantage is that equipment outlay is not as high as in most other health professions.

Optometrists

There are about 25,000 practicing optometrists in the United States and only about five percent are women. But here, too, the 15 optometry schools are showing a greatly increased number of women students. Most optometrists are self-employed generalists, but there are some who specialize.

Schooling is similar to the other health professions as are the rewards and problems. Optometry is another good field for women.

Pharmacists (Druggists)

There are about 140,000 practicing pharmacists in this country and less than 15 percent are women. More women are now entering pharmacy and the nation's seventy-five pharmacy schools now have about 30 percent female enrollment. The old image of the country "doc" or druggist pulverizing pills to make life-saving potions is fading fast. Nowadays, most prescriptions are filled by transferring pills from one bottle to another, and often by female pharmacists. Of far greater importance in pharmacy today is the knowledge about drug actions, reactions, interactions, and side effects.

Training to become a pharmacist is not as extensive as for the other professions. Pharmacy is a good career for a woman but she should be aware of the following:[31]

1. A good "business head" is required as pharmacy (like optometry) is a small business.
2. The hours may be long; one often has to work evenings and weekends. With the help of associates, this is less of a problem.
3. Sometimes one has to be aggressive in business (as when dealing with drug salesmen or delinquent customers).
4. One must constantly keep up with the pharmacology literature, as new drugs are constantly being introduced and old ones are being withdrawn.

But pharmacy has counterbalancing aspects that work to its advantage. For example: Emergencies and life and death situations are rare; part-time employment is feasible; and earnings and working conditions are good. In addition, the pharmacist enjoys excellent prestige and pharmacy can be a life-time occupation.

THE MILITARY[32,33]

In 1975, the service academies were ordered to admit women. There are now female cadets in the Army, Navy, Air Force, Marines, and Coast Guard. As is the case with women in medical and dental schools, women in the academies have suffered sexual and sexist harassment. Women cadets have been harassed about things such as their high-pitched voices being not effective for commands, and their marching strides as not being "military" in style. But as the first classes have graduated, the paths for future women cadets have been made easier. The pay, benefits, and working conditions are good. And the chances and opportunities to remain in good physical condition are excellent.

POLITICS

Golda Meir was the premier of Israel, Indira Gandhi is the Prime Minister of India. In any history of political leaders, they have to be considered among the all-time outstanding politicians. Yet in the United States, women have played a minor role in politics. Whether or not there will ever be a woman president is not known, but many more women are entering politics, making themselves known, and having their influence felt.

A good example of this increased influence is the recent political conventions (1980). The Republicans ignored the Equal Rights Amendment (ERA) and were against abortion. At the Democratic convention, the women "came on strong." Women made up 50 percent of the delegates and were able to get strong profeminist amendments made part of the platform. These included equal pay for women, improved child-care programs, support for boycotts of conventions in states that have not ratified ERA, and denial of party funds for candidates not favoring ERA and Medicaid payments for abortion.[34,35] In light of the Republican victory, the fate of these proposals is left in doubt. Nevertheless, women are becoming politically influential.

Woman politicians do have some problems. In order to get ahead, assertion and aggression (to some extent) is necessary. Aggressive women politicians such as Bella Abzug, may "turn off" some people, as was the case in her encounter with President Carter in which he fired her as cochairperson of the *National Advising Committee for Women*.[36]

But if women stay back, remain passive and "feminine," they often don't get ahead politically. Gloria Steinem put it this way. "No matter in what style you make the demand, what's unwelcome is the demand to tell women that if they just behave nicer, if they shuffle and Uncle Tom a little more, that they will be more successful, is simply not accurate. It's your classic double bind. If you are assertive and aggressive enough to do the job, you're unfeminine and therefore unacceptable; if you're not aggressive, you don't do the job—and in either case, good-by."[36]

As has been shown by the recent Abscam cases, graft and corruption seem to be an integral part of American politics. Women may be more honest, as few of them are involved in corruption or influence-peddling cases. But women entering politics must realize that the temptation will be ever present.

Politics has other stressful aspects. First, there is the severe physical and mental strain of political campaigns. Second, once elected, one has to try and please many different and often opposing constituents. As a result, whatever position a woman takes, she will have political enemies as well as friends. Third, the position is never secure, as every two to four years campaigning and elections have to start again. But the salaries are good; the life-style is exciting; interesting people are met; and there is the opportunity to help people in need.

RELIGION

Introduction

In the various occupations discussed so far, women have made important inroads on their way toward equality with males. However, religion is a different story. It seems that regardless of the religion, women are treated as second-class citizens.

History

From the first recorded writings, we learn that the very concept of God is in terms of Him as a father figure. The Old Testament has Abraham, the first Jew, in a relationship with his "Father" on high. There is also the concept of the long-bearded Jehovah giving the Ten Commandment tablets to Moses on Mount Sinai. All of the Hebrew prophets were males. With the advent of Christianity, it is the trinity: the Father, the Son and the Holy Spirit (Ghost). Jesus and the Apostles were also all males. Mohammed, the founder of Islam was a male, and so were all of the leaders of the Protestant movement (e.g., Calvin, Luther, and Joseph Smith, founder of the Mormons). However, there were some notable exceptions. For example, the Virgin Mary, the biblical Mothers of Judaism (Rachel, Leah, Rebecca, and Sarah), Joan of Arc, and Mary Baker Eddy, the founder of Christian Science.

Current Situation

Of the almost 200,000 ministers in the various Protestant denominations, less than 5 percent are women.[13] However, with the feminist movement, more women are becoming ministers, although they are facing stiff opposition from the church hierarchy.

Being a female minister is not easy. Ministers may have to work long or irregular hours and often have to travel considerably. In addition, in recent years, there has been widespread mergers of Christian denominations and the outlook for new positions is not good. Women ministers must realize that they will be under considerable "pressure" because they are women and must be able to face sexism and other forms of harassment. However, women who have strong religious and moral beliefs may find it worthwhile to be a minister in spite of the potential obstacles.

There are three basic Jewish denominations: Orthodox, Conservative, and Reform. They all have a belief in God as a basic tenet, and the Bible is central in their rituals. The Reform movement is the most liberal.

There are less than 5000 rabbis among all the denominations, and almost all of them are males. At this time, only the Orthodox denomination is holding the line with respect to male rabbis. Recently, the Conservative denomination has accepted females, and the Reform movement has the greatest number. Since less than one-third of the Jewish congregations are Reform, the opportunities for women entering the rabbinate are limited.[13]

As is the case for ministers, being a rabbi can also be hard work for a woman. But for the Jewish woman who has strong moral and religious beliefs and leadership skills, and is not afraid of possible harassment, becoming a rabbi can be an excellent career choice.

Women cannot become priests. Their highest possible ranks in the Roman Catholic hierarchy are those of nun and deacon. Nuns can enter a variety of occupations including teaching, nursing, medicine, and law but they cannot be the spiritual leader of their church and perform priestly duties. Unlike ministers and rabbis, priests and nuns cannot get married and must take vows of celibacy. There may be a great deal of stress in that, but for the individuals concerned the concept of being "married to the church" is of paramount importance and apparently overrides their sexual or maternal desires.

However, nuns are not capitulating on their desire to enter the priesthood. In October 1979, during Pope John Paul II's American tour, Sister Theresa Kane, the president of the *Leadership Conference of Women Religious* (an organization of nuns who are the leaders of the 128,000 Catholic sisters) asked the Pope to allow women to become priests.[37] The Pope turned down the request but the American Sisters have not given up their pressure on the church. In a recent national survey of Roman Catholic sisters, 75 percent favored a changing role for women in the church. More than one-third of American nuns said they were feminists and 85 percent of the nuns favored the feminist movement. Some of the changes that the 75 percent agreed upon were changes in Church structure, liturgy, position on divorce and attitude toward divorced people.[38]

Another recent study showed that 47 percent of the general population believes that women should be allowed to enter the priesthood.[39] However, no one expects immediate action on the nuns' requests, but Sister Theresa Kane believes it will happen eventually.

She concluded in a recent report to a national conference of nun leaders (August 1980) that sexism in the church must be done away with, as keeping women out of the priestly ranks is "a root evil and a social sin which must be eradicated."[37]

It will be interesting to see if the 1980s will be years of change in the attitude of religions toward women. There is no reason that women should suffer sexist harassment in religion as well as in any other area.

In the next section we consider women in professional sports.

WOMEN AND SPORTS

In sports, such as in the case with sexual activities and occupations, there are traditional and nontraditional ways for women to behave. Society always deemed that women should be sexually passive and family oriented, but with permissible occupations such as teaching and nursing. As far as sports are concerned, women were told they should *never*: be competitive; beat a man in any sporting activity (even in jest); engage in any contact sports (they are "unladylike"); use physical force, especially to overcome an opponent; and display strength during sporting activities.

Permissible sports that could be played for "fun" included: tennis; swimming and diving; horseback riding; and gymnastics. Sports definitely to be avoided were: softball and baseball; basketball; football; soccer; lacrosse; track and field; volleyball; boxing; wrestling; and long-distance running.

Theoretically, all of this has changed. Women are now engaged in all of the latter "nonfeminine" sports both as amateurs and as professionals. And they are receiving public acceptance. Yet the underlying biases have hardly changed. In one study, it was found that women retained a more feminine image when they avoided sports that involved face-to-face competition (e.g., basketball), body contact (e.g., wrestling, boxing), handling a heavy object (e.g., shot put, discus throw) and moving over long distances (e.g., cross-country track).[40] To feel "feminine," women stayed with sports such as tennis, gymnastics, racquetball and diving. In another study, a cross-section of five hundred adults was asked which sports would enhance women's femininity. The three rated the highest were swimming, tennis, and gymnastics. Of the sports listed, the three judged as most "unfeminine" were track, basketball, and softball. When female athletes who participated in those sports were asked if they felt that the public attached a stigma to their particular sport, their responses were equated with the public's image. Basketball players and track and field participants were much more likely than swimmers, divers, and gymnasts to perceive their activities as unfeminine. In the same study, 275 women nonathletes were asked if there was a general stigma attached to women's participation in sports. Sixty-five percent of them felt that there was.[40]

Anxieties

As a result of these beliefs, female athletes may suffer certain anxieties about participation in sports. They may question whether they can engage in serious athletic competition and still remain feminine. To try and retain their feminine image, women athletes become extremely conscious of their appearance. For example, in races, female runners often wear attractive hair ribbons, ostensibly to keep the hair out of their faces, but also to present a feminine image. Many professional women tennis players and golfers wear "high fashion" dresses.

Another concern of female athletes is the fear of becoming too muscular. However, this fear is unwarranted. Even when women engage in extensive weight-lifting programs, they do not develop large, unsightly muscles. The main effects are decreases in subcutaneous fat and improvement of body contours.

In a study comparing female athletes with nonathletes, it was found that their physiques were substantially similar. The athletes averaged a one-inch advantage in height (5 foot 6 inches versus 5 foot 5 inches) and three pounds in weight (129 versus 126 pounds).[40] However, women who run or dance extensively may have large and well-defined calf and thigh muscles. But that appearance is not necessarily unattractive or unfeminine.

One other concern women athletes have is fear of becoming injured or ill. They may worry about the effects of being active during their menstrual period, but there is no evidence that sports participation during menses is dangerous. However, there is some evidence that jogging may not be desirable for women contemplating having children. A Chicago gynecologist found that the repeated impact of a woman's heel striking the ground while running can cause a prolapsed uterus and stress incontinence.[41] Nevertheless, many women successfully combine running with motherhood.

In another aspect, women do better than men in running (see Box 17.5).

Many women are now participating in sports that were formally male-dominated, and even in public school girls and boys are participating

BOX 17.5.   Women, Sweat and Stress.

In a study at Temple University, exercise physiologist Albert Paolone found that women who jog during the warm summer days have a higher tolerance for hot, humid weather than do men.[42] It is apparently related to the lesser amount of sweating that women do, as compared to men. However, Paolone advises that neither women nor men should exercise vigorously during hot, humid weather. When the temperature is above 80 degrees F and the humidity exceeds 65–70 percent, then exercise becomes stressful and can result in heat exhaustion, heat stroke, and progressive dehydration.

jointly in sports activities. Is this resulting in more injuries or sicknesses for women? One study addressed this possibility. It was done at West Point and compared hospital admissions for injuries and sicknesses for male and female cadets engaging in intramural and intercollegiate sports.[43] The women cadets were expected to meet men's physical performance standards. The hospital records showed that 3.9 percent of the women and 2.5 percent of the men were admitted for injuries. Twenty-one percent of the women were admitted for diseases while only 7.7 percent of the men were admitted. It was believed that the women's problems were related to chronic fatigue. The women as a group were probably performing at a level close to their maximum physical output in an effort to meet the physical standards. The men seemed to function at a level below their physical maximum. Further studies at West Point revealed that after two years of the same intensive training programs, the women cadets remained about 20 percent below their male classmates in aerobic power and 35 percent below the men in isometric strength.[44]

If the results of these studies can be transferred to other sports in which women participate with men and strength is involved, it may either be advantageous for women to play only with women, or for women to play with men with handicaps given to the men.

An example of this is the age handicap. A younger female tennis champion, Billy Jean King was able to beat senior male tennis champion, Bobby Riggs. The age difference made the match competitive. Even feminists have to agree that the top male tennis players are physically too strong for the top female tennis players in any direct competition.

However, in other sports (if there are ways to test for strength, agility and performance in the particular sport and the women are comparable or superior to the men), women should definitely be encouraged to play against men. Recent evidence has shown that when women receive proper conditioning, training, and medical service, there are no significant differences in injuries between women and men athletes.[45]

At a recent educational conference at Syracuse University, a new problem surfaced regarding women athletes. For years, many male athletes at Syracuse, because of intensive athletic schedules, had difficulties in keeping up with their studies. As a result, some male students had to be tutored and others were forced to drop out of the particular sport. Female sports had always been de-emphasized and the women athletes generally did not have scholastic problems. Currently, women at Syracuse are achieving parity with men in the support and emphasis given to team sports. One result has been an increased number of female athletes requiring help with their studies.[50]

Women often wonder whether they will be able to maintain their athletic ability and endurance after they have had children and as they get older. A recent study revealed that women should not be overly concerned. University of Alabama researchers found that adult men's endurance capacity decreases 10 percent per every ten years of age.[46] With every ten years of increased age, women's endurance capacity decreases only 2 percent. A practical example is: A sixty-year-old man can perform 60 percent of the exercise he could manage at the age of twenty. In contrast, a sixty-year-old woman would be able to perform more than 90 percent of the exercise she could handle at the age of twenty.

Harassment

In 1972, the Education Amendments Act was created. It is popularly known as Title IX and it is supposed to eliminate sex discrimination in athletics. According to the law, females may compete with males in noncontact sports. Contact sports can be limited to men. There are problems with sports that may or may not involve contact. For example, as of this writing, soccer has not yet been clearly established as being either contact or noncontact.

With many sports now being opened to both females and males, in addition to the increased probability of injuries, there is the possibility of both sexual and sexist harassment. However, as is the case with business and the professions, these problems should decrease as men realize that women can more than "hold their own." In some school systems, in order to decrease the harassment and number of injuries, girls and boys are tested and matched according to ability and strength. Then the stronger and more agile girls compete with and against either girls or boys on an "equal footing."

Finances

"Equal pay for equal work" is a feminist theme and it is appropriate. It is now being echoed in increasing numbers by professional female athletes. In recent years, the prize money and salaries have skyrocketed in male sports, but in female sports the rise has been less pronounced. One argument given by sponsors is that the male sports attract more paying and viewing customers. But this is not necessarily true. For example, many male as well as female club tennis players can relate more to the professional women's rallying style of tennis than to the overpowering serve and volley style of the male stars. Women professional tennis matches draw very well. After recent boycotts and threats of boycotts, the women professional tennis players are achieving financial parity. Similar results are occurring in other sports such as golf.

Not only is money important for professional athletics, it is of increasing concern in intercollegiate sports. In 1979, the federal government ruled that proportionate money must be spent on athletic scholarships for both sexes.[47] In the past, many schools spent the majority of their sports' budgets on male sports such as football and basketball, with only "lip service" being given to the female sports. Scholarships were handed out primarily to male athletes. But now, through the activities of the *Association for Intercollegiate Athletes for Women* (AIAW) and recently the *National Collegiate Athletic Association* (NCAA) as well as implementation of Title IX, there is a more equitable distribution of scholarships and school finances. In addition the NCAA has approved women's championships starting in 1981.[48] As a result of these activities, the caliber of female intramural and intercollegiate athletics should greatly improve, and girls who contemplate athletic careers should find the path a lot smoother.

The Athlete's Life Style

Being a professional athlete has potential glory attached to it, but there is a lot of hard work involved. Not everyone is a Chris Evert Lloyd, a Billy Jean King, or a Nancy Lopez-Melton. Many touring "pro's" live out of suitcases, have a disrupted home life, practice for long hours, and don't make a lot of money.* When one plays a sport for fun, it can be just that. When one engages in a sport as a profession, it still may be enjoyable but it can also be hard work. Therefore, women contemplating careers as athletes

---

* One possible problem related to the athlete's life style is the constant living together with female companions. This may have been partly responsible for tennis star Billy Jean King's admitted homosexual affair. An excellent discussion of Billy Jean's disclosure is found in Morrow, L., Why and when and whether to confess. *Time* 91–92, May 18, 1981.

must realize that there is room for very few at the top, and even if one is successful the career lives of professional athletes are very short. "Middle age" begins at around thirty-five. Then the woman must have either saved a lot of money, invested her earnings well or prepared herself for another career such as coaching, recruiting, sports broadcasting, or sports writing.

Courtship, Marriage and Sports

With women participating in athletic training and competition at an early age, and becoming less anxious about appearing unfeminine, they are better able to compete with males. One result is that women are beating men in face-to-face competition. This causes some male "egos" to suffer. Of course, a well-balanced androgynous male wouldn't be upset at losing to a woman, but as of now there aren't too many androgynous males around. Hence, women must realize that in certain instances, they may "turn off" men by beating them. However, this is similar to a situation where a woman or man is playing her (or his) boss or supervisor in a match. Should she or he win, they face the risk of alienating their superior and there may be negative consequences for their job situation.

One potentially stressful occurrence is when couples play as partners in sporting events. There are many instances of verbal abuse between husbands and wives on tennis courts and in bridge games. Divorces have been precipitated by arguments between spouses over losing a match. Hence, it might be practical to play mixed doubles with your friend's husband rather than your own spouse—or to avoid mixed competition altogether.

However, some sporting activities are very beneficial when they are shared. Playing golf, swimming, or riding bicycles together can be very enjoyable. Jogging may or may not be fun. Some men like to sprint ahead of their wives and then the women feel isolated. Sometimes, it's the woman who outdoes the husband. But some couples find enjoyment in running together side-by-side.

Another potentially stressful occurrence with married couples is television sports addiction. Many men love to spend hours watching sports such as basketball, football, and baseball. Women used to think that they would get a respite after the baseball or football season was over, but nowadays sports are on television year round. With cable TV, there is an even greater showing of sporting events. Women have six options in the case of husbands who are TV sports addicts to an extent that the wives become "sports widows":

1. They can insist that it is them or the TV. Either their husbands reduce their TV watching or they will leave them.
2. They can get another TV and watch their own programs while their husbands concentrate on sports.
3. They can join their husbands in the sporting interest and watch the games with them.
4. They can outdo their husbands and watch TV sports even more than their spouses.
5. They can conveniently smash the tubes in all the television sets.
6. They can learn from the enthusiasm of the athletes and take up athletics themselves and at the same time bring their husbands with them.

The best option for both women and men is to be realistic on sports television watching and try to engage in the sporting activities themselves.

The Advantages

Women athletes feel good about themselves. In a recent study, it was found that female athletes rated their bodies much more positively in terms of energy level and health than did nonathletes.[1] The athletes had a more positive body image than did the nonathletes. The female athletes also reported that they "find more happiness in life," are "very satisfied with life," and "generally feel in good spirits" more often than did nonathletes.

Female high-school athletes rated themselves equally or even more "feminine" than did their nonathletic classmates. Another study of collegiate female athletes and nonathletes revealed that both groups of women did not perceive strong competition for women as being unacceptable.[1]

In a study of college women, regardless of their sports activities in college, those who were high-school athletes scored higher than nonathletes in self-confidence and identity. In measures of self-actualization, another group of women college athletes did better than nonathletes.[1] Hence, for women, athletics seem to be a way to instill a sense of well-being and a positive self-image.

Sports have always been viewed as a way to "build men" by developing a sense of team play, that could carry over into other life situations. Other purported positive effects of sports for men are: development of independence; assertiveness; self-control; control over the environment; and motivation to achieve. Although these factors have never been emphasized for women, there is no reason to believe that women cannot find equal results from participation in sports. Many feminists believe that competition in sports can be beneficial to women. It can bring about a sense of mastery and accomplishment that can positively affect their life-styles. Women's participation and success in sports may also diminish society's view of stereotypic roles such as the male athlete and the female cheerleader, and the male achiever and the female admirer.

Diversions

Participating in sports is a wonderful way to decrease stress. The ability to escape from day-to-day stressors by actively engaging in athletics is a great stress reducer. Women are now becoming active in a great variety of sports. There are women sky-divers, skiers, waterskiers, marathon racers, and pool "sharks." (One unique woman athlete is described in Box 17.6.)

Summary

Participation in sports for women: can act as a diversion; can be physically and psychologically beneficial; can act as a stress-relief mechanism; and can be a preparation for one's life-style or career in a particular sport. Be-

BOX 17.6.   Down By the Riverside (With D.M.).

White-water rafting is a particularly stimulating sporting activity. Riding the rapids is just plain fun—even if one occasionally gets thrown into the water. But being a good oarsperson takes a great amount of skill, practice, and some strength. When individuals get proficient in this sport, they may decide to get paid for it by becoming raft guides. The field is dominated by males, but *Pat* is one of the rare female raft guide leaders. I met Pat in the summer of 1980, while rafting down the Shenandoah River. She was the group leader of six other guides and calmly but effectively assured us all of the joys and possible dangers of white-water rafting. Her enthusiasm made all of us a little more excited about the forthcoming trip. As we paddled along awaiting the first Class III rapid (large waves up to four feet in height), she pointed out the historical and ecological highlights. Then we were caught in the first maelstrom and paddled furiously to avoid being thrown out. Luckily we survived that and the subsequent waves and rocks, but all of us, including Pat, got soaked. One thing was certain, Pat handled the oars, steering, and conversation as well or better than the male guides. And when the trip was over, she took her place with the men carrying the raft on her head to its ultimate destination on the truck. Aside from the obvious enjoyment Pat got out of being a raft leader and participant, she emphasized the fact that white-water rafting is excellent for keeping a woman in good physical shape.

ing a female athlete does not make a woman muscular or unfeminine. Rather it can enhance a woman's feminity and improve her figure. As with other activities, however, one should not be an addict and make sports one's whole life. A proper balance of sports, other diversions, work, and social and family life makes for an enjoyable, low-stress life.

In the next chapter, we consider women who suffer a great deal of stress: the minority women; handicapped women, and women criminals.

REFERENCES

1. Associated Press. Female-owned businesses increased by one-third. *Philadelphia Eve. Bull.* B-13, May 27, 1980.
2. Rubin, N. The entrepreneurs: Women who mean business. *New York Times National Recruitment Survey* Sec. 12:56, October 12, 1980.
3. Fletcher, L. Women in business: Top jobs are not out of reach. *Philadelphia Eve. Bull.* NB K-15, February 25, 1980.
4. Gould, H. M., Jr. Women executives: Distaffers point way up corporate ladder. *Philadelphia Inq.* 8-C, 14-C, July 17, 1980.
5. Celender, I. M. Careers in industry for scientifically trained women. *Ann. N. Y. Acad. Sci.* **323**:179–189, 1979.
6. Zimbler Miller, P. Women in business: The truth about the territory. *Philadelphia Eve. Bull.* 15, April 14, 1979.
7. Scott, N. Working women. *Philadelphia Daily News* 23, February 23, 1980.
8. Morse, D. R. and Furst, M. L. *Stress for Success: A Holistic Approach to Stress and its Management.* New York: Van Nostrand Reinhold, 1979.
9. Eisen, E. N. Next: Women in the board room. *Philadelphia Eve. Bull.* NB 13-14, May 21, 1979.
10. Dygert, J. H. Women reshape business travel. *Philadelphia Sunday Bull. Parade Mag.* 18, May 25, 1980.
11. Olson, K. Confessions of an ex-boutique owner. *Philadelphia Inq. Today Mag.* 22,23,25, August 3, 1980.
12. Rice, B. Newsline: Men and women: Sex and the single check. *Psychol. Today* **12**(12):45, 1979.
13. U. S. Dept. of Labor. *Occupational Outlook Handbook, 1978–79 Edition.* Washington, D. C.: U. S. Government Printing Office, 1978.
14. O'Brien, P. Celebrate alone: The lonely woman executive. *Philadelphia Inq.* 15-A, August 25, 1980.
15. Zimmerman, B. and Smith, D. B. *Careers in Health: The Professionals Give You the Inside Picture About Their Jobs.* Boston: Beacon Press, 1978.
16. Serrin, W. Careers: Beating Inflation: Job picture is as cloudy as economy. *New York Times National Recruitment Survey* Sec. 12:1,14,October 12, 1980.
17. McAfee, N. J. Women in engineering revisited. *Ann N. Y. Acad. Sci.* **323**:94–100, 1979.
18. Schmid, R. E. Sign of the times: More women than men in college. *Philadelphia Inq.* 2-A, August 24, 1980.
19. Holden, C. Sex and science. *Science* **205**:670–671, 1979.
20. Sandler, B. R. Women in academe: Why it still hurts to be a woman in labor. *Ann N. Y. Acad. Sci.* **323**:14–26, 1979.

21. Weaver, E. C. Implications of giving women a greater share of academic decision-making. *Ann. N. Y. Acad. Sci.* **323**:257–267, 1979.
22. Abelson, P. H. Women in science-related activities. *Ann. N. Y. Acad. Sci.* **323**:27–34, 1979.
23. Broad, W. J. News and Comment: Ending sex discrimination in academia. *Science* **208**:1120–1122, 1980.
24. Jones, A. B. and Shapiro, E. C. The peak of the pyramid: Women in dentistry, medicine, and veterinary medicine. *Ann. N. Y. Acad. Sci.* **323**:79–93, 1979.
25. U. S. Department of Labor. U. S. Department of Health, Education, and Welfare. *Health Careers Guidebook,* Fourth Ed. Washington, D. C.: U. S. Government Printing Office, 1979.
26. Relman, A. S. Here come the women. *N. Engl. J. Med.* **302**:1252–1253, 1980.
27. Heins, M., Hendricks, J., Martindale, L., Smock, S., Stein, M., and Jacobs, J. Attitudes of women and physicians. *Am. J. Publ. Health* **69**:1132–1139, 1979.
28. Kay, B. C. Women in practice. *J.A.D.A.* **100**:830, 1980.
29. Peterson, S. *Health Careers Series: Preparing to Enter Dental School.* Englewood Cliffs, N. J.: Prentice-Hall, 1979.
30. Morse, D. R. and Furst, M. L. *Stress and Relaxation: Application to Dentistry.* Springfield, Ill.: Charles C. Thomas, 1978.
31. Donelson, J. H. Women in pharmacy—we've only just begun. *Am. J. Pharm.* **150**(5): 165–168, 1978.
32. Editorial. Women: More visible in a changing society. *New York Post* 21, December 12, 1979.
33. Kinzer, N. S. *Stress and the American Woman.* New York: Ballantine Books, 1980.
34. Adams, V. Jane Crow in the Army: Obstacles to sexual integration. *Psychol. Today* **14**(5):50–65, 1980.
35. Goodman, E. Represented: The women made themselves heard. *Philadelphia Inq.* 11-A, August 15, 1980.
36. Editorial. Making quite a difference: Women win two key issues and hold the seats on party councils. *Time* 26, August 25, 1980.
37. Bennetts, L. Women "can't" be aggressive in political role. *Philadelphia Eve. Bull.* 23A, February 15, 1979.
38. Ryan, A. Sister Theresa: Heavenly Hell-raiser. *Philadelphia Journal* 9, August 20, 1980.
39. Loyd, L. Evidence grows: Nuns favor a bigger role. *Philadelphia Inq.* 1-B, 2-B, August 27, 1980.
40. Rohrbaugh, J. B. Femininity on the line. *Psychol. Today* **13**(3):30–42, 1979.
41. Editorial. Good evening: Jogging dangers. *Philadelphia Eve. Bull.* 1, July 9, 1979.
42. Associated Press. Jogging on muggy days can be risky. *Philadelphia Inq.* 10-BJ, July 17, 1980.
43. Protzman, R. R. Women in sports: Can women be overextended in physical conditioning programs? *Amer. J. Sports Med.* **7**(2):145–146, 1979.
44. Knight-Ridder News Services. Females trail in fitness. *Philadelphia Inq.* 2-D, July 10, 1980.
45. Eisenberg, D. D. Focus on women: Proper training reduces injuries. *Philadelphia Eve. Bull.* B-51, May 2, 1979.
46. Editorial. Parade hotline: On physical fitness: Durable women. *Parade Mag.* 35, May 20, 1979.
47. Greenberg, M. Women in sports: NCAA says it's committed to women's sports. *Philadelphia Inq.* 5-D, July 1, 1980.

48. Greenberg, M. Women in the news: A sports empire is hers to build. *Philadelphia Inq.* 1-C, August 19, 1980.
49. The scene: Home, health, family finances. Careers: The corporate ladder has its downs. *Philadelphia Inq.* 2–C, January 13, 1981.
50. Platt, B. Reunion conference of the School of Education. Presented at Syracuse University, May 16, 1981.

18

The Disadvantaged
Women

INTRODUCTION

Women can be members of religious and ethnic minorities and suffer bias and discrimination, as was widespread with Jewish, Italian, and Polish-American women earlier in this century. Members of these and similar religious and national-origin minorities have had the ability to overcome their disadvantages. With hard work, schooling, and governmental help, they have been able to assimilate into the mainstream of American life and have been as successful as most "WASP" women. At times they had to use deception, outright lies, or resort to changing their surnames in order to be accepted. For some, no amount of practice could mask their accents and they still felt the pangs of prejudice. But most of these women had three things in common: they were white; they were not mentally or emotionally impaired; and they did not suffer physical disabilities.

A woman can lose weight, dye her hair, improve her speech patterns, change her name and even improvise a tale about her genealogy (as was the case with Liza Doolittle in *My Fair Lady*). What a person can't do is change her skin color, remove a physical handicap, or eliminate a mental disorder. That is why racial and ethnic minority women, and disturbed and disabled females, have special stress-related problems. Let us now consider these.

RACIAL AND ETHNIC MINORITY WOMEN

The minorities of concern are black Americans, Spanish-surnamed Americans (principally Chicanos and Puerto Ricans), Oriental-Americans (Japanese, Chinese, Filipinos, Vietnamese, Thais and Koreans), American

Indians, Hawaiians, and American Eskimos (principally from Alaska). Although there are variations among the groups, many of these individuals have social, cultural, religious, or ethical beliefs which are different than those of white Americans. When their values come in conflict with those in the mainstream, conflict and stress can result.

Occupations

Many of these minorities hold traditional concepts about the role of women. Women who have strong beliefs about raising a family and managing the household may object to the whole concept of women's liberation. However, even if they decide to be "liberated" women, they often find that the American public is not waiting with "open arms" to offer them jobs. Minority men have an extremely difficult time in getting high status positions, and minority women have it even harder. Let's look at some examples. Blacks represent about 12 percent of the population of the United States, but have only 1 percent of all the academic doctorate degrees held by Americans.[1] Somewhat less than 20 percent of the United States population belongs to a minority group, but only 7 percent of all graduate students (master and doctoral candidates) are minority members.

In 1973, there were 185,000 Ph.D.s in science and engineering in the United States. About 0.5 percent were held by racial and ethnic minorities. Minority-group members represent about 4 percent of the 1–3 million total membership of scientists and engineers. About 2 percent of the physicians, 2.5 percent of the dentists and doctoral level psychologists, 6 percent of sociologists, and about 5 percent of the nurses in America are black.

About 8 percent of the graduate and law school, and 9 percent of medical school candidates are minority members.[2] Even when minority members get a doctorate, it takes minority American citizens an average of 11.3 years to get that doctorate (i.e., from baccalaureate to doctorate). Of the black Ph.D.s, about 20 percent took more than 20 years to get their doctorates. The primary reason for the long time interval is the necessity to earn money for support during school.

When blacks, Latins, and American Indians go for graduate training, most enter the more traditional education field (almost half of all black graduate students are in education as compared to about 25 percent for the total graduate program).[1] In contrast, Orientals are concentrated in business and industry. When the minorities enter education, they generally fill the lower rank positions.[1]

Black average income is less than 60 percent that of whites and black unemployment is almost twice that of whites. Other minorities are in similar circumstances.

All of these findings are present in spite of : (1) laws such as Title VII of the Civil Rights Act (no discrimination allowed in employment based on race, national origin, and sex) and Title IX of the Education Amendments (prohibits sex discrimination in most education programs); (2) active recruitment of minority students; (3) scholarships given to minority students; and (4) tutorial and counseling programs to aid minority students.

There are several reasons why minorities are not sufficiently improving their career outlooks. One major reason is lack of financial resources to cover tuition and related expenses for schooling. Even when they can get scholarships, the students are lost as income-producers to the family for the necessary years of schooling. This factor may prevent the generally low-income minority families from allowing the student to continue her education. Some minority families do not want a "hand-out." If they cannot afford to send their child to school, they would rather not do it.

Some minority students are not adequately prepared educationally to continue their schooling. This may occur because of the lack of governmental and private support to black and minority-based colleges and universities. (About 60 percent of black college students go to black colleges.) That, in turn, limits the equipment and supplies and caliber of educators which can negatively affect the education of the students. One way out of the latter dilemma is the development of postcollege preparatory courses for minority students going to graduate and medical schools (generally six-to eight-week courses given in the summer prior to the start of classes). A second aid would be more governmental and private support, and in these economically bad times that support is not forthcoming.

Another major reason is language. This is a special problem for Spanish and Chinese, Japanese, and Korean-speaking minorities, but it can also be a handicap for black Americans who may be used to a different dialect from standard English in their home community. Here, too, there are two alternative solutions. One is special courses given in English prior to the career-training program. A second is to teach the courses in the native language of the minority student. Although the latter arrangement is done on a limited scale, most educators favor special remedial courses in English.

The impetus for education may be lacking because of family customs, peer pressure, and lack of motivation. This is especially true for women, who as has been mentioned, are generally geared for marriage and family life. Nevertheless, many minority women are forced to work for financial reasons.

Aside from that, minority families often have different sets of values than white middle-class Americans. They often don't believe completely in traditional medicine. They use folk remedies and may have family members involved in diagnosis and treatment. In addition, they may distrust hospitals, doctors, the medical establishment, and Western drugs.

Some Latin groups believe in the concepts of natural disease and supernatural disease and various forms of folk illnesses.[3] Minority members also may have a distrust of science in general (shared by a lot of Americans lately as the result of cloning experiments, nuclear weapons, and pollution). They may believe that nature cannot and should not be understood. This then conflicts with authoritarian teachers' viewpoints. Students from certain minority cultures do not believe in injuring or killing plants and animals. This causes them a great deal of conflict and stress, if for example, they are called upon to do a dissection or do experimental procedures on dogs and cats.

Another problem related to science that can be upsetting to a minority student is Western society's perception and value of pure science. Abstract mathematical, chemical, and physical problems and solutions may mean very little to the minority woman student who often doesn't have two good meals a day or a bed of her own. Applied science would have a lot more meaning to her.

When minority students go to graduate school and opt for a professional career, they may suffer the scorn and ridicule of their peers (especially true for women who are leaving the traditional family role). What is especially frustrating for the minority students who take the brunt from their peers is that they are often not readily accepted by members of the white culture. Hence, they may feel doubly rejected.

Some minority people are not geared to our "high-pressure" working lives. They may prefer a low-keyed, relaxed life-style. For them, happiness may not mean a lot of money, a prestigious career, a new car, or a large house. They may prefer being with their friends in their own community.

The primary way to get minority individuals to upgrade their career aspirations, and to help them achieve "success," is for the involved white majority to have a knowledge of the minority cultures, and their value systems, and to be sensitive to the students who are products of those cultures.

Minority professional organizations are also helping their members to get ahead once they have obtained their degrees. They are also helping prospective professionals plan for careers. For women, one particularly effective organization in that regard is the *National Black Nurses Association.*[4]

In addition to problems minority women face in choosing a career outside of marriage, they also become stressed as a result of their sexual activities.

Sexual and Marital Stressors

Minority women have the same stressors as white American women in terms of the new morality. However, as most of them have a strict upbringing it becomes even more stressful when they have premarital and extramarital sexual relations. When they do "make the break," they often ignore contraceptive advice, and decide *not* to get married.

This is one of the reasons for the higher teen-age pregnancy and out-of-wedlock birth rate for minority women as compared to white women. There is also a higher incidence of venereal diseases among the minority women. In addition, more nonwhites are living together without getting married than are whites. Those that are getting married are getting divorced more frequently than are white women. There is also a higher frequency of abortions in minority women than white women.[5] With the recent cut of federal funding for abortions, the numbers may remain constant—but there undoubtedly will be additional "back street" abortions with ensuing infections and death.

More than three times as many white women as black women receive medical care. This could account for the much higher nonwhite infant and maternal mortality (nonwhite infants have twice the mortality of white infants and nonwhites have over three times the maternal mortality of whites) and the finding that nonwhite infants are of a lower birth weight than white infants. An additional reason may be substandard nutrition of the nonwhites. Another pregnancy-related development is the higher incidence of mental retardation in the minority newborns. This could be related to premature infants (higher in nonwhites) and the poor nutritional state of the nonwhite mothers.

Since the primary role of minority women is that of housewife/mother and since they have a lower use than whites of contraceptives, the birth rate of minority women is one-and-one-half times that of white women.[5]

Another result of the new sexual freedom is the increase of interracial and interreligious marriages. Although the women may marry out of love, the result of the marriages can induce a great amount of stress to themselves, their spouses, their offspring, and especially their families. It is not unusual for an Orthodox Jewish mother to disown her daughter for marrying outside of the faith. Culturally inbred minorities, as well as white families may also display similar perturbations over mixed-race marriages. During times of marital stressors, subliminal prejudice may come to the surface between the partners. This can cause stress for the woman in addition to the harassment she may be getting from her parents. When children of mixed marriages are born, they can suffer prejudice in school. However, mixed marriages are not necessarily stress-inducing and sometimes if people work at them they can be very successful.

Minority women may have certain health problems that white women don't have to face.

Health Stressors

In addition to the previously discussed infant and maternal mortalities, low birth weight and mental retardation, minority women suffer a greater overall mortality rate than white women. They have a predicted longevity of five years less than white women. Minority women have higher rates of certain diseases than white women including cirrhosis of the liver, cervical cancer, diabetes, tooth decay, and nutritional deficiencies.

Nonwhite women see a physician fewer times per year than white women. The minority women more frequently go to out-patient clinics than to doctor's offices as contrasted to white women. Although physicians' house calls are infrequent, more are made to white women than to nonwhite women. Telephone calls are also more frequently made to white than nonwhite women.

There are several reasons for the health problems of minority women. Let us consider them briefly:

1. Generally, the minorities are in the lower income section of the population. They often do not have the finances to get individualized care at physicians' offices and have to resort to clinic care which at times may be less than ideal.

2. Minorities often live in crowded, urban conditions. Crowded conditions increase stress and stress-related diseases such as tuberculosis. Pollution is also increased in center city ghetto areas.

3. Because of the limited finances and lack of health education, many minority women do not regularly frequent medical and dental offices; have less than optimum diets; and rarely practice preventive medicine and dentistry.[6]

4. Some minority women have cultural beliefs that can cause them to

underuse medical facilities. For example, Mexican-Americans may have a fatalistic view of illness and believe the results are in the hands of God.[3] (This is also true with some religions such as Christian Science.) Other Mexican-American health-related beliefs are: belief in the use of folk medicine; the concept of folk illnesses, such as the "evil eye" (mal ojo), "ball in the stomach" (empacho), "fright sickness" (susto), and "witchcraft" (mal puesto).[3]

5. Minority women who are used to persecution and prejudice may distrust hospitals. Hospitals often are viewed as places where people go to die. They disapprove of: the isolation from family and friends; the lack of empathy; the coolness and aloofness of the environment; and the unusual diet (food is different from their ethnic preferences). Specific fears may be present such as: fear of the unknown; fear of bad treatment; fear of not being understood (language barrier); fear of being unconscious; fear of being discriminated against; and fear of dying. They also worry about being unable to meet their family responsibilities and are upset over exposing their bodies for scrutiny.[3]

6. The home is the place to take care of sickness according to many minority people. In many Mexican-American families, women take an active role in diagnosis, treatment, and prevention of illness in family members.[3] This may be helpful for minor ills but may present a problem when major sickness is present.

To help overcome these health problems, health education would be beneficial. However, the language barrier must be breached. Hence, ethnics should preferably work with ethnics. When that is not possible, sympathetic treatment must be rendered. There must be an understanding of the minorities social and cultural beliefs. Whenever possible, folk remedies and folk diagnosis should be incorporated into traditional medicine.

Resolution

Minority women do have special problems but they also have great opportunities. In order to make up for past discrimination policies, industries and colleges are now making special efforts to recruit minority women. Therefore, it it important for minority women to go to school and set their sights on specific goals and work hard to achieve them. Those minority women who don't opt for a career, should try to improve their housewife/mother situations by availing themselves of medical, dental, social, and psychological services. All minority women should use positive methods of stress management which are inexpensive and effective (see Chapters 20–23).

Let's now consider the physical and emotionally disadvantaged women and their particular stressors.

EMOTIONAL, MENTAL AND PHYSICALLY DISADVANTAGED WOMEN

Public Law 94–142 guarantees all handicapped children the right to a free public education in the same facility as other children ("mainstreaming"). The Civil Rights Act (1964) and the Rehabilitation Act (1973) state that "no individual may be discriminated against based upon a handicapping condition in any program receiving federal assistance."[7] These measures have helped to ease the stress for the handicapped women. Let us briefly examine the various types of handicaps and their particular stressors.

Emotionally Disturbed[8]

The emotionally disturbed individual has some form of deviant social behavior. The behavior results from interaction between the person's genetic background and environmental influences (e.g., ingestion of toxic substances; family problems). Emotionally disturbed children and adults often cannot do well in school or maintain a job. They exhibit behavior that ranges from impulsiveness and aggression to depression and withdrawal. They are easily distracted, have short attention spans, lack discipline (oppose authority), have a poor self-image, and are easily frustrated.

About 2 percent of students between five and nineteen years of age in the United States are emotionally disturbed. Although females are found to be emotionally disturbed only one-fourth as frequently as are males, they can grow up to be depressed women unless they are successfully treated. Psychotherapy and physical therapy are most helpful in the management of emotional disturbances.

Learning Disabilities

Learning disabilities result from specific brain damage and environmental factors (e.g., achievement at school). The learning disabled have various problems in talking, writing, reading, spelling, arithmetic, listening, use of language, and cognitive tasks. About 1.5 percent of the American school-age population are afflicted with learning disabilities and are not receiving appropriate education. Most of the learning disabled are males (70 percent).[9] As a result of their dysfunction, the learning disabled are often distractible, impulsive, clumsy, and inconsistent in performance. They may also show hyperactivity.

With many school programs being geared toward the learning disabled, they are learning to use their normal functions to the utmost, and maximizing their abilities in their specific area of dysfunction.

Mental Retardation[10]

The mentally retarded have subaverage general intellectual functioning. Mental retardation originates during the developmental period, has various possible causes (e.g., mongolism; trauma; German measles; malnutrition), and is correlated with impairment in adapted behavior.

In previous classifications, mental retardation was ranked from moron through imbecile to idiot. Nowadays the mentally retarded are categorized as educable (mild), IQ range from 55–70; trainable (moderate), IQ range from 25–55; and severely and profoundly retarded (impaired), IQ range 25 and below. The mentally retarded comprise about 3 percent of the total American population (about 6 million). About 89 percent are mildly retarded, 6 percent are moderately retarded and 5 percent are severely or profoundly retarded. The mentally retarded are inferior to normal individuals in terms of physical, motor, and mental proficiency. The educable mentally retarded can be helped. With the aid of educational programs, these children can adjust socially, master simple skills, and become self-sustaining adults. Many women in this category get married, have children, master housewife skills, and run an efficient home. Other women who do not marry, often can hold down simple factory or farm jobs.

The trainable mentally retarded can often achieve partial independence in daily living activities (self-care), perform simple functions in sheltered or carefully supervised environments, and learn minimal social skills. Hence, as adults, trainable-retarded women may be able to assist in housework and child care, and work at closely supervised job skills.

The severely and profoundly impaired can never function independently and can only perform the most rudimentary self-help tasks. However, they can be made to enjoy their lives within their limited potentials.

Orthopedically Impaired (Physically Handicapped).[11]

There are various types of physical handicaps. With almost all cases, the individuals are mentally alert and aside from the limitations imposed by their handicap, they are physically normal. The major handicaps are cerebral palsy, muscular dystrophy, juvenile rheumatoid arthritis, paraplegia, quadraplegia, spina bifida and other spinal cord injuries, and osteochondroses.

Cerebral palsy occurs in a frequency of 7 per 100,000 and is more common in males. It is a group of permanently disabling symptoms resulting from damage to the child's developing brain. Muscular dystrophy is a genetic disease characterized by progressive degeneration and wasting of muscles. It affects about 200,000 people in the United States and is much more prevalent in males. Juvenile rheumatoid arthritis is a progressive and degenerative chronic inflammation of unknown cause that involves the joint and connective tissues (see Chapter 3). It affects about 175,000 youngsters with the incidence being four times as high in girls as in boys. The cause is unknown, but there are predisposing factors such as infection, trauma, dietary deficiencies, genetics, and environmental stressors. The affected people are often compulsive, introverted, have an inferiority complex, and are depressed.

Spinal cord injuries affect about 175,000 individuals each year in this country and can cause paraplegia (partial or complete paralysis of both legs and the lower trunk), or quadraplegia (partial or complete paralysis of the arms and legs and the trunk). Osteochondroses and osteochondritises are severe degenerations and inflammations around joints that cause impairments of movements, especially walking.

Physically handicapped women may enter many careers including that of wife and mother. Knowing that there are special considerations given to them at work, school, in the home, in automobiles, and in public transportation should reduce the stress that normally would occur from being handicapped.

Visually Handicapped

In the United States, there are approximately 6.4 million people with some form of visual impairment. Of these, 1.7 million are "legally blind" (20/200 or less vision).[12] Blind individuals can often be integrated into regular classrooms and can work at many jobs and careers with the help of their employers and co-workers, and certain modifications of the facilities. Blind women can also be homemakers and mothers with the help of their spouses, families and environmental modifications.

Blind people may suffer a negative self-image but this can be improved if some commonsense suggestions are followed such as these:

1. Always address the person by name.
2. Remove hazardous objects from the work, play, living, or study area.

3. Acquaint the person with the physical characteristics of the immediate surroundings.
4. Indicate your presence in the room by speaking to the blind person.
5. Do not display a patronizing attitude or show pity.
6. Guide the individual, if necessary, but allow for as much independent movement as possible.
7. Have all required learning materials available (e.g., Braille instructional materials).

Hearing Impairment (Auditory)

Approximately 35 out of every 1000 people have an auditory handicap. Almost 6 percent of all school-age children have a hearing impairment (approximately 377,000; of these, 30,000 are totally deaf and 347,000 are partially deaf).[13]

Deaf and hard-of-hearing people have problems with self-awareness, interpersonal relations, social development and are more emotionally unstable. They may become disciplinary problem cases in school and may be reluctant to participate in activities. Suggestions to help the auditory disabled overcome their lowered self-image are:

1. Use additional modes of stimulation whenever possible such as visual and tactile.
2. Provide individual attention.
3. Be patient.
4. Face the person when speaking.
5. Be considerate and empathetic.

Hearing-impaired women who are treated in this way should be able to function effectively in society either as a housewife/mother or in employment of various types. The reward of being productive should help overcome any feelings of inferiority.

Multihandicapped

Some unfortunate individuals have two or more of the aforementioned physical, mental, or emotional disturbances. They are considered multihandicapped. Cerebral-palsied individuals may have other handicaps such as mental retardation, blindness, deafness, speech difficulties, and *epilepsy*.[14] There are two major types of epilepsy: *petit mal* (loses consciousness from a few seconds to about a minute) and *grand mal* (a violent seizure of the whole body).

To reduce the epileptic's stress, it would be helpful if people would follow these simple suggestions:

1. Do not express horror.
2. Remain calm.
3. Do not restrain the epileptic.
4. The surroundings should be cleared so that injuries don't take place.
5. The epileptic should be permitted to complete the uncontrolled movements.
6. The epileptic should be permitted to rest and be gently reassured.

Epileptics under drug control can and should be allowed to participate in school, work and family life.

Another multihandicap is blindness and deafness combined. If left alone, these individuals spend their lives in asylums but with treatment and support (as shown by the amazing Helen Keller), the deaf-blind can lead extremely productive lives.

Other Health-Impaired

There are various diseases and disorders that can cause disabilities. These include postural disorder (e.g. scoliosis; i.e., a rotary lateral curvature of the spine), heart defects (e.g., rheumatic fever; a heart and joint disease), and hyperactivity.[15] People with postural disorders can feel inferior, unloved, or depressed because of their physical appearance. However, physical educators can help with exercises, and chiropractic adjustments may also prove beneficial. Patients with heart defects can be treated with antibiotics and/or surgery and may be able to live relatively normal lives.

Hyperactive children have been a problem in the classroom. Instead of the use of drugs, the Feingold diet (elimination of food additives) has proven successful in many cases.

SUMMARY

Although none of these emotional, mental, and physical disabilities are limited to females, when women have them they add to the stress of being a female. Fortunately, the government, educators, and employers are pooling their resources to decrease the stress from being handicapped.

Another group of women who are disadvantaged are women criminals. This is especially true for prostitutes.

THE ILLEGAL PROFESSIONS: PROSTITUTION
AND ASSORTED CRIMINAL ACTIVITIES

Women criminals used to be rare. The ratio of male-to-female arrests was eight to one in 1960. In 1973, it was six to one, and currently it is even closer. Women are committing more crimes and are being arrested more frequently. For example, from 1965 to 1973, female arrests for robbery increased 187 percent.[16]

Even in this "free" society with the general letdown of social inhibitions and widespread drug use, there are still many fewer female than male criminals. One of the reasons is that the housewife/mother (still the principal roles of women) has a lesser opportunity to commit a crime.

Women do commit minor crimes such as shoplifting but these are just an aside to their regular roles. Women bank robbers are increasing but most often women stay in the background. They may act as instigators of crimes committed by men. However, there is one profession that is considered to be criminal that is dominated by women: prostitution.

PROSTITUTION

Aspects

Prostitution has been called the oldest profession. In various ancient cultures, it was associated with religious ceremonies since it was known as "sacred" or "temple" prostitution. Throughout history, prostitution has existed and persisted in one form or another, even though there have been numerous attempts to eradicate it. Prostitution is characterized by frequent sexual activity by women with a variety of male partners (usually unknown to the women on a personal basis). As with other occupations, the women receive a predetermined fee for their services. There is usually no emotional involvement by the prostitutes.

Although oral sex, anal intercourse, and adultery are defined as felonies in most states, the only sexual act for which women are regularly prosecuted is prostitution. This is another area in which women are unfairly persecuted. Prostitution exists only because men are willing to pay for it. And men (in large part) write and administer the laws that define prostitution as being illegal. Women are arrested for their participation but male clients are rarely arrested. In most states, using the services of a prostitute is not considered as a crime. However, other males involved in the business of prostitution such as pimps (solicit customers), panderers (coerce women into prostitution), taxicab drivers (transport customers), and landlords (supply the premises) are culpable and do get prosecuted.

Employment

Prostitutes have five kinds of employment. The first and most widespread is *solitary street walking*. Most prostitutes are arrested when they solicit customers on streets or in public places such as bars or hotels. Undoubtedly, this is quite stressful for the inexperienced prostitute. The experienced prostitute couches her invitations in vaguely worded phrases such as: "Do you want to have a good time?" "Would you like to have some fun?" "Do you want a date?" She also does not directly ask for fees for service but may ask for help to "support her sick children" or "dying mother." However, even if the prostitute is arrested and convicted, it is merely superficial "treatment." She is often booked and released and then resumes her normal practice.[18]

Many prostitutes do not solicit their own customers but rely on a pimp to procure for them. The pimp then gets a fee (akin to an agent in that respect), or the pimp collects the money and doles out a salary to the prostitute. In one study, it was found that 80 to 85 percent of prostitutes had pimps.[19] Women who don't have pimps are highly respected in the subculture of prostitution but it is extremely difficult to operate without a pimp.

The interaction with the pimp is an extremely stressful one. Prostitutes often have strong love-hate relationships with their pimps. The pimp often is the recipient of the love that the prostitute had lost or never had at home. Prostitutes tend to "mother" their pimps and pimps may simultaneously act as a mother figure for the child-like prostitutes.[17] Masochism is part of the pimp-prostitute relationship. It is accepted in the subculture that the prostitute will be abused and even physically beaten by the pimp. Prostitutes often have a sexual liaison with their pimps and they are frequently emotionally attached to them. Many prostitutes like the expensive clothing they receive and enjoy going to "fancy" night clubs and bars. They may consider the life as a lawbreaker to be exciting and fast paced. Prostitutes may also get "kicks" out of being "partners in crime" with their pimps and taunting the police (offshoot of their earlier taunting of their parents).

Prostitutes often get jealous of their pimps who frequently employ more than one prostitute. There can be disharmonious relations among prostitutes working with the same pimp. Should the prostitute attempt to sever her relations with the pimp, she may be threatened or intimidated to such an extent that she just maintains the status quo.

"Streetwalkers" have other stressors aside from police and pimps. They have little or no background information on their clients. Prostitutes may be robbed, beaten, or even killed by their clients. They also must be concerned about receiving or transmitting venereal diseases and getting pregnant. From a psychological viewpoint, prostitutes may also become stressed from having "sex" with men of all sizes, shapes, and personalities. They may be asked to perform a variety of bizarre sexual acts. Their clients may be sick, drunk, drugged, or psychotic. Almost invariably, prostitutes do not achieve orgasm or derive enjoyment from their sexual activities. This places them in the category of women who do not work for enjoyment, but for the money.

In addition to the money, there is one other possible positive aspect of being a prostitute. That is, the feeling of power prostitutes can get from being able to sexually "turn on" men. They may also like being admired by their male customers. "High-class" prostitutes don't take advantage of their customers but many other prostitutes would not hesitate to rob their clients under the proper circumstances.[17] No matter how they get the money, prostitutes have one advantage over most employed individuals; that is, they don't pay taxes on their income. One might consider the fines they pay when arrested to be sort of a nuisance tax.

Aside from "streetwalking," many prostitutes work in *brothels*. Here the prostitute is an employee working for an employer (i.e., the "madam") and she receives a salary. There are certain benefits from working in a brothel ("whorehouse"). The "girls" have regular jobs, definite hours, good pay, fine living quarters, many acquaintances, and, in the better establishments, receive free medical examinations and treatments (less chance to become pregnant and get or transmit venereal diseases). The customers are also screened by the madam so there is less danger of the prostitute being hurt or robbed.

Prostitutes who have seniority also have the right to refuse unacceptable customers. The relationship of the madam to her "girls" is an employer-employee relationship, but it can also be a substitute mother-daughter one. The prostitutes can develop "sister-sister" relationships among themselves and lesbian activity is not uncommon (up to 80 percent in one study).[20] In fact, most prostitutes experience orgasm only through masturbation or lesbian activities.[21]

Houses of prostitution may be helpful in the community in certain ways. They tend to keep the streets "clean" as there is less streetwalking. The brothels should also reduce the incidence of syphilis, gonorrhea, and other venereal diseases. (In the better "houses," the prostitutes have medical examinations twice a week.)

Another argument for brothels is that with regular outlets available married men would have less affairs. The belief is that going to a prostitute does not involve emotional attachments. However, for equality's sake, there should also be male brothels.

Theoretically, brothels can also help the town's economy. The "girls" spend a lot of money buying clothes, food, furnishings, and for entertainment. The male customers should be happier and less likely to commit crimes. When the local brothel was closed in the town of Deadwood, South Dakota, the town's economy suffered.[22]

A third source of employment for prostitutes is in business establishments such as *massage parlors, nude photography studios, "nude counseling" services,* and *escort services.* Some of these businesses are legitimate but others are fronts for prostitution. In these establishments, the prostitutes are able to select their clients. Other advantages are similar to brothels, such as regular hours and good wages. In addition, the women can legitimize their chosen careers by stating that they are masseuses, photographers, or escort service employees. As there are no madams involved, the "mother-daughter" relationship is missing, and it becomes a strict business arrangement. Owners of these establishments, as well as brothels, may have to "pay off" the police in order to stay in business.

The most successful prostitutes work as *"call girls"* at hourly rates of $100, $200, or more. They deal only with referrals and by appointment (much like professionals in medicine and law; see Box 18.1). These women may work part-time and in general have the most relaxed life-style of any prostitute. Some expensive call-girls become the exclusive mistress of a rich man and are given exquisite clothes, a well-decorated apartment, and the finest food and entertainment.

Another "legitimate" prostitute is the *sexual surrogate.* She works for a sex therapist and for a fee helps clients improve their sexual performance.

Background of Prostitutes

Who becomes a prostitute? Most prostitutes go into their field as adolescents. They generally come from a broken, chaotic home with problems such as alcoholic, drug-addicted, and extra-maritally sexually active parents. Many prostitutes suffer as children from parental separation, child abuse, incest and gross neglect.[20] They often feel alone, unprotected, unloved, and suffer from bouts of depression.[17] Prostitutes frequently have a history of delinquency, drug abuse, and frequent sexual activity.[19]

In one study, it was found that about 80 percent of prostitutes are mentally retarded,[23] but this was not corroborated in a more recent study.[17] One characteristic attributed to prostitutes is mania (abnormal elation) that seems to go along with their high activity level.[24] Other prostitutes suffer from schizophrenia, and many are reported as being masochistic.[17]

Box 18.1: Pity the Poor Prostitute by LF.

In my youth I chose to "play" rather than work. In those days my wants were simple, and I found that the "best things in life are free." On critical occasions, I took whatever job was available to meet immediate needs . . . like eating. Such "positions" literally ranged from dishwasher and ditchdigger to sanitation man. In retrospect I can say that these humbling experiences must have been "good for my soul" since I still take out the garbage without complaint!

Shortly thereafter I realized that it would take more than "survival" money to complete my undergraduate education at Northwestern University. Under the circumstances, I was lucky to get a job working nights as a desk clerk at a sleazy hotel which not only allowed me to take daytime courses but provided extra money. For instance, I earned 25¢ for each bed that I "made up." (While this doesn't sound like much money per unit, it was a windfall considering the volume.) It was standard practice for this "hotel" to rent each room several times in the course of an evening, and such "quickies" tended to tip generously. And it was obvious that street-walkers in the neighborhood brought their "John's" to this "hotel."

After several stints in such settings, I was approached by a "recruiter." Apparently my clean-cut appearance and attention to "business" had not gone unnoticed. (I had none of the drinking and gambling habits that were common among the seedy characters who typically held such jobs.) Thus, I "graduated" to one of the "finer" establishments in Chicago.

The hotel "organization," via its network, expected me to abide by its basic rules and regulations (e.g., never talk openly to strangers, particularly those who ask questions; and *never* discuss "business" over the phone). As I think about it, the system was virtually foolproof: To make direct contact with "management" was a no-no. Johnny, the pimp, made the arrangements. Frank, the "muscle," took care of security. And Larry, the desk clerk, gave the correct room to the "client" according to a prearranged code ("Do you have a room with a Southern exposure?"). He then alerted the call girl by a coded phone message. ("Your 'luggage' is on the way up to 814".)

I was amazed at the clientele; it ranged from the most distinguished-looking gentlemen to famous people that I recognized from pictures in newspapers. There were sports figures, business tycoons, and politicians and, on rare occasions, men of the cloth. The well-heeled clients enjoyed many advantages: (1) insurance against robbery, violence, and blackmail; (2) efficient and "clean" call girls; and (3) no emotional entanglements.

In time I came to know some of the high-class call girls and I learned much more about life and people from them than from any of the courses I was taking in college.

The sex act itself is short compared to other human activities like eating and sleeping. Thus, many times I was invited to "visit" with them in order to break up the monotony. (I was considered part of the "family.") The conversations generally ranged from small talk to discussions of literature, music, art, and politics. Sometimes I even learned about sensitive matters from important "clients" well before the knowledge became public.

When the high-class call girls spoke of their earlier lives, I expected to hear stories of fathers who drank, gambled, and deserted, and of mothers who were slovenly, unkempt, and sexually active. It wasn't anything like that. The young women were invariably beautiful and intelligent. Typically, they had either been a "runner up" in a local beauty contest or had not quite "made it" in Hollywood. In both instances, it was common to hear about a "casting couch" or a "try out."

The young women were simply capitalizing on their natural assets, "living for the moment," and waiting for the "big break." They considered that there was nothing wrong with meeting the "finest" and most "cultured" men, and being admired and loved for their beauty and intelligence. They enjoyed being exposed to literature, music and art, and savoring the best of food and drink.

Looking back at these experiences, I realize that stress was ever present for everyone. There was a fear of getting caught, a fear of contracting a venereal disease, and anxiety about money. But as far as the "poor" prostitute was concerned, she seemed superrich in terms of men and material things. From what I observed her "career" was short—but it sure seemed "sweet" at the time. As for myself, if things ever get "bad" in the field of psychology, I just might reapply for a position as "desk clerk" in a "fancy" hotel.

Prostitution as a Career

Why do women become prostitutes? One reason is to escape an unhappy home life; a second reason is to become independent. As they often have no training, they go into the only endeavor with which they are familiar, sexual activity. Another reason for entering prostitution is to earn money to support a drug or alcohol addiction. The money may also be used for food, clothes, shelter, and to support children, parents or lovers. Some prostitutes believe or rationalize that they are performing an important service as a sexual therapist. Others consider that prostitution is no better or worse than any other job. Nevertheless, prostitutes do suffer stress-related problems. Many of them abuse drugs and alcohol and suffer bouts of anxiety, rage, helplessness, deprivation, and depression. The rate of attempted suicide is very high among prostitutes.[17] Some of the causes for these stress-related problems are: (1) the love-hate relationship between prostitutes and pimps; (2) the anxiety about arrest, disease, pregnancy, injury, and death; (3) the short-term career of prostitutes (usually lasts for no more than ten years[17]; (4) the unstable life style of prostitutes; and (5) the lack of financial security. (Many prostitutes squander their money as fast as it comes in.)

Overall, prostitution cannot be considered a good career. The money may be good temporarily and some retired prostitutes can "graduate" and become madams, but there are so many potential stressors that it is not worth the risk. Women who want to leave prostitution have had success with psychotherapy but only if they were committed to a change.

In the next section, we consider the various ways that women who are committed to change can help themselves cope with stress.

REFERENCES

1. Melnick, V. L. and Hamilton, F. D. (eds.), *Minorities in Science: The Challenge for Change in Biomedicine.* New York: Plenum Press, 1977.
2. Cadbury, W. E., Jr., Cadbury, C. M., Epps, A. C., and Pisano, J. C. (eds.), *Medical Education: Responses to a Challenge.* Mount Kisco, New York: Futura, 1979.
3. Jaurez, M. and Gronseth, E. The Mexican American woman: Stress related to health, health beliefs and health practices. *In* Kjervik, D. K. and Martinson, I. M. (eds.), *Women In Stress: A Nursing Perspective.* New York: Appleton-Century-Crofts, 1979, pp. 157–170.
4. Branch, M. F. and Paxton, P. P., (eds.), *Providing Safe Nursing Care for Ethnic People of Color.* New York: Appleton-Century-Crofts, 1976.
5. U. S. Department of Health, Education, and Welfare. *Health Status of Minorities and Low-Income Groups.* Washington, D. C.: U. S. Government Printing Office, 1979.
6. McElmurry, B. L. Health appraisal of low-income women. *In* Kjervik, D. K. and Martinson, I. M., (eds.), *Women In Stress: A Nursing Perspective.* New York: Appleton-Century-Crofts, 1979.
7. Horgan, J. S. and Porretta, D. L. *Project: Stop-Gap. Curriculum Resource Guide: General Considerations Public Law 94-142.* Philadelphia: Temple University, 1979–80.
8. Horgan, J. S. and Porretta, D. L. *Project: Stop-Gap. Curriculum Resource Guide: Emotionally Disturbed.* Philadelphia: Temple University, 1979–80.
9. Horgan, J. S. and Poretta, D. L. *Project: Stop-Gap. Curriculum Resource Guide: Specific Learning Disabilities.* Philadelphia: Temple University, 1979–80.
10. Horgan, J. S. and Poretta, D. L. *Project: Stop-Gap. Curriculum Resource Guide: Mental Retardation.* Philadelphia: Temple University, 1979–80.
11. Horgan, J. S. and Poretta, D. L. *Project: Stop-Gap. Curriculum Resource Guide: Orthopedically Impaired.* Philadelphia: Temple University, 1979–80.
12. Horgan, J. S. and Poretta, D. L. *Project: Stop-Gap. Curriculum Resource Guide: Visually Handicapped.* Philadelphia: Temple University, 1979–80.
13. Horgan, J. S. and Poretta, D. L. *Project: Stop-Gap. Curriculum Resource Guide: Hearing Impaired.* Philadelphia: Temple University, 1979–80.
14. Horgan, J. S. and Poretta, D. L. *Project: Stop-Gap. Curriculm Resource Guide: Multi-Handicapped.* Philadelphia: Temple University, 1979–80.

15. Horgan, J. S. and Poretta, D. L. *Project: Stop-Gap. Curriculum Resource Guide: Other Health Impaired.* Philadelphia: Temple University, 1979–80.
16. Williams, J. H. *Psychology of Women: Behavior in a Biosocial Context.* New York: W. W. Norton, 1977.
17. MacVicar, K. and Dillon, M. Childhood and adolescent development of ten female prostitutes. *J. Am. Acad. Child. Psychiat.* **19:**145–159, 1980.
18. Katchadourian, H. A. and Lunde, D. T. *Human Sexuality,* Second ed. New York: Holt, Rinehart & Winston, 1975.
19. Davis, N. J. The prostitute. *In* Henslin, J. M. (ed.), *Studies in the Sociology of Sex.* New York: Appleton-Century-Crofts, 1971, pp. 297–322.
20. Maerov, A. S. Prostitution. *Psychiat. Quart.* **39:**675–701, 1965.
21. Caprio, F. and Brenner, D. *Sexual Behavior: Psychological Aspects.* New York: Citadel Press, 1961, p. 251.
22. Interview with Pam Holliday. *AM/PM, KYW-TV.* Philadelphia, September 3, 1980.
23. Glover, E. The psychopathology of prostitution. *In* Glover, E. (ed.), *The Roots of Crime: Selected Papers on Psychoanalysis.* New York: 1960, pp. 244–267.
24. Spalt, L. Sexual behavior and affective disorders. *J. Dis. Nerv. Syst.* **36:**644–647, 1975.

PART VI
STRESS
MANAGEMENT
FOR WOMEN

Stress can be managed negatively or positively. In Chapter 19, a review is given of the negative methods which include smoking, drinking, "pill popping," improper eating, and defensive psychological methods such as rationalization and denial. Chapter 20, is concerned with the positive psychological methods including mental preparation and group therapy along with the deep relaxation methods such as meditation and hypnosis. In Chapter 21, the physical methods of heat, massage, and exercise are emphasized. Balanced nutrition is the theme of Chapter 22. How diversions can help in stress control is taken up in Chapter 23. In Chapter 24, a self-analysis of female stress and its management is given in a comprehensive questionnaire.

19
The Wrong Ways: Negative Coping Methods

INTRODUCTION

In Chapter 4, we examined how stress can lead to disorders such as alcoholism, drug addiction, caffeinism, chain-smoking, obesity, anorexia nervosa, and destructive oral habits such as gum chewing and nail biting. These stress-related disorders can be considered negative coping methods. Although they may be temporarily effective in relieving or reducing stress they can lead to serious or even fatal medical disorders.*

The major dangers with drugs are dependence, addiction, overdosage, and interactions. The fact that drugs such as Valium work well to reduce anxiety compounds the effect. Rather than work at trying to analyze and solve the problems, all one has to do is take a pill. And if the worry doesn't recede, then another pill may be taken. Soon one becomes habituated or addicted to the drug.[1,2]

Often a drink or two is mixed in, and then dangerous or fatal drug interactions can occur. Of major importance for women is the fact that their intake of alcoholic beverages and drugs is increasing at an alarming rate.[3] Whether the result is "slow" suicide (e.g., from drinking or cigarette smoking) or "rapid" suicide (e.g., from mixing tranquilizers with alcohol), drug intake must be stopped. If not, women will achieve equality and even surpass men in the use of destructive stress-coping methods.

Overeating can be as dangerous as taking drugs. It merely takes a little

---

* The long-term result of using addictive stress-coping methods can be serious diseases, but even for the short-term, the outcome is negative. At the start, there is a "rush" or euphoria, but this soon turns to opposite effects such as pain, depression, and withdrawal symptoms. This is the basis of the *opponent-process theory*. Leo, J. Behavior: A painful theory on pleasures. *Time* **112**, November 10, 1980.

longer for the effects to be manifested (e.g., heart attacks, diabetes). Starving oneself to look slim (anorexia nervosa) can be just as destructive.* It is not life-threatening to put all kinds of objects into one's mouth and then bite, chew, or suck on them, but teeth can be seriously injured, and teeth are important for esthetics, proper digestion, and good speech.

Aside from these improper physical coping methods, there are negative methods of psychological coping. These defense methods are now considered with specific examples geared toward women.

DEFENSE MECHANISMS[4-7]

Defense mechanisms are the means that all of us use to protect ourselves from anxiety, "soften" failures, and maintain feelings of adequacy, equilibrium, and personal worth. However, these mechanisms involve a high degree of self-deception and reality distortion. In addition, they are rigid, automatized, and inflexible.

Defense mechanisms generally operate on an unconscious** level and therefore, are not subject to normal conscious control. Generally, the more intense the stress situation, the greater the use of defense mechanisms. The more one uses defense mechanisms, the more persistent and less appropriate are the responses. In a sense, one becomes addicted to the use of defense mechanisms, and the resultant disturbances to the individual can be as damaging as is the repeated use of drugs to control stress. Let us now examine the major defense mechanisms.

Denial of Reality

When a disagreeable situation faces us, we may not want to accept it and so we deny its reality. This escapism can be extremely dangerous and life-threatening. People who repeatedly use denial feel either omnipotent or have the philosophy that "it can't happen to me." Women have lost their

---

* Recently, a less well-known variation on anorexia nervosa has been discussed. It is known as *bullimarexia* (from the Greek, meaning ox and hunger). It is also known as the *gorge-purge syndrome* and *bulimia nervosa*. The affected individuals (mainly women) alternately go on "eating binges" and then induce vomiting and take laxatives. They tend to be extroverted and perfectionists. They eat as a stress outlet and purge themselves to stay slim. Unfortunately, this is a very poor coping method. Psychotherapy may be helpful. Behavior, Eating binges: Anorexia's sister ailment. *Time,* 94, November 17, 1980.

** In Freudian terms, the unconscious denotes that part of consciousness that is not under willful knowledge or control. However, it has never been pinpointed in the human nervous system, and many psychological researchers question the existence of the unconscious. We use the term in connection with defense mechanisms although it is realized that it is a questionable concept.

Box 19.1. Denial and its Dangers.

Women may use denial to preserve a floundering marriage by ignoring tell-tale evidence of their husband's adulterous behavior. For example, they see lipstick marks on his shirt collars and tell themselves that they are food stains. When he repeatedly comes home from a business meeting at 3 A.M., they accept his devious explanations.

One unusual case of denial is the following. A mother had a nine-year old son diagnosed as being mentally retarded. The mother refused to acknowledge the fact, and developed the firm belief that her son was a member of a new species which matured at a very slow rate and would eventually achieve a high level of mental development.[4]

lives because of denying the possibility that the small lump in the breast could be breast cancer.[8] Other examples are given in Box 19.1.

Occasionally, denial may be helpful in allowing us to live for the present. If we always think about pollution, nuclear warfare, radiation, artificial additives in our foods, inflation and recession, equal rights, and safety in the streets, we would have no time to pursue our daily activities.

Denial may also be helpful in buying preparation time such as when one has a serious disease or is dying. By denying reality, the person gives herself time to adjust to the changes at a gradual pace.[7]

Fantasy

When people have frustrated desires that need gratification, they may resort to fantasy. In fantasy, a woman can achieve her goals and gratify her needs but in an unreal fashion. Fantasizing is usually a wish-fulfilling activity that does nothing to promote achievement. When things get too "tough," people may retreat into a dream world. (See Box 19.2 for some examples.)

Box 19.2. Women Who Fantasize.

Consider these fantasies: The woman who is overweight and doesn't want to diet and exercise, fantasies herself as a princess with a beautiful figure and does nothing constructive about her body shape. The rich, homely widow fantasies that her beaux are telling the truth when they tell her how beautiful she is. The lonely woman fantasizes that the automobile salesman really means it when he tells her that owning a Porsche will insure that everyone will become her friend.

Sometimes fantasy can prove beneficial. If a woman is envious of her neighbor's three cars, luxurious home, and twenty-four-foot sailboat, rather than display her envy and have a hostile neighbor, she can fantasize that her own material possessions are vastly superior. Many women find that they become bored staying at home and doing housework. A very popular way to fantasize is to escape from the drudgeries of being a housewife by submerging oneself into the afternoon TV soap operas.

Fantasizing can occasionally prove productive. Some get-rich schemes were the result of creative imagination, but unfortunately most of the ideas that we come up with in our dream worlds are doomed to failure.

Compensation

People compensate when they feel inferior or inadequate as the result of real or imagined defects or weaknesses. They also use compensation when failures or setbacks occur. However, compensation can be beneficial. See Box 19.3 for some examples.

Identification

Another way people try to enhance their own prestige is to identify themselves with others. We all do this to an extent. We belong to political

Box 19.3. Compensating Women.

People with handicaps often compensate. Helen Keller was a perfect example. She compensated for her blindness and deafness by becoming a great teacher and humanitarian. A well-known example of compensation is the unattractive girl who becomes a brilliant student or develops a lovable personality.

In a similar vein is the "devil-may-care" attitude of many obese women. Dress manufacturers are well aware of compensation. They design clothes to make short women look taller and fat women look thinner. Cosmetic companies use similar compensatory mechanisms to make a drab-looking woman appear glamorous.

Undoubtedly, quite often people use compensation in a negative way. Consider the lonely unloved female who compensates by eating rich desserts. Another example is the woman who wouldn't spend the time or effort to go back to school and develop a career of her own. Instead she basks in the glory of her husband's or children's accomplishments.

parties and religious, social, and community groups. We may "root" for college or professional teams either because we are alumni or are natives of the particular city. Many people identify with their employers especially if the companies or universities are prestigious. Identification can be damaging if we become too engrossed in others and forget ourselves. When the home-town team loses, we may get noticeably upset. When our boss loses an account, we may get the ulcer. Some women identify with the heroines in daily soap operas to such an extent that they neglect their own needs and responsibilities.

As with compensation, married women can identify themselves so much with their husband's accomplishments that they completely ignore their own desires. When identification becomes extreme, a person can become psychotic and believe that she is someone special (e.g., Joan of Arc).

Introjection (Internalization)

Sometimes people take the values and concepts of others with whom they don't agree and internalize them as if they were their own beliefs. The rationale is that it would be useless to try to fight or overcome the others. Their motto would be, "If you can't defeat your foes, then join them." Some women who do not support ERA are accused by many feminists of doing such a thing—joining their enemies. Brainwashing may have some elements of introjection. After a while, the victim accepts the values of the group in order not to be at its mercy any longer. Patty Hearst may have suffered brainwashing and used introjection as a defense mechanism. Women who suffer from repeated abuse from their husbands may learn to accept it because of internalizing their husband's notion of a wife's role. As is obvious from these examples, introjection is a surrender-type mechanism and, although it may temporarily be useful, the end result is humiliation and a loss of the possibility of personal achievement.

Projection

By projection one transfers the blame for one's own shortcomings, faults, misdeeds, or mistakes onto others. Another aspect of projection is attributing to others one's own unacceptable thoughts, wishes, and impulses. Some examples are given in Box 19.4.

Projection can be temporarily helpful in protecting our self-esteem but it is self-defeating since we cannot accept blame and pull ourselves up by our own efforts.

Box 19.4. Projecting Women.

1. A female student legitimately fails an examination and says it was because of sexist discrimination, even though the exam was graded by a computer and the other women in the class did well.
2. This one we are guilty of: the tennis player who misses a ball completely and then stares at the racket with a puzzled look as if there was a hole in it.
3. The woman who goes to a bar, has a drink or two and ends up in a compromising position in a strange apartment—and blames it on the alcohol.
4. A woman who has lesbian tendencies accuses other women of trying to seduce her.
5. A woman who is always punctual, honest, and conscientious projects this behavior on others—and then becomes stressed when people she deals with are late for appointments, tell lies, and continually procrastinate.
6. The woman who always is blaming her failures on "bad luck," fate, or the will of God.
7. When projection is carried to an extreme, the woman has delusions of persecution—everyone is working against her. (Such a psychosis is known as paranoia.)

Rationalization

Rationalization involves the use of logical, socially approved reasons for one's past, present, or future behavior even though the reasons are only a "cover up" for the individuals own shortcomings. Rationalization helps people justify their behavior and beliefs and can also reduce the disappointment connected with not reaching planned goals. By rationalizing, individuals invent "good" reasons to discount their failures. In Box 19.5 some examples of rationalization are given.

Rationalization can help protect us against unnecessary frustrations and aid us in maintaining our self-image. However, it leads to self-deception and doesn't let us profit from our own mistakes or learn how to face situations squarely. If rationalization is used continuously, it can lead to a life full of delusions.

Repression

Suppression is a method of excluding painful or dangerous thoughts and desires from one's conscious awareness. The material is not really forgotten; it just becomes repressed. It is kept submerged because if it is

Box 19.5. Rationalizing Women.

Common examples of rationalization are:

1. The woman who marries a rich old widower because of his wonderful personality (the rationalization for marrying for money).
2. The minority woman who cheats on an examination, and justifies it by telling herself that she was persecuted all her life and this is her way of "getting even."
3. A woman finds out that the man she was in love with has married someone else. She rationalizes her disappointment by convincing herself that he was too short, too conceited, and too domineering (although she never considered those factors before). This latter behavior is an example of "sour grapes" rationalization.*
4. The widow who never had a job is living in abject poverty. She comforts herself in her poverty by rationalizing that "money is the root of all evil" and she enjoys her neighborhood and wouldn't want to live near those "rich snobs." This is an example of "sweet lemon" rationalization. (The slum home is better than a new home in an upper-class neighborhood.)

remembered the knowledge could be extremely distressful and the individual couldn't cope with it. (See Box 19.6 for an example.)

Suppression can temporarily allow someone to overcome a crisis but if repression continues it can lead to psychosomatic disturbances and prevent a realistic working out of one's problems.

Box 19.6. Repression and Headaches.

A woman sees an acquaintance who was walking towards her being run over by a passing vehicle. The experience is so traumatic that it is excluded from her consciousness. She then develops selective amnesia for the incident and never discusses this former acquaintance with anyone. However, as the result of the repression, the woman gets unbearable migraine headaches. She goes for therapy; the psychologist hypnotizes her and uncovers the repressed memory. As a result, the woman faces the reality of her acquaintance's death, and the headaches disappear. She does suffer grief but after a few weeks she can carry on her daily activities without the headaches and guilt feelings.

* The "sour grapes" mechanism is based on the fable of the fox who unsuccessfully tries to reach clusters of luscious-appearing grapes. The fox finally gives up and decides that the grapes were sour anyway and not worth getting.[4]

Reaction Formation

Sometimes people are so upset by their own desires, wishes or attitudes that they repress them and develop conscious attitudes and behavior patterns that are exactly the opposite. See Box 19.7 for some examples.

Reaction formation can help us keep our antisocial attitudes in check and allow us to act like good citizens. But as is the case with the other defense mechanisms, it causes self-deception. In addition, it can result in excessive harshness in dealing with others and prevents a realistic resolution of one's problems.

Displacement

With displacement, a person who becomes emotionally aroused by another person, object, or situation vents the emotion on the other person or object. The discharge of aroused emotion is toward a neutral or less dangerous object or person. A young girl who has been spanked by her mother kicks her little sister or smashes her doll. A housewife/mother who has had her day filled with broken dishes, screaming children, and intrusive salespeople lashes out at her "Casper Milquetoast" husband when he opens the front door. A woman who hates her husband and has repressed fears of murdering him may displace them onto the fear of all types of dangerous weapons such as guns, knives, and toxic chemicals.

Displacements can prevent individuals from carrying out dangerous actions against people whom they either love, respect, or fear. Unfortunately, displacement exacts a stiff penalty. The child that kicks her sister will have an angry sister with whom to contend. Broken dolls may be replaceable but psychologically the "hurt" may go deep. The salesman may not become stressed but the woman's vented anger at her husband may make the meek

Box 19.7. Women's Reactions.

A daughter unconsciously detests her mother but consciously she makes every effort to appear concerned with her mother's comfort and health. A militant crusader against lesbianism is often fighting her own repressed homosexual impulses. A vociferous equal rights advocate may be holding in check her own impulses to be a housewife/mother.

The woman who craves affection and admiration for her beauty deliberately dresses like a "slob." The woman who detests her boss is extremely polite to him. Shakespeare gave us a good example of reaction formation when one of his characters said, "The lady doth protest too much, methinks."

man retaliate, and the marriage could suffer irreparable damage. And the fear of weapons may save her husband's life but it could be the the cause of the woman's death when she can't use a gun to defend herself against an intruder. Generally, it is better to face and work through anxiety and hostility-producing situations whenever possible rather than avoid them through displacement.

Emotional Insulation

When people have had repeated episodes of disappointment and frustration, they may react to new anxiety-producing situations by withdrawing themselves into a "shell." This is known as emotional insulation. Sometimes it may be beneficial to do nothing. For instance, every time you speak to your friend about nuclear energy, you have a violent argument. You have all the necessary information to substantiate your beliefs and you invariably "win" the argument but one result is a pounding headache and your blood-pressure level rises several points. It may be more advantageous to politely change the subject and insulate yourself from the stress that could result from "winning."

Most often emotional insulation is disadvantageous. Some examples follow.

A young lady is so disappointed after the loss of the "love of her life" that she decides never to be emotionally involved with men again. People who have been "burned" by others in love, business, or politics may become cold, passionless, detached, and aloof individuals. Some people become despondent and give up trying. They may wind up as poverty-stricken recluses.

Another way some women use insulation is to avoid competition of any type. They want to protect themselves from the unpleasantness and self-devaluation that might result from not performing well, or the reverse, performing too well. Women may then avoid things such as going to college (they may feel more secure as homemakers); taking up sports (afraid to appear "unladylike" or beat a man); entering the business world (again fear of losing a feminine image); and becoming politically active (don't want to appear aggressive). As a result the women have prevented themselves from choosing both a vocation and leisure activities for which they might be well suited.

Isolation (Intellectualization, Dissociation)

Isolation is a defense method in which one tries to lessen the hurt of a situation by distorting or cutting off the emotional impact. One unconsciously isolates or dissociates one attitude from the other. Some examples will help clarify this mechanism.

The impact of the death of one's mother is lessened by saying things such as she lived a "full" life; she had a painless death; and it was the "will of God."

Isolation is also used to justify one's antisocial behavior. A woman may be ruthless and dishonest in her business deals but she "makes up for it" by being a dedicated churchgoer and contributes money to charitable causes. A woman can dissociate her behavior to the point that she almost believes it is not happening. One prostitute reported that she felt as if she was not even aware of having sexual activities. She was not actively taking part in it. It was merely happening to her. Her mind was drifting away and cooly calculating how much money she needed for a new coat.[4]

Some people can dissociate as during a hypnotic trance and it may well be that people who use isolation put themselves into a trance.

Isolation can be helpful in reducing emotional conflicts, but in the long run it is self-defeating as it prevents one from facing the true situation and dealing with it constructively. If isolation becomes extreme, it can lead to a multiple personality formation.

Regression

An individual who regresses, retreats to a more primitive, infantile mode of behavior. If the stress situation is severe enough, even normal, well-adjusted adults may revert to child-like behavior. Let's consider some examples.

A frustrated man who can't get his own way may resort to having a temper tantrum which was effective for him as a child. In contrast, a frustrated woman may have a crying fit which was her way of gaining attention as a child. As the result of marriage-induced stress, a woman may go home to her mother for comfort and consolation. Older individuals often use regression when they tend to live in the past when they were happy and successful.

In daydreaming, regression can occur and under hypnosis people can be induced to regress to earlier stages of development. In the latter instance, regression can be helpful because it may uncover the causes of neurotic behavior.

However, regression is generally a method of escaping the stressors of the present. Retreating to the successful methods used in the past is a negative response because it prevents one from dealing with the present or the future. When regression becomes extreme, it can lead to psychoses in which adults become so infantile in their behavior that they are unable to dress, feed, and wash themselves.

Undoing (Atonement)

The concept of undoing or atoning for one's sins is one of the most well-ingrained defense mechanisms. Apologizing for wrongs done to others, doing penance, being repentant, and accepting punishment are all examples of undoing. It is almost as if we take an eraser and wipe out our misdeeds. Once the apology is accepted, as soon as the punishment is completed, or right after the restitution occurs, the misdeed is negated—at least that is what we anticipate. We hope that by saying we are sorry and by offering to do a substitute action, we can overcome and escape rejection and punishment. So the unfaithful husband brings his wife presents or the unfaithful wife makes an elaborate dinner for her husband. In the same vein, the mother who spanks her daughter goes out to the store and buys her toys.

Sometimes people feel that only by accepting punishment will they be granted atonement. Hence, the, "gallivanting" husband tells his wife about his affairs. This may clear his conscience, but it may wreck the marriage. People who believe that their sins are so great may feel that they can only atone for them by ending their lives—so they commit suicide. People commit misdeeds all the time—many are minor and are ignored. When people worry over all their actual or potential misdeeds, they may end up by renouncing their normal lives and live as recluses. They can also blame themselves to such an extent, that they become manic-depressive psychotics.

Sublimation

Sublimation is a means of substituting a socially acceptable goal for a drive or a goal that is blocked. A female who is unsuccessful at marriage may find a substitute sexual outlet as a masseuse. A person with sadistic tendencies may become a surgeon or dentist.

Sublimation has some value as it allows a woman not to dwell on her frustrations and it sidetracks her from carrying out potentially harmful activities such as sadistic behavior. Yet it can be harmful because one may be suppressing basic drives such as sexual urges. Nowadays women have much more leeway in their sexual and career choices. Therefore, they don't have to sublimate sexual desires just because of a broken marriage. They may decide to live with someone, engage in homosexual activities, or have sexual relations at their own convenience. It is no longer a stigma to be unmarried or a career woman.

Sympathism

People who are continually frustrated in their efforts have a poor self-image. Unless they can have their ego bolstered, they will continue to suffer stress. One way they try to overcome their own failures is to enlist the sympathy of others. To do this the individuals may build up "tales of woes," embellish on a series of tough breaks, or describe serious illnesses that have held them back. In other words, they play on the sympathy of others.

When others express sympathy, they then feel a little better about themselves. We all do this to an extent. (See Box 19.8 for an example.)

Unfortunately, sympathism is generally a cover-up and people must learn not to hide their problems, but face them realistically.

Acting-Out

The final defense mechanism to be considered is acting-out. In this method, a person tries to reduce the anxiety aroused by forbidden desires by actually permitting their expression. Thus, it is the opposite of repression in which the desires are kept submerged. Acting-out is not consciously done because the individuals would be subjecting themselves to social disapproval and the possibility of enhanced guilt feelings. Some people with weak ethical and reality controls may use this method. Also under the influence of drugs, alcohol or hypnosis, people can act out to relieve their frustrations.

Box 19.8. Sympathetic Tennis.

You're about to have an important tennis match and you just twisted your knee. So you wrap it up with a thick bandage and bemoan your fate to your opponent. Sometimes this technique is quite effective. Your opponent feels so sorry for your injury that she plays a tentative game (doesn't want to hurt you any further) and you win the match.

This is an example of sympathism, but it is generally not that effective. It gives us a scapegoat to blame, e.g., the injured knee, bad luck, or tough breaks. But as with the other defense mechanisms, we fail to face the real reason for our problems and then can never realistically cope with them.

Two examples of acting-out are:

1. A woman has strong sexual desires but she normally keeps them in check. She sees this "sexy" guy walk by her office every day. Finally, the images become overwhelming and she foolishly sends him a letter confessing to her passion.
2. Another woman has had a strife-ridden marriage for twenty years, but she has never complained to her husband. One day, he says something that upsets her and it is "the straw that broke the camel's back." She lashes out at him and unleashes her sadistic tendencies. He winds up with a slashed arm and she winds up in court.

It is obvious that "acting-out" is an inappropriate defense mechanism. It would be far better to face one's own sexual or hostile desires and try to find appropriate outlets for them. In that regard, psychotherapy might be helpful. Taking it out on a punching bag or a golf ball might be another effective method.

CONCLUSION

Now that we have dealt with the major defense mechanisms, it should be apparent that they are generally inappropriate methods of dealing with anxiety-inducing situations. They all involve self-deception and reality distortion, and if unchecked could lead to neuroses, psychoses, and even suicide. A far better way to deal with stressful situations is to use conscious, rational methods of psychological coping. These are dealt with in the next chapter. Methods of deep relaxation are also covered in Chapter 20.

REFERENCES

1. Hughes, R. and Brewin, B. *The Tranquilizing of America: Pill Popping and the American Way of Life.* New York: Harcourt, Brace, Jovanovich, 1979.
2. Gordon, B. *I'm Dancing As Fast As I Can.* New York: Harper & Row, 1979.
3. Sandmaier, M. *The Invisible Alcoholics: Women and Alcohol Abuse in America.* New York: McGraw-Hill Book Co., 1980.
4. Coleman, J. C. *Abnormal Psychology and Modern Life,* Second Ed. Chicago: Scott, Foresman, 1956.
5. Krech, D., Crutchfield, R. S., Livson, N., and Krech, H. *Psychology: A Basic Course.* New York: Knopf, 1976.

6. Mischel, W. *Introduction to Personality,* Second Ed. New York: Holt, Rinehart & Winston, 1976.
7. Kagan, J. and Havermann, E. *Psychology: An Introduction,* Fourth Ed. New York: Harcourt, Brace, Jovanovich, 1980.
8. Lazarus, R. S. and Goleman, D. Positive denial: The case for not facing reality. *Psychol. Today* 13(6):44–57, 1979.

20

The Positive Mental Methods: Psychological Coping, Consultations, and Deep Relaxation

INTRODUCTION

In the last chapter, two ways of coping with stress were considered; i.e., the use of drugs and the reality-distorting, self-deceptive defense methods. In both of these, there is a lack of clear, conscious activity. Drugs cloud the consciousness and defense mechanisms work primarily on an unconscious level. In this chapter, we consider psychological methods of stress coping that involve conscious effort and allow for flexibility and choice. In the second half of the chapter, the deep relaxation methods which can effectively counteract the stress response are examined.

AVOIDANCE

The best way to cope with stressors is to avoid them. (See Box 20.1 for a few possibilities.)

Box 20.1. The Art of Avoidance.

> You love Chinese food, but the monosodium glutamate (MSG) in the food causes you all sorts of aches and pains. Avoid the distress by either going to a restaurant that will cook without MSG or try Italian food.
>
> You drive to work every day, but the traffic jams, smog, noise, and discourteous drivers give you a headache. Although it may take a few minutes longer, take public transportation and either read, nap, meditate, or watch the scenery.

The Iranian hostages, the battle over ERA, the Mideast crisis, the Russian threat—does listening to the news about these and similar situations depress you? Well, rather than hear it, watch it, and read it, why not ignore the news for a day or two? Instead, read a book, go to a movie, or watch a humorous TV show.

You'd like to take a certain course that's given in the city. But this term it is given in the evening session. Already there have been four rapes in that section of the city. Although the obvious choice would be to take another course during the day—or wait until the desired course is given as a day course—many people are persistent and still would take the evening course. Unfortunately, some women have been raped because of making *just* that decision.

EVASION

Delay or evasion may prevent undesirable results or can increase stress. Hence, evasion should be used with caution. Box 20.2 gives two examples that may help clarify these divergent possibilities.

GOAL SELECTION

Another important way to avoid stress is to be selective about goals. When a person has attainable goals, frustrations are greatly diminished. Even with attainable goals, one must not be impatient. Everyone is clamoring for a "piece of the pie," and the hue and cry is, "I want it now." It is true that

Box 20.2.   The Art of Evasion.

As a receptionist for a busy doctor, you must try to be diplomatic on the phone. Occasionally, you have an irate patient calling. Knowing the circumstances, you realize the patient is in error, but this does not prevent you from getting extremely upset as a result of the phone call. Rather than arguing with the caller, it would be preferable to inform the patient that you must discontinue the conversation since you have to assist the doctor, and will call back in an hour. This will give you time to prepare a calculated response and give the patient time to "cool off."

You have a job offer that looks promising. The potential employer is impressed by you and asks for your decision. You can't make up your mind and ask for a week's delay. He reluctantly agrees—but in the interim he interviews someone else and hires her. The next week you give him your affirmative response but it is too late. As a result, you have to settle for a less prestigious job. In this instance, evasion was not helpful.

there has been a great deal of discrimination against women, but trying to get it all back in "one fell swoop" can only engender stress for all concerned.

On the other hand, procrastination and delay can also be stress-inducing. If you really want to go back to school, don't put it off until the children are in college. Find a way to do it soon, even if you only take one course at a time.

When goals which originally seemed appropriate, later become unattainable, it is worthwhile changing goals (see Box 20.3).

Another reason for changing goals or careers is monotony. Monotony is stressful.* Studies have shown that people who do repetitive procedures are bored and develop a high incidence of stress-related diseases (see Box 20.3). Hence, if you find your career (or being a housewife) to be extremely monotonous, it is time to consider a change. However, one must be selective, for frequent career changes can also be stressful. The stress can result from indecision, moving, meeting new people, breaking old ties, and facing unknown situations.

It must be realized that even if a woman reaches her goals, she may still have stress. Quite often things are never quite like what they seemed to be when you were on the outside looking in. If you don't expect perfection and bliss, you can reduce stress. Finally, one must be willing to compromise. Not everyone can get into Harvard, and a Mercedes must obey the same 55 mph speed limit as a Chevrolet.

Box 20.3.   Goals, Occupations, and Stress.

> Many women have started off as housewives, and then gone back to school envisioning a professional career, perhaps as a physician. For one woman, the intense competition of medical school caused extreme anxiety which helped precipitate a gastric ulcer. Rather than continue her medical career, she went on to graduate school and became a very successful (and calm) microbiologist.
>
> In one study of twenty-three occupations, it was found that assembly-line workers had the highest incidence of irritation, physical illness, and depression.[1] In another study of thirty occupations, it was found that hospital workers (primarily women) and waitresses (along with waiters) had the highest incidence of admission to mental hospitals.[2]

* Strictly speaking, boredom *per se* does not induce the stress response (see Chapter 2), but when monotony is combined with high levels of alertness, considerable stress can be elicited. In addition, boredom can have adverse effects on morale, performance and workmanship. Thackray, R.I. The stress of boredom and monotony. A consideration of the evidence. *Psychosom. Med.* **43**: 165–176, 1981.

SOLO COPING

A person can avoid stress for a time, but sooner or later one must confront stressors and that is when positive psychological coping methods are most useful. First to be considered is mental preparation.

Mental Preparation

To be prepared is one of the best ways to reduce stress. If you are going for a job interview, find out ahead of time about the qualifications required for the position. If at all possible, learn something about the idiosyncracies of the employer. It is common sense that is often ignored, but studying for examinations reduces the stress of taking the exams. Knowing one's material makes it much easier to face an audience and answer questions.

A simple thing like examining a map before taking a trip can diminish the stress from driving. (The *American Automobile Association* (AAA) is aware of that; which is why their tour guides packets are so successful.)

Rehearsal

It is beneficial to plan ahead and rehearse before one acts. It may be helpful to review one's past actions to help in future activities. However, one should not dwell in the past or worry about the future. The key is to concentrate on the present. See Box 20.4 for an example.

Box 20.4. Past, Present, and Future Tennis.

It is match point. You have just hit the previous shot into the net. As you stand waiting to return the serve, these thoughts are crowding your mind: "What a jerk I am for not bending my knees. Why did I keep my racquet down and blow that last point? Now I better not overhit the next shot or I'll lose the point, the game, and that'll be the match. How then will I face my friends?" Doing this mentally, there is a good chance that you will miss the point and lose the match. To be effective in the present one must avoid concentrating on the past and contemplating the future.

There are a few ways to block out those distressing thoughts. One is to listen to your own breathing. Concentrating on each inhalation and exhalation while keeping your eyes "glued" on the approaching ball can be quite helpful.[3] Another method is to silently repeat a sound or word to yourself. The repetition of the word will exclude the distracting thoughts (discussed further under *Meditation*.) A third way is to mentally concentrate on a positive image. For example, you can visualize yourself hitting through the ball with perfect form.

Box 20.5.   "Great Expectations."

You arrive home early in the afternoon. You notice that the front window shade is completely raised. It is your usual practice to leave the shades partly raised during the day. Now you might dismiss your observation by telling yourself, "Oh, I must have pulled the shade up by accident," or "The shade must have snapped open by itself." You could further reassure yourself, "No stranger would enter my house in the middle of the day. After all it is a good neighborhood and the police patrol here regularly." Thus, you enter the house and are confronted by a robber. Had you trusted your first observation and had not been influenced by expectations and biases, you would have gone to your neighbor's and informed the police about your suspicions.

Vigilance

To reduce stress a woman must be vigilant and use all of her senses to the maximum. Only by concentrating can you *really* see, hear, feel, and smell. Don't let your expectations or biases influence your observations.[4] See Box 20.5. for an example.

Effective Action

Once a woman is prepared and uses her senses to the maximum she should then take effective action. The action varies with the situation but it should be appropriate. See Box 20.6 for a few possibilities.

Sometimes stress comes from your perception of the situation. You may go into it with a pessimistic viewpoint and as a result things will turn out

Box 20.6.   Taking Action.

A mugger with a knife confronts you and shouts, "Your money or your life." Your quick appraisal of the situation reveals that he is serious. Here the best action might be to surrender. However, as a karate expert, or if you possessed mace, you might choose an aggressive response.

If you are in a situation where your only chance for survival is to run away, then that is your only choice. (It would help if you were an experienced jogger.) Tears can also be an effective weapon and if necessary they should be used.[5] However, women should not shy away from being assertive. Here, too, there are appropriate and inappropriate times to be assertive. While being attacked by a rapist, calling him a big bully and demanding that he stop, is not a recommended strategy.

Box 20.7.   The Art of Losing.

It is not critical that you win every Mah-Jongg game or tennis match. There may be less stress for all concerned if you occasionally lose. If you are late for a movie, it's not something that should aggravate an ulcer or precipitate a migraine—but often those results occur. If you are criticized, your first inclination might be to return the criticism. But if the criticism is justified, you would be better off by accepting it. Anger would then be replaced by acceptance. Rather than raise your blood pressure, you might even be able to stabilize or lower it.[4]

If a woman confronts you in an angry mood, by saying something complimentary to her, or agreeing with her (as long as it is not a crucial matter), it is possible to defuse her anger and reduce your stress.

badly. However, if you can see some potential good, things may turn out better. You should make every effort to see the "glass as half full rather than half empty." It is important not to magnify things out of proportion (see Box 20.7).

Facing Severe Stressors

There are certain stressors that can neither be avoided nor evaded. One must merely accept them. Examples are aging and death. Yet a person can age gracefully and if one has lived a well-rounded life, it is possible to face the inevitability of death. Other stressors are traumatic and unforeseen and require the use of all of the resources that have previously been built up. Death of a loved one is one of the most severe stressors, especially when it is unexpected and there is no time for preparation. Grief is normal and seeking the comfort and support of others can be very helpful.

After a few weeks, in order to avoid a double tragedy, it is necessary to resume one's normal activities. Deeply religious people and fatalists appear to handle tragedies well, but that may merely be a cover-up. The only real consolation a grieving person can have is that the deceased had some moments of happiness and that sooner or later everyone must meet the same fate.

CONSULTATIONS

As just mentioned, sudden severe stressors may so overwhelm a woman that she needs the support of others. Some women need support to handle even minor stressors. Men traditionally are supposed to bear up well under tragedy but that also may be a cover-up. It is well-known that women seek professional consultations at a much higher rate than do men. This can have both benefits and disadvantages. It depends upon both the therapist and the woman involved. We've previously discussed the alarmingly high rate of women taking tranquilizers. Since these are prescription drugs, their use results from medical consultations. On the other hand, many women receive psychotherapeutic help in managing stressors without the use of drugs. For them, the results can be beneficial without the possibility of addiction.

Some physicians prescribe drugs because it is the "easy way out" but some women insist on drug help and their physicians merely oblige them. Knowledgeable women are now insisting on nondrug therapy whenever possible. They are also trying alternative types of consultations including group therapy, family therapy, and behavior modification. There are also various encounter groups in which women are participating with increased frequency. Many are excellent, but others are questionable on scientific grounds. And what is helpful for one person may be stressful to another.

Some examples of these methods are: est; Esalen; Gestalt: Life Spring; assertiveness training; transactional analysis; Reality; Psychocybernetics; Bioenergetics; Rational-Emotive; Psychodrama: Silva Mind Control; and Primal Scream Therapy.[6]

It is not always essential to turn to psychotherapists or eclectic encounter groups for consultation aid. Sometimes, the help is forthcoming from one's own family, friends, or relatives. Quite often a clergyman, or the family physician, dentist, or chiropractor can offer the necessary advice and comfort. (Other examples are given in Box 20.8.)

Box 20.8.   Dogs and Other Companions.

Family pets can be helpful as companions. Researchers have known for a long time that heart disease is more common in people who live alone. Now new evidence has shown that heart-attack victims live longer if they have a pet. It doesn't matter what type of pet either. It can be a dog, a cat, birds, gerbils, and even lizards.[7]

Consultations and companions are helpful, not only with disease, but also during childbirth. Women with (female or male) companions were found in a recent report to have faster and simpler births than women without companions.[8] They had faster deliveries, fewer complications, and were more affectionate with their offspring. Interestingly enough, mature women were found to be better companions than husbands, because they were more likely to remain calm.

The important thing to remember with all consultations and companions is that the mere act of talking to others (including animals) can be cathartic, and seeking advice or help is not an admission of sickness or weakness.

SUMMARY

The best psychological way to cope with stressors is the use of conscious control. Those stressors that can safely be avoided or evaded should be managed in that manner. To reduce stress, one should select realistic goals and set a reasonable time period in which to achieve them. If necessary, goals can and should be changed. When faced with stressors that must be dealt with, being prepared is the first criterion and rehearsal is advantageous. It is essential to be vigilant and with the use of all one's resources, effective action should be taken. When dealing with potentially stressful situations, it is helpful to try to see them in the best possible light. This may change a negative outcome into a positive one. There is no easy way to deal with calamitous events but with time and the help of others, it is possible to overcome the anguish and carry on a normal life. Consultations with others may be helpful in dealing with minor stressors as well as with the consequences of major life stress events.

In addition to psychologically coping with stressors, a very effective method of managing stress is to counteract the effects of stress. This entails the use of deep relaxation methods.

DEEP RELAXATION METHODS

In Chapter 2, the stress response was examined. With the deep relaxation methods, the relaxation response* is elicited, and effects are just the opposite of those produced by the stress response. In Chapter 2, we examined the three components of the stress equation:

$$Stressors + Individual\ Makeup = Stress\ Response$$
In similar fashion:
$$Relaxors + Individual\ Make\text{-}up = Relaxation\ Response$$

Relaxors

A relaxor is any stimulus or technique that induces deep relaxation. Similar to stressors, there are physical, psychological, and social relaxors but the

*In this section a simplified description of the relaxation response is given. For a more detailed presentation, see: Morse, D.R. and Furst, M. L. *Stress For Success: A Holistic Approach To Stress and Its Management.* New York: Van Nostrand Reinhold, 1979.

types are often combined. Some examples follow. Tai Chi is a physical form of meditation and it is also social, being an expression of the Taoist religion. With the use of a series of slow fluid movements and positions, deep relaxation is induced. Aikido is another physical form of meditation. Sufi and Zen meditation combine psychological and social techniques. Some purely psychological relaxors are Autogenic Training and self-hypnosis, while Progressive Relaxation combines physical and psychological techniques.

Individual Makeup

Relaxors are used to counteract the effects of stress but an individual's makeup determines which techniques may be of advantage. In our several studies of hypnosis, meditation and relaxation therapy, the effectiveness of techniques was related to: (1) the individual's previous experience; (2) the kind of technique used; (3) the length of time the technique was used; (4) the subject's personality and mood; and (5) the amount of reinforcement given.[9-11]

Previous Experience. In these studies, it was found that individuals trained in Transcendental Meditation (TM) preferred meditation to self-hypnosis and instructed relaxation. Subjects trained in hypnosis preferred that modality. Subjects who were trained in neither hypnosis nor meditation had variable preferences. Nevertheless, the preliminary findings show one female-male difference (see Box 20.9).

Kind of Technique Used. Furthermore, most untrained subjects preferred meditation to unstructured relaxation. Nevertheless, there were about 13 percent of the subjects who found that the repetition of the sound

Box 20.9. ''Sexy'' Words.

Preliminary data analysis of a recent study by the authors on meditation and personality shows an interesting correlation with sex.[11] Of the forty available words for meditation, the single most popular word selected was ''love'' (15.7 percent of the subjects chose it). Next in order were ''om,'' ''shirim'' (the latter two are well-known sanskrit meditation words; i.e., mantras), ''lum'' (a nonsense word), ''fly,'' and ''relax.'' Words with an *m* or *n* ending were most popular (40 percent of the selected words, e.g., shiri*m*, o*m*, lu*m*, o*n*e). The selection of ''love'' showed an interesting sex difference. Almost 23 percent of the women selected ''love'' as the best meditation word while only 12.5 percent of the men did so.

during meditation interfered with their relaxation. They relaxed better when they merely closed their eyes. The majority of the subjects were stressed when they had to do a mental task with their eyes closed (i.e., repeating a series of numbers). However, there were a few subjects who found the mental work to be relaxing.

Length of Time Per Session. In the first study, it was observed that when subjects either meditated or used self-hypnosis for twenty minutes or more, after a number of repetitions they became irritated and definitely showed signs of stress.[9] In contrast, when the subjects used each technique for five to six minutes at a time, deep relaxation was induced. This seems to show that just like drugs and food, too much relaxation can be harmful.

Subjects Personality and Moods. In the last two studies, it was observed that an individual's personality and mood can determine which words are preferred for meditation. In the study comparing the use of the emotionally charged words "love" and "hate" with the neutral word "one," it was found that most subjects preferred "love" (25 of 48). It was surprising that more people did better with "hate" than with "one" (11 to 6).[10] The psychologist, Patricia Carrington reported similar findings. Comparing the use of pleasant and unpleasant-sounding terms, she found that most subjects preferred the pleasant-sounding terms (e.g., "lohm"). However, a few subjects did better with the unpleasant-sounding terms (e.g., "grik"). Carrington reported that some depressed people used those negative terms to help them get rid of their negative feelings.[12]

In our most recent study correlating personalities and moods with words selected for meditation, we have not yet completely analyzed the data.[11]

Just as personalities and moods can affect word selection for meditation, they can also affect whether or not meditation is beneficial. Religious individuals may prefer religious forms of meditation. Members of the Jewish and Christian faiths may object to Zen Meditation (since it is a Buddhist technique). Atheists might find any form of religious meditation to be stressful. Some individuals fear loss of control. For them, any form of meditation or self-hypnosis could cause distress. They would do better with simple relaxation or napping. As previously discussed, migraine headaches are more common in women. There is evidence that attacks can be precipitated during relaxation. Hence, meditation or self-hypnosis may not be beneficial for migraine sufferers.

Most people relax best when they are in a quiet room and are alone, but others require the support of others. For them, group meditation or group hypnosis would be better. Just as the effectiveness of a drug is partly based on the assurance of the doctor and the patient's belief in the drug's potency (known as the placebo effect), so, too, is the effectiveness of meditation and hypnosis. These techniques are rarely effective for skeptics or those who are negativistic. Fortunately, there are many techniques available for deep relaxation, and very few individuals find that none are applicable to them. For the rare person who cannot use any relaxor, alternative stress-relieving methods should be used (e.g., exercise; positive psychological coping methods; and sleep).

Reinforcement. As far as reinforcement is concerned, techniques in which individuals receive continuing knowledge of results, such as biofeedback, seem to be more beneficial than nonreinforcement techniques. In unpublished observations, the authors found that TM subjects had a lower drop-out rate than those subjects who were taught meditation and did not receive any follow-up instruction or check-ups. Let us now consider the changes that occur under deep relaxation, the relaxation response.

The Relaxation Response

The easiest way to understand the relaxation response is to consider it to be the opposite of the stress response. The relaxation response can be thought of as the body's way of "turning down the rheostat," of "discharging excess steam," or of "cooling off the engine." Similar mechanisms are involved as in the case with the stress response (see Figures 2.3 and 2.4) In this particular instance, the stress hormones are "turned off" and the relaxation hormone, acetylcholine, is "turned on" (see Figures 2.4 and 20.1).

Physiological Changes. The usual results are the following:[6,9,10] (1) Slowed down breathing rate; decreased intake of oxygen and release of carbon dioxide; (2) decreased heart rate and lowered blood pressure (occurs after several months of use);[15] (3) decreased energy expenditure (lower blood lactate; i.e., a waste product of glucose metabolism);[13] (4) reduced sweating (early aspects measured by skin resistance changes); (5) decreased blood cholesterol level (may be beneficial in prevention of heart attacks);[16] (6) reduced flow of blood to muscles and decreased skeletal muscle activity; (7) constriction of the pupils (visual acuity not needed); (8) increased flow of saliva as digestion can now proceed normally;[17,25] and (9) production of alpha and theta brain wave patterns which are indicative of deep relaxation.

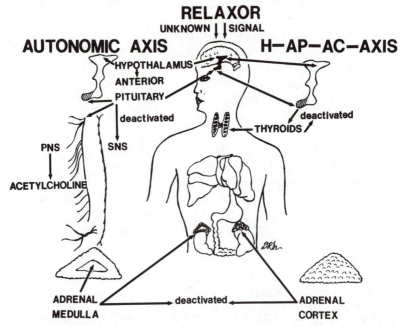

Fig. 20.1.   Major physiological changes of the relaxation response. pns = parasympathetic nervous system; sns = sympathetic nervous system. An unknown signal from the hypothalamus activates the pns, deactivates the sns, and probably also deactivates the H–AP–AC (hypothalamus–anterior pituitary-adrenal cortex) axis. As a result of pns activation, acetylcholine is released. (The resultant physiological changes are described in the text.)

Subjective Changes. Along with the aforementioned physiological changes, most people report subjective changes during the relaxation response. Some commonly described feelings are: warmth; tingling; numbness; floating; drowsiness; lightness; out of body sensation; dissociation (feeling as if one were in two places at once, or the mind and body were separate); and euphoria (extreme pleasure). People also report various mental images and they generally verbalize feelings of peace and tranquility.

Benefits[18-20]

Regular practice of deep relaxation has many possible benefits. Reported changes include: decreased blood pressure in hypertensives; reduction in the incidence of heart arrhythmias (see Chapter 3); improvement in asthmatic conditions; improved psychological health; decreased aggression; less anxiety; better study and work habits; and overall improvement in interpersonal relationships.

There are various relaxors, but techniques that are especially effective are hypnosis and meditation. Let us now consider them a little further.

Hypnosis

Hypnosis is an altered state of awareness in which a person achieves deep relaxation, subjective changes in body image, certain distortions of reality, and the ability to exert some control over autonomic nervous system functions. The hypnotic state is induced by the repetitive action of some constant stimulus (e.g., the sound of a monotonous voice; the sight of a flickering flame).

A hypnotized woman is not a "zombie"; she is not under someone else's control; she will not do anything against her will; and she would not permanently stay in the trance (even if the hypnotist were to die).

However, some people who are psychotic or prepsychotic may have bizarre reactions under hypnosis. That is why it is preferable for the hypnotist to be a doctor who is trained in managing medical and psychological complications. This is of special importance when hypnosis is used for medical and psychological problems such as for pain control, obesity, smoking, alcoholism, drug addiction, and neuroses.

It is possible to learn self-hypnosis for deep relaxation by reading a book or going to a hypnotist. An easily learned technique for self-hypnosis for relaxation is given in Box 20.10.

Hypnosis can also be helpful in improving study habits, recalling information, overcoming shyness and stage fright, making oneself more assertive and improving performance in sporting events. However, with all of its benefits, hypnosis is only effective if the subject is motivated. If a woman is "hooked" on cigarette smoking and doesn't really want to "kick the habit," hypnosis will not work. Similarly, an obese woman who insists her problem is a sluggish thyroid (even though she has an enormous appetite) will not be helped by hypnosis.

Even with motivation, there must be rapport between the subject and the hypnotist (see Box 20.11).

Finally, the subject must have a degree of suggestibility to be hypnotized. There are simple tests for suggestibility, and within a few minutes, the hypnotist would be able to give the individual a good idea of whether or not she would be a good subject. Most people can enter a light to medium trance during which they are deeply relaxed. But only about 15 percent of

Box 20.10.   Relaxation-Self Hypnosis.

Sit semi-inclined in a comfortable chair. Loosen your clothes, take off your shoes, watch, and jewelry. Choose an object to stare at. It should be slightly above your eye level so that you have to look upward to see it. The object should be about three to five feet away and could be fixed like a chandelier or picture, or moving like a pendulum or candle flame.

As you stare, concentrate and don't move your head. Soon the object will appear fuzzy and your eyelids will seem heavy. Your eyes may blink, become watery and you may begin to see double. When it becomes difficult to keep your eyes open, let them close. Once your eyes close, mentally concentrate on your toes. Flex the muscles and then relax them completely. Do the same thing with your ankles, calves, and thighs. Let this surge of concentration-relaxation spread until it reaches the top of your scalp. Your whole body should feel completely relaxed.

Now it is time to take a mental trip. See and feel yourself going into an elevator on the tenth floor. Then let yourself descend floor by floor. As you go down, feel your body sinking into the chair, and feel yourself getting more and more relaxed. When you reach the first floor, get out and get into the awaiting cab. It will take you to your destination; that is your special place for comfort, peace, tranquility, and relaxation. As you travel toward your special place, you will feel your troubles melt away, your anxieties will lessen and you will feel at peace. Stay in this peaceful place for about twenty minutes. Then call for the cab and let it take you back to the awaiting elevator. When you reach the tenth floor, you will get out and will awaken feeling completely relaxed and refreshed ready to face the rest of the day.

One can use variations on this theme. You can take an escalator going down or you can descend a mountain. Instead of a cab, you can take a boat or an airplane ride. You can relax your muscles in the reverse order, from the scalp to the toes. You can even close your eyes right away and listen to the sound of a waterfall or the pitter-patter of raindrops to induce you into a trance. Use whichever method is easiest. However, people find it best to first be hypnotized by someone else who will then teach them self-hypnosis. Whatever way one learns, relaxation-type hypnosis is a very effective method to bring on the relaxation response and reduce the effects of distress.

the population can achieve sufficient depth to be able to undergo dental or surgical treatment without anesthesia.[29] Fortunately, for stress reduction, only a light to moderate trance is necessary. Let us now consider meditation.

Box 20.11.　The Funny Trance.

A friend of ours told us that she really was motivated to lose weight. She went to an internationally known psychiatrist, but when he started to induce the trance, she burst out laughing. It seemed he had a strong foreign accent and mispronounced several words. Since the would-be subject was an English teacher, she found his speech amusing rather than trance-inducing. So be certain that you and your hypnotist have a positive interaction.

Meditation

Similarly to hypnosis, meditation is an altered state of awareness in which a person achieves deep relaxation, subjective changes in body image, certain distortions of reality, and the ability to decrease autonomic nervous system functions. It, too, is induced by the repetitive action of a constant stimulus (such as staring at an object—contemplative meditation); fixating on a mental image (concentrative meditation); chanting and rhythmic dancing (physical meditation); and silent repetition of a sound, word or phrase (mantra meditation).

Physiologically, there are no apparent major differences between hypnosis and meditation but subjective differences are reported. In hypnosis, one tries to control various body functions. For example, a good hypnotic subject can achieve deep relaxation, analgesia (pain control), bleeding control, and a reduction of salivation and sweating. With meditation, one does not try to control anything. As a result of the deep relaxation achieved, the body's functions slow down. There is another difference between the most popular methods of hypnosis and meditation. In eye-fixation hypnosis, the subject stares at an object until the eyes close and trance is achieved. With mantra meditation, the eyes close immediately and the individual begins to silently repeat the mantra. As a result, during the induction phase, there is greater muscle activity during hypnosis than meditation.[9]

Meditation can be associated with religious practices. Yoga is part of Hinduism; Zen is derived from Buddhism; Sufism is an Islamic practice; and there are meditative techniques involved with Judaism, Christianity, Taoism, Confucianism, and Shintoism. TM is purported not to be religious but it is derived from Yoga, and Hindu Sanscrit dialogue is used in the initiating ceremony. In contrast, hypnosis is not specifically associated with any religious practice.

With the traditional forms of meditation, as the result of repeated use, an individual is supposed to expand and purify her consciousness, to achieve higher states of consciousness, to attain an increased self-understanding and self-enlightenment, and to ultimately achieve unity with the cosmos. Modern forms of meditation such as Benson's method,[18] Clinically Standardized Meditation (CSM—a home instruction method taught on taped cassettes by Princeton University psychologist Patricia Carrington)[21]* and the authors' simple-word technique (see Box 20.12) lay no claim to the achievement of higher states of consciousness. The same is true for hypnosis. Mantra meditation (the most popular type) is generally practiced twice a day (before breakfast and before dinner) for approximately twenty-minute sessions. Some people find they can only do it once a day and they, too, find it beneficial. Most individuals find the evening session (either before dinner or about two hours after dinner) to be more satisfactory than the early morning meditation. However, an early morning relaxation-break is helpful, because although sleep can be rejuvenating, quite often there are fitful periods of sleep and one is not completely rested upon awakening.

Box 20.12.   Meditation for Women.

Meditation is generally engaged in twice a day, but extra meditations are useful in anticipation of stressful situations or immediately after a stressful situation. The twice-daily meditations last about twenty minutes per session but the extra meditations can be brief—anywhere from 2–5 minutes.

For the "quickie" or "minimeditations" (Carrington's term), you should find a place where you will not be disturbed (e.g., you might take the phone off the hook at home). As a last resort, you can even go to a toilet stall at work and meditate.

Now let us consider the standard meditation technique. First of all, it is important to relieve yourself, as fullness of the bladder or rectum interferes with meditation. The same is true for pains or aches. If you have a headache or stomachache you may be able to eliminate it by meditation, but if it is severe enough it may prevent you from meditation. Therefore, if you have medication available, take it and when the pain has subsided, you can begin your meditation. However, you should not take tranquilizers and mind-altering drugs, alcoholic drinks, and caffeinated beverages right before meditation as they will interfere with the technique.

If you are thirsty and hungry, take a drink and small snack and wait at least one-half hour before meditation. If you have eaten a full meal wait

* Information on CSM home instruction courses can be obtained from: Pace Systems, P.O. Box 113, Kendall Park, N.J. 08824.

two hours before beginning meditation. Experience has shown that for most people an empty or a full stomach interferes with meditation.

When you are ready, go to a quiet, dark room away from distractions such as a radio, TV, and the telephone. The room should be of moderate temperature, well-ventilated, and clean. Now sit partially inclined in a comfortable chair (lying down completely while meditating can bring on sleep and may be something for insomniacs to consider). As with self-hypnosis, loosen clothing and remove jewelry. Keep the arms and legs uncrossed with the feet flat on the floor and the hands by the sides or on the lap. Now close your eyes, take a few deep breaths, and silently repeat a word. In our just-completed study of words for meditation, it was observed that the most popular meditation word for women was "love" (almost 28 percent of the subjects chose it). The next most popular words chosen by women were "sky," "fly," "drive," "women" and "between." Each of those words was chosen by 10 percent of the female subjects. Nevertheless, you can repeat any word or sound that seems relaxing to you and use it as your mantra (meditation word). Some words that are popular are "flower," "shirim," "om," "lum," "relax," "one," "beautiful," and "boulder."

You can repeat the word at any pace (e.g., to your heart beat, to your breathing rate, to some outside sound, or any way that feels comfortable). The word may become distorted after a time but that does not matter. As you repeat the word, thoughts and visualizations may come and go. Complete the thought or observation and when you realize it, go back to the repetition of the word.

That is the whole technique—that's all there is to it. You just repeat a word and let yourself relax. After a while you may feel various body sensations such as warmth, floating, tingling, numbness, lightness, heaviness and out-of-body sensations. You may feel as if your mind and body are dissociated and the sensations are often very pleasurable (euphoria).

Keep a watch nearby. Don't use an alarm clock or the noise will jolt you. After about twenty minutes, gradually arouse yourself. Stretch and slowly open your eyes. You should feel relaxed and refreshed and possibly a little lightheaded. This technique is effective for most people and can be used for a lifetime. It is one of the best ways to counteract the daily stressors.

Meditation can be beneficial. There have been reports of meditation yielding reduced blood pressure in hypertensives, decreased anxiety and other psychological symptoms, reduction in number of headaches and asthma attacks, fear and pain control in dentistry, improved interpersonal relations, increased job productivity, improved athletic performance, better grades in school, and decreased use of alcohol, drugs, and cigarettes.[6,18,19,21,22,26,27]

However, as with hypnosis, it can be dangerous for prepsychotic and psychotic individuals.[23] The feeling of loss of control can be quite upsetting to those people. For most people, prolonged periods of meditation can lead to hallucination, insomnia, depression, and other nervous system symptoms.[6,18,21]

Time

"That's all well and good but with young children and a house to take care of, where am I going to get the time to meditate (or use self-hypnosis)?" This is a common and justifiable complaint of many housewife/mothers. Wives or husbands who go outside to work often can "free up" the needed time to meditate or practice self-hypnosis. For example, they can meditate on the bus, train, or trolley on the way to and from work. During work, they may be able to take a meditation break instead of a coffee break. In the evening, they can take a relaxation session while their spouses prepare dinner. But how about the spouses who stay home? When can they have their relaxation breaks?

First of all, before a woman gets married she should insist that she receive the same opportunities after marriage as her husband. This includes time off to exercise and relax and may necessitate a maid, housekeeper, or mother's helper. For the family that cannot afford this arrangement, possible family members (mothers, fathers, in-laws) can help out during specified periods of the day. Another possibility is for the woman to make arrangements with a neighbor to watch each others' children during certain daily time periods.

If none of these arrangements are feasible, then other possibilities depend upon the ages of the children. With young children, after the children are put to sleep, the mother can take her first relaxation break (hopefully they can remain asleep for about twenty minutes). Slightly older children can play with the neighbor's children under her supervision (and this arrangement can be reciprocated). With school-age children, the mother can take her relaxation session when the children have left for school.

In the evening, the housewife can either prepare the dinner early and let it simmer or have her husband watch the pots while she takes her second relaxation break. If he drives to and from work and doesn't have a chance to relax on the way home (never meditate or use self-hypnosis while driving or you won't get home safely), then different arrangements should be made. For instance, couples can alternate. One evening the husband would be in charge of either preparing the dinner or overseeing the cooking. His wife would then relax and he would have his relaxation session about two hours after dinner. The next evening they can reverse the situation, unless one member would prefer either of the two time periods on a regular basis.

Single, divorced, or widowed women with children will have to try to make arrangements with family, friends, neighbors, babysitters, or child-care centers to free up the time to relax.

Nevertheless, one should not be compulsive about relaxing. Although meditation and hypnosis are extremely helpful, it is self-defeating if a person becomes stressed over missing a relaxation session. Skipping meditation or hypnotic sessions on occasion is of little consequence.

Alternatives

It is not essential to use hypnosis or meditation to bring forth the relaxation response. Some people are excellent nappers and for them a couple of daily short naps is all that is needed.[24] Other people can just close their eyes and relax.* However, there are individuals who can neither relax, nap, meditate, nor use self-hypnosis. For them, a possible alternative is the use of biofeedback.[28]

Biofeedback is a method of controlling autonomic nervous system activity with the help of a signal from an electronic unit. An illustrative example is given in Box 20.13.

Box 20.13.   Feedback from the Frontalis.

> One of the principal places that muscle tension shows up is in the frontalis muscles of the forehead (the typical wrinkling of the brow). Electrodes are put in a band that is placed over the forehead. The other termination of the electrodes is a biofeedback unit that connects to an FM radio. The subject is then told to try and relax the forehead muscles (a visualization technique of floating in a tub of water may be used). As the muscles relax, the signal is picked up and transferred to the FM radio. The music that had been playing loudly now gets quieter and when the muscles are completely relaxed, the music becomes inaudible. The subject is then told to tense the forehead muscles and the music becomes louder. In this manner, the sound of the music (loud or soft) gives the subject the "feedback" about whether or not the forehead muscles are being relaxed. Later on when the person gets proficient, relaxation can be done without the use of the machine.

* A recent study done at the University of Pennsylvania showed that watching moving fish in a fish tank was an excellent relaxation technique as shown by a lowering of blood pressure. Cory, C. T. Newsline: Age of aquari-om. *Psychol. Today* **15**(5): 14, 1981.

In addition to psychologically coping and bringing forth the relaxation response, another major method of coping with stress is exercise. This and other physical methods are discussed in the next chapter.

REFERENCES

1. Pelletier, K. R. *Mind as Healer Mind as Slayer: A Holistic Approach to Preventing Stress Disorders.* New York: Dell Publishing, 1977.
2. Colligan, M. J., Smith, M. J., and Hurrel, J.J., Jr. Occupational incidence rates of mental health disorders. *J. Hum. Stress* **3**(3):34–39, 1977.
3. Gallwey, T. *The Inner Game of Tennis.* New York: Random House, 1974.
4. Selye, H. *Stress Without Distress.* Philadelphia: J. B. Lippincott, 1974.
5. Shatzman, M. Shedding new light on the fine art of crying. *Philadelphia Eve. Bull.* BK 24, June 13, 1980.
6. Morse, D. R. and Furst, M. L. *Stress For Success: A Holistic Approach to Stress and its Management.* New York: Van Nostrand Reinhold, 1979.
7. Editorial. Pet lovers live longer. *Family Health* **11**(4): 16, 1979.
8. Sosa, R., Kennell, J., Klaus, M., Robertson, S., and Urrutia, J. The effect of a supportive companion on perinatal problems, length of labor and mother-infant interaction. *N. Engl. J. Med.* **303**:597–600, 1980.
9. Morse, D. R., Martin, J. S., Furst, M. L., and Dubin, L. L. A physiological and subjective evaluation of meditation, hypnosis and relaxation. *Psychosom. Med.* **39**:304–324, 1977.
10. Morse, D. R., Martin, J. S., Furst, M. L., and Dubin, L. L. A physiological and subjective evaluation of neutral and emotionally-charged words for meditation. *J. Am. Soc. Psychosom. Dent. Med.* **26**:31–38, 56–62, 106–112, 1979.
11. Morse, D. R. and Furst, M. L. Psychosomatic effects of words used for meditation. *J. Am. Soc. Psychosom. Dent. Med.* In Press, 1981.
12. Carrington, P. New directions in meditation research. Read before the symposium on Meditation Related Therapies. St. Louis, October 28–29, 1977.
13. Benson, H. Your innate asset for combatting stress. *Harvard Bus. Rev.* **52**(4):49–60,1974.
14. Wallace, R. K. Physiological effects of transcendental meditation. *Science* **167**: 1751–1754, 1970.
15. Frumkin, K., Nathan, R. J., Prout, M. F., and Cohen, M. C. Nonpharmacologic control of essential hypertension in man: A critical review of the experimental literature. *Psychosom. Med.* **40**:294–320, 1978.
16. Cooper, M. J. and Aygen, M. M. A relaxation technique in the management of hypercholesterolemia. *J. Hum. Stress* **5**(4):24–27. 1979.
17. Morse, D. R., Schacterle, G. R., Furst, M. L., and Bose, K. Stress, Relaxation, and Saliva: A Pilot Clinical Study involving endodontic patients. *Oral Surg.* In Press 1981.
18. Benson, H. *The Relaxation Response.* New York: William Morrow, 1975.
19. Bloomfield, H. H., Cain, M. P., and Jaffe, D. T. *TM* Discovering Inner Energy and Overcoming Stress.* New York: Delacorte, 1975.
20. Kroger, W. S. and Felzer, W. D. *Hypnosis and Behavior Modification: Imagery Conditioning.* Philadelphia: J. B. Lippincott, 1976.
21. Carrington, P. *Freedom in Meditation.* Garden City, New York: Doubleday, 1977.
22. Morse, D. R. and Furst, M. L. *Stress and Relaxation: Application to Dentistry.* Springfield, Ill.: Charles C. Thomas, 1978.

23. Otis, L. S. If well-integrated but anxious, try TM. *Psychol. Today* 7(4):45–46, 1974.
24. Evans, F. J., Cook, M. R., Cohen, H. D., Orne, E. C., and Orne, M. T. Appetitive and replacement naps: EEG and behavior. *Science* 197:687–688, 1977.
25. Morse, D. R., Schacterle, G. R., Furst, M. L., and Bose, K. Stress, relaxation, and saliva: A follow-up study involving clinical endodontic patients. *J. Hum. Stress,* Sept. 1981. In Press.
26. Mills, W. W. and Farrow, J. T. The transcendental meditation technique and acute experimental pain. *Psychosom. Med.* **43:** 157–164, 1981.
27. Morse, D. R., Schacterle, G. R., Furst, M. L., Brokenshire, J., Butterworth, M. and Cacchio, J. Examination-induced stress in meditators and non-meditators as measured by salivary protein changes. *Stress.* In Press, 1981.
28. Burish, T.G. and Schwartz, D. P. EMG biofeedback training, transfer of training, and coping with stress, *J. Psychosom. Res.* **24:** 85–96, 1980.
29. Morse, D. R. and Wilcko, J. M. Nonsurgical endodontic therapy for a vital tooth with meditation-hypnosis as the sole anesthetic: A case report. *Am. J. Clin. Hyp.* **21:**258–262, 1979.

21
The Physical Methods:
Exercise, Energy, and Massage

INTRODUCTION

The major physical method of dealing with stress is exercise. Exercises to be considered are of three types: aerobic, strength-building, and collaborative. Also examined as forms of exercise are laughing, crying, shouting, screaming, singing, and whistling.

Under "energy," the various forms of heat are covered. These include warm baths, hot tubs, steam baths, saunas, Jacuzzi® whirlpools, and float tanks. In addition, cold showers, sound waves, and ions are considered. The final physical method examined is massage.

EXERCISE

Purposes

Exercise serves seven major purposes in stress management. The first is strengthening of the body's muscles, tendons, and bones. This allows for an increased capacity to deal with stressors and helps prevent bone breakdown.* Women are now becoming more involved in weight training and calisthenics. With these exercises, women can increase the strength of their muscles without developing large-sized muscles.[1] This could conceivably help them overcome physical assaults. It certainly would help

---

*In a recent study of women over forty-five it was shown that exercise can help prevent osteoporosis (bone loss). There was a decrease in body calcium in the sedentary women while there was an increase in calcium in the exercising women. Uhlaner, J. Exercise keeps you young and quick. *Prevention* 32(8): 70–76, 1980.

women handle minor emergencies such as jacking up a car to change a flat tire.

The second stress-management purpose of exercise is to promote cardiovascular fitness. This improves endurance and would also help a woman cope with stressors. For instance, she might be able to run away from a burning building or flee an attacker.

With the continual use of cardiovascular fitness exercises (e. g., running, swimming, bicycling), women can decrease their chances of getting heart attacks and other stress-related diseases and increase their life-span. Recent studies have shown that regular practice of fitness exercises leads to: (1) lower blood concentration of triglycerides (a type of fat) and LDLs (dangerous type of cholesterol; see Chapter 3 under heart disease); (2) increased levels of protective HDLs (beneficial type of cholesterol); (3) lower blood pressure (high blood pressure is a high risk factor for heart attacks); (4) slower heart rate (considered to be more efficient); (5) larger bore coronary arteries (blood flows easier, less chance of clot); (6) increased ability to break down blood clots (decreased chance of heart attacks);[2] (7) weight reduction (beneficial in preventing heart disease, diabetes, kidney disease, and backaches); (8) increased sensitivity to insulin (may be helpful in managing diabetes and obesity);[3] (9) improved mood, thinking, and behavior; and (10) increased physical work capacity.[4]

There have been several studies that have shown that people who use vigorous exercise over a period of years have a decreased incidence of heart attacks.[4,5] In a major study of longevity factors, it was found that women who exercise regularly had a much lower mortality rate than those who never exercised.[6]

The third stress-management purpose of exercise is to allow for communication and companionship. In the last chapter, we discussed the advantages of consultations and companionship. By participating in group activities such as golf, bowling and doubles tennis, women have the opportunity to interact with other people in a pleasant and relaxing manner (unless they take winning too seriously). The only disadvantage to this aspect of exercise is that the talking may be distracting to others who are concentrating on hitting a ball or knocking down pins.

By learning a new sport (e.g., racquetball, white-water rafting, cross-country skiing), a woman has the opportunity to acquire a new skill which can be ego-enhancing. In addition, she can acquire new friends and become part of a group (to identify with) which can also be psychologically rewarding as well as giving a new potential for communication.

A fourth stress-management purpose of exercise is diversionary. In Chapter 23, the use of diversions for stress-management is highlighted. At this point, let us merely mention that any form of exercise can act as a diversion; i.e., takes one's mind off of "pressing" problems.

Not only does exercise act as a diversion, it can be a physical outlet for stress. Hence, the fifth stress-management use of exercise is as release for a physical stressor. For example, you have had a hard day at home or in the office. You've built up stress levels but have not vented them. An excellent way to release the pent-up pressures is to "let it all out" by doing exercises such as hitting a ball (tennis, racquetball, golf), swinging a bat (softball), punching a bag, throwing or rolling a ball (softball, bowling), and practicing karate or judo. Although these various forms of exercise are in themselves stressful (i.e., heart rate and blood pressure increase as occurs during any stressful activity), they are beneficial because they act as a vent for built-up anxieties, and over a period of time, they improve cardiovascular fitness.

A sixth stress-management role of exercise is enhancement of relaxation. Muscles relax better after a good work-out and it is easier to mentally relax as well. Our clinical experience has shown that people who exercise regularly find it easier to meditate or practice self-hypnosis, and they have less problems in getting to sleep and staying asleep.

When people sit around for long periods of time as when watching television or movies and riding in airplanes, trains and buses, blood pools in their legs. The legs can become numb, and varicosities and blood clots can develop. In addition, people may feel tired and sluggish, and with long airplane flights, they can develop jet lag. Therefore, the seventh stress-management purpose of exercise is to prevent the development of disorders related to inactivity. Exercises for this purpose can be simple such as bending over to touch the toes, walking in the aisles, opening and closing the jaw, rising up and down on the toes and stretching the arms in front of the chest and over the head. These exercises can also relieve the boredom of traveling and can act as a diversion. It gives an individual something else to do aside from eating, drinking, and reading.

Female-Male Differences[1]

Women can generally engage in the same types of exercise as do men with a few minor variations. The differences which are now presented are based on averages. Therefore, they will not apply to all women, but at least give an idea of possible limitations for women in certain physical activities.

Women possess about half the amount of lean muscle mass as men; hence, they cannot lift as much weight or supply as much power in sporting activities. With equal size, women are about 80 percent as strong as men. Estrogen is believed to inhibit the development of muscle mass.

The elbow joint of males and females is different. With females, the arms form an "X" from the shoulders. With men the arms are parallel from the shoulders. This apparently is a slight handicap for women in sports requiring maximum leverage. Such sports include tennis, racquetball, gymnastics, and discus and javelin throwing.

Women have a lower center of gravity than men. This is advantageous as it gives them better balance. Hence, they would be less likely to fall off their feet in a sporting activity (important in ice- and roller-skating, roller derby, dancing, and acrobatics).

Women have more body fat than men. This gives them greater buoyancy than men for floating and swimming, but less strength and speed. Women have shorter leg length than men and this negatively affects their speed of movement. However, women are excellent in sports and activities that require flexibility.

Women have a smaller heart than men. As compared to men, they have: less stroke volume (amount of blood forced out from the heart per beat); a decreased vital capacity (related to oxygen retention ability in the lungs); a faster heart rate; lower hemoglobin (oxygen-containing component in the red blood cells); fewer red blood cells; and fewer sweat glands (less effective dissipation of body heat). Working outside in hot weather, women are at a disadvantage, but in humid weather they do better than men.[7]

Types of Exercises

Weight Training. Weight training can strengthen a woman's muscles without greatly increasing their size. Weight training can reduce excess fat and recontour the body into a firmer figure. Weight training improves performance in sports and activities that require strength and flexibility. It can also strengthen the abdominal and chest muscles to help prevent injuries, and also allow for easier deliveries.

Collaborative. Golf, doubles tennis, bowling, and various forms of dancing can be considered collaborative forms of exercise. There is time for socialization and one is free to enjoy the acitivities especially if there is not strong competitive push. Square dancing is a good example of an activity that combines social interplay with exercise. Other fun-type collaborative activities are white-water rafting, miniature golf, and par-3 golf. The latter two forms of golf are easier to play, and generally less competitive than conventional golf. People take them less seriously and they are excellent diversions.

Aerobics. Aerobics is a term coined by Kenneth Cooper.[8,9] It refers to a variety of exercises that stimulate heart and lung activity for a sufficient time to produce beneficial bodily changes. The beneficial changes are: (1) more efficient heart activity (lower blood pressure, greater stroke volume, slower heart rate); (2) greater oxygen-carrying capacity by the lungs; (3) more efficient exchange of oxygen and carbon dioxide (waste gas); (4) improved general blood circulation (lower blood pressure, more red blood cells, more hemoglobin); (5) better mental outlook (can include feeling of euphoria; intense pleasure); and (6) better ability to concentrate (possibly related to improved circulation in the brain).

Before any woman engages in aerobic exercises, she should have a medical checkup to detemine that she has no heart or lung problems or any other medical condition that would prevent her from doing sustained exercises. Once she is "cleared," there are a variety of excellent aerobic activities that she can engage in. A few are considered in Box 21.1.

Fast walking is an excellent aerobic exercise for women with few potential problems. A good pair of shoes is essential to prevent foot injuries. Jogging is also effective, but women should gradually work themselves into a regimen and not go too rapidly into a strenuous pace. This will prevent back, leg, foot, and endurance problems. Here, too, good shoes are a must and one should not walk or jog too long in hot, humid weather.

Walking and jogging can also serve as collaborative activities since people can carry on a conversation while "on the move." Some husbands and wives or lovers walk or run together. That may either be stressful or relaxing. If one member continually outpaces the other, that could be a problem. If they get into arguments while in motion that, too, is not relaxing. However, if the partners go side-by-side and exchange pleasantries, these can be positive activities.

There are some misconceptions about women and running. First of all, running is not dangerous to a woman's ovaries. The ovaries are well-protected inside a fluid sac. The man's testicles are much more vulnerable to injury. Second, jogging does not cause sagging breasts.[1] The breasts are well-supported and will not be detached by jogging or running. A brassiere, however, will prevent sagging or bouncing. In this context, there are two kinds of brassieres. The "fashion" bra is worse than useless in preventing sagging or bouncing. The "active support" bra not only prevents sagging and bouncing, but is also comfortable. One danger of running in the cold

Box 21.1.   Aerobic Activities.

With Cooper's system, if you get 30 points a week you are achieving a beneficial aerobic effect. Some examples are:

1. Walking 4 miles in 1 hour gives 11 points.
2. Running 3 miles in 36 minutes also yields 11 points.
3. Riding a bicycle (divided equally between uphill and downhill and with and against the wind) for 8 miles in 32 minutes yields 10.5 points.
4. Swimming 1000 yards in 25 minutes gives 10.33 points.
5. Playing the following sports continuously without a break for 1 hour yields 11 points: handball, racquetball, squash, basketball, hockey, lacrosse, soccer.
6. Running in place 70–80 steps per minute for 25 minutes yields 10.5 points.
7. Riding a stationary bicycle at 17.5 mph and 65 rpm with moderate resistance for 55 minutes gives 11 points.
8. Skipping rope at 70–90 steps per minute for 25 minutes yields 10.5 points.
9. Rowing continuously with 2 oars at 20 strokes per minute for 45 minutes yields 10.5 points.
10. Playing singles tennis with a player of equal ability for 2 hours yields 9 points.
11. Engaging in cross-country skiing for 30 minutes yields between 9 and 12 points (the higher amount for the more severe terrain).
12. Roller-skating or ice-skating for 2 hours yields 8 points; for speed skating in 1 hour, you would get 12 points.
13. Two hours of volleyball are worth 8 points.
14. For women wrestlers 25 minutes of activity yields 10 points.
15. Aerobic dancing is now very popular with women; one half-hour of active continous dancing is worth 8 points.

without support is frost bite of the nipples. Hence, women should wear protective clothing while running in the winter.

Riding a bicycle is a very popular aerobic activity for women. It can be more rewarding than running because one can more easily combine aerobic exercise with arriving at a destination. It is less strenuous than running. There is greater freedom in choosing one's route as there are more bicycle paths than running paths. It is also somewhat less hazardous to ride a bike on main streets than it is to jog on those streets. However, riding a bicycle or running on busy thoroughfares can be dangerous both for the risk of being hit by a car or truck and the inhalation of noxious gases (such as carbon monoxide) emitted by vehicle exhausts. Since there is the possiblility of an accident, injury, or even a heart attack occurring while a woman is bicycling or running, it is important that she carry an identificaton card on her. A few cases have occurred of runners with medical emergencies being brought to hospital emergency rooms in critical condition without any means of identification.[10]

One disadvantage of intense commitment to running (e.g., marathons) or bicycling (e.g., long bike races) is that it can negatively affect one's personal relationships. Several cases of divorce being precipitated by overcommitted runners have been reported.[34]

Women who cannot run or ride a bicycle because of leg problems may be able to swim very effectively. Swimming is another popular aerobic activity for women and can be done all year round with the large number of indoor pools now available.

Racquetball is becoming an extremely popular sport. It combines an exciting game with effective aerobic activity. The major problems are related to possible injury. The ball moves very fast and in the small confines of the court, people can be hit in the eye, face, mouth, and genitals by either the ball or racquet. If you become a racquetball fan, be prudent and careful and don't forget to duck.

Running in place, stationary bicycling, and skipping rope are all effective, but they can also be boring. One way to overcome the boring aspect is to engage in those activities while watching TV or listening to music. In Box 21.2, another approach is given.

Cross-country skiing is an excellent, exhilarating winter sport. It combines good aerobics with strength-building action. The paths are usually scenic and the air can be stimulating.

Finally, aerobic dancing is another popular women's areobic activity. It too combines several features. There is the benefit of music, the collaborative effect of the group and the strenuous nature of the activity. There are several dances that can be learned and hence, it tends not to be boring. As dancing is "natural" for many women, aerobic dancing gives women the benefits of aerobics with the enjoyment of dance.[11] A somewhat similar popular program is *Jazzercise* in which there are choreographed musical exercises.[12] To get the minimal amount of 30 points in Cooper's system, a woman can do any of the exercises that rate for 10 points or more for three sessions a week. She can also combine different activities.

For example, do aerobic dance one day, swimming another day, and bicycle riding on a third day. A great deal of time is not needed. For most of these activities, no more than thirty minutes per session are adequate. A good practical program could be to have three days of aerobic activities

Box 21.2 Up the Down Escalator

Researchers at the University of Pennsylvania Medical School recently investigated another "aerobic" exercise frequently done by women; that is, climbing up stairs. The investigators first watched 45,000 people in three commercial establishments. The people had the choice of using a crowded escalator or walking up an adjacent, uncrowded flight of stairs. Only 5 percent chose the stairs. They then placed a sign at the escalator/stairway crosspoint which emphasized the cardiovascular benefits of climbing the stairs. Stairway usage then tripled for the 15 day duration of the sign's placement. One month later, stair utilization was back to 5 percent. This was unfortunate as the researchers found that using stairs is an excellent means of expending energy. In the same amount of time, stair-climbing burns off 250 percent more calories than swimming, 400 percent more than walking, 23 percent more than running, 94 percent more than racquetball and 150 percent more than tennis (but who wants to climb steps for one-half hour or more continuously?). Guthman, E. Climbing the steps to a hearty (puff) exercise plan. *Philadelphia Inq.* 9–1, February 15, 1981.

(e.g., Monday, Wednesday, and Friday) interposed with two days of strength-building work-outs. The latter could be two forty-five minute sessions at a health club (e.g., on Tuesday and Thursday). For a complete well-rounded program one could play doubles tennis, golf, or bowling on one of the weekend days. One can occasionally miss a session of exercise but it is better to try and keep up the three aerobic sessions. It is all too easy to get out of condition and just a week or two of inactivity puts a person almost back to the baseline.

Time

As with relaxation techniques, women may also find a lack of time to exercise. Here, too, women should have equal opportunities with men for exercise time. Actually not too much time is needed. The actual work-out is usually about thirty to forty-five minutes; with another thirty minutes for before and after preparation. The total time is approximately one to one-and-a quarter hours. Some affluent people are now placing gymnasiums and swimming pools into their homes, and various businesses are incorporating health clubs into their facilities. Although they were originally planned with males in mind, facilities are now allowing for female participation.[13]

Exercise should become a part of every woman's life-style. Along with activities such as eating, sleeping, and toothbrushing, both exercise and deep relaxation techniques should be a habitual part of daily living.

Let's now consider the emotional forms of exercise such as laughing, crying, shouting and screaming.

Laughing and Crying

Laughing is an excellent means to "let off steam" and it may have a health benefit as well. Norman Cousins, the noted editor, was suffering from a chronic, generally fatal disease, ankylosing spondylitis. By using a combination of laughter and vitamin C, he was able to overcome the disease and almost twenty years later he is alive and well.[14] Laughing is "catching" and can help in the collaborative aspect of stress-management (see Chapter 2).

As mentioned before, crying is a positive stress coping method. One concept is that emotionally induced stress produces toxic substances and that crying helps remove them from the system.[15] Emotionally produced tears are different than irritant-induced tears (as from peeling onions). In addition to removing harmful substances, crying is also beneficial psychologically. One often feels better after a "good cry." Crying, like laughing, is a means of communication and is a call for help. Finally, recent evidence has shown that tears contain anti-infective substances that can inactivate viruses.[16] Hence, women should not hold back their tears.

Shouting and Screaming

It's better to "let it out" then "hold it in." Many women are taught to suppress their anger and "hold in" their emotions.[31] But as discussed in Chapter 2, this can be dangerous. Screaming and shouting at others may be temporarily useful, but it makes for increased hostility.[17] Continually venting anger can also raise one's blood pressure.[18] A better method is to have controlled screaming as in *Primal Scream Therapy* where people can scream at their own pace and not at other people.

Singing and Whistling

Whistling "dixie" and singing for "one's supper" are well-known phrases, but whistling and singing are both ways to release inner "tension," overcome anxiety, and are methods of communication. Whistling "in the dark" can help overcome loneliness and it's even good exercise for the oral muscles and the lungs. The same is true for singing and when one is proficient in these oral activities, there is a great sense of satisfaction.

Let us now examine the "energy" aspects of stress management.

ENERGY

Under the concept of energy are included heat, cold, whirlpools, and sound waves. The most popular are the various techniques involving heat.

Heat

Extreme prolonged heat is a physical stressor but high heat for short periods of time or moderate heat, can be relaxing. The oldest methods used are *hot tubs* and *warm baths*. (See Box 21.3 for some examples.) Especially popular with women is the "bubble bath" that together with a good book and background music makes for a relaxing experience.

Steam, and *sauna baths* are popular. Not only can they be used at health clubs, but they are available in some hotel and motel rooms. People are now installing steam and sauna baths in their homes. (A portable steam bath can be installed in a shower or bath tub.) Steam and sauna baths can cause the loss of excess salts, toxins, metabolic products and water.[20] But

Box 21.3.   Hot Baths Throughout the Ages and Throughout the World.

Charlemagne, the ruler of the Holy Roman Empire, was reported to hold court sessions while immersed in a tub of warm water. For centuries, the Arapesh women of New Guinea have immersed the lower part of their bodies into a vat of extremely hot water for the purpose of easing menstrual discomfort. The Uzbekistan peasants in central Asia place the lower half of their bodies into hot tubs as a method of treatment for backaches and constipation.

For many years, the people in the Eastern European countries such as Yugoslavia, Greece, and Rumania have treated chronic rheumatism with a ten minute hot bath before bedtime. The Slavic peoples ease the withdrawal symptoms of alcoholics by giving them warm baths every three hours. In Western countries, the most popular form of heat has been the warm bath (97°-104°F). The purposes have been to induce relaxation and to treat rheumatism, neuralgia, and irritated muscles. A warm bath before bedtime has been a standard method for relieving insomnia.[19] Probably the main reason for the popularity of hot baths is their relaxing effect.

the weight loss is temporary and is regained by drinking liquids. Steam and saunas are effective in inducing relaxation, easing the pain of stiff and sore muscles, and reducing the pain symptoms of arthritis and rheumatism. A sauna is a well-known remedy for a hangover. However, one should wait at least one hour after drinking since the high heat can speed up the circulation and speed the alcohol throughout the blood stream (and make the individual feel even more drunk).[21] People often feel euphoric from the effects of a steam or sauna bath.

Nevertheless, steam and sauna baths can be dangerous. The high heat can be harmful for cardiac patients and patients with excessive thyroid activity.[22] Prolonged heat can also result in dizziness, ringing in the ears, and fainting. Pregnant women are advised to avoid steam and sauna baths or only stay in for a few minutes. (For example, a maximum of seven minutes in a sauna.) These warnings are based on a recent study that showed that the high heat of saunas may damage the nervous system of newborns.[23] For women, at other times, steam and sauna baths are both refreshing and relaxing.

Jacuzzi® whirlpool baths are an excellent combination of moderate heat and massage. By moving around, one can direct the pulsating water to various parts of the body. The effects are invigorating as well as relaxing, but people with high blood pressure must be careful and check with their physicians first.

The newest heat-related technique is the *float tank*. With this method, a woman dunks herself in a small tank containing 250 gallons of salt water heated to 93.5°F.[24] The tanks are eight feet long, four feet high and contain ten inches of water. The person is enclosed in total darkness for an hour or more. The experience combines sensory deprivation with moist heat and salt water. Some people initially feel claustrophobic and dislike the smell, but those negative aspects are soon dissipated. Other initial problems are smarting of nicks and scratches and stinging of the eyes (from the salts). These sensations are also short-lived. Most people report the experience as being pleasant and even euphoric. Tanks are available in various centers and are also sold for home consumption. (Samadhe Tank Center of Beverly Hills, Float to Relax Inc. of Denver). The use of float tanks appears to be another effective method to induce tranquility, and like other forms of heat, it can be helpful in treating various aches and pains.

However, float tanks may not be indicated for some people. Recently, one of us (MF) was on a panel that reviewed the movie *Altered States* (in which a float tank played a prominent part). Subsequently, MF appeared with Robert Goodman, the Philadelphia entrepreneur of *Float to Relax,* on the Phil Donahue segment of the *Today* show (April 7, 1981). Although the beneficial aspects of floating were emphasized, MF suggested the following precautions:

1. Some people who do not like confinement might panic.
2. The "spaced-out" feeling may last after one leaves the tank. Therefore, the individual should wait until she feels back to normal before she goes out to drive (to prevent an accident).
3. A psychotic episode may be precipitated in those people who are predisposed to "mental breakdown," severe neuroses and psychoses. (A mental health clearance should first be obtained for those individuals.)
4. Medically compromised people (e.g., epileptics, hypertensives) should have a medical clearance first to prevent untoward physical changes.

Taking into consideration the above precautions, the average woman should find the float tank to be both relaxing and rewarding.

Cold

Cold can act as a stressor but paradoxically it can also be relaxing. Probably the cold shocks the system and then as a rebound, relaxation occurs. As with heat, the sudden shock of the cold can be dangerous for cardiac patients. Cardiac patients should also avoid the rapid changes from hot to cold and vice versa. (For example, going from a steam bath to a cold shower and then into a sauna.) Women in good health would likely find the combination of alternating hot and cold to be stimulating, refreshing, and relaxing.

Sound

Ultrasound is a form of high-frequency sound waves. The vibrations when placed in different parts of the body have been used by physicians and physical therapists to relieve pain and promote healing in muscles and joints.[19] Most people report the sensations to be pleasant.

Recently, certain sound frequencies have been synthesized and incorporated into an hour long tape cassette. The sounds are known as *astral sounds* and they are theorized to simulate the sounds and frequencies present inside the central nervous system of individuals who are in a euphoric state.*[25] Although no controlled studies are available (as far as we are aware), testimonials describe the effects of listening to the tapes as being

---

*Available as Astral Sounds Cassettes from S. Cunningham, Box 3387, Hollywood, CA 90028

relaxing, pleasurable, euphoric, sensual, and capable of diminishing pain. People have also reported feeling vibrations and visions of light and color. The concept sounds interesting. It appears to us to be related to meditation and hypnosis in its effects on the central nervous system.

Ions

Atmospheric ions are small, chemically charged (positive or negative) particles that are found in the air as a result of cosmic rays, radioactivity, movement of dry, hot winds, and waterfall activity. A sudden severe concentration of postitive ions, as can occur during wind storms, can cause people to become ill. The opposite effect, making people feel good and relieving anxiety, is believed to occur when negative ions are in the atmosphere.[26] There are now negative ion-generating machines being produced with the expressed purpose of reducing anxiety. The verdict is not yet in on their effectiveness.[27,32]

Let us now look at a more well-known way of reducing anxiety and inducing relaxation, the use of massage.

MASSAGE

With the physical method of massage, the muscles, tendons, joints, skin, and fat tissues are manipulated. The primary purpose is to relieve partial muscle contractions (knots) and subsequently induce relaxation.[28] Massage can also help improve circulation and aid in inducing sleep. There are various forms of massage. The most well-known is *Swedish massage* where the entire body is manipulated. Women generally get massaged by masseuses while men have their massages by masseurs. When the roles are reversed (e.g., woman being massaged by a man) the results may be more stimulating than relaxing.

Other forms of massage are (1) self-use of *hand-held vibrators; (2) hydromassage* (water under pressure) which is generally done in health clubs; (3) the somewhat similar *shower massage* (e.g., the Shower Massage by Water Pik®); (4) massage that is built into either *reclining* chairs or mattresses (e.g., Contour® by Contour Chair Lounge, Inc.); (5) *scalp massage* (often done in beauty shops); (6) *facial massage* (also a beauty shop procedure); (7) concentrated foot massage (known as *reflexology* and purportedly helpful in the relief of systemic aches and pains);[29] and (8) *rolfing* (a form of a deep massage that may be painful at times but is reported to be extremely effective in reducing anxieties and in improving body posture and contour).[30]

Other manipulative procedures are the basis of therapies such as osteopathy, chiropractic, kinesiology, myotherapy and acupuncture. Although each technique has its specific indication, in many instances the effects on the body yield relaxation, and in some instances, euphoria and pain relief.[33]

SUMMARY

When a woman is able to get out to a health club (preferably should be about three times a week), she should make it an enjoyable experience. To do this, she can combine the three major physical methods. First is to have a good work-out (aerobic or strength-building on alternate days). Next, she should have a shower and sauna (or steam bath). Then, at least once a week, she should complete the experience with a good massage. Then wouldn't it be "heavenly" if her husband or friend picked her up at the health club and drove her home while she meditated in serene bliss.

In the next chapter, nutrition and stress management is discussed.

REFERENCES

1. Darden, E. *The Superfitness Handbook*. Philadelphia: George F. Stickley, 1980.
2. Williams, R. S., Logue, E. E., Lewis, J. L., Barton, T., Stead, N. W., Wallace, A. G., and Pizzo, S. V. Physical conditioning augments the fibrinolytic response to venous occlusion in healthy adults. *N. Eng. J. Med* 302:987–991, 1980.
3. Soman, V. R., Koivisto, V. A., Deibert, D., Felig, P., and De Frongo, R. A. Increased insulin sensitivity and insulin binding to monocytes after physical training. *N. Engl. J. Med.* 301:1200–1204, 1979.
4. Paffenbarger, R. S. and Hyde, R. T. Exercise as protection against heart attack. *N. Engl. J. Med.* 302:1026–1027, 1980.
5. Morse, D. R. and Furst, M. L. *Stress for Success: A Holistic Approach to Stress and its Management*. New York: Van Nostrand Reinhold, 1979.
6. Belloc, N. B. Relationship of health practices and mortality. *Prev. Med.* 2:67–81, 1973.
7. Associated Press. Jogging on muggy days can be risky. *Philadelphia Inq.* 10-BJ, July 17, 1980.
8. Cooper, K. H. *The Aerobics Way*. New York: M. Evans, 1977.
9. Cooper, K. H. and Cooper, M. *Aerobics for Women*. New York: M. Evans, 1972.
10. Newsline. Recreation 1: Joggers anonymous. *Psychol. Today* 12(9):26–27, 1979.
11. Sorensen, J. and Bruns, B. *Aerobic Dancing*. New York: Rawson, Wade, 1979.
12 Los Angeles Times Service. Jazzing up exercise paid off. *Philadelphia Inq.* 3-D, August 26, 1980.
13. Geannette, G. Inside the corporate gymnasium. *American Way* 12(1):20–25, 1979.
14. Cousins, N. *Anatomy of an Illness*. New York: W. W. Norton, 1979.
15. Gottlieb, W. Have a good cry. *Prevention* 32(8):126–130, 1980.
16. Langford, M. P., Yin-Murphy, M., Ho, Y. M., Barber, J. C., Baron, S., and Stanton, G.

J. Human fibroblast interferon in tears of patients with picornovirus epidemic conjunctivitis. *Infect. Immun.* **29**:995–998, 1980.

17. Varro, B. What's this? Don't vent our anger? *Philadelphia Eve. Bull.* A:17, August 8, 1978.
18. Harburg, E., Blakelock, E. H., Jr., and Roeper, P. J. Resentful and reflective coping with arbitrary authority and blood pressure. Detroit: *Psychosom. Med.* **41**:189–202, 1979.
19. Shaw, L. Healing with heat. *Prevention* **31**(11):55–59, December 1979.
20. Foley, W. J. Stress from many sources affects your health and well being. *Dent. Stud.* **55**(8):34–35, 1977.
21. Johnson, T. and Miller, T. *The Sauna Book.* New York: Harper & Row, 1977.
22. Parade hotline. On physical fitness: Hot but not healthy. *Parade* 27, May 4, 1980.
23. Editorial. Heat is on saunas as possible teratogens. *Med. World News* **19**(6):37, March 20, 1978.
24. Living. Nirvana in a dank, dark tank: Seeking tranquility? Slip into a watery coffin. *Time* 77, March 24, 1980.
25. Cunningham, S. *A Natural High.* Hollywood, Calif.: The American Research Team, 1979.
26. Krueger, A. P. and Read, E. J. Biological impact of small air ions. *Science* **193**:1209–1213, 1976.
27. Sun, M. Ion generators: Old fad, new fashion. *Science* **210**:31–32, 1980.
28. Gottlieb, B. Release your tension with massage. *Prevention* **29**(2):134–142, 1977.
29. Reibstein, L. Foot rubs a cure for ills? *Philadelphia Sunday Bull.* N C:3, August 6, 1978.
30. Rolf, I. P. *Rolfing: The Integration of Human Structures.* Santa Monica, Calif.: Dennis-Landman, 1977.
31. Sifford, D. Women should learn how to express anger, she says. *Philadelphia Inq.* 3-C November 17, 1980.
32. Bissell, M., Diamond, M.C., Ellman, G.L., Krueger, A.P., Orenberg, E.K., Sigel, S.S.R.G., Yost, M., and Moore, A.D. Air ion research. *Science* **211**:1114–1116, 1981.
33. Prudden, B. *Pain Erasure: The Bonnie Prudden Way.* New York: M. Evans, 1980.
34. Warshaw, R. Mile after mile, putting distance in relationships. *Philadelphia Inq.* 1-G, April 26, 1981.

22
Nutrition and Stress: A Feminine Approach

INTRODUCTION

When a woman is face-to-face with stressors, she must cope with them in one way or another. We've already discussed the physical methods of fighting and running away from a confrontation, and the psychological methods of mental rehearsal, planning, vigilance, and unbiased observations. Whether one reacts physically, psychologically or a combination of both, it is essential that the brain and body be maximally supplied with nutrients and oxygen.

An analogy is a sparkling new automobile with a superb engine and a crash-resistant body. If that car is fueled with a low octane gasoline mixture, it will develop "knocks" and sputter just like a decrepit vehicle. With proper high octane gasoline the automobile would ride as if it were floating on air. The same holds true with women and their ability to cope with stress. With optimum levels of vitamins, minerals, carbohydrates, fats, proteins, water, and fiber, women will have the best "fuel" to physically and psychologically deal with stressful situations. Unfortunately, most people take better care of their cars than they do of their own bodies.

Although women and men both need optimum nutrition to cope with stress throughout life, there are certain differences between them. The stressors of menstruation have already been discussed (see Chapter 6). During menses and premenses there are both physical and psychological stressors. The loss of blood can create a temporary anemia and contribute to nutritional deficiencies. Replacement of the blood and the internal metabolism necessary for the rejuvenation of the next cycle with formation of a mature egg both require increased nutrients (especially vitamins).

If pregnancy occurs, there are severe physiological changes taking place inside the woman's body that greatly increase her nutritional demands. The developing fetus requires additional nutrients. Pregnancy often induces psychological stressors that place further nutritional demands upon her body. Failure to have ample nutrients (especially vitamin C) can have disastrous results on the developing fetus. It can contribute to: miscarriage; stillbirths; prematurities; underweight infants; disabilities and retardations; and infant mortalities. The nursing mother requires additional vitamins and other nutrients. Many women take diuretic drugs to remove excess fluid accumulated during menstruation, pregnancy and lactation. The flushing action removes many water-soluble vitamins. Hence, additional supplementation is necessary. Prior use of the "pill" affects the baby's metabolism and there is evidence that vitamin-supplementation is needed.[1]

Once a woman's reproductive years are over, she faces the challenge of menopause (see Chapter 8). Since this time period can be stressful to women because of hormonal changes and psychological stressors, optimum nutrition is essential. This is especially true since women's natural resistance to stress-related diseases, such as heart attacks, is lost following menopause.

With these factors in mind, let us now consider each of the nutrients as they relate to female stress. The water-soluble vitamins, C and the B complex, are the first to be examined. These vitamins are preferably incorporated into a combined pill or capsule, which must be taken once a day with water or juice since they are not stored by the body. For specific indications, vitamin C can be taken separately.

VITAMIN C (ASCORBIC ACID)

Without going into the controversies over the use of vitamin C for disease prevention and treatment (e.g., common cold, influenza, and cancer),[2-7] let us consider how vitamin C may help in dealing with stress. Studies have shown that under stressful conditions, there is an excessive outpouring of vitamin C into the urine.[8-9] There is some evidence that vitamin C acts as a coenzyme (works along with an enzyme to speed up a chemical reaction) for the manufacture of the stress hormone cortisone.[1,8] Since cortisone increases during stress, it may be that extra vitamin C is needed for cortisone mobilization.

In stress responses induced by infection, the body's immune system is called into play. Vitamin C appears to play a part in activating the white blood cells that act to destroy bacteria and viruses.[8,10,11] Vitamin C specifically helps these white blood cells migrate to the site of infection and when there to phagocytize (engulf) the infectious organisms.[11]

In Chapter 3, the HDLs were discussed as being related to heart disease prevention and it was mentioned that vitamin C ingestion can elevate these protective HDLs.[12] Vitamin C acts as an antioxidant that protects other vitamins and body tissues from physical stressors such as pollutants, poisons, and free radicals (substances produced by aging cells). There is also some evidence that vitamin C prevents the conversion of food nitrites (found in processed meats such as frankfurters, salami, and bologna) into cancer-causing nitrosamines.[1]* Cigarette smoking has been shown to reduce the body's supply of vitamin C.[8] Hence, this is another negative aspect of smoking in stress management.

Women should have an optimal level of vitamin C at all times, but especially during premenses, menses, pregnancy, lactation, other potentially stressful periods, and while taking birth-control pills. The adult U.S. Recommended Daily Allowance (RDA) for vitamin C is only 60 milligrams but many nutritionists believe that this dose is merely for scurvy prevention and is far too low as an optimum amount.[1,6-9,13]

It was the work of Linus Pauling, the two-time Nobel Prize Laureate, that originally questioned the U.S. RDA for vitamin C. A renowned biochemist-nutritionist, Robert Benowicz, recommends the optimum level of vitamin C for women to be between one and three grams (1000 to 3000 milligrams) a day.[1] Although vitamin C is practically nontoxic (excess amounts are excreted in the urine), there is the possibility of development of kidney stones (crystalluria). The use of a time-release capsule (e.g., Cevi-Bid®, Geriatric Pharmaceutical Corp.) purportedly prevents that occurrence.

VITAMIN B₁ (THIAMINE)

Thiamine is another vitamin that plays a role in stress and its management. It is an essential coenzyme for reactions that require release of energy from carbohydrates (starches). Hence, it is important for the energy needed in physically coping with stress (e.g., fighting or running). Vitamin B₁ is required for the formation of acetylcholine (see Figure 2.4). As discussed in Chapters 2 and 20, acetylcholine is an important hormone that acts as a neurotransmitter (transfers nerve messages) in the parasympathetic and central nervous system (activates muscles and glands). A dietary lack of vitamin B₁ can lead to fatigue, irritability, depression, and insomnia.[1,13,14]

---

* In 1978, based on some animal experiments, the FDA decided that nitrites, by themselves, could cause cancer. Just recently, based on new information, the FDA rescinded the warning against nitrites. Hilts, P.J. The nitrite case: How science and politics mix. *Philadelphia Inq.* 1-H, 4-H, May 3, 1981.

For women, extra vitamin B_1 is needed during pregnancy and lactation. The adult RDA for thiamine is 1.5 milligrams per day, but Benowicz recommends between 50 and 200 milligrams as being optimum for women.[1] Thiamine along with other members of the B complex (discussed next) should be taken together in balanced quantities to prevent masking symptoms of certain anemias. There is no indication of toxicity from taking too much vitamin B_1. Unused amounts are excreted in the urine.

VITAMIN B_2 (RIBOFLAVIN)

Riboflavin's role in stress is related to its function as a coenzyme in releasing energy from proteins. In addition, vitamin B_2 specifically helps in the synthesis of stress hormones such as growth hormone (STH), thyroxine, ACTH, and insulin (see Chapter 2). A deficiency of riboflavin can cause symptoms of anxiety and fatigue. Vitamin B_2 is also needed in extra amounts during pregnancy. The adult RDA is 1.7 milligrams per day. The Benowicz recommendation for women is between 50 and 200 milligrams per day.[1] Unused riboflavin is lost in the urine.

VITAMIN B_3 (NIACIN, NIACINAMIDE, NICOTONIC ACID, NICOTINAMIDE)

Niacin acts as a coenzyme in energy reactions involving carbohydrates, proteins, and fats. It, too, is active in the synthesis of stress hormones such as STH, thyroxine, and insulin. A lack of vitamin B_3 can cause stress-related symptoms such as irritability, depression, and headache.[1,13] High quantities of vitamin B_3 have been used with some degree of success in treating the stress-related diseases: migraine headaches, angina pectoris, and schizophrenia.[1,15] The adult RDA is 20 milligrams per day and the Benowicz recommendation for women is 100–400 milligrams per day. Only in large amounts (3–4 grams per day) have signs of toxicity been observed.[1] Normal excesses are removed via the urine.

VITAMIN B_6 (PYRIDOXINE, PYRIDOXAL, PYRIDOXAMINE)

Pyridoxine acts as a coenzyme that partakes in fat and protein metabolism and niacin formation. It is involved in energy production and resistance to stressors. Women who are taking oral contraceptives and cortisone suffer a loss of vitamin B_6. In one study, vitamin B_6 was effective in overcoming the depression associated with the taking of birth-control pills.[16]

Pregnant and lactating women also require extra pyridoxine. The adult RDA is 2 milligrams per day but Benowicz considers 100–300 milligrams per day to be ideal for women. Toxicity has been reported only in huge doses (exceeding 1 gram per pound of body weight per day).[1] In recommended amounts, any excess is excreted in the urine.

VITAMIN B$_{12}$ (COBALAMINE, CYANACOBALAMINE)

Cobalamine also functions as a coenzyme. It is involved in the synthesis of proteins, fats, and nucleic acids (DNA is the substance of genes, and RNA is the precursor of proteins). Vitamin B$_{12}$ helps regulate the formation of red blood cells (important in the transport of oxygen for energy-requiring reactions). Symptoms of vitamin B$_{12}$ lack are mood changes and depression. Improvement of mood and feeling was attained in one study after the administration of vitamin B$_{12}$ as contrasted to a control group that received a placebo.[17] There is evidence that women taking oral contraceptives have a higher requirement for vitamin B$_{12}$.[1]

The adult RDA is 6 milligrams per day and Benowicz's suggestion for women is 50–200 milligrams per day.[1] Vitamin B$_{12}$ is nontoxic. In one study, it was found that excess vitamin C can cause destruction of vitamin B$_{12}$. However, this has not been corroborated by others.[1,8] One should not take an excess of folic acid (another B vitamin) since it can mask the symptoms of vitamin B$_{12}$ deprivation. Vegetarians who eat neither meat nor milk products (vegetans) will have a deficiency of vitamin B$_{12}$ and require supplementation.

FOLIC ACID (FOLACIN, FOLATE)

Folate is another B vitamin that acts as a coenzyme and partakes in the synthesis of nucleic acids and acetylcholine (see Figure 20.1). Symptoms of folate deficiency include irritability, sleeplessness, and depression.[19] Folate has analgesic (pain-reducing) activity and may help in naturally overcoming pain. Folate supplementation has also been shown to relieve mild depression and fatigue.[20] Pregnant women and women taking oral contraceptives typically require additional folic acid. There is some evidence that folate deficiency during pregnancy can cause problems with the pregnancy.[19] The adult RDA of folate is 400 milligrams per day and Benowicz's recommendations for women is 500 to 1000 milligrams per day. There are no reports of toxicity related to excessive dosage.

PANTOTHENIC ACID (PANTOTHENATE)

Pantothenate is yet another B vitamin that has coenzyme activity. It functions in carbohydrate, fat, and protein metabolism. Its specific stress role is related to its action in the synthesis of cortisone, STH, and actylcholine.[1,21] Deficiencies can yield stress-related symptoms such as headache, fatigue, and depression.[13,21] It has been used to treat dizziness related to general debilitation. In animal experiments pantothenate-supplemented groups swam longer, were less affected by radiation, and lived longer than nonsupplemented groups.[22] The adult RDA is 10 milligrams per day while the Benowicz recommendation for women is 100–300 milligrams per day.[1] There is no evidence of pantothenate toxicity.

CHOLINE

The major stress role of the B-vitamin, choline, is related to its function in the synthesis of the neurotransmitter, acetylcholine. Choline also functions in the synthesis of fats. There is no RDA, but it is believed that normal diets provide about 500–900 milligrams of choline per day. Choline is found in high levels in beef liver, eggs, wheat germ, peanuts, and brewer's yeast. No symptoms of toxicity have been reported.[1]

BIOTIN

Biotin is still another member of the B complex that acts as a coenzyme in the metabolism of fats, carbohydrates, and proteins. Biotin maintains the sweat glands (active during stress) and hair quality (affected by stress). The adult RDA is 200 milligrams per day and in this instance Benowicz recommends less for women (50–200 milligrams per day).[1] There is no evidence of toxicity.

INOSITOL

Inositol is a contested member of the B complex. The FDA does not recognize it as a vitamin. Inositol is involved in fat metabolism and is apparently effective in reducing cholesterol deposits. Deficiency symptoms are not known in humans but inositol is believed to play a role in the stress response. It helps improve muscle tone and function.[1]

Animals lacking inositol have deficient growth and lose their hair.[13] Although there is no guarantee that women who are losing their hair will be helped by inositol, there is some evidence that inositol, along with biotin, choline, folic acid, and PABA (discussed next), can help restore natural hair coloring to those who are prematurely gray.[13] Benowicz recommends an adult female daily dose of 100 to 300 milligrams.[1] There is no known toxicity.

PABA (PARA-AMINOBENZOIC ACID)

PABA is another contested member of the B complex that is also not recognized as a vitamin by the FDA. It is a constituent of folic acid and acts as a coenzyme in protein metabolism and the synthesis of red blood cells. PABA's function is not known in humans but its deficiency causes a loss of hair color in mice. As in the case with inositol, it has been occasionally effective in restoring natural color to prematurely gray hair.[13] There is more than one reason for hair to fall out and turn gray but stress and lack of B vitamins are definite factors.

Another finding of interest to women who enjoy sunbathing is that PABA has been found to be an effective sunscreen against the ultraviolet rays of the sun (a potential severe physical stressor).[13,23]

Benowicz suggests a daily dose of 50 to 200 milligrams for adult females.[1] Toxicity is unknown.

PANGAMIC ACID (PANGAMATE, VITAMIN B$_{15}$)

Pangamate is another contested B vitamin that is unapproved by the FDA. Biochemically it functions as a coenzyme and is involved in oxygen transport, protein synthesis, and steroid hormone activation.[1,13] Therefore, it would be important in the energy required for the stress response. It is not known to be toxic except in extremely high doses (50,000-100,000 times the usual dosage). One researcher contends that one of the components of vitamin B$_{15}$ induces genetic mutations which may cause cancer.[24,51] However, this has neither been proven nor shown for the complete vitamin. Benowicz suggests a daily dose for women of 25 to 75 milligrams.

LAETRILE (AMYGDALIN, VITAMIN B$_{17}$)*

Laetrile is considered by some investigators to be a member of the B complex. It is found in many seeds (e.g., apricots, apples, cherries, peaches, nectarines, and plums). As it contains cyanide (a severe toxin), the FDA considers Laetrile to be a drug. Laetrile is used for cancer therapy in several countries (e.g., Mexico, France, Germany) but the FDA has banned its use in the United States (it is currently being tested in several major U.S. health centers).** There is no knowledge on its relationship to stress and, therefore, it will not be considered further.

* Another little-known member of the B-complex is *lipoic acid* (thioctic acid). Its need in human nutrition is not known; hence, there is no recommended dosage.

** The first results are in on the FDA-initiated research on Laetrile. The patient population consisted of terminally-ill cancer patients being treated at the Mayo Clinic and other major

BIOFLAVINOIDS (VITAMIN P, FLAVONES, FLAVONOLS)

The bioflavinoids are part of the natural vitamin C complex. They are not recognized by the FDA as separate vitamins. They apparently help in the utilization of vitamin C.[13] Benowicz considers 50 to 100 milligrams to be an optimal daily dose for women. A deficiency may exacerbate the edema (fluid retention) associated with the menses.

Let us now examine the fat-soluble vitamins beginning with a discussion of vitamin E and stress.

VITAMIN E (TOCOPHEROLS)

The fat-soluble vitamins are vitamins E, A, D, and K. They must be dissolved in fat before they can be absorbed through the intestinal membrane. Hence, they should be taken with milk or at the conclusion of a meal in which some fat has been ingested.

Vitamin E plays an important role in stress related to its various physiological functions. Vitamin E maintains the integrity of cell membranes; thereby ensuring proper functioning of the respiratory, circulatory, nervous, digestive, excretory, and muscular systems.[1,25] Vitamin E acts as an antioxidant (scavenger of toxic peroxides, free radicals, and other breakdown products of aging and worn-out cells). This, in turn, helps protect the body against physical stressors such as pollutants, radiation, and toxic substances. There have been several studies relating vitamin E and physical stressors. Thomas Cureton, Jr., world-renowned physical educator, showed that athletes who ingested a wheat-germ oil supplementation (high in vitamin E) prior to their work-outs did significantly better and had less fatigue than a control group who exercised without the supplements.[26]

In animal studies, vitamin E-supplemented groups as contrasted with controls: had less lung damage when exposed to ozone (an atmospheric pollutant); had less toxicity when overexposed; had fewer gastric ulcers when confounded in a maze; and lived longer.[22]

As a result of its detoxifying and antioxidant effects, theoretically vitamin E supplementation should help protect body cells from the damaging effects of distress reactions and should delay aging.[27,28] Vitamin E is not considered to be toxic but very high doses may increase blood pressure.[1]

U.S. health centers. There was no significant improvement for the Laetrile-using patients. The results were predictable according to both Laetrile proponents and opponents. Kilpatrick, J.J. Harmless Substance: Laetrile should be a private matter. *Philadelphia Inq.* 15-A, May 14, 1981.

Therefore, individuals who are hypertensive should restrict their intake of vitamin E.

For women, extra vitamin E is needed during pregnancy and lactation and when on oral contraceptives. The adult RDA is 30 I.U.* per day. Benowicz recommends a dosage for women of 100–660 I.U. per day. [1]

VITAMIN A (RETINOL)

Vitamin A is another fat-soluble vitamin that plays a role in stress. Biologically, vitamin A acts as a coenzyme in the retina, skin, bone, liver, and in the adrenal glands where the stress hormones, cortisone and adrenaline are produced. It is needed for protein metabolism. Vitamin A aids in the detoxification of physical stressors such as poisons and air pollutants.[1,29] There have been several animal studies showing that vitamin A can protect against physical stressors. In one study, mice pretreated with vitamin A had a much lower incidence of tumors than mice not given the supplement.[30]

In a human study, it was found that vitamin A-supplemented burn victims had less than one-third the ulcer incidence of a similar group of burn patients who had not received vitamin A supplementation.[31] Vitamin A is one vitamin that can be toxic at high doses. Ingestion of 100,000 I.U. per day may cause symptoms such as headache, profuse sweating, lethargy, and abdominal pain. The Benowicz recommendation for women is 5–1500 I.U. per day as contrasted to the adult RDA of 2,500–8,000 I.U. per day.[1]

VITAMIN D (CALCIFEROL, CHOLECALCIFEROL, ERGOSTEROL)

Vitamin D is involved in calcium and phosphorus metabolism and as such is required for proper growth and repair of bone and formation of teeth. Hence, vitamin D is essential in coping with the results of physical stressors such as surgery, infection, and injury in which bone is destroyed. The pregnant woman needs additional supplies of vitamin D since in fetal bone and teeth formation some of her supplies are removed. Vitamin D can also be toxic in excessive amounts. Doses of 1000 I.U. per pound per day can cause toxic manifestations such as calcification of blood vessels, skin, and kidney tissues, and symptoms such as excessive thirst, a great need to urinate, and vomiting and diarrhea.[1,13]

* I.U. = International Units.

The adult RDA is 200–400 I.U. per day while the Benowicz recommendation is 400–800 per day.

OTHER VITAMINS

Vitamin K is essential for blood coagulation (clotting) but it is rarely lacking. It may be deficient because of the intake of antibiotics or anticoagulants. Therefore, it is one vitamin that should not be self-administered. Supplements should be under the direction of a physician.

Another possible vitamin has been designated Vitamin Q. It also appears to be essential for blood coagulation. It is not yet available. One other potential vitamin is known as vitamin U (metionic acid). It was isolated in Russia and has been used for prevention and treatment of stress-related ulcers.[13] It, too, is not yet available in the United States.

Let us now consider minerals and stress.

MINERALS

Unlike vitamins, minerals are generally adequately supplied in average daily diets. However, there are occasions when extra intake is important. When one anticipates working or exercising in hot, humid weather, extra salt (sodium chloride) may be needed. But too much salt is a risk factor for coronary heart disease and hypertension. *Potassium* is required for nerve transmission. Hypoglycemia and muscular weakness may result from potassium lack.

Calcium is needed for nerve conduction, muscle contraction, bone and teeth formation, and blood coagulation.[22] Calcium is also considered to have a sedative and hypnotic (sleep-inducing) effect.[25] The warm glass of milk which helps promote sleep for some people, is rich in calcium. *Phosphorus* is involved in the same processes as calcium. It is also essential for energy reactions (important in the stress response).

Magnesium is required for nerve conduction, muscle contraction, and bone and teeth formation. Deficiencies of magnesium have been associated with "nervousness," irritability, and abnormal heart rhythms (arrhythmias; see Chapter 3) that can lead to fatal heart attacks.[32] Kenneth Cooper (of "Aerobics" fame) contends that many Americans have a magnesium deficiency and should be supplemented with 350 milligrams per day. Good natural sources are in seeds and nuts.[33]

Zinc is needed for repair and it may play a role as a scavenger of lead (antipollutant effects).[34] However, the body level of zinc must be carefully monitored as there is evidence that too much can reduce the blood level of the protective HDLs (see Chapter 3).[35] This negative effect was found in doses of approximately 160 milligrams of zinc per day which is quite high as the average daily intake is about 12 milligrams per day.

Iron is needed for muscle functioning and oxygen transport (both important in the stress response). A lack of iron can lead to iron deficiency anemia. Women need more iron than men because of the loss of blood during menses. *Copper* lack can also result in anemia. *Iodine* is necessary for the functioning of the thyroid hormones (needed in the stress response; see Chapter 2).

Selenium plays a role with vitamin E in antioxidation, and in scavenging aging and injured cells.[13] *Manganese* and *fluoride* are required for normal bone formation. Fluoride also provides for decay-resistant teeth. However, excess fluoride can cause toxic symptoms. The average concentration of fluoride in fluoridated water is one part per million.*

Along with vitamins and minerals, stress management requires an adequate intake of proteins, carbohydrates and fats.

PROTEINS

Physical stressors of injury, infection, radiation, and surgery cause cellular damage which must be repaired. Protein is needed for repair of injuries and wounds and for replacement of cells. For women, protein is especially important to repair the damage that takes place each month following menses. During pregnancy, extra protein is needed for both the developing fetus and the woman's expanding abdomen and enlarging breasts.

Protein can also be used for energy but only after carbohydrates and fats have been used up. Best sources of protein that do not contain unneeded excessive fat are fish, poultry, veal, skim-milk products, and egg whites. One additional advantage of fish is that, according to recent evidence, cold water fish (e.g., mackerel) contains an anti-clot factor that appears to be protective against heart attacks. That may be the reason why fish-eating Eskimos rarely have heart attacks.[54]

There are twenty amino acids (constituents of proteins) of which eight

---

* Some representative vitamin and mineral supplements are: Albee® with C; Z Bec® (A. H. Robins); Stresstabs® 600 with Iron (Lederle); B C-Bid® (Geriatric Pharmaceutical Corp.); Alpha E® (Barth Vitamin Corp.); All® (Westpro); Diet-Tab 21® (Vitamerica); Feminine® (Mead Johnson); Fortespan® (Smith, Kline & French); Maxim-All® (Am. Diet Aids); Mi-Cebrin T® (Dista); Myadec® (Parke-Davis); Natalins® (Mead Johnson); V-Complete® (Schiff); One A Day plus Minerals® (Miles); Vita Kaps M® (Abbott); Unicap Therapeutic® (Upjohn); Therovite M® (Natural Sales); Theragram-M® (Squibb); Stuart Formula® (Stuart).

are essential. Vegetables do not contain all eight amino acids but a mixture of vegetables, seeds, and nuts can provide the requisite amino acids.

Tryptophan is a particular amino acid that is of interest in stress management. It is one of the essential amino acids. Tryptophan is converted in the brain to serotonin, a neurotransmitter that among its various functions can induce deep relaxation and sleep.[22] Tryptophan may also act to inhibit pain and may induce hallucinogenic changes in susceptible individuals.[13,36]* When calcium was discussed, it was mentioned that the calcium content of milk may be the reason why a warm glass of milk can be sleep-inducing. Milk also contains tryptophan and it may be the tryptophan content that is more important in that regard. [37]

An average woman should do well on about 85 grams of protein per day (slightly higher during pregnancy).[38] Recent evidence suggests that too much protein can result in obesity.[52]

CARBOHYDRATES

Carbohydrates are the principal source of energy and energy is of major importance in the stress response. Carbohydrates should form the bulk of the diet for the average woman. About 300–400 grams per day (depending upon physical activity) is considered ideal by some authorities (i.e., up to 75 percent of the total caloric intake).[22,38] The principal form of carbohydrate used for energy is glucose (a simple or single sugar; monosaccharide). Sucrose (refined sugar; either white, brown or found in syrup and honey) is a double sugar (disaccharide) which is converted to glucose by the body. Although sucrose is an available form of energy, it has no other value and can be damaging if taken in excess.

For example, sucrose in the form of candies and cakes is cariogenic (causes tooth decay).[39] High sucrose intake is a predisposing factor for diabetes, can lead to hypoglycemia, is considered by some to be a risk factor for coronary heart disease and has been implicated in "irritability and confused thinking".[25,39-41]

Complex carbohydrates (polysaccharides; starches) are an excellent source of energy and they have none of the deleterious effects of glucose. Readily available forms are bread, pasta (spaghetti, macaroni), potatoes (white and sweet), and pizza. The more active the woman is, the greater would be her need for complex carbohydrates. According to Pritikin, a diet

---

* Current findings show that tryptophan and tyrosine (another amino acid) may protect the heart against dangerous cardiac ventricular arrhythmias (abnormal heart rhythms; see Chapter 3). Scott, N.A., DeSilva, R.A., Lown, B. and Wurtman, R.J. Tyrosine administration decreases vulnerability to ventricular fibrillation in the normal canine heart. *Science* 727–729, 1981.

high in starches, low in sucrose, low in fat (discussed next), and relatively low in protein is the perfect diet.[42] It should help maintain an ideal body weight while greatly decreasing the chances of getting a heart attack.

While not everyone agrees with the concept and strictness of the Pritikin diet, it seems to be rational and the basis of a good nutritional life-style. Nevertheless, women should not become stressed over their diet. An occasional slice of pie, piece of candy or ice cream soda would probably be less harmful than constantly worrying about everything that is being eaten. In the same vein, it seems logical to buy foods without artificial flavors, colors and preservatives, but in some instances the chemically treated food is healthier. For example, some natural foods contain arsenic, which can be removed by processing. Hence, read labels but don't become stressed by an occasional additive.

FATS (LIPIDS)

Fats also play a role in stress. They are the most concentrated form of energy available to the body but carbohydrates are used first. A certain amount of fat is needed to absorb and transport the fat-soluble vitamins (A,D,E, and K). In addition, fats are needed to form a layer of tissue to cushion and protect the body's internal organs.[43] Women have a greater layer of subcutaneous fat than do men. It serves a protective function (e.g. cushions the blow of a physical stressor) and enhances the soft, feminine appearance (as contrasted to the hard, muscular, masculine appearance).

Although fat has these important physiological roles, most Americans take in too much fat. The average American ingests about 105 grams of fat daily, most of which is in the form of animal fat (i.e., about 40 percent of the total caloric intake). Animal fats are of the saturated type (e.g., activate cholesterol in the form of VLDLs and LDLs) and have been implicated in coronary heart disease.[53] Americans ingest about 800 milligrams of cholesterol per day and one egg yolk contains about 240 milligrams. Saturated fat is high in beef, pork, lamb, bacon, ham, and dairy products.[22]

Nevertheless, dietary fat is not the only way blood cholesterol can be formed (see Figure 2.1) and there are contrasting studies on blood cholesterol levels and coronary heart disease.[44,45] Vegetable fats usually contain no saturated fats. Exceptions are palm and coconut oils and cocoa butter. Vegetable oils that are high in polyunsaturated fats are safflower, cottonseed, corn and soybean. The only essential fatty acid is linoleic acid and this is found in those oils.

An intake of only unsaturated vegetables fats can lower blood cholesterol, but the evidence that this intake can prevent heart attacks is inconclusive. However, in one study in Finland, both blood cholesterol and heart disease incidence decreased in the group of patients receiving a diet high in polyunsaturates.[46] Studies have also shown that polyunsaturated fat intake can raise the level of the protective HDL-cholesterol.[47] But an intake of polyunsaturated fats can also be dangerous. There is some evidence that they can promote the development of cancer.[47]

It seems reasonable to cut down on the daily intake of fats for several reasons:

1. Fat is not essential for energy; carbohydrate is more important.

2. A high fat intake leads to obesity and that is definitely related to heart disease, diabetes, and other problems.

3. There is some relationship between high fat intake (vegetable as well as animal fats) and the incidence of bowel and breast cancer.[47,48]

4. Excess fat tends to accumulate in unsightly places (e.g., for women in the hips, thighs, buttocks, and abdomen).

5. Being overweight makes it more difficult to physically cope with stressors.

6. In this society being overweight induces psychological stressors (but one must bear in mind that ingesting excess fat is only one way to become obese).

Considering the deleterious effects of accumulated fat, some investigators suggest that fat intake should be no more than 55 grams per day (about 20 percent of the daily calories).[38] Pritikin suggests even less.[42] As with carbohydrates, it is believed that an occcasional "slip" will not be fatal. Having eggs or steak once or twice a week is not harmful and may be less stressful than constantly being on guard about everything one eats.

Some dietary suggestions for women are: If there are no associated medical problems, have a daily dietary intake of 15–20 percent of fat (mainly of the vegetable type), 70 percent carbohydrate (mainly of the starch type), and 10–15 percent protein (containing all of the essential amino acids). During pregnancy and lactation, the protein content should be increased about 10 percent at the expense of carbohydrates.*

LECITHIN

Lecithin is a unique fatty substance. It is a combination of two B vitamins, choline and inositol, along with the mineral phosphorus and some unsaturated fats (principally linoleic acid). The stress-related roles of choline,

---

* Our recommendations are based on a review of the current literature and discussions with authorities. However, if there are any medical or psychiatric problems, women should follow the advice of their physicians in terms of their nutritional intake. This is also true during pregnancy.

inositol, phosphorus, and linoleic acid have already been discussed, but the combined product has other important positive functions. Some studies have shown that lecithin can decrease blood levels of the dangerous LDLs and raise the blood levels of the protective HDLs.[47,48] A good natural source of lecithin is soybeans. Egg yolk also contains lecithin and possibly could compensate for the high cholesterol content of the yolk. So far, three nutrients, vitamin C, polyunsaturated fats, and lecithin apparently have the property of increasing the beneficial HDL-cholesterol.

Although not usually considered to be a nutrient, water has important stress-related benefits.

WATER

We came from the sea (evolutionarily speaking) and the sea is inside us (all of our tissues are bathed in a salt solution). Water is required for all our metabolic activities including the stress response. Women who work or exercise outside during warm weather need extra water when faced with the physical stressors of high heat and humidity (even though they sweat less than men).

In Chapters 4 and 19, the negative coping method of drinking caffeinated beverages was discussed. But drinking warm beverages can have a soothing and relaxing effect. Some nutritious and tranquilizing beverages are: Postum®, Non-Caf® (both are made from cereal grains); soups (e.g., Campbell's®, Heinz®, Progresso®, and homemade chicken soup); decaffeinated coffee (e.g., Sanka®, Taster's Choice®, Nescafe®), and various types of herbal teas.[49] In regard to herbal teas, there are many different types. Some contain caffeine and tannic acid and may even have toxic substances. Hence, one should read labels and check out the ingredients before routinely drinking herbal teas.

Aside from nutrients, roughage also plays a role in stress.

ROUGHAGE (FIBER)

With age, some women develop problems with their bowel movements. The principal problem is constipation. The straining that occurs while trying to force a movement acts as a severe physical stressor. This can cause marked increases in blood pressure and in susceptible individuals may result in a heart attack or stroke.

Constipation can easily be prevented in most instances. The key is to increase the roughage (fiber) in the diet. Fiber adds bulk. The bulk material swells up in the digestive tract and helps move food along. Substances rich in fiber include bran, rice, leafy vegetables, and fresh fruits. Studies have shown that fiber can play a preventive role against diseases such as diverticulitis (an inflammatory disease of the large intestine), appendicitis, gastrointestinal tract cancer, and peptic ulcers.[13,42,50]

To insure adequate roughage in the diet, a woman can start off the day with a bran cereal. During the other meals, she can have leafy salads and fresh fruits for dessert. Another bonus of having adequate fiber in the diet is that it can be filling and yet is not absorbed (all of it is eliminated unchanged in the feces). Therefore, the woman who is concerned about her diet can eat enough, feel satisfied, help her intestinal tract, and often not gain weight.[42,50]

Eating away from home is an excellent way to reduce stress. Almost every housewife likes to "eat out" and eating out in restaurants is one of the diversionary methods to cope with stress—the subject of the next chapter.

REFERENCES

1. Benowicz, R. J. *Vitamins & You*. New York: Grosset & Dunlap, 1979.
2. Kline, R. Vitamin C and common sense. *Prevention* 32(1):94–98, 1980.
3. Cameron, E. and Pauling, L. Ascorbic acid as a therapeutic agent in cancer. *J.Internat. Acad. of Prev. Med.* 5(1):8–29, 1978.
4. Creagan, E. T., Moertel, C. G., O'Fallon, J.R., Schutl, A. J., O'Connell, J., Rubin, J., and Frytak, S. Failure of high-dose vitamin C (ascorbic acid) therapy to benefit patients with advanced cancer: A controlled trial. *N. Engl. J. Med.* 301:687–690, 1979.
5. Anderson, T. W., Reid, D. B. and Beaton, G. H. Vitamin C and the common cold: A double blind trial. *Can. Med. Assoc. J.* 107:503–508, 1972.
6. Pauling, L. *Vitamin C, The Common Cold and the Flu*. San Francisco: W. H. Freeman, 1976.
7. Cameron, E., Pauling, L., and Leibovitz, B. Ascorbic acid and cancer: A review. *Cancer Res.* 39:663–681, 1979.
8. Riccitelli, M. L. Vitamin C: A review and reassessment of pharmacological and therapeutic uses. *Conn. Med.* 39:609–614, 1975.
9. Hodges, R. E. The effect of stress on ascorbic acid metabolism in man. *Nutr. Today* 5(1):11–12, 1970.
10. Shaw, L. Vitamins that pick up a sagging defense. *Prevention*:32(4):151–154, 1980.
11. Manzella, J. P. and Roberts, N. J., Jr. Human macrophage and lymphocyte responses to mitogen stimulation after exposure to influenza virus, ascorbic acid, and hyperthermia. *J. Immun.* 123:1940–1944, 1979.
12. Editorial. Vitamin C, HDL and a healthier heart. *Prevention* 30(2):86–90, 1979.
13. Passwater, R. *Supernutrition: Megavitamin Revolution*. New York: Dial press, 1975.
14. Gottlieb, B. Make up your mind—eat more thiamine. *Prevention* 32(4):130–138, 1980.
15. Ross, H. M. Vitamin pills for schizophrenics. *Psychol. Today* 7(4)83–88, 1974.
16. Shaw, L. B₆ for common and uncommon ailments. *Prevention* 32(2)88–93, 1980.
17. Elis, F. R. and Nasser, S. A pilot study of vitamin B₁₂ in the treatment of tiredness. *Brit. J. Nutr.* 30:277–283, 1973.

18. Herbert, V. and Jacob, E. Destruction of vitamin B$_{12}$ by ascorbic acid, *J.A.M.A.* **203**:241–242, 1974.
19. Pechter, K. Peak energy: Iron's not enough. *Prevention* **32**(9):142–147, 1980.
20. Botez, M.I., Young, S. N., Bachevalier, J, and Gauthier, S. Folate deficiency and decreased brain 5—hydroxytryptamine synthesis in man and rat. *Nature* **278**:182–183, 1979.
21. Feltman, J. A nutritional shield against the arrows of stress. *Prevention* **28**(9):88–93, 1976.
22. Morse, D. R. and Furst, M. L. *Stress for Success: A Holistic Approach to Stress and its Management.* New York: Van Nostrand Reinhold, 1979.
23. Shaw, L. Tan without burning with PABA. *Prevention* **32**(6):110–113, 1980.
24. Solomon, N. The high P/S rations are best. *Philadelphia Inq.* 4-C, September 24, 1980.
25. Rosenberg, H. and Feldzamen, A. N. *The Doctor's Book of Vitamin Therapy: Megavitamins for Health.* New York: G. P. Putnam's Sons, 1974.
26. Cureton, T. K., Jr. *Physical Fitness and Dynamic Health,* Second Ed. New York: Dial Press, 1973.
27. Di Cyan, E. *Vitamin E and Aging.* New York: Pyramid Books, 1972.
28. Kugler, H. *Slowing Down the Aging Process.* New York: Pyramid Books, 1973.
29. Gottlieb, B. A and C: Vitamins for a toxified world. *Prevention* **32**(2):72–77, 1980.
30. Seifter, E. Of stress, vitamin A, and tumors. *Science* **193**:74–75, 1976.
31. Chernov, M. S., Hale, H. W., Jr., and Wood, M. Prevention of stress ulcers. *Am. J. Surg.* **122**:674–677, 1971.
32. Classen, H. G. Magnesium and cardiac necroses: Experimental data and their significance for human pathology. *J. Inter. Assoc. Prev. Med.* **6**(1):118–138, 1980.
33. Cooper, K. H. Levels of Physical Fitness and Selected Coronary Risk Factors. Presented to the Monmouth-Ocean County Dental Society, Neptune, New Jersey, April 18, 1979.
34. Rodale, R. The healthful touch of zinc. *Prevention* **30**(6):25–30, 1978.
35. International Medical News Service. Zinc tied to decline in "antiatherogenic" high-density lipoprotein. *Int. Med. News* **13**(8):3, 31, April 15, 1980.
36. Cory, C. C. Newsline: Pain: The promise of drugless pain control. *Psychol. Today* **12**(12):26–27, 1979.
37. Wiley, D. B. Sleep: Too much or too little, it's a problem. *Philadelphia Eve. Bull.* A:37,42, August 17, 1978.
38. Connor, W. E. and Connor, S. L. The key role of nutritional factors in the prevention of coronary heart disease. *Prev. Med.* **1**:49–83, 1972
39. Morse, D. R. Sucrose: A common enemy. *J. Am. Soc. Prev. Dent.* **2**(5):27–28, 1972.
40. Cheraskin, E., Ringsdorf, W. M., and Clark, J. W. *Diet and Disease.* Emmaus, Pa.: Rodale Books, 1968.
41. McCamy, J. C. and Presley, J. *Human Life Styling: Keeping Whole in the 20th Century.* New York: Harper & Row, 1975.
42. Pritikin, N. and McGrady, P. M., Jr. *The Pritikin Program for Diet and Exercise.* New York: Grosset & Dunlap, 1979.
43. Howard, R. B. and Herbold, N. H. *Nutrition in Clinical Care.* New York: McGraw-Hill Book Co., 1978.
44. Stamler, J., Farinaro, E., Mojonnier, L. M., Hall, Y., Moss, D., and Stamler, R. Prevention and control of hypertension by nutritional-hygienic means. *J.A.M.A.* **243**:1819–1823, 1980.
45. Brody, J. E. Panel reports healthy Americans need not cut intake of cholesterol. *New York Times* A1, A16, May 28, 1980.
46. Turplinen, O. Effect of cholesterol-lowering diet on mortality from coronary heart disease and other causes. *Circulation* **59**:1–7, 1979.

47. Sherman, C. Jack Sprat had the right idea. *Prevention* **32**(2):133–142, 1980.
48. Hems, G. The contribution of diet and childbearing to breast-cancer rates. *Brit. J. Cancer* **37**:974–982, 1978.
49. Wheeler, A. C. Try a tisane for tranquility. *Prevention* **24**(6):142–146, 1972.
50. Siegel, S. *Dr. Siegel's Natural Fiber Permanent Weight-Loss Diet.* New York: Dial Press, 1975.
51. Check, W. A. Vitamin B_{15}—Whatever it is, it won't help. *J.A.M.A.* **243**: 2473, 2480, 1980.
52. Donald, P., Pitts, G. C., and Pohl, S. L. Body weight and composition in laboratory rats: Effects of diets with high or low protein concentrations. *Science* **211**: 185–186, 1981.
53. Brown, M. S., Kovanen, P. T., and Goldstein, J. L. Regulation of plasma cholesterol by lipoprotein receptors. *Science* **212**: 628–635, 1981.
54. Van, J. Researchers find out why fish is helpful in heart-patient diet. *Philadelphia Inq.* 9-D, February 4, 1981.

23
Leaving The Pots and Pans for Exotic Lands: The Diversionary Methods

INTRODUCTION

Day in and day out doing the same thing, whether it is working in the kitchen or doing exotic experiments in a research lab, "all work and no play" can be self-destructive. Women need to escape from the routine even if the routine is interesting.

Meeting stressors on a daily basis—even when coping is successful—can induce fatigue and sluggishness. That is another reason to escape. There are various means of escape from reading a book to taking a vacation in a foreign country.

DAILY DIVERSIONS

It is no secret that people vary in their likes and dislikes. How many times have you told a friend to read a certain book or see a particular movie—and then have her berate you for wasting her time. Hence, a detailed list of what would be guaranteed effective daily diversions cannot be given. It can only be said that a person should do what they like as a diversion. Things that may be enjoyable are going to the theater, movies, concerts, and sporting events.

Reading books, listening to music, playing instruments, engaging in physical activities, and playing cards and games (e.g., Mah-Jongg, Backgammon) and delving into needlepoint, crewel, and découpage are other interesting hobbies. Some women find going to the beauty parlor to be a very effective diversion. Drawing, painting, sculpting, carving, photography, collecting (stamps, coins, antiques, etc.), writing and composing are other enjoyable diversions.

One diversion that is shared by millions of American women is watching "soaps" on television. That can be fine, but some women get so involved with the TV soap operas that they have their whole lives revolve around the "TV screen" episodes. Women have changed jobs just so that they would not miss the daily dramas. When people become stressed over missing a TV program, then watching television is no longer a diversion.[1] It then becomes an addiction. And addictions of any sort, from drugs to gambling, are damaging and should be avoided.

One wonderful diversion for both the harried housewife and the female executive (among others) is going to restaurants. Nowadays, one can combine entertainment and dining with the various dinner theaters available. But even "eating out" can be overdone. In that case, a good home-cooked meal can be the exciting diversion (especially if it is prepared by one's mother, spouse, or date). It has also been shown that eating in a relaxed atmosphere with family or friends results in better digestion and absorption of the food.[2]*

The sex act can also be considered a diversion. Some married couples have sexual relations so infrequently that when they do have "sex" it becomes a diversion. Other people seek their sexual diversions outside of the marriage. As discussed in Chapters 7 and 10, this form of diversion can be distressful rather than stress-reducing.

VARIETY

Variety is one method to achieve diversion. As boredom may precipitate stress, changing either the procedural order or adding other procedures can decrease monotony and reduce stress. See Box 23.1 for a few possibilities with women in mind.

---

*Whether a woman "eats out" or eats at home, quite often she is "on guard" about calories and overeating. One way to cut down on overeating is to examine your plates. That's right—look at the dishes. A recent finding is that the color of the dishes can affect one's eating. Plates with warm colors such as red, yellow and orange make food look more appetizing. However, cool color dishes like blue and green help curb the appetite. The scene. Home, health, family finances. Dieting: I'll have the blue plate special. *Philadelphia Inq.* 2-D, May 18, 1981.

Box 23.1. Women's Diversions.

Simple things like changing the schedule of daily routines can make them stimulating, at least for a while.

One can go to the supermarket in the evening instead of the morning, or go to the hardware store and let one's husband (or friend) do the supermarket shopping. Another diversion might result from seeing the variety of different groceries he brings home.

On the job, it may be possible to change either working days or hours. If one avoids the normal rush-hour traffic, that could be a double bonus. First, one is relieved of the stress involved in fighting traffic. Second, the different hours can act as a diversion; e.g., seeing the sun at another view and passing or meeting other people. In New Jersey, the concept of "flex-itime" has been introduced to state employees.[3] It permits them to have a certain degree of freedom in choosing their working hours.

Other ways to achieve variety are changing locations or adding new furnishings to a home or office. Changing wardrobes, varying hairstyles, taking courses at schools, and getting part-time jobs are other helpful methods.

Gambling is another diversion, but at times it may be stress-inducing rather than stress-relieving. Men generally gamble at the race track, in casinos (e.g., black jack, craps) and in the stock market. Women also gamble in casinos (mainly slot machines) and tend to play the lottery, bingo, and the recent craze, the "Money Game." (A pyramid game is played in people's homes in which each player brings in $250–$1000 dollars and then must call in others to join in order to move up on the charts and eventually make money.)

VACATIONS

In addition to daily and regular diversions, it is necessary to break away for vacations. Vacations can be a great means to turn off the regular daily pressures; to give oneself a chance to meet other people; to observe different cultures; and to just get an opportunity to literally do nothing.[4] For vacations to be maximally effective in stress reduction, there are certain rules to follow.

1. Don't take your work with you on the vacation. Don't worry about who's "watching the shop." It is important to realize that whatever the business or activity, it can exist without you. So don't mentally concentrate on your home or office and don't physically bring office or school work with you. However, if you have an avocation that you hadn't had the time to work on at home, you may want to work on it in a relaxed vacation at-

mosphere. It could be anything from painting a landscape to writing a book.

2. Don't program your vacation to the point that you have to be at a certain place at a definite time to participate in a specific activity. The stressful nature of doing something like that was vividly portrayed in the movie, "If It's Tuesday It Must Be Belgium." Vacations should be free-floating and relaxing.

3. Depending upon your inclination and financial means, you may find it relaxing to take a vacation in a trailer and "cook in," or you may prefer motels and hotels and "eat out." As with books, movies and plays, people differ in their choice of sites for vacations. Hence, try to get a consensus with the other people in your party.

4. Don't go to a place just because it's the "in" thing. Just as was discussed in the section on psychologically dealing with stressful situations, preparation is important. Therefore, plan your vacation; read about the area; ask others who have been there; and inquire from travel agencies. But remember travel agencies always emphasize the virtues of a particular place. Try to get a well-rounded picture before *you* make the final decision.

5. To reduce stress, don't expect too much from a vacation. Vacations don't automatically bring back honeymoons (years of living together can change people's attitudes toward each other). Nevertheless, vacations can make people think more clearly and see the other person's viewpoint. It is also important to realize that facilities are generally superior in the United States and Western countries as compared to many other foreign lands. Don't expect quick telephone service or excellent bathroom facilities, and in some countries a meal can last for a few hours.

6. When you return home, don't be stressed by the pile of mail or the list of telephone messages. Just take your time and gradually attend to them (unless there are major decisions that have to be considered immediately).

7. Finally, don't plan your next vacation as soon as you get home. It's good to consider future plans, but give yourself some time. If you are so keen on getting away again the moment you arrive home, then you should reconsider your life-style. If your life, marriage or occupation is so stressful that you can't wait to get away, then you should seriously consider making a change.

CONCLUSION

Daily diversions and regular vacations are essential if one is to be able to successfully cope with stress on a regular basis. This is especially true for women with large families and women who have the double burden of a family and a career. Although most diversions cost money, it is still possible to visit parks, go to free concerts, take books and records out of libraries, and go to free beaches. Maybe the best things in life are not really free, but there are still some free diversions available. The authors hope that the reading of this book has acted as a diversion from your regular life-style and will help you deal with stress in a more positive manner.

To see how well you are coping with stress, answer the questionnaire in the next chapter.

REFERENCES

1. Bricklin, M. This year make time for fun. *Prevention* **30**(1):32–42, 1977.
2. Baird, P.C. and Schutz, H.G. Dietary and nutritional status: Life-style correlates. *J. Am. Dietet. Assoc.* **76**:228–235, 1980.
3. Morse, D.R. and Furst, M.L. *Stress for Success: A Holistic Approach to Stress and its Management.* New York: Van Nostrand Reinhold, 1979.
4. Tracy, L. Doing nothing is an art. *Philadelphia Eve. Bull.* A-23-24, September 1, 1979.

24
The Personalized Assessment
Stress System
for Women
Pass (W)

INTRODUCTION

To effectively manage stress, women must first recognize their stress symptoms, analyze their ways of reacting to stressors, and then come up with a plan for coping with stressors. The three aspects have been discussed in the previous chapters but a brief review is now in order.

Consider how you feel and what happens to you when you are under stress. Does your heart start to thump in your chest? Do you breathe rapidly? Do you grit your teeth? Is a pounding headache the first sign? Do you make a tight fist or grasp the sides of a chair? Can you feel the muscles in your forehead pull tight? Do you get sweaty palms and a dry mouth? Does your voice crack or do you stutter? Is a stomachache your reaction or do you get diarrhea? Do you feel dizzy and faint? Do you begin to make mistakes and forget things? Or do you keep it in and let your blood pressure slowly and insidiously rise?

Whatever the signs and symptoms, learn to recognize them. That is the first step in managing stress.

Next consider your personality type. Are you a Type A who is always doing too many things at once? Do you thrive on stress? Would you be bored silly if you didn't have "job pressures"? Or are you the type that gets upset over minor occurrences? Does it "bug" you when people are late for appointments or do you take it in stride? Remember, what is a stressor for one person can be a relaxor for another. Try to put things in proper perspective and not magnify them out of proportion. There are enough unavoidable stressors without us adding to the list by our negative interpretations of minor occurrences.

Finally, draw up a plan to cope with and counteract stressors on a daily basis. The plan should have five parts to it. First, there are the psychological methods. Avoid stressors whenever possible and evade them until you are better prepared. Then take the time to prepare yourself mentally so that you would be in a better position to deal with unavoidable stressors.

Second, there are the physical methods. Build yourself up physically so that you could confront physical stressors in a reasonable manner. Practice aerobic exercise on a regular basis to give you cardiovascular fitness and a physical outlet for the stress response. Don't tie yourself down to one activity (unless you find no other one to be enjoyable). Try to engage in one or more of the following aerobic activities at least three times a week: Swimming, bicycling, aerobic dancing, running, walking, racquetball, vigorous tennis, rope skipping, and skating.

Third, use the deep relaxation methods. Twice a day is best, but once a day is still beneficial. Choose any of the previously discussed methods. Give your body and mind a regular relaxation break.

Fourth, is the nutritional approach. Keep away from the junk foods. Try to have three regular meals with the emphasis on low fat, low sugar, moderate protein, high starch, and high fiber. Take a B complex, C, and E vitamin supplement daily (only if there are no medical contraindications), but don't become upset if you occasionally miss a vitamin or eat a piece of cake. Moderation is still the key.

The fifth and last part of the stress management plan is diversions. Learn a hobby; break up the routine, do something different; get out of the house. When you have the time and finances, get away for a trip. Don't put it off for retirement. It's helpful to save for the future, but it is also beneficial to enjoy yourself in the present.

Now that you know what stress is—and how to deal with it—take the following stress assessment questionnaire so that you can rate yourself and see how you can improve.

THE TEST

The test is not primarily designed to be a "doomsayer," but rather an indicator on which areas of your life need most to be changed so that you can begin to move toward the good life; relaxed, calm, and in control. The weight given to the various factors in the female stress assessment system was not obtained by an impartial scientific evaluation. Rather it is based on our interpretation of the available information. It gives women a guide to their stress-coping abilities and directions on how to improve their performance.

There are 41 factors in the test and the 5-point scales run from 0 (the best) to 4 (the worst) for each factor. Each woman who wants to evaluate herself should take a blank sheet of paper and number it from 1 through 41. Then she should read the description for each factor and judge (as best as possible) where she "fits." With some factors, the reader may find nothing "fits." In that case, an educated guess is the best response. Remember this is only a guide. The point value determined for each factor should then be placed next to the appropriate factor number (1–41). When all 41 factors are listed, the values should be summed and a total obtained. The reader should then see where her total score falls according to the following ranges. This will give her an idea of her stress level and her stress-management capabilities.

Excellent	Very Good	Good	Average	Poor	Bad
0–34	35–69	70–103	104–137	138–171	172–205

STRESSORS

Physical (See Chapter 2)

Rate the frequency of the following physical stressors in your life at the present time.

1. Loud Noise (e.g., typewriters, loud music, drills, vacuum cleaners, shouts, screams).
   _____ (0) never
   _____ (1) rarely (less than once a week)
   _____ (2) occassionally (about once a week)
   _____ (3) often (3–5 times per week)
   _____ (4) regularly (every day)

2. Pollution (e.g., air as from others smoking, car exhausts, occupational chemicals, smog)
   _____ (0) never
   _____ (1) rarely
   _____ (2) occasionally
   _____ (3) often
   _____ (4) regularly

3. Trauma (e.g., get into accidents; get "beat up" by spouse or lover; injured from occupation; contact sports)
_____ (0) never
_____ (1) rarely
_____ (2) occasionally
_____ (3) often
_____ (4) regularly

4. Radiation (e.g., excessive heat, cold, light, x-rays, laser beams)
_____ (0) never
_____ (1) rarely
_____ (2) occasionally
_____ (3) often
_____ (4) regularly

5. Infections (e.g., colds, flu, sinusitis, sore throat)
_____ (0) never
_____ (1) rarely
_____ (2) occasionally
_____ (3) often
_____ (4) regularly

6. Drugs (other than tranquilizers and sedatives)
_____ (0) never or rarely (about once a month)
_____ (1) between once a week and once a month
_____ (2) 2–5 times a week
_____ (3) daily: one medication
_____ (4) daily: two or more medications

Social (See Chapter 2)

7. Rate the frequency of social stressors within the last year.
_____ (0) none
_____ (1) one "moderate" (e.g., change in residence, school, working hours, recreation or social activities; start of a job; trouble with boss; son or daughter leaving home).
_____ (2) two "moderate."
_____ (3) one "severe" (e.g., death of a spouse, a close family member or friend; divorce or separation; jail term; injury or illness; loss of a job; forced move; retirement; menopause onset; marriage; pregnancy; sex difficulties; getting raped; severe

financial problems; having an affair; finding out about spouse's affair); or three or more "moderate" (see (1) above).

_____ (4) two or more "severe."

Psychological (See Chapter 2)

Rate the frequency of the following psychological stressors in your life at the present time.

8. Frustration

_____ (0) never

_____ (1) rarely (less than once a week)

_____ (2) occasionally (about once per week)

_____ (3) often (3–5 times per week)

_____ (4) regularly (every day)

9. Guilt or Shame

_____ (0) never

_____ (1) rarely

_____ (2) occasionally

_____ (3) often

_____ (4) regularly

10. Anxiety, Fear, Worry, Phobia, Panic

_____ (0) never

_____ (1) rarely

_____ (2) occasionally

_____ (3) often

_____ (4) regularly

11. Anger or Resentment

_____ (0) never

_____ (1) rarely

_____ (2) occasionally

_____ (3) often

_____ (4) regularly

12. Hate or Disgust

_____ (0) never

_____ (1) rarely

_____ (2) occasionally

_____ (3) often
_____ (4) regularly

13. Feelings of Inferiority, Worthlessness, or Self-pity
_____ (0) never
_____ (1) rarely
_____ (2) occasionally
_____ (3) often
_____ (4) regularly

14. Sadness, Malaise (the "blahs"), and/or Depression
_____ (0) never
_____ (1) rarely
_____ (2) occasionally
_____ (3) often
_____ (4) regularly

15. Happiness, Joy, Feeling Good
_____ (0) regularly
_____ (1) often
_____ (2) occasionally
_____ (3) rarely
_____ (4) never

16. Love
_____ (0) regularly
_____ (1) often
_____ (2) occasionally
_____ (3) rarely
_____ (4) never

INDIVIDUAL MAKEUP

17. Sexual Preference (See Chapters 10 and 12)
_____ (0) heterosexual (one partner)
_____ (1) homosexual (one partner); asexual voluntarily (e.g., nun with
          no homosexual activities)
_____ (2) heterosexual (more than one partner)
_____ (3) bisexual; homosexual (more than one partner)
_____ (4) asexual involuntarily (inability to have "sex")

18. Age (See Chapter 2)
_____ (0) 1–12; the young girl
_____ (1) 21–34; the "sexy" years
_____ (2) 50–64; menopause and beyond
_____ (3) 13–20 the juvenile years; 34–49, the "mid-life crisis"
_____ (4) 65+; the stressors of aging

19. Ethnic Background (See Chapter 2)
_____ (0) Protestant, white
_____ (1) Catholic, white
_____ (2) Jewish, Moslem, white
_____ (3) Oriental; American Indian
_____ (4) Black; Hispanic

20. Mental Health (See Chapters 18, 19, and 20)
_____ (0) above average to gifted: IQ 117+
_____ (1) average intelligence: IQ 85–116
_____ (2) borderline: IQ 70–84
_____ (3) educable and trainable retarded: IQ 36–69
_____ (4) severe and profound retarded: IQ below 35

21. Physical Health (See Chapter 21)
_____ (0) excellent physical condition
_____ (1) good physical condition
_____ (2) average physical condition
_____ (3) poor physical condition
_____ (4) extremely poor physical condition

22. Stress Related Symptoms and Signs (See Chapters 2 and 3)
_____ (0) rarely have stress manifestations such as pounding heart,
           sweating palms, tension headaches, gritting teeth, dry mouth,
           stomachaches, nausea and dizziness
_____ (1) occasionally
_____ (2) once or twice a week on the average
_____ (3) 2–5 times per week
_____ (4) daily

23. Body Weight (See Chapters 4, 21 and 22)
_____ (0) 1–5 pounds below normal weight
_____ (1) (+) or (−) 5 pounds from normal
_____ (2) 6–15 pounds above normal weight

_____ (3) 16-29 pounds over normal weight; 6-25 pounds under normal weight

_____ (4) grossly overweight or underweight (30 pounds $\pm$ normal weight)

24. Physical Appearance (See Chapters 6 and 18)
_____ (0) good-looking features, no bodily deformities
_____ (1) average looking features, no bodily deformities
_____ (2) beautiful face and figure (the stress of being beautiful)
_____ (3) "ugly duckling" (the stress of being ugly)
_____ (4) physical handicap

25. Personality Types (See Chapter 2). At least one in each category.
_____ (0) internal, relaxed life-style; type B; self-assured
_____ (1) noncompetitive
_____ (2) passive-dependent; extrovert
_____ (3) introvert: external; obsessive-compulsive; dependent-passive; narcissistic; hysterical; masochistic
_____ (4) type A: aggressive; rheumatoid arthritis; ulcerative colitis; migraine; depressive; accident-prone; ulcer; cancer; sociopathic

26. Negative Attitudes (See Chapters 2 and 3)
_____ (0) 0-3 negative attitudes (e.g., feel neglected, mistreated, overwhelmed, deprived, threatened, nagged at, frustrated)
_____ (1) 4-8 negative attitudes
_____ (2) 9-13 negative attitudes
_____ (3) 14-18 negative attitudes
_____ (4) 19-24 negative attitudes

27. Religious Affiliations and Personal Image (See Chapters 17 and 20)
_____ (0) devout or excellent self-image
_____ (1) regularly attends services or good self-image
_____ (2) agnostic or unsure of one's self
_____ (3) atheist or have negative self-image
_____ (4) neither believes in God nor in oneself

28. Occupation (See Chapters 13-18)
_____ (0) no financial problems and free to engage in diversions
_____ (1) scientist; artist; entertainer; writer; fashion model; housewife with "help" (any of these)

_____ (2) housewife with "help" and part-time job or "female occupation (teacher, librarian, nurse, etc.)

_____ (3) in "male" occupation (harassment on job) or full-time housewife with two or more children, and no "help"

_____ (4) housewife and full-time job, children at home; or prostitute

29. Location (See Chapter 2)

_____ (0) home and job or schooling in rural area

_____ (1) home and job or schooling in suburbs

_____ (2) home and job or schooling in small city (50–250,000)

_____ (3) work full-time during day in large city and live in suburbs

_____ (4) live in crowded center city apartment and work in crowded center city environment

30. Marital Status (See Chapters 7–10)

_____ (0) happily married, living together or single (happy at it)

_____ (1) happily married or second marriage or living together (2nd time)

_____ (2) tolerable marriage or living together arrangement

_____ (3) single (unsuccessful in marital quest) or divorced or widowed

_____ (4) twice divorced or widowed

STRESS MANAGEMENT METHODS

31. Drinking Alcoholic Beverages (See Chapters 4 and 19)

_____ (0) a glass of wine per day

_____ (1) complete abstainer; one cocktail, 1 beer or 2 glasses of wine daily

_____ (2) 2 cocktails, 2 beers or 3 glasses of wine daily

_____ (3) one-half bottle of hard liquor; 6 beers; a bottle of wine per day

_____ (4) alcoholic

32. Drugs (See Chapters 4 and 19)

_____ (0) none

_____ (1) an occasional tranquilizer, sedative, stimulant or illegal drug (e.g., marijuana)

_____ (2) once a week

_____ (3) 3-5 times a week
_____ (4) daily intake

33. Caffeinated Products (See Chapters 4 and 19)
_____ (0) none
_____ (1) occasional tea, cocoa, cola, piece of chocolate cake, or chocolate bar
_____ (2) 1-2 cups of coffee daily; 3-4 cups of tea or cocoa; 1-2 colas daily; a couple of pieces of chocolate cake or candy bars
_____ (3) 3-4 cups of coffee daily or 5-6 cups of tea or cocoa daily
_____ (4) 5 or more cups of coffee daily; 7 or more cups of tea or cocoa daily; 5 or more colas daily; half a chocolate cake or 16 ounces of chocolate candy daily; (any combination of the above)

34. Cigarette Smoking (See Chapters 4 and 19)
_____ (0) none
_____ (1) rarely
_____ (2) half a pack or less per day
_____ (3) up to two packs per day
_____ (4) over two packs per day

35. Eating (See Chapters 4, 22 and 23)
_____ (0) low fat, low sugar, high starch, moderate protein, low salt, no junk food, regular eating habits, vitamin supplements
_____ (1) little fat, low sugar, low salt, high starch, moderate protein, no snacks, regular eating, no vitamin supplements
_____ (2) moderate fat, sugar, salt, starch, and protein, some snacks, regular eating, no vitamin supplements
_____ (3) moderate fat, sugar, salt, starch and protein, high snacks, irregular eating, no vitamin supplements
_____ (4) high fat, sugar, protein and salt, high snacks, no vitamin supplements, irregular eating habits

36. Defense Methods (See Chapter 19)
_____ (0) rarely use defense methods (e.g., rationalization, denial, regression)
_____ (1) occasionally
_____ (2) a couple of times a week

_____ (3) 3–5 times a week
_____ (4) daily

37. Positive Psychological Methods (See Chapter 20)
_____ (0) regularly use methods such as mental preparation, rehearsal, avoidance, reasonable goals, positive attitudes
_____ (1) usually use positive methods
_____ (2) occasionally use positive methods
_____ (3) rarely use positive methods
_____ (4) never use positive methods

38. Consultations (See Chapter 20)
_____ (0) consult regularly with family, friends, professionals, clergy
_____ (1) a few time a week
_____ (2) on occasion as in crisis situations
_____ (3) rarely, have few friends or acquaintances
_____ (4) never, a "loner"

39. Physical Methods (See Chapter 21)
_____ (0) regularly use combination exercises, (e.g., running, calisthenics, bowling), massage, and heat
_____ (1) regularly use combination exercises, rarely other physcial methods
_____ (2) work out twice a week
_____ (3) work out once a week or less
_____ (4) never exercise or use other physical methods

40. Relaxation Response (See Chapter 20)
_____ (0) twice daily, use meditation, self-hypnosis, biofeedback, or other relaxation method
_____ (1) once a day
_____ (2) once every other day
_____ (3) once a week
_____ (4) never; or more than 3 hours a day

41. Diversions (See Chapter 23)
_____ (0) daily regular diversions such as hobbies, shows, movies, restaurants; regular vacations
_____ (1) daily regular diversions, occasional vacations
_____ (2) rarely get away, few diversions
_____ (3) never get away, few diversions
_____ (4) never get away and have no diversions

CONCLUSION

Now that you have taken the test, if you fall in the category of "good" or better, you should be enjoying your life and managing stress relatively well. However, try to improve those factors in which your score is too high. If you fall in the "bad" to "average" range, it is necessary for you to seriously consider changing your habits and life-style.

You might find that after a few weeks of involvement in one or two specific areas, your scores in other areas will begin to come down. For example, if you begin a formal learning program in relaxation or exercise, you may discover yourself having more companionship or sleeping better.

But there is no need to push too quickly. Easy does it. You are not in a race here. You are learning to improve the quality of your life by discovering your areas of greatest interest. Then through gently working at them, you will discover a spillover effect which can relate to other aspects of your living.

After six months of positive stress management, take the test again. You should note an improved score and feel better.

Best of luck and the best of health!

SUGGESTED READINGS

Women's Stress

1. Kjervik, D. K. and Martinson, I. M. (eds.), *Women in Stress: A Nursing Perspective.* New York: Appleton-Century-Crofts, 1979.
2. De Rosis, H. *Women and Anxiety: A Step-by-Step Program to Overcome Your Anxieties.* New York: Delacorte, 1979.
3. Kinzer, N. S. *Stress and the American Woman.* New York: Ballantine Books, 1980.
4. Scarf, M. *Unfinished Business: Pressure Points in the Lives of Women.* Garden City, New York: Doubleday, 1980.
5. Chesley, P. *Women and Madness.* New York: Avon, 1973.

Women's Life Stressors

1. Gornick, V. and Moran, B. K. (eds.), *Women in Sexist Society: Studies in Power and Powerlessness.* New York: Basic Books, 1971.
2. Sheehy, G. *Passages: Predictable Crises of Adult Life.* New York: Dutton, 1976.
3. Friday, N. *My Mother/My Self: The Daughter's Search for Identity.* New York: Dell Publishing, 1978.
4. Bardwick, J. *In Transition: How Feminism, Sexual Liberation and the Search for Self-Fulfillment Have Altered America.* New York: Holt Rinehart & Winston, 1978.
5. Kaplan, A. *Psychological Androgyny: Further Considerations.* New York: Human Sciences Press, 1979.
6. O'Kelly, C. *Women and Men in Society.* New York: Van Nostrand Reinhold, 1980.

Drugs, Alcohol And Women

1. Greenblatt, M. and Schuckett, M. A. (eds.), *Alcoholism Problems in Women and Children.* New York: Grune & Stratton, 1976.
2. Corea, G. *The Hidden Malpractice.* New York: William Morrow, 1977.
3. Gordon, B. *I'm Dancing as Fast as I Can.* New York: Harper & Row, 1979.
4. Sandmaier, M. *The Invisible Alcoholics: Women and Alcohol Abuse in America.* New York: McGraw-Hill Book Co., 1980.

Menstruation And Menopause

1. Weidger, P. *Menstruation and Menopause: The Physiology and Psychology, The Myth and the Reality.* New York: Knopf, 1976.
2. Dalton, K. *The Premenstrual Syndrome and Progesterone Therapy.* Chicago: Year Book Med. Publ. Inc., 1977.

3. Shuttle, P. and Redgrove, P. *Wise Wound: Eve's Curse and Everyman*. New York: R. Marek, 1978.
4. Reitz, R. *Menopause: A Positive Approach*. New York: Penguin Books, 1979.

Women's Psychology And Health

1. Sherman, J. *On the Psychology of Women*. Springfield, Ill: Charles C. Thomas, 1971.
2. Horney, K. *Feminine Psychology*. New York: W. W. Norton, 1973.
3. Williams, J. H. *Psychology of Women: Behavior in a Biosocial Context*. New York: W. W. Norton, 1977.
4. Blum, H. P. (ed.), *Female Psychology: Contemporary Psychoanalytic Views*. New York: International Universities Press, 1977.
5. The Boston Women's Health Book Collective. *Our Bodies, Ourselves*. New York: Simon & Schuster, 1979.
6. Donelson, E. and Gullahorn, J. E. (eds.), *Women: A Psychological Perspective*. New York: Wiley, 1977.
7. Brodsky, A.M. and Hare-Mustin, R. (eds.), *Women and Psychotherapy*. New York: Guilford Pr., 1980.

Female Sexuality

1. Kinsey, A. C., Pomeroy, W. B., Martin, C. E., and Gebhard, P. H. *Sexual Behavior in the Human Female*. Philadelphia: W. B. Saunders, 1953.
2. Masters, W. H. and Johnson, V. E. *Human Sexual Response*. Boston: Little, Brown, 1966.
3. Sherfey, M. J. *The Nature and Evolution of Female Sexuality*. New York: Random House, 1972.
4. Hunt, M. *Sexual Behavior in the Seventies*. Chicago: Playboy Press, 1974.
5. Kaplan, H. S. *The New Sex Therapy*. New York: Brunner/Mazel, 1974.
6. Hite, S. *The Hite Report: A Nationwide Study of Female Sexuality*. New York: Macmillan, 1976.

Rape And Wife Beating

1. Brownmiller, S. *Against Our Will: Men, Women and Rape*. New York: Simon & Schuster, 1975
2. Roy, M. (ed.), *Battered Women: A Psychosociological Study of Domestic Violence*. New York: Van Nostrand Reinhold, 1978.
3. Burgess, A. W. and Holmstrom, L. L. *Rape: Crisis and Recovery*. Bowie, Md.,: Robert J. Brady Co., 1979.

Marriage And Its Alternatives

1. De Lora, J. S. and De Lora, J. R. (eds.), *Intimate Life Styles: Marriage and its Alternatives*. Pacific Palisades, Calif.: Goodyear, 1972.
2. O'Neill, G. and O'Neill, N. *Open Marriage*. New York: Avon, 1972.
3. Johnston, J. *Lesbian Nation: The Feminist Solution*. New York: Simon & Schuster, 1973.
4. Rosen, D. H. *Lesbianism: A Study of Female Homosexuality*. Springfield, Ill.: Charles C. Thomas, 1974.

5. Martino, M. *Emergence.* New York: Crown, 1977.
6. Barkas, J. L. *Single in America.* New York: Atheneum-Scribners, 1980.

Working Mothers

1. Lopata, H. Z. *Occupation: Housewife.* New York: Oxford University Press, 1971.
2. Oakley, A. *Women's Work: The Housewife, Past and Present.* New York: Random House, 1974.
3. Hoffman, L. W. and Nye, F. I. *Working Mothers.* San Francisco: Jossey-Bass, 1974.
4. Curtis, J. *Working Mothers.* Garden City, New York: Doubleday, 1976.
5. Fader, S. S. *From Kitchen to Career: How any Woman Can Skip Low-Level Jobs and Start in the Middle or at the Top.* New York: Stein and Day, 1977.
6. Roland, A. and Harris, B. (eds.), *Career and Motherhood: Struggles for a New Indentity:* New York: Human Sciences Press, 1979.

Working Women

1. Janeway, E. *Man's World Woman's Place: A Study in Social Mythology.* New York: Dell, 1971.
2. Carone, P. A., Kieffer, S. N., Krinsky, L. W., and Yolles, S. F. (eds.), *Women in Industry.* Albany, New York: State University of New York Press, 1977.
3. Seidman, A., (ed.), *Working Women: A Study of Women in Paid Jobs.* Boulder, Colorado: Westview Press, 1978.
4. The Staff of Catalyst. *Marketing Yourself: Women's Guide to Successful Résumés and Interviews.* New York: C.P. Putnam's Sons, 1980.
5. Hyatt, C. *Women and Work: Honest Answers to Real Questions.* New York: M. Evans, 1980.

Women And Economics

1. Auerback, S. *A Woman's Book of Money: A Guide to Financial Independence.* Garden City, New York: Doubleday, 1976.
2. Ahern, D. D. and Bliss, B. *Economics of Being a Woman.* New York: Macmillan, 1976.
3. Chesler, P. and Goodman, E. J. *Women, Money and Power.* New York: William Morrow, 1976.
4. Welch, M. S. *Networking: The Great New Way for Women to Get Ahead.* New York: Harcourt, Brace, Jovanovich, 1980.

Stress Management For Women

1. Cooper, K. H. and Cooper, M. *Aerobics for Women.* New York: M. Evans, 1972.
2. Carrington, P. *Freedom in Meditation.* Garden City, New York: Doubleday, 1977.
3. Benowicz, R. J. *Vitamins and You.* New York: Grosset & Dunlop, 1979.
4. Sorenson, J. and Burns, B. *Aerobic Dancing.* New York: Rawson, Wade, 1979.
5. Oglesby, C. A. (ed.), *Women and Sport: From Myth to Reality.* Philadelphia: Lea & Febiger, 1978.
6. Kaplan, J. *Women and Sports.* New York: Viking Pr., 1979.

Name Index

Subject Index